Remedies for Torts and
Breach of Contract

Remedies for Torts and Breach of Contract

Second edition

Andrew Burrows MA (Oxon), BCL, LLM (Harvard)

Barrister,
Fellow of Lady Margaret Hall, Oxford

Butterworths
London, Dublin, Edinburgh
1994

United Kingdom	Butterworth & Co (Publishers) Ltd, 88 Kingsway, LONDON WC2 6AB and 4 Hill Street, EDINBURGH EH2 3JZ
Australia	Butterworths, SYDNEY, MELBOURNE, BRISBANE, ADELAIDE, PERTH, CANBERRA and HOBART
Canada	Butterworths Canada Ltd, TORONTO and VANCOUVER
Ireland	Butterworth (Ireland) Ltd, DUBLIN
Malaysia	Malayan Law Journal Sdn Bhd, KUALA LUMPUR
New Zealand	Butterworths of New Zealand Ltd, WELLINGTON and AUCKLAND
Puerto Rico	Butterworth of Puerto Rico, Inc, SAN JUAN
Singapore	Butterworths Asia, SINGAPORE
USA	Butterworth Legal Publishers, CARLSBAD, California; and SALEM, New Hampshire

A CIP Catalogue record for this book is available from the British Library.

First edition 1987

ISBN 0 406 50713 9

Typeset by M Rules, London
Printed by Clays Ltd, Bungay, Suffolk

For Rachel ~~Seedher~~

Preface to the second edition

In the seven years since the first edition of this book, there have been many relevant developments. This has necessitated extensive updating and rewriting of the text.

Perhaps the most important change has been the regime for recouping state benefits in personal injury cases contained in the Social Security Administration Act 1992 Part IV. Statute has also abolished that long-standing anachronism, the rule in *Bain v Fothergill*.

Of the many new cases, my own 'top twenty', in terms of interest and significance, are (in the order dealt with in the text): *Hotson v East Berkshire HA* (proof of loss); *Royscot Trust Ltd v Rogerson* (remoteness under s 2(1) of the Misrepresentation Act 1967); *Vesta v Butcher* (contributory negligence in contract); *Hussey v Eels* and *Hussain v New Taplow Paper Mills Ltd* (compensating advantages); *The Alecos M* and *Dean v Ainley* (basic pecuniary loss caused by breach of contract); *East v Maurer* (damages for deceit); *Hunt v Severs* (gratuitously rendered services); *Stanley v Saddique* and *Hayden v Hayden* (s 4 of the Fatal Accidents Act 1976); *Hayes v Dodd* and *Watts v Morrow* (mental distress damages for breach of contract); *AB v South West Water Services* (exemplary damages); *Ministry of Defence v Ashman* (restitution for torts); *Surrey CC v Bredero Homes Ltd* (restitution for breach of contract); *Jobson v Johnson* and *Philips Hong Kong Ltd v A-G for Hong Kong* (penalty clauses); *Powell v Brent London BC* (specific performance); and *Warren v Mendy* (injunction amounting to indirect specific performance).

The above are all decisions of the House of Lords, Court of Appeal or Privy Council. Of the noteworthy Commonwealth cases, *Commonwealth of Australia v Amann* (a decision of the High Court of Australia primarily on contractual reliance damages) is the most important.

The Law Commission has also been busy in this area producing two consultation papers ('Structured Settlements and Interim and Provisional Damages', and 'Aggravated, Exemplary and Restitutionary Damages') and, very recently, a report (following a working paper) on 'Contributory Negligence as a Defence in Contract'.

From the new academic literature, two books should be mentioned here. Harris *Remedies in Contract and Tort* (1988) covers much the same subject matter as this book but analyses the law from an economic perspective; and Treitel *Remedies for Breach of Contract* (1988) has no equal as a comparative account of the law on contractual remedies.

I would like to thank all those who reviewed the first edition or who wrote to me with encouraging comments. I have gratefully adopted many of the suggestions made for the book's improvement. After a great deal of thought I have, however, resisted the idea of expanding the book to include self-help remedies. In my view, such remedies not only raise significantly different issues from judicial remedies but are also very wide-ranging. A full and proper treatment would require a separate book.

The manuscript was submitted at the end of October 1993 and, subject to a few amendments at proof stage, the law is stated as at that date.

Andrew Burrows
10 December 1993
Oxford

Preface to the first edition

The aim of this book is to clarify and assess the principles applied by the courts in providing redress for a defendant's tort or breach of contract. While principally designed for students' use it is hoped that it will also be of assistance to practitioners.

Although there are several books dealing with one (or more) of the remedies for torts and breach of contract, as well as sections on remedies in books on contract, tort and equity respectively, this is the first book to treat the area as a coherent whole. This has the great advantage of enabling the many similarities, as well as the differences, between tortious and contractual remedies and their governing principles to be fully appreciated.

Moreover, it is a sad fact that many of the important and fascinating issues raised in this area have in the past escaped the attention of students, owing to the tendency in traditional contract and tort courses to concentrate on the cause of action rather than the remedies side of the law. It is therefore hoped that as well as being used in 'Remedies' courses this book will encourage greater concentration on remedies in the teaching of contract and tort, whether taught separately or as part of a joint 'Obligations' or 'Common Law' course.

In considering judicial remedies for torts and breach of contract only, an important objective has been to avoid the problems of superficiality and lack of context and structure that tend to beset attempts to examine all remedies. But having said that this book could happily be used alongside those on the law of restitution to provide an exposition of almost all civil law remedies. The temptation to expand this book to include all restitutionary remedies has, however, been resisted for three main reasons. First, knowledge of what constitutes a tort or breach of contract is basic to all law students, usually by the end of their first year and certainly by the end of their studies, whereas the same cannot be said of what constitutes an unjust enrichment. Secondly, in contrast to remedies for wrongs, it is unhelpful to consider separately the remedies for unjust (non-wrongful) enrichment and the unjust enrichment itself. Finally, the recent expansion of the tort of negligence and the acceptance of concurrent liability between tortious negligence and breach of contract – as well as academic challenges to the division between tort and contract – have already rendered it commonplace for tort and contract to be taught as closely related subjects.

In writing this book I have been helped by many people. Peter Bromley first gave me encouragement with the project. Philip Davies, Peter Birks, John Davies, Alan Evans and Stephen Moriarty kindly read and made invaluable comments on various chapters. Five years of Manchester University third-year 'Remedies' students inspired and challenged my thoughts. Colleagues in the law faculty there were stimulating companions and friends over those years and furthermore generously allowed me study leave in Lent Term 1986. A research grant from the British Academy enabled me to make the best use of that time as well as helping with typing and other expenses. Jane Andrews and Gladys Allsop did most of the typing and made a splendid job of it. My parents provided support and encouragement throughout. Finally and most of all I would like to thank my wife Rachel, without whom, quite simply, this book would never have been written.

Andrew Burrows
5 November 1986
Oxford

Contents

Table of statutes

References in this Table to *Statutes* are to Halsbury's Statutes of England (Fourth Edition) showing the volume and page at which the annotated text of an Act may be found.

Table of cases

PAGE

F

PAGE

M

PAGE

PAGE

P

PAGE

PAGE

PAGE

T

PAGE

Chapter 1

Introduction

1. JUDICIAL REMEDIES

Judicial remedies are remedies given by the courts. They can be contrasted with self-help remedies, which are remedies that are available without coming to court, for example, out of court settlements, termination of a contract, and the ejection of trespassers. This book is solely concerned with judicial remedies.[1] Put another way, it examines what the courts can do to counter an infringement (or threatened infringement) of the plaintiff's legal rights, by a tort or breach of contract; but it is not concerned with any other legally permissible options open to the plaintiff to counter such an infringement.

A judicial remedy may be either coercive or non-coercive,[2] that is, it may be either a court order to do or not to do something, backed up by enforcement procedures,[3] or a court pronouncement indicating or altering what the parties' rights or duties are or were. Examples of the former are damages, specific performance, injunctions and the award of an agreed sum while the declaration is the most obvious example of the latter.

---

1 For introductory examinations of some self-help remedies see, eg, Harris *Remedies in Contract and Tort* chs 2 and 19; Lawson *Remedies of English Law* (2nd edn, 1980) chs 1–2. A third group of remedies, namely those awarded by quasi-judicial bodies, such as tribunals, are also excluded from this book's scope although such remedies are in any event hardly ever (if at all) awarded for torts or breach of contract. They do, however, form an interesting source of comparison.
2 Lawson *Remedies of English Law* (2nd edn, 1980) pp 12–4.
3 An undertaking given by a defendant to the court and accepted in place of an injunction is enforceable and hence coercive even though it does not comprise a court order.

2. PROCEDURE

Our concern will be with the substantive law governing judicial remedies and not with the adjectival law dictating the procedure by which those remedies are obtained. For that, reference should be made to *The Supreme Court Practice* and *The County Court Practice*. It will also be assumed throughout that an English court has jurisdiction in respect of the claim[4] and that the plaintiff is proceeding within the appropriate English civil court.[5]

3. ENFORCEMENT

There is a distinction between the coercive remedies granted by the courts for a tort or breach of contract, and the enforcement or execution of those remedies which may require further court orders. This book is not concerned with the latter secondary realm of judicial involvement. Suffice it to say that for some non-monetary remedies, such as injunctions and specific performance, enforcement is by proceedings for contempt of court, with the ultimate sanction being imprisonment; whereas for monetary remedies, such as damages and the award of an agreed sum, there are several methods of enforcing payment, examples being a writ of *fieri facias* (or, in the county court, a warrant of execution) an attachment of earnings order, a garnishee order or a charging order.

To give some general perspective to the role of the judicial remedies, two further points on enforcement are worth emphasising. First, enforcement of judicial remedies is at the plaintiff's discretion. This means that, even after he has been granted a judicial remedy, a plaintiff has the choice of settling for a different resolution of the dispute.[6] Secondly, even judicial methods may not succeed in enforcing the remedy. For example, a defendant who has insufficient assets cannot comply with a monetary remedy; and imprisoning or fining a defendant for failing to carry out an order of specific performance does not guarantee his performance. But it seems true to say that, generally speaking, the fact that a court has granted a remedy is in itself sufficient to ensure compliance.

---

4 Morris *The Conflict of Laws* (3rd edn, 1984) ch 6 and pp 337–43.
5 Eg a personal injury action worth less than £50,000 must be brought in a county court. All the remedies covered in this book can be awarded by both the High Court and the county courts: County Courts Act 1984, s 38.
6 The possibility of bargaining round non-monetary remedies has recently attracted much academic interest—see infra, p 14.

4. ORDERS MADE TO ASSIST THE PLAINTIFF IN COLLECTING EVIDENCE TO ESTABLISH HIS CASE

Although the case that the plaintiff is trying to establish involves a tort or breach of contract, orders made to assist the plaintiff in collecting evidence, like discovery and interrogatories, cannot realistically be described as remedies for a tort or breach of contract; rather, in so far as it is at all sensible to describe such orders as remedies, they are remedies to help the plaintiff in his attempt to show that a tort or breach of contract has been committed. Or, to put it another way, on the assumption that a tort or breach of contract has been committed or is threatened, such orders are not the relief that the plaintiff seeks but rather are means towards obtaining that relief. They are therefore not considered in this book.

5. TORTS AND BREACH OF CONTRACT

Tortious and contractual obligations are the two main types of obligations recognised in English law. A contractual obligation arises where one person makes a promise to another, provided generally that that promise is supported by consideration or is made by deed, and is not invalidated on grounds such as mistake, misrepresentation or frustration. The promisor is under an obligation to perform his promise and should he fail to do so the promisee has a cause of action against him for breach of contract. A tortious obligation, on the other hand, is an obligation not to wrong another by conduct that the different torts specify to be wrongful. Should a person break such an obligation, the person wronged has a cause of action against him for the tort.

This book will, generally, not be concerned with the plaintiff's establishing such causes of action, ie it will not in general be concerned with how the plaintiff establishes the defendant's tort or breach of contract. Rather it will focus on the judicial remedies available to a plaintiff assuming that he can establish a tort or breach of contract or, more rarely, a threatened tort or breach of contract.

There are two major qualifications to this. The first is that in relation to torts actionable only on proof of damage, like negligence (as opposed to breach of contract and torts actionable per se such as trespass to land), some of the principles that are concerned with establishing relevant damage, and hence generally[7] with establishing

---

7 Sometimes the damage and hence the tort is clearly established and the dispute concerns further damage. One is then concerned only with compensatory damages.

the tort, are principles of compensatory damages for an established liability in relation to torts actionable per se and breach of contract. Examples are factual causation, intervening cause, remoteness, and the restrictions on recovery for mental distress. So as to provide a rounded picture of such principles, chapters 2 and 3 include cases dealing with them, even where they concern the establishment of a tort actionable only on proof of damage.

Secondly, for reasons there explained, liquidated damages and similar clauses are discussed in chapter 7 on the award of an agreed sum, even though the essential question is whether the clause is valid, and hence whether the defendant is contractually liable to pay the agreed sum.

6. CONCURRENT LIABILITY BETWEEN THE TORT OF NEGLIGENCE AND BREACH OF CONTRACT[8]

On the same facts and in relation to the same loss, the plaintiff may be able to show not only that the defendant has broken his contract but also that he has committed the tort of negligence. For example, where a carrier contracts to carry goods for the owner, it will usually be a term of the contract that he takes reasonable care of the goods in transit. If he then negligently damages the goods, he is not only in breach of contract but is also liable to the owner for the tort of negligence. The number of potential overlaps between breach of contract and the tort of negligence has increased in recent times. This is particularly so since the tort of negligence has been expanded to allow the recovery in some situations of pure economic loss (that is economic loss not consequent on physical damage).[9]

Clearly what the plaintiff cannot here do is to recover damages both for the breach of contract and for the tort of negligence for this would be to recover double damages for the same loss. Moreover it

8 See, eg Reynolds (1985) 11 NZULR 215; Markesinis (1987) 103 LQR 354; Holyoak (1990) 6 PN 113.
9 See, eg *Hedley Byrne & Co Ltd v Heller & Partners Ltd* [1964] AC 465; *Midland Bank Trust Co Ltd v Hett, Stubbs and Kemp* [1979] Ch 384; *Junior Books Ltd v Veitchi Co Ltd* [1983] 1 AC 520; *White v Jones* [1993] 3 All ER 481. But the recovery of pure economic loss for tortious negligence is still very restricted: see, eg *Candlewood Navigation Corpn Ltd v Mitsui OSK Lines Ltd* [1985] 2 All ER 935; *Muirhead v Industrial Tank Specialities Ltd* [1985] 3 All ER 705; *Leigh & Sillavan Ltd v Aliakmon Shipping Co Ltd* [1986] 2 All ER 145; *Murphy v Brentwood DC* [1991] 1 AC 398.

may be unacceptable for the tort of negligence to impose a standard of liability that is more onerous that that laid down by the express or implied terms of the contract.[10] But if the standard of liability is not more onerous, there should in principle be no objection to the plaintiff choosing to obtain judgment either for the breach of contract or for the tort of negligence, depending on which is more favourable to him. This was traditionally accepted where the defendant was exercising a 'common calling', for example if he were a carrier, innkeeper, bailee or farrier, but where he was a professional person, such as a solicitor or architect, the rule was that where there was a contract between the parties, the plaintiff could recover judgment only for breach of contract.[11] That restrictive rule has been departed from in numerous subsequent cases and, although dicta of Lord Scarman giving the judgment of the Privy Council in *Tai Hing Cotton Mill Ltd v Liu Chong Hing Bank Ltd*[12] has caused some confusion, the better view is that the courts fully accept concurrent consistent liability for breach of contract and the tort of negligence.[13]

7. SHOULD ONE CONTINUE TO DISTINGUISH TORTS AND BREACH OF CONTRACT?

The acceptance of concurrent liability and the expansion of the tort of negligence to allow the recovery of pure economic loss in some

---

10 *Tai Hing Cotton Mill Ltd v Liu Chong Hing Bank Ltd* [1986] AC 80, 107; *National Bank of Greece SA v Pinios Shipping Co No 1, The Maira* [1989] 1 All ER 213; *Greater Nottingham Co-op Soc Ltd v Cementation Piling & Foundations Ltd* [1989] QB 71; *Reid v Rush & Tomkins Group plc* [1989] 3 All ER 228; *Johnstone v Bloomsbury HA* [1991] 2 All ER 293; *Scally v Southern Health & Social Services Board* [1991] 4 All ER 563; *Lancashire and Cheshire Association of Baptist Churches Inc v Howard & Seddon Partnership* [1993] 3 All ER 467.
11 *Groom v Crocker* [1939] 1 KB 194; *Clark v Kirby-Smith* [1964] Ch 506; *Bagot v Stevens Scanlon & Co Ltd* [1966] 1 QB 197.
12 [1986] AC 80, 107.
13 See, prior to *Tai Hing, Esso Petroleum Co Ltd v Mardon* [1976] QB 801; *Midland Bank Trust Co Ltd v Hett, Stubbs and Kemp* [1979] Ch 384; *Ross v Caunters* [1980] Ch 297; *Perry v Sidney Phillips & Son* [1982] 1 WLR 1297; *Pirelli General Cable Works Ltd v Oscar Faber & Partners* [1983] 2 AC 1. See, subsequent to *Tai Hing, Forsikringsaktieselskapet Vesta v Butcher* [1988] 2 All ER 43, 47; *Smith v Eric S Bush* [1990] 1 AC 831, 870; *Caparo Industries plc v Dickman* [1990] 2 AC 605, 619; *Youell v Bland Welch & Co Ltd (No 2)* [1990] 2 Lloyd's Rep 431; *Murphy v Brentwood DC* [1991] 1 AC 398; *Punjab National Bank v de Boinville* [1992] 3 All ER 104; *Lancashire and Cheshire Association of Baptist Churches Inc v Howard & Seddon Partnership* [1993] 3 All ER 467. Cf *Lee v Thompson* [1989] 2 EGLR 151; *Bell v Peter Browne & Co* [1990] 2 QB 495.

situations raise the question whether the traditional division between torts and breach of contract (ie tort and contract) can be sensibly maintained. In particular, one interpretation of some of the cases allowing the recovery of pure economic loss in the tort of negligence[14] is that the courts are now recognising that a negligent breach of promise is a tort, enabling the recovery of damages, even by a third party, to fulfil expectations engendered by the promisor. If this is so, the rationale of the division between torts and breach of contract is largely undermined. That rationale is that contract alone deals with promissory liability, and that such separate treatment of promissory liability is sensible, for while ultimately all liabilities are imposed, promissory liability seeks to fulfil the expectations of the promisee engendered by the other party. In many, probably most, cases this will also uphold what the promisor intended or willed. On the other hand, non-promissory liability is imposed irrespective of the promisee's engendered expectations or the promisor's will. Promissory liability can, therefore, be regarded as meriting separate treatment because it respects the parties' private intentions and arrangements, and is in this sense more laissez-faire based than are tortious (or other) liabilities.

However, despite these developments in tort, this book continues to use the distinction between torts and breach of contract for a number of reasons:

(i)   The judges continue to think and talk in terms of distinct actions for torts and breach of contract.

(ii) As regards remedies, while there are clearly many similarities between remedies for torts and breach of contract—for example, damages and injunctions are both available for torts and breach of contract, and most of the principles governing their grant are common to both causes of action—there remain significant differences. The following are some of them. First, remedies such as specific performance and the award of an agreed sum are available only for breach of contract. Secondly, some principles of compensatory damages, such as remoteness and contributory negligence, and some types of loss, like mental distress and loss of reputation, are dealt with differently for torts than for breach of contract. Thirdly, exemplary damages can be awarded for certain torts but not for breach of contract. Fourthly, restitutionary remedies are more readily available for torts than for breach of contract.

---

14 Eg *Midland Bank Trust Co Ltd v Hett, Stubbs and Kemp* [1979] Ch 384; *Junior Books Ltd v Veitchi Co Ltd* [1983] 1 AC 520.

(iii) The view that some tort cases rest on recognising that a negligent breach of promise is a tort may not be their only possible explanation. Certainly there is little indication of the judges using promissory liability to explain the negligence liability; and where the defendant is liable to the plaintiff for breach of contract it may be thought odd to recognise a concurrent tortious liability resting on what is, on this view, essentially the same basis, ie breach of promise.

(iv) Even if the 'negligent breach of promise as a tort' interpretation is correct, an action for breach of contract still formally differs from the tort action in that it accrues before 'damage', making it less favourable for the plaintiff as regards limitation periods. Furthermore a non-negligent breach of promise can still only be sued on by an action for breach of contract. In particular, this means that it will still only be for breach of contract that one can recover pure economic loss for non-negligent breach of an obligation, at least where that obligation is a positive one. Indeed strict liability, breach of a positive obligation, and pure economic loss are the standard features of most actions for breach of contract.

(v) Even if the courts are treating a negligent breach of promise as a tort, one can of course argue that it is unsatisfactory for them to do so. In accordance with the sensible reason for distinguishing contract and tort, explained above, an action for negligent breach of promise should be regarded as contractual and not tortious. Only the unfortunate traditional insistence on consideration and privity is hindering acceptance of this, and as such, those doctrines should no longer be regarded as central to contract law.

8. THE PRIMARY FUNCTIONS OF JUDICIAL REMEDIES FOR TORTS AND BREACH OF CONTRACT

At a very general level, the usual function of the remedies[15] is to relieve the plaintiff rather than to punish the defendant. This follows from the fact that torts and breach of contract are part of civil and not criminal law. The major exception is that exemplary damages,

---

15 This book does not discuss public law judicial remedies (certiorari, prohibition and mandamus) even though arguably they can be awarded for a tort or breach of contract committed by a public authority—see, eg *Ex p Napier* (1852) 18 QB 692 at 695. Such remedies are better considered in books on administrative law. See Craig *Administrative Law* (2nd edn, 1989) ch 13.

designed to punish the defendant, can be awarded for certain torts. Restitutionary remedies concerned to reverse enrichments wrongly made by the defendant, are also available for some torts and, in an exceptional case, for breach of contract.

At a more particular level, the primary functions of the remedies can be expressed as follows: compensation, restitution, punishment, compelling performance of positive obligations, preventing wrongful acts, compelling the undoing of a wrong, declaring rights. A diagram (see below) is helpful to indicate which remedies correspond to which function.

These functions will be referred to throughout the book. This is not meant to suggest that there is no other way of expressing the primary functions; eg one can equally well regard most of the remedies for breach of contract as having the common function of fulfilling expectations engendered by the contractual promise. But taking into account all judicial remedies for torts and breach of contract, the scheme below is considered the most helpful for understanding the role of and links between the remedies.

Primary Function	Remedies
Compensation	Compensatory damages.
Restitution	Restitutionary damages. Account of profits. Award of money had and received.
Punishment	Exemplary damages.
Compelling performance of positive obligations	Specific performance. Award of an agreed sum. Mandatory enforcing injunction. Appointment of a receiver and manager.
Preventing wrongful acts	Prohibitory injunction. Delivery up for destruction or destruction on oath.
Compelling the undoing of a wrong	Mandatory restorative injunction. Delivery up of goods.
Declaring rights	Declaration. Nominal damages. Contemptuous damages.

9. LEGAL AND EQUITABLE REMEDIES

References will be made throughout to remedies being either legal or equitable. This is historical labelling indicating that the remedy was developed in the common law courts or in the Court of Chancery prior to their fusion by the 1873–5 Judicature Acts. As a legacy of history, legal remedies, in contrast to equitable remedies are almost all monetary. But of particular importance is the fact that legal remedies cannot be refused once liability has been established, whereas equitable remedies can be; ie legal remedies are available as of right whereas equitable remedies are discretionary. So, for example, some damages, although of course not necessarily the amount claimed, must be awarded for a tort or breach of contract, and there is at present no discretion to refuse an award of an agreed sum if there is a breach of a valid contractual obligation to pay it; whereas, despite liability, specific performance or an injunction can be refused by the courts. But it is a grave error of some books and courses to perpetuate the historical division by treating equitable remedies separately from legal remedies as if they have no connection with each other.

One of the purposes of this book is to emphasise that both legal and equitable remedies may be available to a plaintiff for a legal wrong, whether a tort or breach of contract. Indeed, in certain situations, the legal and equitable remedies perform the same or similar functions, eg an account of profits and the award of money had and received or restitutionary damages effect restitution, and specific performance and the award of an agreed sum compel performance of positive contractual obligations.

10. EQUITABLE WRONGS

The fact that both legal and equitable remedies are available for the common law wrongs is one good reason for treating law/equity as a purely historical and not a rational division. It is worth briefly deviating from the main theme of this book to emphasise that the pattern of remedial functions set out above suggests another attack on that divide; for while it is still essentially true, as the non-fusionists stress, that only equitable remedies are available for equitable wrongs, it is also true that the same or similar functions are performed by the equitable remedies awarded for equitable wrongs, as by the remedies for torts and breach of contract.

So if we take the two main types of equitable wrong (other than breach of confidence),[16] namely proprietary estoppel and breach of fiduciary duty, we find that the remedies granted are analogous to those for breach of contract and torts respectively.

16 Infra, p 11.

Taking proprietary estoppel first, the primary remedies are orders to convey land[17] and declarations of rights over another's land,[18] which correspond respectively to the contractual remedies of specific performance and declaration. In other cases, monetary awards corresponding to compensatory damages have been secured for a plaintiff by, for example, an equitable lien[19] or by a conditional possession order.[20] Throughout, the remedies can also be regarded as fulfilling the expectations engendered in the promise.[1] To imagine, then, that markedly different principles are being applied to remedies for proprietary estoppel, than to remedies for breach of contract, is incorrect. If tomorrow proprietary estoppel were to be treated as a breach of contract, giving rise to solely contractual remedies, the range of remedial functions would barely differ.

For breach of fiduciary duty, of which the prime example is breach of trust, the main remedies are accounting for loss[2] (otherwise referred to as equitable compensation) the prohibitory injunction[3] and an account of profits.[4] The first of these corresponds directly to compensatory damages, while the last two are also remedies for torts (albeit that an account of profits and other restitutionary remedies are as yet only available in relation to certain torts). Again, therefore, there is no wide gulf between the judicial remedies awarded for torts and those for breach of fiduciary duty, so that to treat breach of fiduciary duty as a tort, giving rise to purely tortious remedies, would produce little change in the range of remedial functions.

17 *Dillwyn v Llewellyn* (1862) 4 De G F & J 517; *Pascoe v Turner* [1979] 1 WLR 431.
18 *Inwards v Baker* [1965] 2 QB 29; *Crabb v Arun District Council* [1976] Ch 179.
19 *Hussey v Palmer* [1972] 1 WLR 1286.
20 *Dodsworth v Dodsworth* (1973) 228 Estates Gazette 1115.
 1 *Dodsworth v Dodsworth* (supra), is a rare exception, in effect protecting the plaintiff's reliance interest.
 2 Eg *Fry v Fry* (1859) 27 Beav 144; *Nocton v Lord Ashburton* [1914] AC 932; *Re Dawson* [1966] 2 NSWR 211; *Wallersteiner v Moir (No 2)* [1975] QB 373; *Bartlett v Barclays Bank Trust Co (No 2)* [1980] Ch 515; *Re Bell's Indenture* [1980] 1 WLR 1217. Davison (1982) 13 Melb Univ LR 349; Gummow, Essay 2 in *Equity, Fiduciaries and Trusts* (ed Youdan); Tilbury *Civil Remedies* (1990) paras 3247–3254.
 3 Eg *Fox v Fox* (1870) LR 11 Eq 142; *Dance v Goldingham* (1873) 8 Ch App 902; *Wheelwright v Walker* (1883) 23 Ch D 752; *Waller v Waller* [1967] 1 All ER 305. Mandatory enforcing injunctions have also been granted—*Foley v Burnell* (1783) 1 Bro CC 274; *Fletcher v Fletcher* (1844) 4 Hare 67.
 4 Eg *Keech v Sandford* (1726) 2 Eq Cas Abr 741; *Reading v A-G* [1951] AC 507, *Boardman v Phipps* [1967] 2 AC 46, *English v Dedham Vale Properties Ltd* [1978] 1 WLR 93. For discussion of the idea of a constructive trust as a proprietary remedy for breach of fiduciary duty and breach of confidence, see Burrows *The Law of Restitution* pp 35–45, 405–18. See also *A-G for Hong Kong v Reid* [1994] 1 All ER 1.

It follows that those who argue against the fusion of law and equity merely seek to perpetuate an historical rather than a rational division,[5] and that it will not be at all surprising if torts and breach of contract ultimately absorb equitable wrongs. In the meantime, and in using this book, it should always be remembered that alongside judicial remedies for torts and breach of contract there are remedies performing essentially the same functions for equitable wrongs.

11. BREACH OF CONFIDENCE

Although breach of confidence is still probably best viewed as an equitable wrong[6] it is included within this book and is examined alongside torts. This is for two main reasons. First, the exact jurisdictional basis of breach of confidence is controversial. While the damages awarded are probably best viewed as equitable damages granted in addition to or in lieu of an injunction for an equitable wrong, a case such as *Seager v Copydex Ltd*[7] has been interpreted as recognising breach of confidence as a tort leading to common law damages. Secondly, the Law Commission in its report on Breach of Confidence[8] recommended that breach of confidence should be made a statutory tort. In short, breach of confidence has come within a 'hair's breadth' of being treated as a tort.

12. COMBINING REMEDIES

In general there is no objection to a plaintiff being awarded more than one remedy for a tort and/or breach of contract. This free choice of the plaintiff to combine remedies is subject to two main restrictions. First, the function or aim of the remedies must not be inconsistent: ie the remedies must not be mutually exclusive. For example, a plaintiff cannot recover compensatory damages for a tortious misrepresentation inducing a contract, aimed at putting the plaintiff into as good a position as if the contract had not been made, plus compensatory (expectation) damages for breach of that

---

5 For a discussion of fusion, see Hanbury and Martin *Modern Equity* (14th edn, 1993) pp 21–5. *United Scientific Holdings Ltd v Burnley Borough Council* [1978] AC 904 esp at 924–25 (per Lord Diplock) supports fusion.
6 *A-G v Guardian Newspapers (No 2)* [1990] 1 AC 109, 286 (per Lord Goff). Cf *Aquaculture Corpn v New Zealand Green Mussel Co Ltd* [1990] 3 NZLR 299.
7 [1967] 1 WLR 923. Infra, pp 246–7.
8 Report No 110 (1981).

contract aimed at putting the plaintiff into as good a position as if the contract had been performed. The two aims are inconsistent. Secondly, the remedies must not afford the plaintiff double recovery. For example, one cannot recover compensatory damages for a tort and compensatory damages for a breach of contract so as to recover twice over for the same personal injury.

If either of those restrictions is in play, so that the plaintiff must make a choice of judicial remedy, that choice need not be made until judgment (and, even then, can be changed if the defendant fails to comply with the remedy).[9]

13. ECONOMIC ANALYSIS, BARGAINING AROUND NON-MONETARY REMEDIES AND THE CONSUMER SURPLUS

Over the past twenty years or so, there has been widespread interest by academic lawyers, especially in the United States, in the economic analysis of law, which examines how far the law promotes economic efficiency. Indeed a good deal of economic analysis writing has focused on the civil law remedies considered in this book. Some commentators even seem to come close to using efficiency as the only important criterion for critically assessing the law, but this surely overplays its importance. The common law is best regarded as a coherent system of principle, reflecting a complex mix of 'moral rights' reasoning, modified and tempered by the desire to pursue certain long-term social policies. One important social policy is efficiency; but its place is alongside, not as a replacement for, moral rights reasoning, and this is how it is used in this book.

On a more detailed level, several other criticisms can be levelled at traditional economic analysis. To understand these, it is as well to set out very briefly how economists have tended to look at tort and contract.[10] There can be said to be three important steps in the reasoning. The first is that a system is efficient where those who place the highest value on resources have the use of those resources. Free market voluntary exchanges, by which resources are moved to successively more valued uses, are therefore the necessary means for efficiency. The second step is the Coase Theorem,[11] stating that in

9 See, generally, *United Australia Ltd v Barclays Bank Ltd* [1941] AC 1, 19, 21, 30. See also infra, pp 385–6 (specific performance).
10 See also Harris *Remedies in Contract and Tort* pp 6–14.
11 (1960) 3 J Law & Econ 1.

the absence of transaction costs it does not matter what legal rights and remedies there are because the parties as rational maximisers of value will negotiate round them to produce the most efficient result. Say, for example, A's factory produces smoke ruining B's enjoyment of his land. If the value of the factory to A as it is (that is, the value attributable to the smoke) is £100,000 and the enjoyment of B's land is worth £70,000 to him, the efficient allocation of resources is to allow A to continue polluting. According to the Coase Theorem, even if A is legally ordered to stop the factory emitting such smoke, he will carry on as before, by paying B £70,000, or indeed up to £99,999. If we reverse the figures, then by the same reasoning the smoke will be stopped even if B is given no injunction because, according to Coase, B will pay A between £70,000 and £99,999 to stop the smoke. The final step is then economic analysis confronting the fact that in the real world there are transaction costs. Hence the allocation of legal rights and remedies can be expected to affect efficiency. Free bargaining will not necessarily take place to correct 'errors' and, even if it does, transaction costs will be incurred. The courts should therefore strive to promote efficiency by deciding on legal rights and remedies that on a general level promote voluntary exchanges, and more specifically mimic the voluntary exchanges that the parties as rational maximisers of value would make.

This economic approach is troubling in several respects. First, the methodology being used is most unappealing to lawyers, who are used to dealing at a specific level with concrete facts and issues. In particular, lawyers are likely to be unhappy with individuals being portrayed as solely concerned to maximise value, when this does not correspond to the reality of human motivation. Secondly, it can be argued that efficiency is not a value-free notion, and that the approach outlined above rests on nothing more than right-wing, free market ideology. Thirdly, even though applying the same general approach, economists differ as to whether particular legal rules are efficient or not. To give an example from the law in this book, it was for several years argued that it was efficient for specific performance to remain a secondary remedy to damages, but more recently the opposing view has been fervently put forward. It should not be thought, therefore, that the law can always turn to clearly agreed conclusions as to what is and what is not efficient. Finally, many of the arguments turn on the extent of transaction or other costs and yet there is little empirical data to support the views expressed.

For reasons such as these there seems little to be gained from detailed economic analysis. Moreover it should be reiterated that

14 *Introduction*

even where used at a general and relatively uncontroversial level, efficiency should in no sense be regarded as the sole criteria for assessing the law. Indeed it can be argued that, in the remedies field, the most significant contribution of the economic analysis movement lies not in showing that particular legal principles do or do not promote efficiency but rather in highlighting two legally important notions that might otherwise not have received the attention they deserve.

One is what economists term the 'consumer surplus', namely the subjective value that a consumer places on particular property or services, over and above the objective market value.[12] This is a useful way of explaining, for example, why a person having a wall built for privacy is, in the event of breach, unlikely to be put into as good a position as if the contract had been performed if he is simply awarded damages reflecting the difference in market value of his land with and without the wall; or why it is essential for the courts to award mental distress damages to compensate fully for a ruined holiday; or why specific performance is a preferable remedy to damages for someone buying a particular home.

The other notion is that the parties may well bargain around non-monetary remedies, like injunctions and specific performance, whether pre- or post-judgment.[13] Indeed, in some areas, such as nuisance, empirical data indicates that they are very likely to do so. Two views can be suggested as to the effect this should have on the remedies awarded. First, there is the view that the possibility of post-judgment bargaining should have no effect on a court's reasoning. The court should rather reach a decision according to what it thinks is just, and should regard it as entirely a matter for the parties if they then prefer a different solution. After all, the court cannot know in advance whether the parties will embark on post-judgment bargaining. Alternatively, it can be argued that the courts should be wary of granting non-monetary remedies, precisely because the plaintiff who has been or will be awarded an injunction or specific performance is placed in too strong a position in pre- or post-judgment bargaining; for to the extent that the defendant's gains from the wrong will exceed the plaintiff's loss, it will be in each party's interest to negotiate a deal whereby the plaintiff takes a share in the defendant's gains in return for the defendant being free to commit the 'wrong'. Moreover, there will be every incentive for the plaintiff to demand a huge share of those gains, going far

12 Harris, Ogus and Phillips (1979) 95 LQR 581.
13 Sharpe *Injunctions and Specific Performance* (1992, 2nd edn) paras 1.150–1.170, Thompson (1975) 27 Stan LR 1563.

beyond the compensation needed to cover the value to him of the right infringed. Both the consumer surplus and bargaining around the remedies are ideas that will be returned to at various stages in this book.

14. THE LAYOUT OF THE BOOK

The general approach adopted is to look at each judicial remedy in turn, starting with the monetary remedies and moving through to the (largely) non-monetary remedies. So chapters 2–4 deal with compensatory damages, chapter 5 examines non-compensatory damages, most notably exemplary damages, and chapter 6 links together several remedies all concerned to effect restitution. The following three chapters consider respectively the award of an agreed sum, specific performance and injunctions. The final chapter deals with other remedies on which the material is insufficient to merit separate chapters. The aim throughout is to elucidate and assess critically the functions of, principles governing and relationship between the various judicial remedies.

Chapter 2

Compensatory damages I: general principles of assessment

An award of damages is almost always a common law remedy and by it a sum of money assessed by the court is ordered to be paid by the defendant to the plaintiff for a tort or breach of contract. Damages for breach of contract usually aim to fulfil the plaintiff's expectations by putting him into as good a position as he would have been in if the contract had been performed. For tort, damages usually aim to put the plaintiff into as good a position as he would have been in if no tort had been committed. The principles can be linked by saying that the usual function of damages is compensation,[1] that is, the award of a sum of money to cover the plaintiff's loss.

This chapter and the following two are solely concerned with usual compensatory damages, while less common non-compensatory damages, such as nominal, contemptuous and exemplary damages are examined in chapter 5.

This chapter is designed to equip one with all that is basically needed to assess compensatory damages, whatever the type of loss in question, and is divided into four main sections. The first examines the compensatory aims themselves, including their theoretical underpinnings and the notions of factual causation and proof of loss that are necessarily involved in their application. The second looks at the principles that limit (or may limit) compensatory damages for both torts and breach of contract—remoteness, intervening cause, the duty to mitigate, contributory negligence and impecuniosity. The following section considers two principles that limit compensatory damages solely for breach of contract—the refusal to award damages beyond the defendant's minimum contractual obligation and the restriction where the only obligation broken is to pay money. Finally, several general points on the assessment of compensatory damages are examined—the form of damages, the date for assessment, compensating advantages and taxation.

1 Or that damages seek the *restitutio in integrum*.

1. THE COMPENSATORY AIMS

(1) Classic authorities

Before proceeding any further it is as well to refer to the classic authorities laying down that the usual aim of contractual and tortious damages is respectively to put the plaintiff into as good a position as he would have been in if the contract had been performed, or if no tort had been committed. So in *Robinson v Harman*[2] Parke B said:

The rule of common law is that where a party sustains a loss by reason of a breach of contract he is, so far as money can do it, to be placed in the same situation with respect to damages as if the contract had been performed.

Lord Blackburn's statement in *Livingstone v Rawyards Coal Co*,[3] a case concerning trespass to goods, is probably the most cited tort authority on this. He said that the measure of damages was:

. . . that sum of money which will put the party who has been injured, or who has suffered, in the same position as he would have been in if he had not sustained the wrong for which he is now getting his compensation or reparation.

Many subsequent cases contain equally clear expressions of these central principles.[4]

(2) Theoretical underpinnings

(a) Breach of contract

Fuller and Perdue in their seminal article 'The Reliance Interest in Contract Damages'[5] labelled the principle of putting the plaintiff

---

2 (1848) 1 Exch 850 at 855.
3 (1880) 5 App Cas 25 at 39.
4 Eg for breach of contract, *Wertheim v Chicoutimi Pulp Co* [1911] AC 301 at 307; *British Westinghouse Co v Underground Electric Rlys Co of London Ltd* [1912] AC 673 at 689; *Monarch SS Co Ltd v Karlshamns Oljefabriker* [1949] AC 196 at 220; *The Heron II* [1969] 1 AC 350 at 414; *Doyle v Olby (Ironmongers) Ltd* [1969] 2 QB 158 at 167; *Tito v Waddell (No 2)* [1977] Ch 106 at 328–334; *Radford v De Froberville* [1977] 1 WLR 1262 at 1268. For torts, see, eg *Shearman v Folland* [1950] 2 KB 43 at 49; *British Transport Commission v Gourley* [1956] AC 185 at 187; *Lim Poh Choo v Camden and Islington Area Health Authority* [1980] AC 174 at 186 et seq; *Dodd Properties (Kent) Ltd v Canterbury City Council* [1980] 1 WLR 433 at 456; *Swingcastle Ltd v Alastair Gibson* [1991] 2 AC 223.
5 (1936–37) 46 Yale LJ 52 and 373.

into as good a position as if the contract had been performed as that of protecting the plaintiff's expectation interest. They regarded this, on the face of things, as a queer kind of compensation since it often puts the plaintiff into a better position than if no contract had been made. Hence the central question raised by Fuller and Perdue was, why should contractual damages usually protect the plaintiff's expectation interest? Why, for example, should damages not be restricted to ensuring that the plaintiff is made no worse off than if the contract had not been made— in Fuller and Perdue's terminology why should not damages be restricted to protecting the plaintiff's reliance interest?[6]

A famous illustration of the distinction between damages protecting the plaintiff's expectation and reliance interests is provided by the United States case of *Hawkins v McGee*.[7] The plaintiff had burnt his hand and the defendant, who was a surgeon interested in skin grafting, contractually promised the plaintiff to restore his hand to a perfect condition by an operation. The operation went wrong and, instead of having a perfect hand, the plaintiff's hand was made worse than it was before the operation. Two possible ways in which the damages for the breach of contract could be assessed were examined. The first was to deduct from the value of the hand before the operation the value of the hand as it was after it—in Fuller and Perdue's terminology this would protect the plaintiff's reliance interest. The second was to deduct from the value of a perfect hand the value of the hand after the operation—this would protect the plaintiff's expectation interest. The court held that for breach of contract the plaintiff was entitled to be put into as good a position as if the contract had been performed; hence the second measure of damages was awarded. In other words the plaintiff's expectation interest was protected.

Fuller and Perdue ultimately thought that at least for bargain promises—promises supported by consideration—protection of the expectation interest could be justified on two main grounds. First, that the expectation interest is the best measure of the plaintiff's reliance interest given that the latter is difficult to prove, particularly with regard to the forgoing of opportunities to enter other bargains. But this seems a weak argument since it is often just as difficult to prove what position the plaintiff would have been in if the contract had been performed as it is to prove what position he would have been in if no contract had been made. Moreover, difficulty of proof

---

6 An alternative way of expressing this is to ask why should not contractual obligations always be negative rather than positive?

7 84 NH 114, 146 A 641 (1929).

does not justify picking what on this reasoning would be an arbitrary measure.

Fuller and Perdue's second justificatory argument is, in contrast, a forceful one. This is that protecting the plaintiff's expectation interest for promises supported by consideration encourages people to perform their side of a bargain, thereby upholding the working of the market economy under which goods and services find their way to where they are most wanted. If parties could only recover their reliance interest there would be no such incentive to perform. Indeed one can go further and argue that protection of the expectation, but not the reliance interest, encourages parties to enter into bargains in the first place.

A similar approach is taken by the economics and law theorists, like Posner,[8] who argue that contract law is a system of rules and principles furthering economic efficiency and hence overall social welfare. As expectation damages for bargain promises give the plaintiff no less and no more than the value he has placed on the defendant's performance, they provide the defendant with an incentive to exchange resources with those who place the highest value on them; the efficient result is thereby promoted. Say, for example, A contracts to sell to B for £100,000 a machine that is worth £110,000 to B (ie that would yield him a profit of £10,000). Before delivery C comes to A and offers him £109,000 for that machine. A would be encouraged to break the contract with B were he not liable to pay B £10,000 expectation damages. Given that damages do protect the expectation rather than the reliance interest, C will not be able to induce a breach of A's contract with B unless he offers A more than £110,000 thereby indicating that the machine really is worth more to him than to B. The expectation rule thus assures that the machine ends up where it is most valuable.

In contrast to the above justification is Fried's theory of 'Contract as Promise'.[9] This is essentially a revival of the will theory of contract whereby a contractual obligation as against, for example, a tortious obligation is regarded as resting on the defendant's voluntary acceptance of that obligation. On this approach the expectation interest is the obvious and natural measure of damages for all promises, even if gratuitous, since it represents the monetary equivalent of the defendant's promised performance. Fried expresses this as follows:

---

8 *Economic Analysis of Law* (4th edn, 1992) ch 4. See also Birmingham (1970) 24 Rutgers LR 273; Beale *Remedies for Breach of Contract* (1980) (hereinafter cited as *Remedies*) pp 159–64.
9 *Contract as Promise* (1981); see Burrows (1985) CLP 141.

If I make a promise to you, I should do as I promise: and if I fail to keep my promise to you, it is fair that I should be made to hand over the equivalent of the promised performance . . . In contract doctrine this proposition appears as the expectation measure . . . [it] gives the victim of a breach no more or less than he would have had had there been no breach.[10]

Fried's approach has much to commend it but it is submitted that it is not a complete justification for expectation damages since, in many situations, particularly given the central objective test of intention, expectation damages are awarded for breach of contract even though it cannot sensibly be said that the defendant has voluntarily undertaken an obligation. As such, a more complete theory of contract as promise is that promises are prima facie morally binding not because of the promisor's will, but precisely because it is wrong to disappoint a promisee's expectations and thereby to abuse the trust and confidence that the promisor has instilled in the promisee. On this view, the expectation measure is again the natural measure of recovery, since it accords directly with the underlying morality of promise-keeping; and on this sort of approach, Fuller and Perdue's market economy and Posner's economic efficiency explanations provide merely additional reasons for protecting the plaintiff's expectation interest, where the promise is a bargain promise.

However, it should be stressed that all the above approaches, purporting to justify the protection of the expectation interest, run counter to the important writings of Atiyah.[11] A major thrust of Atiyah's work is that while protecting the expectation interest may have been justified in the nineteenth century, when people strongly believed in the moral bindingness of promises, and in upholding the free market economy, it is far more difficult to justify in today's welfare state. He would therefore prefer protection of the reliance interest to be the normal rule and, while he has recently backtracked to some extent,[12] his predominant view has been that traditional contract law protecting the expectation interest and built up on nineteenth-century laissez-faire values is dead or at least in its final death throes.

But his attack grossly overstates the position; for while the law does and should enable a promisor to escape from a contract more easily than in the past—reflecting a greater concern in today's age

10 Ibid, p 17.
11 *The Rise and Fall of the Freedom of Contract* (1979); *Promises, Morals and Law* (1981); essays 2 and 7 in *Essays on Contract* (1987). Similar views are put forward by Gilmore *The Death of Contract* (1974). See also Collins *The Law of Contract* (2nd edn, 1993) pp 371–85.
12 *An Introduction to the Law of Contract* (4th edn, 1989) pp 30–9, 457–80.

for the weak—there is still a large area where the expectation interest is and should be protected for breach of a binding promise. Indeed the development of promissory estoppel and attacks on privity potentially open the way for many more promises to be legally enforceable. Moreover, while in the United States Restatement of Contracts, restriction to the reliance interest is suggested as a possibility under promissory estoppel or where there is a disproportion between the consideration and the defendant's liability,[13] there is no indication in England of the courts preferring to measure contractual damages by the reliance rather than the expectation interest.[14] It is therefore submitted that contract law, and its central protection of the promisee's expectation interest, remains fully alive and is in no sense dying.

One final point, which concerns Fuller and Perdue's interest analysis, is that it does not seem particularly helpful and indeed may be downright confusing to subdivide the expectation interest into damages protecting the (subsidiary) reliance and expectation interests, although this is an approach now commonly adopted by commentators. All possible confusion is best avoided by using the expectation and reliance interests to refer only to the overall interest that the damages are seeking to protect. If so confined, *there is no question of combining the different interests since they are mutually inconsistent.*[15] Hence in this book there will be no discussion of the reliance interest until examination of contractual damages' central compensatory aim of protecting the expectation interest has been completed.[16]

(b) Torts

In the tort realm (with the minor exception of misrepresentation)[17] the theoretical underpinnings of compensation have not been discussed in relation to any controversy over what the compensatory aim should be. On the contrary it is accepted without dispute that the compensatory aim is and should be to put the plaintiff into as good a position as if no tort had been committed. Nevertheless the justification for tort compensation is equally hotly debated, with attention being particularly concentrated on the most fundamental

13 Sections 87, 90 and 351(3). See also ss 158(2), 272(2) dealing with recovery of reliance loss where a contract is unenforceable. Generally, see Young (1981) Col LR 19. On s 90, see Slawson (1990) 76 Cornell LR 197.
14 This is so even for non-bargain promises; Burrows (1983) 99 LQR 217, 241.
15 Burrows (1983) 99 LQR 217, 223–224.
16 Reliance damages for breach of contract are therefore examined in chapter 4.
17 Infra, pp 172–6.

question of all—should tort compensation (at least in the realm of accidents) be abolished altogether?[18]

Most of the theoretical discussion has had in mind the usual type of tortious obligation, which is the imposed *negative* obligation; that is, the obligation not to make the plaintiff worse off. However, not all tortious obligations are negative, and arguably there is a growing trend to impose positive tortious obligations, that is, obligations to benefit the plaintiff. This will be discussed later. For the present, sole concentration will be on the justification for imposing on a defendant negative obligations and corresponding compensatory damages.

One explanation is again offered by economics and law theorists, like Posner,[19] who argue that tort compensation promotes economic efficiency. By making a defendant responsible for costs he has caused, it encourages him to take precautions to prevent those costs unless the costs of the precautions outweigh the costs caused to the plaintiff. The general tort standard of negligence precisely fixes liability on those who act inefficiently by not taking cost-justified precautions. The approach to negligence taken in *United States v Carroll Towing Co*[20] is particularly focused on as showing such economic reasoning. Judge Learned Hand there said, 'If the probability be called P: the injury L: and the burden B: liability depends upon whether B is less than L multiplied by P: ie whether $B < PL$.'[1] For Posner then, the liability to pay compensation for negligence promotes economic efficiency by deterring uneconomical accidents.

A different and more elaborate economic efficiency justification is advocated by Calabresi in his 'market deterrence' theory.[2] According to this, the costs of accidents will be reduced, and indeed, will reach the optimum level in terms of efficiency, where the cheapest cost avoider, who is a cause of an accident, is made strictly liable to compensate the injured party. It is essential to this theory that while the defendant's ability to spread the loss is an important factor in deciding liability, the aim is not loss-spreading per se, but rather the reaching of the most efficient level of accidents by making the defendant bear the costs of the accident. So while for

---

18 See generally, Williams & Hepple *Foundations of the Law of Tort* (2nd edn, 1984) ch 7; England *The Philosophy of Tort Law* (1993) chs 1–6; Cane (1982) 2 Ox JLS 30; Klar (1983) 33 UTLJ 80; Hutchinson and Morgan (1984) 22 Osgoode Hall LJ 69; Ogus (1984) 37 CLP 29.

19 *Economic Analysis of Law* ch 6.

20 159 F 2d 169 (1947).

1 Ibid, p 173.

2 Eg *The Costs of Accidents* (1970); see Cane *Atiyah's Accidents Compensation and the Law* (5th edn, 1993) pp 374–94.

Calabresi 'non-fault enterprise liability' should replace the present legal emphasis on fault, the tort system of individual responsibility for accident compensation is preferable to a state compensation scheme. As Blum and Kalven put it, Calabresi's view is that: 'Social security "externalises" from the activities that produce accidents the costs of those accidents—bringing in its wake a loss of "general deterrence"'.[3]

In contrast to such economic justifications for tort compensation is an explanation in terms of individualistic morality. It can be argued that it is a basic principle of corrective justice that, while one should generally be free to carry out one's own activities, one should not be free to interfere with or harm others by those activities; hence if one does cause harm, one should compensate the injured party. On this view, the traditional insistence on fault is arguably unnecessary and may merely add further moral weight to an already sufficient case for compensation: it is perhaps best explained (like consideration in contract) as being concerned to confine legal intervention in individuals' lives to the strongest cases.[4]

The leading modern theorist advocating a strict liability corrective justice approach to tort compensation is Epstein.[5] He states his aim as being, '. . . to show how . . . tort law can be viewed usefully as a system of corrective justice appropriate for the redress of private harms.'[6] His central proposition is that he who causes harm by affirmative action should be strictly liable to compensate the victim, subject to certain limited defences. On this view causation is crucial and, while not developing any general theory of causation, Epstein offers four examples of sufficient causal connections; A hit B; A frightened B; A made B hit C; A created a dangerous condition that resulted in B's harm. Epstein's approach is both simple and clear, but its prime importance, as far as we are here concerned, is that it emphasises that tort compensation can be justified on the basic moral principle of corrective justice albeit that, contrary to the present law, strict liability rather than negligence is regarded as the central standard of liability.

---

3 (1967) 34 U of Chi LR 239, 243.
4 For a corrective justice theory requiring fault, see Weinrib (1989) 34 McGill LJ 403.
5 *A Theory of Strict Liability* (1980). Cf Epstein (1987) 63 Chicago Kent Law Review 653. For a different moral explanation of strict liability, which rests on the fairness of bearing responsibility for the results of bad luck, see Honoré (1988) 104 LQR 530. For criticisms of Epstein's theory, and strict liability in general, see Stoljar *Essays on Torts* (ed Finn) (1989) ch 11; and Weinrib (1989) 34 McGill LJ 403, 411–12. See also Fletcher (1972) 85 Harv LR 537.
6 Ibid, p 71.

Strict liability for accidents has also been widely advocated by those who view loss distribution as a justification in itself for tort compensation.[7] Stemming directly from dissatisfaction with the fault system, this approach calls upon the courts to take into account insurance and other methods of spreading losses such as a manufacturer charging higher prices for its goods. Strict liability should then fall on whichever of the parties was most capable of spreading the loss or, as it can alternatively be expressed, on the party who was better able to guard against the risk of damage. The underlying rationale is that while it is fair that individuals who have suffered loss from the activities of others should be compensated, it is also fair that the burden of compensation should not fall on one pair of shoulders, but should be distributed. Fleming explains this as follows:

[I]f a certain type of loss is looked upon as the more or less inevitable by-product of a desirable but dangerous activity, it may well be just to distribute its costs among all who benefit from that activity, although it would be unfair to impose it upon each or any one of those individuals . . .[8]

Although the courts have traditionally purported to ignore insurance considerations, advocates of this theory regard some areas of traditional tort law, most notably vicarious liability, as best justified by loss distribution.

The major problem with this approach, as a justification for tort compensation, is that to apply it fully would undermine tort compensation altogether; for if loss distribution is the sole objective, a state compensation scheme where the loss can be widely distributed among, for example, all taxpayers would be the best way forward. In other words, the 'fairness' underlying loss distribution is that of distributive justice but, followed to its true conclusion, distributive justice requires compensation by the state, and to leave it to tort compensation is to adopt an unsatisfactory half-way house.

This leads finally to those, like Atiyah,[9] who consider that a state compensation scheme on the lines, for example, of the industrial injuries scheme, should replace tort compensation for accidents at least where causing personal injury or death. In contrast to all the above theories, this approach considers that distributive justice dictates state compensation, and that there is here no justification for the tort system based as it is on individual responsibility. Support for this is particularly sought in the vagaries and expense of

7 Eg Jolowicz (1968) CLJ 50.
8 *The Law of Torts* (8th edn, 1992) p 9.
9 *Atiyah's Accidents, Compensation and the Law* (5th edn, 1993) esp ch 19.

the present fault system. But arguably the tort system would be harder to attack if strict liability were to replace negligence as the general standard of liability for accidents. Moreover, it should be realised that a state compensation scheme would have no deterrent effect at all on harmful actions or activities though if this were considered a defect it could perhaps be overcome by, for example, extending the criminal law.

All in all, within the realm of accidents (and few would ever seek to deny the need for tort compensation outside that realm, for example, in the area covered by intentional torts) it is submitted that the basic moral corrective justice principle of compensating those whom one's activities have harmed, has traditionally justified, and provides a convincing reason for continuing to impose on a defendant, negative tort obligations and corresponding compensation. However there is room for debate (and it may here be relevant whether specific deterrence arguments, like Posner's, are thought valid) as to whether fixing the general standard of liability at negligence is an unsatisfactory cut-off point short of strict liability.

So far our discussion has been confined solely to negative tort obligations. But some tortious obligations, particularly those imposed by the torts of negligence or breach of statutory duty, are positive; that is, the obligation is to put the plaintiff into a better position than he would have been in if the defendant had done nothing. For example, there is often a tortious obligation to use reasonable care to ensure that a person within your control,[10] or property belonging to you,[11] does not cause personal injury or property damage to others. Again, there is often a tortious obligation to use reasonable care to ensure that a person within your control does not himself suffer personal injury or property damage;[12] and there is sometimes an obligation to use reasonable care to perform properly services that are beneficial to a plaintiff with whom one is in a relationship of close proximity.[13]

What then is the justification for positive tortious obligations, and hence for the compensatory damages for breach of them? There has been relatively little consideration of this. What there has been

---

10 Eg *Carmarthenshire County Council v Lewis* [1955] AC 549; *Home Office v Dorset Yacht Co Ltd* [1970] AC 1004. Cf *Smith v Littlewoods Organisation Ltd* [1987] AC 241.

11 Eg *Goldman v Hargrave* [1967] 1 AC 645; *Leakey v National Trust* [1980] QB 485; Occupiers' Liability Act 1957.

12 Eg *Kasapis v Laimos Bros* [1959] 2 Lloyds Rep 378; *McCallion v Dodd* [1966] NZLR 710.

13 Eg *Midland Bank Trust Co Ltd v Hett Stubbs and Kemp* [1979] Ch 384; *Junior Books Ltd v Veitchi Co Ltd* [1983] 1 AC 520.

has tended to concentrate on the classic hypothetical example of whether there should be a duty of care to rescue a drowning child. Posner[14] considers that there should be such a duty, wherever the costs of the intervention are less than the costs of the injury, ie wherever it is economically efficient to confer the benefit. Epstein, confining himself to corrective justice, considers that there should be no such duty.[15] But perhaps the courts' approach is best regarded as applying the moral principle of altruism, albeit to a limited extent. In most of the situations where a positive duty of care has been imposed, the defendant has been in a particularly good position to prevent personal injury or property damage being suffered by the plaintiff, and it is not merely efficient, but also accords with minimum altruism, that the defendant should use reasonable care to prevent such harm. Applying this, a defendant in a particularly good position to rescue a drowning child should be under a legal duty of care to do so.

Where pure economic loss is in issue the justification for imposing positive obligations seems less obvious. One possible explanation of the cases is that the courts are recognising that a negligent breach of promise is a tort, and that the promisee's expectations are being fulfilled as in an action for breach of contract. If so, it may be thought preferable to recognise the action as one for breach of contract and not for tort.[16] An alternative explanation is to say that irrespective of any promissory or expectations-engendered reasoning, the courts are applying a more extensive principle of altruism, so that those with particular skill or knowledge should use reasonable care to benefit those who are closely proximate; and that this kind of extension of legal altruism reflects the welfare-orientated values of the twentieth century. But it is submitted that such an imposed obligation of altruism would go too far in infringing an individual's freedom of action and that the preferable justification is the promissory one.

(3) Factual causation

A requirement that can be regarded as inherent in the compensatory aims is that the defendant's tort or breach of contract has been *a* cause of the plaintiff's loss. So the words, '. . . as if the tort or breach of contract had not been committed' correlate to the usual 'but for' or *sine qua non* test of factual causation; that is, the

---

14 *Economic Analysis of Law* (4th edn) pp 189–91.
15 *A Theory of Strict Liability* ch 4.
16 Supra, p 7.

plaintiff must establish that but for the tort or breach of contract he would not have suffered the loss.

It should be emphasised that for torts actionable only on proof of damage, factual causation is a factor more often concerned with whether a tort has been committed than with damages. But to provide a rounded analysis of the courts' approach, examples of factual causation are included even where they do go to liability rather than damages.

The approach to factual causation does not differ whether the plaintiff is suing for a tort or breach of contract. Nevertheless nearly all the important cases concern torts. This is because factual causation is usually a disputed issue only in respect of damages for personal injury or property damage, and such damages are generally sought in tort.

(a) The 'but for' test

The best known case showing a straightforward application of the 'but for' test is *Barnett v Chelsea and Kensington Hospital Management Committee.*[17] A night-watchman, the plaintiff's husband, called early in the morning at the defendant's hospital complaining of vomiting after drinking tea. The nurse on duty consulted a doctor by telephone and he said that the night-watchman should go home and consult his own doctor in the morning. Five hours later he was dead as a result of arsenic poisoning. In failing to examine the deceased the doctor was in breach of his duty of care but the plaintiff's action failed because she could not establish on a balance of probabilities that the doctor's negligence had been a cause of the death since, even if the deceased had been properly examined and treated, he would almost certainly still have died.

(b) Additional sufficient events

Where a tort or breach of contract was sufficient in its own right to bring about the loss and yet there was an additional sufficient event, application of the 'but for' test to each event would produce the result that neither was a cause of the loss. That result offends common sense. In this situation, therefore, the courts have departed

---

17 [1969] 1 QB 428. For other good recent examples, see *JEB Fasteners Ltd v Marks Bloom & Co* [1983] 1 All ER 583; *Tate & Lyle Industries Ltd v Greater London Council* [1983] 1 All ER 1159; *Rigby v Chief Constable of Northamptonshire* [1985] 2 All ER 985; *Wisher v Essex Area Health Authority* [1988] AC 1074; cf *McGhee v NCB* [1973] 1 WLR 1. In *Messenger Newspapers Group Ltd v National Graphical Association* [1984] IRLR 397, expenditure incurred in anticipation of a tort was held recoverable: the 'but for' test shows that this cannot be correct.

from simply applying the 'but for' test and have relied on other reasoning to decide that each event, or one or other, was a cause of the loss. This therefore represents a minor qualification to the compensatory aim being to put the plaintiff into as good a position as if the tort or breach of contract had not been committed.

Additional sufficient events may be either concurrent or successive. The classic hypothetical illustration of the former is where two independent fires, negligently started by D_1 and D_2 respectively, converge on a house and demolish it, each being sufficient on its own to demolish it. Applying the 'but for' test neither defendant's breach of duty would be regarded as a cause because each could say that the plaintiff's home would have been burnt down even if he had not committed his breach of duty.

However, it has been established that the 'but for' test is not applied in situations of concurrent sufficient events and that D_1 and D_2 can both be held liable for the loss. For example in *Crossley & Sons v Lightowler*[18] it was held to be no defence to an action for nuisance against the defendant for wrongfully polluting a river that the river was also being wrongfully polluted by others so that the plaintiffs would not have had water in a fit state for use even if the defendant had not polluted it. One can say that the justification for this is that there is no more reason to pin the loss on one tortfeasor than on the other, and hence both should be liable.

Although there is no direct authority, analogous reasoning from successive sufficient events[19] suggests that where the concurrent event is not a breach of duty but rather a natural event—for example, if one of the fires in the above example started naturally—the 'but for' test will be applied to the breach of duty so that the defendant will not be liable for the loss.

The facts of *Baker v Willoughby*[20] beautifully illustrate the problem of successive sufficient events. As a result of D_1's negligence the plaintiff suffered an injury to his left leg. Later he was the victim of an armed robbery during which he was shot in the left leg by D_2. The leg had to be amputated. D_1 argued that he was liable only for loss suffered from having an injured leg until the date of the robbery: after that time D_1's breach could not be regarded as a factual cause of that loss. But the House of Lords rejected that argument and held that as regards an action against D_1 in a situation of successive sufficient causes the 'but for' test should not be applied; D_1 should therefore be liable for the loss suffered from having an injured leg without any reduction on the ground of D_2's breach. In other words, D_1 was held liable to pay full compensation for the difference between a good and an injured leg. On the other hand, the House of Lords did consider that D_2 would only have been liable for depriving the plaintiff of an already damaged leg, which represents an acceptance of the 'but for' test in relation to D_2. This aspect is further supported by the earlier case of *Performance Cars Ltd v Abraham*.[1] The plaintiff's car was involved successively in two collisions brought about by the negligence of D_1 and D_2 respectively, and each necessitated a respray of the lower part of the bodywork. The car had not had this work done to it in between the two collisions. D_2 was held not liable, because he had not caused any additional loss in relation to what was an already damaged car.

The *Baker* approach in respect of D_1 again shows the rejection of the 'but for' test. Of the three possible solutions left of pinning the relevant loss (that is, the loss for which D_1's and D_2's acts were sufficient—here the loss suffered from an injured leg after the date of the robbery) either on D_1 alone, or on D_2 alone, or on both D_1 and D_2, the Lords in *Baker* were taking the first alternative. This seems correct. It cannot be right for the plaintiff to be worse off, as regards damages, by being the victim of two torts than if he had suffered just the first of them. And to hold D_2 liable for more than the *additional* injury would infringe the normal principle, applied in *Performance Cars Ltd v Abraham*, that whether for better or worse one takes one's victim as one finds him, a principle that attaches greater importance to events that happen first in time.

On the facts a further possible reason for favouring the first alternative was that D_2 was a man of straw. But as a matter of principle that should be irrelevant: *Baker* should still have been decided in the same way even if D_1 had been the man of straw.

But what if one of the successive sufficient events is a natural event rather than a breach of duty? In *Jobling v Associated Dairies Ltd*[2] the defendants' breach of statutory duty had caused the plaintiff to suffer a back injury which meant that he could thereafter do only light work. Three years later and before trial he was found to be suffering from a spinal disease (myelopathy) unrelated to and arising after the accident but which in itself rendered him wholly unfit to work. The defendants argued that the onset of the myelopathy ended their liability for his loss of earnings resulting from the back injury; applying the 'but for' test to the breach of duty it could not be said that the plaintiff would not have suffered the loss of

1 [1962] 1 QB 33.
2 [1982] AC 794.

earnings but for the defendants' breach of duty. Moreover, they argued that this approach is implicitly accepted in the courts' practice of reducing damages for future pecuniary loss to take account of the 'vicissitudes of life'. The plaintiff, on the other hand, contended that *Baker v Willoughby* should be analogously applied, so that the defendants remained liable for the loss of future earnings as if no spinal disease had occurred.

The House of Lords found for the defendants. Much of the reasoning in *Baker v Willoughby* was heavily criticised, but it was left open whether that decision may remain valid for successive sufficient breaches of duty. All their Lordships accepted the 'vicissitudes of life' argument and in effect therefore accepted the 'but for' test as applied to the breach of duty, but not to the natural event. But most of them also emphasised that at root the question was one of policy, and that it was only fair that the defendants' liability should here be cut down. Unfortunately there was little clear articulation of why this solution was considered fair. Lord Wilberforce thought it relevant whether or not the plaintiff would be compensated from other sources. But irrespective of that, it would seem that the fairness of the decision rests on the notion, firmly embedded in the common law, that an individual has no right to compensation for natural injury and disease. In McGregor's words:

It is one thing to protect the victims of multiple torts from falling between two stools: it is quite another to afford protection from non-tortious loss while our legal system continues to adhere to the principle that adequate compensation for injury and disease should be available only to those whose injury or disease has been tortiously inflicted.[3]

Where the successive sufficient events comprise a natural event followed by the defendant's breach of duty, the 'but for' test will be applied to the breach of duty so that the defendant will not be liable. This follows from the notion of taking one's victim as one finds him and is consistent with *Baker* and *Jobling*. It is directly supported by *Kerry v England*[4] where a druggist supplied tartar emetic (a fatal poison), instead of bismuth, for an attack of 'flu to a fatally sick patient. Damages were reduced to nil on the basis that the tartar emetic had not accelerated to any appreciable extent an already imminent death.

---

3 (1970) 33 MLR 378 at 382–3.
4 [1898] AC 742. See also *The Ferdinand Retzlaff* [1972] 2 Lloyds Rep 120 at 128.

(4) Proof of loss

(a) Standard of proof

(i) Past facts and future or hypothetical events

In applying the compensatory aims, what standard of proof of loss is required?[5]

Where in proving loss one is concerned with past facts the usual civil standard of 'proof on the balance of probabilities' is deemed appropriate. That usual standard is thought apt for facts which must be either true or false. But where in proving loss one is concerned with future or hypothetical events—the position the plaintiff will be in in the future or would have been in had there been no tort or breach of contract—the balance of probabilities standard is inapt. Instead full damages are only awarded if the plaintiff can prove his loss with reasonable certainty. Below that, damages—sometimes referred to as 'speculative damages'—can be awarded in proportion to the chance of that loss. No damages at all are recoverable where the chance of the loss is entirely speculative.

In *Mallett v McMonagle*[6] Lord Diplock summarised the law as follows:

In determining what did happen in the past a court decides on the balance of probabilities. Anything that is more probable than not it treats as certain. But in assessing damages which depend upon its view as to what will happen in the future or would have happened in the past, the court must make an estimate as to what are the chances that a particular thing will or would have happened and reflect those chances, whether they are more or less than even, in the amount of damages which it awards.

The leading case (and one which has commonly been misinterpreted) is *Hotson v East Berkshire Area HA*.[7] The plaintiff injured his hip in a fall. The medical staff at the defendant's hospital incorrectly diagnosed his injury and he was sent home. After five days of severe pain he returned to the hospital where the medical staff realised its earlier mistake. The plaintiff developed a permanent hip disability and brought an action for negligence against the defendant claiming that if his injury had been properly diagnosed at the start his permanent disability would have been avoided. Simon Brown J found that even if the defendant had treated the plaintiff properly there

---

5 See generally Cooper (1972–3) 37 Sask LR 193.
6 [1970] AC 166, 176.
7 [1987] AC 750. See also *Davies v Taylor* [1974] AC 207, esp at 212–13, 219–20; *Malec v JC Hutton Pty Ltd* (1990) 169 CLR 638.

was still a 75% chance that his disability would have developed. Nevertheless he awarded the plaintiff damages (of 25% of the full damages) for being deprived by the defendant's negligence of the 25% chance of avoiding the disability.

In overturning that award the House of Lords stressed that what was in question was a matter of past fact to which the all or nothing balance of probabilities standard of proof applied. Lord Bridge said, 'This was a conflict, like any other about some relevant past event, which the judge could not avoid resolving on a balance of probabilities.'[8] In Lord Ackner's words, '. . . the judge had determined as a matter of fact, on the balance of probabilities, that the compression and blocking of the blood vessels had had no effect on the plaintiff's ultimate condition. In determining what happened in the past the court decides on the balance of probabilities. Anything that is more probable than not is treated as certainty . . .'[9] And according to Lord Mackay, '. . . the fundamental question of fact to be answered in this case related to a point in time before the negligent failure to treat began. It must, therefore, be a matter of past fact. It did not raise any question of what might have been the situation in a hypothetical state of facts.'[10]

So applying the balance of probabilities test to the judge's findings, the Lords concluded that the plaintiff's claim failed in that he had not established that the negligence of the defendant had caused his hip disability.

Simon Brown J had regarded the crucial question as being whether causation or quantification of damage was in issue (with the all or nothing balance of probabilities approach applying to the former but not to the latter). And he had come to the conclusion that on the facts quantification, not causation, was in point. The House of Lords disagreed. But the very distinction between causation and quantification may be misleading in that it does not perfectly match the true distinction—applied by the Lords — between past fact and hypothetical or future events. For example, if a plaintiff who has indisputably been injured by the defendant's negligence claims damages for pain suffered and expenses incurred, the questions of whether that pain has been suffered or the expenses incurred must be decided on the balance of probabilities albeit that they are most naturally regarded as going to quantification rather than causation. And while in almost all cases the question of whether a personal injury has been *caused by* the defendant's breach

8 Ibid at 782.
9 Ibid at 792.
10 Ibid at 785.

of duty (whether a tort or breach of contract) is one of past fact, this is not invariably so. For example, it may be that an illness would have been averted if a doctor had been promptly called and had prescribed one particular type of medicine. If the uncertainty on causation revolves around whether the doctor would have exercised his judgment to choose the one type of medicine, damages could be awarded for the loss of the chance of avoiding the illness.

(ii) Where the uncertainty concerns future or hypothetical events

At the top end of the scale full damages can be awarded for a loss that is proved to a standard of reasonable certainty. So in *Ratcliffe v Evans*[11] Bowen LJ said:

> As much certainty and particularity must be insisted on, both in pleading and proof of damage, as is reasonable, having regard to the circumstances and to the nature of the acts themselves by which the damage is done. To insist upon less would be to relax old and intelligible principles. To insist upon more would be the vainest pedantry.

This means that full damages may be awarded for a loss even though there is some doubt whether that loss has been or will be incurred. Reasonable certainty is therefore a notch down from absolute certainty.

Interestingly, in the United States in the nineteenth century some types of loss, especially contractual loss of profits, had to be proved with certainty. As such, and in contrast to England, certainty played a vigorous role in restricting damages alongside limiting principles, like remoteness and the duty to mitigate. During the twentieth century this high standard has been relaxed so that, in the United States too, the standard required is now one of reasonable certainty.[12]

Even though a loss cannot be proved with reasonable certainty, some damages may be awarded in proportion to the chance of loss. The leading case is *Chaplin v Hicks*.[13] The defendant, a theatrical manager, in a newspaper beauty competition, offered theatrical engagements to those 12 contestants whom he should choose after interview from the 50 who secured the greatest number of votes of the newspaper's readers. 6,000 people entered the contest and the plaintiff succeeded in becoming one of the 50 to be interviewed. However, because of the defendant's breach, the plaintiff was not

---

11 [1892] 2 QB 524 at 532–3.
12 Farnsworth *Contracts* (2nd edn, 1990) p 922; *McCormick on Damages* (1935) ch 4.
13 [1911] 2 KB 786. See also *Hall v Meyrick* [1957] 2 QB 455 (reversed on other grounds); *Kitchen v Royal Air Force Association* [1959] 1 WLR 563; *Mulvaine v Joseph* (1968) 112 Sol Jo 927.

informed of the interview in time and the 12 winners were chosen in her absence from the remaining 49. The Court of Appeal held that while the plaintiff could not recover for the loss of a theatrical engagement, since she could not establish to the required degree of proof that she would have been one of the 12, nevertheless she should be given damages for the loss of the chance of being one of the 12 (ie about a 25% chance).

The same approach of awarding damages in proportion to the lost chances of gain is commonly shown in personal injury and death cases by future earnings and dependency awards which take into account the contingencies of life.[14]

However, the plaintiff cannot recover any damages if he cannot establish that the chance of the gain was more than very small ie if the chance of the gain was entirely speculative. The classic hypothetical example was given by Erle CJ in *Priestley v Maclean*:[15] '. . . supposing a lady to have been injured and disfigured in a railway accident, she could not say that she ought to recover damages because she was prevented from going to a ball, at which she might have met a rich husband.' In *Davies v Taylor*[16] the principle was applied in relation to a claim under the Fatal Accidents Act by a wife, who had deserted the deceased husband, and the latter had begun divorce proceedings against her. It was held that she had no claim because she could show nothing more than a 'speculative possibility'[17] of a reconciliation, and hence a pecuniary gain, had the husband lived.

The above examples have all concerned lost chances of gain, but the same approach of awarding damages in proportion to the chance of loss also applies where it is the chance of a worsening of the plaintiff's existing position that is in issue. The most common examples are in personal injury cases, where there is a chance of the plaintiff developing epilepsy or osteo-arthritis.[18] Presumably again, there must be more than a mere speculative possibility of the illness or disability developing.

(iii) Is the conventional distinction satisfactory?

Although the distinction between the approach to past fact and to future or hypothetical events is now well-established, it can be

14 Infra, pp 200, 215.
15 (1860) 2 F & F 288 at 289.
16 [1974] AC 207. See also *Fielding v Variety Inc* [1967] 2 QB 841—the Court of Appeal reduced damages for injurious falsehood from £10,000 to £100 because the loss was almost entirely speculative.
17 Ibid at 219 (per Viscount Dilhorne).
18 *Jones v Griffiths* [1969] 1 WLR 795 at 801.

criticised as too simplistic. If the state of medical and scientific knowledge is such that past facts necessarily cannot be determined with certainty, wherein lies the justification for treating them differently from future or hypothetical events? In his masterly dissenting judgment in *Commonwealth of Australia v Amann Aviation Pty Ltd*,[19] which concerned reliance damages for breach of contract, Deane J said the following:

> It is true that Lord Reid's reasons for rejecting the balance of probability test in the circumstances of *Davies v Taylor* could be applied equally to some categories of case in which a court is concerned with the determination of past facts. That does not mean, however, that the traditional approach for determining past facts should be applied to a case requiring the assessment of damages on the basis of what would have happened or will happen. To the contrary, it lends support for the view that there is a need for modification or reassessment in some categories of case of the conventional approach that, in assessing damages for what has occurred in the past, a court decides on the balance of probabilities and assumes certainty where none in truth exists.

It remains to be seen whether, in line with Deane J's dicta, the courts will consider it necessary to carve out exceptions to the all or nothing approach to past facts. But it may be doubted whether it is possible to recognise exceptions without shattering the conventional distinction altogether.

(iv) Sometimes loss is presumed

In several types of case English law eases the burden on the plaintiff by presuming that loss has been suffered: in other words, damages are sometimes 'at large'. The tort of defamation is probably the most important in this respect,[20] but the same applies, for example, to trespass to goods,[1] and inducing breach of contract.[2] Very similar is the tort of injurious falsehood, where although loss will not be presumed, proof of general loss of business is sufficient and the plaintiff does not need to prove the loss of any particular customer or contract.[3] The one clear case of loss being presumed for breach of contract is in respect of pecuniary loss of reputation, caused by the defendant's failure to honour the plaintiff's cheques.[4]

---

19 (1991) 66 ALJR 123, 147. See also, eg Fleming (1991) 70 CBR 136, 140–41.
20 *Tripp v Thomas* (1824) 3 B & C 427; *Ley v Hamilton* (1935) 153 LT 384.
1 *GWK Ltd v Dunlop Rubber Co Ltd* (1926) 42 TLR 376.
2 *Exchange Telegraph Co Ltd v Gregory & Co* [1896] 1 QB 147; *Goldsoll v Goldman* [1914] 2 Ch 603.
3 *Ratcliffe v Evans* [1892] 2 QB 524.
4 *Rolin v Steward* (1854) 14 CB 595; *Wilson v United Countries Bank Ltd* [1920] AC 102.

(b) Difficulty of assessment is not a bar

Where loss or a more than speculative chance of loss has been proved or is presumed, a court will do its best to assess damages even if the assessment is difficult and is necessarily imprecise. So in *Chaplin v Hicks*[5] Vaughan Williams LJ said:

> . . . it may be that the amount [of damages] . . . will really be a matter of guesswork. But the fact that damages cannot be assessed with certainty does not relieve the wrongdoer of the necessity of paying damages for his breach of contract.

The most obvious example of difficulty of assessment is in respect of damages for non-pecuniary loss, such as loss of amenity or pain and suffering. Lord Halsbury LC emphasised the point in *The Mediana*:[6]

> How is anybody to measure pain and suffering in moneys counted? Nobody can suggest that you can by arithmetical calculation establish what is the exact sum of money which would represent such a thing as the pain and suffering which a person has undergone by reason of an accident . . . But nevertheless the law recognises that as a topic upon which damages may be given.

But the same sort of approach applies also to pecuniary loss. For example, in *Simpson v London and North Western Rly Co*,[7] the plaintiff was a manufacturer who displayed samples of his goods at shows in order to attract custom. The defendants in breach of contract failed to deliver the samples in time for a particular show. The plaintiff recovered damages from the defendants for loss of custom and the defendants' argument that damages for the loss of custom could not be awarded because the amount of damages could not be precisely assessed was rejected.

2. PRINCIPLES LIMITING COMPENSATORY DAMAGES

There can be said to be five[8] principles limiting compensatory damages (ie which reduce the damages that full adherence to the compensatory aims would dictate) for both torts and breach of

5 [1911] 2 KB 786 at 792.
6 [1900] AC 113 at 116.
7 (1876) 1 QBD 274.
8 Consent, *volenti non fit injuria* and *ex turpi causa* are not considered because these defences are practically always concerned with liability rather than with damages. Exclusion and limitation clauses are also omitted because, taken together, they are not purely concerned with restricting remedies and, in any

contract, and the role played by each can be briefly described as follows:

Remoteness—A plaintiff cannot succeed if the loss was too remote from the breach of duty.[9] The tests for remoteness centre on reasonable foreseeability or contemplation of the loss.

Intervening cause—A plaintiff cannot succeed if an intervening cause is so much more responsible for the loss than the defendant's breach of duty that it breaks the chain of causation between the breach of duty and the loss.

Duty to mitigate—A plaintiff cannot succeed if subsequent to the tort or breach of contract he could reasonably have avoided the loss.

Contributory negligence—Damages are reduced where the plaintiff's negligence has contributed to, ie been a partial cause of, his loss. But this principle is not applicable to some torts and is generally inapplicable to breach of contract.

Impecuniosity—In *The Liesbosch*[10] (a tort case), the House of Lords held that loss flowing from the plaintiff's lack of financial means was irrecoverable. The validity of this is now in doubt.

Five introductory points need to be made regarding these principles. First, for torts actionable only on proof of damage, such as negligence, and in contrast to torts actionable per se and breach of contract, remoteness and intervening cause are often concerned with establishing whether a tort has been committed (ie liability) rather than with damages. But in order to provide a full picture of the courts' approach to those principles they will here be examined even when they are concerned with establishing tort liability.

Secondly, since all these principles are concerned to limit compensatory damages it is not at all surprising that the same result may often be reached by applying more than one of them. So, for example, in *Compania Financiera Soleada SA v Hamoor Tanker Corpn Inc, The Borag*,[11] where the issue was the recoverability of interest charges paid on a loan taken out by the plaintiff as a consequence of the defendant's breach of contract, Templeman LJ said, '. . . in the present case if the interest charges were unreasonable, they were too

---

event, space prevents an adequate examination of them. See generally Treitel *The Law of Contract* (8th edn) ch 7. Also not examined are special statutory provisions limiting damages: eg Merchant Shipping Act 1979, s 17; Carriage by Air Act 1961, Sch 1, art 22; Carriage of Passengers by Road Act 1974, Sch 1, art 13(1).

9 Breach of duty is throughout used as shorthand for breach of contract, tort actionable per se, or in the case of a tort actionable only on proof of damage, breach of duty.

10 *Owners of the Dredger Liesbosch v Owners of SS Edison* [1933] AC 449.

11 [1981] 1 All ER 856.

remote: they were not caused by the breach; they were not part of a reasonable form of mitigation; all these matters hang together.'[12] But normally just one of these principles will be used to limit damages.

Thirdly, the distinction between remoteness and intervening cause is often not drawn and both principles are dealt with under the one head, whether labelled 'remoteness' or 'legal causation' or 'proximate cause'. This is perfectly acceptable since both principles are essentially concerned with the same policy, namely that, as explained by Lord Wright in *The Liesbosch*, '. . . the law cannot take account of everything that follows a wrongful act: it regards some subsequent matters as outside the scope of its selection . . . In the varied web of affairs, the law must abstract some consequences as relevant not perhaps on grounds of pure logic, but simply for practical reasons.'[13] In Ogus' words, 'A line has to be drawn somewhere so that the burden of liability will not crush those who have to pay the bill.'[14] However in this book it has been considered helpful to separate remoteness and intervening cause for not only has each got a different focus of attention but also the principles applied to each are not the same.

Fourthly, where the plaintiff's unreasonable conduct subsequent to the tort or breach of contract has been a cause of his suffering loss, both the duty to mitigate and intervening cause *can* be regarded as denying damages for exactly the same reason. Hence in this situation the courts sometimes use the principles interchangeably.[15] But generally they are distinguished by using the duty to mitigate for the plaintiff's unreasonable inaction, ie his failure to minimise loss, while using intervening cause breaking the chain of causation for the plaintiff's unreasonable action, ie his augmenting of loss.[16] However, where the unreasonable action comprises incurring expense, this is generally viewed as an aspect of the duty to

12 Ibid at 864.
13 [1933] AC 449 at 460.
14 *The Law of Damages* (1973) (hereinafter cited as *Damages*) p 67.
15 Eg *Compania Naviera Maropan SA v Bowaters Lloyd Pulp and Paper Mills Ltd* [1955] 2 QB 68; *The Borag* [1981] 1 All ER 856 (per Templeman LJ); *Emeh v Kensington and Chelsea and Westminster Area Health Authority* [1984] 3 All ER 1044; *Schering Agrochemicals Ltd v Resibel NV SA* (26 November 1992, unreported) (per Purchas LJ).
16 For express recognition of this, see *Schering Agrochemicals Ltd v Resibel NV SA* unreported (per Nolan LJ). A different distinction was drawn by Scott LJ in that case and by Phillips J in *Youell v Bland Welch & Co (No 2)* [1990] 2 Lloyd's Rep 431, 461–2 to the effect that a duty to mitigate only arises once the plaintiff has actual knowledge of the breach: for criticism of that, see Burrows (1993) 109 LQR 175.

mitigate rather than intervening cause. These general usages are adopted in this book.

The role of contributory negligence (if applicable to the tort or breach of contract in question) also needs to be clarified in this situation. In particular it should be realised that contributory negligence has been applied to the plaintiff's negligence occurring subsequently to, as well as prior to or contemporaneously with, a tort.[17] Therefore the essential distinction between contributory negligence on the one hand, and intervening cause and the duty to mitigate on the other, is that the former is a partial defence while the latter two are total defences; ie if a plaintiff has broken the chain of causation to the loss, or has failed in his duty to mitigate that loss, he cannot recover any damages for it, whereas if he has been contributorily negligent in relation to that loss, his damages are merely reduced to the extent that this is thought just and equitable.[18]

Finally, the authorities are unclear (except with regard to contributory negligence)[19] as to who has the burden of proof in relation to these limiting principles.[20] In terms of policy probably the best view is that once the plaintiff has proved a breach of duty, factual causation and his loss—that is, once he has shown that prima facie he merits compensation—it should be for the defendant to prove that one of these limiting principles applies to reduce the damages.

(1) Remoteness

A principal restriction on compensatory damages is that the loss must not be too remote from the breach of duty. The tests formulated for deciding on this have centred on whether the loss was (in contract) reasonably contemplated or (in tort) reasonably foreseeable by the defendant. While broadly similar these tests have, in their detail, been traditionally regarded as having significant

---

17 *The Calliope* [1970] P 172.
18 It is for this reason that *Tennant Radiant Heat Ltd v Warrington Development Corpn* [1988] 1 EGLR 41 is controversial as a decision on causation (as opposed to contributory negligence).
19 *SS Heranger (Owners) v SS Diamond (Owners)* [1939] AC 94 at 104 (burden on defendant).
20 Putting the burden on the plaintiff are eg *SS Singleton Abbey (Owners) v SS Paludina (Owners)* [1927] AC 16 (intervening cause); *Selvanayagam v University of West Indies* [1983] 1 All ER 824 (duty to mitigate). Putting the burden on the defendant are eg *Philco Radio and Television Corpn of Great Britain Ltd v Spurling Ltd* [1949] 2 KB 33 (intervening cause); *Roper v Johnson* (1873) LR 8 CP 167; *Garnac Grain Co Inc v Faure & Fairclough Ltd* [1968] AC 1130n (duty to mitigate).

differences. The full recognition of concurrent liability, and the expansion of the recovery of pure economic loss in the tort of negligence, have rendered these differences particularly interesting, important, and controversial. Moreover, some doubt has fairly recently been cast on the traditional view by the Court of Appeal in *H Parsons Ltd v Uttley Ingham & Co Ltd*,[1] a contract case. The *Parsons* case, and this central issue of whether the tests are different, will be examined in depth in the contract section.

In policy terms the remoteness restriction is based on the view that it is unfair to a defendant, and imposes too great a burden, to hold him responsible for losses that he could not have reasonably contemplated or foreseen. It has also been regarded as having an economic efficiency rationale in encouraging the disclosure of information regarding unusual potential losses, so that the defendant with full knowledge of the risks involved can plan and act rationally.[2]

(a) Torts

(i) The Wagon Mound test

Remoteness for torts has been primarily discussed judicially in relation to the tort of negligence; but as is explained below, it seems that with the exception of deceit, and the possible exception of the other intentional torts, the test applied to negligence applies to all other torts.

The old test for remoteness was that laid down in *Re Polemis and Furniss Withy & Co*:[3] according to this, a defendant was liable for all the direct consequences of his negligence suffered by the plaintiff whether a reasonable man would have foreseen them or not. But *Re Polemis* was effectively overruled by *Overseas Tankship (UK) Ltd v Morts Dock & Engineering Co Ltd, The Wagon Mound*[4] which established that consequences are too remote if a reasonable man would not have foreseen them. Here the defendants carelessly discharged oil from their ship into a harbour. Over two days later, molten metal from the plaintiff's welding operations on the wharf set fire to the oil on the water. The plaintiff's wharf was severely damaged. The Privy Council held that the defendants were not liable in

---

1 [1978] 1 All ER 525.
2 Posner *Economic Analysis of Law* (4th edn) pp 126–8; Beale *Remedies* p 180.
3 [1921] 3 KB 560. Davies (1982) 45 MLR 534.
4 [1961] AC 388.

negligence because, while they could have reasonably foreseen damage to the wharf by fouling, they could not have reasonably foreseen that the wharf would be damaged by fire when they carelessly discharged the oil. Viscount Simonds said: 'It is the foresight of the reasonable man which alone can determine responsibility. The *Polemis* rule by substituting "direct" for "reasonably foreseeable" consequence leads to a conclusion equally illogical and unjust.'[5] The illogicality he was referring to was that under *Re Polemis* the test for the extent of the defendant's liability (directness) differed from that for the existence of liability (reasonable foreseeability).

However, in applying the *Wagon Mound* the courts have chosen not to restrict the defendant's liability to the degree indicated by the reasoning of Viscount Simonds. Rather 'reasonable foreseeability' has been loosely adhered to, so that the results produced differ little from those that would have been reached under *Re Polemis*. This represents a policy view that fairness to the defendant does not dictate quite such a rigid cutting off point as that favoured by Viscount Simonds. Five features of this loose case-law application of the *Wagon Mound* merit particular consideration.

First, so long as the type of physical damage which has resulted was reasonably foreseeable at the time of the negligence, neither the actual manner in which it came about nor its actual extent needs to have been reasonably foreseeable.[6] *Hughes v Lord Advocate*[7] is the classic illustration. Post office workmen left an open manhole, in which they had been working, covered by a shelter tent and surrounded by warning paraffin lamps. The plaintiff, aged eight, was playing with one of the lamps when he stumbled over it and knocked it into the hole. An explosion followed and the plaintiff was thrown into the manhole and was severely burned. The defendants were held liable because while it was not reasonably foreseeable that a child would be burned as a result of the actual sequence of events that had occurred, it was reasonably foreseeable that a child could be burned by playing with one of the gas-lamps. Nor did it matter that the burns were more serious than those that were reasonably foreseeable. Similarly in *Vacwell Engineering Co Ltd v BDH Chemicals Ltd*,[8] the defendants supplied a chemical and carelessly failed to attach a warning that it was liable to explode in water. A scientist working for the plaintiffs placed a consignment in

---

5 Ibid at 424.
6 *Doughty v Turner Manufacturing Co Ltd* [1964] 1 QB 518 is difficult to reconcile with this principle.
7 [1963] AC 837.
8 [1971] 1 QB 88.

a sink and a violent explosion ensued causing extensive damage. The defendants were held liable because a minor explosion causing some property damage was reasonably foreseeable, and it did not matter that the magnitude of the explosion and the actual extent of the damage could not reasonably have been foreseen.

Goff LJ's judgment in the negligence case of *Muirhead v Industrial Tank Specialities Ltd*[9] contains an excellent passage stressing the need for only the type of physical damage to be reasonably foreseeable:

. . . the true question to which the judge should have addressed his mind was simply whether damage of the relevant *type* was reasonably foreseeable by the manufacturers, ie physical harm to fish stored in a tank at a fish farm . . . If he had found that damage of that type was reasonably foreseeable, then the fact that, by reason of the full stocking of the relevant tank, the fish died more quickly or in greater quantity was of no relevance, unless it could be said that overstocking of the tank constituted the sole or contributory cause of the disaster which took place.[10]

Applying this, the manufacturers of defective circulation pumps were held liable for the loss of the plaintiff's entire stock of lobsters.

Secondly, the notion that it is the type of physical damage that needs to be reasonably foreseeable allows the courts considerable discretion in how wide to extend the defendant's liability, for opinions can differ as to how to divide up types of damage. Two cases can be usefully contrasted. In *Bradford v Robinson Rentals Ltd*[11] the defendant employers exposed the plaintiff van driver to extreme cold in the course of his duties and in consequence he suffered frostbite. It was held that a common cold, pneumonia or chilblains were reasonably foreseeable and since frostbite was of the same type of harm as these the defendants were liable. On the other hand, in *Tremain v Pike*,[12] the rat population on the defendants' farm was allowed to become unduly large and the plaintiff, a herdsman on the farm, contracted a rare disease, Weil's disease, through coming into contact with rat's urine. Payne J held that the defendants were not liable, for while the effects of a rat bite or food poisoning from contaminated food were reasonably foreseeable, Weil's disease was not and was 'entirely different in kind'[13] from such consequences.

Thirdly, the 'thin skull' principle, that the defendant takes his

9 [1986] QB 507. See also *Ogwo v Taylor* [1988] AC 431, 444–5.
10 Ibid at 532.
11 [1967] 1 All ER 267.
12 [1969] 1 WLR 1556.
13 Ibid at 1561.

victim in the physical condition he finds him in, survives. A good example of it is *Smith v Leech Brain & Co Ltd*[14] in which a negligently inflicted burn on the plaintiff's husband's lip resulted in his dying of cancer, because he was suffering from pre-malignant cancer and this was caused to develop by the burn. The defendants were held liable for his death. Lord Parker CJ's reasoning suggests that the thin-skull principle is merely an aspect of the principle looked at above: that so long as the type of damage which has resulted was reasonably foreseeable, its actual extent need not have been; but it is probably preferable, so as to avoid deciding whether the type of damage is the same as that which could have been reasonably foreseen, to regard the thin-skull principle as separate.

Fourthly, the *Wagon Mound* has not affected the principle that it is no bar to recovery that the pecuniary value of property damage or the loss of earnings/dependency resulting from personal injury or death is far greater than could reasonably have been foreseen.[15] So if the defendant negligently injures a millionaire or negligently damages an antique vase, it is no defence that he could not reasonably have foreseen that the loss of earnings or pecuniary value would be so great and he will be liable so long as the personal injury or property damage was reasonably foreseeable. One *can* say that this follows logically because the damage itself is foreseeable, and it is merely the quantum that is unexpectedly high. But the line between damage and quantum is not an easy one to draw. Ultimately then the principle is best seen as a policy decision that such loss should not be regarded as too remote, even though unforeseeable. However, it is doubtful whether this principle extends to profits consequent on physical damage or to other pecuniary loss.[16]

Finally, what degree of likelihood of the loss occurring is required under the *Wagon Mound* test? This has rarely been discussed in the tort cases themselves. The main exception was *The Wagon Mound (No 2)*,[17] which arose out of the same fire that produced *The Wagon Mound*. In this case, however, the plaintiffs were the owners of the damaged ship rather than the wharf owners, and they sued in nuisance and negligence. Somewhat different evidence was presented than in the first case and the Privy Council decided that the damage to the ship by the fire was not too remote, since it was reasonably

14 [1962] 2 QB 405. See also *Brice v Brown* [1984] 1 All ER 997.
15 The usually cited authority is the dictum in Scutton LJ's dissent in *The Arpad* [1934] P 189 at 202.
16 But see *The Liesbosch* [1933] AC 449 at 463–4; *The Argentino* (1889) 14 App Cas 519 at 523.
17 *Overseas Tankship (UK) v Miller SS Co Pty Ltd (The Wagon Mound No 2)* [1967] 1 AC 617.

foreseeable. One *can* distinguish the two *Wagon Mound* decisions because of the different facts found, but it does appear from the use of phrases like 'real risk' that in the second case, in contrast to the first, the Privy Council considered that only a low degree of likelihood of the loss occurring need be reasonably foreseeable in order for the loss to be recoverable. Thus Smith has written that *The Wagon Mound (No 2)*, 'makes a substantial change in *The Wagon Mound* rule in that it limits . . . the test of foreseeability of damage to possibility rather than to probability.'[18] Furthermore the House of Lords in *The Heron II*[19] (a contract case), in contrasting the contract and tort remoteness tests, emphasised that the tort test requires only a low degree of likelihood of the loss to be reasonably foreseeable. Similarly, in *H Parsons Ltd v Uttley & Co Ltd*[20] (a contract case) Lord Denning MR said that the *Wagon Mound* test was reasonable foreseeability at the time of the breach of the type of loss occurring *as a slight possibility*.

(ii) Is the Wagon Mound *the test for remoteness for all torts?*

The *Wagon Mound* test was applied to the tort of nuisance in *The Wagon Mound (No 2)*. It has also recently been applied by the House of Lords to liability under *Rylands v Fletcher*[1] in *Cambridge Water Co v Eastern Counties Leather plc*.[2] These cases strongly suggest that the *Wagon Mound* test is the appropriate remoteness test for all unintentional torts even though the liability is strict (as under *Rylands v Fletcher* and, arguably, nuisance) in the sense that the defendant may be held liable despite the fact that he has taken all reasonable care to avoid harm to others.[3]

However, as far as the tort of deceit is concerned the Court of Appeal in *Doyle v Olby (Ironmongers) Ltd*[4] considered that reasonable foreseeability was too restrictive a test. Lord Denning said: 'the defendant is bound to make reparation for all the actual damages directly flowing from the fraudulent inducement . . . All such damages can be recovered: and it does not lie in the mouth of the fraudulent person to say that they could not reasonably have been

18 *Studies in Canadian Tort Law* (ed Linden) (1968) p 102.
19 *Koufos v Czarnikow Ltd, The Heron II* [1969] 1 AC 350.
20 [1978] 1 All ER 525.
 1 (1868) LR 3 HL 330.
 2 [1994] 1 All ER 53.
 3 This is also supported by *Winfield & Jolowicz on Tort* (13th edn, 1989) pp 142, 440–1, 463–4; and *Clerk & Lindsell on Torts* (16th edn, 1989) para 10-156. For a contrary view in respect of liability under the Animals Act 1971, see North *The Modern Law of Animals* (1971) pp 47, 58, 107–8.
 4 [1969] 2 QB 158.

foreseen.'[5] This seems to indicate the survival of the *Polemis* test for the tort of deceit and it may be that the same should apply to other intentional torts on the ground that there is less justification for showing leniency and limiting compensatory damages where the defendant intentionally committed the tort.

Unfortunately the remoteness test laid down in *Doyle v Olby* was applied by the Court of Appeal in *Royscot Trust Ltd v Rogerson*[6] to a claim for negligent misrepresentation brought under s 2(1) of the Misrepresentation Act 1967. This was on the ground that the 'fiction of fraud' wording used in the subsection left the court with no alternative but to apply the same test of remoteness as for deceit. This is a most unsatisfactory approach for it cannot be sensible to apply a different remoteness test under the Act than to the closely analogous common law tort of negligent misrepresentation. And the rejection of the *Wagon Mound* only seems justifiable where, as in deceit, there is a high degree of blameworthiness by the tortfeasor. Moreover the words in s 2(1) do not need to be read as dictating that the rules applicable to assessing damages for deceit apply in exactly the same way in every respect to claims under s 2(1).[7]

(iii) The effect of H Parsons Ltd v Uttley Ingham & Co Ltd[8]

It is arguable that the judgments in the Court of Appeal in this contract case suggest that even for torts for which it is indisputably the general test, such as negligence, the *Wagon Mound* should not always be the tort test. For example, perhaps a stricter test should be applied where loss of profit is in issue, or where there is a contractual (or similar) relationship between the parties. This is discussed further in the next section.

(b) Breach of contract[9]

(i) What is the test for remoteness and how does it relate to the Wagon Mound *test?*

The contract remoteness test has been dealt with in four main cases. The first was *Hadley v Baxendale*.[10] The plaintiff's mill was

5 Ibid at 167.
6 [1991] 2 QB 297.
7 For an historical argument to the contrary, written before the *Royscot* case, see Cartwright (1987) Conv 423 .
8 [1978] 1 All ER 525.
9 For an excellent discussion, see Beale *Remedies* pp 179–87. See also Whincup (1992) NLJ 389, 433. For a comparative account, see Treitel *Remedies for Breach of Contract* pp 150–62.
10 (1854) 9 Exch 341. Danzig (1975) 4 J Legal Studies 249.

brought to a standstill by a broken crank-shaft. The plaintiff engaged the defendant carrier to take it to Greenwich as a pattern for a new one, but in breach of contract the defendant delayed delivery. The plaintiff claimed damages for loss of profit arising from the fact that the mill was stopped for longer than it would have been if there had been no delay. All the carrier knew was 'that the article to be carried was the broken shaft of a mill and that the plaintiffs were millers of that mill.'[11] The court held that the loss of profit was too remote and that therefore the carriers were not liable for it.

The test for remoteness was laid down in two rules by Alderson B. He said:

Where two parties have made a contract which one of them has broken, the damages which the other party ought to receive in respect of such breach of contract, should be such as may fairly and reasonably be considered, either arising naturally, ie according to the usual course of things from such breach of contract itself, or such as may reasonably be supposed to have been in the contemplation of both parties, at the time they made the contract as the probable result of the breach of it.[12]

On the facts neither of these two rules was satisfied; the loss was not the natural consequence because it was felt that in the great multitude of cases the absence of a shaft would not cause a stoppage at a mill as usually a mill-owner would have another shaft in reserve or be able to get one; nor was the loss in the contemplation of both parties because the special circumstance that the mill could not re-start until the shaft came back was not known to the defendant.

In the second case of the quartet, *Victoria Laundry (Windsor) Ltd v Newman Industries Ltd*,[13] the plaintiffs, launderers and dyers, decided to extend their business and contracted to buy a boiler from the defendants. The defendants knew that the plaintiffs wanted the boiler for immediate use in their business, but in breach of contract delivered the boiler five months late. The plaintiffs claimed damages for the loss of profits that would have resulted from using the boiler, including damages for the exceptional loss of profits that they would have been able to gain from contracts made with the Ministry of Supply. The Court of Appeal held, applying *Hadley v Baxendale*, that damages should be awarded for ordinary loss of profits but not for the exceptional loss of profits. The exceptional profits were too remote because they did not arise naturally

11 Ibid at 355.
12 Ibid at 354.
13 [1949] 2 KB 528.

and were not in the contemplation of the parties at the time of contracting since the defendants knew nothing about the Ministry of Supply contracts. What is particularly interesting is that Asquith LJ rightly took the view that the two rules of *Hadley v Baxendale* could be reformulated as a single rule, centring on reasonable contemplation or, as he preferred, reasonable foreseeability, if one remembered that it was not only what the defendant actually contemplated or foresaw that was important, but also what he should have reasonably contemplated or foreseen if he had thought about the breach at the time of contracting.

In *Heron II*[14] a ship was chartered to carry sugar from Constanza to Basrah. At the time of contracting the plaintiff charterer intended to sell the sugar as soon as it reached Basrah. The defendant shipowner did not actually know this but did know that there was a market for sugar at Basrah. In breach of contract the shipowner reached Basrah nine days late. During those nine days the market price of sugar at Basrah fell and the plaintiff claimed damages for the profit lost by reason of that fall. The House of Lords held that he should recover such damages because the loss of profit was not too remote. Concentration focused on what degree of likelihood of the loss occurring was required to have been reasonably contemplated by the defendant at the time of the contract and, in particular, whether it was the same degree of likelihood of loss occurring that was required under the tort test of remoteness laid down in *The Wagon Mound*. The Law Lords agreed that a higher likelihood of the loss occurring was required in contract than in tort, but unfortunately there was no clear consensus as to how that higher degree of likelihood should be expressed. However, perhaps the best way of expressing what was said, which fits in with Lord Denning's interpretation in *Parsons v Uttley Ingham*,[15] is that while a slight possibility of the loss occurring is required in tort, a serious possibility is required in contract; so losses that are too remote in contract may not be too remote in tort. Taking this view the full contract test applied in *Heron II* can be regarded as follows: loss is too remote if the defendant could not reasonably have contemplated that loss as a serious possibility, if he had thought or did think about the breach at the time the contract was made.

Finally, we come to the complex case of *Parsons v Uttley Ingham*. The defendants supplied to the plaintiffs a hopper for storing pig food; in breach of contract they failed to provide for proper ventilation so that food became mouldy and many of the plaintiffs' pigs

14 [1969] 1 AC 350.
15 [1978] 1 All ER 525.

died from a rare intestinal disease. The plaintiffs claimed damages for the loss of the pigs in contract. All three Court of Appeal judges agreed that such loss was not too remote. But the reasoning of Lord Denning differed from that of the majority, Scarman and Orr LJJ.

To take Lord Denning's reasoning first, in his opinion there are two contract remoteness tests depending on the nature of the loss.[16] To loss of profit, the stricter so-called contract test should be applied; '. . . the defaulting party is only liable for the consequences if they are such as, at the time of the contract, he ought reasonably to have contemplated them as a serious possibility or real danger'.[17] As *Hadley v Baxendale, Victoria Laundry*, and *Heron II* all dealt with loss of profits, this was why, according to Lord Denning, the stricter test was there applied. On the other hand, as regards physical damage, ie personal injury or damage to property, or expenses incurred, Lord Denning considered that the less strict *Wagon Mound*, so-called tort test, should be applied. By this '. . . the defaulting party is liable for any loss or expense which he ought reasonably to have foreseen at the time of the breach as a possible consequence even if it was only a slight possibility'.[18] As this case was concerned with physical damage (loss of pigs) Lord Denning applied the *Wagon Mound* (and *Hughes v Lord Advocate*[19] to stress that it was the type, rather than the extent or manner of the damage that was important) and thereby arrived at the decision that the defendants were liable for the loss of the pigs, which in his view they would not have been if the stricter so-called contract test had been applied.

So for Lord Denning the important distinction is not so much the cause of action—contract or tort—but rather the nature of the loss—loss of profit as against physical damage or expense. In particular, he went on to emphasise that where a defendant is liable for physical damage to one man in contract and to another in tort—and he cited as examples, product liability, occupier's liability and medical negligence—there should be no difference in the remoteness test applied: 'Instances could be multiplied of injuries to persons or damage to property where the defendant is liable for his negligence to one man in contract and to another in tort. Each suffers like damage. The test of remoteness is, and should be, the same in both.'[20] One can go further to point out that a defendant can be

16 Lord Denning drew his analysis from Hart and Honoré *Causation In The Law* (1st edn, 1959) pp 281–7.
17 [1978] 1 All ER 525 at 532.
18 Ibid at 533.
19 [1963] AC 837.
20 [1978] 1 All ER 525 at 534.

liable for physical damage to one and the same plaintiff in both contract and tort. Indeed in *Parsons* itself, the defendants would surely also have been liable in the tort of negligence had the plaintiffs so framed their claim.

There are two issues left unclear by Lord Denning's judgment. The first is what test he would apply to loss of profit in tort. He adopts two tests for remoteness in contract, but he does not say whether a dual test for remoteness would also apply in tort. Would he, in other words, adopt a stricter test than the *Wagon Mound* for tortious loss of profit? The acceptance of pure economic loss recovery in the tort of negligence makes this an important issue. The simplest, neatest view is that Lord Denning would apply the *Heron II* stricter test to tortious loss of profit (albeit with references to the time of the contract replaced by appropriate substitutes, such as the time of the work commencing). The nature of the loss would then be the sole and simple determinant of the remoteness test to be applied, whether in tort or contract. If loss of profit, the stricter *Heron II* would be applicable; if physical damage or expense, the *Wagon Mound*. Against this view is that in *Spartan Steel and Alloys v Martin & Co Ltd*,[1] Lord Denning had earlier been happy to assume that the *Wagon Mound* was the appropriate test for tortious loss of profit, although admittedly there was no dispute in that case over which was the appropriate remoteness test to apply. But if the *Wagon Mound* is to continue to apply in a *Spartan Steel* type situation, a further possibility in accordance with Lord Denning's judgement, is to say that where there is a contractual or similar relationship between the parties *Heron II* should be applied to tortious loss of profit, but otherwise the *Wagon Mound* applies to such loss. These alternatives will be returned to when looking at the policy justification for Lord Denning's loss of profits and physical damage or expense distinction.

The second uncertainty is where the exact division lies between Lord Denning's two categories. However it seems safe to assume— particularly given his express reliance on the distinction drawn in the tort of negligence between pure economic loss and other economic loss—that Lord Denning's reference to loss of profit is to 'pure' loss of profit (as was in issue in *Hadley v Baxendale*, *Victoria Laundry* and *Heron II*) and not to loss of profit consequent on personal injury or damage to one's property.

What about the majority's judgment, given by Scarman LJ with whom Orr LJ agreed? They disagreed with Lord Denning's reasoning because they did not think that his distinction between the

1 [1973] QB 27.

remoteness test for loss of profit and for physical damage was supported by the authorities. Rather, they considered that *Heron II* provides the single test for remoteness in contract but stressed that, in applying it, it is the type and not extent of loss that must be reasonably contemplated as a serious possibility at the time of contracting. Scarman LJ said:

> It does not matter . . . if they thought that the chance of physical injury, loss of profit, loss of market, or other loss as the case may be, was slight or that the odds were against it, provided they contemplated as a serious possibility the type of consequence, not necessarily the specific consequence, that ensued on breach.[2]

Applying that test to the facts, as it was reasonably contemplated by the parties at the time of the contract that by reason of the failure to provide a hopper fit for storing pig food, there was a serious possibility that the pigs would become ill, and since illness could be said to be the same type of loss as death, it did not matter that the extent of that illness (that is the death of many pigs) was not reasonably contemplated as a serious possibility. Ultimately, therefore, the majority arrived at the result that the loss of the pigs was not too remote.

Three main points should be made regarding the majority's approach. First, it did not say how types of loss are to be divided up. One could argue, for example, that since illness and death of pigs were regarded as the same type of loss, and merely differed in extent, the majority's approach is irreconcilable with *Victoria Laundry*; for one could argue that the type of loss in issue there was loss of profits, and that the exceptional profits were merely a greater extent of that same type of loss. Presumably, the majority's answer to this would be that its test allows the courts a discretion as to how to divide up types of loss, and that *Victoria Laundry* is reconcilable by regarding the ordinary loss of profits as a different type of loss from the exceptional loss of profits. But such discretion and flexibility in the test is only achieved at the expense of certainty. However, some support for the majority's approach does derive from Megarry J's earlier holding in *Wroth v Tyler*[3] that the extraordinary and uncontemplated rise in the market price of houses was not too remote because the type of loss—a difference between the market and contract prices—had been contemplated. But it is submitted that the case is better regarded as turning on the fact that the plaintiffs were 'consumers' who wanted the house to live in, rather

2 [1978] 1 All ER 525 at 541.
3 [1974] Ch 30.

than businessmen. As such their loss was most accurately described as the loss of a home of a certain standard, rather than a loss of profit. Viewed in this way, the loss was clearly contemplated, and remoteness and the type/extent distinction were not in issue.

Secondly, Scarman LJ's approach differed from Lord Denning's in that in applying his test to the facts, he regarded the breach not as that of supplying a hopper with inadequate ventilation but rather that of supplying a hopper unfit for the purpose of storing pig food. So that instead of asking, 'was it reasonably contemplated at the time of contracting as a serious possibility that supplying a hopper with inadequate ventilation would make the pigs ill?' to which the answer was clearly 'no', Scarman LJ asked, 'was it reasonably contemplated at the time of contracting as a serious possibility that supplying a hopper unfit for the purpose of storing pig food would make the pigs ill?' to which he was able to answer 'yes'. In other words, Scarman LJ's approach shows that, by defining the breach more generally, the loss is less likely to be judged too remote. Although both these approaches are reconcilable with the *Heron II*—and indeed reveal an inherent discretion in applying that test— it would seem that Lord Denning's, which concentrates more closely on the breach that has actually occurred, is more in line with the *Heron II* approach.

A third point is that there are passages where Scarman LJ seems at least to suggest that where there is a contractual (or similar) relationship between the parties, there should be no difference between the remoteness tests in contract and tort. For example he says:

... the law must be such that in a factual situation where all have the same actual or imputed knowledge ... the amount of damages recoverable does not depend on whether, as a matter of legal classification, the plaintiff's cause of action is breach of contract or tort. It may be that the necessary reconciliation is to be found, notwithstanding the strictures of Lord Reid in *Heron II*, in holding that the difference between 'reasonable foreseeability' (the test in tort) and 'reasonably contemplated' (the test in contract) is semantic not substantial. Certainly Asquith LJ in *Victoria Laundry v Newman Industries* and Lord Pearce in *Heron II* thought so; and I confess I think so too.[4]

But the difference between *Heron II* and the *Wagon Mound* tests is not to do with the terms foreseeable or contemplation; ie we can agree that the difference in these terms is semantic and not substantial; rather, even if one modifies the *Heron II* in the way that Scarman LJ does, it differs from the *Wagon Mound* as to the degree

4 [1978] 1 All ER 525 at 536.

of likelihood of loss required—the *Heron II* test requiring a higher degree—and as to the time at which the contemplation or foreseeability is judged, being at the time the contract is made under the *Heron II* and at the time of the breach of duty under the *Wagon Mound*. It is submitted therefore that this 'reconciliation' between the tort and contract tests is nothing of the kind. As such a reconciliation fails, this passage and others like it[5] must be interpreted in one of two ways. First, as suggesting that assimilation of tests *would* be desirable where there is a contractual (or similar) relationship between the parties, while at the same time leaving the law without any such assimilation; or, secondly, as bringing about assimilation by laying down that where there is a contractual (or similar) relationship between the parties, the *Parsons* majority test applies, even as the test in tort—that is, as there replacing *The Wagon Mound*.

Before moving on to look at policy, the law can be summarised by saying that there are three main views of the remoteness test in contract and its relationship with the *Wagon Mound* remoteness test in tort. First, the *Heron II* view that a different test applies in contract, the contract test being stricter than the *Wagon Mound* test. Secondly, the majority's view in *Parsons* which basically follows *Heron II*, but with the emphasis being placed on the type (rather than the extent) of the loss. On one interpretation, this test is also meant to apply to tort, where there is a contractual or similar relationship between the parties. Thirdly, Lord Denning's view in *Parsons* that there is the same test in contract and tort for cases of physical damage, the less strict so-called tort *Wagon Mound* test, but in contract claims for loss of profit the stricter *Heron II* test applies.

(ii) What are the policies behind the three different views?

The *Heron II* is based on the simple view that in contract the plaintiff has the chance to throw the risk of unusual losses on to the defendant by informing the defendant of that risk prior to the contract whereas in tort the plaintiff has no such opportunity. Hence one should be less willing to grant the plaintiff compensation for unusual losses in contract than in tort. In *Heron II* Lord Reid said that there was good reason for the difference between the remoteness test in contract and tort because:

In contract, if one party wishes to protect himself against a risk which to the other party would appear unusual, he can direct the other party's attention to it before the contract is made, and I need not stop to consider in what circumstances the other party will then be held to have accepted

5 Ibid at 535.

responsibility in that event. In tort however, there is no opportunity for the injured party to protect himself in that way and the tortfeasor cannot reasonably complain if he has to pay for some very unusual but nevertheless foreseeable damage which results from his wrongdoing.[6]

The possible policies underlying Lord Denning's view in *Parsons v Uttley Ingham* are more complex. Clearly Lord Denning thought that the *Heron II* does not provide a satisfactory policy justification for having a distinction between the remoteness tests for tort and contract. One obvious explanation for this is that the plaintiff and defendant in a tort action are often not strangers prior to the tort, so that the plaintiff has had just as good an opportunity to inform the defendant of unusual losses as if they had been in a contractual relationship. Indeed they may even be in a contractual relationship. Furthermore, Lord Denning clearly considered that, at least for physical damage or expense, there is no other good reason to have a different remoteness test in contract than in tort.

But how can one justify having a different remoteness test for physical damage or expense and loss of profit? There are three main possible answers. The first is to say that loss of profit is less serious than physical damage or expense; for this reason the courts should be less willing to protect the plaintiff against loss of profit than physical damage, and hence a stricter test should be applied to the former than to the latter. A second, and similar argument, is to say that, as loss of profit is more speculative and uncertain than physical damage or expense, a stricter test should be applied. Put another way, loss of profits is always to some extent in the realm of the hypothetical, in contrast to physical damage and expense which is a matter of past fact. The third is to say that, as a generalisation, it is realistic as regards loss of profit, but unrealistic as regards physical damage or expense, to take into account the possibility of a contracting party informing the other of the risk of unusual losses prior to the contract, since contracting parties think about loss of profit but not about physical damage or expense.

It is important to note that whichever of these justifications is preferred helps to answer the question posed earlier as to which test Lord Denning would apply for tortious loss of profit. The first two justifications indicate that the *Heron II* should also be applied to tortious loss of profit whereas the last indicates the application of the *Wagon Mound* for such loss, other than where the parties are in a contractual (or similar relationship) where the *Heron II* would be applied.

---

6 [1969] 1 AC 350 at 385–6. See similarly at 411 (per Lord Hodson) and at 422–3 (per Lord Upjohn).

The majority's modification of *Heron II*, by the type of loss emphasis, presumably rests on the view that to look for a contemplation of the extent as well as the type of loss is to make the remoteness test too generous to the defendant. But, in general, the majority appear to accept the *Heron II* policy justification for different tests in contract and tort. However, they do realise that that justification cannot apply where the parties are in a contractual or similar relationship since there they are plainly not strangers to each other. On one interpretation, then, they advocate that the *Parsons* test should be applied in that situation, whether the cause of action be contract or tort.

(iii) Which is the best approach?

Since the parties are often in a contractual or similar relationship it is clear that the *Heron II* policy reasoning cannot validly justify always having a different remoteness test in contract and tort. All the judges in *Parsons* recognise this, but their attempts to grapple with the consequences produce different approaches. Lord Denning's is the clearer although he does leave open the test to be applied for tortious loss of profit. Ultimately, however, the validity of his views stands or falls on whether it is justifiable here to distinguish loss of profit and physical damage or expense. The majority's approach is, by contrast, more vague and it is only on one interpretation that they can be said to have produced any assimilation at all between the contract and tort tests.

There has been no judicial clarification of these issues. In subsequent cases the courts have largely been content simply to apply *Hadley v Baxendale* and *Heron II* without any consideration of the difficulties raised in *Parsons*. For example, in *Kemp v Intasun Holidays Ltd*[7] a defendant holiday firm, in breach of contract with the plaintiffs, substituted inferior holiday accommodation to that booked. The plaintiffs, who were husband and wife, were held entitled to mental distress damages for their loss of enjoyment but the husband was held not entitled to damages for the asthmatic attack brought on by dirt in the hotel room. That 'loss' was held to be too

---

7 [1987] 2 FTLR 234. See also, eg, *Rumsey v Owen, White and Catlin* (1978) 245 Estates Gazette 225; *The Pegase* [1981] 1 Lloyd's Rep 175; *Seven Seas Properties Ltd v Al-Essa (No 2)* [1993] 3 All ER 577. Cf *The Borag* [1981] 1 All ER 856 (in which Lord Denning relied on his own judgment in *Parsons*); *The Rio Claro* [1987] 2 Lloyd's Rep 173 (in reliance on *Parsons*, the type of loss was stressed, albeit that the loss was held too remote); *The Forum Craftsman* [1991] 1 Lloyd's Rep 81 (in which an argument that the loss was not too remote, based on the 'type' emphasis in *Parsons*, was rejected).

remote in accordance with *Heron II*. *Parsons* was not even discussed, albeit that on the facts the asthmatic attack would presumably not have been too remote on Lord Denning's approach and might not have been too remote applying the majority's view.

On one view, clarification of the issues raised by *Parsons* is unnecessary and indeed even undesirable; rather the law must remain inconsistent and uncertain in order to allow the courts the discretion to achieve justice on the remoteness question. However that approach seems totally unacceptable. It may well be that considerable discretion must be allowed to the courts, for example in dividing up the types of loss. But the present law is unsatisfactory because in leaving unclear what the appropriate test is (other than for tortious physical damage where the parties are strangers) it leaves unclear what the area of discretion is. Either of the two approaches in *Parsons* presents an acceptable way forward, assuming one adopts the assimilation interpretation of the majority's judgment.[8]

(iv) Is the test too harsh on a defendant?

In the above discussion, geared towards the currently crucial issue of whether the contract and tort tests should be assimilated, it has been assumed that, if anything, the contract test is too kind to a defendant. But it can be argued that the reverse is true, especially where the loss in question is loss of profit, for whichever of the three approaches is adopted the test of remoteness does not take into account the amount of the contractual consideration to be received by the defendant. In other words, the fact that the plaintiff's losses are out of all proportion to what the defendant was to receive under the contract is an irrelevant factor in judging remoteness. For example, in *Hadley v Baxendale* itself, the fact that the plaintiff's loss of profits from delay were out of all proportion to the price to be paid to the defendant for carrying the mill-shaft was irrelevant. In the United States this point has led commentators and courts frequently to suggest that the *Hadley v Baxendale* test does not restrict liability enough.[9] In accordance with this, the Second Restatement of Contracts, s 351 (3) states: 'A court may limit damages for foreseeable loss . . . if it concludes that in the circumstances justice so requires in order to avoid disproportionate compensation'; and by comment (f) 'disproportionate' means 'an

---

8 For a different approach, see Cooke (1978) CLJ 288 (advocating a wide judicial discretion, albeit with articulated considerations to be taken into account).
9 Eg *Lamkins v International Harvester Co* 182 SW 2d 203 (1944); Farnsworth (1970) Col LR 1145, 1209.

extreme disproportion between the loss . . . and the price charged by the party whose liability for that loss is in question.'[10]

Similarly, in a few English cases, particularly concerning carriers, the courts have applied a different more restrictive test than that of *Hadley v Baxendale*. For example, in *British Columbia and Vancouvers Island Spar, Lumber and Saw-Mill Co Ltd v Nettleship*[11] it was held that a carrier would not be liable even if told of special circumstances unless he agreed to accept liability for the unusual risk as a term of the contract. Willes J said:

Take the case of a barrister on his way to practise at the Calcutta bar, where he may have a large number of briefs awaiting him; through the default of the Peninsular and Oriental Company he is detained in Egypt or in the Suez boat, and consequently sustains great loss: is the company to be responsible for that, because they happened to know the purpose for which the traveller was going?[12]

The answer was considered to be 'no' applying the approach that one needs both knowledge and actual acceptance of the risk. However this approach has clearly been rejected, not only impliedly by the approval of *Hadley v Baxendale* in *Heron II*, but also specifically by the Court of Appeal in *GKN Centrax Gears Ltd v Matbro Ltd.*[13]

Moreover, it is submitted that the traditional English approach is to be preferred. Once the defendant has been given notice of unusual potential losses, he can act accordingly, whether by refusing to contract, or by raising the price, or by reducing the probability of breach, or by excluding liability. Given such a choice, it seems perfectly fair and not unduly harsh to hold him responsible for reasonably contemplated losses flowing from what, after all, was his breach of contract. In any event, an approach like that advocated in the Second Restatement creates unacceptable uncertainty.

(v) The principle in Cory v Thames Ironworks Co[14]

Where the plaintiff's actual loss of profit is too remote, and hence irrecoverable, he is still entitled to recover a lesser sum measured by the loss of profit that would have been non-remote. The leading authority on this often overlooked principle is *Cory v Thames*

---

10 See Kniffin (1988) 63 Notre Dame LR 247; see also supra, p 21, fn 13.
11 (1868) LR 3 CP 499. See also *Horne v Midland Rly Co* (1873) LR 8 CP 131.
12 Ibid at 510.
13 [1976] 2 Lloyd's Rep 555. See also Lord Upjohn in *Heron II* [1969] 1 AC 350 at 422. Cf *The Pegase* [1981] 1 Lloyd's Rep 175, 183–4; Treitel *The Law of Contract* (8th edn) pp 860–2.
14 (1868) LR 3 QB 181.

Ironworks Co in which the defendants were in breach of contract in failing to deliver the hull of a boat on time. The plaintiffs, who were coal merchants, intended to use the hull in a novel way unknown to the defendants. The defendants assumed that the plaintiffs intended to use the hull for the usual purpose of storing coal. It was held that, while the loss of profit flowing from the special use was too remote, the lesser profit that would have been lost from applying the hull for usual purposes was recoverable. That was so even though the plaintiffs had suffered no such loss in the sense that they would not have used the hull for storage.[15] Cockburn J said:

> The buyer has lost the larger amount, and there can be no hardship or injustice in making the seller liable to compensate him in damages so far as the seller understood and believed that the article would be applied to the ordinary purposes to which it was capable of being applied. [16]

This must be correct. To overcome the objection that the plaintiff recovers for a loss that he has not suffered, the principle is best rationalised by saying that the plaintiff recovers that part of his actual loss of special profit that is *equivalent* to the ordinary profit that would have been lost.

(2) Intervening cause[17]

Even though the defendant's breach of duty is a cause of the plaintiff's loss, the plaintiff may not recover damages for it because an intervening cause,[18] combining with it to produce the loss,[19] is regarded as breaking the chain of causation between the defendant's breach of duty and the loss. The underlying policy behind this restriction is that where an intervening cause is much more

---

15 *Victoria Laundry (Windsor) Ltd v Newman Industries Ltd* [1949] 2 KB 528, supra, pp 46–7, was significantly different in that the plaintiffs had suffered a loss of both ordinary and exceptional profits.

16 (1868) LR 3 QB 181, 190.

17 The leading discussion on causation is Hart and Honoré *Causation In The Law* (2nd edn, 1985). The analysis in this book is in agreement with theirs that causal limits should be kept distinct from other limits on responsibility such as remoteness; but it differs from theirs in regarding intervening cause as depending on a policy decision rather than on the largely factual question of whether there is causation in the ordinary commonsense meaning of that term.

18 Ie a factual cause subsequent to the breach of duty. A factual cause prior to or contemporaneous with the defendant's breach of duty cannot be correctly described as intervening so as to come within this section. But such a factual cause does not merit separate treatment elsewhere since it is very rarely regarded as the sole legal cause of the damage.

19 Contrast sufficient causes, supra, pp 27–30.

responsible for the loss than is the defendant's breach of duty, it is considered unfair on the defendant and is imposing too great a burden on him to hold him liable for the loss.

The principles upon which the decisions in this area are based have rarely been clearly articulated, and some judges have even resorted to saying that it is simply a matter of instinct.[20] However, unarticulated instinct is hardly a satisfactory basis for legal decision-making and therefore an attempt will be made to indicate the main principles that underlie the decisions in relation to each of the three main types of intervening cause, namely natural events (that is, where the event is not caused by any identifiable person), conduct of a third party and conduct of the plaintiff.

(a) Intervening natural events

A natural event only breaks the chain of causation if the sole contribution that the defendant's breach of duty makes to the plaintiff's loss is that he (the plaintiff) or his property is in the place where, at the time when, the natural event intervenes. Even then the natural event will not break the causal chain if it was likely to intervene.

This is illustrated by the well-known hypothetical examples of the plaintiff who, having been injured by the defendant's negligence and while on the way to hospital, is further injured by a falling tree or roof-tile or, while in hospital, suffers further injury because of a fire there.[1] In each of these situations the sole contribution of the breach of duty to the further loss is that the plaintiff is at the place where, at the time when, the natural event intervenes; since, in addition, none of these natural events was likely to intervene the causal chain is broken. Similarly in *Carlslogie SS Co Ltd v The Royal Norwegian Government*[2] the plaintiff's ship was damaged in a collision for which the defendant was wholly responsible. After temporary repairs rendering the ship seaworthy, she set out on a voyage to the United States. On that voyage she suffered extensive damage due to heavy weather. The House of Lords considered that there was certainly no question of the defendant being liable for the heavy weather damage. Viscount Jowitt said that it '. . . was not in any sense a consequence of the collision, and must be treated as a supervening

---

20 Watkins LJ in *Lamb v Camden London Borough Council* [1981] QB 625 at 647.
 1 See *Hogan v Bentinck West Hartley Collieries (Owners) Ltd* [1949] 1 All ER 588 at 601 (per Lord Macdermott).
 2 [1952] AC 292.

event occurring in the course of a normal voyage'.[3] More specifically it can be said that the chain of causation was broken because the sole contribution of the breach of duty to the heavy weather damage was that the plaintiff's ship was in the Atlantic at the time of that heavy weather, and moreover that heavy weather was unlikely to intervene.

On the other side of the fence, let us suppose that the defendant negligently sets fire to the plaintiff's field and later, fanned by gale-force winds, the fire spreads to and destroys the plaintiff's house; the winds do not break the chain of causation because the contribution of the defendant's negligence to the burning down of the house clearly has nothing to do merely with the plaintiff's property being in the place where, at the time when, the natural event intervenes. On the contrary without the defendant's breach of duty there would have been no fire at all.

A further example of a natural event not breaking the causal chain is provided by *Monarch SS Co Ltd v A/B Karlshamms Oljefabriker*.[4] The defendant's breach of contract in failing to provide a seaworthy ship for the carriage of the plaintiff's cargo of soya beans meant that the voyage was delayed, and that the ship could not reach her destination in Sweden before the Second World War broke out. The ship was ordered by the Admiralty to discharge the soya beans at Glasgow. The plaintiffs thereupon had to pay for the beans to be forwarded to Sweden in neutral ships. They claimed damages for the cost of that transhipment. One issue was whether that transhipment was too remote in the sense discussed in the last section, but another was whether the intervening events, in particular the outbreak of war, broke the causal connection between the defendant's breach and the transhipment. It was held that the chain of causation was not broken. Although the sole contribution of the defendant's breach to the transhipment was that the ship was within waters patrolled by the British Navy when the war broke out, that intervention, as Lord Porter stressed, was likely.[5]

This principle for natural events sets a fairly high standard for establishing that the chain of causation is broken and it should be contrasted with the approach to wrongful intervention by a third party or the plaintiff's own unreasonable conduct. The difference reflects sound policy; a defendant cannot attach blame to anyone else in the case of natural events.

3 Ibid at 299.
4 [1949] AC 196.
5 Ibid at 215.

(b) Intervening conduct of a third party

(i) The duty was to guard against such a third party intervention

Clearly in this situation the third party should not be regarded as having broken the chain of causation, and this is shown in a number of contract cases. In *London Joint Stock Bank v Macmillan*,[6] for example, the defendant customer of the plaintiff bank, in breach of his contractual duty to the plaintiff not to draw cheques so as to facilitate fraud, signed for a trusted clerk a cheque for £2 drawn in such a way as to enable the clerk readily to alter the amount to £120; the clerk then obtained this sum from the bank and absconded. The House of Lords held that the defendant was liable to the plaintiff for the forged sum. Lord Finlay LC said 'The fact that a crime was necessary to bring about the loss does not prevent it being the natural consequence of the carelessness.'[7] More specifically, one can say that the reason why the intervening acts of the third party, albeit criminal, did not break the chain of causation was that the duty broken was to guard against a third party fraudulently obtaining money from the bank.

Stansbie v Troman,[8] in which the cause of action is probably best rationalised as breach of contract,[9] is a further and very clear example. A decorator was at work in a house and left it for two hours to get wallpaper. He was alone and had been told by the plaintiff householder to lock the front door if he ever left. Instead he left the door unlocked and during his absence a thief entered and stole some jewellery and clothes. The Court of Appeal held that the defendant was liable for the loss: the third party intervention did not break the chain of causation because the duty broken was clearly to prevent what had occurred. As Tucker LJ said, '. . . the act of negligence itself consisted in the failure to take reasonable care to guard against the very thing that in fact happened.'[10]

Similarly in *Home Office v Dorset Yacht Co Ltd*[11] the majority of their Lordships, with the notable exception of Lord Reid, framed the issue in terms of whether a duty of care in the tort of negligence was owed by borstal officers to the owners of nearby yachts damaged by escaping borstal boys. Having decided that there was such a duty, and that it had been breached, it obviously followed that the

---

6 [1918] AC 777. See also *De La Bere v Pearson* [1908] 1 KB 280.
7 Ibid at 794.
8 [1948] 2 KB 48.
9 See *P Perl (Exporters) Ltd v Camden London Borough Council* [1983] 3 All ER 161 at 170.
10 [1948] 2 KB 48 at 52.
11 [1970] AC 1004.

chain of causation was not broken by the intervention of the borstal boys. As Oliver LJ said in *P Perl (Exporters) Ltd v Camden London Borough Council*[12] in which the defendant was held to owe no duty of care to a neighbour whose premises had been burgled by thieves gaining access through the defendant's premises:

... the question of the existence of a duty and that of whether the damage brought about by the act of a third party is too remote are simply two facets of the same problem: for if there be a duty to take reasonable care to prevent damage being caused by a third party then I find it difficult to see how damage caused by the third party consequent on the failure to take such care can be too remote a consequence of the breach of duty.[13]

The same sentiment was expressed by Lord Goff in *Smith v Littlewoods Organisation Ltd*[14] in which it was decided that no duty of care was owed to neighbours whose property had been damaged as a result of vandals setting fire to the defendant's derelict cinema. 'Of course, if a duty of care is imposed to guard against deliberate wrongdoing by others, it can hardly be said that the harmful effects of such wrongdoing are not caused by such breach of duty.'[15]

The controversial decision in *Weld-Blundell v Stephens*[16] seems to be out of line with the principle being discussed and it is submitted that, for this reason alone, the minority view is to be preferred. The plaintiff, when employing the defendant accountant to investigate the affairs of the company, libelled certain officials of the company in his letter of instructions to the defendant. The defendant negligently left the letter at the company's office, where it was read by a third party who related its contents to the officials, who successfully sued the plaintiff for libel. The plaintiff brought an action against the defendant for breach of contract, claiming compensation for those damages and the costs. The House of Lords held by a bare majority that the third party's act broke the chain of causation and that the plaintiff could therefore recover no more than nominal damages. The main ground of reasoning was expressed as follows by Lord Sumner:

In general ... even though A is in fault he is not responsible for injury to C which B, a stranger to him, deliberately chooses to do. Though A may have given the occasion for B's mischievous activities, B then becomes a new and independent cause ... It is hard to steer clear of metaphors.

12 [1983] 3 All ER 161.
13 Ibid at 167.
14 [1987] AC 241.
15 Ibid at 272.
16 [1920] AC 956. The case was distinguished in *Slipper v BBC* [1991] 1 QB 283.

Perhaps one may be forgiven for saying that B snaps the chain of causation; that he is no mere conduit pipe through which consequences flow from A to C, no mere part of a transmission gear set in motion by A; that in a word, he insulates A from C.[17]

Such a generalisation is misleading and did mislead the majority in the case, for it fails to indicate that where, as on the facts of this case, the duty broken is to guard against such a third party intervention as occurred, even a criminal act of the third party, let alone a non-wrongful act as here, does not break the chain of causation. In the dissenting words of Viscount Finlay, '. . . the very thing happened which it was [the defendant's] duty to guard against'.[18]

(ii) Third party intervention other than where there was a duty to guard against it

Rationalisation of the case law is here particularly difficult. However it would seem that where the third party's intervention comprises wrongdoing it breaks the chain of causation unless it was a likely, or in the case of intentional wrongdoing, a very likely consequence of the defendant's breach of duty. Non-wrongful conduct of a third party will probably only break the chain on the same principle as for natural events. The policy is therefore one of showing more leniency towards the defendant, if a third party's intervening conduct has been wrongful, so that the plaintiff can claim against him, than if non-wrongful. Moreover, the greater the culpability of the third party's wrong, the greater the leniency.

Two cases involving multiple collisions can be used to illustrate a third party's non-intentional wrongdoing. In *Rouse v Squires*[19] D_1 negligently jack-knifed his lorry across a motorway. D_2 driving his lorry negligently, collided into D_1's lorry and killed the plaintiff's husband who was assisting at the scene. D_2 was held liable to the plaintiff. D_2 now brought third party proceedings against D_1. The question that arose was whether that intervening negligence of D_2 broke the chain of causation between D_1's negligence and the death of the plaintiff's husband. The Court of Appeal held that that chain of causation was not broken. Cairns LJ said that where a driver:

. . . so negligently manages his vehicle as to cause it to obstruct the highway and constitute a danger to other road users, including those who are driving too fast or not keeping a proper look-out, but not those who deliberately or

17 Ibid at 986.
18 Ibid at 974.
19 [1973] QB 889.

recklessly drive into the obstruction,[20] then the first driver's negligence may be held to have contributed to the causation of an accident of which the immediate cause was the negligent driving of the vehicle which because of the presence of the obstruction collides with it.[1]

Moreover, on these facts, once D_1 had negligently jack-knifed, it was likely that another negligently-driven vehicle would collide causing injury or death to those on the scene.

On the other hand, in *Knightley v Johns*[2] D_1 negligently over-turned his car thereby blocking a tunnel. D_2, a police inspector, was held to be negligent in not immediately closing the tunnel and in ordering the plaintiff, a constable, to ride back along the tunnel against the traffic in order to close it. While doing so, the plaintiff collided with D_3's oncoming car and was injured. The primary question was whether the intervening negligent acts of D_2 broke the chain of causation between D_1's negligence and the plaintiff's injuries. Stephenson LJ said that the test to be applied was '. . . reasonable foreseeability, which I understand to mean foreseeability of something of the same sort being likely to happen.'[3] Applying that the Court of Appeal, not surprisingly, reached the conclusion that D_2's negligent acts broke the chain of causation and that therefore D_1 was not liable for the plaintiff's injuries. Some types of risk-taking and even negligence by the police were likely to intervene; but the same could not be said of the acts of negligence that D_2 had actually committed.

The well known case of *The Oropesa*[4] concerned non-wrongful intervention. A ship of that name negligently caused a collision with another ship. The master of the latter ship decided to cross to 'The Oropesa' in a small boat. The boat overturned and the plaintiff's son was killed. The question was whether the death was caused by the negligence of 'The Oropesa' or whether the master's action in taking to the boat broke the chain of causation. It was held that the chain of causation was not broken. Lord Wright said:

To break the chain of causation it must be shown that there is something which I will call ultroneous, something unwarrantable, a new cause which

---

20 These words were expressly relied on by the Court of Appeal in *Wright v Lodge* [1993] 4 All ER 299 in holding that the *reckless* driving in question broke the chain of causation.
1 Ibid at 898.
2 [1982] 1 WLR 349.
3 Ibid at 366.
4 [1943] P 32.

disturbs the sequence of events, something which can be described as either unreasonable or extraneous or extrinsic.[5]

This is typical of reasoning in the area of intervening cause in not articulating the exact principle; but it does indicate that non-wrongful conduct will rarely break the chain. It is submitted that in accordance with this and with the approach to natural events, the underlying principle is that third party non-wrongful acts will only break the chain if the sole contribution that the defendant's breach of duty makes to the plaintiff's loss is that the plaintiff is in the place where, at the time when, the third party intervenes. Even then the causal chain will not be broken if the intervention was likely. Applying this to the facts of *The Oropesa* the causal chain was not broken because the defendant's breach of duty contributed to the master taking out the boat, and its contribution was therefore not solely that the plaintiff was in the boat when it overturned. Similarly it is submitted that, had the events considered above under natural events[6] been caused by a third party's non-wrongful act, the same decisions on causation would be reached.

Where the third party's conduct comprises intentional wrongdoing, the intervention will break the chain of causation, unless it was a very likely consequence of the defendant's breach of duty. In *Home Office v Dorset Yacht Co Ltd*[7] Lord Reid who, unlike the majority, regarded the primary issue as one of intervening cause rather than as one of duty, said:

. . . where human action forms one of the links between the original wrong-doing of the defendant and the loss suffered by the plaintiff, that action must at least have been something very likely to happen if it is not to be regarded as *novus actus interveniens* breaking the chain of causation. I do not think that a mere foreseeable possibility is or should be sufficient, for then the intervening human action can more properly be regarded as a new cause than as a consequence of the original wrong-doing.[8]

Since on these facts it was very likely that as a result of the defendant's negligence the boys would escape and damage nearby yachts, the chain of causation was not broken.

Lord Reid's dictum was subsequently applied by Oliver LJ in *Lamb v Camden London Borough Council*,[9] albeit that he recast

5 Ibid at 39.
6 Supra, pp 58–9.
7 [1970] AC 1004.
8 Ibid at 1030.
9 [1981] QB 625.

Lord Reid's test in terms of 'reasonable forseeability' and regarded intervening cause as an aspect of remoteness, The defendants had negligently caused the subsidence of the plaintiff's house with the result that the plaintiff had to leave it unoccupied. The question was whether in addition to their admitted liability in nuisance for the subsidence the defendants should be held responsible for the loss caused by the action of squatters occupying and looting the home. The Court of Appeal unanimously held that the defendants should not be liable for that further loss. Oliver LJ, applying Lord Reid's test, in effect held that as the third party's intervention was unlikely the chain of causation was broken. On the other hand the reasoning of the other judges is unhelpful with regard to intervention by a third party. Least satisfactory was Watkins LJ who regarded the loss as too remote because his instinct told him so. Rather more satisfactory was Lord Denning's primary reasoning by which he in effect decided the issue in terms of the plaintiff's failure to act (that is, the duty to mitigate) rather than intervening third party conduct; the plaintiff had unreasonably failed to secure adequately the empty house even after an initial intrusion by squatters.

Unfortunately even Oliver LJ thought that Lord Reid's test might not be stringent enough, and he said, 'There may . . . be circumstances in which the court would require a degree of likelihood amounting almost to inevitability before it fixes a defendant with a responsibility for the act of the third party over whom he has and can have no control.'[10] The hypothetical example worrying the Court of Appeal was that of an escaping borstal boy stealing a car and committing a burglary hundreds of miles from the borstal. While this was thought very likely, it was considered that the Home Office ought not to be held liable for it. But there is surely no need to qualify or reject Lord Reid's test to reach that result for it can be argued that the Home Office would owe no duty of care to the plaintiff in that situation. In other words Lord Reid regarded *Dorset Yacht* as raising particular difficulties over intervening cause rather than the duty of care, but he could still regard the duty of care as the problem issue on other facts.

In *Ward v Cannock Chase District Council*[11] there was no such qualification of Lord Reid's dictum which was applied, along with Oliver LJ's reasoning in *Lamb*, to reach the decision that the defendant council (which admitted negligence) was liable for damage to

---

10 Ibid at 644.
11 [1985] 3 All ER 537.

the plaintiff's house resulting initially from vandalisation of the defendant's empty house next door and later from direct vandalisation of the plaintiff's then unoccupied house. The chain of causation was held to be unbroken as it was very likely that unoccupied houses in that area would be vandalised.

(c) Intervening conduct of the plaintiff

The position here seems to be that, where there has been a tort[12] or breach of contract, unreasonable conduct of the plaintiff breaks the chain of causation (unless the duty was to guard against that intervention)[13] whereas reasonable conduct does not. In accordance with the distinction explained above,[14] cases where the plaintiff has unreasonably failed to take action, or has unreasonably incurred expenses, are not discussed here but under the duty to mitigate.

(i) Unreasonable acts

The classic case is *McKew v Holland and Hannen and Cubitts*.[15] The pursuer had suffered an injury for which the defenders were tortiously liable, and as a result he occasionally lost control of his left leg. Some days after the accident he was descending a steep staircase without a handrail and without the available assistance of his wife and brother-in-law when he lost control of his left leg and, in jumping to save himself falling, broke his ankle. The House of Lords held that the further injury was brought about by the pursuer's own actions, because in placing himself unnecessarily in a position where he might be injured the pursuer was acting unreasonably; and even though unreasonable conduct was not unlikely or unforeseeable, it nevertheless broke the chain of causation. Lord Reid said, '. . . it is not at all unlikely or unforeseeable that an active man who has suffered such a disability will take some quite unreasonable risk but if he does, he cannot hold the defender liable for the consequences'.[16]

12 Separate consideration is not given to the plaintiff's conduct subsequent to a breach of duty but prior to a tort (that is, where there is as yet no damage and the tort is not actionable per se) because here even unreasonable conduct rarely breaks the chain of causation and usually amounts to contributory negligence. Exceptions are *Rushton v Turner Bros Asbestos* [1960] 1 WLR 96, and *Jayes v IMI Ltd* [1985] ICR 155 (but in the latter the incorrect term '100% contributory negligence' was used).
13 Eg an accountant may be under a duty to prevent his client's negligent errors.
14 Supra, pp 38–9.
15 [1969] 3 All ER 1621.
16 Ibid at 1623.

Two contract cases similarly illustrate the principle. In *Quinn v Burch Bros (Builders) Ltd*[17] the defendants in breach of contract failed to supply a step-ladder to the plaintiff, a sub-contractor. The plaintiff injured himself when he fell from an unfooted trestle which he had made use of in the absence of a step-ladder. The Court of Appeal held that the defendants were not liable for the plaintiff's injuries because their breach of contract did not cause them: the plaintiff's own unreasonable acts broke the chain of causation between the breach of contract and his injuries.

Again in *Lambert v Lewis*[18] a dealer supplied a defective trailer coupling to a farmer, who negligently went on using it after it was obviously broken. There was an accident resulting in injuries to other parties, when the coupling gave way. The farmer was found liable for those injuries and in an action for breach of contract against the dealer sought to recover an indemnity for the damages he had had to pay. The House of Lords held, however, that he should not be so indemnified because his negligence in continuing to use the coupling knowing of its condition had broken the chain of causation between the dealer's breach of contract and the accident.

(ii) Reasonable acts

The contract case of *Compania Naviera Maropan v Bowaters*[19] illustrates that the chain of causation will not be broken by reasonable intervening acts of the plaintiff. The defendant charterers were in breach of contract with the plaintiffs by nominating an unsafe loading place for their ship. The master of the plaintiff's ship thought that the place nominated was unsafe, but placed reliance on the assurance of safety given by the defendants' experienced pilot. The ship was damaged and the question that arose was whether the master's actions had broken the chain of causation between the breach of contract and the damage to the ship. It was held that they had not because he had acted reasonably in the circumstances. Hodson LJ said:

The question is one of causation. If the master by acting as he did, either caused the damage by acting unreasonably in the circumstances in which he was placed or failed to mitigate the damage, the charterers would be relieved accordingly, from the liability which would otherwise have fallen upon them.[20]

17 [1966] 2 QB 370.
18 [1982] AC 225.
19 [1955] 2 QB 68.
20 Ibid at 99.

Similarly in *Wieland v Cyril Lord Carpets Ltd*[1] the defendants negligently inflicted neck injuries on the plaintiff so that she had to wear
a collar. She later fell down some stairs because she could not use
her bifocal spectacles with her usual skill. Eveleigh J held that she
was entitled to recover for her further injuries from the defendants
because her own acts did not break the chain of causation. Again we
can say this was because the plaintiff was not acting unreasonably
when she fell down the stairs.

(iii) Contributory negligence?

The all or nothing division between reasonable and unreasonable
acts leaves out of account the possibility that contributory negligence subsequent to the tort or breach of contract might not break
the chain of causation while allowing a reduction of damages. For
breach of contract this mid-position is generally unavailable because
the Law Reform (Contributory Negligence) Act 1945 does not generally apply to breach of contract.[2] But there is no such reason for
forcing tort cases into the all or nothing straitjacket and contributory
negligence has been applied to acts subsequent to a tort. In *The
Calliope*,[3] a ship of that name sustained damage in a collision in the
river Seine with another ship, attributable to the negligence of both.
In view of the damage she had sustained it was decided to turn the
'Calliope' round and proceed up river to an anchorage to await the
ebb-tide. The next day she was to be turned round again to proceed
down river. Unfortunately, when the ship was being turned round
for the second time she sustained further damage. Brandon J found
that this would not have occurred but for the negligence of the
'Calliope' but he held that this negligence did not break the chain of
causation between the other ship's negligence and the further damage; rather, some damages for that further damage should be given,
albeit of a reduced amount for the 'Calliope's' contributory negligence.[4] He said:

Looking at the question from the point of principle, I cannot see any logical reason for denying to the court the right to apportion . . . liability in the
circumstances contemplated. Where all relevant negligence on both sides
precedes the original casualty the fact that A's negligence occurs later than
B's negligence, and possibly also in a different place, does not prevent an
apportionment of liability for such casualty. The view that it did so was

1 [1969] 3 All ER 1006.
2 Infra, pp 80–7.
3 [1970] P 172.
4 As the 'Calliope' had been contributorily negligent in relation to the original accident, there was a sub-apportionment.

enshrined in the so-called last-opportunity rule, which is, to this extent, dead and buried. I find it difficult to see why, as a matter of principle, it should make any difference that, in relation to a particular part of the damage arising or alleged to arise, from the casualty, the later negligence of B should follow rather than precede the casualty itself. Why should later negligence of B before the casualty be held not necessarily to break the chain of causation but later negligence of his after the casualty be held necessarily to do so?[5]

This is an eminently sensible approach, and it is therefore surprising that contributory negligence was not even discussed let alone applied in the *McKew* case.[6]

(3) The duty to mitigate

The duty to mitigate is a further restriction on compensatory damages.[7] On the one hand a plaintiff should not sit back and do nothing to minimise loss flowing from a wrong but should rather use his resources to do what is reasonable to put himself into as good a position as if the contract had been performed or the tort not committed. On the other hand, he should not unreasonably incur expense subsequent to the wrong. The policy is one of encouraging the plaintiff, once a wrong has occurred, to be to a reasonable extent self-reliant or, in economists' terminology, to be efficient, rather than pinning all loss on the defendant.[8]

The term 'duty to mitigate' should not be thought to indicate that the plaintiff can himself be sued for failure to comply with his duty: rather the consequence of such a failure is simply that no damages are given for the avoidable loss.[9] The duty is best regarded as comprising two principles, the first focusing on unreasonable inaction, the second on unreasonable action.

---

5 [1970] P 172 at 181–2.

6 Millner (1971) 22 NILQ 168, 178–9.

7 The duty to mitigate is also sometimes used as a positive reason for awarding damages, ie one can recover reasonable expenses incurred in seeking to minimise loss. But it is simpler to view this proposition as a natural consequence of there being no relevant restriction limiting the compensatory principle.

8 Bridge (1989) 105 LQR 398 argues that several policies are at play in explaining the duty to mitigate.

9 Theoretically, contributory negligence should apply as a mid-position to *reduce* damages but this defence is generally inapplicable to breach of contract, and as regards tort, no case has been found allowing contributory negligence as an alternative to the duty to mitigate: cf supra, pp 68–9.

(a) The first principle—unreasonable inaction

A plaintiff must take all reasonable steps to minimise the loss to him. The classic judicial formulation of this is Viscount Haldane LC's in *British Westinghouse Electric v Underground Electric Railways Co of London Ltd*[10] (a contract case), who said that the principle '. . . imposes on a plaintiff the duty of taking all reasonable steps to mitigate the loss consequent on the breach and debars him from claiming any part of the damage which is due to his neglect to take such steps.'

Clearly whether steps should reasonably have been taken to minimise loss depends on the particular facts in question. However some indication can be given of the sort of factors that have been considered important in past cases in deciding this.

(i)   Where the plaintiff has been wrongfully dismissed he need not accept an offer of re-employment from his former employer if factors like the following are present: the new work would involve a reduction in status; employment elsewhere would be more likely to be permanent; the plaintiff has no confidence in his employers because of their past treatment of him. Such factors were present in *Yetton v Eastwoods Froy Ltd*,[11] and it was therefore held that the plaintiff had not failed in his duty to mitigate by refusing his former employer's offer of re-employment. The opposite decision was reached in *Brace v Calder*,[12] where such factors were not present.

(ii) If in a contract of sale the defendant makes an offer of alternative performance, it will generally be unreasonable for the plaintiff to turn it down if acceptance would have reduced his loss. So in *Payzu Ltd v Saunders*[13] the defendants, who had contracted to deliver goods to the plaintiffs in instalments, refused to deliver the second and subsequent instalments unless the plaintiffs would pay cash on delivery. The plaintiffs refused this offer and sued the defendants for breach, claiming damages based on the difference between the market and contract prices, the market having risen. It was held that although the defendants were in breach, the plaintiffs had failed in their duty to mitigate, and they recovered merely £50 damages for the period of credit they would have lost by paying the cash on

10 [1912] AC 673 at 689.
11 [1967] 1 WLR 104.
12 [1895] 2 QB 253.
13 [1919] 2 KB 581. See also *Sotiros Shipping Inc v Sameiet Solholt, The Solholt* [1983] 1 Lloyds Rep 605. These decisions are criticised by Bridge (1989) 105 LQR 398.

delivery rather than when stipulated in the contract. Contrasting with this is *Strutt v Whitnell*,[14] where the defendants offered to repurchase from the plaintiff a house, which they could not transfer to him with vacant possession. The plaintiff's refusal of the offer was held not to amount to a failure to mitigate; the offer was not of an alternative performance but of no performance at all and was in effect merely equivalent to an offer by the defendants to pay the plaintiff damages.

(iii) The plaintiff's conduct is unreasonable if he refuses an operation contrary to firm medical advice. In *McAuley v London Transport Executive*[15] the plaintiff, having been injured by the defendants, refused to have an operation strongly recommended by a doctor which, if successful, would have restored him to his previous earning capacity. It was held that his refusal was unreasonable, and the plaintiff was therefore able to recover his loss of earnings only until the time when he would have recovered had he undergone the operation. On the other hand in *Selvanayagam v University of West Indies*[16] the Privy Council upheld the trial judge's decision that the plaintiff had not been unreasonable in refusing to undergo a neck operation. A doctor had recommended the operation but, given the plaintiff's diabetic condition, the recommendation had not been a strong one.

(iv) It will generally be unreasonable for the plaintiff to refuse offers of help which would have prevented further property damage. In *Anderson v Hoen, The Flying Fish*[17] the plaintiff's ship was damaged by the negligence of those in charge of the defendant's vessel. After the collision, the plaintiff's captain refused aid and in consequence the ship was destroyed. The plaintiff was able to recover for the damage caused by the collision but not for the additional loss when the ship was destroyed.

(v) The plaintiff need not take action which will put his commercial reputation or good public relations at risk. In *James Finlay & Co Ltd v Kwik Hoo Tong*[18] the seller under a cif contract tendered to the buyer a bill of lading which incorrectly stated the date of shipment. The buyer was unaware of this and entered into sub-contracts but the sub-purchasers, realising

---

14 [1975] 1 WLR 870.
15 [1957] 2 Lloyds Rep 500.
16 [1983] 1 All ER 824.
17 (1865) 3 Moo PCCNS 77.
18 [1929] 1 KB 400.

the error on the bill of lading, refused in breach of contract to take delivery. The buyer sued the seller for breach of contract and recovered substantial damages, the Court of Appeal holding that the buyer was not bound to reduce its loss by suing the sub-purchasers because to do so, when knowing of the error on the bill of lading, might seriously injure its commercial reputation. Similarly in *London and South of England Building Society v Stone*[19] borrowers from the plaintiff building society had covenanted to keep the house being purchased in good repair. In fact the house suffered from serious subsidence and was valueless and the plaintiff undertook repairs at a cost to itself of £29,000. The plaintiff had made the loan on the strength of the defendant valuer's report which had negligently failed to disclose the subsidence. In an action brought in contract and tort against the defendant valuer the plaintiff recovered as damages the sum lent (£11,880). The Court of Appeal rejected the defendant's argument that there should be a deduction of £3,000, as the amount the plaintiff could have recovered from the borrowers by enforcing the repair covenant because, to maintain its good public relations, it was reasonable for the plaintiff not to call upon the borrowers to pay for any part of the repairs.

(vi) The plaintiff need not take steps which would involve him in complicated litigation. In *Pilkington v Wood*[20] the plaintiff bought a house but when he came to sell it he discovered that his vendor had given him a defective title. The plaintiff sued the defendant, his solicitor, for contractual negligence and recovered damages based on the difference in value between the property with and without good title. The defendant's argument that the plaintiff should have mitigated by suing his vendor was rejected by Harman J because, '. . . the so-called duty to mitigate does not go so far as to oblige the injured party . . . to embark on a complicated and difficult piece of litigation against a third party.'[1]

(vii) The plaintiff need not take steps which he cannot financially afford, ie impecuniosity is an excuse for failure to mitigate. This is examined in a later section.[2]

19 [1983] 3 All ER 105.
20 [1953] Ch 770.
 1 Ibid at 777.
 2 Infra, p 87–92.

(b) The second principle—unreasonable action

Unreasonable action subsequent to a wrong is normally regarded as an aspect of intervening cause. But the unreasonable incurring of expense subsequent to the wrong is generally viewed as an aspect of the duty to mitigate.[3]

The principle is that a plaintiff should not unreasonably incur expense subsequent to the wrong.[4] As with the first principle, what is unreasonable depends on the facts, but a number of illustrations can be given in most of which the expense was held to be reasonably incurred.

So, for example, in *Holden Ltd v Bostock & Co Ltd*,[5] the defendants had sold sugar to the plaintiffs for brewing beer. Unfortunately the sugar had contained arsenic. To prevent any loss of business the plaintiffs advertised that they had changed their brewing methods. In an action against the defendants for breach of contract, the plaintiffs were awarded, inter alia, the advertising costs. Again in *Bacon v Cooper (Metals) Ltd*[6] the high hire-purchase interest charges paid for a rotor to replace that damaged beyond repair because of the defendants' breach of contract were held to be reasonably incurred and recoverable. No doubt the most common example of recoverable reasonable expenses are the medical, hospital and nursing expenses undertaken following personal injury.[7]

A particularly colourful illustration is provided by *Banco de Portugal v Waterlow & Sons Ltd*.[8] Here the defendants contracted to print banknotes for the plaintiff bank. In breach of contract they delivered a large number of these to a criminal, who put them into circulation in Portugal. On discovering this, the bank withdrew the issue. It then undertook to exchange all the notes illegally circulated for others. In an action brought against them for breach of contract the defendants argued that they were only liable for the cost of printing new notes, which amounted to £8,922, and that the further heavy loss was due to the bank's own act in giving value for the notes. But the House of Lords, by a majority, rejected this argument and held the defendants liable for the further loss because the conduct of the bank was reasonable, having regard to its commercial

3 Supra, p 38.
4 Although there appears to be no case in point, the principle of *Cory v Thames Ironworks Co* (1868) LR 3 QB 181, supra, pp 56–7, may apply by analogy: ie even though the actual expenses were unreasonably incurred a lesser amount, equivalent to what would have been reasonable expenses, may be recoverable.
5 (1902) 18 TLR 317.
6 [1982] 1 All ER 397.
7 Infra, p 192.
8 [1932] AC 452.

obligations towards the public. Lord MacMillan emphasised that no great weight should be attached to the defendant's argument that cheaper measures could have been taken:

> It is often easy after an emergency has passed to criticise the steps which have been taken to meet it, but such criticism does not come well from those who have themselves created the emergency . . . [The plaintiff] will not be held disentitled to recover the cost of such measures merely because the party in breach can suggest that other measures less burdensome to him might have been taken.[9]

On the other hand, in *Compania Financiera Soleada SA v Harmoor Tanker Corpn Inc, The Borag,*[10] the plaintiffs in seeking to gain the release of a ship detained in breach of contract took out a loan requiring very high interest charges. It was held by the Court of Appeal that such high interest charges should not be compensated since the plaintiffs had not acted reasonably in incurring them.

It should also be stressed that the fact that the incurring of expense has overall augmented the loss, rather than minimised it, ie it has not been a success, does not mean that it was unreasonably incurred and is irrecoverable. A statement to this effect in the twelfth edition of *Mayne and McGregor on Damages* was cited with approval in *Lloyds and Scottish Finance Ltd v Modern Cars and Caravans (Kingston) Ltd.*[11] *Esso Petroleum Co Ltd v Mardon*[12] may be said to illustrate it. Here the plaintiff had been induced to enter into a tenancy agreement for a petrol station by the defendant's false estimates of the potential throughput of petrol. In an action for negligent misrepresentation, or breach of a warranty that the estimate was made using reasonable care, the plaintiff was held able to recover all the loss he had suffered, until he gave up possession. This included the loss after he had entered into a fresh tenancy agreement. In the Court of Appeal's opinion, in view of the loss already suffered, the plaintiff was acting reasonably in attempting to mitigate some of that loss by entering into that new agreement: the fact that he actually suffered further loss as a result did not prevent recovery.

---

9 [1932] AC 452 at 506. This passage was approved in *Bacon v Cooper* [1982] 1 All ER 397 at 399, and *London and South of England Building Society v Stone* [1983] 3 All ER 105 at 121.
10 [1981] 1 All ER 856.
11 [1966] 1 QB 764.
12 [1976] QB 801. See also *Hoffberger v Ascot International Bloodstock Bureau Ltd* (1976) 120 Sol Jo 130. *Banco de Portugal v Waterlow & Sons Ltd* [1932] AC 452 may be a further example, depending on what was regarded as the value of the bank's commercial obligations to the public. Somewhat similar is *Gebruder Metalmann GmbH & Co KG v NBR (London) Ltd* [1984] 1 Lloyds Rep 614.

(c) When does the duty to mitigate arise in relation to the anticipatory repudiation of a contract?

Indisputably there is a duty to mitigate once there has been an actual breach of contract. This is reflected, for example, in the general rule that one assesses the market value of property at the date of the breach of contract. But the traditional approach is that, following an anticipatory repudiation, there is no duty to mitigate,[13] unless the plaintiff chooses to accept the anticipatory repudiation.[14] It is submitted that the better view is that economic efficiency should override the wishes of the innocent party to hold the contract alive and that, as in the United States,[15] the duty to mitigate should arise once there has been an anticipatory repudiation. Such a reform is supported by recent departures from *White & Carter (Councils) Ltd v McGregor*[16] regarding the analogous question of the extent to which a plaintiff is entitled to outflank the duty to mitigate by an action for the agreed price.

(4) Contributory negligence

At common law, although it was unclear whether it applied as such to breach of contract, contributory negligence was a complete defence to many torts. In other words, where applicable, it nullified the causal potency of the defendant's breach of duty.[17] However, the Law Reform (Contributory Negligence) Act 1945 made contributory negligence a partial defence, by which damages are reduced but not completely denied. Section 1(1) of that Act provides:

Where any person suffers damage as a result partly of his own fault and partly of the fault of any other person or persons, a claim in respect of that damage shall not be defeated by reason of the fault of the person suffering the damage, but the damages recoverable in respect thereof shall be reduced to such extent as the court thinks just and equitable having regard to the claimant's share in the responsibility for the damage.

---

13 *Tredegar Iron & Coal Co v Hawthorn Bros & Co* (1902) 18 TLR 716; *Shindler v Northern Raincoat Co Ltd* [1960] 1 WLR 1038.

14 As in *Melachrino v Nickoll & Knight* [1920] 1 KB 693. See also *Gebruder Metalmann GmbH & Co KG v NBR (London) Ltd* [1984] 1 Lloyds Rep 614.

15 Uniform Commercial Code, s 2–610a, s 2–723(1). But see Goetz & Scott (1983) 69 Vir LR 967, 993–5.

16 [1962] AC 413. See infra, pp 317–22.

17 Where subsequent to the breach of duty contributory negligence was therefore indistinguishable from saying that the intervening conduct of the plaintiff broke the chain of causation or, where a negligent failure to act followed a tort, from saying that the plaintiff failed in his duty to mitigate.

As far as breach of contract is concerned, the crucial question is whether the Act, and hence the defence of contributory negligence, applies at all. This will be examined after looking at the operation of the defence for torts, where generally it is clear that the Act applies.

(a) Torts

(i) What must the defendant establish?

In order for the defence to apply the defendant must establish three points. First, the plaintiff must have been at fault or negligent towards himself. To illustrate this by reference to cases of personal injury or death, the plaintiff is most obviously negligent towards himself if he negligently causes an accident (involving himself) or puts himself in an inherently dangerous position or renders an inherently non-dangerous position dangerous by failing to take safety precautions. The first situation is illustrated by the commonest of contributory negligence examples, where two motorists negligently collide. Examples of the second situation are riding on the towbar at the back of a 'traxcavator', as in *Jones v Livox Quarries Ltd*,[18] accepting a lift with someone who you know to have been drinking heavily, as in *Owens v Brimmell*,[19] or accepting a lift in a car knowing that the brakes are defective, as in *Gregory v Kelly*.[20] The classic examples of the third situation are failing to wear a seat-belt while travelling in the front seat of a car, as in *Froom v Butcher*,[1] or failing to wear a crash helmet while riding a motor-bike, as in *O'Connell v Jackson*.[2] It should be added that the courts are reluctant to find that a child has been negligent towards himself—and the younger the child the greater the reluctance.[3]

Secondly, the plaintiff's negligence must have been a factual cause of his loss. The usual 'but for' test is used to decide this. So, for example, where two motorists negligently collide, as each person's negligent driving is a factual cause of the collision, so necessarily it is a factual cause of the loss suffered by each. A case like *Froom v Butcher* stressed that while not wearing a seat-belt could of course not be said to be a factual cause of the collision, it was a factual cause of the loss, and this was what was important. On the other hand in *Owens v Brimmell* the plaintiff's negligence in not

18 [1952] 2 QB 608.
19 [1976] 3 All ER 765.
20 [1978] RTR 426.
 1 [1976] QB 286.
 2 [1972] 1 QB 270.
 3 Eg *Yachuk v Oliver Blais Co Ltd* [1949] AC 386; *Gough v Thorne* [1966] 1 WLR 1387.

wearing his seat-belt was not established to be a factual cause of his injuries—they were no worse than if he had been wearing one.

Thirdly, the plaintiff's negligence must have exposed him to the particular risk of the type of damage suffered. In the standard negligent driving case there is no difficulty in establishing this since in driving negligently or in not wearing his seat-belt the plaintiff is clearly exposing himself to a particular risk of suffering personal injury in a crash. This principle, which can be regarded as analogous to remoteness, was discussed in some detail in *Jones v Livox Quarries Ltd.* There the plaintiff was riding on the towbar at the back of a quarry vehicle. Another vehicle belonging to the defendants was negligently driven into him and the plaintiff was injured. By so riding, the plaintiff exposed himself not only to the particular risk of falling off the vehicle but also to the particular risk of being crushed—as had happened. The plaintiff was therefore found to be contributorily negligent, although Denning LJ said that this would not have been the case if, whilst riding on the towbar, the plaintiff had, for example, been hit in the eye by a shot from a negligent sportsman—he was not exposing himself to a particular risk of suffering that type of damage by riding on the towbar.

(ii) How do the courts decide the extent to which the damages should be reduced?

Section 1(1) of the Law Reform (Contributory Negligence) Act 1945 says that where contributory negligence applies, the damages '. . . shall be reduced to such extent as the court thinks just and equitable having regard to the claimant's share in the responsibility for the damage.' How exactly the courts apply these words is difficult to clarify; but what can be said as stressed by Denning LJ in *Davies v Swan Motor Co (Swansea) Ltd*,[4] is that the courts consider both the causal potency and the comparative blameworthiness of the parties' conduct.[5]

Where the defendant is held strictly liable, it might be thought difficult to apply comparative blameworthiness, since the defendant is not blameworthy at all. But Ogus[6] thinks that one can still talk in terms of comparative blameworthiness by asking how far short of the standard imposed by law did the conduct of each party fall.

4 [1949] 2 KB 291 at 326.
5 For a suggested principled approach in applying these criteria, see Gravells (1977) 93 LQR 581.
6 *Damages* p 105.

In *Froom v Butcher*[7] Lord Denning, recognising the difficulty of deciding to what extent to reduce damages and in a desire to avoid prolonging cases, suggested standard figures for reducing damages where the plaintiff has been contributorily negligent by not wearing a seat-belt. If the damage would have been prevented altogether a reduction of 25% should be made and if it would have been considerably less severe a reduction of 15% should be made. To have standard figures for very common instances of contributory negligence sensibly produces certainty and uniformity but it can only be adopted where, as with seat-belts, the blameworthiness of the contributory negligence varies hardly at all from case to case.

In *Capps v Miller*[8] the plaintiff moped-driver was severely brain-damaged when a car negligently ran into him. The plaintiff was wearing a crash helmet but, contrary to the Motor Cycles (Protective Helmet) Regulations 1980, the chin strap was unfastened and the helmet came off before the plaintiff's head struck the ground. Damages were reduced by 10% for contributory negligence in not fastening the strap. In arriving at that figure Lord Denning's guidelines were relied on but it was felt (Croom-Johnson LJ dubitante) that the true analogy to not fastening a seat-belt was not wearing a helmet at all. Wearing a helmet but not fastening the chin-strap was less blameworthy than not fastening a seat-belt (or not wearing a helmet at all) so that 10% rather than 15% was the appropriate reduction.

In deciding on the appropriate reduction contributory negligence must be kept distinct from the issue of contribution between tort-feasors. In *Fitzgerald v Lane*[9] the plaintiff was hit by two cars one after the other on a pelican crossing. The plaintiff and each of the drivers was found to have been equally to blame for the plaintiff's injuries. It was held by the House of Lords that the appropriate reduction for contributory negligence should have been 50% and not 33⅓%. In Lord Ackner's words:

. . . the determination of the extent of each of the defendants' responsibility for the damage is not made in the main action but in the contribution proceedings between the defendants, inter se, and this does not concern the plaintiff.[10]

What has to be contrasted is the plaintiff's conduct on the one hand with the totality of the tortious conduct of the defendants on the other.

7 [1976] QB 286.
8 [1989] 1 WLR 839.
9 [1989] AC 328.
10 Ibid at 345.

(iii) Contributory negligence subsequent to the tort

As has been discussed above,[11] in *The Calliope*[12] Brandon J applied contributory negligence in respect of the plaintiff's conduct subsequent to the tort. In terms of policy this is a sensible approach and there seems to be nothing in the 1945 Act to restrict the defence to contributory negligence prior to or contemporaneously with the tort.

(iv) Is contributory negligence applicable to all torts?[13]

The crucial words are those in s 4 which define fault in s 1(1) as meaning '. . . negligence, breach of statutory duty or other act or omission which gives rise to a liability in tort, or would, apart from this Act, give rise to the defence of contributory negligence'.

For reasons discussed under 'breach of contract',[14] it is best to read this as comprising two limbs, the first—'. . . negligence, breach of statutory duty or other act or omission which gives rise to a liability in tort'—referring to the defendant's fault and the second—any act or omission which '. . . would apart from this Act, give rise to the defence of contributory negligence'—referring to the plaintiff's fault.

In this context, the first limb creates no difficulties; the defendant is at fault, whenever he is liable for a tort and it makes no difference which tort. So whether contributory negligence is inapplicable to some torts turns solely on the second limb of s 4. One interpretation of the second limb is that it all depends whether, in relation to the tort for which the plaintiff is now suing, his (the plaintiff's conduct) would have given rise to the total defence of contributory negligence at common law. Since contributory negligence was probably not a defence at common law to intentional torts, like deceit and intentional trespass to the person, this view means that contributory negligence continues not to apply to such torts. That was the approach taken by Mummery J in *Alliance & Leicester Building Society v Edgestop Ltd*[15] in denying that contributory negligence can apply to the tort of deceit. But an alternative interpretation is that the conduct of the plaintiff must be of the sort that at common law would have given rise to the total defence of contributory negligence, if the plaintiff had been suing for a tort to which the defence

11 Supra, p 68.
12 [1970] P 172.
13 See Glanville Williams *Joint Torts and Contributory Negligence* (1951) pp 318–9, 326–8; Hudson (1984) 4 LS 332.
14 Infra, p 83.
15 [1993] 1 WLR 1462.

indisputably applied, for example the tort of negligence. On this view contributory negligence applies to all torts. In terms of policy this latter view is to be preferred. If principles such as intervening cause and the duty to mitigate apply to all torts, and mean that the plaintiff can be held totally responsible for his own loss, there must logically be room for a mid-position where his damages are merely reduced. This is supported by the indications in *Murphy v Culhane*[16] that contributory negligence is a defence to intentional trespass to the person. It may also derive some support from *Gran Gelato Ltd v Richcliff (Group) Ltd*[17] in which it was held that contributory negligence applies to the statutory tort of negligent misrepresentation in s 2(1) of the Misrepresentation Act 1967. Unfortunately Sir Donald Nicholls VC thought it important that the defendant was also concurrently liable for the tort of negligence at common law and drew an analogy with the approach to contributory negligence as a defence to breach of contract laid down in *Forsikringsaktieselskapet Vesta v Butcher*.[18] On the best view, that analogy is inapt given that, in contrast to where the action is for breach of contract, there is no difficulty here about the *defendant* being at fault (within the first limb of s 4).

Whichever interpretation of the second limb of s 4 is taken, there is one area of torts to which contributory negligence definitely does not apply. The Torts (Interference with Goods) Act 1977, s 11,[19] specifically lays down that contributory negligence is not a defence to conversion or intentional trespass to goods. It is submitted that, for the reason of policy just discussed, there is no sound justification for this.

(b) Breach of contract—does contributory negligence apply?[20]

In *Forsikringsaktieselskapet Vesta v Butcher*[21] the difficult question of whether contributory negligence is a defence to breach of contract was for the first time examined in detail by an appellate court. And although the Court of Appeal's discussion was obiter dicta, that is

16 [1977] QB 94. This case also supports the view that provocation, although formerly treated as a separate defence, can be regarded as a form of contributory negligence.
17 [1992] 1 All ER 865.
18 [1988] 2 All ER 43: see the next subsection.
19 This must be read subject to s 47 of the Banking Act 1979.
20 Swanton (1981) 55 ALJ 278; Palmer & Davies (1980) 29 ICLQ 415; Chandler (1989) 40 NILQ 152; Glanville Williams *Joint Torts and Contributory Negligence* pp 328–32.
21 [1988] 2 All ER 43; affd without discussion of contributory negligence [1989] AC 880, HL.

now the leading case.[1] Before examining it, it is helpful to set out briefly the three contrasting views taken in the decisions and dicta prior to *Vesta v Butcher.*

A first view was that contributory negligence never applies as a defence to an action for breach of contract. That view was supported by Stanwick J in *Sole v Hallt Ltd*,[2] where the defence was held not to apply to an occupier's breach of his contractual duty of care to a visitor; by Donaldson LJ's dictum in *Acrecrest Ltd v WS Hattrell & Partners*,[3] where he said that he was assuming that the Act did not apply to claims in contract; and, after a detailed examination, by Neill LJ, sitting as a judge in the Queen's Bench Division, in *Marintrans AB v Comet Shipping Co Ltd*,[4] which concerned the breach of a contractual duty of care to stow cargo properly.

A second view was that contributory negligence does apply as a defence to breach of contract provided the breach is of a contractual duty of care rather than the breach of a strict contractual duty. This was supported by Paull J at first instance in *Quinn v Burch Bros (Builders) Ltd*[5] and, most clearly, by Brabin J at first instance in *De Meza v Apple*,[6] where contributory negligence was held to apply to the breach of a contractual duty of care owed by an auditor to his client even though there was no concurrent liability in tort. Both cases went to the Court of Appeal which expressed no opinion on the correctness of those views.

A third view was that contributory negligence does apply as a defence to breach of contract provided the breach is of a contractual duty of care and also renders the defendant liable for the tort of negligence. This is probably supported by the Court of Appeal in *Sayers v Harlow UDC*,[7] where damages for the breach of a contractual or tortious duty of care owed by an occupier to his licensee were reduced because of contributory negligence, Lord Evershed saying that nothing turned on the foundation of liability. Unfortunately

---

1 It has been applied in *Bank of Nova Scotia v Hellenic Mutual War Risks Assoc (Bermuda) Ltd, The Good Luck* [1989] 3 All ER 628, 672; *Youell v Bland Welch & Co Ltd (No 2)* [1990] 2 Lloyd's Rep 431; *Gran Gelato Ltd v Richcliff (Group) Ltd* [1992] 1 All ER 865. It was also applied, but then unsatisfactorily evaded by using causation, in *Tennant Radiant Heat Ltd v Warrington Development Corpn* [1988] 1 EGLR 41.
2 [1973] QB 574.
3 [1983] 1 All ER 17 at 31.
4 [1985] 3 All ER 442.
5 [1966] 2 QB 370.
6 [1974] 1 Lloyd's Rep 508. See also *Artingstoll v Hewen's Garages Ltd* [1973] RTR 197.
7 [1958] 1 WLR 623 at 625.

there was no detailed reasoning on the point and it is possible to interpret the decision as alternatively favouring the second view above. The third view is more clearly favoured by Pritchard J in his influential judgment in the New Zealand case of *Rowe v Turner, Hopkins & Partners*.[8] In *Basildon District Council v JE Lesser (Properties) Ltd*[9] that decision was heavily relied on by Judge Newey QC who felt that he could not improve upon Pritchard J's words. But his support for the third view was then somewhat obscured by his ambiguous conclusion (on the face of it supporting the first view) that, 'The Act does not apply to contract.'[10]

Vesta v Butcher concerned the reinsurance of underlying insurance that the plaintiffs had given in respect of fish lost on a fish farm in Norway. The plaintiffs asked their brokers, who were the defendants, to sort out the reinsurance for them. They specifically told them in a telephone call that they did not want one of the terms in the underlying insurance (requiring a 24-hour watch over the fish) to be relevant to the reinsurance contract. But in breach of their contractual (and tortious) duty of care to the plaintiffs, the defendants failed to delete that term in the offer of reinsurance.

Ultimately it was held by the Court of Appeal, and upheld by the House of Lords, that the reinsurers were liable to pay the plaintiffs for what they had had to pay out in respect of a loss of fish irrespective of the '24-hour watch' term. The defendants' breach of contract did not therefore cause the plaintiffs any loss. But if that term had been crucial the plaintiffs would have had an action for substantial damages against the defendants for breach of contract. And it was in relation to that action that contributory negligence was discussed, as obiter dicta, by the Court of Appeal (there was no examination of the point by the Lords): for the defendants argued that the plaintiffs were contributorily negligent in relying on just the one telephone call to bring about the deletion of an important contract term, especially as the plaintiffs had asked for confirmation that the deletion was acceptable to the reinsurers and the defendants had never given that confirmation.

The Court of Appeal thought that contributory negligence could here apply because the defendants were liable not only for breach of a contractual duty of care but were also liable in the tort of negligence. Hobhouse J's reduction of damages by 75% at first instance was approved as was his threefold classification of cases for dealing with contributory negligence. A 'category 1' case is where the

8 [1980] 2 NZLR 550; revsd on liability [1982] 1 NZLR 178.
9 [1985] QB 839.
10 Ibid at 818.

defendant is in breach of a strict contractual duty. A 'category 2' case is where the defendant is in breach of a contractual duty of care. A 'category 3' case is where the defendant is in breach of a contractual duty of care and is also liable for the tort of negligence (or would be so liable, if pleaded). In terms of that classification, the Court of Appeal's view was that contributory negligence applies to breach of contract in a category 3 case only. In other words, the third of the views considered above was preferred and, in reaching that conclusion, *Sayers v Harlow*, *Rowe v Turner*, and *Basildon v Lesser* were relied on. Significantly, one of the three judges was Neill LJ who accepted that he was going back on what he had said in the *Marintrans* case.

Is the approach in *Vesta v Butcher* correct?

The central problem that has had to be faced in all the cases—and which renders this topic so complex—is that the Law Reform (Contributory Negligence) Act 1945 makes no express reference to breach of contract. Whatever one might like the law to be, one is constrained by the words of the Act. The issue is therefore one of statutory interpretation: and the crucial words are those of s 4, set out above,[11] which define 'fault' in s 1(1).

The initial problem is whose fault does s 4, or the different parts of s 4, refer to? The best view is that taken by Pritchard J in *Rowe v Turner*,[12] which was relied on by Judge Newey QC in *Basildon v Lesser* and was in effect approved by the Court of Appeal in *Vesta v Butcher*.[13] According to Pritchard J the first limb of s 4—'. . . negligence, breach of statutory duty or other act or omission, which gives rise to a liability in tort'—refers to the defendant's fault: while the second limb—any act or omission which '. . . would apart from this Act, give rise to the defence of contributory negligence'—refers to the plaintiff's fault. To divide s 4 in this way is sensible: for on the one hand, it is hard to see how any act or omission which '. . . would apart from this Act, give rise to the defence of contributory negligence' can refer to the defendant's fault, since such an act or omission might not even be actionable; and on the other hand, it seems irrelevant to establishing the plaintiff's fault whether his acts or omissions give rise to a liability in tort.

But so to divide s 4 is merely the start of the problem of statutory interpretation, for each of the two limbs can be interpreted in various ways.

11 Supra, p 79.
12 See also Glanville Williams *Joint Torts and Contributory Negligence* p 318.
13 But, while stressing that the practical effect would be the same, O'Connor LJ preferred to regard both parts of s 4 as applying to the *plaintiff's* fault: [1988] 2 All ER 43, 49.

Taking first the second limb defining the plaintiff's fault, on one interpretation the essential issue is whether the plaintiff's conduct would have given rise to the total defence of contributory negligence at common law had the plaintiff been suing, as he is now is, for breach of contract. Assuming, as seems correct, that contributory negligence was not a defence at common law, this interpretation concludes that the Act does not apply to breach of contract. This was the approach taken by Neill LJ in the *Marintrans* case. He said, '. . . once it is conceded that there was no defence *eo nomine* before the Act where the claim against the defendant lay in contract, it seems to me to follow that if the claim is in contract, there can be no relevant "fault [of the plaintiff]"'.[14]

However, there are at least two alternative interpretations according to which the second limb sometimes does apply to breach of contract, even accepting that contributory negligence was not a defence to breach of contract at common law. One of these, or an equivalent, must have been adopted in *Rowe v Turner* and *Vesta v Butcher*.

The first is that where the defendant is concurrently liable in tort, then if the plaintiff's conduct would have been a total defence at common law to that tort, had the plaintiff framed his action in tort, the Act applies even though the plaintiff has now framed his action in contract.[15] The second interpretation is that it is irrelevant to consider the defendant's actual conduct, or what the plaintiff is suing for in the instant case. Rather the second limb refers to the plaintiff's conduct being of the sort that at common law would have given rise to the total defence of contributory negligence, if the plaintiff had been suing for a cause of action to which the defence indisputably applied, eg the tort of negligence. On this second interpretation, the plaintiff's fault in the second limb is kept rigidly distinct from the defendant's fault in the first limb.

The common feature of these alternative interpretations is that the second limb of s 4 does sometimes apply to breach of contract, so that the applicability of contributory negligence rests on the first limb of s 4 defining the defendant's fault. So turning now to the first limb (which was primarily focused on in *Rowe v Turner* and *Vesta v Butcher*) does 'negligence, breach of statutory duty, or other act or omission which gives rise to a liability in tort' include the defendant's breach of contract?

One approach is to regard the first limb as comprising three

---

14 [1985] 3 All ER 442, 447.
15 Palmer & Davies (1980) 29 ICLQ 415, 445; cf Swanton (1981) 55 ALJ 278, 280–1.

separate clauses, ie 'which gives rise to a liability in tort' does not qualify 'negligence'. On this view, breach of a contractual duty of care can simply be regarded as included within 'negligence'. This accords with Brabin J's view in *De Meza v Apple*.[16] More controversially, one could even say that a negligent breach of a strict contractual duty is included within 'negligence'.

But such an approach seems to ignore the word 'other', and in *Rowe v Turner* and *Vesta v Butcher* (and *Marintrans v Comet Shipping*) it was considered that 'negligence' (and 'breach of statutory duty') is qualified by 'which gives rise to a liability in tort'. Taking that interpretation, the most natural conclusion, and the one adopted by Neill LJ in *Marintrans*, is that, as breach of contract is not liability in tort, the Act does not apply to breach of contract. But in *Rowe v Turner* and *Vesta v Butcher* it was considered that the words do cover where the defendant is being sued only for the breach of a contractual duty of care provided he would also be liable for the tort of negligence on the ground that that is then 'negligence . . . which gives rise to a liability in tort'.

So much for the technicalities in construing the 1945 Act. How satisfactory as a matter of policy is the 'category 3' only approach of *Vesta v Butcher*?

Two main criticisms can be made.

The first is that it encourages an odd reversal of roles in that a blameworthy plaintiff will be better off, as regards contributory negligence, if he can establish that the defendant was merely liable for breach of a contractual duty of care (or the breach of a strict contractual duty) and was not also liable for the tort of negligence. In other words, as far as contributory negligence is concerned, the plaintiff will be trying to show that the defendant was not also liable in the tort of negligence, while the defendant will be trying to show that he was also liable in the tort of negligence.

Secondly, it would seem that contributory negligence ought to apply as a defence to breach of contract, irrespective of whether the defendant is concurrently liable in the tort of negligence and even if the duty broken was strict. If the plaintiff's unreasonable conduct can sometimes result in his recovering no damages, through the principles of intervening cause or mitigation, it must be sensible for there to be a mid-position where his negligence results in a mere reduction of damages. This is most obviously so where the defendant is in breach of a contractual duty of care, for then the plaintiff's and the defendant's fault are both in the same range, ie there is clear

16 [1974] 1 Lloyds Rep 508.

negligence/blameworthiness on both sides. But the same argument applies even where there is the breach of a strict contractual duty. After all, contributory negligence is applicable to torts of strict liability.[17]

In line with that argument, the Law Commission in its Working Paper *Contributory Negligence as a Defence in Contract*[18] provisionally recommended that contributory negligence should be an available defence to the breach of all contractual obligations, including strict obligations. In other words, the provisional suggestion was that the defence should be extended from cases within category 3 to categories 1 and 2.

The recent decision of the Court of Appeal in *Schering Agrochemicals Ltd v Resibel NV SA*[19] constitutes a classic illustration of the injustice that the present law can cause. It provides the best possible support for the Law Commission's provisional proposals.

The plaintiffs manufactured and bottled certain inflammable chemicals. The defendants supplied them with equipment that heat-sealed caps on to bottles. The equipment contained a safety alarm system whereby the heat sealer would be switched off if a bottle was stationary for too long and thereby exposed to excessive heat. Two months after the equipment was operational, there was a serious fire at the plaintiffs' premises owing to a defect in the safety system of the heat sealer. On appeal, the defendants accepted that they were in breach of a strict contractual duty in supplying equipment that was not reasonably fit for its purpose, contrary to s 14(3) of the Sale of Goods Act 1979. The crucial fact in what would otherwise have been a simple case was that three weeks before the fire there had been an incident, observed by two of the plaintiffs' employees and reported to a supervisor, in which the safety system did not switch off when it should have done, resulting in a small explosion in one or more of the bottles and an orange flash. The supervisor took no action in response to that report.

The Court of Appeal held that the plaintiffs' unreasonable failure to investigate that incident (which would have revealed the defect) or to close down the bottling line pending investigations meant that no damages at all should be awarded for the loss caused by the fire: the plaintiffs had failed in their duty to mitigate their loss or had broken the chain of causation.[20]

---

17 See, eg *Cork v Kirby MacLean Ltd* [1952] 2 All ER 402; *Mullard v Ben Line Steamers Ltd* [1970] 1 WLR 1414 (breach of statutory duty).
18 (No 114, 1990).
19 (26 November 1992, unreported).
20 *Supra*, p 38.

Nolan LJ observed that the defendants were fortunate that the present state of the law ruled out apportionment. Had the Law Commission's provisional recommendations been law, the plaintiffs would have been entitled to damages for the loss resulting from the fire but with an appropriate reduction, as in tort, for contributory negligence. It is submitted that that would have been a more just and principled outcome.

Of course to extend the scope of contributory negligence so that it can act as a defence to all types of breach of contract runs the risk of turning many straightforward claims for contractual damages into heavy disputes about comparative blameworthiness and causative potency and hence about the appropriate reduction that should be made. It can be argued, therefore, that principle should to some extent give way to the policy of not creating uncertainty. One obvious compromise would be merely to extend contributory negligence to category 2. An alternative compromise might be to extend contributory negligence to category 1, while restricting to a few fixed percentages (say 25%, 50%, and 75%) the possible reductions for contributory negligence.

In its report the Law Commission has bowed to the fear of too much uncertainty (hence making settlements more difficult to achieve, payments into court harder to assess, and trials longer and more expensive) by backtracking from its provisional proposals and recommending that contributory negligence be extended merely to category 2.[1] This compromise reform would have the great merit of removing the reversal of role oddity: and unlike the provisional proposals it limits the risk of complicating straightforward damages claims. But in abandoning pure principle it leaves in play the 'all or nothing' injustice forced upon courts in cases like *Schering*. And it should be realised that, if it is correct that the courts fully accept consistent concurrent liability,[2] very few, if any, cases fall within category 2 and not category 3 so that the proposed reform would be largely cosmetic.

(5) Impecuniosity

According to the House of Lords decision in *Owners of Dredger Liesbosch v Owners of Steamship Edison, The Liesbosch*,[3] loss resulting from the plaintiff's weak financial position is irrecoverable. Here the

---

1 Report No 219 (1993) 'Contributory Negligence as a Defence in Contract'.
2 Supra, p 5.
3 [1933] AC 449. Davies (1982) JBL 21.

dredger, 'Liesbosch', was fouled and sunk by the negligent navigation of the 'Edison'. The owners of the 'Liesbosch' were under contract to complete work within a certain time. Although a substitute dredger could have been bought and fairly quickly adapted for use, the owners of the 'Liesbosch' could not afford to buy a substitute at once and had to hire a replacement. This was more expensive to use than a substitute dredger would have been, as it required the attendance of a tug and two barges. The House of Lords held that the plaintiffs could recover the market price of a comparable dredger, the expenses that would have been incurred in adapting the dredger for use, and the loss on the contract between the date of the sinking and the date on which the substitute dredger could reasonably have been ready for work. But they could not recover their greater actual loss including, in particular, the hire fee and expenditure incurred in using the hire vessel, because that resulted from their impecuniosity. Lord Wright rationalised this decision on grounds of either intervening cause or remoteness. He said that the extra loss arose from the plaintiffs' '. . . impecuniosity as a separate and concurrent cause, extraneous to and distinct in character from the tort', and, '. . . if the financial embarrassment is to be regarded as a consequence of the tort, I think it is too remote, but I prefer to regard it as an independent cause.'[4] However, since by applying normal principles of causation (and more arguably remoteness) to the facts the loss from impecuniosity should have been recoverable, Lord Wright was in reality treating impecuniosity as a reason in itself for limiting damages.

At the same time Lord Wright accepted Lord Collins' dictum in *Clippens Oil Co Ltd v Edinburgh and District Water Trustees*[5] to the effect that if a plaintiff failed to mitigate his loss because of impecuniosity this did not act to reduce the amount of damages he would recover ie no argument based on mitigation could prevent full recovery by an impecunious plaintiff. Lord Collins had there said, '. . . the wrongdoer must take his victim *talem qualem*, and if the position of the latter is aggravated because he is without the means of mitigating it, so much the worse for the wrongdoer.'[6]

The denial of recovery for loss flowing from impecuniosity seems unjustified in terms of policy. As Sir Patrick Bennett QC said at first instance in *Perry v Sidney Phillips & Son*:[7]

I find it difficult to understand why, if you harm somebody who is a

4 Ibid at 460.
5 [1907] AC 291.
6 Ibid at 303.
7 [1982] 1 All ER 1005 at 1013.

millionaire and thereby increase the damages you have to pay, or a talented musician whose hands are damaged, which also increases the damages you have to pay, when the victim is impecunious . . . that fact is used via *The Edison* decision to reduce the damages.

Moreover it is mystifying how Lord Wright could regard the whole issue as being treated differently if viewed in terms of the duty to mitigate. Although *The Liesbosch* has never been overruled, it is therefore not surprising that the courts have often not followed it.[8]

In *Muhammad Issa El Sheikh Ahmed v Ali*[9] and *Trans Trust SPRL v Danubian Trading Co Ltd*[10] loss flowing from impecuniosity was held to be recoverable so long as it satisfied the normal test for remoteness and *The Liesbosch* was ignored. In the latter case Denning LJ said, 'It was said that the damages were the result of the impecuniosity of the sellers and that it was a rule of law that such damages are too remote. I do not think there is any such rule.'[11] It is true that both these cases were contract cases, and the courts may therefore have felt more free to depart from *The Liesbosch*, that being a tort case. But there is no reason in principle why the decision is any less applicable in contract than tort; and in purporting to reconcile the *Muhammad v Ali* case with *The Liesbosch*, Lord Wright in *Monarch SS Co v A/B Karlshamns Oljefabriker*[12] did say that '. . . the difference in result did not depend on the differences (if any) between contract and tort.'

In other cases, the issue has been viewed in terms of the duty to mitigate so that in accordance with *The Liesbosch* the loss due to impecuniosity could be compensated. In *Robbins of Putney Ltd v Meek*,[13] for example, the defendants in breach of contract refused to accept a 1967 Bentley T series car from the plaintiff sellers. The plaintiffs sold the car to another buyer at a lower price, largely because they were short of funds and as a result did not want to wait for a higher price. The plaintiffs were awarded damages based on the original contract price minus the price obtained from the substitute buyer. This was so, even though the loss could be said to flow from the plaintiffs' impecuniosity, because viewed in terms of the duty to mitigate and following *The Liesbosch* and *Clippens Oil* the plaintiffs had acted reasonably.

---

8 In addition to the cases discussed below, see *Burns v MAN Automotive (Aust) Pty Ltd* (1986) 69 ALR 11 (esp per Gibbs CJ).
9 [1947] AC 414.
10 [1952] 2 QB 297.
11 Ibid at 306.
12 [1949] 1 All ER 1 at 14.
13 [1971] RTR 345.

In other cases *The Liesbosch* has been distinguished. In *Dodd Properties v Canterbury City Council*[14] the plaintiffs' building had been seriously damaged by the defendants' pile-driving operations. The plaintiffs sued in negligence and nuisance and were held to be entitled to the cost of repairs. The controversial question, however, was at what date should the cost of repairs be assessed—soon after the cause of the action arose (1970) or at the date of the hearing (1978) by which time the repair costs had almost trebled? The plaintiffs had not carried out any repairs because, inter alia, they could not afford to do so unless they knew that the defendants would be legally liable for the repair cost. Cantley J at first instance had awarded the 1970 cost of repairs on the ground that *The Liesbosch* prevented him awarding the 1978 cost since this would be to allow recovery for loss flowing from impecuniosity. The Court of Appeal however overturned this decision and awarded the 1978 cost of repairs. *The Liesbosch* was distinguished because here the plaintiffs' impecuniosity was not the only reason why they had delayed in carrying out the repairs: the other was that it would not have made commercial sense to repair the building without first knowing whether they would be compensated for the repairs, ie if they were not to be compensated it may have made commercial sense not to bother repairing the building because the profits to be made might not cover the costs of repair.[15] Alternatively, the Court of Appeal said that the case should be viewed in terms of the duty to mitigate and, in accordance with *Clippens Oil* and *The Liesbosch*, it had not been unreasonable to delay repair on the basis of impecuniosity.

Similarly in *Perry v Sidney Phillips*[16] the Court of Appeal judges went out of their way to distinguish *The Liesbosch*. The plaintiff had purchased a house in reliance on a survey report prepared by the defendants. After completion he discovered serious defects which had not been mentioned in the report. He could not afford to carry out repairs and the overall result was that he suffered a good deal of mental distress. The defendants were held to be both negligent and in breach of contract. One of the questions that arose on appeal was whether mental distress damages should be awarded given that the plaintiff's impecuniosity was a cause of that distress. The Court of Appeal held that the mental distress should be compensated and *The Liesbosch* was distinguished. Most radical was Lord Denning who felt that *The Liesbosch* should be restricted to its particular facts

14 [1980] 1 All ER 928.
15 See similarly, *Martindale v Duncan* [1973] 1 WLR 574.
16 [1982] 3 All ER 705.

and not generally applied. Oliver LJ distinguished it on similar grounds to that adopted in the *Dodd Properties* case, namely that impecuniosity was not the only reason for failing to carry out the repairs: the other was that the defendants were disputing their legal liability to pay any damages. Finally Kerr LJ distinguished *The Liesbosch* on the ground that there the loss due to impecuniosity was too remote whereas here, being reasonably foreseeable, it was not.

It was on this last ground that *The Liesbosch* was distinguished in *Archer v Brown*,[17] where the plaintiff had been induced by the defendant's fraudulent misrepresentation to buy shares from the defendant which the defendant had already sold. In order to finance the purchase the plaintiff had taken out a bank loan. In an action for deceit, he claimed, inter alia, damages of £13,528 which was the amount of the interest charges paid on the loan. Peter Pain J rejected the defendant's argument that such a loan was irrecoverable because it flowed from the plaintiff's impecuniosity, and said that, applying a reasonable foreseeability test, '. . . it must have been plain to the defendant that his deceit was putting the plaintiff in a position where he could not repay the bank. This was quite different from *The Liesbosch* case, where the parties were complete strangers before the accident which gave rise to the claim.'[18]

Finally, in distinguishing *The Liesbosch* in *Mattocks v Mann*,[19] in which the claim was for the tort of negligence, Beldam LJ said, '. . . it is only in an exceptional case that it is possible or correct to isolate impecuniosity . . . as a separate cause and as terminating the consequences of a defendant's wrong'.

In still other cases loss flowing from impecuniosity has been compensated without the judges making any mention of the problem.[20]

It would be tempting to conclude from all this that loss flowing from impecuniosity is nowadays as recoverable as any other loss. But unfortunately there is still the odd case in which *The Liesbosch* is applied. For example, in *Ramwade Ltd v W J Emson & Co Ltd*[1] the plaintiffs' lorry had been written off in a road accident. Negligently and in breach of contract the defendant insurance brokers had failed to provide the plaintiffs with comprehensive insurance so that they were not covered for the lorry. In an action against the defendants in contract and tort the plaintiffs were at first instance awarded damages for the lorry's value and for the cost of

17 [1984] 2 All ER 267.
18 Ibid at 277.
19 [1993] RTR 13.
20 Eg *Wroth v Tyler* [1974] Ch 30; *The Borag* [1981] 1 All ER 856; *Wadsworth v Lydall* [1981] 1 WLR 598; *Bacon v Cooper Metals Ltd* [1982] 1 All ER 397.
 1 [1987] RTR 72.

hiring substitute lorries (except for the first six weeks) which would not have been incurred had the plaintiffs been insured (the assumption being that an insurance company would have paid over the lorry's value, enabling replacement, after about six weeks). However the Court of Appeal overturned the award in relation to the hiring charges, one of the grounds being that in so far as that loss flowed from the plaintiffs' impecuniosity it was irrecoverable under *The Liesbosch*. This was a most unsatisfactory decision not only in terms of policy but also because none of the cases distinguishing or ignoring *The Liesbosch* was referred to. Nevertheless it does serve as a useful reminder that, until formally overruled and however unsatisfactory its continued existence, *The Liesbosch* cannot simply be written off.

3. PRINCIPLES LIMITING COMPENSATORY DAMAGES SOLELY FOR BREACH OF CONTRACT

Apart from the five general principles limiting compensatory damages for both torts and breach of contract, there are two principles which limit compensatory damages solely for breach of contract.[2]

(1) No damages beyond the defendant's minimum contractual obligation

Where a contract entitles the defendant to perform in alternative ways or, as it is sometimes expressed, the defendant has a discretion as to the contractual benefits to be conferred on the plaintiff, damages are generally assessed on the basis that the defendant would have performed in the way most favourable to himself. As Maule J said in *Cockburn v Alexander*,[3] 'Generally speaking, where there are several ways in which the contract might be performed, that mode is adopted which is the least profitable to the plaintiff and the least burthensome to the defendant'; and in *Lavarack v Woods of Colchester Ltd*,[4] Diplock LJ said, 'The first task of the assessor of damages is to estimate as best he can what the plaintiff would have

---

2 A third—the rule in *Bain v Fothergill* (1874) LR 7 HL 158—was abolished by the Law of Property (Miscellaneous Provisions) Act 1989, s 3. For the old law, see *Remedies for Torts and Breach of Contract* (1st edn) pp 83–4.
3 (1848) 6 CB 791 at 814.
4 [1967] 1 QB 278.

gained . . . if the defendant had fulfilled his legal obligation and had done no more.'[5]

The cases provide a number of illustrations of the application of this principle. As shown in *Kaye Steam Navigation Co v W & R Barnett*,[6] for example, if in a contract for the carriage of goods by sea the cargo-owner has the right to choose between a number of different ports for the cargo to be unloaded, damages for his failure to provide the cargo to the carrier will be based on the assumption that he would have chosen the most distant port for unloading. In *Re Thornett & Fehr and Yuills Ltd*,[7] it was held that in a contract for the sale of goods, where the seller has an option as to the exact quantity to be delivered (in this case, '200 tons, 5% more or less') damages for non-delivery are based on the assumption that he would have delivered the smallest quantity, ie here 190 tons. Wrongful dismissal actions provide a particularly rich source of examples.[8] So, as held in *British Guiana Credit v Da Silva*,[9] where an employee could have been dismissed with notice, but has been dismissed without notice, damages for his loss of earnings are restricted to the period of notice. Again where it is at the employer's discretion to make certain payments, no damages should be awarded for them in a wrongful dismissal action: so, in *Lavarack v Woods of Colchester Ltd*, no damages were awarded in relation to bonuses under a service contract that still had two years eight months to run; and in *Beach v Reed Corrugated Cases Ltd*[10] no damages were awarded for the fees that the employee, a director, could have been paid. Similarly in *Withers v General Theatre Corpn Ltd*,[11] an actor who had been wrongfully dismissed recovered no damages for the loss of the opportunity to enhance his reputation by appearing at a famous theatre, because the defendant had the option as to the theatres at which the plaintiff should appear.

A very difficult question is whether the usual principle is infringed by the courts' assessment of damages in hire-purchase agreements

5 Ibid at 294.
6 (1932) 48 TLR 440. See also *Phoebus D Kyprianou Co v Wm Pim Jnr & Co* [1977] 2 Lloyd's Rep 570; *The Rija* [1981] 2 Lloyd's Rep 267; *Spiliada Maritime Corpn v Louis Dreyfus Corpn* [1983] Com LR 268; *Kurt A Becher GmbH v Roplak Enterprises SA, The World Navigator* [1991] 2 Lloyd's Rep 23.
7 [1921] 1 KB 219.
8 But as shown in *Rigby v Ferodo Ltd* [1988] ICR 29 the principle has no application where the defendant has continued to employ the plaintiff, while underpaying him. It would contradict the facts to postulate that it would have been cheaper for the defendant to have dismissed the plaintiff.
9 [1965] 1 WLR 248.
10 [1956] 2 All ER 652.
11 [1933] 2 KB 536.

where the debtor repudiates the contract. As established in *Yeoman Credit v Waragowski*,[12] damages are assessed on the assumption that the debtor would have gone on to pay off the instalments, albeit without exercising his option to purchase. So the creditor is entitled to recover the unpaid balance of the hire-purchase price, less the sum fixed as the fee for exercise of the option to purchase, the proceeds of resale of goods repossessed or their value, and a discount to allow for acceleration of payment.[13]

It can be argued that that contradicts the usual principle: as the debtor had the option to terminate the contract lawfully at any time, the creditor's damages should be restricted to those to which he would have been entitled if the debtor had terminated.[14] But the difficulty is that usually in such contracts the debtor in choosing to terminate (other than for the creditor's breach) would be bound by a minimum payment clause that would dictate payment of a sum at least as great as judicially assessed damages. It follows that, unless the minimum payment clause is invalid as a penalty (even though there is no breach in issue),[15] the assessment in *Waragowski* does not normally exceed the defendant's minimum contractual obligation.

In applying the usual principle there are two qualifications that must be borne in mind. The first is that where, on the construction of the contract, the court considers that it was the parties' intention that the defendant's discretion should be exercised reasonably, damages will be assessed on the basis of the defendant's minimum *reasonable* performance. In *Abrahams v Herbert Reiach Ltd*,[16] the defendants, a firm of publishers, agreed with the plaintiffs, authors of a series of articles on athletics, to publish the articles in a book, paying the authors 4d for every copy of the book sold. The number of copies to be printed and other details regarding the publication

---

12 [1961] 3 All ER 145.
13 This follows from the *Waragowski* case, as modified by *Overstone Ltd v Shipway* [1962] 1 WLR 117.
14 See *Financings v Baldock* [1963] 2 QB 104, 113 (per Lord Denning MR). But the decision in *Baldock* distinguished between the creditor accepting a repudiatory breach (*Waragowski* damages recoverable) and the creditor terminating for breach under an express term (damages only recoverable for breaches before termination). That untenable distinction has been applied subsequently (see, eg *Charterhouse Credit Co Ltd v Tolly* [1963] 2 QB 683) but, fortunately, it has in effect been emasculated by *Lombard North Central plc v Butterworth* [1987] QB 527. See the excellent article by Opeskin (1990) 106 LQR 293 (cf Treitel (1987) LMCLQ 143); Goode *Hire Purchase Law and Practice* (2nd edn, 1970) pp 400–2; *McGregor on Damages* (15th edn, 1988) paras 862–5.
15 Infra, pp 331–4.
16 [1922] 1 KB 477.

were left to the publishers' discretion. They refused to publish the book. In an action for breach of contract, the Court of Appeal seems to have held that damages should be assessed on the basis not that the defendants would have published the minimum number of copies that could be described as a publication, but rather that they would have printed the minimum number that was reasonable in all the circumstances. Similarly in *Paula Lee Ltd v Robert Zehil & Co Ltd*[17] the plaintiffs, who were dress manufacturers, entered into a contract by which they appointed the defendants the sole distributors for the sale of their garments in a certain territory. The defendants undertook to purchase not less than 16,000 garments each season. The defendants repudiated the contract with two seasons left to run. In an action for that breach of contract, Mustill J held that there was an implied term that the garments would be selected in a reasonable manner and that it would not have been reasonable for the defendants to select the 32,000 cheapest garments because some variation of style, size and colour would be necessary to fulfil buyers' desires. Damages should therefore be assessed, applying *Abrahams v Herbert Reiach Ltd*, in terms of that reasonable selection which would be the cheapest for the defendants to buy.

The second qualification is that while a particular performance may be the least burdensome to the defendant when judged solely according to the contract, this may not be the basis upon which damages are assessed because the courts judge the defendant's least burdensome performance by taking all other potential losses into account. The classic expression of this was in *Lavarack v Woods of Colchester Ltd*,[18] where Diplock LJ said, '. . . one must not assume that he [the defendant] will cut off his nose to spite his face and so [act] as to reduce his legal obligations to the plaintiff by incurring greater loss in other respects'.[19] The decision in *Bold v Brough, Nicholson and Hall Ltd*[20] is probably best explained on this basis. There the plaintiff, who had been wrongfully dismissed by the defendant, claimed for the loss of pension rights. Phillimore J held that the plaintiff should be compensated for this loss even though the defendant had the right to terminate the pension scheme on notice because it was unlikely that it would have taken 'a step so

17 [1983] 2 All ER 390.
18 [1967] 1 QB 278.
19 Ibid at 295.
20 [1963] 3 All ER 849. See also *Commonwealth of Australia v Amann Aviation Pty Ltd* (1991) 66 ALJR 123 (in assessing reliance damages it was assumed by all their Honours, with the exception of Toohey J, that the defendants would have exercised an option to renew the contract so that there was no need for a discount for the chance of non-renewal).

disastrous to its relations with all its employees solely to defeat a claim by this plaintiff.[1]

It would seem that the rationale for giving no damages beyond the defendant's minimum contractual obligation is that people generally do not do more than they are legally bound to do and this therefore represents the most realistic assessment of the way in which the defendant would have performed; the plaintiff is thereby being put most closely into the position he would have been in if the contract had been performed. But such an approach is not always satisfactory, for there are situations where there is at least a reasonable chance that the defendant would have gone beyond his bare legal obligation. A good example is provided by *Lavarack v Woods of Colchester Ltd*[2] in relation to the bonus payments. Applying the normal principle, damages were not awarded for these even though there was a good chance that they would have been paid. It was for this reason that Lord Denning dissented on the point: he would have awarded damages to the plaintiff for his lost chance of gaining the bonuses: '. . . the compensation is to be based on the probabilities of the case—on the remuneration which the plaintiff might reasonably be expected to receive—and not on the bare minimum necessary to satisfy the legal right'.[3] Lord Denning's approach seems preferable.[4] The aim should always to be put the plaintiff most closely in the position he would have been in if the contract had been performed, and the present approach of assessing damages according to the performance least burdensome to the defendant should be regarded merely as being *generally* the best way to achieve that aim.

An analogous (or, on another view, the same) principle as that being discussed in this section applies where the plaintiff would himself have committed a repudiatory breach had the contract continued. In *The Mihalis Angelos*[5] charterers were entitled to cancel a charterparty if the ship was not ready to load by July 20. On July 17, when it was clear that the ship would not be ready to load by July 20, the charterers purported to terminate the contract. It was held

1 Ibid at 856.
2 [1967] 1 QB 278.
3 Ibid at 288.
4 But a strong argument based on this approach was rejected in *The World Navigator* [1991] 2 Lloyd's Rep 23.
5 [1971] 1 QB 164. See also *Commonwealth of Australia v Amann Aviation Pty Ltd* (1991) 66 ALJR 123 (in assessing reliance damages it was held by the majority that the *Mihalis Angelos* principle did not affect the result because there was merely a 20% chance that the defendants would otherwise have validly cancelled the contract for the plaintiffs' own breach).

that they were entitled to do so and were therefore not liable in damages. But in dicta the Court of Appeal discussed what the position would have been had that termination by the charterers constituted an anticipatory repudiation which had been accepted by the owners. It was thought that the owners' damages would have been nominal because the charterers would otherwise have exercised their option to terminate on July 20. In Edmund Davies LJ's words:

> The assumption has to be made that, had there been no anticipatory breach, the defendant would have performed his legal obligation and no more . . . [I]t is beyond dispute that, on the belated arrival of the Mihalis Angelos at Haiphong, the charterers not only could have elected to cancel the charterparty, but would certainly have done so. The rights lost to the owners by reason of the assumed anticipatory breach were thus certain to be rendered valueless.[6]

(2) The only obligation broken is to pay money

London, Chatham and Dover Rly Co v South Eastern Rly[7] has traditionally been regarded as House of Lords authority for the rule that where the only obligation broken is to pay money, no damages can be awarded and the sole remedy is the award of the agreed sum.

However this rule has never been regarded as affecting the plaintiff's right to terminate the contract and sue for damages for the defendant's repudiatory breach, presumably on the ground that a repudiatory breach always goes beyond merely being the breach of an obligation to pay money. So of course, a seller of goods can sue the buyer for non-acceptance, and a wrongfully dismissed employee can sue for lost earnings. Similarly damages are recoverable for a debtor's failure to pay so many hire-purchase instalments as to constitute a repudiation of the contract.[8]

But there were two respects in which the rule did formerly disadvantage the creditor. First, he could recover no compensation for loss of the general use of the money during a delay before the agreed sum was paid: in other words he could recover no interest. Secondly, he could recover no compensation for other losses caused by not receiving the agreed sum or receiving it late.

Subsequent developments have reduced or removed these disadvantages. As regards the first, the courts' statutory power to

---

6 Ibid at 203.
7 [1893] AC 429.
8 *Yeoman Credit Ltd v Waragowski* [1961] 3 All ER 145. In addition the rule does not prevent a promisee recovering damages where the promise is to pay money to a third party: infra, p 317.

award interest on an agreed sum has gradually been extended. The law is now contained in s 35A of the Supreme Court Act 1981,[9] and by s 35A(3) interest can be awarded even where the agreed sum was paid before judgment. However this power does not extend to where the sum was paid before proceedings started. In *Tehno-Impex v Gebr van Weelde Scheepvartkantoor BV*[10] the Court of Appeal held that arbitrators at least could get round this, by awarding damages to compensate for the loss of the use of the money in this situation. But in *President of India v La Pintada Compania Navigacion SA*[11] the House of Lords overruled *Tehno-Impex* and applied *London, Chatham and Dover Rly*. The consequence is that where the agreed sum is paid before proceedings to recover it have begun, the creditor remains disadvantaged because he cannot recover compensation for loss of the general use of the money during a delay before the payment.

The second disadvantage has been entirely, or almost entirely, removed by the decision in *Wadsworth v Lydall*[12] (following earlier doubts cast on it in *Trans Trust SPRL v Danubian Trading Co Ltd*).[13] When the defendant failed to pay all the agreed sum, the plaintiff had to take out a mortgage in order to finance a contract to purchase some land and also incurred legal costs. He was awarded damages for interest charges paid on the mortgage and for his legal costs, even though these followed from the defendant's failure to pay a sum of money. The Court of Appeal distinguished *London, Chatham and Dover Rly* on the ground that, while it prevents general damages for failure to pay a sum of money, it does not prevent special damages. The exact scope of the decision rests on what is here meant by the terms general and special damages. The Lords in the *President of India* case regarded them as referring to the first and second rules, respectively, in *Hadley v Baxendale*.[14] But an alternative interpretation, which is to be preferred in that it limits further the traditional rule, is that special damages refers to any loss other than the general loss of use of the money (that is, other than the loss

9 Infra, p 256. See generally Mann (1985) 101 LQR 30.
10 [1981] QB 648.
11 [1985] AC 104. For criticism, see Wooldridge and Insley (1985) 4 CJQ 97.
12 [1981] 1 WLR 598. Approved by the House of Lords in the *President of India* case [1985] AC 104 at 125–7. In so far as the traditional rule rested on grounds similar to those denying damages for loss from impecuniosity, *Wadsworth* is consistent with the recent departures from *The Liesbosch* [1933] AC 449: supra, pp 87–92.
13 [1952] 2 QB 297.
14 (1854) 9 Exch 341. Cf *International Mineral & Chemical Corpn v Karl O Helm AG* [1986] 1 Lloyds Rep 81 in which currency exchange losses were held recoverable as special damages.

involved in the first disadvantage) so that the second disadvantage has been removed altogether.

The effect of these developments is that a creditor will now rarely be disadvantaged by the traditional limiting rule, and this is to be welcomed for there is nothing in terms of policy to justify that rule. Nevertheless it is to be regretted that the House of Lords in the *President of India* case did not take the golden opportunity presented to rid the law of the remaining disadvantages by removing *London, Chatham and Dover Rly* altogether.[15]

4. GENERAL POINTS ON THE ASSESSMENT OF COMPENSATORY DAMAGES

(1) The form of damages

(a) The once-and-for-all rule

This rule can be expressed as follows: a court must assess in a lump sum all past, present and prospective loss resulting from the particular tort or breach of contract being sued for, because no damages can be later given for a cause of action on which judgment has already been given. The classic authority is *Fitter v Veal*,[16] where the plaintiff had been awarded £11 damages against the defendant in an action for assault and battery. His injuries proved to be more serious than at first thought and he had to undergo an operation on his skull. It was held that he could not recover for this further loss in a new action.

Naturally, this rule does not prevent a different cause of action later being brought, and in deciding what amounts to a different cause of action it should be remembered that a single act may give rise to more than one cause of action. A leading case is *Brunsden v Humphrey*,[17] which involved a road accident injuring the plaintiff

---

15 See also, from a comparative perspective, Treitel *Remedies for Breach of Contract* p 205; and for developments in Australia and New Zealand, see Davis *Essays on Damages* (ed Finn) pp 142–8.

16 (1701) 12 Mod Rep 542. For more recent examples, see *Buckland v Palmer* [1984] 3 All ER 554; *Burke v Tower Hamlets HA* (1989) Times, 10 August.

17 (1884) 14 QBD 141. See also *Darley Main Colliery Co v Mitchell* (1886) 11 App Cas 127; *O'Sullivan v Williams* [1992] 3 All ER 385. The decision in *Brunsden* has been criticised in eg *Talbot v Berkshire CC* [1993] 4 All ER 9; cf *The Indian Endurance* [1993] 1 All ER 998, 1006 (per Lord Goff). For continuing wrongs (even apparently where the defendant commits no further acts) a fresh cause of action accrues *de die in diem* and hence 'prospective loss' is irrecoverable (at common law) as being caused by a future rather than an already committed tort or breach of contract: eg *Battishill v Reed* (1856) 18 CB 696.

and damaging his vehicle. It was held that the plaintiff had two separate causes of action, one for his personal injury and another for his property damage.

The purpose of the once-and-for-all rule is to prevent continual litigation. But it carries with it the problem of the court having to make an assessment of future loss, which must necessarily involve guesswork and usually produces inaccuracy. As Lord Scarman said in *Lim Poh Choo v Camden and Islington Area Health Authority*,[18] 'Knowledge of the future being denied to mankind, so much of the award as is to be attributed to future loss and suffering . . . will almost surely be wrong. There is really only one certainty: the future will prove the award to be either too high or too low.' While an assessment of damages generally involves some speculation in judging what position the plaintiff would have been in if no tort or breach of contract had been committed, to have to assess once-and-for-all what position the plaintiff will from now on be in requires additional speculation about the uncertain.

For personal injury, prospective loss is often an important head of assessment, and it is here that the question has been hotly debated of whether the once-and-for-all rule should be departed from by introducing provisional damages, or, more radically, reviewable periodic payments.[19] The difficulties of assessing the future are particularly obvious in this field—common questions that arise, for example, are whether further operations will be necessary, whether brain damage will lead to epilepsy, when the plaintiff will die or when he will be fit to return to work. In all such instances provisional damages or reviewable periodic payments would make the courts' task easier and would enable them to put the plaintiff more closely into the position he would have been in if the tort or breach of contract had not been committed.

A rather different criticism of the once-and-for-all rule in relation to future pecuniary loss following on personal injury or death is that the lump sum award, which is intended to be sufficient to provide for the plaintiff's pecuniary needs over the years, may be quickly and foolishly dissipated and may hence not fulfil its purpose. Periodic payments would overcome this. Moreover, periodic payments correspond more closely than does a lump sum to the continuing loss of income, for which the damages are generally intended to compensate.

However, it should not be thought that the arguments are all

---

18 [1980] AC 174 at 183.
19 See, eg Law Commission Report No 56, HC 373 (1973), paras 231–44; Pearson Commission Report Vol 1, Ch 14.

one way. The finality produced by the once-and-for-all rule enables the defendant and his insurers to be certain where they stand and minimises judicial expense and time. Furthermore, a once-and-for-all award contains no disincentive for the plaintiff to recover from an injury, puts an end to any 'compensation neurosis' (which is a recognised medical illness), rules out any difficulties produced by the defendant's subsequent insolvency, and renders unnecessary continued investigation of the plaintiff's condition and lifestyle, sometimes possible only by intrusive 'spying'.

What also influenced the Law Commission[20] in its conclusion that at least periodic payments should not be introduced was that plaintiffs prefer lump sums and that therefore even if the courts were to award periodic payments, plaintiffs would simply settle for lump sums out of court. However, the Law Commission did recommend the less radical exception to the once-and-for-all rule of allowing the courts to award provisional damages.

The majority of the Pearson Commission,[1] on the other hand, concluded that the advantages of periodic payments outweighed any disadvantages and recommended such a system for future pecuniary loss in cases of serious or lasting injury or death. The award of periodic payments would be the normal practice in those cases but, on the application of the plaintiff, there would be a judicial discretion to award a lump sum instead. The payments would be reviewable to take account of changes in the plaintiff's medical condition and would be automatically revalued annually in line with the movement of average earnings.

The legislature has preferred the Law Commission's recommendations. By s 32A of the Supreme Court Act 1981, as inserted by s 6 of the Administration of Justice Act 1982, where there is a chance that at some time in the future the injured person will develop some serious disease or suffer some serious deterioration in his physical or mental condition, as a result of the act or omission which gave rise to the cause of action, he may be awarded damages assessed on the assumption that the disease or deterioration will not occur, and further damages at a future date if it does occur.[2] RSC Ord 37, rr 7–10,[3] accompany these provisions. By r 8(2) an order for an award of provisional damages shall specify the disease or type of deterioration in respect of which an application may be made at a future

---

20 Report No 56, para 28.
 1 Vol 1, Ch 14.
 2 See generally Law Commission Consultation Paper No 125 (1992) 'Structured Settlements and Interim and Provisional Damages' Part V.
 3 For county courts, see County Courts Act 1984, s 51; CCR Ord 6, r 1B, Ord 22, r 6A.

date and will normally specify the period within which such application may be made although, by r 8(3), the period may be extended on an application by the plaintiff. By r 10(6) only one application for further damages may be made in respect of each disease or type of deterioration specified in the order for the award of provisional damages.[4] It should also be stressed that by r 8(1)(a) the plaintiff must plead a claim for provisional damages before the courts can award provisional damages: in other words, plaintiffs may still opt for damages to be assessed on the usual once-and-for-all basis. In practice, and not surprisingly, most plaintiffs choose to forgo the possibility of higher damages in the long-term under the new scheme, in preference for what at trial will be a higher award under the once-and-for-all approach.

In the leading reported case on provisional damages, *Willson v Ministry of Defence*,[5] such damages were refused on the ground that 'serious deterioration' refers to a clear and severable event rather than an ordinary continuing deterioration as in a typical osteoarthritic case. It was further said by Scott Baker J that s 32A is concerned with a measurable rather than a fanciful chance of deterioration.

Interim damages—that is, damages awarded at an interlocutory (pre-trial) stage—can also be regarded as an exception to the once-and-for-all rule in that they obviously do not prevent further damages being awarded at trial for the same cause of action. By the Supreme Court Act 1981, s 32, and RSC Ord 29, r 11,[6] an interim payment of damages can be ordered by the High Court if the defendant has admitted liability or the plaintiff has obtained pre-trial judgment against the defendant or if the court is satisfied that the plaintiff will obtain judgment for substantial damages against that defendant at trial.[7] The interim payment comprises such amount as is thought just, not exceeding a reasonable proportion of the damages the plaintiff is likely to recover. But in a personal injury action, an interim award can only be made if the defendant is insured in respect of the claim, is a public authority or is a person whose means and resources would enable him to make the interim payment. The policy behind interim payments is that if he so wishes the plaintiff should be relieved of immediate financial worries where there is a strong case on liability.[8]

---

4 This is criticised for certain situations in the Law Commission's Consultation Paper No 125 (1992) para 5.12.
5 [1991] 1 All ER 638.
6 For county courts, see County Courts Act 1984, s 50; CCR Ord 13, r 12.
7 For the standard of proof of this, see *British and Commonwealth Holdings plc v Quadrex Holdings Inc* [1989] QB 842; *Andrews v Schooling* [1991] 1 WLR 783.
8 Winn Committee Report (1968) Cmnd 3691, paras 71–110.

Mention should also be made of a very important recent development in relation to out-of-court settlements of personal injury and death cases: the structured settlement.[9]

The crucial point of such a settlement is that it represents a way of avoiding the tax that the plaintiff would pay on the income from investing a lump sum of damages. If the defendant's insurer purchases an annuity for the plaintiff it has been accepted by the Inland Revenue that the plaintiff's payments from the annuity are tax free (ie they are treated as capital not income). It follows that the defendant has to pay less to produce the same (or a greater) stream of money for the plaintiff. (The appropriate discount made by defendants from what would be the lump sum appears to run at 10%–15% which presumably includes the defendant's insurer's administrative and other costs as well as the tax saving.) Moreover such a settlement avoids the risk of the plaintiff dissipating the lump sum of damages: he is instead, with expert evidence, guaranteed a stream of 'income'. Structured settlements are therefore favourable to defendants and the state (which is saved having to support those who squander lump sums of damages) and they are in the best interests of plaintiffs. They also accord more precisely to the compensatory ideal.

The structuring of settlements relates to future pecuniary loss only. Non-pecuniary loss and past pecuniary loss will be paid in the usual form of a lump sum. But structured settlements are flexible so that part of the future pecuniary loss can be paid in a lump sum or paid into a contingency fund to deal with unexpected emergencies. More than one annuity can be bought depending on the plaintiff's likely future needs: eg deferred annuities could commence at the appropriate time for education, housing, marriage and children. Most annuities are index-linked so that the plaintiff is protected against inflation. Although an annuity would normally cease on the plaintiff's death (as the compensatory principle would suggest) it is usual to incorporate a guaranteed minimum time period (eg 10 years) of payments: plaintiffs might otherwise be loathe to forgo the windfall to their dependants that occurs under the lump sum system where the plaintiff unexpectedly dies after being awarded damages. However, it should be stressed that, while structured settlements guarantee periodic payments, they are not reviewable. With the exception of index-linking they seem as prone to inaccuracy as a lump sum.

9 See generally Allen (1988) 104 LQR 448; Lewis (1991) CJQ 212; Whitfield (1992) 142 NLJ 135; Kemp and Kemp *The Quantum of Damages* Vol I, ch 6A; Law Commission Consultation Paper No 125 (1992) Part III.

While structured settlements have principally been used for large claims, settlements as low as £53,000 have been structured. Any restriction appears to be based simply on the idea that the future pecuniary loss must be large enough to justify the administrative costs involved.

At present a court has no power to structure an award of damages. Structured settlements are therefore not a development within the law on judicial remedies so as to fall for detailed treatment within this book. Judicial involvement is confined to those settlements that require court approval because of, eg the plaintiff's disability or infancy.[10] It appears to be the case that structured settlements lose their tax benefits even if a judicial consent order incorporating a structured settlement is made. If so, that is plainly unsatisfactory and, accordingly, the Law Commission has provisionally recommended its reform.[11] But on the wider issue the Law Commission has left open whether courts should be given power to structure damages.[12] It seems that the best view is that they should not. To break with the traditional form of damages may at first sight appear attractive but if the parties cannot themselves agree on a structured settlement it is invidious for the courts to choose and impose a particular package. It is surely inappropriate for a court to be deciding such administrative questions as which life assurance company the annuity should be purchased from and what the rate of discount from the lump sum of damages should be. And from whom would the courts seek the necessary expert advice in setting up the structure and who would pay for that advice? At least at this stage it seems preferable to leave structuring to the parties.

(b) Damages must be awarded unconditionally

The leading case is *Banbury v Bank of Montreal*,[13] where the defendant was held liable for negligently advising the plaintiff to invest in certain securities. The jury's verdict on damages was 'for £25,000 and all securities to be returned to the defendant bank.' The finding of liability was overturned by the House of Lords, but three of their Lordships considered that in any event the award was improper because of the condition attached.

The main reason for having this principle is that it brings finality to litigation. Another possible explanation is the inappropriateness

---

10 See, eg *Kelly v Dawes* (1990) Times, 27 September.
11 Law Comm No 125 (1992) para 3.38.
12 Ibid at para 3.88.
13 [1918] AC 626.

of sanctions in the event of non-compliance by the plaintiff with the condition. But in some personal injury cases involving gratuitous nursing services rendered or expenses incurred by a relative, or gratuitous payments made by an employer, damages have been made conditional on the plaintiff paying them over to,[14] or holding them on trust for,[15] the relative or employer. Unfortunately, despite the convenience of these techniques in this sort of case, the force of these decisions is diminished by there having been no discussion of the principle against unconditional awards. It should also be noted that, at least in respect of gratuitous nursing services, the justification for such an award has been controversially removed by the courts' more recent approach of regarding the loss as the plaintiff's rather than the third party's.[16]

(2) The date for the assessment of damages

This heading, although commonly used, is rather ambiguous and in order to understand the issues involved, it is helpful to distinguish two questions raised by it. Is there a time after which the court assessing damages is barred from taking into account events that have already occurred? Which value of money, property or services do the courts apply in assessing damages?

(a) Is there a time after which the court assessing damages is barred from taking into account events that have already occurred?

As regards a court of first instance the answer to this question is in the negative; a trial judge can avail himself of evidence of all events that occur *prior to the date of judgment*. One of the clearest judicial statements on this is that of Lord Macnaughten in *Bwllfa and Merthyr Dare Steam Collieries Ltd v Pontypridd Waterworks Co*,[17] albeit that he was there dealing with an arbitrator's assessment of statutory compensation. He said:

. . . the arbitrator's duty is to determine the amount of compensation payable. In order to enable him to come to a just and true conclusion, it is his duty . . . to avail himself of all information at hand at the time of

---

14 Eg *Dennis v London Passenger Transport Board* [1948] 1 All ER 779; *Schneider v Eisovitch* [1960] 2 QB 430.
15 Eg *Cunningham v Harrison* [1973] QB 942.
16 Eg *Donnelly v Joyce* [1974] QB 454.
17 [1903] AC 426.

making his award which may be laid before him. Why should he listen to conjecture on a matter which has become an accomplished fact?[18]

For contractual pecuniary loss relevant events commonly arising subsequent to breach but prior to judgment include payments that the plaintiff has had to make to a third party because of the breach, or subsequent 'mitigation' of his loss, for example by obtaining another job having been wrongfully dismissed. In the field of personal injuries, illustrations include a deterioration of the plaintiff's medical condition after the initial injury, a wage-rise in the job that the plaintiff would have been in but for his injuries, and the death of the injured person (in a claim by the estate).

By RSC Ord 59, r 10 the Court of Appeal (and by analogy the House of Lords) has the power to admit evidence of events occurring since the judgment at first instance. But so as not to undermine finality in litigation, some restraint is exercised in using this power. Lord Wilberforce laid down a few guidelines in *Mulholland v Mitchell*:[19]

Negatively, fresh evidence ought not to be admitted when it bears upon matters falling within the field or area of uncertainty, in which the trial judge's estimate has previously been made. Positively, it may be admitted if some basic assumptions, common to both sides have clearly been falsified by subsequent events, particularly, if this has happened by the act of the defendant.[20] Positively, too, it may be expected that courts will allow fresh evidence where to refuse it would affront common sense, or a sense of justice. All these are only non-exhaustive indications . . .[1]

A good example of where fresh evidence was admitted was *Lim Poh Choo v Camden and Islington Area Health Authority*.[2] There the trial judge had assessed damages on the assumption that the plaintiff would be looked after abroad by her mother, but since then her mother had become ill and the plaintiff had been transferred to a nursing home in England. The House of Lords admitted such fresh evidence, so that the cost of future care was reassessed. Lord Scarman's comments are of interest. He said:

The device of granting the parties leave to adduce fresh evidence at the appellate stages of litigation can, as in the present case, mitigate the injustices of a lump sum system by enabling the appellate courts to bring the

18 Ibid at 431.
19 [1971] AC 666.
20 Eg *Murphy v Stone-Wallwork (Charlton) Ltd* [1969] 2 All ER 949.
 1 [1971] AC 666 at 679–80.
 2 [1980] AC 174. See also *Curwen v James* [1963] 1 WLR 748; *Jenkins v Richard Thomas and Baldwin Ltd* [1966] 1 WLR 476; *Perry v Sidney Phillips & Son* [1982] 1 WLR 1297; cf *Hunt v Severs* [1993] 4 All ER 180.

award into line with what has happened since trial. But it is an unsatisfactory makeshift, and of dubious value in any case where the new facts are themselves in issue.[3]

(b) Which value of money, property or services do the courts apply in assessing damages?

It is this question that is usually in mind when one refers to the date for the assessment of damages. The traditional general rule has been stated in one of two ways. Either that damages are assessed (that is the value is taken) at the date of the loss for which the damages are being awarded, or at the date of the accrual of the cause of action. So in *Philips v Ward*[4] Denning LJ said, 'The general principle of English law is that damages must be assessed as at the date when the damage occurs',[5] whereas in *Dodd Properties (Kent) v Canterbury City Council*[6] Donaldson LJ commented that '. . . the general rule is that damages fall to be assessed as at the date when the cause of action arose.'[7] The two normally correspond but where they do not, for example, as regards pecuniary losses in personal injury cases, the former seems to be the more accurate.

However, the trend more recently—reflecting high inflation and a decline in the external value of sterling—has been to recognise exceptions to the rule. Indeed the exceptions are such that it is now arguable that assessment at the date of loss no longer represents the general rule. In examining the details of the law it is convenient to consider separately changes in the value of property or services or in the internal value of money and changes in the external value of money.

(i) Changes in the value of property or services or in the internal value of money

Over the last 25 years or so, the major relevant factor here has been the dramatic fall in the internal value of money because of inflation. But of course the value of property or services may additionally fluctuate because of ordinary market movements.

Looking first at non-pecuniary loss, it would seem that until fairly recently the traditional general rule applied, so that any internal fall in the value of money between loss and judgment was ignored. So,

---

3 Ibid at 183.
4 [1956] 1 WLR 471.
5 Ibid at 474.
6 [1980] 1 All ER 928.
7 Ibid at 939.

for example, in *Bishop v Cunard White Star Co Ltd v The Queen Mary*,[8] Hodson J did not think that the conventional figure of £200 laid down for loss of expectation of life in *Benham v Gambling*[9] should be altered despite the fall in the value of the pound since that decision and since the accident in the case. But the courts' approach has since changed. In *Yorkshire Electricity Board v Naylor*,[10] the conventional figure for loss of expectation of life was raised to £500 because of inflation. That head of loss has now been abolished but the same approach is shown in the application of the 'tariff' system for loss of amenity and pain and suffering. There are several judicial statements recognising this. In *Mitchell v Mulholland (No 2)*[11] Widgery LJ said:

No one doubts that an award of damages must reflect the value of the pound sterling at the date of the award and conventional sums attributed to, say, the loss of an eye, have been adjusted in recent years on that account. Inflation which has reduced the value of money at the date of the award must, thus, be taken into account.[12]

Again, in *Walker v John McLean & Sons Ltd*,[13] where the issue was the level of damages for non-pecuniary loss because of paraplegia, Cumming-Bruce LJ said:

We cannot distinguish any principle recognised in the law of damages which suggests that damages for non-pecuniary loss are in this regard different from damages for pecuniary loss. And in the case of damages for future pecuniary loss the award is assessed by reference to the value of money at the date of trial, and not some other lower sum calculated by reference to an earlier and higher value of the pound.[14]

Finally in *Wright v British Railways Board*[15] Lord Diplock, in deciding that interest on personal injury non-pecuniary loss should be kept at a low rate, regarded the judges as having a duty to assess damages for such loss '. . . in the money of the day at the date of the trial.'[16]

Although there is no express authority, it can be assumed that

8 [1950] P 240.
9 [1941] AC 157.
10 [1968] AC 529.
11 [1972] 1 QB 65.
12 Ibid at 83.
13 [1979] 1 WLR 760.
14 Ibid at 765.
15 [1983] 2 AC 773. See also *Cookson v Knowles* [1977] QB 913 at 921, CA; *Dodd Properties v Canterbury City Council* [1980] 1 All ER 928 at 939; *Housecroft v Burnett* [1986] 1 All ER 332 at 337.
16 Ibid at 782.

awards for other non-pecuniary loss, such as mental distress, similarly reflect the value of money at the date of judgment, rather than any earlier value. Analogously, one would expect that the Lord Chancellor would use his discretion to keep the sum for bereavement under the Fatal Accidents Act 1976 (at present £7,500) in line with inflation.

All such adjustments are necessary in order that the plaintiff be fully compensated for the loss he has suffered. Although money can never be perfect compensation for non-pecuniary loss, it is the best that the law can offer. If £X was the right compensation for a particular non-pecuniary loss, when £1 was worth 10% more than at the date of trial, it must be right to award £X + 10% for that loss.

Turning to pecuniary loss, past recurring pecuniary loss, such as loss of earnings and medical expenses in personal injury cases, is assessed, applying the general rule, according to the value of money at the date of the loss. So if £50 was spent on medical expenses, £50 will be awarded, irrespective of whether £50 is worth less at the date of judgment than at the date when spent. Future pecuniary loss has to be assessed according to the value of money at the date of judgment since there is no sound basis for choosing any other date; but it is less obvious why the courts refuse to increase damages for future pecuniary loss to take into account future inflation. This is discussed in chapter 3.[17]

In relation to other pecuniary loss, the application of the traditional rule is shown, for example, in the prima facie rules for assessing damages under the Sale of Goods Act 1979, which take the market value of the goods at the date of the breach of contract, and by cases such as *General and Finance Facilities Ltd v Cooks Cars (Romford) Ltd*[18] and *Chubb Cash Ltd v John Crilley & Son*,[19] which show that for conversion, the value of the goods is generally to be assessed at the time of the conversion. On the other hand in several recent cases the traditional rule has been departed from.

In *Wroth v Tyler*,[20] for example, Megarry J was concerned to assess damages given in lieu of specific performance[1] for the breach of a contract to sell a bungalow. Applying the usual formula of market price minus contract price, the question arose whether the market price should be that at the date of the breach (£7,500) or

---

17 Infra, pp 198–9.
18 [1963] 1 WLR 644.
19 [1983] 1 WLR 599. See also, eg *BBMB Finance (Hong Kong) Ltd v Eda Holdings Ltd* [1990] 1 WLR 409. See generally Tettenborn (1991) NLJ 452.
20 [1974] Ch 30.
 1 Ie equitable damages; see infra, pp 242–7.

that at the date of judgment (£11,500). Megarry J considered that where damages were being given in lieu of specific performance the usual date of breach rule did not necessarily apply, and here, since the plaintiffs in view of their lack of funds could not have been expected to mitigate their loss by going into the market, the market price at the date of judgment was chosen. Furthermore, Megarry J indicated in dicta that even for ordinary common law damages the date of breach rule might not be inflexible.

In *Radford v De Froberville*[2] the defendant in breach of contract failed to build a wall. In assessing the plaintiff's damages one issue was the date at which the cost of building a wall should be assessed. Oliver J considered that the decision in *Wroth v Tyler* was equally applicable to ordinary common law damages, and indeed went so far as to say that '. . . the proper approach is to assess the damages at the date of the hearing unless it can be said that the plaintiff ought reasonably to have mitigated by seeking an alternative performance at an earlier date.'[3] Ultimately, however, Oliver J did not reach a decision as to which date was appropriate, because there was insufficient evidence to enable him to decide whether the plaintiff should have mitigated earlier.

This move in favour of fixing the date for assessment more flexibly so as to accord with when the plaintiff ought reasonably to have or has mitigated his loss has been authoritatively confirmed by the House of Lords in *Johnson v Agnew*,[4] where it was the vendor of land who was plaintiff in a situation where mortgagees had sold the land off at a low value subsequent to the date of breach. The vendor had initially obtained an order for specific performance but the defendant purchaser had delayed in complying with the order with the consequence that the vendor's mortgagees became entitled to sell off his land. The vendor therefore now sought damages for the purchaser's breach of contract. Having emphasised that damages in lieu of specific performance and ordinary common law damages should be assessed on the same basis, Lord Wilberforce went on to say the following:

The general principle for the assessment of damages is compensatory, ie that the innocent party is to be placed, so far as money can do it, in the same position as if the contract had been performed. Where the contract is one of sale, this principle normally leads to assessment of damages as at the date of breach—a principle recognised and embodied in s 51 of the Sale of Goods Act 1893. But this is not an absolute rule; if to follow it would give

2 [1977] 1 WLR 1262.
3 Ibid at 1286.
4 [1980] AC 367.

rise to injustice, the court has power to fix such other date as may be appropriate in the circumstances. In cases where a breach of contract for sale has occurred, and the innocent party reasonably continues to try to have the contract completed, it would to me appear more logical and just rather than tie him to the date of the original breach to assess damages as at the date when otherwise than by his default the contract is lost.[5]

Accordingly, it was decided that the market value of the land should be assessed not at the date of the purchaser's original breach, but rather when the vendor's reasonable attempts to have the contract enforced failed: ie when the mortgagees, as they were entitled to do, contracted to sell the land to another party hence making it impossible for the plaintiff vendor to comply with his side of the contract.

Johnson v Agnew was applied, and its approach very clearly summarised, in *Suleman v Shahsavari*.[6] This concerned actions by a prospective purchaser of a house against the vendors for specific performance or, in the event of the contract for purchase being held invalid, against the vendors' solicitor for damages for breach of a warranty that he had authority to bind the vendors. Andrew Park QC, sitting as a deputy judge of the High Court, held that the contract was invalid because the vendors' solicitor had had no authority to sign the contract on their behalf. Specific performance against the vendors was therefore denied. The question then arose whether the damages for the solicitor's breach of warranty of authority should be calculated according to the difference between the contract price and the market price on the completion date (£9,500 plus interest) or the difference between the contract price and the market price at the date of judgment, nearly two-and-a-half years later, which was £29,500. On a straightforward application of *Johnson v Agnew* the judge awarded £29,500.

Again in *Naughton v O'Callaghan*[7] Waller J relied on *Johnson v Agnew* in awarding damages (for a negligent misrepresentation and breach of a contractual warranty) calculated according to the price paid for a horse (26,000 guineas) minus its value (£1,500) nearly two years later after it had proved a failure on the racecourse and hence lost most of its value. The plaintiffs would not have bought the horse but for the vendor's misrepresentation as to its pedigree and had they discovered the error straightaway they would have sold the horse at its then value. Moreover, and in line with the crucial importance to the date of assessment of the duty to mitigate, it is

5 Ibid at 401.
6 [1989] 2 All ER 460.
7 [1990] 3 All ER 191.

clear that the plaintiffs could not reasonably have mitigated their loss until they discovered the error nearly two years after purchase.

In *Dodd Properties v Canterbury City Council*[8] a similar approach was adopted in relation to the time at which the cost of repairing damaged property should be assessed in an action for tortious negligence or nuisance. Having said that the general rule was that the cost of repairs should be assessed at the date of the tort, the Court of Appeal went on to emphasise that this was not an inflexible rule, and that here the cost of repairs should be assessed at the date of the hearing. The reason for preferring this later date was that, having regard to all the circumstances and in particular the plaintiff's impecuniosity, it was the date when it was first reasonable for the plaintiff to have undertaken the repairs.

It should further be noted that apart from these important departures from the traditional general rule, the earlier decision in *Sachs v Miklos*,[9] while leaving the date of conversion as the date for assessing the value of the chattel, apparently accepted that subsequent increases in the market value of the converted chattel could be recovered as consequential loss. The defendant, having gratuitously stored the plaintiff's goods from 1940 to 1943, twice wrote to the plaintiff requesting their removal. Receiving no reply he sold them for £15. In 1946 the plaintiff demanded the goods. The defendant tendered the £15 but the market value having risen to £115, the plaintiff claimed and was seemingly held able to recover the extra £100 as consequential damages for conversion (on the assumption that he had never received the letters). In essence this again was a departure from the general rule albeit by a different route.

Waddams criticises the new more flexible approach and considers that it would be preferable to stick more rigidly to assessment at (or shortly after) the date of the loss.[10] He offers several arguments in support: postponement of assessment hampers desirable finality to litigation: it encourages the plaintiff to be inefficient; interest awarded on the damages acts as an adequate counter to inflation; and assessment at an early date tends to reduce the total cost of litigation. But finality of litigation in the sense, seemingly intended, of

---

8 [1980] 1 All ER 928. See also *Forster v Silvermere Golf & Equestrian Centre Ltd* (1981) 42 P & CR 255 (breach of contract).

9 [1948] 2 KB 23. See also *Empresa Exportadora De Azucar v Industria Azucarera Nacional, The Playa Larga* [1983] 2 Lloyds Rep 171, 181; *IBL Ltd v Coussens* [1991] 2 All ER 133 (conversion damages for value of cars—under what would previously have been an action for detinue—to be assessed at a date fixed flexibly, although prima facie at the date of judgment).

10 (1981) 97 LQR 445; *The Law of Damages* (2nd edn,1991), hereinafter cited as *Damages*, paras 1.650–1.1100, 7.60–7.70.

litigation not going on beyond trial is no more achieved by a date of loss than a date of trial assessment; and the second argument is countered by the fact that the courts would consider that a plaintiff who had unreasonably delayed allowing values to rise could have mitigated earlier, and his damages would therefore be assessed at that earlier date.[11] While it is true that interest rates do reflect inflation, so that assessment of damages at an early date plus full interest will often achieve much the same result as assessment at a later date plus reduced or no interest until that date,[12] interest rates reflect price rises only very roughly and clearly they are not attuned to fluctuations (whether up or down) in the value of particular property. Finally, although rigid adherence to the date of loss rule may save litigation costs, because that approach is clear and simple (but without empirical data the extent of the cost-saving is unclear) this is at the expense of effecting true compensation. Tossing a coin is the cheapest way of deciding a dispute but it hardly represents justice.

The above discussion on pecuniary loss has assumed that it is advantageous for the plaintiff to have damages assessed at a later date than that of loss. But what if it is disadvantageous? Say, for example, the plaintiff is a buyer and that the value of property has fallen since the date of the vendor's breach; or that the defendant has converted the plaintiff's goods, which have since fallen in value. In these situations, assessment at the date of the breach of contract or conversion would be more advantageous to the plaintiff than assessment at a later date. Although the few cases on this[13] assess damages at the date of loss, they do predate the recent developments. It is submitted that logical symmetry, avoidance of overcompensation, and adherence to the duty to mitigate dictate that the same flexibility should be adopted as where assessment at a later date is to the plaintiff's advantage. Waddams again disagrees and in particular focuses on a situation where the plaintiff buyer or owner of converted goods may wish to establish that he would have mitigated against a fall in the value of the property by, for example, selling off the goods at an early date. He writes, 'The cost of inquiry into how the plaintiff would have used his property had the defendant not deprived the plaintiff of it outweighs the cost of overcompensation . . .'[14] Once more therefore Waddams is expressing a

---

11 As in *Malhotra v Choudhury* [1980] Ch 52.
12 For the relationship between date for assessment and interest, see infra, pp 260–1.
13 *Aronson v Mologa Holzindustrie A/G Leningrad* (1927) 32 Com Cas 276; *Solloway v McLaughlin* [1938] AC 247.
14 *Damages* para 1.660.

preference for rough-and-ready often inaccurate compensation produced by rigid adherence to the date of loss rule as against the true compensation produced by the more flexible approach, on the ground that the former is much cheaper, albeit that no empirical data is offered to indicate the extent of the cost-saving.

(ii) Changes in the external value of money—foreign money liabilities

It should be stressed at the outset that the law here applies to the award of an agreed sum,[15] as well as to damages. Indeed the recent legal changes were initially concerned solely with the former remedy. In order to provide a coherent exposition, the law will be looked at as a whole, rather than simply examining the damages aspect of it.

The traditional assessment date rule meant that the conversion into sterling of agreed sums payable or damages calculable in foreign money was made according to the rates applicable at the time of the loss.[16] Also of relevance in understanding this area of the law was the rule that a money judgment had to be expressed in sterling.[17] The Law Commission[18] has referred to these two rules taken together as the sterling-breach-date rule, although sterling-loss-date is, strictly speaking, more accurate.

The problem with that rule was that, where the value of sterling had changed in relation to the relevant foreign currency between the date of loss and the date of judgment, the plaintiff was left under- or overcompensated. This began to bother the courts when sterling weakened as a currency, so that plaintiffs were being undercompensated. An example will make this clearer. Say D owes P 1000 units of foreign currency and at the date of loss those units are worth £100 (ie £1 = 10 units), but at the date of judgment they are worth £200 (ie £1 = 5 units). In other words, the value of sterling has declined. Clearly if P is given only £100 he is undercompensated. But assessment at the date of loss will overcompensate P if the value of sterling has increased. Say the units at the date of judgment are worth £50 (ie £1 = 20 units). By being given £100 P is overcompensated.

---

15 Infra, ch 7.
16 Eg *Di Fernando v Simon, Smits & Co* [1920] 3 KB 409 (contractual damages); *SS Celia (Owners) v SS Volturno (Owners)* [1921] 2 AC 544 (tort damages); *Tomkinson v First Pennsylvania Banking and Trusts Co* [1961] AC 1007 (agreed sum).
17 Eg *Manners v Pearson & Son* [1898] 1 Ch 581 at 587.
18 Report No 124 Private International Law—Foreign Money Liabilities (1983) Cmnd 9064.

Given this defect with conversion at the date of loss, what were the alternatives? One obvious alternative was to convert at the date of judgment. But this would leave injustice where the value of sterling changed between judgment and actual payment of the agreed sum or damages. The ideal solution was therefore for conversion to be made at the rates prevailing at the date of payment. But the rule that judgment had to be in sterling was here a stumbling-block, for it was very difficult to see how one could have the judgment expressed in sterling, while converting into sterling at the date of payment. On the other hand, if judgments could be expressed in foreign currency this would free the way for the ideal solution of conversion into sterling at the date of payment: ie the order could then be for the defendant to pay the plaintiff X units of the foreign currency or the sterling equivalent at the time of payment. It should be stressed that for two reasons to allow judgment in a foreign currency would not prevent the need for a conversion date rule: first, English execution necessarily yields value in sterling; secondly, there seems no reason why a defendant should not have the option of satisfying an English court's judgment in sterling.

Miliangos v George Frank (Textiles) Ltd[19] is the classic case in which the House of Lords departed from the 'sterling-breach-date' rule and held that for some foreign agreed sums a judgment can be expressed in foreign currency, and that conversion into sterling can be made at the date of payment, meaning the date of actual payment or, if earlier, the date on which the court authorises enforcement of the judgment. The facts concerned the non-payment of a contract price for yarn. The money of account (ie the currency by which the debtor's obligation was measured) and the money of payment (ie the currency in which the payment was to be tendered) was Swiss francs, and the proper law of the contract was Swiss. The defendants were ordered to pay in Swiss francs or the equivalent in sterling at the time of payment.

Lord Wilberforce explained that because of the instability of sterling:

. . . instead of a situation in which changes of relative value occurring between the 'breach date' and the date of judgment or payment being the exception, so that a rule which did not provide for this case could be generally fair, this situation is now the rule. So the search for a formula to deal with it becomes urgent in the interest of justice.[20]

But Lord Wilberforce confined his departure from the long-

19 [1976] AC 443.
20 Ibid at 463.

established rule to agreed sums: 'In my opinion, it should be open for future discussion whether the rule applying to money obligations, which can be a simple rule should apply as regards claims for damages for breach of contract or for a tort.'[1] However, the policy underlying *Miliangos* does not differ whether one is talking of agreed sums or damages, and in *Services Europe Atlantique Sud v Stockholms Rederiaktiebolag SVEA, The Folias*[2] and *The Despina R*,[3] *Miliangos* has been extended to claims for contractual and tortious damages respectively. It is therefore now clearly accepted that a foreign currency liability should be expressed in foreign currency and that the date for conversion into sterling is the date of payment.

It is important to realise that although the *Miliangos* reform was triggered by plaintiffs being undercompensated where sterling had declined in value since the date of loss, it was not solely concerned with preventing undercompensation. Rather it was concerned that judgment should be expressed in the most appropriate currency, whether this was to the benefit or detriment of the plaintiff in comparison with the sterling-breach-date rule. Thus in *Miliangos* Lord Wilberforce explained: 'The creditor has no concern with pounds sterling: for him what matters is that a Swiss franc *for good or ill* should remain a Swiss franc.'[4] And in *The Despina R*, he said, 'To fix such a plaintiff with sterling commits him to the risk of changes in the value of a currency with which he has no connection; to award him a sum in the (appropriate) currency . . . gives him exactly what he has lost and commits him only to the risk of changes in the value of that currency.'[5] It follows that where the appropriate foreign currency loses value in relation to sterling, the plaintiff should not be able to resort to the sterling-breach-date rule. This point is firmly expressed by the Law Commission:

Although there is little authority on the point it is clear that to allow the plaintiff to seek judgment in sterling in the case of a foreign-currency claim would be contrary to the principle in *Miliangos* . . . [therefore] a plaintiff should not be able to obtain judgment in sterling in the case of the enforcement of a claim which ought properly to be expressed in a foreign currency.[6]

However, the Law Commission does accept that where the plaintiff can show that he would have converted the appropriate foreign

1 Ibid at 468.
2 [1979] AC 685.
3 Ibid.
4 [1976] AC 443 at 466 (italics inserted).
5 [1979] AC 685 at 697.
6 Report No 124, para 3.9. See also para 2.5.

currency into sterling, and thereby reaped the benefit of the increase in sterling's value, he should be able to recover damages for such exchange losses, subject to remoteness.[7] This is the basis of the Commission's interpretation of the difficult case of *Ozalid Group (Export) Ltd v African Continental Bank Ltd.*[8] Here the defendant had delayed in paying a contract price of US dollars to the plaintiffs. By exchange control regulations the plaintiffs were obliged to convert US dollars into sterling and would have done so if the money had been paid. During the period of delay sterling rose in value against the dollar. The plaintiffs claimed the difference in value between sterling at the time payment should have been made and when it was made. Donaldson J held that the plaintiffs were entitled to that amount.

The Law Commission's interpretation of the decision is that damages were being awarded for non-remote exchange losses consequent on the defendant's delay in making payment. This was therefore an example of the *Wadsworth v Lydall*[9] 'special damages' exception to the *London, Chatham & Dover Rly Co v South Eastern Rly Co*[10] rule that no damages can be awarded for breach of an obligation to pay money. But an alternative interpretation was that the appropriate currency was not US dollars at all but was sterling; and that where a plaintiff's loss was really suffered in sterling rather than a foreign currency—and that sterling loss was not too remote—conversion according to the sterling-breach-date rule is appropriate.

Both interpretations seem acceptable: indeed they are simply different legal analyses of the same ideas. The crucial common point is that the plaintiff does not have a free choice to have the sterling-breach-date rule applied; rather he must have suffered a non-remote loss of sterling.

Some commentators criticise the *Miliangos* reform. Waddams, for example, thinks that it neglects the fact that many plaintiffs can perfectly well mitigate against a decline in sterling.[11] But surely there is nothing in *Miliangos* to undermine normal mitigation principles so that if the defendant can show a failure to mitigate the plaintiff would not be entitled to full loss assessed according to *Miliangos*. More forceful are the arguments first, that introducing flexibility as against the certainty of the sterling-breach-date rule is paid for by higher litigation costs; and secondly, that the injustice to plaintiffs of

7 Ibid, paras 2.34–2.35, 3.58–3.61.
8 [1979] 2 Lloyds Rep 231; Cf *International Minerals & Chemical Corpn v Karl O Helm AG* [1986] 1 Lloyds Rep 81 at 105.
9 [1981] 1 WLR 598. Supra, pp 98–9, esp fn 14.
10 [1893] AC 429.
11 *Damages* paras 7.250–7.300.

the sterling-breach-date rule has been overstated, since interest rates will generally increase in response to a decline in the currency's value; hence the sterling-breach-date rule plus interest at sterling rates will produce much the same result as expressing judgment in foreign currency, converted at the date of payment, plus interest at the rate for that foreign currency.[12] In similar vein, Waddams argues that, as regards an increase in the home currency's value, it is better to risk overcompensation than to encourage costly investigation of how the plaintiff would have used the foreign currency.[13] Analogous arguments have been considered earlier[14] and again it is submitted that the courts are right to effect true compensation rather than favouring a less costly approach (and the extent of the cost-saving is unclear) of rough-and-ready justice.

Finally, while not concerning the date for assessment as such, it is convenient to consider briefly two further questions of central importance. When is sterling considered a less appropriate currency than a foreign currency? And where more than one foreign currency is involved, which is the more appropriate foreign currency? The answers can be indicated in five points.

(i)   For the judgment to be expressed in foreign currency the loss in question must be pecuniary loss. As laid down in *Hoffman v Sofaer*[15] non-pecuniary loss, such as pain and suffering and loss of amenity in a personal injury action, does not raise foreign currency problems; rather such a loss is calculated and expressed in sterling whatever the plaintiff's nationality or wherever the injury or loss occurred.

(ii) In *Miliangos*, Lord Wilberforce confined departure from the sterling-breach-date rule to where the proper law of the contract was foreign, but in subsequent cases *Miliangos* has been applied to contracts whose proper law was English.[16]

(iii) As regards agreed sums where the money of account and payment are of the same foreign money, as in *Miliangos* itself, it is clearly appropriate for judgment to be expressed in that foreign currency. Lord Wilberforce confined departure from the old

---

12 Bowles & Whelan (1982) 45 MLR 434 at 442, 444. For the relationship between foreign currency judgments and interest, see infra, pp 261–2.

13 *Damages* paras 7.180–7.200.

14 See supra, pp 112–4.

15 [1982] 1 WLR 1350.

16 *Barclays Bank International Ltd v Levin Bros (Bradford) Ltd* [1977] QB 270; *Federal Commerce and Navigation Co v Tradax Export, The Maratha Envoy* [1977] QB 324; *Veflings Rederi A/S v President of India* [1979] 1 WLR 59; *The Folias* [1979] AC 685.

approach to this situation, but in *Veflings Rederi A/S v President of India, The Bellami,*[17] Donaldson J at first instance held that where the money of payment and account are of different countries, and even if the money of payment is English, judgment can be expressed in the currency of the money of account.

(iv) As laid down in *The Folias,*[18] for contract damages, unless there is a 'currency of the contract'—that is, an appropriate currency expressly laid down in the contract—the appropriate currency will be that in which the loss was felt or which most truly expresses the plaintiff's loss. This may or may not be the currency in which the loss first and immediately arose and depends on ordinary principles of proof and remoteness.

(v) A similar approach to that adopted in *The Folias* was applied for tort damages in *The Despina R.*[19] The only main difference is that with no contract in play, the currency of the contract is obviously not a possibility.

(3) Compensating advantages

The compensatory aims require the courts to assess not only the position the plaintiff would have been in if the breach of contract or tort had not been committed but also his actual position as a result of the tort or breach of contract, so that damages can make up the difference. Where the plaintiff's actual position has been, or will be, improved by benefits acquired subsequent to and as a result of the tort or breach of contract, one might expect (in accordance with the compensatory aims) that such benefits would be taken into account—if they are ignored the plaintiff will be left in a better position than if the contract had been performed or if no tort had been committed. In a nutshell, one might expect 'compensating advantages' to be deducted or, as it is sometimes alternatively expressed, that losses mitigated would not be compensated. But in

---

17 [1978] 1 WLR 982. On appeal CA held that US dollar was money of account and payment: [1979] 1 WLR 59.

18 Followed in, eg *President of India v Taygetos Shipping Co SA, The Agenor* [1985] 1 Lloyd's Rep 155 (cf *President of India v Lips Maritime Corpn* [1985] 2 Lloyd's Rep 180 at 187–8 per Staughton J, [1988] AC 395, 426, HL); *Société Française Bunge SA v Belcan NV, The Federal Huron* [1985] 3 All ER 378; *Metaalhandel JA Magnus BV v Ardfields Transport Ltd* [1988] 1 Lloyd's Rep 197; *A-G of the Republic of Ghana v Texaco Overseas Tankships Ltd, The Texaco Melbourne* (1994) Times, 16 February.

19 Followed in *The Lash Atlantico* [1987] 2 Lloyd's Rep 114; *The Transoceanica Francesca and Nicos V* [1987] 2 Lloyd's Rep 155.

fact compensating advantages are often not deducted. Our concern here is to indicate when this is so.

However, it is first essential to stress that to be a compensating advantage the benefit in question must arise from the breach of contract or tort; that is, the breach of contract or tort must be a cause of the benefit according to the 'but for' test of factual causation. So, for example, if the plaintiff is injured by the defendant's negligence but completes his football pools coupon as usual, and wins the pools, that benefit is not a compensating advantage since he would have won the pools even if there had been no tort. Upjohn J in *WL Thompson Ltd v Robinson (Gunmakers) Ltd*[20] can similarly be viewed as applying the 'but for' causation test in deciding that a subsequent gain was not a compensating advantage. The issue was whether a purchaser who had broken his contract to buy a car should be made to pay damages for the vendor's loss of profit on the sale even though he had since sold the car at the same price to someone else. It was held that, because supply exceeded demand, if the purchaser had not broken the contract the vendor would have made two profits and not one; hence the subsequent sale was not a compensating advantage and the purchaser had to pay damages for the vendor's lost profit on his sale.

Having stressed the factual causation inherent in the notion of a compensating advantage, we can now attack the question, when are compensating advantages ignored?

Leaving aside claims under the Fatal Accidents Act 1976,[1] there are two general principles of non-deduction; and it can be taken that a compensating advantage that does not fall within either principle is normally deducted in accordance with the compensatory aims,[2] common examples being the expenses of performance saved by a plaintiff because of the defendant's breach of contract and the earnings the plaintiff has acquired under a new job following his wrongful dismissal or dismissal necessitated by his personal injury.

---

20 [1955] Ch 177.
1 Compensating advantages following the death are now almost entirely covered by s 4 of the Fatal Accidents Act 1976, ordering non-deduction. For full discussion see infra, pp 217–9.
2 A good example is *Westwood v Secretary of State for Employment* [1985] AC 20. One exception is the non-deduction of the price at which goods have been resold, above the market price, in cases like *Slater v Hoyle and Smith Ltd* [1920] 2 KB 11 and *Campbell Mostyn (Provisions) Ltd v Barnett Trading Co* [1954] 1 Lloyds Rep 65, infra, pp 144, 147.

(a) Indirect compensating advantages are not deducted

'Directness' puts a limit on the extent to which compensating advantages are deducted on the policy ground that it is unfair that a plaintiff should have his damages reduced by a benefit that is far removed from the wrong and is essentially coincidental to it. Directness therefore plays an analogous but reverse role to remoteness and intervening cause; they counter a rigid adherence to the compensatory principle by limiting the plaintiff's damages, whereas directness here counters compensation, as strictly applied, by increasing the plaintiff's damages.

A useful hypothetical example, illustrating an indirect and non-deductible compensating advantage, is of a plaintiff who, because he has more time on his hands as a result of his wrongful dismissal or negligently-caused injuries, fills in a winning football pools coupon, which he would otherwise not have had time to do. Even though the defendant's tort or breach of contract has been a factual cause of the plaintiff's pools win, that benefit should not be deducted because it was too indirectly related to the tort or breach of contract.

Turning to the cases, it is submitted that those dealing with compensating advantages provided by third parties shed little light on the directness principle since the judges have used the terminology of directness for decisions that are clearly better justified on other grounds.[3] This leaves as prime examples cases where the compensating advantages have been gained from actions taken by the plaintiff subsequent to the tort or breach of contract; and here the test for directness appears to turn on whether the compensating advantage derived from actions taken by the plaintiff *to avoid* the consequences of the wrong. In McGregor's words, '. . . the basic rule is that the benefit to the plaintiff, if it is to be taken into account in mitigation of damages, must arise out of the act of mitigation itself.'[4]

A leading case, albeit that the advantage was considered direct and therefore deductible, is *British Westinghouse v Underground Electric Rlys Co of London Ltd.*[5] The defendants in breach of contract supplied to the plaintiffs turbines which were defective. The plaintiffs subsequently replaced them with other turbines. The replacement turbines turned out to be more efficient and profitable

---

3 Infra, p 124.
4 *McGregor on Damages* para 253.
5 [1912] AC 673. See also *Erie County Natural Gas & Fuel Co Ltd v Carroll* [1911] AC 105; *Bellingham v Dhillon* [1973] QB 304; *Techno Land Improvements Ltd v British Leyland (UK) Ltd* (1979) 252 Estates Gazette 805.

than the old turbines would have been if non-defective. In fact the extra profit gained from the replacement turbines being more efficient amounted to more than the losses caused by the original turbines being defective. The House of Lords held that the plaintiffs were entitled only to nominal damages for the defendants' breach of contract because their losses had been completely mitigated by the extra profit gained from the plaintiffs' steps taken to avoid the consequences of the breach. Viscount Haldane LC said, 'When in the course of his business he [the plaintiff] has taken action arising out of the transaction, which action has diminished his loss, the effect in actual diminution of the loss he has suffered may be taken into account even though there was no duty on him to act.'[6]

An excellent illustration of the distinction between direct and indirect compensating advantages is provided by *Lavarack v Woods of Colchester Ltd*.[7] The plaintiff was wrongfully dismissed from his employment with the defendants and so freed from a provision in his contract with them that he should not, without their written consent, be engaged or interested in any other business. After his dismissal the plaintiff took employment with a company called Martindale at a lower salary than he had earned with the defendants, acquired half the shares in the Martindale company and bought shares in a company called Ventilation. The value of both the Martindale and Ventilation shares increased. The Court of Appeal held that while his new salary and the profit from the Martindale Co shares should be deducted, the profits from the Ventilation Co shares should not be. Lord Denning said:

I realise that the plaintiff was only at liberty to invest in Ventilation because his employment was terminated. But nevertheless the benefit from that investment was not a direct result of his dismissal. It was an entirely collateral benefit . . . for which he need not account to his [former] employers . . . [his shareholding in] Martindale stands on a little different footing . . . it looks as if he was getting a concealed remuneration by a profit on his shares in the company.[8]

In other words, while the profit on the Ventilation shares was a compensating advantage, it should not be deducted because it was too indirectly related to the breach, as it did not follow from action taken to avoid its consequences. On the other hand, the profit on the Martindale shares was more directly related, as it followed from

---

6 Ibid at 689.
7 [1967] 1 QB 278. See also *Hodge v Clifford Cowling & Co* [1990] 2 EGLR 89 (compensatory advantage not deducted because the mitigating conduct, in acquiring another ship, was not connected with the wrong).
8 Ibid at 290–1.

actions taken to avoid being without employment, and could not be clearly distinguished from the plaintiff's salary with Martindale.

A more difficult example of a compensating advantage that was not deducted is provided by *Hussey v Eels*.[9] The plaintiffs were induced to buy a bungalow from the defendants by a negligent misrepresentation that the property had not been subject to subsidence. It was estimated that the plaintiffs had paid £17,000 more than the bungalow was worth given its actual subsidence problems. Rather than effecting repairs or reselling straightaway, the plaintiffs sought planning permission to replace the bungalow with two new ones. After two-and-a-half years they finally succeeded in obtaining that permission and sold the bungalow and land with planning permission for nearly £23,000 more than they had paid for it. The trial judge held that the plaintiffs were not entitled to any damages for the negligent misrepresentation because they had fully mitigated their loss by the favourable resale. But that decision was overturned by the Court of Appeal which awarded £17,000 damages. The reasoning of Mustill LJ, giving the leading judgment, was that the resale profit was too indirect a consequence of the tort:

Did the negligence which caused the damage also cause the profit, if profit there was? I do not think so. It is true that in one sense there was a causal link between the inducement of the purchase by misrepresentation and the sale two-and-a-half years later, for the sale represented a choice of one of the options with which the plaintiffs had been presented by the defendants' wrongful act. But only in that sense . . . It seems to me that when the plaintiffs unlocked the development value of their land they did so for their own benefit, and not as part of a continuous transaction of which the purchase of land and bungalow was the inception.[10]

This is controversial because, although there was a considerable time lag, the seeking and obtaining of planning permission and subsequent sale were clearly actions taken to avoid the subsidence problems. It is difficult to accept that those actions were too indirectly related. While the plaintiffs might have been entitled to damages because of the general increase in prices over that two-and-a-half year period (ie the loss of opportunity to buy an equivalent bungalow that would have increased in value), they had not produced evidence supporting such a claim. Certainly there is no reason to think that the £17,000 bore any relationship to such price increases.

9 [1990] 2 QB 227.
10 Ibid at 241.

(b) Some compensating advantages provided by third parties in response to the consequences of a tort or breach of contract are not deducted or are only partly deducted

The compensating advantages in issue here may be provided by the state in the form, for example, of social security benefits; or by an insurance company or employer by the terms of an existing contract with the plaintiff; or gratuitously by the plaintiff's relatives, friends, employer, trade union or indeed by the public at large. Usually arising in respect of personal injury, it is the deduction or non-deduction of this type of compensating advantage that has given rise to the most discussion and controversy.[11] Before looking at the details of the law, it is helpful to examine the factors that influence the courts.

(i)   Traditionally, the commonest explanation offered for the non-deduction of this type of compensating advantage is that it was too indirectly related to the tort or breach of contract. For example, in relation to accident insurance it has been said that the contract of insurance, rather than the accident, was the cause of the compensating advantage.[12] The same idea is often alternatively expressed by saying that the compensating advantage is a *res inter alios acta* or is collateral,[13] although the latter term invites confusion since all compensating advantages provided by third parties are commonly labelled collateral, whether deductible or not. But the essential objection to this traditional reasoning is that a compensating advantage provided in response to the consequences of a tort or breach of contract cannot realistically be said to be too indirect so as to be non-deductible under the first principle examined above. In *Parry v Cleaver*,[14] the usage of remoteness and causation in this context was criticised and overall it is clear that the terminology of cause, collateral and *res inter alios acta* is here merely a shroud for decisions really justified on other grounds.

(ii)   Much of the traditional inconsistency in this area of the law appears to stem from the courts' willingness to punish the

---

11 (1964) 77 Harv LR 741; McGregor (1965) 28 MLR 629; Cane *Atiyah's Accidents, Compensation and the Law* (5th edn) pp 322–30; Fleming *Int Encyc of Comparative Law* vol XI. For an economic analysis, see Posner *Economic Analysis of Law* (4th edn) pp 201–2.

12 *Bradburn v Great Western Rly Co* (1874) LR 10 Exch 1.

13 *Parsons v BNM Laboratories Ltd* [1964] 1 QB 95 at 141; *McGregor on Damages*, para 245.

14 [1970] AC 1.

defendant, rather than merely to compensate the plaintiff. Hence there is often reference to the defendant being a wrong-doer who ought to pay and who does not deserve to be benefited by the compensating advantage.[15] But, if punishment is desired, it is surely better to administer it through exemplary damages, where the punishment is explicit and where the amount awarded can be fixed in accordance with the extent to which it is felt the defendant deserves punishment. But in any event it is strongly arguable that punishment should not be an aim of the civil law. Certainly, exemplary damages are not awarded for breach of contract, and in *Rookes v Barnard*,[16] the ambit of exemplary damages in tort was significantly reduced.

(iii) Parliament has sometimes laid down whether these compensating advantages are or are not to be deducted. For example, the Social Security Administration Act 1992 Part IV dictates full deduction of nearly all social security benefits (the 'relevant benefits') from damages for personal injury for five years (or until an earlier final settlement payment) under a system whereby the state recoups the amount of those benefits from the tortfeasor. After five years the relevant benefits are not to be deducted. And for personal injury damages of £2,500 or less, the amended s 2(1) of the Law Reform (Personal Injuries) Act 1948 dictates half deduction of relevant benefits for five years.

(iv) The courts sometimes regard the fact that the plaintiff has paid for, and in that sense earned, the advantage as a reason for not deducting it. In *Parry v Cleaver*, for example, this was part of Lord Reid's justification for not deducting a disability pension. If this were not so, it would mean that, as events have turned out, the plaintiff's payments would be rendered unnecessary, since he would have recovered the same compensation without those payments. Put another way, the person who has been a spendthrift should not be treated as well as someone who has used his money to guard against the unfortunate event that has occurred.

(v) The purpose of the compensating advantage is often regarded as relevant; for example, in *Parry v Cleaver* this partly underlay Lord Reid's explanation of why gratuitous payments are not deducted. But it is questionable whether this factor does provide much real assistance. In relation to any of these

15 Eg *Yates v Whyte* (1838) 4 Bing NC 272 at 283.
16 [1964] AC 1129. Infra, ch 5.

compensating advantages one can say that the purpose is to benefit the plaintiff as opposed to relieving the wrongdoer. But the real question is whether the purpose is to overcompensate the plaintiff and the answer to that is generally unclear. Indeed to answer it properly would require analysing the intention of, for example, each gratuitous donor or each insured plaintiff, and clearly the courts do not attempt this. So a better underlying explanation of the approach to gratuitous payments, albeit unarticulated, is that the courts do not want to discourage benevolence.

(vi) Leaving aside an indemnity insurer's subrogation rights,[17] there is rarely any question at common law of the third party (X) recovering the value of the benefit conferred on the plaintiff (P) from P, assuming the compensating advantage has not been deducted, or from the defendant (D), assuming the deduction has been made.

X has no restitutionary claim against P in that he has rendered the benefit, either as a volunteer, or under a valid contractual or statutory obligation owed to the plaintiff. Therefore the only possibility of recovery is where there is an undertaking by P to reimburse X in the event of recovering damages. At present, that undertaking is only generally exacted by an employer providing sick pay, and significantly, in this situation, the courts do indeed appear to depart from the general approach to sick pay by not deducting it from the damages.[18] The possibility of the court itself exacting an undertaking from P to use part of the damages to reimburse X has generally not found favour, being contrary to the usual rule that damages must be awarded unconditionally.[19]

Where a deduction has been made, X does not have a

---

17 Street *Principles* p 105. Property insurance is indemnity insurance, accident insurance is not.

18 *Browning v War Office* [1963] 1 QB 750 at 777; *IRC v Hambrook* [1956] 2 QB 641 at 656–7. See also *Berriello v Felixstowe Dock & Rwy Co* [1989] 1 WLR 695 (payments from Italian state welfare fund held not deductible because under Italian law the state would recover from P if P recovered the same loss from D); *Cosemar SA v Marimarna Shipping Co Ltd* [1990] 2 Lloyd's Rep 323 (owners able to recover voyage expenses from time charterers even though paid by third party because, on recovery from time charterers, owners bound to reimburse third party). Cf *Design 5 v Keniston Housing Assoc* (1986) 34 BLR 92 in which it was thought that a state grant given by the Department of the Environment was non-deductible: the best explanation for that otherwise controversial view was that the grant would probably have to be repaid.

19 Supra, pp 104–5. Contra, eg is *Dennis v London Passenger Transport Board* [1948] 1 All ER 779.

restitutionary claim at common law against D, even where he has provided the benefit non-voluntarily, because, as laid down in *Metropolitan Police District Receiver v Croydon Corpn*,[20] X has not discharged any liability of D, since if the damages were reduced by the compensating advantage D was not liable to pay any higher amount.

The importance of X rarely having any rights at common law against P or D is that the courts almost always regard the question of deducting these compensating advantages, as solely involving P and D, so that the choice is either to overcompensate P or to relieve D. Hence, in the leading case of *Parry v Cleaver*, there was no mention of X's rights. It can be argued that, while more expensive (for example, extra litigation would be likely),[1] it would be better to deduct these compensating advantages, other than gratuitous payments, and to allow X to recover from D the value of that benefit deducted by, for example, extending subrogation rights or reversing *Metropolitan Police v Croydon Corpn*.

This approach to reform has now been accepted by the Legislature vis-à-vis state benefits. The strategy of the Social Security Administration Act 1992 Part IV is precisely for there to be full deduction of compensating benefits provided by the state (X) but for the state to be able to recoup the value of those benefits from D. In effect this represents a reversal, within the limits of the statute, of *Metropolitan Police v Croydon Corpn*.

Having examined the factors influencing the courts, we can now look at whether particular benefits are deducted, not deducted or partly deducted.

(i) State benefits

In respect of damages for personal injury the law on the deduction of social security benefits has been transformed by the radical and complex provisions contained in the Social Security Administration Act 1992 Part IV accompanied by the Social Security (Recoupment) Regulations 1990.

The basic approach of the new regime is that 'relevant benefits', which comprise nearly all social security benefits, paid or likely to be

---

20 [1957] 2 QB 154. See Goff and Jones *Law of Restitution* (4th edn) pp 355–9.
 1 For other objections, see *Atiyah's Accidents Compensation and the Law* (5th edn) pp 320–2; Street *Principles* p 106.

paid during the 'relevant period' to the victim in respect of the injury or disease, are to be fully deducted from the compensation but that the state recoups the amount of those benefits from the tortfeasor: ie the tortfeasor is obliged to deduct the full amount of the relevant benefits and to pay them over to the Secretary of State. The scheme therefore means that the victim is properly and not over-compensated while at the same time the tortfeasor's liability is not reduced overall by the provision of state benefits to the victim. The key pillars in the administration of the scheme are a certificate of total benefit furnished by the Secretary of State to the tortfeasor (the 'compensator') and a certificate of deduction furnished by the tortfeasor to the victim (the 'intended recipient').

The 'relevant benefits' are listed in rule 2 of the recoupment regulations and comprise attendance allowance, disablement benefit, family credit, income support, invalidity pension and allowance, mobility allowance, benefits payable under schemes under the Old Cases Act, reduced earnings allowance, retirement allowance, severe disablement allowance, sickness benefit, statutory sick pay, and unemployment benefit. By s 81(1) of the Act the 'relevant period' for full deduction is five years or, if shorter, the period to a final settlement payment, from the day following the accrual of the cause of action (or, in the case of disease, from the victim's first claim for a relevant benefit). It appears from s 81(5) that after five years the relevant benefits are not to be deducted (subject to any other enactment to the contrary).

By ss 81(3)(a) and 85 the new regime does not apply to a 'small payment' which, by rule 3 of the recoupment regulations, means compensation of £2,500 or less. For such 'small payments' the relevant governing provision is s 2(1) of the Law Reform (Personal Injuries) Act 1948, as amended by para 22 of Sch 4 to the Social Security Act 1989. According to this, half of the value of 'relevant benefits' paid or likely to be paid within the first five years are to be deducted. Again by s 81(5) the benefits are not to be deducted after the five years.[2]

It is disappointing that, in the course of such a radical overhaul of the previous law, the Legislature did not see fit to abolish altogether the 'half deduction for five years' approach of the 1948 Act. That approach represented a compromise following the Monkton Committee's report,[3] in which a majority considered that all social security benefits should be deducted. But that was an unsound

2 That was also the position at common law: *Haste v Sandell Perkins Ltd* [1984] QB 735; *Jackman v Corbett* [1988] QB 154.
3 Committee on Alternative Remedies (1946) Cmnd 6860.

compromise for there is no good policy reason not to apply the basic principle that compensation dictates deduction: punishment is not justified, the plaintiff has not directly paid for such benefits, and there is no question of deduction discouraging private benevolence. The Pearson Commission recommended that social security benefits should be fully deducted[4] and this is strongly supported by the reasoning of the House of Lords in *Hodgson v Trapp*[5] in which, prior to the new legislative regime, it was held that attendance and mobility allowance were fully deductible in assessing damages for personal injury. Even if there were a valid objection to extending the recoupment provisions to small sums of damages (eg the expense of the administration), the second-best option would have been to have repealed s 2(1) altogether and to have laid down that all social security benefits are fully deductible.

In similar vein it is unfortunate that by reason of s 81(5) of the 1992 Act social security benefits paid after a five year period are non-deductible.

In practice, the common law approach to the deductibility of social security benefits is now only of relevance to claims for wrongful dismissal. In accordance with correct principle the cases establish that social security benefits paid as a result of the dismissal (eg unemployment benefit) are fully deducted.[6]

A further example of what can be regarded as a state benefit is dealt with in s 5 of the Administration of Justice Act 1982. By this, any saving to the injured plaintiff which is or will be attributable to his maintenance by the National Health Service is to be set off against his loss of earnings.[7] This will leave the plaintiff unjustifiably overcompensated to the extent that he has suffered no loss of earnings or a loss of earnings lower than the expense saved. The section should be amended to require a set off against any of the damages.

---

4 Pearson Report paras 467–98; cf para 494. See also the more radical argument in Cane's *Atiyah's Accidents, Compensation and the Law* (5th edn) at p 327: '. . . tort damages and social security benefits . . . are paid for by much the same group of people (that is, a significant section of the public), and there is no rational justification for paying double compensation for the same loss at the expense of the same group.'
5 [1989] AC 807.
6 *Parsons v BNM Laboratories Ltd* [1964] 1 QB 95; *Westwood v Secretary of State for Employment* [1985] AC 20.
7 Section 5 was enacted following the Pearson Commission's recommendation, paras 510–12, that *Daish v Wauton* [1972] 2 QB 262 should be reversed.

(ii) Non-state benefits

In *Bradburn v Great Western Rly Co*[8] it was held that sums received
under an accident insurance policy should not be deducted, and in
Parry v Cleaver[9] the House of Lords decided, by a three – two
majority, that sums received under a disability pension scheme
should also not be deducted. In essence this rested on the view
that such a pension scheme is more akin to insurance than to wages
and hence, in accordance with *Bradburn*, no deduction should be
made. Lord Reid said:

As regards moneys coming to the plaintiff under a contract of insurance, I
think that the real and substantial reason for disregarding them is that the
plaintiff has bought them and that it would be unjust and unreasonable to
hold that the money which he prudently spent on premiums and the benefit from it should enure to the benefit of the tortfeasor . . . Then I
ask—why should it make any difference that he insured by arrangement
with his employer rather than with an insurance company?[10]

But while the analogy drawn between the disability pension and
accident insurance is justified, the controversial issue is whether
accident insurance payments should be non-deductible. It is submitted that *Bradburn* is right on this, because a plaintiff who has
paid for benefits in the event of misfortune has earned those benefits over and above full damages from a defendant.

In *Smoker v London Fire and Civil Defence Authority*[11] the House of
Lords held that the non-deduction principle of *Parry v Cleaver*
remained good law and was applicable even where the employer
operating the disablement pension scheme was the tortfeasor. And in
Hopkins v Norcross plc[12] the same principles were applied by David
Latham QC, sitting as a deputy high court judge, in holding that a
retirement pension was not to be deducted in assessing damages for
a wrongful dismissal. He said, 'It seems to me that there is no
room . . . for a different approach to the question of deductibility of
a pension dependent upon whether the claim is in contract or tort.'[13]

Gratuitous payments are not deducted.[14] Non-deduction here is
fully supported by *Parry v Cleaver* where Lord Reid said:

8 (1874) LR 10 Exch 1.
9 [1970] AC 1.
10 Ibid at 14.
11 [1991] 2 AC 502.
12 [1993] 1 All ER 565; affd (1993) Times, 13 October, CA.
13 Ibid at 572.
14 *Redpath v Belfast & County Down Rly* [1947] NI 167 (public appeal); *McCamley
    v Cammell Laird Shipbuilders Ltd* [1990] 1 All ER 854 (accident insurance policy
    taken out by employer for employees).

It would be revolting to the ordinary man's sense of justice and therefore contrary to public policy, that the sufferer should have his damages reduced, so that he would gain nothing from the benevolence of his friends or relatives or the public at large, and that the only gainer would be the wrongdoer.[15]

At a deeper level, as suggested earlier, the best explanation for this non-deduction is that the courts do not want to discourage benevolence. But, if that is correct, gratuitous payments *made by the tortfeasor* should normally be deducted.[16]

Wages, salary and sick pay are generally deducted[17] and rightly so, for there is here no reason not to apply the 'compensation dictates deduction' principle. In *Hussain v New Taplow Paper Mills Ltd*[18] the injured plaintiff was entitled under his contract of employment to full sick pay for 13 weeks and thereafter to half pay under his employers' permanent health insurance scheme. The House of Lords held that payments under the scheme should be deducted in assessing damages for loss of earnings. They were indistinguishable from the sick pay paid during the first 13 weeks and were the antithesis of the pension in *Parry v Cleaver* which was payable only after employment ceased. Moreover it was the employers, not the plaintiff, who had paid the insurance premiums under the scheme. In an excellent summary of the law, Lord Bridge explained that while there are two well-established exceptions of first, moneys under an insurance policy paid for by the plaintiff and, secondly, money received from the benevolence of third parties, the rule is that 'prima facie the only recoverable loss is the net loss.'[19] And he went on to say:

It positively offends my sense of justice that a plaintiff, who has certainly paid no insurance premiums as such, should receive full wages during a period of incapacity to work from two different sources, his employer and the tortfeasor. It would seem to me still more unjust and anomalous where, as here, the employer and the tortfeasor are one and the same.[20]

An exception to the deduction of sick pay is where the plaintiff is

---

15 [1970] AC 1 at 14.
16 This is supported by dicta of Lloyd LJ in *Hussain v New Taplow Paper Mills Ltd* [1987] 1 All ER 417, 428. See also *Hunt v Severs* [1993] 4 All ER 180: infra, p 194. But Lloyd LJ's dicta was distinguished in *McCamley v Cammell Laird Shipbuilders Ltd* [1990] 1 All ER 854.
17 *Parry v Cleaver*, ibid; *Turner v Ministry of Defence* (1969) 113 Sol Jo 585.
18 [1988] AC 514.
19 Ibid at 527. See also his very similar comments in *Hodgson v Trapp* [1989] AC 807 (which concerned state benefits: see supra, p 129).
20 Ibid at 532.

under an obligation to refund the sick pay to his employer in the event of recovering full damages. In such a situation the courts do not make a deduction, and this seems a sensible way of both compensating the plaintiff and reimbursing his employer.[1]

In accordance with the general principle of deduction, where the plaintiff has been made redundant as a result of his injuries and has received a redundancy payment that payment is deducted.[2]

(4) Taxation

The question here is, in assessing damages for the gains that the plaintiff has been prevented from making by the defendant's tort or breach of contract, do the courts deduct income tax that the plaintiff would have paid on those gains?

(a) The *Gourley* principle

Applying the usual compensatory aims it would seem that tax that would have been paid on the gains should be deducted since, if liabilities which the plaintiff would have otherwise incurred are ignored, he will be put into a better position than he would have been if the contract had been performed or the tort not committed.

However, until 1955, it was considered that, other than in Fatal Accidents Act actions,[3] tax considerations should be ignored. But in that year in the now famous case of *British Transport Commission v Gourley*,[4] the House of Lords held that, in assessing damages in a personal injuries action for loss of earnings, the tax which the plaintiff would have paid if he had been working for those earnings must be deducted. In Lord Goddard's words:

I cannot see on what principle of justice the defendants should be called upon to pay [the plaintiff] more than he would have received, if he had remained able to carry out his duties . . . Damages which have to be paid for personal injuries are not punitive, still less are they a reward. They are simply compensation.[5]

The *Gourley* principle has since been applied to actions for wrongful

---

1 Supra, p 126, fn 18.
2 *Colledge v Bass Mitchells & Butlers Ltd* [1988] 1 All ER 536. Cf *Mills v Hassall* [1983] ICR 330 where the plaintiff would have been made redundant irrespective of his injury.
3 *Zinovieff v British Transport Commission* (1954) Times, 1 April.
4 [1956] AC 185.
5 Ibid at 207–8.

dismissal,[6] for trespass and conversion[7] and for libel,[8] and it can therefore be regarded as a general principle in assessing compensatory damages.

In *Gourley* itself, however, it was emphasised that the deduction should apply only if the damages themselves were not to be taxed, on the basis that otherwise the plaintiff would be taxed twice. This has created particular difficulties in wrongful dismissal actions, where awards of damages of less than a certain amount, at present £30,000, are exempt from income tax, whereas awards over that amount are taxable. The approach traditionally adopted is that where the award (not having applied *Gourley*) is less than £30,000, *Gourley* must then be applied to reduce the damages, but that where the award of damages (not having applied *Gourley*) is greater than £30,000, *Gourley* must be applied to £30,000 of it but not to the excess.[9] But more recently, Sheen J in *Shove v Downs Surgical plc*[10] adopted a more satisfactory approach. He took the view that whether the damages are themselves to be taxed or not, one should apply *Gourley* to work out first the plaintiff's loss, net of tax. The damages award is then the sum, taking into account the tax to be paid on the damages, which ensures that the plaintiff receives that amount of net loss. So on the facts of the case the plaintiff's net loss, applying *Gourley* was £60,729. To ensure that the plaintiff recovered that loss, given that the damages were themselves taxable, the plaintiff was awarded £83,477.

(b) Is the *Gourley* principle satisfactory?

It should not be thought that the *Gourley* principle has been accepted as satisfactory by everyone. On the contrary, there has been a good deal of criticism of it and the Canadian courts,[11] for example, have refused to follow it.

Apart from the clearly unsatisfactory punitive view that the defendant does not deserve to be benefited by a reduction in damages, three main arguments have been put against deducting tax.[12] First,

6 *Beach & Reed Corrugated Cases Ltd* [1956] 2 All ER 652.
7 *Hall & Co Ltd v Pearlberg* [1956] 1 All ER 297n.
8 *Rubber Improvement Ltd v Daily Telegraph Ltd* [1964] AC 234.
9 *Parsons v BNM Laboratories Ltd* [1964] 1 QB 95, and particularly *Bold v Brough, Nicholson & Hall Ltd* [1964] 1 WLR 201.
10 [1984] 1 All ER 7. See also *Stewart v Glentaggart* 1963 SLT 119.
11 *R v Jennings* (1966) 57 DLR (2d) 644. See also *North Island Wholesale Groceries Ltd v Hewin* [1982] 2 NZLR 176. But in Australia *Atlas Tiles v Briers* (1978) 144 CLR 202, which had rejected *Gourley*, was overturned by *Cullen v Trappell* (1980) 146 CLR 1.
12 Ogus *Damages* pp 113–15.

it means that judges and practitioners, who are not tax experts, are required to argue and decide complex questions of how much tax the plaintiff would have paid, and on the *Shove* approach, what grossed-up amount is now needed to ensure that the plaintiff is compensated for his loss net of tax. But if *Gourley* has justice on its side, such an argument of impracticality can hardly be regarded as a good reason for not applying it. Moreover, there has been little evidence post-*Gourley* of lawyers being unable to cope with its consequences, and nowadays there is, in any event, greater legal education in tax matters.

Secondly, *Gourley* means that the Inland Revenue loses tax revenue that it would otherwise have gained. But as this was also true pre-*Gourley* it is not an argument against *Gourley* in itself but is rather an argument for legislation to be introduced ordering tax to be paid on all damages awards.[13] In any case, the point does not necessarily hold true; for example, a defendant employer may have replaced the injured or dismissed plaintiff employee.

A third argument is that without further adjustment *Gourley* would leave the plaintiff undercompensated. Damages awards are reduced where the plaintiff would not otherwise have had a capital sum to invest. But if he does invest the damages he will have to pay tax on the investment income. The pre-*Gourley* approach was a rough-and-ready way of taking this tax liability into account. So Waddams writes:

> The Canadian rule of ignoring income tax is . . . justified as a short-cut to the complex and uncertain process of deducting first, the tax that the plaintiff would have had to pay on his income, and then adding back the tax the plaintiff will presumably have to pay on the income from the investment of the award.[14]

But the objection to this short-cut is that it cannot hope to be as accurate as applying *Gourley* and also taking account of the presumed tax payable on the investment income. That standard rate tax will be paid on investment income is assumed in the fixing of the appropriate multiplier for assessing future pecuniary loss. Unfortunately the House of Lords in *Hodgson v Trapp*[15] has overruled *Thomas v Wignall*[16] in laying down that there should be no increase in the normal multiplier to take account of higher rate tax

---

13 This is strongly advocated by Bishop and Kay (1987) 103 LQR 211.
14 *Damages* para 3.980.
15 [1989] AC 807; criticised by Burrows (1989) 105 LQR 366 and Anderson (1989) 52 MLR 550. See also Law Commission Consultation Paper No 125 (1992) paras 2 .40–2.41.
16 [1987] QB 1098.

payable on the investment income from large awards: ie there should be no '*Gourley* in reverse' as Lord Reid termed it in *Taylor v O'Connor*.[17]

While *Hodgson v Trapp* is to be deplored, the arbitrariness it introduces should not be matched by an equally arbitrary refusal to deduct tax in the first place. Whatever the fate of *Hodgson v Trapp*, *Gourley* must stand. There is little force in objections put to it and, despite the greater complexity involved in the assessment of damages, the *Gourley* principle adheres to the compensatory aims and is fully justified.

17 [1971] AC 115 at 129.

Chapter 3

Compensatory damages II: damages for the different types of loss

1. INTRODUCTION—PECUNIARY AND NON-PECUNIARY LOSS AND A FURTHER SUBDIVISION

The previous chapter equipped one with all that is basically needed to assess compensatory damages for a tort of breach of contract. This chapter now seeks to put some flesh on those bare bones.

One way of doing this would be to divide torts and breach of contract and then to examine compensatory damages for each of the different torts and contracts respectively. But there are many common approaches to compensation, whether the cause of action be tort or breach of contract, and in order to bring these out it has been considered preferable to examine compensatory damages in respect of the different types of loss with the tort/breach of contract divide then being recognised, where helpful, under each of those types.

In looking at types of loss there is a fundamental division between pecuniary and non-pecuniary loss. Money can be complete compensation for the former but not for the latter. As Lord Diplock said in *Wright v British Railways Board*,[1] '[Non-pecuniary] loss is not susceptible of *measurement* in money. Any figure at which the assessor of damages arrives cannot be other than artificial . . .'

This distinction does not mean that there are never any difficulties in assessing pecuniary loss; for while in some cases compensation for monetary loss is mathematically obvious and exact (for example, pre-trial expenditure), in most instances the uncertainties of what would have happened but for the wrong, and of what will happen in the future, make the assessment of even the loss of monetary income (eg loss of earnings) problematical.

---

1 [1983] 2 All ER 698 at 699. For similar judicial statements, see *The Mediana* [1900] AC 113 at 116; *West & Son Ltd v Shephard* [1964] AC 326 at 346; *Fletcher v Autocar and Transporters Ltd* [1968] 2 QB 322 at 335, 339–40, 363.

Similarly, while reliance on market values is often the most accurate method of assessing pecuniary loss for, for example, property damage, any attempt to put a value on anything, other than money itself, involves some approximation. So the distinction is not between losses where the compensation is precise and losses where it is imprecise. Rather it is between losses which are of wealth, and can therefore be readily translated into money, and other losses.

But as non-pecuniary losses are not losses of wealth, how exactly are they viewed and compared? The traditional judicial approach is to treat some heads of non-pecuniary loss, namely loss of amenity, physical inconvenience, and loss of reputation, as analogous to proprietary losses and as losses over and above the plaintiff's distress or loss of happiness; such heads of loss, in contrast to pain and suffering and mental distress, are therefore assessed objectively with the severe distress of the plaintiff or his unconsciousness being regarded as irrelevant. On this approach, while pain and suffering and mental distress are compared in terms of the degree of distress suffered by the plaintiff, the other non-pecuniary losses are compared by examining the extent of the interference with, and the importance of, the 'personal asset' affected.

An alternative and preferable view is that to treat any non-pecuniary loss as analogous to a property loss is unrealistic and that ultimately all non-pecuniary loss is concerned with the plaintiff's distress or loss of happiness. Taking this approach the different heads of non-pecuniary loss must simply be regarded as different types of distress with the head of 'mental distress' being a residual category. In practice this approach would rarely lead to different results than the traditional judicial one for the courts would need to treat a particular personal injury or physical inconvenience or loss of reputation as affecting individuals' happiness in essentially the same way, just as they already do, for example, in assessing pain and suffering damages. So adoption of the alternative approach would not mean that the plaintiff who has made the best of his misfortune would be likely to recover less than the plaintiff who has not, nor that a plaintiff would be encouraged to present a long face to the court. But the alternative view does provide a sound theoretical explanation for non-pecuniary loss and hence for why, for example, some non-pecuniary losses are regarded as more serious than others. Moreover, there would be at least two practical differences. First, severe distress suffered by the plaintiff would merit higher damages under any of the heads of non-pecuniary loss and, secondly, an unconscious plaintiff would recover nothing for non-pecuniary loss.

Whichever of the two approaches is taken—and as yet there is little judicial support for any departure from the first traditional view—there ought to be uniformity between awards. In other words, similar awards should be made for similar non-pecuniary losses and more serious losses should be compensated by higher awards. This is dictated by the essential justice of like cases being treated alike. It also gives some certainty to the law which in turn aids out-of-court settlements.

Since the virtual elimination of jury trials in personal injury cases, uniformity has indeed become the prime feature of damages for pain and suffering and loss of amenity, with judges relying on a tariff system. Similarly in Fatal Accidents Act cases there is a fixed statutory sum for bereavement. There would also seem to be an awareness of the need for uniformity in respect of other non-pecuniary losses, such as mental distress, although the survival of jury trials in defamation cases hampers putting this into effect for tortious loss of reputation.

Of course the emphasis on uniformity in no sense explains how the level of award is reached in the first place. Why, for example, should damages for loss of amenity and pain and suffering resulting from blindness be assessed at (say) £100,000 rather than £100? The courts are generally content to say merely that the level of awards must be fair and reasonable,[2] should keep pace with the times,[3] and should in no sense reflect the plaintiff's wealth.[4] This may be all that can be sensibly said. However, economists have suggested that a value can be put on injury or life by, for example, asking what people would be prepared to pay to avoid incurring that injury, or what they would be willing to accept to incur it.[5] But in general it is hard to see how either question can produce anything more than further guess-work and the latter would, in any event, produce astronomically high awards. Perhaps more hopeful is to think in terms of the cost of substitute pleasures; that is, a plaintiff should be enabled to buy whatever can in some sense be regarded as making up for the loss he has suffered or will suffer so that, for example, a blind man should at the very least be able to buy hi-fi equipment and compact discs, and the person disabled from skiing should be able to buy holidays in the sun.

---

2 Eg *Rowley v London and North Western Rly Co* (1873) LR 8 Exch 221 at 231; *Scott v Musial* [1959] 2 QB 429 at 443; *Gardner v Dyson* [1967] 1 WLR 1497 at 1501.
3 Supra, pp 107–9.
4 *Fletcher v Autocar and Transporters Ltd* [1968] 2 QB 322 at 340–1.
5 See *Atiyah's Accidents, Compensation and The Law* (5th edn) p 139.

It follows from this discussion that one way to divide the types of loss for the purposes of examining compensatory damages is simply to divide between pecuniary and non-pecuniary loss. But ultimately it has been considered preferable in this chapter to make a different and more detailed division of types of loss which, it is believed, accords more with the way lawyers are used to confronting and thinking about compensatory damages. The division adopted is therefore as follows: pecuniary loss (except consequent on personal injury, death or loss of reputation); personal injury losses; losses on death; loss of reputation; physical inconvenience (except consequent on personal injury); and mental distress (except consequent on death or the plaintiff's personal injury).[6]

2. PECUNIARY LOSS (EXCEPT CONSEQUENT ON PERSONAL INJURY, DEATH OR LOSS OF REPUTATION)

Breach of contract damages are normally sought and awarded for this type of loss. It is therefore not surprising that there is a host of different ways of analysing and subdividing it. Here the approach adopted will be to divide between basic pecuniary loss, which will be primarily concentrated on, and which focuses on the benefit to which the plaintiff was contractually entitled and of which he has been wholly or partially deprived by the defendant's breach, and additional pecuniary loss.[7]

On the other hand, for torts, where the central focus is on wrongful interference rather than a failure to benefit, it has been considered more helpful to adopt a division which gives some flavour of the interference in question. This type of tortious pecuniary loss is therefore examined under three heads:[8] damage to property, including destruction; wrongful interference with goods or land, other than causing property damage; and pure economic loss.

---

6 This chapter's viewing of tort and breach of contract cases alongside one another under these particular heads has no direct equivalent in other works on damages.
7 This is similar to Farnsworth's analysis (1970) 70 Col LR 1145, 1160–75.
8 Other examples of such pecuniary loss are the expenses of gaining release from a false imprisonment in *Prichet v Boevey* (1833) 1 Cr & M 775, and the legal costs of defending a malicious prosecution in *Savile v Roberts* (1699) 1 Ld Raym 374 and *Berry v British Transport Commission* [1962] 1 QB 306.

(1) Breach of contract—basic pecuniary loss

(a) The content of the promise

It is crucial to keep constantly in mind what the defendant contractually promised, so as not to put the plaintiff in a better or worse economic position than if the contract had been performed.

A good illustration of how easy it is to drift away from the basic compensatory principle is where a surveyor contracts to survey a house for a prospective house purchaser. Subject to any express term, the surveyor will be taken to have promised contractually to use reasonable care in making the survey. He will not be taken to have warranted either that the house is worth any particular price or that it is free from any defects other than those reported. It follows that if in reliance on the survey the purchaser goes ahead and buys the house and it transpires that the survey was made in breach of contract, because the surveyor did not report reasonably discoverable defects, the aim of damages will be to put the plaintiff into as good a position as if reasonable care had been used in making the survey and the report; they are not aimed at putting the plaintiff into any (other) warranted position. There are two possible positions the plaintiff may claim that he would have been in if reasonable care had been used in making the survey and report. Either he would not have bought the house at all or he would have bought it but for less than he paid. Applying the former, the plaintiff's basic loss will be the purchase price paid minus the house's actual value. Applying the latter, the basic loss will be the same if one assumes that the plaintiff would have paid the actual value of the house. Alternatively, the court might take the cost of repairs as a convenient starting point for the deduction in price the purchaser would actually have made from the purchase price if he had known of the defects.

The principles have been clearly and correctly applied by the Court of Appeal in cases such as *Perry v Sidney Phillips & Son*[9] and *Watts v Morrow*[10] but in other cases concerning negligent surveys the court's failure to reason from the basic compensatory principle is shown not so much by wrong decisions but rather by statements suggesting that damages are to be calculated according to the warranted value or condition of the property minus its actual value.[11]

---

9 [1982] 1 WLR 1297.
10 [1991] 1 WLR 1421. See similarly *Swingcastle Ltd v Alastair Gibson (a firm)* [1991] 2 AC 223.
11 Eg *Philips v Ward* [1956] 1 WLR 471 at 473; *Simple Simon Catering Ltd v Binstock Miller & Co* (1973) 117 Sol Jo 529.

(b) Difference in value or cost of cure

There is often a choice between awarding the difference in value or the cost of cure. The former directly awards the plaintiff the financial advantage he has lost by being deprived, partially or wholly, of the benefit to which he was contractually entitled. The cost of cure, on the other hand, seeks to award the plaintiff the additional financial sacrifice he would have to incur to put himself into as good a position as if he had received the benefit to which he was contractually entitled.

In many situations the difference in value is in practice the only possible measure because no replacement benefit is available at any cost: for example, the party in breach may alone be capable of performing the contract or the delay may have made the performance impossible. Where both are possible measures, which will be awarded is a central question of interest and will be constantly referred to when looking at examples of the measures of basic pecuniary loss applied. But it is useful here to point to three of the factors that should and do influence the courts in making this choice. First, the plaintiff's duty to mitigate means that he will recover the cost of cure where he has, or ought to have, incurred that cost in reasonably seeking to minimise his losses. Secondly, the fact that the plaintiff has cured or intends to cure may be a decisive factor favouring the cost of cure. Thirdly, the plaintiff's purpose for wanting performance may be relevant; so if the plaintiff wanted performance primarily to reap economic gain, the difference in value will fully compensate him; that is, he will obtain the profits he wanted. But if performance was wanted for other reasons, difference in value will not, or not as fully, compensate him.

(c) The general formulae for assessing basic pecuniary loss

From what has already been said it can readily be seen that, taking into account the advantages as well as the disadvantages resulting from the breach, the plaintiff's basic pecuniary loss can be represented as follows: the value to the plaintiff of the benefit he should have received (minus the value of any benefits gained under the contract or that have, or ought to have, been gained as a result of the breach) minus the cost he has, or ought to have, avoided as a result of the breach; *or* the cost required to put himself into as good a position as if he had received the benefit minus the cost he has, or ought to have, avoided as a result of the breach; put shortly, *difference in value minus cost avoided* or *cost of cure minus cost avoided*.

The beauty of such formulae is that they can be applied whatever the nature of the benefit contracted for: that is, whether it comprised the delivery of goods, the transfer of land, the rendering of services, or the payment of money.

(d) Examples of the measures of basic pecuniary loss applied

These examples show the above general formulae in operation in respect of two of the most common types of contract—contracts for the sale of goods (examples (i)–(vii)) and contracts for the building or repairing of real property (examples (viii)–(x)).

(i) Breach by seller failing to deliver goods wanted for resale

The buyer's duty to mitigate generally dictates that he should buy substitute goods in the market so as to make his resale profit. Therefore, as laid down in s 51(3) of the Sale of Goods Act 1979, the generally appropriate measure is market price at time fixed for delivery minus contract price, with the market price here referring to the market buying price.[12] This is a cost of cure rather than a difference in value measure, with the contract price, assuming unpaid or recovered, being deducted as a cost avoided.

A higher resale price (that is, the price at which the buyer has contracted to sell the goods) clearly does not displace the market price, since it does not affect the buyer's duty to mitigate. More controversial is a lower resale price. Several cases indicate that this should also be ignored. The leading one is *William Bros Ltd v Agius Ltd*[13] where the defendant contracted to sell coal to the plaintiff at 16s 3d per ton. The plaintiff agreed to resell the coal to a third party for 19s per ton. The defendant failed to deliver. The market price at the date of breach was 23s 6d. The plaintiff claimed and was awarded damages of 7s 3d per ton, that is 23s 6d minus 16s 3d. The defendant's argument that the damages should have been only 2s 9d per ton, that is 19s minus 16s 3d, was rejected. Although most commentators support this decision,[14] it would seem that ignoring the resale wrongly overcompensated the plaintiff. True, it is often reasonable, given the plaintiff's potential liability to the sub-buyer, to buy at a higher market price. But on the facts the plaintiff had not done so and there was no question of liability on

---

12 Ogus *Damages* p 324.
13 [1914] AC 510. See also *Rodocanachi v Milburn* (1886) 18 QBD 67. Cf *A-G of the Republic of Ghana v Texaco Overseas Tankships Ltd, The Texaco Melbourne* (1994) Times, 16 February.
14 Eg Waddams *Damages* paras 1.30–1.40, 1.1940, and more generally Simon and Novack (1979) 92 Harv LR 1395.

the resale contract. Nor is it satisfactory to say that, if the contract had been performed, other goods could still have been bought to fulfil the resale leaving the plaintiff free to sell the goods that should have been delivered by the defendant at the market selling price; for those other goods would still have to be bought at the higher market price and resold at the lower resale price, thereby producing an identical loss. So, it is submitted that a lower resale price should displace the market buying price, except where the plaintiff has reasonably bought substitute goods to fulfil the resale, in which case damages should be the price paid for the substitutes minus the original contract price.

Where the plaintiff cannot mitigate by buying substitute goods in the market, he is entitled to a difference in value measure. A good example is *Re R & H Hall and W H Pim, Jr & Co's Arbitration*.[15] The plaintiffs could not mitigate because they had contracted to resell the specific cargo of grain, and no other, to be delivered by the defendant. They were held entitled, subject to remoteness, to the actual resale price, which was higher than the market price, minus the contract price.

(ii) Breach by seller failing to deliver goods wanted for use

The buyer's duty to mitigate means that he should generally buy substitute goods in the market so as to make his user profit and again, therefore, as laid down in s 51(3) of the Sale of Goods Act 1979, the generally appropriate measure is market buying price at time fixed for delivery minus contract price. However, where the buyer cannot so mitigate and cannot mitigate in other ways, for example by having substitute goods manufactured and adapted,[16] he will generally be awarded his lost user profit as the difference in value measure.[17]

Exceptionally, a buyer is awarded the market resale price of goods (minus the contract price if unpaid or recovered). This will be so where the cost of replacing the goods exceeds that resale value, the plaintiff has no intention of replacing the goods, and there is no obvious lost user profit. In *Sealace Shipping Co Ltd v Oceanvoice Ltd, The Alecos M*[18] the defendants contracted to sell a ship, including its spare parts, to the plaintiffs. However, when it was delivered, the

---

15 (1928) 139 LT 50. However, Viscount Haldane's judgment is misleading on remoteness; see Goode *Commercial Law* (1982) p 343.
16 See, by analogy, *Hall Ltd v Barclay* [1937] 3 All ER 620; infra, p 168.
17 See, by analogy, *Cullinane v British Rema Manufacturing Co Ltd* [1954] 1 QB 292.
18 [1991] 1 Lloyd's Rep 120. The decision seems correct but it is criticised by Treitel (1991) 107 LQR 364.

ants failed to also deliver its spare propeller. The arbitrator
awarded $1,100 for that breach on the grounds that the plaintiffs
were not interested in buying a replacement spare propeller (which
would cost $121,000) and that, as there was no commercial market
in second-hand propellers, the resale value of a propeller was its
scrap value of $1,100. Steyn J disagreed and awarded $121,000 but
the Court of Appeal allowed an appeal by the defendants and
restored the lower award made by the arbitrator.

(iii) Breach by seller delivering defective goods wanted for resale[19]

While one can imagine situations[20] in which the duty to mitigate
would dictate that the buyer should render the goods non-defective
before reselling, hence entitling him to the cost of cure, a difference
in value measure is here generally applied. As laid down in s 53(3)
of the Sale of Goods Act 1979 the buyer is generally awarded the
market price that the goods would have had if of the contracted-for
quality, less the market price of the goods actually delivered and it
is clear that the market price here refers to the market selling price.[1]
The contract price is not deducted because it is payable by the
buyer and is therefore not a cost avoided.

   Resale prices here seem relevant in two senses. First, if prior to
the breach the buyer had made a resale contract of the goods, one
would expect the resale selling price to displace the market selling
price of the goods had they been of contracted-for quality.
Secondly, if after breach the buyer had sold the goods, one would
expect the resale price to displace the market selling price of the
goods actually delivered if the former was higher. But in the leading
case of *Slater v Hoyle and Smith*,[2] where a resale concluded prior to
breach had been carried through after breach, resale prices were
considered irrelevant, whether prior or subsequent, and the plaintiff
was held entitled to the normal measure under s 53(3) of the Sale
of Goods Act 1979. The plaintiff bought cotton cloth from the
defendant to fulfil a contract of sale already made. The cloth delivered was of inferior quality than warranted, although the plaintiff
was able to use it as intended to fulfil his sub-contract and received
the full contract price from the sub-buyer. The price paid by the
sub-buyer was greater than the market selling price of the cloth
delivered but less than the market selling price of the cloth as

19 It is assumed here and in examples (iv)–(vi) that the buyer has reasonably
   accepted the goods. If not, the damages are assessed as for non-delivery.
20 Eg where the cost of cure is much lower than the difference in market value.
 1 Ogus *Damages* p 324.
 2 [1920] 2 KB 11.

warranted. The defendant contended that the plaintiff's damages should be nominal because the resale contract price concluded prior to breach minus the resale contract price received subsequent to breach amounted to nil. But the Court of Appeal rejected this, considered cases like *Williams Bros v Agius Ltd*[3] to be correct, and awarded the plaintiff damages assessed according to s 53(3). Again while most commentators support this approach,[4] it is submitted that it cannot be justified on compensatory reasoning and leaves the plaintiff in a better position than if the contract had been properly performed.

(iv) Breach by seller delivering defective goods wanted for use

While one can imagine situations[5] where the duty to mitigate would dictate that the buyer should render the goods non-defective, hence entitling him to the cost of cure, a difference in value measure is here generally applied whereby the buyer is normally entitled to his lost user profit. For example, in *Cullinane v British Rema Manufacturing Co Ltd*,[6] the defendants sold and delivered to the plaintiff a clay pulverising machine warranting that it would process clay at six tons per hour. In fact it could process clay at only two tons per hour. The plaintiff claimed damages, inter alia,[7] for his lost user profit and throughout the judgments it was taken for granted that the buyer was so entitled.[8] Jenkins LJ said:

The plant having been supplied in contemplation by both parties that it should be used by the plaintiff in the commercial production of pulverised clay, the case is one in which the plaintiff can claim as damages for the breach of warranty, the loss of the profit he can show that he would have made if the plant had been as warranted.[9]

(v) Breach by seller making late delivery of goods wanted for resale

A difference in value formula is generally applied whereby, as laid down in *Elbinger Aktiengesellschaft v Armstrong*,[10] the plaintiff is entitled to the market selling price at the time when the goods should

---

3 [1914] AC 510.
4 Eg *McGregor on Damages* para 331; Waddams *Damages* paras 1.2570–1.2580.
5 Eg where the cost of cure is much lower than the lost user profits.
6 [1954] 1 QB 292. See also *Gull v Saunders* (1913) 17 CLR 82.
7 The plaintiff also claimed damages for some of his wasted expenses. The majority (Morris LJ dissenting) refused these. But this seems wrong since the profits awarded were not gross; see Ogus *Damages* pp 352–4; Macleod [1970] JBL 19.
8 [1954] 1 QB 292 at 303, 308, 316.
9 Ibid at 308.
10 (1874) LR 9 QB 473.

have been delivered minus the market selling price at the time when they were actually delivered. As regards resale prices, in *Wertheim v Chicoutimi Pulp Co*[11] a resale after breach was taken into account but a resale prior to breach was not; ie the higher resale price received subsequent to breach displaced the market selling price of the goods when actually delivered but the lower resale price concluded prior to breach did not displace the market selling price of the goods at the time when they should have been delivered. The case concerned a contract for the sale of a number of tons of wood pulp. Applying the normal measure of market selling price at the time when the goods should have been delivered (70s per ton) minus the market selling price when actually delivered (42s 6d), the plaintiff would have been entitled to damages of 27s 6d per ton. However, the Privy Council awarded damages of 5s per ton on the ground that the plaintiffs had subsequently resold the same goods at 65s per ton (ie 70s minus 65s). It would seem, however, that the Privy Council was taking an unsatisfactory mid-position. Either the *Slater v Hoyle and Smith Ltd*[12] approach of ignoring resale prices applies, in which case the plaintiffs should have been entitled to 27s 6d per ton or, and preferably, resale prices of goods both prior and subsequent to breach are taken into account—in which case the plaintiffs should have been entitled to merely nominal damages (ie 65s minus 65s).

(vi) Breach by seller making late delivery of goods wanted for use

A difference in value measure is here generally applied, whereby the buyer is normally entitled to his lost user profit. An illustration of this is provided by one of the classic cases on remoteness, *Victoria Laundry (Windsor) Ltd v Newman Industries*,[13] where the plaintiffs were awarded damages for loss of their ordinary (but not exceptional) user profit following the defendants' breach of contract in delivering five months late a boiler to be used in the plaintiffs' business.

(vii) Breach by buyer refusing to accept the goods

The duty to mitigate generally dictates that the seller should sell the goods to another buyer. Therefore, as laid down by s 50(3) of the

11 [1911] AC 301.
12 [1920] 2 KB 11.
13 [1949] 2 KB 528.

Sale of Goods Act 1979, the general measure is the contract price minus the market price at the date of breach.

This is a difference in value measure—the contract price represents the value to the plaintiff of the defendant's performance as it should have been and the market price is the market selling price[14] and represents the benefit the seller has or ought to have gained by selling the goods to another buyer.

If the seller resells the goods at a price higher than the market selling price, one would expect that this resale price—being the benefit gained—would displace the market selling price as the sum deducted from the contract price. Unfortunately, in *Campbell Mostyn (Provisions) Ltd v Barnett Trading Co*[15] (as analogously in relation to a buyer's damages for non- or defective delivery) it was held that the resale price should be ignored. The defendants had refused to accept 350 cases of tinned ham, which they had contracted to buy from the plaintiffs. The plaintiffs were awarded damages of the contract price minus the market price at the date of breach, even though they had subsequently sold the goods at or above the contract price. This approach leaves the plaintiff in a better position than if the contract had been performed and therefore unjustifiably runs contrary to the avowed compensatory goal.

Where the seller cannot mitigate by selling in the market—for example, where supply exceeds demand—s 50(3) does not apply, and the plaintiff will instead be basically entitled to his loss of profit on that sale (ie contract price minus cost avoided) without any deduction of the market selling price.[16] This is shown by *W L Thompson Ltd v Robinson (Gunmakers) Ltd*[17] in which there was a contract to sell a Vanguard car. The supply of those cars exceeded the demand and therefore when the buyer refused to take the car the seller was held entitled to his loss of profit on the sale even though there was no difference between the contract price and the market selling price at the date of breach. A particularly clear analysis of *Thompson v Robinson* was made by Jenkins LJ in *Charter v Sullivan*.[18] There, because demand exceeded supply, *Thompson v Robinson* was distinguished and s 50(3) applied entitling the seller of a Hillman Minx car to merely nominal damages. Jenkins LJ said:

14 Ogus *Damages* p 324.
15 [1954] 1 Lloyd's Rep 65.
16 See similarly US Uniform Commercial Code, s 2–708(2); Goetz and Scott (1979) 21 Stan LR 323.
17 [1955] Ch 177. Supra, p 120.
18 [1957] 2 QB 117.

The number of sales he [the plaintiff] can effect and consequently the amount of profit he makes, will be governed, according to the state of the trade, either by the number of cars he is able to obtain from the manufacturers or by the number of purchasers he is able to find. In the former case demand exceeds supply, so that the default of one purchaser involves him in no loss, for he sells the same number of cars as he would have sold if that purchaser had not defaulted. In the latter case, supply exceeds demand so that the default of one purchaser may be said to have lost him one sale . . .[19]

and later he went on to say:

Upjohn J's decision in favour of the plaintiff dealers in *Thompson*'s case was essentially based on the admitted fact that the supply of the cars in question exceeded the demand and his judgment leaves no room for doubt that if the demand had exceeded the supply, his decision would have been the other way.[20]

It should further be added that, as laid down in *Lazenby Garages Ltd v Wright*,[1] *Thompson v Robinson* cannot be applied to sales of second-hand cars, because one cannot say of such cars that supply exceeds demand, or that a subsequent sale does not mitigate the seller's loss of profit. As Lord Denning said, '. . . it is entirely different in the case of a second-hand car. Each second-hand car is different from the next, even though it is the same make.'[2]

(viii) Breach by builder refusing to carry out work or carrying it out defectively

One obvious possibility is that the owner will here be awarded the difference in value (ie difference in market selling price) between his property as it should have been if the contract had been performed and its actual value.[3] However the cost of cure, ie the cost of engaging someone to complete the work, is often awarded instead. This may be because the cost of cure is less than the difference in the property's value and hence the owner's duty to mitigate dictates that he should recover only the cost of cure. But even where the cost of cure greatly exceeds the difference in the property's value, the owner has been held entitled to that cost provided he has cured or

19 Ibid at 124–5.
20 Ibid at 130.
 1 [1976] 1 WLR 459.
 2 Ibid at 462.
 3 Where the owner intended to use the property to make a profit, the difference in value measure could alternatively (at least in theory) refer to his loss of user profits.

intends to cure;[4] the three most important cases on this are now *Tito v Waddell (No 2)*,[5] *Radford v De Froberville*,[6] and *Dean v Ainley*.[7]

In the first case, a British company mining for phosphate on Ocean Island, a small island in the Pacific, had contractually promised to restore the land mined by replanting trees but had failed to do so. One of the questions that arose was whether the islanders would be entitled as damages to the cost of cure (ie the cost of replanting the land) which ran into thousands of pounds, or merely to the difference in value between the land as it was and as it would be if replanted, which at most ran to a few hundred pounds. Megarry V-C thought that the fundamental issue was whether the plaintiff had already cured or intended to cure. If so, the higher cost of cure would be awarded. He said, '. . . if the plaintiff establishes that the contractual work has been or will be done, then in all normal circumstances, it seems to me that he has shown that the cost of doing it is, or is part of, his loss and is recoverable as damages.'[8] Of course, where the court is basing itself on the plaintiff's intention to cure it cannot be absolutely sure that this is what the plaintiff will do but Megarry V-C thought that probable intention would be sufficient and he suggested that in cases of doubt the court might be satisfied if the plaintiff gave an undertaking to do the work.[9] On the facts of the case it was held that there was not a sufficiently clear intention on the part of the islanders to use the damages to replant Ocean Island. In particular this was because they were now living on a different island. Damages based on the lower difference in the property's value were therefore awarded.

In *Radford v De Froberville* the plaintiff had sold a plot of land to the defendant on terms, inter alia, that the defendant would erect a wall on the plot so as to divide it from the plaintiff's land. The defendant had failed to do so. One question was whether the plaintiff was entitled to damages assessed according to the cost of cure (ie the cost of building a wall on his land) which at the time of trial would have cost £3,400 and at the time of breach £1,200, or

---

4 There has been much academic discussion of this situation; eg Harris, Ogus and Phillips (1979) 95 LQR 581, 589–94, 601–3; Beale *Remedies* pp 173–7; Farnsworth (1970) 70 Col LR 1145, 1167–75; Tettenborn (1978) 42 Conv 366; Marschall (1982) 24 Ariz LR 733; Muris (1983) 12 J Legal Studies 379.
5 [1977] Ch 106, 328–38.
6 [1977] 1 WLR 1262. See also *Mertens v Home Freeholds Co* [1921] 2 KB 526.
7 [1987] 3 All ER 748.
8 [1977] Ch 106 at 333.
9 Cf supra, p 105, fn 14.

according to the difference in the land's value with and without the wall, which was almost nil. Oliver J, applying *Tito v Waddell (No 2)*, held that the plaintiff was entitled to the cost of cure. He said, 'In the instant case, I am entirely satisfied that the plaintiff genuinely wants this work done, and that he intends to expend any damages awarded on carrying it out.'[10]

In *Dean v Ainley* the majority of the Court of Appeal approved the 'intention' approach. By the terms of a contract for the sale of a house by the defendant to the plaintiff, the defendant covenanted to carry out work to prevent the leaking of water from the patio into a cellar underneath. In breach of contract the defendant failed to do that work properly. In fact the water was seeping into the cellar from areas other than the patio. Waterproofing the patio as the defendant had covenanted to do would cost about £7,500 but would keep out only about 30% of the water. Instead the plaintiff intended to stop leakage from all areas by 'tanking' the cellar which would cost about £10,500. The majority (Glidewell LJ and Sir George Waller) applied *Radford v De Froberville* in holding that the plaintiff was entitled to £7,500. In Glidewell LJ's words, '. . . . [The plaintiff] gave a firm undertaking that, if damages were awarded to him, he would carry out the work of tanking the cellar internally.'[11] Although the plaintiff was clearly not entitled to the £10,500 (because, as Kerr LJ explained, the covenant was merely to stop water leaking from the patio) the decision shows that a plaintiff is not barred from recovering cost of cure damages by the fact that he is intending to effect more extensive work than that contracted for. No reference was made to the difference in value (selling price) between the house with the cellar as it was and the house with the cellar made drier by about 30% but, in line with the trial judge's award of nominal damages, that difference was probably minimal.

In contrast Kerr LJ thought that the plaintiff's intentions were irrelevant and he preferred instead to look for a 'real economic loss'. 'It would have made no difference if he had said that he intended to sell the property or that it was uncertain whether he would do so or not.'[12] With respect such reasoning lacks clarity; and it is hard to understand how, on his reasoning, Kerr LJ managed to arrive at the same figure for damages as the majority.

Earlier cases support the 'intention' approach. For example,

---

10 [1977] 1 WLR 1262 at 1284. In *Minscombe Properties Ltd v Sir Alfred McAlpine & Son Ltd* (1986) 279 Estates Gazette 759 an intention to effect the cure was held sufficient even though it was conditional on obtaining planning permission.
11 [1987] 3 All ER 748, 753.
12 Ibid at 755.

while s 18(1) of the Landlord and Tenant Act 1927 lays down that, for a tenant's breach of a covenant to repair, the measure of damages is the extent by which the market value of the reversion at the end of the lease is diminished by the want of repair, cases like *Smiley v Townshend*[13] and *Haviland v Long*[14] have awarded the cost of repairs that have been or are intended to be carried out, albeit under the pretence that the cost of repair represented the diminution in value. In *Haviland v Long* Denning LJ said:

The measure of damage is the extent by which the market value of the reversion at the end of the lease was diminished by the want of repair. That depends on whether the repairs are going to be done or not. In cases where they have been or are going to be done the cost of repair is usually the measure of damage . . .[15]

Clearly the danger of this approach, where the plaintiff has not yet effected cure, is that he may not use the damages as he appears to intend, and will thereby end up with a windfall. But the main alternative, commonly adopted in the United States, of awarding difference in value if the cost of cure is far higher and therefore 'economically wasteful',[16] fails to compensate a plaintiff fully, wherever he has contracted for a purpose not reflected in the objective market value, ie this often fails to recognise properly the 'consumer surplus'[17] such as the plaintiff's interest in privacy in *Radford*. For this reason the English reliance on the plaintiff's intention generally seems preferable. However, one qualification, which was not discussed in the above cases, is that where the plaintiff wanted the contractual performance solely to make a profit (so that the difference in value can fully compensate him) and the cost of cure is far higher than the difference in value, the duty to mitigate should override the plaintiff's intention to effect cure and the lower difference in value only should be awarded.

It finally remains to consider three further approaches that have been advocated for this situation where the cost of cure far exceeds the difference in value.

The first is to award damages according to the cost the defendant has saved by not performing. These damages are restitutionary, reversing the defendant's unjust enrichment, and are discussed in chapter 6.[18]

---

13 [1950] 2 KB 311.
14 [1952] 2 QB 80.
15 Ibid at 84.
16 Eg *Peevyhouse v Garland Coal Mining Co* 382 P 2d 109 (1962).
17 Harris, Ogus and Phillips (1979) 95 LQR 581.
18 Infra, pp 307–14.

The second is to award a figure representing what the plaintiff would have accepted to release the defendant from his contractual obligation or, similarly, the alteration to the price that, at the time of contracting, the plaintiff would have accepted for the relevant contractual obligation to have been omitted.[19] This approach was specifically rejected in *Tito v Waddell* and rightly so for it is a mere fiction to pretend that damages can here be assessed according to what the parties would themselves have agreed. For even if it is realistic to imagine that the plaintiff would have accepted a price for releasing the defendant, that price cannot be sensibly fixed.

The third is akin to the second but removes the fiction by simply asserting that a reasonable sum, in between the cost of cure and difference in value, should be awarded.[20] But this has no clear basis in principle and would leave uncertain how the reasonable sum should be fixed. Indeed it may simply disguise a desire to reverse (part of) the defendant's unjust enrichment. If so this should be stated openly. It would also mean that this approach merges with the first mentioned above.

(ix) Breach by builder in carrying out work late

There are no authorities on the measure of damages in this situation, but presumably the owner is entitled to either the value (market selling price) of the property at the time the work should have been completed minus its value at the time the work was actually completed, or if he intended to use the property for profit, the loss of user profit in the interim period of delay.

(x) Breach by owner refusing to allow work to proceed

There are again no cases on the measure of damages in this situation. However, applying the general difference in value formula (and assuming no other profitable work has or should have been taken on in the time now left free) the builder should be entitled to the contract price minus the cost avoided because of the breach. So, for example, if a house-owner has contracted with a builder for the building of an extension for £2000 payable on completion, and it will cost the builder £800 for materials and £1000 on labour to complete the job, and the owner repudiates when the job is three-quarters of the way through, the builder will be basically entitled to

19 Beale *Remedies* p 177.
20 See, eg Farnsworth (1970) 70 Columbia LR 1145, 1175.

damages of £1550, ie contract price (£2000) minus cost avoided (£200+£250).[1]

(e) Contracts for the benefit of third parties

The doctrine of privity generally prevents actions for breach of contract by third parties. But what is the measure of damages if the promisee chooses to sue on a contract made for another's benefit?

Applying the normal expectation principle, the plaintiff is entitled to be put into as good a position as *he* would have been if the contract had been performed; ie the relevant loss is the plaintiff's not the third party's. Subject to a few exceptions,[2] this has now been accepted as the correct approach and Lord Denning's reasoning to the contrary in *Jackson v Horizon Holidays Ltd*[3] has been rejected.[4]

However – and again as the authorities have made clear – this does not mean that the promisee is necessarily restricted to nominal damages.[5] On the contrary, one would expect that in many, or even most, contracts made for a third party's benefit, the defendant's failure to benefit the third party will constitute a substantial pecuniary loss to the promisee.[6] This may be, for example, because the promisee required the defendant to pay the third party in order to pay off a debt owed by the promisee to the third party. Or the promisee may have stood to gain from the use to be made by the third party of the promised benefit. Moreover, by analogy to the cases allowing a cost of cure in excess of a difference in value,[7] the plaintiff should be entitled to substantial damages (measured by the cost of cure) where he has subsequently conferred the benefit on the third party or intends to do so.[8]

---

1 Simplistically this assumes that the builder at the time of breach has used three-quarters of the required materials and labour.
2 Eg actions by trustees. See also *The Albazero* [1977] AC 774 and *Linden Gardens Trust Ltd v Lenesta Sludge Disposals Ltd* [1993] 3 All ER 417 in which the House of Lords controversially recognised an exception where the third party is a subsequent owner of property to which the loss relates.
3 [1975] 1 WLR 1468.
4 *Woodar Investment Development Ltd v Wimpey Construction UK Ltd* [1980] 1 WLR 277. See also *Coulls v Bagot's Executor and Trustee Co Ltd* [1967] ALR 385, 410–11 (per Windeyer J).
5 See the two cases cited in the previous footnote; and Lord Pearce's judgment in *Beswick v Beswick* [1968] AC 58.
6 This leaves aside the additional possibility of mental distress damages being awarded on the ground that the predominant object of the contract is the plaintiff's mental satisfaction: infra, pp 232–7. One rationalisation of *Jackson* given in *Woodar* was that the damages were purely for the plaintiff's mental distress.
7 See, eg supra, pp 148–51.
8 Briggs (1981) NLJ 343.

To accept that the normal expectation principle will often dictate the award of substantial damages for the contracting party does not necessarily mean that the damages are the same as the third party's expectation loss. In particular, on an unexecuted contract the contracting party's own saved cost of performance must be deducted whereas this need not be so in calculating a third party's loss. Of course on the present state of the law, where privity holds sway, it is rarely of relevance to assess a third party's loss. That would no longer be true if privity were abolished, so that the third party could himself sue, as has been provisionally recommended by the Law Commission.[9]

(2) Breach of contract—additional pecuniary loss

To put the plaintiff into as good a position as if the contract had been performed, all other pecuniary loss caused to the plaintiff by the defendant's breach and not ruled out by limiting principles, such as remoteness and the duty to mitigate, must be added to the basic measures of pecuniary loss so far discussed.

Loss of user profit may be an additional pecuniary loss: for example, where the plaintiff is basically awarded the costs of replacing and adapting goods, he is also entitled to any interim loss of user profit. Additional pecuniary loss may also comprise—albeit fairly rarely—damage to or destruction of the plaintiff's property. So, for example, in *Harbutt's Plasticine Ltd v Wayne Tank and Pump Co Ltd*[10] the defendant's breach of contract in installing an unsuitable heating system and insulating the pipes with unsafe material led to the plaintiffs' factory burning down. Such damage to property is directly analogous to tortious damage to property and it has therefore been considered preferable to discuss the few contract cases in that tort subsection.[11]

But the commonest form of additional pecuniary loss is expenses caused by the breach, other than those that have been awarded within a cost of cure measure.[12] These expenses are referred to in

---

9 Consultation Paper No 121 (1991) 'Privity of Contract: Contracts for the Benefit of Third Parties'.
10 [1970] 1 QB 447. See also *Bacon v Cooper (Metals) Ltd* [1982] 1 All ER 397.
11 Infra, pp 156–67.
12 One can regard expenses *wasted* because of breach as an additional loss. But in protecting the expectation interest (as opposed to the reliance interest—infra, chapter 4) such expenses are only recoverable if the basic measure has been calculated according to net rather than gross difference in value. Since the basic measure can always therefore take wasted expenses into account it seems unnecessarily complex to consider them separately here. But for claims framed in this

the United States Uniform Commercial Code as giving rise to 'incidental damages'. By s 2–710 a seller's incidental damages include 'any commercially reasonable charges, expenses or commissions incurred in stopping delivery, in the transportation, care and custody of the goods after the buyer's breach, in connection with return or resale of the goods or otherwise resulting from the breach.' By s 2–715 a buyer's incidental damages include '. . . expenses reasonably incurred in inspection, receipt, transportation and care and custody of goods rightfully rejected, any commercially reasonable charges, expenses or commissions in connection with effecting cover and any other reasonable expense incident to the delay or other breach.' Two common examples following a seller's breach are compensation paid to a sub-buyer and the costs incurred in defending a sub-buyer's claim. *Henry Kendall & Sons v William Lillico & Sons Ltd*[13] provides an example of the former. The buyer bought groundnut extractions from the seller, which were then used for making a poultry food, that the buyer sold to a game farm. The groundnut extractions were contaminated and many of the game farm's poultry died or grew up stunted. The buyer was liable to pay damages to the game farm but it successfully claimed compensation in respect of those damages from the seller. An example of the latter is the award in *Hammond & Co v Bussey*.[14] There the plaintiffs bought coal from the defendants and resold it with the same description to C who used it for steamships. The defendants knew that it was the plaintiffs' business to supply coal to steamships. The coal delivered by the defendants was, however, not of the warranted quality. The defendants admitted responsibility in respect of the plaintiffs' liability to pay damages to C, but disputed that they should also have to pay damages for the plaintiffs' legal costs in defending C's action against the plaintiffs. The Court of Appeal held however that the defendants were liable to pay such damages, because not only were those costs not too remote, but also the plaintiffs had not failed in their duty to mitigate by defending C's action, since the defect in the coal was discoverable only by C's using the coal and not by mere inspection, and hence there was some doubt as to C's claim.

way, see *Hydraulic Engineering Co Ltd v McHaffie, Goslett & Co* (1878) 4 QBD 670; *Cullinane v British Rema Manufacturing Co Ltd* [1954] 1 QB 292.
13 [1969] 2 AC 31. See also *Re Hall Ltd and Pim* (1928) 139 LT 50.
14 (1887) 20 QBD 79. See also *Agius v Great Western Colliery Co* [1899] 1 QB 413.

(3) Torts—damage to property, including destruction

This section is concerned with where the defendant's tort (such as trespass to land or goods, negligence, nuisance or conversion)[15] has caused damage to the plaintiff's existing property, whether real or personal. Cases where damage to property is an additional pecuniary loss consequent on a breach of contract will also be considered.[16] Whether for torts or breach of contract, the general compensatory aims dictate that the plaintiff should be put into as good a position as if his property had not been damaged. This was emphasised in relation to tortious damage to a ship in *The Liesbosch*,[17] where Lord Wright said:

> . . . the owners of the vessel are entitled to what is called *restitutio in integrum* which means that they should recover such sum as will replace them, as far as can be done by compensation in money, in the same position as if the loss had not been inflicted on them . . .[18]

A basic choice is generally presented between awarding diminution in value of the property or cost of cure. The former compensates the plaintiff for his loss of financial advantage in being deprived of his property, while the latter compensates him for the cost of putting himself into as good a position as if his property had not been damaged. This choice is analogous to that presented in assessing compensation for tortious interference with goods by misappropriation or loss and in assessing basic pecuniary loss for breach of contract (the damaged property corresponds to a deprivation of the contractual benefit). The decision therefore similarly rests on factors such as the plaintiff's duty to mitigate, whether he intends to cure, and for what purpose he owned the property.

The details of the law are best examined by dividing between damage to real and personal property. Separate consideration will also be afforded to the so-called 'betterment' question.

(a) Damage to real property

The diminution in value of real property is normally assessed by taking the difference between the market selling price of the

---

15 In respect of goods the relevant torts come within the Torts (Interference with Goods) Act 1977. Liability under the Consumer Protection Act 1987 Pt I extends, under s 5, to property damage subject to restrictions (eg that the property is for private use and that the damages exceed £275).
16 Supra, p 154.
17 [1933] AC 449.
18 Ibid at 459.

damaged and undamaged property, while the cost of cure normally comprises the cost of repair or, as a more appropriate term where a building has been destroyed, the cost of reinstatement. The cost of cure might alternatively comprise the market cost of buying or building replacement property elsewhere, minus the selling value of the plaintiff's damaged property, but in view of the nature of real property, this is rarely a realistic option in practice.[19]

A useful dictum on the choice between diminution in value and cost of cure is Donaldson LJ's in *Dodd Properties v Canterbury City Council*,[20] a case where the plaintiff's building had been damaged by the defendants' pile-driving. In an action for negligence and nuisance, the defendants conceded that they were liable for the cost of repairs. Donaldson LJ however took the opportunity to explain the law on damages for property damage. Having said that there are two possible measures he went on:

> The first is to take the capital value of the property in an undamaged state and to compare it with its value in a damaged state. The second is to take the cost of repair or reinstatement. Which is appropriate will depend on a number of factors, such as the plaintiff's future intentions as to the use of the property and the reasonableness of those intentions. If he reasonably intends to sell the property in its damaged state, clearly the diminution in capital value is the true measure of damages. If he reasonably intends to continue to occupy it and to repair the damage, clearly the cost of repairs is the true measure. And there may be in-between situations.[1]

There have been several cases in which a decision between the two measures has had to be made. In *Hollebone v Midhurst and Fernhurst Builders Ltd*[2] the plaintiff's dwelling-house had been damaged by fire due to the admitted negligence of the defendant. The plaintiff was awarded the cost of repairs (£18,991 5s 8d) rather than the difference between the value of the house in its undamaged and damaged state (£14,850). This was an undoubtedly correct decision as the plaintiff had already carried out the repairs and it was reasonable for him to have done so given that he owned the house for living in. Similarly in *Harbutt's Plasticine Ltd v Wayne*

---

19 An exception, on unusual facts, was *Ward v Cannock Chase District Council* [1985] 3 All ER 537, 561–3. See also *Dominion Mosaics and Tile Co Ltd v Trafalgar Trucking Co Ltd* [1990] 2 All ER 246.
20 [1980] 1 All ER 928.
 1 Ibid at 938.
 2 [1968] 1 Lloyd's Rep 38. See also *Heath v Keys* (1984) Times, 28 May. In *Jones v Stroud District Council* [1986] 1 WLR 1141 the cost of repairs was awarded to the plaintiff even though the cost had been borne by a third party (cf infra, p 164, fn 14). See also *Linden Gardens Trust Ltd v Lenesta Sludge Disposals Ltd* [1993] 3 All ER 417, 422–3 (per Lord Griffiths).

Tank and Pump Co Ltd,[3] the plaintiffs' factory was burnt down as a result of the defendant's breach of contract. The plaintiffs were awarded the cost of building and equipping a new factory (£146,581) rather than the diminution in value (£116,785). Again the plaintiffs had already had the factory rebuilt and, given that the factory was owned for business, it was not only reasonable to do so but, as stressed by the Court of Appeal, necessary in order to keep their business going.

The cost of reinstatement was also preferred, though subject to an important qualification, in *Ward v Cannock Chase District Council*.[4] Here the defendant council's negligence in failing to maintain their houses in a particular terrace had led, through the activities of vandals, to the destruction of the plaintiff's two houses where he had been living with his large family. Scott J held that the cost of reinstatement should be awarded, provided that the plaintiff could obtain planning permission to rebuild the houses. If not, and if permission was also refused to convert another of the plaintiff's houses nearby,[5] he should instead be awarded the diminution in value of the properties.

Again in *Dominion Mosaics and Tile Co Ltd v Trafalgar Trucking Co Ltd*,[6] in which the plaintiffs' business premises had been burnt down because of the defendants' negligence, the Court of Appeal followed *Harbutt's Plasticine* and awarded a cost of cure measure (albeit the cost of leasing property elsewhere rather than the cost of reinstatement). Salient points were that the plaintiffs had leased other property, that it was reasonable for them to do so to mitigate their loss of use, and that the cost of the lease was significantly less than the cost of rebuilding. The plaintiffs were awarded £390,000, as the cost of the lease, even though the diminution in the value of the site was estimated at merely £60,000.

Contrasting with those four decisions is *CR Taylor (Wholesale) Ltd v Hepworths Ltd*,[7] where the plaintiffs' disused billiard hall was destroyed by fire. The cost of reinstating it was agreed at £28,957.

---

3 [1970] 1 QB 447.
4 [1985] 3 All ER 537.
5 Supra, fn 19. The issue was being tried as a preliminary question of law: had Scott J been awarding damages he could not have left open the question of planning permission because of the rule that damages must be awarded unconditionally (supra, pp 104–5).
6 [1990] 2 All ER 246.
7 [1977] 1 WLR 659. See also *Jones v Gooday* (1841) 8 M & W 146; *Moss v Christchurch RDC* [1925] 2 KB 750; *Munnelly v Calcon Ltd* [1978] IR 387; *Farmer Giles Ltd v Wessex Water Authority* [1988] 2 EGLR 189.

The diminution in value of the site was notionally £2,500, although in the event of sale for redevelopment this would be completely off-set by the beneficial effect of the fire in saving the expense of clearing the site. May J held that the diminution in value measure should here be preferred (and hence no damages were awarded under this head). This was because the site and billiard hall were owned by the plaintiffs as an investment, which in time would be sold off for redevelopment. The plaintiffs had no intention, prior or subsequent to the fire, of rebuilding the billiard hall.

A further issue, that arose at first instance in the *Dodd Properties* case,[8] is what exactly is meant by repair (or reinstatement). Cantley J said:

The plaintiffs are entitled to the reasonable cost of doing reasonable work of restoration and repair. They are, of course, not bound to accept a shoddy job or put up with an inferior building for the sake of saving the defendants expense. But I do not consider that they are entitled to insist on complete and meticulous restoration when a reasonable building owner would be content with the less extensive work which produces a result which does not diminish to any or any significant extent the appearance, life or utility of the building, and when there is also a vast difference in the cost of such work and the cost of meticulous restoration.[9]

Applying this, the lower cost of non-meticulous repair was awarded and there was no appeal against this. So, in other words, while generally repair or reinstatement means to produce as close a restoration to the original condition as is reasonably possible it will mean a lesser restoration where this will serve the plaintiff's purposes just as well and will cost far less.

Finally, in addition to the diminution in value or cost of cure all other pecuniary losses resulting from the property damage should be recoverable subject to the usual limiting principles, such as remoteness and mitigation. So, for example, in *Grosvenor Hotel Co v Hamilton*,[10] the plaintiffs' expenses in moving their hotel business from the damaged property were recovered: and in the *Dodd Properties* case[11] the plaintiffs were awarded the potential loss of profits on their car business for the time during which the repairs would be carried out.

8 [1979] 2 All ER 118.
9 Ibid at 124.
10 [1894] 2 QB 836.
11 [1980] 1 All ER 928. See also *Rust v Victoria Graving Dock Co* (1887) 36 Ch D 113.

(b) Damage to goods

As in relation to damage to real property there is a basic choice between, on the one hand, awarding the diminution in value of the property—normally the market selling price of the goods as undamaged minus, if the goods are still in existence, their market selling price as damaged—and, on the other hand, the cost of cure, comprising the cost of replacing or, if possible, repairing the goods.[12]

But damage to goods does differ from damage to land or buildings in that here the cost of replacement is often a realistic cost of cure measure. Indeed it is convenient to distinguish between the destruction of goods (including 'constructive total loss') where the cost of replacement is *the* cost of cure measure, repair being out of the question, and mere damage to goods, where both cost of replacement and cost of repair are potential cost of cure measures. Although most of the cases concern ships, it has been said on several occasions that the same principles of assessment apply to all goods.[13]

(i) Destruction of goods

Although the measure of damages chosen has sometimes been obscured by the courts' ambiguous references to damages being assessed according to the value of the chattel, early cases generally seemed to prefer the market selling price (ie diminution in value), while more modern cases have generally preferred the market replacement cost (ie cost of cure). In either case, if anything is left of the chattel, its salvage value (ie market selling price in its present condition) must be deducted.[14]

Illustrative of the earlier cases is *The Clyde*,[15] in which the market selling price was applied. In Dr Lushington's words, 'It is the market price which the Court looks to, and nothing else, as the value of the property. It is an old saying, "the worth of a thing is the price it will bring."'[16] But for goods owned for use rather than sale (such as ships) this is generally a less appropriate measure than the market replacement cost, which was awarded in the modern leading case *The Liesbosch*.[17] There the plaintiffs were using their

---

12 For what is meant by replacement or repair, see supra, p 159.
13 Eg *The Hebridean Coast* [1961] AC 545 at 562 (per Devlin LJ).
14 See, eg *The Fortunity* [1960] 2 All ER 64.
15 (1856) Sw 23.
16 Ibid at 25.
17 [1933] AC 449. See also *Clyde Navigation Trustees v Bowring SS* (1929) 34 Ll L Rep 319; *Jones v Port of London Authority* [1954] 1 Lloyds' Rep 489; *Dominion Mosaics and Tile Co Ltd v Trafalgar Trucking Co Ltd* [1990] 2 All ER 246 (paternoster machines).

dredger 'The Liesbosch' to carry out work at Patras harbour, when it was sunk owing to the defendants' negligence. The plaintiffs were awarded, inter alia, the market price of a replacement dredger, and the costs of adapting it for their use and of transporting it to Patras.

Where damages are based on the chattel's market selling price at the time of destruction, additional damages for loss of use should not be recoverable: this theory of assessment rests on the assumption that the plaintiff could have otherwise sold his chattel at the time of destruction and clearly he could not both have sold it and used it. As Lord Wright said in *The Liesbosch*:

The value of prospective freights cannot simply be added to the market value but ought to be taken into account in order to ascertain the total value for purposes of assessing the damage, since if it is merely added to the market value of a free ship, the owner will be getting pro tanto his damages twice over. The vessel cannot be earning in the open market, while fulfilling the pending charter or charters.[18]

However, these principles have not always been correctly adhered to and in some cases loss of profit on the voyage the ship was on,[19] or even on all other engagements already fixed,[20] has been awarded in addition to the market selling price at the date of the destruction.

On the other hand, where damages are based on the cost of replacement, damages for loss of use during the period until use could be made of the replacement are and should be recoverable subject to the usual limiting principles. As Street wrote, 'The ratio nale of . . . claims for loss of profits is that they are allowable for that period which would elapse before a replacement is procurable.'[1] So in *The Liesbosch*[2] the House of Lords held that additional damages should be awarded for the loss of user profit for the period between the dredger's sinking and the time at which the substitute dredger could reasonably have been available for use in Patras. In Lord Wright's words, 'The true rule seems to be that the measure of damages in such cases is the value of the ship to her owner as a going concern at the time and place of loss.'[3] He then regarded the

---

18 Ibid at 464.
19 *The Llanover* [1947] P 80.
20 *The Philadelphia* [1917] P 101; *The Fortunity* [1960] 2 All ER 64 (cf Hudson *Interests in Goods* (eds Palmer & McKendrick) p 549, fn 16 who appears to construe the latter case as having awarded the cost of replacement rather than the market selling price).
1 *Principles of the Law of Damages* (1962) p 195. See, generally, Knott (1993) LMCLQ 502.
2 [1933] AC 449.
3 Ibid at 464.

combination of replacement costs and loss of user profit, as opposed to the market selling price, as representing that value.

The other most obvious consequential losses that are prima facie recoverable are the reasonable hiring charges of a substitute chattel in the interim period before the replacement chattel can be used.[4] These costs will often mitigate any loss of use and, indeed, where they ought to have been incurred to mitigate such loss of use, they will presumably be awarded instead of damages for loss of use.

(ii) Mere damage to goods

No case has been traced in which diminution in value (ie market selling price as undamaged minus market selling price as damaged) has here been awarded although if the goods were owned for sale rather than use and the repair or replacement costs are a lot higher, the diminution in selling price should be the preferred measure.

Under the cost of cure, there is a decision to be made here between awarding the replacement cost (minus the market selling price of the damaged chattel) and the cost of repairs.[5] Two pairs of cases may be contrasted to illustrate the courts' approach.

In *O'Grady v Westminster Scaffolding Ltd*,[6] the plaintiff's MG car was damaged by the defendant's admitted negligence. The plaintiff repaired the car at a cost of £253 and also incurred costs of about £208 in hiring a substitute car in the interim. The defendant argued that the plaintiff should have written the car off and replaced it which, according to the defendant, would have cost him about £145, ie market price of replacement (£180) minus scrap value of MG (£35). But Edmund Davies J held that the plaintiff was entitled to damages based on the cost of repair (plus hiring charges) because he had acted reasonably in carrying out the repairs; this was particularly because the car, lovingly named 'Hortensia' by the plaintiff, was his pride and joy, which he had spent a lot of time and effort maintaining and it could not really be replaced.

On the other hand in *Darbishire v Warran*[7] the plaintiff, who had repaired his car for £192 (plus hiring charges) preferring to keep a car he knew to be reliable and suitable for his needs, was restricted to damages based on the market cost of a replacement, namely £85 (plus hiring charges). The Court of Appeal held that the plaintiff

---

4   But such costs were not recoverable in *The Liesbosch*, because they flowed from impecuniosity—see supra, pp 87–8. See also *Moore v DER Ltd* [1971] 3 All ER 517, where no replacement cost was being awarded.
5   For what is meant by replacement or repair, see supra, p 159.
6   [1962] 2 Lloyds Rep 238.
7   [1963] 1 WLR 1067.

had failed to take reasonable steps to mitigate his loss by buying a replacement and *O'Grady v Westminster Scaffolding* was distinguished on the ground that there, unlike here, the car in question was unique.

Another contrasting pair of cases concerns damaged ships. In *Italian State Rlys v Minnehaha*[8] the plaintiffs' ship was damaged. They had it repaired for about £37,000 (and had also incurred some relatively minor consequential expenses during the repairing period). It was decided that the value of the ship when repaired, which it was assumed equalled the market cost of replacement, was £53,000. Its value, that is its market selling price, in its damaged condition had been £20,000. The Court of Appeal held that the plaintiffs were only entitled to the replacement cost minus market selling price, which equalled £33,000. It had been unreasonable to incur the greater expense of repair, for the plaintiffs had failed to establish that there was anything particularly special about the ship. Instead they should have sold it off in its damaged state. Lord Sterndale MR said, '. . . unless there is some circumstance to justify him the shipowner does not act reasonably in repairing the ship if the repaired value is very much less than the cost of repairing her'.[9]

In contrast in *Algeiba v Australind*,[10] the cost of repairing the ship was awarded which, including lost profits during repair, amounted to £31,000. This was so even though this exceeded the cost of a replacement (£30,000) minus the selling price as damaged (£6,000), amounting to £24,000. It was held to have been reasonable to repair because it was not easy to obtain a replacement at that time and the ship was particularly well equipped for the plaintiff's work.

These pairs of cases show that the duty to mitigate dictates that whichever is the cheaper of the cost of repair and the replacement cost (also taking into account consequential loss) will generally be preferred. However, if the plaintiff has chosen to repair and there is good reason for him to have done so—because of the special value to him of the chattel and the difficulty of replacing it—the repair cost will be awarded even if well in excess of the replacement cost. There must however be some limit to the discrepancy between repair and replacement cost that will be tolerated. Admittedly, in *O'Grady v Westminster Scaffolding* the cost of repairs and consequential loss was three times the replacement cost, but this was still only a matter of hundreds and not thousands of pounds.

8 (1921) 6 Ll L Rep 12.
9 Ibid at 13.
10 (1921) 8 Ll L Rep 210.

In the light of the above cases *The London Corpn*,[11] which is often cited for there being a general rule that the cost of repairs will be awarded, must be approached with caution. There the damaged ship had been sold off and not repaired yet the cost of repairs was awarded. Greer LJ said, 'Prima facie, the damage occasioned to a vessel is the cost of repairs.'[12] But assuming that a replacement had been bought, or was intended to be, the measure should have been the replacement cost, unless the cost of repairs was cheaper.

In addition to the cost of repair or replacement, all other pecuniary losses resulting from the property damage are recoverable, subject to the usual limiting principles like remoteness and mitigation. So, as already briefly mentioned, in *O'Grady v Westminster Scaffolding Ltd*,[13] damages were awarded for the charges of hiring a car while the plaintiff's car was being repaired, as they were in *Darbishire v Warran*[14]—although this was presumably on the basis that the plaintiff would have had to incur such charges even if he had bought a replacement.

Loss of user profit for the period while the goods are being repaired or replaced is also recoverable.[15] But if the chattel would have been operating at a loss during that period no such damages should be awarded.[16]

Particularly interesting are the cases allowing damages for loss of use where non-profit-earning ships have been damaged. In *The Greta Holme*,[17] for example, the damage was to a dredging boat owned by a harbour authority for removing silt from the sea bed and in *The Mediana*[18] the damage was to a harbour authority's light-ship. In addition to the cost of repairing these service ships the plaintiffs were held entitled to damages for the loss of their use. In the latter case, this was held to be so even though the plaintiffs always maintained a substitute light-ship as cover in the event of damage to the main ship. The justification for such damages for loss of use is not at all obvious. In *The Mediana* Lord Halsbury LC

---

11 [1935] P 70.
12 Ibid at 77.
13 [1962] 2 Lloyds Rep 238.
14 [1963] 1 WLR 1067. In *McAll v Brooks* [1984] RTR 99, on an analogy with the personal injury case of *Donnelly v Joyce* [1974] QB 454, hiring charges were awarded even where a third party and not the plaintiff had incurred them: see, similarly, *Giles v Thompson* [1993] 3 All ER 321.
15 *The Argentino* (1889) 14 App Cas 519; *The World Beauty* [1970] P 144.
16 *The Bodlewell* [1907] P 286.
17 [1897] AC 596. See also *The Marpessa* [1907] AC 241; *Admiralty Comrs v SS Susquehana* [1926] AC 655; *The Hebridean Coast* [1961] AC 545.
18 [1900] AC 113. See also *Birmingham Corpn v Sowsbery* [1970] RTR 84.

drew an analogy with tortious misappropriation: '. . . supposing a person took away a chair out of my room and kept it for 12 months, could anybody say you had a right to diminish the damages by showing I did not usually sit on that chair, or that there were plenty of other chairs in the room.'[19] That analogy is misleading. In misappropriation cases the justification for damages can be said to be either that they compensate for the loss of the fee that the plaintiff would have charged if he had been approached by the defendant or, perhaps more realistically, that they reverse the defendant's unjust enrichment.[20] But in the case of damage to chattels those justifications are not in play. Furthermore, even though the plaintiffs would have been entitled to damages to compensate for the additional costs of hiring a temporary replacement if incurred, they clearly could not be said to have suffered that loss where not incurred. Nor had the plaintiffs suffered a loss in terms of the depreciation of the ships or the costs incurred (for example, the crew's wages) during repair or replacement, because there would have been that depreciation and those costs would have been incurred even if the ships had not been damaged.

Reflecting these problems of justification is the difficulty of how to assess damages for loss of use in this type of case. In *The Marpessa*[1] the House of Lords held that damages should be assessed according to the costs of working and maintaining the dredger that would have been incurred, plus its depreciation, during the period of repairs. In *The Hebridean Coast*[2] the House of Lords awarded a reasonable rate of interest on the value of the ship, as if it had been invested as capital money for the repair period, plus a sum of depreciation. A further possibility would be to award what it would have cost to hire a temporary replacement.[3]

Overall the approach of the courts in these cases cannot be supported. References to loss of use merely serve to obscure the truth that no pecuniary (or non-pecuniary)[4] loss had been suffered by the plaintiffs. This was particularly clear in *The Mediana* where there was a cover ship. No damages should therefore have been awarded under this head in these cases and the plaintiffs should have been confined to recovering the cost of repair or replacement.

---

19 Ibid at 117.
20 Infra, chapter 6.
1 [1907] AC 241. *Birmingham Corpn v Sowsbery* [1970] RTR 84.
2 [1961] AC 545. *Admiralty Comrs v SS Chekiang* [1926] AC 637.
3 Suggested in *The Bodlewell* [1907] P 286 at 292 (per Bargrave Deane J).
4 But where the owner is an individual, damages for loss of use are justifiable as compensating for non-pecuniary loss, ie physical inconvenience or mental distress.

(c) The betterment question

The courts have sometimes been criticised[5] for purportedly leaving the plaintiff overcompensated by not deducting from the full repair or replacement cost of property damaged or destroyed by the defendant's tort or breach of contract an amount for 'betterment'; that is, for the fact that the replacement or repaired property is in a better condition than the property before it was damaged or destroyed. So, for example, in *The Gazelle*[6] the plaintiff's ship was damaged in a collision with the defendant's ship caused by the defendant's negligence. In the plaintiff's action for damages for the costs of repairing his ship and replacing items destroyed, the assessors of the damages had deducted one-third from those costs because the plaintiff was getting new for old. But Dr Lushington overruled this. He said, '. . . if that party derives incidentally a greater benefit than mere indemnification, it arises only from the impossibility of otherwise effecting such indemnification without exposing him to some loss of burden, which the law will not place upon him.'[7] Again, in *Harbutt's Plasticine Ltd v Wayne Tank and Pump Co Ltd*[8] where the plaintiffs' factory was burnt down as a result of the defendants' breach of contract, it was held that the plaintiffs were entitled to the cost of building and equipping a new factory and that no deduction would be made for the fact that the new factory would be better than the old one. Similarly in *Bacon v Cooper (Metals) Ltd*,[9] where the defendants were in breach of contract in supplying the plaintiffs with the wrong kind of scrap metal which then broke the rotor of the plaintiffs' fragmentiser, the plaintiffs were held entitled to the hire-purchase cost of a new rotor and no deduction was made for the fact that the new rotor had an expected life of seven years, whereas the old rotor had had only 3¾ years' expected life left.

But it is submitted that these cases do not contradict the compensatory principle, because it is not at all clear that the betterment represented a real benefit to the plaintiff. In *The Gazelle* and *Harbutt's Plasticine* the plaintiff would only realise a gain from the betterment if the ship and factory respectively were to be sold, and there was little likelihood of that. Similarly in *Bacon v Cooper* there was no certainty that having a new rotor would benefit the plaintiff more than the old one since by the time the old rotor would have

5 Ogus *Damages* p 134.
6 (1844) 2 Wm Rob 279.
7 Ibid at 281.
8 [1970] 1 QB 447. See also *Hollebone v Midhurst and Fernhurst Builders Ltd* [1968] 1 Lloyds Rep 38; *Dominion Mosaics and Tile Co Ltd v Trafalgar Trucking Co* [1990] 2 All ER 246.
9 [1982] 1 All ER 397.

worn out, the fragmentiser itself might have become outmoded. So these cases should not be read as an unjustifiable commitment to not deducting for a true benefit; and where the plaintiff has clearly benefited from the new for old—and it should probably be for the defendant to show this—an appropriate deduction should be made. That this will be so is supported by Cantley J's view in *Bacon v Cooper* that it would be absurd to allow the full cost of replacing a rotor that had only a few days of useful life left.

(4) Torts—wrongful interference with goods or land, other than causing property damage

(a) Goods

Wrongful interference with the plaintiff's goods, without causing property damage, comprises misappropriation or loss of those goods whether by conversion[10] trespass to goods or negligence.[11]

In aiming to put the plaintiff into as good a position as he would have been in if no misappropriation or loss had occurred, as the general compensatory aim dictates, then where the goods have been permanently misappropriated or lost the courts are generally content to say simply that damages are assessed according to the value of the goods.[12] But this is a rather ambiguous phrase. For example, even if there is a market for the goods there may be a variation between the market selling and buying prices. Indeed there is often a basic choice between directly awarding the plaintiff his lost financial advantage from not having the goods (diminution in value) and, on the other hand, awarding him the costs of acquiring substitute goods (cost of cure). This choice is analogous to that presented in assessing compensation for damage to goods and in assessing basic pecuniary loss for breach of contract (the lost property corresponds to a deprivation of the contractual benefit).

It is also noteworthy that in some of the leading cases the

---

10 Conversion was extended and detinue abolished by the Torts (Interference with Goods) Act 1977, s 2.
11 See supra, p 156, fn 15.
12 Eg *Re Simms* [1934] Ch 1; *Caxton Publishing Co Ltd v Sutherland Publishing Co* [1939] AC 178 at 192 (per Lord Roche). The relevant date for assessing the value has been in issue in several conversion cases: see supra, pp 109, 112. For the damages recoverable by those with a limited interest in the goods, see *McGregor on Damages* (15th edn) paras 1342–56; eg the creditor under a hire-purchase agreement is restricted to the unpaid instalments if lower than the goods' value: *Wickham Holdings Ltd v Brooke House Motors Ltd* [1967] 1 All ER 117; *Chubb Cash Ltd v John Crilley & Son* [1983] 2 All ER 294.

defendant had contracted to deliver the goods in question to the plaintiff, and the plaintiff's action in conversion (property in the goods having passed to him) was therefore alternative to that for breach of contract for non-delivery. Subject to differences in limiting principles, like remoteness and contributory negligence, the damages do not differ according to which action is chosen.

So the plaintiff's duty to mitigate means that normally the value of the goods is the market buying price of replacements. However, if there is no such market and if the plaintiff's purpose in having the goods was to sell them, the goods' value will be represented by the profit that would have been made on sale, ie by the market selling price or the actual resale price. The market selling price was awarded in *The Arpad*.[13] There the plaintiffs had bought a quantity of wheat and had resold it at 36s 6d a quarter. The market price had since fallen considerably. The defendant shipowners failed to deliver some 47 tons. In an action for conversion (and breach of contract) the plaintiffs were awarded damages only for the market selling price of the 47 tons at the time fixed for delivery, ie 23s 6d per ton, on the ground that the actual resale price was too remote. On the other hand, in *France v Gaudet*[14] the actual resale price was awarded in a situation where the defendant had failed to deliver champagne. It is submitted that the latter decision is to be preferred since if there is no market for buying replacements, as in these two cases, an award of the actual resale price puts the plaintiff more closely into the position he would have been in if the goods had not been misappropriated or lost; moreover it is hard to see why the resale loss was regarded as too remote in *The Arpad*. Significantly, Scrutton LJ dissented in that case.

Where the plaintiff's purpose in having the goods was for use, and there is no market for buying replacements, the plaintiff is likely to be awarded the cost of manufacturing a replacement plus adaptation costs. This was awarded, for example, in *J and E Hall Ltd v Barclay*,[15] where the defendant converted the plaintiff's machinery and there was no market for buying such machinery. Where the plaintiff cannot even mitigate by replacement manufacture he will presumably be awarded his lost user profits.

In addition to the diminution in value or cost of cure, all other pecuniary losses resulting from the misappropriation or loss of the goods should be recoverable, subject to the usual limiting principles. So, most obviously, where the plaintiff is having replacement goods

13 [1934] P 189.
14 (1871) LR 6 QB 199.
15 [1937] 3 All ER 620.

manufactured, any loss of interim user profit or any charge reasonably incurred in hiring a temporary replacement should be recoverable.

Where the plaintiff gets his goods back he will still be entitled to some damages for having been temporarily deprived of them. So, for example, in *Hillesden Securities Ltd v Ryjak Ltd*,[16] where the plaintiff's car had been returned at the commencement of the trial, the plaintiff was awarded damages under s 3 of the Torts (Interference with Goods) Act 1977 for the temporary loss of use based on the commercial hire fee that it would otherwise have gained during the weeks before the date of the conversion and the date of the car's return. *Strand Electric and Engineering Co Ltd v Brisford Entertainments Ltd*[17] was followed. There the defendants had wrongfully detained the plaintiffs' electrical theatrical equipment. In a detinue action, the defendants were ordered to return the goods or pay their value (at the time of judgment) and additionally the plaintiffs were awarded damages assessed according to a reasonable hiring charge for the period until judgment. The trial judge found, however, that the plaintiffs would not themselves have realised the full hire during that period. Therefore the decision may be best viewed as compensating the plaintiffs for loss of the fee that they would have charged the defendants for legitimate use of their goods or, as Denning LJ but not the majority preferred, as reversing the defendants' unjust enrichment rather than compensating the plaintiffs' loss of use.[18]

(b) Land

Wrongful interference with land is mainly covered by the torts of trespass and nuisance. Normally a plaintiff is concerned with a temporary loss of use of his land, either because of wrongful occupation or use (and here the damages are often referred to as 'mesne profits')[19] or because the defendant's activities off the land have prevented the plaintiff using the land as desired.

Damages for the temporary loss of use of land attempt to compensate the plaintiff's lost user profit (a diminution in value measure). This will often comprise the rent or fee which would have been obtained if the defendant had not wrongfully interfered.

16 [1983] 2 All ER 184.
17 [1952] 2 QB 246.
18 Infra, pp 294–5.
19 Eg *Clifton Securities Ltd v Huntley* [1948] 2 All ER 283; *Morris v Tarrant* [1971] 2 QB 143.

For example, in *Hall & Co Ltd v Pearlberg*,[20] where the defendant had wrongfully occupied the plaintiffs' two farms, the plaintiffs were awarded, inter alia, £650 damages for trespass, representing the one year's rent that they would otherwise have been able to charge an incoming tenant. In other cases damages have been given for the loss of custom caused by the defendant's wrongful interference. For example in *Fritz v Hobson*[1] damages were awarded for the plaintiff's loss of custom caused by the defendant's nuisance in carrying on building operations which prevented free access along a public passage to the plaintiff's shop. Similarly in *Andreae v Selfridge & Co Ltd*[2] damages were awarded, inter alia, for the plaintiff's loss of hotel custom attributable to those building operations of the defendant which constituted a nuisance. Of course the loss of user profit is only recoverable to the extent that it does not infringe limiting principles, like remoteness and the duty to mitigate.

Sometimes, however, damages are based on what is regarded as a reasonable rent or fee irrespective of whether the plaintiff would have otherwise acquired that sum by letting to a third party.[3] Those damages can only sensibly be regarded as compensating loss of use if it is realistic to think that the plaintiff would have charged the defendant that sum for legitimate use of the land. The damages can alternatively be viewed as reversing the defendant's unjust enrichment, and in some cases this seems the only realistic analysis.[4]

Where a plaintiff has been and *will be* prevented from using his land or using it as desired (that is, the deprivation is permanent)— for example, where no injunction is granted to restrain smells or noise or to remove buildings blocking lights—damages (in lieu of an injunction) will normally be measured by the diminution in the market selling price of the land.[5] But in *Bracewell v Appleby*[6] and *Carr-Saunders v Dick McNeil Associates Ltd*[7] the courts have recently assessed damages according to what would have been a fair sum for the plaintiffs to have accepted for granting the defendants a right of way and a right to obstruct light respectively. In both cases the judges spoke of the damages being awarded for the plaintiff's 'loss

20 [1956] 1 All ER 297n.
 1 (1880) 14 Ch D 542.
 2 [1938] Ch 1.
 3 Eg *Whitwham v Westminster, Brymbo, Coal & Coke Co* [1896] 1 Ch 894; *Swordheath Properties Ltd v Tabet* [1979] 1 WLR 285.
 4 Infra, pp 295–8.
 5 Eg *Griffith v Clay & Sons Ltd* [1912] 2 Ch 291.
 6 [1975] Ch 408.
 7 [1986] 2 All ER 888.

of amenity'.[8] But in the former Graham J's emphasis on the profits the defendant had made from building his home (which was accessible only by using the plaintiff's road) makes it preferable to regard the damages in that case as restitutionary, reversing the defendant's unjust enrichment.[9]

(5) Torts—pure economic loss

The term 'pure economic loss' is well-known in the realm of tortious negligence where it refers to economic loss that is not consequent on physical damage. Physical damage most obviously comprises personal injury or property damage but its 'spirit' also includes death, damage to reputation and wrongful interference with goods or land (other than property damage). Hence, for our purposes, pure economic loss will be taken to comprise economic loss not consequent on any of the above kinds of 'physical damage'.

In looking at compensatory damages for pure economic loss it is convenient to divide between four general heads of tortious liability: misrepresentation; wrongful infringement of intellectual property rights; wrongful interference with business or contract; acts or omissions under the tort of negligence.

It is important to realise that the recovery of damages for pure economic loss was, until 30 years ago, severely restricted in that, other than for infringement of intellectual property rights, there was no liability for negligently inflicted pure economic loss; deceit and the torts concerning interference with contract or business require intentional or reckless conduct. But more recently this restriction has been eased, initially by the development of the tort of negligent misrepresentation allowing the recovery of pure economic loss in *Hedley Byrne & Co Ltd v Heller & Partners Ltd*[10] and later by the recognition that, where there is close proximity between the parties, a defendant can be liable in the tort of negligence for acts or omissions causing pure economic loss.

(a) Misrepresentation

A misrepresentation is the basis of a cause of action in tort where made fraudulently, as in the tort of deceit, or negligently, as in the tort of negligent misrepresentation. Similarly a negligent

8 [1975] Ch 408 at 420, [1986] 2 All ER 888 at 896.
9 Infra, p 297.
10 [1964] AC 465.

misrepresentation inducing the making of a contract between the parties is a statutory tort under s 2(1) of the Misrepresentation Act 1967.

(i) What is the aim of the damages?

Most discussion regarding damages for tortious misrepresentation has centred on what the compensatory principle here requires. [As the tort consists of fraudulently or negligently making a false statement misleading the plaintiff, the aim should be to put the plaintiff into as good a position as if no statement misleading him had been made.] Although the contrary has sometimes been suggested, the aim is not and should not be to put the plaintiff into as good a position as he would have been in if the statement had been true, for this would go beyond the essence of the tort. To put it another way, fulfilling the misrepresentee's expectations would usually put him into a better position than if the tort had not been committed and would therefore be punishing the defendant rather than compensating the plaintiff.

Damages for tortious misrepresentation are therefore fundamentally distinct from damages for breach of contract, where the plaintiff's expectations are fulfilled by putting him into as good a position as if the contract had been performed. At a deeper level the distinction between the two rests on the difference between lying and breaking one's promise, with the latter, unlike the former, generally comprising the breaking of a positive rather than a negative obligation. It is hence essential to distinguish between mere representations, where the sole action is for tortious misrepresentation, and warranties, where the plaintiff can sue for breach of contract; or, to put it another way, between [statements merely inducing the making of a contract and the terms of the contract.]

A number of cases show that the aim of damages for tortious misrepresentation is indeed to put the plaintiff into as good a position as if no statement had been made, rather than as if the statement had been true. For fraudulent misrepresentation the leading authority is *Doyle v Olby (Ironmongers) Ltd*.[11] The plaintiff had bought a business from the defendant company. He was induced to do so by various fraudulent misrepresentations. The critical one was that the trade of the business was 'all over the counter', when in fact half of it was obtained by a traveller going out to canvass customers. The judges, particularly Lord Denning, indicated that there is a difference between damages for the tort of deceit and for breach of contract. Lord Denning said:

11 [1969] 2 QB 158. See also *East v Maurer* [1991] 1 WLR 461.

It appears therefore that the plaintiff's counsel submitted and the judge accepted that the proper measure of damages was the 'cost of making good the representation' or what came to the same thing, 'the reduction in value of the goodwill' due to the misrepresentation. In so doing, he treated the misrepresentation as if it were a contractual promise, that is, as if there were a contractual term to the effect, 'The trade is all over the counter. There is no need to employ a traveller.' I think it was the wrong measure. Damages for fraud and conspiracy are assessed differently from damages for breach of contract . . . On principle, the distinction seems to be this: in contract, the defendant has made a promise and broken it. The object of damages is to put the plaintiff in as good a position as far as money can do it, as if the promise had been performed. In fraud, the defendant has been guilty of a deliberate wrong by inducing the plaintiff to act to his detriment. The object of damages is to compensate the plaintiff for all the loss he has suffered, so far again, as money can do it.[12]

Winn and Sachs LJJ agreed with Lord Denning, and Winn LJ specifically approved the passages in the 12th edition of *Mayne and McGregor on Damages*[13] which emphasised that damages for deceit aim to put the plaintiff into the position he would have been in if no statement had been made. The learned authors there relied, as Lord Denning did in *Doyle v Olby*, on cases such as *McConnel v Wright*[14] and *Clark v Urquhart*[15] which had established that, when the plaintiff is induced to buy shares by a fraudulent misrepresentation, the measure of damages is not the value of the shares if the representation had been true less their actual value but rather the purchase price paid less their actual value.

Doyle v Olby was applied but, it is submitted, the wrong result reached in *Smith Kline & French Laboratories Ltd v Long*.[16] The plaintiff was induced by the deceit of the defendant, the managing director of Swift Exports Ltd, to sell to Swift 16,800 packs of tablets at a price of £56.66 per pack. The fraudulent misrepresentation was to the effect that Swift would sell the tablets in Central Africa. In fact they were sold in Holland. Swift paid all but £157,028 of the agreed contract price but then became insolvent. Whitford J dismissed the claim on the ground that the plaintiff had suffered no loss as a result of the fraud. The Court of Appeal reversed that decision and awarded £157,028.

That award would only have been correct if the plaintiff would have sold the tablets at the same price to someone else had it not

12 Ibid at 166–7.
13 (12th edn, 1961) paras 955 et seq.
14 [1903] 1 Ch 546.
15 [1930] AC 28.
16 [1989] 1 WLR 1.

been induced to sell to Swift. Yet the plaintiff conceded that it could have supplied whatever quantity of tablets was needed to meet demand (and that it could be assumed that the tablets had cost nothing to produce). It should have followed that the contract with Swift could not be treated as having deprived the plaintiff of the opportunity to sell those tablets (at the same price) to someone else: and that there was no true analogy with cases on wrongful interference with goods which have awarded damages based on the value of the goods.[17]

Moving on to the tort of negligent misrepresentation, as established in *Hedley Byrne & Co v Heller & Partners Ltd,*[18] *Esso Petroleum Co Ltd v Mardon*[19] shows the application of the same principle. Here a tenant was induced to take a lease of a petrol station from an oil company by a statement made by an experienced salesman on the company's behalf, as to the potential throughput of petrol at that station. The Court of Appeal held that the defendant was liable, inter alia, for its salesman's pre-contractual negligent misrepresentation. As regards the damages, Lord Denning said:

> Mr Mardon is not to be compensated for 'loss of a bargain'. He was given no bargain that the throughput would amount to 200,000 gallons a year. He is only to be compensated for having been induced to enter into a contract which turned out to be disastrous for him. Whether it be called breach of warranty or negligent misstatement, its effect was not to warrant the throughput, but only to induce him to enter into the contract. So the damages in either case are to be measured by the loss he suffered . . . It is to be measured in a similar way as the loss due to a personal injury. You should look into the future so as to forecast what would have been likely to happen if he had never entered into the contract; and contrast it with his position as it now is, as a result of entering into it.[20]

Shaw LJ agreed with Lord Denning over these principles, and while Ormrod LJ did not clearly adopt this approach his comments on the computation of damages are consistent with it.

Similarly in *Box v Midland Bank Ltd,*[1] which concerned a negligent misrepresentation made by a bank's employee regarding the plaintiff's chances of getting a large loan from the bank, Lloyd J had the following to say on the question of how to assess the damages:

17 Supra, pp 167–9.
18 [1964] AC 465.
19 [1976] QB 801.
20 Ibid at 820–1.
  1 [1979] 2 Lloyd's Rep 391. See also *Naughton v O'Callaghan* [1990] 3 All ER 191, 196–8.

The damages claimed amount to just under £250,000 but a very large part of that represents the gains that the plaintiff would have made if the Manitoban contract had been successfully carried through and the Churchman Newton group saved. Once the claim in contract had been abandoned, Mr Box could not hope to recover for loss of his bargain and [his counsel] rightly abandoned that part of the claim. Instead he says that Mr Box is entitled to be put in the position he would have been in if the negligent misstatement had not been made. That always involves questions of the greatest difficulty. It was difficult in *Doyle v Olby*; it was difficult in *Esso v Mardon*; it is even more difficult here.[2]

Applying this principle Lloyd J ultimately assessed damages at £5,000.

With regard to statutory liability under s 2(1) of the Misrepresentation Act 1967, it is also now clear (contrary to early cases suggesting that the plaintiff should be put into as good a position as if the representation had been true)[3] that the basic principle is to put the plaintiff into the position he would have been in if no statement has been made. In *F & B Entertainments Ltd v Leisure Enterprises Ltd*,[4] Walton J ordered an inquiry as to damages under s 2(1) saying that, "The measure of damages, quite clearly, is the same as those in an action for damages for deceit.'[5] In *André & Cie SA v Ets Michel Blanc & Fils*[6] Ackner J similarly said of s 2(1), 'To my mind, the subsection puts the victim of the innocent misrepresentation in the same position, relative to his claim for damages, as the victim of the fraudulent misrepresentation. To his claim, the measure of damages appropriate to claims in tort has to be applied'. In *McNally v Welltrade International Ltd*,[8] Sir Douglas Franks QC, in assessing damages under s 2(1) applied *Doyle v Olby* and said, 'The plaintiff's position before the inducement should be compared with his position at the end of the transaction.'[9] And in *Cemp Properties (UK) Ltd v Dentsply Research & Development Corpn*,[10] in which the Court of Appeal awarded damages under s 2(1) to a purchaser of land, Bingham LJ regarded it as 'the cardinal rule of damages in this field that the plaintiff should be put in the

2 Ibid at 399.
3 *Gosling v Anderson* (1972) 223 Estates Gazette 1743; *Davis & Co (Wines) Ltd v Afa-Minerva (EMI) Ltd* [1974] 2 Lloyds Rep 27; *Watts v Spence* [1976] Ch 165.
4 (1976) 240 Estates Gazette 455.
5 Ibid at 461.
6 [1977] 2 Lloyds Rep 166.
7 Ibid at 181.
8 [1978] IRLR 497.
9 Ibid at 499.
10 [1991] 2 EGLR 197, 201.

same financial position as if the misrepresentation had not been made.' Furthermore Balcombe LJ in *Royscot Trust Ltd v Rogerson*[11] expressly disapproved the early cases describing them as 'initial aberrations' and said, '[I]t is difficult to see how the measure of damages under [s 2(1)] could be other than the tortious measure and . . . that is now generally accepted.'

This must be correct. As has been explained above, it follows from the very nature of the wrong of misrepresentation. Moreover, it would be nonsensical to award the plaintiff the expectation measure under s 2(1) when he is confined to being put into as good a position as if no statement had been made under the very similar tort of negligent misrepresentation and under the more blameworthy tort of deceit.

It follows from the above reasoning that damages that can be awarded for even a purely innocent misrepresentation in lieu of rescission under s 2(2) of the Misrepresentation Act 1967 should not go beyond putting the plaintiff into as good a position as if no statement had been made.[12]

(ii) Expenses caused and gains forgone

To put the plaintiff into as good a position as if no representation had been made he can recover damages for all the expenses caused by and gains forgone because of the misrepresentation, subject to the usual limiting principles.

Dealing first with expenses caused, a useful example is *Richardson v Silvester*.[13] The defendant inserted in a newspaper an advert for the letting of a farm which, as he knew, he had no power to let. In reliance on the advert the plaintiff incurred expenses by himself inspecting the property and in employing other persons to inspect and value it. It was held that the plaintiff had an action for deceit enabling him to recover his expenses.

Where the expenses take the form of a contract price paid under a contract induced by a misrepresentation, the damages are assessed according to the contract price paid minus the value of what has been received under the contract. This is well illustrated by cases

---

11 [1991] 2 QB 297, 304–5. See also *Chesneau v Interhome Ltd* (1983) Times, 9 June; *Sharneyford Supplies Ltd v Edge* [1987] Ch 305, 323 (per Balcombe LJ); *Naughton v O'Callaghan* [1990] 3 All ER 191, 196–8; *Gran Gelato Ltd v Richcliff (Group) Ltd* [1992] 1 All ER 865, 876.

12 See generally *William Sindall plc v Cambridgeshire CC* (1993) Times, 8 June: the specific point in the case was that, whether recoverable under s 2(1) or not, loss due to the sharp fall in the market value of the land subsequent to its purchase by the plaintiff could not be included within damages under s 2(2).

13 (1873) LR 9 QB 34.

where the misrepresentation induced the purchase of shares, such as *McConnel v Wright*,[14] *Clark v Urquhart*[15] and *Archer v Brown*.[16] So, in the last of these, the purchase price of £30,000 was recovered as damages because the plaintiff received no shares in return, the defendant having already sold them to someone else. The plaintiff also received damages of £13,528 in respect of the interest payable on a bank loan taken out to buy the shares. Similarly in *Naughton v O'Callaghan*,[17] in which the plaintiffs had been induced to buy a horse by a negligent misrepresentation as to its true pedigree, the damages awarded were the difference between the price paid (26,000 guineas) and the horse's value nearly two years later when the misrepresentation was discovered and the horse had proved a failure on the racecourse (£1,500); plus £9,820 expenses incurred in training and keeping the horse.

A more complex illustration of damages based on expenses caused minus benefits accruing is provided by *Doyle v Olby*.[18] The expenses amounted to £12,500, and comprised the purchase of business and stock (£9,500) and interest on a loan and overdraft plus rates (£3,000). The benefits amounted to £7,000 and comprised the sale of the business and stock (£4,300) and salary and living accommodation (£2,700). The damages awarded were therefore £5,500 (£12,500 minus £7,000).

Turning to gains forgone, there are very few examples. One is *Burrows v Rhodes*,[19] where the plaintiff joined a private army invading the South African Republic in reliance on the defendant's fraudulent misrepresentations that protection was needed for women and children, that the invasion would be reinforced by other lawful troops, and that the plan had the sanction of HM Government. It was held that the defendant had a good action in deceit enabling him to recover, inter alia, his loss of earnings while involved in the invasion. Another example is *East v Maurer*,[20] in which the plaintiff had been induced to buy a hair salon by the vendor's fraudulent misrepresentation that he would not be continuing to run a competing salon. In an action for deceit, the plaintiff was awarded not only the price paid minus the selling price, plus the trading losses, plus the expenses incurred in buying and selling

14 [1903] 1 Ch 546.
15 [1930] AC 28.
16 [1984] 2 All ER 267. See also *Smith New Court Securities Ltd v Scrimgeour Vickers (Asset Management) Ltd* (1994) Times, 8 March.
17 [1990] 3 All ER 191. See also supra, p 111.
18 [1969] 2 QB 158.
19 [1899] 1 QB 816.
20 [1991] 1 WLR 461.

and carrying out improvements, but also £10,000 for profits forgone. It was explained by the Court of Appeal (in reducing the sum that had been awarded under the last head by the trial judge) that the recoverable profits forgone were what the plaintiff might have been expected to make in another similar hairdressing business and *not* the profits that would have been made in this particular business had the vendor's representation been true. The latter could only have been justified in an action for breach of a contractual warranty.

(b) Wrongful infringement of intellectual property rights[1]

The torts concerned with the wrongful infringement of intellectual property rights are the infringement of a trade-mark, patent, design, or copyright and passing-off.[2] The equitable wrong of breach of confidence will also be examined here. To put the plaintiff into as good a position as if there had been no wrongful infringement he can recover damages for all the expenses caused by and gains forgone because of the infringement, subject to the usual limiting principles.

There are no clear examples of cases in which expenses caused by the defendant's infringement of the plaintiff's intellectual property rights have been compensated. However in *A-G Spalding Bros v AW Gamage Ltd*[3] the defendants had sold some of the plaintiffs' old and discarded footballs as their new goods and in a passing-off action the plaintiffs were awarded damages, inter alia, for what it would have cost to counter-advertise. It clearly follows that if they had incurred expenses in counter-advertising these would have been recoverable.

In contrast there have been numerous cases compensating for the plaintiff's lost profits. The profits that have most commonly been lost have been from the reduction in sales of goods or materials as a result of the defendant's unlawful competition.[4] The assessment

---

1 See Brown (1977) 3 Auck Univ LR 188.
2 A non-negligent wrongdoer is not liable for damages (but may be subject to an injunction) for infringement of a patent or copyright or primary infringement of a design right: see the Patents Act 1977, s 62(1); the Copyright, Designs and Patents Act 1988, ss 97(1), 233(1). It would appear that a non-reckless wrongdoer is not liable for damages (but may be subject to an injunction) for infringement of a trade mark or passing off: *Edelsten v Edelsten* (1863) 1 De GJ & Sm 185; contra is *Clerk and Lindsell on Torts* (16th edn) paras 30-26, 30-42.
3 (1918) 35 RPC 101.
4 *United Horse-Shoe and Nail Co Ltd v Stewart & Co* (1888) 13 App Cas 401 (patent infringement); *Draper v Trist* [1939] 3 All ER 513 (passing-off);

of those lost profits is often very difficult and the courts frequently resort to rough estimation. Certainly it cannot simply be assumed that the sales made by the defendant from selling infringed goods or materials correspond to the plaintiff's lost sales, that is, that there is equivalence between the diversion of customers from the plaintiff and the customers buying from the defendant.[5] In particular one is concerned only with profits lost from (that is, factually caused by) the infringement and not the profit that would in any event have been lost because of lawful competition. Furthermore the defendant's profits may have resulted from special exertions which the plaintiff would not have undertaken.

Some lost sale profits may also have been the result of the plaintiff lowering his prices to counter the defendant's unlawful competition. Damages for such losses were awarded in the patent infringement case of *American Braided Wire Co v Thomson*,[6] but were denied in *United Horse-Shoe and Nail Co Ltd v Stewart*[7] on the ground that the plaintiffs would have lowered their prices irrespective of the patent infringement.

However, the plaintiff may not have lost sales profits; rather he may have lost the profits from licensing his intellectual property. This loss is assessed by determining the lump sum or royalties the plaintiff would have received for granting a licence to the defendant. A detailed examination of the assessment of such damages was made by the House of Lords in *General Tire Co v Firestone Tyre Co Ltd*,[8] an infringement of patent case. Ultimately damages were assessed on the basis of a royalty rate of 3/8th of a US cent, the Lords holding that there was sufficient evidence indicating that this 'going rate' (that is the rate at which other licences for the patent had been granted) was the rate for which the plaintiffs would have

---

Aktiebolaget Manus v Fullwood & Bland Ltd (1954) 71 RPC 243, 250 (infringement of trademark); *Catnic Components Ltd v Hill & Smith Ltd* [1983] FSR 512 (patent infringement). In *Sutherland Publishing Co Ltd v Caxton Publishing Co Ltd* [1936] Ch 323, 336, Lord Wright said that for copyright infringement, 'The measure of damages is the depreciation caused by the infringement to the value of the copyright, as a chose in action.' Taking this approach the lost sale profits represent the depreciation in value.

5 *United Horse-Shoe and Nail Co* case, ibid. But there was taken to be this equivalence in *American Braided Wire Co v Thomson* (1890) 44 Ch D 274.

6 (1890) 44 Ch D 274. *Alexander v Henry* (1895) 12 RPC 360 (infringement of trademark).

7 (1888) 13 App Cas 401.

8 [1975] 1 WLR 819. *Meters Ltd v Metropolitan Gas Meters Ltd* (1911) 28 RPC 157 at 164–5 (patent infringement); *Stovin-Bradford v Volpoint Properties Ltd* [1971] Ch 1007 (infringement of copyright); *Catnic Components Ltd v Hill & Smith Ltd* [1983] FSR 512.

granted the patent licence to the defendants. Lord Wilberforce did however stress that:

Before a 'going rate' of royalty can be taken as the basis on which an infringer should be held liable, it must be shown that the circumstances in which the going rate was paid are the same as or at least comparable with those in which the patentee and the infringer are assumed to strike their bargain.[9]

In *Watson, Laidlaw & Co v Pott, Cassels & Williamson*,[10] an infringement of patent case, Lord Shaw suggested that even where the plaintiff can show neither loss of sales profit, because, for example, he could not have sold patented machines in the particular area where the defendant has sold them, nor loss of licensing profit, because he would not have granted a patent licence, he can still recover substantial damages. Lord Shaw drew an analogy with taking someone's horse, using it and returning it in the same condition, and said:

Each of the infringements was an actionable wrong, and although it may have been committed in a range of business or of territory which the patentee might not have reached, he is entitled to hire or royalty in respect of each unauthorised use of his property. Otherwise, the remedy might fall unjustly short of the wrong.[11]

However, it is difficult to view this approach as being concerned to put the plaintiff into as good a position as if no tort had been committed, and it looks rather as if it is based on reversing the defendant's unjust enrichment, with the royalties representing either the expense the defendant saved in not having to acquire an equivalent patent licence or a fair proportion of the defendant's profits.[12] However, in the *General Tire* case the House of Lords disapproved a similar sort of approach adopted by the Court of Appeal in that case, Lord Wilberforce saying:

Given that the respondents were not claiming an account of profits, the consequence of departing from the conception of loss can only be to discover a *tertium quid* defined, it seems, by reference to what the infringer ought fairly to have paid. But there is no warrant for this on authority or principle.[13]

It finally remains to examine how damages, best viewed as

9 Ibid at 825.
10 (1914) 31 RPC 104.
11 Ibid at 120.
12 Infra, pp 293–9.
13 [1975] 1 WLR 819 at 833.

equitable damages, are assessed for breach of confidence. This merits separate treatment, for in *Seager v Copydex Ltd (No 2)*,[14] which dealt with a breach of confidence claim in respect of a carpet grip, the Court of Appeal put forward an approach that differs somewhat from the above general approach to assessing damages for intellectual property infringement. Drawing an analogy with damages for conversion, Lord Denning viewed the issue in terms of the 'value' of the confidential information. He went on to say that the value depended on the nature of the confidential information. If there was nothing special about it, ie it was the sort of information which could be obtained by employing any competent consultant, the value was the fee which a consultant would charge for it because, by taking the information, the defendant has merely saved himself the time and trouble of employing a consultant. But if the information was special, for example, if it involved some inventive step, its value would be far higher: '. . . not merely a consultant's fee, but the price which a willing buyer—desirous of obtaining it—would pay for it. It is the value as between a willing buyer and a willing seller.'[15] It was suggested that this price might be calculated by a capitalisation of the royalties which the court thinks the defendant would have had to pay the plaintiff for the information.

But this approach is controversial for at least two reasons. First, Lord Denning's emphasis on the expense the defendant has saved himself makes it appear that he was more concerned to reverse the defendant's unjust enrichment than to compensate the plaintiff's loss.[16] Secondly, assuming that he was concerned with compensation, there may be no reason to think that the plaintiff would have sold the special information rather than keeping it for his own use. In such a situation, the plaintiff's loss is likely to be better represented, as in other intellectual property cases, by the lost profits from sales of goods or materials produced with the information.

It is therefore no surprise that the Court of Appeal in *Dowson & Mason Ltd v Potter*[17] has distinguished *Seager v Copydex (No 2)* in holding that, where the plaintiffs are manufacturers who would not have licensed the use of the information, the appropriate measure, in accordance with the usual compensatory aim of damages, is the plaintiffs' lost sales profits. This decision therefore rightly puts the

---

14 [1969] 2 All ER 718. This case also indicates that the standard of liability for damages for breach of confidence may be strict: cf supra, p 178, fn 2.
15 Ibid at 720.
16 Infra, p 299.
17 [1986] 2 All ER 418. See also *Talbot v General Television Corpn Pty Ltd* [1980] VR 224.

assessment of damages for breach of confidence on the same footing as for other cases of intellectual property infringement.

(c)Wrongful interference with business or contract

Wrongful interference with the plaintiff's business or contract is the basis of several torts, for example, inducing breach of contract, intimidation, interference by unlawful means, conspiracy and injurious falsehood. To put the plaintiff into as good a position as if there had been no such interference he can recover damages for all the expenses caused by and gains forgone because of the interference, subject to the usual limiting principles.

As regards expenses caused, *British Motor Trade Association v Salvadori*[18] provides a good example. The plaintiff trade association, in an attempt to keep down the price of certain cars, required all purchasers of those cars to covenant not to resell within twelve months. The defendants with the intention of breaking the system induced certain purchasers to break the covenant. In an action for inducing breach of contract and conspiracy Roxburgh J held that the plaintiffs could recover, inter alia, the expenses incurred in 'unravelling and detecting the unlawful machinations of the defendants.'[19]

But where the defendant has interfered with the plaintiff's business or contract, the plaintiff is usually primarily concerned to recover damages for the profit lost as a result of such interference. So, for example, in *Goldsoll v Goldman*[20] the defendant induced an employee of the plaintiff to break his contract with the plaintiff by setting up a rival jewellery business close to the plaintiff's. In an action for inducing breach of contract damages were awarded for the plaintiff's general loss of business.

Less commonly the gains forgone may comprise a loss of earnings. In *Morgan v Fry*[1] the plaintiff lockman had been dismissed by his employers under pressure from the defendant. In an action for intimidation the plaintiff was at first instance awarded the earnings he would have made as a lockman (and it was assumed that he would not have continued in that job for more than another five years) minus his present wages working in a different job.

It should be noted that damages awarded for tortious interference with contract will not necessarily be the same as for breach of that contract. In particular, principles like remoteness and contributory negligence do not apply in the same way and in the tortious claim

18 [1949] Ch 556.
19 Ibid at 569.
20 [1914] 2 Ch 603.
1 [1968] 1 QB 521; rvsd on liability [1968] 2 QB 710.

there is no role for the two special principles limiting damages for breach of contract.[2]

(d) Acts or omissions under the tort of negligence

Pure economic loss caused by negligent acts or omissions is now sometimes recoverable in the tort of negligence. However, it is far from being the case that damages for pure economic loss are as freely recoverable as for, for example, property damage or personal injury. On the contrary, cases since the radical and controversial decision of the House of Lords in *Junior Books Ltd v Veitchi Co Ltd*,[3] have rejected its wide reasoning and have construed the decision narrowly, and the traditional fears of an indeterminate liability to an indeterminate number and of undermining contractual terms have been re-emphasised.

In looking at how damages should be assessed for negligently caused pure economic loss, it seems helpful to divide between (i) negligent interference with contract or business and (ii) negligent performance of services beneficial to the plaintiff.[4]

(i) Negligent interference with contract or business

No English case has yet allowed the recovery of damages for pure economic loss caused by a negligent interference with contract or business. The situation is exemplified by the pure economic loss claim in *Spartan Steel and Alloys v Martin & Co (Contractors) Ltd*.[5] In that case, the defendants had negligently damaged an electricity cable, thereby cutting off the electricity supply to the plaintiff's factory for 14 hours. As a result the 'melt' then in the furnace was damaged. The plaintiffs were able to recover damages for the damaged melt (£368) and the loss of profit that would have been made on that melt (£400), but not for the profit on four further melts (£1,767) that would have been put through the furnace if the electricity supply had not been cut off. The last head was denied because it amounted to pure economic loss.

For a time the influential Australian case of *Caltex Oil (Australia) Pty Ltd v Dredge 'Willemstad'*[6]—which allowed the plaintiffs to recover the costs of transporting oil by other means when the defendants' dredger negligently damaged an underwater pipeline used,

2 Supra, pp 92–9.
3 [1983] 1 AC 520.
4 For a similar division, see MacGrath (1985) Ox JLS 350.
5 [1973] QB 27.
6 (1976) 136 CLR 529.

but not owned, by the plaintiffs—and the decision in *Junior Books*—albeit that that was directly concerned with the negligent performance of services beneficial to the plaintiff—cast doubt on whether the denial of damages for pure economic loss in *Spartan Steel* was correct. But in *Candlewood Navigation Corpn Ltd v Mitsui OSK Lines Ltd*[7] the Privy Council reaffirmed the traditional position, rejecting the tests in *Caltex Oil* and treating *Junior Books* as irrelevant in this context.

As regards the assessment of damages, the important point is that if negligently caused pure economic loss were to be recoverable in English law in this situation, it should be seen alongside the earlier section on wrongful (intentional) interference with business or contract and damages should be assessed in basically the same way; ie in aiming to put the plaintiff into as good a position as if the defendant had not negligently interfered, expenses caused, as in *Caltex,* and particularly gains forgone, as claimed for in *Spartan Steel,* should be compensated in so far as not ruled out by limiting principles such as remoteness. In the same vein it should be added that this aspect of pure economic loss recovery for tortious negligence does not raise problems for the distinction between tort and contract because it is within traditional tort reasoning in imposing a negative obligation not to interfere making someone worse off rather than imposing a positive obligation to confer a benefit.

(ii) Negligent performance of services beneficial to the plaintiff

Most of the cases on negligently inflicted pure economic loss have so far been concerned with this situation. It occurs, for example, where a professional person, such as a solicitor,[8] surveyor,[9] or an engineer,[10] fails to advise his client properly. The client has an action against him in the tort of negligence to compensate for the pure economic loss caused.

The client will also almost always have a prima facie concurrent claim for breach of the professional's contractual duty of care[11] although in several cases the tortious claim was relied on because the contractual action was time-barred. Subject to differences in limiting principles, such as remoteness and contributory negligence, the assessment of damages will be the same for breach of the

---

7 [1985] 2 All ER 935.
8 Eg *Midland Bank Trust Co Ltd v Hett, Stubbs & Kemp* [1979] Ch 384; *Forster v Outred & Co* [1982] 1 WLR 86.
9 Eg *Perry v Sidney Phillips & Son* [1982] 1 WLR 1297.
10 Eg *Pirelli General Cable Works Ltd v Oscar Faber & Partners* [1983] 2 AC 1.
11 Supra, pp 4–5.

tortious as for the breach of the contractual duty of care with the basic aim being to put the plaintiff into as good a position as if the defendant had performed the services using reasonable care. For example, in *Perry v Sidney Phillips & Son*,[12] if the survey had been properly carried out, the purchaser would not have bought the house or at least would not have paid more for it than its true market value. Hence damages for both breach of contract and the tort of negligence were assessed according to the purchase price of the house minus its actual market value (difference in value measure); and Lord Denning, having said that the aim of damages for breach of contract is 'to put the plaintiff in the same position as he would have been in if the contract had been properly performed' continued, 'Even if the claim be laid in tort against the surveyor, the damages should be on the same basis.'[13] It is important to realise that while one can see this as being in line with the usual compensatory aim of putting the plaintiff into as good a position as if no tort had been committed, the tortious obligation here is a positive one to benefit the plaintiff by performing the services non-negligently.

But the tortious action may also be available where the defendant is performing the services under a contract with a party other than the plaintiff, so that privity prevents the plaintiff suing for breach of contract. Although the tide of dynamic change has been halted,[14] it can be said that where there is close proximity between the plaintiff and the defendant, the plaintiff can recover damages for pure economic loss resulting from negligent performance of the services. This was the situation in *Junior Books*, where the owners of a new factory were held able to recover damages from sub-contractors, against whom they had no contractual rights, for pure economic loss caused by the sub-contractors' negligence in laying a floor in the factory, which was defective and had now started to crack. Slightly wider was *White v Jones*,[15] in which those who would have benefited under a will, had it been changed as instructed by the testator, were held able to recover their loss from the negligent solicitor. Although in contrast to *Junior Books* there was no reliance by the plaintiffs on the defendant, it was held that there was a sufficiently proximate relationship between them and that it was fair, just and reasonable to impose the duty. In particular the plaintiffs

---

12 [1982] 1 WLR 1297.
13 Ibid at 1302.
14 See, eg *Muirhead v Industrial Tank Specialities Ltd* [1985] 3 All ER 705; *Leigh & Sillivan Ltd v Aliakmon Shipping Co Ltd* [1986] 2 All ER 145; *Murphy v Brentwood DC* [1991] 1 AC 398.
15 [1993] 3 All ER 481. This decision approved *Ross v Caunters* [1980] Ch 297.

were a small number of identified people and there would otherwise be no sanction in respect of the solicitor's breach of professional duty.

Assuming that a defendant is held tortiously liable (and in a book on remedies this is the starting point) then, as where the parties are in a contractual relationship, the damages should be assessed according to the position the plaintiff would have been in if the services had been performed non-negligently. In other words, subject to differences in limiting principles, the approach should be the same as for contractual pecuniary loss. For example, in *Junior Books* the factory-owner was entitled to the cost of cure—namely the cost of replacing the defective floor (ie of putting in a floor as specified in the plans)—plus loss of user profit (ie lost production) while the floor was being relaid. And in *White v Jones* the plaintiffs were held entitled to the £9,000 each that they would have received under the amended will had the solicitor carried out his instructions properly.

A final general comment is that if the policy behind allowing tortious negligence claims in this situation ultimately rests on there being a breach of promise, as it may do, it would have been preferable to have treated these actions as being for breach of contract with attendant modifications to consideration and privity.[16]

3. PERSONAL INJURY LOSSES

Personal injury includes disease and illness, both physical and mental,[17] as well as the more obvious cuts, bruises, broken bones and loss of limbs. Nervous shock, as 'a recognised psychiatric illness',[18] is included, as also are 'symptomless' personal injuries, such as pleural plaques caused by inhaling asbestos dust.[19] Damages have also been awarded for the physical and mental effects of a rape or sexual assault.[20]

Claims for personal injury are nearly always founded on a tort (and usually the tort of negligence or breach of statutory duty) but

16 Supra, p 7.
17 Examples are nervous breakdown, as in *Collard v Saunders* (1972) 222 Estates Gazette 795, and compensation neurosis, as in *Malyon v Lawrence, Messer & Co* [1968] 2 Lloyd's Rep 539.
18 *Hinz v Berry* [1970] 2 QB 40 at 42; *Brice v Brown* [1984] 1 All ER 997 at 1005–6; *McLoughlin v O'Brian* [1983] 1 AC 410, 418, 431; *Attia v British Gas Plc* [1988] QB 304, 317.
19 *Church v Ministry of Defence* (1984) 134 NLJ 623; *Sykes v Ministry of Defence* (1984) Times, 23 March.
20 *W v Meah* [1986] 1 All ER 935.

they can also be founded on a breach of contract.[1] Subject to differences in relation to some of the limiting principles, like remoteness and contributory negligence, the principles applied are and should be the same whether founded on tort or breach of contract.

(1) Claims by the injured plaintiff

The general compensatory aims dictate that damages should put the plaintiff into as good a position as if the personal injury had not occurred. In so doing, damages are awarded for several heads of loss, both pecuniary and non-pecuniary. Before examining these, three introductory points should be made.

First, as laid down in *Jefford v Gee*,[2] awards must be itemised, at least into non-pecuniary loss, pre-trial pecuniary loss and future pecuniary loss. This itemisation was held to be required, because of the differing awards of interest payable or non-payable under these three heads.[3] So, as regards non-pecuniary loss, interest on damages is awarded at the rate of 2% from the date of service of the writ to the date of trial.[4] Interest on pre-trial pecuniary loss awards is normally payable from the date of the accident until trial and the normal rate is half the average rate on the special investment account over that period.[5] No interest is payable on damages for future pecuniary loss.[6]

An undoubted consequence of itemisation has been an increase in the damages awarded for personal injury. Indeed in several cases in recent years awards of over £1 million have been made to plaintiffs requiring constant care. But as rightly stressed in *Lim Poh Choo v Camden and Islington Area Health Authority*[7] it is no ground for appeal that the global award is too high; rather rationality dictates that a particular item of damages should be challenged.

A second point is that reference is often made to a distinction between special and general damages. In the context of personal injury, special damages now appear to refer to damages awarded for all pecuniary loss, including future pecuniary loss. General damages

---

1 *Summers v Salford Corpn* [1943] AC 283; *Matthews v Kuwait Bechtel Corpn* [1959] 2 QB 57; *Kralj v McGrath* [1986] 1 All ER 54.
2 [1970] 2 QB 130.
3 Interest is discussed infra, chapter 4.
4 *Wright v British Railways Board* [1983] 2 AC 773.
5 *Jefford v Gee* [1970] 2 QB 130; *Cookson v Knowles* [1979] AC 556.
6 *Jefford v Gee*, ibid. In Australia non-pecuniary loss is further itemised into pretrial and future loss, with no interest being payable on the latter: see *Fire and All Risks Insurance Co Ltd v Callinan* (1978) 140 CLR 427.
7 [1980] AC 174.

refer to damages for non-pecuniary loss. By RSC Ord 18, r 12(1A–C),[8] the amount of the special damages claimed, and the details, must be pleaded: ie the plaintiff must serve with his statement of claim 'a statement giving full particulars of the expenses and losses already incurred and an estimate of any future expenses and losses (including loss of earnings and of pension rights).' The amount and details of general damages claimed do not have to be pleaded.

Finally, the first break with lump sum awards has been made in this field, for s 32A of the Supreme Court Act 1981, as inserted by s 6 of the Administration of Justice Act 1982, empowers courts to award provisional damages.[9]

(a) Non-pecuniary loss

Although it is usual for one sum to be awarded for both loss of amenity and pain and suffering, it is helpful for the purpose of exposition to examine each separately.

(i) Loss of amenity[10]

Damages are here given for the injury itself and its effect on the ability to enjoy life as an objective loss.[11] The amount of damages is awarded in accordance with a tariff system whereby the courts are guided by awards made for similar personal injuries in other cases. This system has in the past depended on the publication (in, for example, *Current Law* and Kemp & Kemp *The Quantum of Damages*) of judicial awards listed under the different types of personal injury (such as deafness, loss of thumb, loss of leg, quadraplegia) with brief details of the plaintiff's circumstances.[12] The tariff or bracket of damages for that injury, which the previous cases have laid down (making adjustments for inflation), will provide the basic award (or range of award) in the instant case; but it is the loss of amenity of the individual plaintiff that is being compensated, so the basic award may then be varied to take account of the plaintiff's life expectancy[13] and any particular deprivations, for

8 For county courts, see CCR Ord 6, r 1(5–7).
9 For discussion, see supra, pp 99–102.
10 See Ogus (1972) 35 MLR 1.
11 Ie irrespective of the plaintiff's feelings. Loss of amenity (as traditionally viewed) is a purely objective loss if one regards the subjective awareness of disability and its consequences as an element of suffering (now like loss of expectation of life).
12 An important example was *Housecroft v Burnett* [1986] 1 All ER 332—£75,000 for non-pecuniary loss for average tetraplegia as at April 1985.
13 Eg *Rose v Ford* [1937] AC 826 where £2 only was awarded for amputation of the deceased's leg the day before she died.

example, that the plaintiff who has lost a hand was a pianist,[14] that the injuries prevent sexual intercourse,[15] or that the plaintiff has lost the comfort and companionship of marriage.[16]

In an attempt to produce greater consistency in awards, the Judicial Studies Board in 1992 produced a report entitled *Guidelines for the Assessment of General Damages in Personal Injury Cases* which sets out the brackets for various injuries based on, but without mentioning the names of, cases reported up to September 1991. This has reduced, while not eliminating, the need to refer to particular past cases although, apart from making adjustments for inflation, periodic updating of the guidelines will presumably be required if they are to retain their authoritative status.

Taking the traditional objective approach, a majority of the Court of Appeal in *Wise v Kaye*[17] and of the House of Lords in *West & Son Ltd v Shephard*[18] upheld a loss of amenity award of £15,000, and a loss of amenity and pain and suffering award of £17,500 respectively, for plaintiffs who had been reduced to 'human vegetables' and were totally, or almost totally, incapable of appreciating their loss. Similarly, in *Lim Poh Choo v Camden and Islington Area Health Authority*[19] the House of Lords refused to overrule *West v Shephard* and upheld an award of £20,000 under loss of amenity and pain and suffering for the plaintiff's brain damage even though she was largely unaware of her deprivation. As Lord Morris said in *West v Shephard*:

An unconscious person will be spared pain and suffering and will not experience the mental anguish which may result from knowledge of what has in life been lost or from knowledge that life has been shortened. The fact of unconsciousness is therefore relevant in respect of and will eliminate those heads or elements of damages which can only exist by being felt or thought or experienced. The fact of unconsciousness does not, however, eliminate the actuality of the deprivations of the ordinary experiences and amenities of life which may be the inevitable result of some physical injury.[20]

Such an approach has been criticised[1] and there were strong dissenting judgments by Diplock LJ in *Wise v Kaye* and by Lords

---

14 Eg *Moeliker v Reyrolle and Co Ltd* [1977] 1 All ER 9 (fishing).
15 Eg *Cook v J L Kier and Co Ltd* [1970] 2 All ER 513.
16 *Hughes v McKeown* [1985] 3 All ER 284.
17 [1962] 1 QB 638.
18 [1964] AC 326. Also see *Andrews v Freeborough* [1967] 1 QB 1.
19 [1980] AC 174.
20 [1964] AC 326 at 349.
1 See *Skelton v Collins* (1966) 115 CLR 94, and Pearson Commission Report Vol I, paras 393–8.

Devlin and Reid in *West & Son Ltd v Shephard*.[2] A main line of criticism is that for loss of amenity the courts should be seeking to compensate for the plaintiff's distress or loss of happiness and hence where the plaintiff cannot feel any distress or unhappiness no damages should be awarded under this head. In other words, critics of these decisions are mainly advocating what has been referred to above[3] as the alternative view of non-pecuniary loss, by which all such loss is ultimately viewed in terms of distress or of loss of happiness. This contrasts with the traditional judicial approach by which the heads of loss of amenity, loss of reputation and physical inconvenience are regarded as analogous to proprietary losses, and as losses over and above any distress caused. While the alternative view seems preferable, it is important to realise that not only has it been rejected by these decisions, but also consistent application of it would require more than just refusing an unconscious plaintiff damages for non-pecuniary loss. For example, all of the heads of non-pecuniary loss would, on this approach, have to be viewed as simply types of distress and, under each, severe distress of the plaintiff would merit higher damages.

(ii) Pain and suffering

Under this head, the courts award damages for all the mental distress that the plaintiff has suffered and will suffer in the future as a result of the personal injury: for example, pain caused by the injury or its treatment, the awareness of physical disability and its consequences, the fear of future incapacity, and embarrassment at disfigurement. Clearly this is a subjective loss and hence no damages were awarded for it in the total human vegetable case of *Wise v Kaye*. But having said that, the courts do use the tariff system to produce uniformity—by this, awards given for similar injuries will represent the basic award, which may then be varied to take account, for example, of the plaintiff's life expectancy or his unusually severe pain and suffering.

Where the plaintiff's expectation of life has been reduced by the injury an objective fixed sum, additional to loss of amenity and pain and suffering, used to be awarded for 'loss of expectation of life'. This was abolished by s 1(1) (a) of the Administration of Justice Act 1982, although by s 1(1) (b) the courts are ordered to take into account in assessing damages for the plaintiff's pain and

---

2 Unfortunately these minority judges still thought that some damages should be awarded for loss of amenity to an unconscious plaintiff.
3 Supra, p 137.

suffering, '. . . any suffering caused or likely to be caused to him by awareness that his expectation of life has been reduced.'

Three less common examples of what can be included under 'suffering' are provided by: *Rourke v Barton*,[4] where the court took into account that the plaintiff, because of her injuries, was unable to help her husband, who had cancer, as much as she would have liked; by *Ichard v Frangoulis*,[5] where the plaintiff, injured in a motor accident while on holiday, was awarded compensation within his general damages for the loss of enjoyment of his holiday; and by *Meah v McCreamer*,[6] where Woolf J included within the plaintiff's general damages, damages for his being imprisoned on the ground that but for the brain damage received in a car accident for which the defendant was responsible, and his resulting personality change, the plaintiff would not have committed the sexual and violent crimes for which he was serving a sentence of life imprisonment.[7]

(iii) Should damages for non-pecuniary loss be restricted?

The Pearson Commission recommended that no damages should be awarded for non-pecuniary loss suffered during the first three months after the injury.[8] Its reasoning was, first, that the primary concern of the tort system should be with compensating pecuniary loss and, secondly, that excluding such damages would save the system a great deal of expense. But such a reform is unlikely to be implemented, and thankfully so, for it contradicts not only the basic compensatory aims but also other areas of the law, such as mental distress damages, where the compensation of non-pecuniary loss (at least in tort) is being extended rather than cut back. Even if it is right that the present system is too expensive, there are better ways to proceed than tinkering arbitrarily and inconsistently with basic common law principles.[9]

In any discussion on abolishing or restricting non-pecuniary loss it is also of interest to realise that in many Communist countries damages for non-pecuniary loss have been denied altogether on the

---

4 (1982) Times, 23 June.
5 [1977] 2 All ER 461.
6 [1985] 1 All ER 367.
7 But in *Meah v McCreamer (No 2)* [1986] 1 All ER 943 Meah was refused damages indemnifying him against his liability to victims of his sex attacks on the grounds of remoteness and public policy. There seems no satisfactory distinction between the two cases.
8 Report, paras 362, 382–9.
9 Eg procedural reform—see Civil Justice Review (1988) Cm 394.

ground that it undermines human dignity to have life and injuries valued economically.[10] But this is puzzling since it surely shows even less respect and an even more materialistic approach to regard only pecuniary losses flowing from personal injury as worthy of compensation.

(b) Pre-trial pecuniary loss

(i) Loss of earnings

This rarely produces any difficulty. The plaintiff is entitled to the net earnings[11] he would have made but as a result of his injury has not made.[12] In principle the expenses involved in earning, which have been saved (eg the costs of travelling to work), should be deducted, although in general this appears not to be the practice.[13]

(ii) Cost of care

The plaintiff can recover all medical, nursing and hospital expenses where reasonably incurred. It follows that if the plaintiff does not incur these expenses because he makes use of the NHS, he cannot recover what he would have had to pay if he had had private treatment.[14] So as not to overcompensate, ordinary living expenses saved are deducted from the cost of staying in a private hospital or home[15] and by s 5 of the Administration of Justice Act 1982 any saving to the plaintiff which is or will be attributable to his maintenance by the NHS is to be set off against his loss of earnings.[16] In *Rialas v Mitchell*[17] it was held that, where the plaintiff continues to live at home, the fact that it would be much cheaper to provide medical and nursing expenses in a private institution does not prevent the full recovery of such expenses. By s 2(4) of the Law Reform (Personal Injuries) Act 1948 the possibility that the plaintiff could have avoided expenses by using the facilities of the NHS

---

10 McGregor *Int Encyclopedia of Comparative Law* Vol XI, ch 9, para 46.
11 Ie taking into account the tax (*British Transport Commission v Gourley* [1956] AC 185), national insurance contributions (*Cooper v Firth Brown Ltd* [1963] 1 WLR 418), and pension payments (*Dews v National Coal Board* [1988] AC 1) he would have paid from his gross earnings.
12 Benefits in kind are included alongside earnings, eg a company car in *Kennedy v Bryan* (1984) Times, 3 May.
13 *Dews v National Coal Board* [1988] AC 1, 12–3.
14 *Cunningham v Harrison* [1973] QB 942; *Lim Poh Choo v Camden and Islington Area Health Authority* [1980] AC 174.
15 *Shearman v Folland* [1950] 2 KB 43; *Lim Poh Choo* case ibid.
16 Supra, p 129.
17 (1984) 128 Sol Jo 704.

is to be disregarded. The Pearson Commission has recommended the repeal of s 2(4)[18] but so long as there is a private system, offering an arguably better service, it is hard to see how it can be unreasonable to opt for it.

There is still a valid claim for nursing expenses even though they may be rendered by a wife, as in *Cunningham v Harrison*[19] or a mother as in *Donnelly v Joyce*[20] and *Housecroft v Burnett*,[1] or someone else who is performing the services voluntarily. In the latter two cases the Court of Appeal attempted to fit this within the normal compensatory principle by regarding the plaintiff's loss, not as the incurring of nursing expenses but rather as the need for care. On this approach damages are then assessed according to the proper and reasonable cost of supplying that need, with the commercial rate providing the ceiling, and it being considered essential that the plaintiff has enough to pay reasonable recompense to the third party, including making up for any lost wages.

But it is hard to resist the view that in reality—as Lord Denning had accepted in *Cunningham v Harrison*—the courts are here seeking to compensate the third party and that the presentation of the damages as covering the plaintiff's own loss is artificial, given that the plaintiff has not incurred any expenses (nor any liability for expenses). Moreover, and with respect to Cane and Harris,[2] it does not seem helpful to regard these latter decisions as representing an underlying theoretical shift from compensating the plaintiff's loss to providing for his needs; for, using 'needs' terminology, damages are unnecessary for the provisions of those needs, since they are and will be supplied gratuitously irrespective of the award. It is submitted therefore that the latter cases merely adopt a different technique for compensating a third party to that adopted by Lord Denning in *Cunningham v Harrison*. He had said that the damages should be held on trust for the third party, whereas these decisions remove that legal obligation to hand over the damages and rather overcompensate the plaintiff in the hope and belief that he will feel morally obliged to use the award to compensate the third party.

If there had been a true loss to the plaintiff in these cases, the gratuitous services rendered by the third party could be naturally viewed as a non-deductible compensating advantage, like a gratuitous payment to the plaintiff by a third party. But without a real

18 Report, para 342.
19 [1973] QB 942.
20 [1974] QB 454. Reliance was placed on the earlier case of *Roach v Yates* [1938] 1 KB 256.
1 [1986] 1 All ER 332. See also *Croke v Wiseman* [1982] 1 WLR 71.
2 (1983) 46 MLR 478, 482–3.

194 Compensatory damages II: damages for different types of loss

loss, talk of a compensating advantage (that is, a benefit compensating that loss) is artificial.

In *Hunt v Severs*[3] the Court of Appeal decided that the plaintiff can still claim the cost of nursing services where they have been rendered *by the defendant tortfeasor* who, on the facts, was the plaintiff's husband. Although no weight was attached to the fact that the defendant was insured, the argument that the defendant would be 'paying' twice over was rejected on the grounds that it was likely that the defendant would, at least indirectly, benefit from the damages. In addition it was felt that plaintiffs would otherwise be given an incentive to rely on the paid help or the voluntary services of third parties rather than the voluntary services of family defendants or, alternatively, would enter into contracts for services with family defendants (thereby incurring a clear pecuniary loss). On the other hand, it was accepted that where a tortfeasor gratuitously supplies a wheelchair to the plaintiff he has injured, or gratuitously repairs the bodywork of a car that he has damaged, or gratuitously replaces and re-erects a fence that he has destroyed, the plaintiff cannot claim the value of those goods and services. Relying on the words of Lord Bridge in one of the leading cases on compensating advantages, *Hussain v New Taplow Paper Mills Ltd*,[4] Sir Thomas Bingham MR said, 'It would positively offend our sense of justice ... if this were permissible.' Yet the precise distinction between the facts of *Hunt v Severs* and those hypothetical examples is not easy to pinpoint. Perhaps the core idea is that it is in the interests of plaintiffs to have nursing services provided by family and friends, rather than strangers, and that any possible disincentive to such care should therefore be removed. Or the thinking may be that some tortfeasors, especially spouses rendering nursing services are highly likely to receive reimbursement, at least indirectly, out of the damages whereas this is not so with regard to other tortfeasors, eg strangers rendering gifts or one-off services.

Two further types of recoverable expenses concerned with the plaintiff's care deserve mention. First, the plaintiff can recover the cost of buying, fitting out and moving to special accommodation, but the capital cost of a new house (as opposed to the cost of the capital) is not awarded since the plaintiff still has that capital in the form of the house.[5] In *Roberts v Johnstone*[6] it was laid down that the plaintiff can recover 2% per annum of the capital cost of the purchase as the cost of the capital. Secondly, a sum was agreed between

---

3 [1993] 4 All ER 180.
4 [1988] AC 514, 532; see generally supra, p 131.
5 *George v Pinnock* [1973] 1 All ER 926; *Cunningham v Harrison* [1973] QB 942; *Moriarty v McCarthy* [1978] 1 WLR 155; *Roberts v Johnstone* [1989] QB 878.
6 [1989] QB 878.

the parties in cases like *Donnelly v Joyce* and *Walker v Mullen*[7] to cover the costs of hospital visits by a spouse or mother. Although in the former the Court of Appeal regarded this as an aspect of the plaintiff's need for care, and hence as part of the plaintiff's loss, those costs are clearly more naturally viewed as the third party's loss. The actual decision in *Walker v Mullen* concerned the further question of whether the plaintiff could recover damages in respect of his father's lost earnings, where his father had not gone back to his job in Jordan so as to be with his wife and the plaintiff while the latter was in hospital. Comyn J reluctantly refused such damages, on the ground that the loss was too remote. But surely that type of loss was foreseeable; and applying the *Donnelly* approach at least some part of the father's loss of earnings should have come within the reasonable and proper cost of supplying the plaintiff's needs. Nevertheless, taking the view that the loss in these sorts of cases is really the third party's, and hence that allowing the plaintiff to recover is highly exceptional, the decision is perhaps justified as confining recovery to a narrow range of claims.

(iii) Other pecuniary losses

All other pre-trial pecuniary losses should be recoverable provided the usual limiting principles, such as remoteness and the duty to mitigate, are not infringed.

A potentially important example, recognised at first instance in *Daly v General Steam Navigation Co Ltd*,[8] is a plaintiff's 'loss of housekeeping capacity', which Brandon J equated with a loss of earnings by someone in paid employment. But in a confused decision in the Court of Appeal[9] it was held that while this loss could be compensated for the future, irrespective of whether any expenses in employing a housekeeper would be incurred or whether a third party would gratuitously carry on the duties, it was only recoverable for the past either where the plaintiff actually had employed someone or where a third party, in this case the husband, had given up earnings so as to help gratuitously with the housekeeping. Otherwise it was thought that past loss of housekeeping capacity should be regarded as a non-pecuniary loss, which was recoverable at least where the plaintiff had struggled on with her housekeeping despite

---

7 (1984) Times, 19 January. See also the award of travelling expenses in *Hunt v Severs* [1993] 4 All ER 180.

8 [1979] 1 Lloyd's Rep 257. Cf Pearson Commission, paras 352–8 recommended that damages should be recoverable by an injured person for loss of capacity gratuitously to render services to the family.

9 [1980] 3 All ER 696.

her injury. But this approach seems hopelessly inconsistent: it criticises the artificiality of regarding the housewife as having always suffered a past pecuniary loss in respect of housekeeping incapacity, while applying that artificiality to the future.

It is submitted therefore that the correct compensatory principles are as follows (assuming that, in line with the nursing services cases, the plaintiff can claim for a third party's loss in gratuitously carrying out the housekeeping): the plaintiff may herself suffer a recoverable pecuniary loss by incurring the expense of employing someone to carry out her housekeeping services; even if not, she can recover a third party's loss where a third party gratuitously carries out those services, especially if the third party suffers a loss of earnings; the plaintiff is entitled to damages for loss of housekeeping capacity as a non-pecuniary loss, at the very least where she struggles on with the housekeeping despite her injury; these principles are just as applicable to the past as to the future.

Jones v Jones[10] formerly provided a further important example of an additional recoverable pecuniary loss. There the plaintiff's marriage broke up as a result of the injuries he sustained in an accident for which the defendant was responsible. The plaintiff was held able to recover for the pecuniary loss of £15,000 resulting from the divorce, ie for the fact that he had to provide his ex-wife with a large lump sum payment as well as maintenance payments. Unfortunately a different Court of Appeal in *Pritchard v J H Cobden Ltd*[11] departed from *Jones v Jones* and held that, even though a divorce has foreseeably resulted from the plaintiff's injury, pecuniary 'loss' on that divorce is irrecoverable.

There were three main grounds for this surprising decision. The first was that where the financial consequences of a divorce have not yet been decided on in the Family Division, a judge in a personal injury action would be placed in the invidious position of having to make an assessment of the outcome of those proceedings. But this merely supports non-recovery where the loss cannot be proved and provides no reason for refusing damages where the divorce provision proceedings have already taken place, as in *Jones v Jones* and in the *Pritchard* case itself (where the two proceedings were heard together by the same judge).

Secondly, it was thought that to allow compensation for this sort of loss would produce a 'vicious circle' in deciding on the orders to be made after divorce, for the potential assets of the parties, including any claims for damages, are taken into account in making those

10 [1985] QB 704. See also *Oakley v Walker* (1977) 121 Sol Jo 619.
11 [1988] Fam 22.

orders. However the obvious and right way out of this difficulty is not to deny damages for this head of loss but rather to exclude from consideration in making the divorce orders any damages that the plaintiff might be entitled to for loss on divorce. After all, the purpose of the damages is to compensate the plaintiff and not to benefit the other spouse or the children of the marriage.

Finally, talk of loss on divorce was in any case thought inapt on the ground that the financial consequences of a divorce are based on a distribution of the parties' assets taking into account various factors. But this objection is difficult to understand since if the plaintiff can prove that he (or she) is in a worse financial position than if there had been no divorce, he is surely naturally viewed as having suffered a pecuniary loss. Indeed, that this is so is supported by the majority's judgment which went on to assess the recoverable loss on divorce should it be thought that their rejection of *Jones v Jones* was wrong.

(c) Future pecuniary loss

Before examining the sub-heads of recoverable loss three introductory points should be made. First, to estimate what the plaintiff's future pecuniary loss will be is clearly a very difficult task. As such one might have expected the courts to make use of actuarial evidence and this is generally so in other common law jurisdictions.[12] But the traditional approach of the English courts has been to resist such evidence.[13] Typical of the judiciary's traditional attitude is Oliver LJ's statement in *Auty v National Coal Board*[14] that in this context, '. . . the predictions of an actuary can be only a little more likely to be accurate (and will almost certainly be less entertaining) than those of an astrologer.'

Commentators have long criticised this attitude[15] and in 1982 a joint working party of lawyers and actuaries was set up to produce tables specifically geared to the assessment of damages for future pecuniary loss in personal injury and death actions. These tables were published in 1984,[16] shortly after the Court of Appeal's

---

12 Eg *Andrews v Grand & Toy Alberta Ltd* (1978) 83 DLR (3d) 452.
13 Eg *Taylor v O'Connor* [1971] AC 115; *Mitchell v Mulholland (No 2)* [1972] 1 QB 65; *Croke v Wiseman* [1982] 1 WLR 71; *Auty v National Coal Board* [1985] 1 All ER 930.
14 [1985] 1 All ER 930 at 939.
15 Eg Prevett (1972) 35 MLR 140, 257; Kemp and Kemp *The Quantum of Damages* Vol 1, ch 8. But *Atiyah's Accidents, Compensation and the Law* (5th edn) pp 133–4 is more cautious.
16 *Actuarial Tables for Use in Personal Injury and Fatal Accident Cases* HMSO May 1985. See Prevett (1985) LS Gaz 2640.

decision in *Auty*. Perhaps their most significant feature is the presumption that plaintiffs will invest their damages in index-linked Government stocks, so that multipliers are based on the rate of discount corresponding to the yield on such stocks at the date of assessment. This makes it unnecessary to speculate as to the future rate of inflation. While even these tables were initially not regarded as acceptable evidence in their own right,[17] the decision of the Court of Appeal in *Hunt v Severs*[18] may mark a turning-point. Sir Thomas Bingham MR said:

> There is . . . a good deal to commend [the tables] as avoiding dispute and tending towards certainty . . . we think it right to accept the submission that, when the amount and timing of future payments are known—or assumed to be known—the multiplier should be chosen on a mathematical basis. And if there is an element of uncertainty which can best be allowed for by choosing a multiplier in that way and then adjusting it, that too should be done.

This more enlightened approach may obviate the need to implement the Law Commission's provisional recommendation that legislation should be introduced 'to encourage the general use of these tables'.[19]

Secondly, the difficulty of assessing the plaintiff's future pecuniary loss led the Pearson Commission to recommend that the main form of award for future pecuniary loss should be periodic payments rather than a lump sum award. However, this idea had earlier been rejected by the Law Commission and the legislature has preferred the Law Commission recommendation for a less radical break with lump sum awards by empowering the award of 'provisional damages' in a personal injury claim.[20]

Thirdly, the courts ordinarily ignore the effect of future inflation.[1] This is for two main reasons. First, it is very difficult to estimate what any future rate of inflation will be. As Lord Scarman said in *Lim Poh Choo v Camden and Islington Area Health Authority*,[2] '. . . it is pure speculation whether inflation will continue at present, or higher rates or even disappear. The only sure comment one may make upon any inflation prediction is that it is as likely to be falsified

---

17 *Spiers v Halliday* (1984) Times, 30 June.
18 [1993] 4 All ER 180. See also *O'Brien's Curator Bonis v British Steel Corpn* 1991 SLT 477.
19 Law Commission Consultation Paper No 125 (1992) para 2.22.
20 For discussion see supra, pp 99–102.
 1 Apart from the cases cited in this paragraph, see *Mallett v McMonagle* [1970] AC 166; *Taylor v O'Connor* [1971] AC 115; *Auty v National Coal Board* [1985] 1 All ER 930.
 2 [1980] AC 174 at 193.

as to be borne out by the event.' Secondly, high inflation has in recent years been accompanied by high interest rates: as an award calculated by the multiplier method assumes that investment of the award will yield only the low rates of interest related to a stable currency, one can regard this as countering the effects of future inflation without any further allowance. As Lord Fraser put it in *Cookson v Knowles*:[3]

. . . inflation and the high rates of interest to which it gives rise is automatically taken into account by the use of multipliers based on rates of interest related to a stable currency. It would therefore be wrong for the court to increase the award of damages by attempting to make a further specific allowance for future inflation.

But in practice there has clearly been no such rough-and-ready balancing out; for while the courts have been basing multipliers on 4½% interest,[4] the effect of high inflation has meant that the real rate of return on investments has generally been lower than that.[5] Many commentators[6] have sensibly suggested that there is now a way out of this difficulty, since a plaintiff can completely protect himself against inflation by investing in index-linked securities. By basing multipliers on the rate of interest on those securities at the date of assessment, the courts would realistically avoid the need to speculate on inflation. In practice this would result in a substantial increase in the multipliers currently applied.

(i) Loss of future earnings

The judicial approach to converting future loss of earnings into a present capital sum is to multiply a multiplicand by a multiplier. The multiplicand is basically the plaintiff's present annual loss of net earnings, ie the annual net sum the plaintiff would at present have been earning minus what he actually is earning. This figure is then adjusted to take account, for example, of lost promotion prospects. Where there is no present loss of earnings, as in the case of a child plaintiff, it has been held acceptable to take the national average earnings during early working years as the multiplicand (or the basis for working out the multiplicand).[7]

---

3 [1979] AC 556 at 577.
4 As stressed in *Cookson v Knowles*, ibid, and *Robertson v Lestrange* [1985] 1 All ER 950.
5 Indeed this is the basis of the decisions that there should be only a 2% rate of interest on damages for non-pecuniary loss: infra, pp 260–1.
6 Eg Kemp (1985) 101 LQR 556.
7 *Croke v Wiseman* [1982] 1 WLR 71.

The starting point for the multiplier is the estimated number of years of disability from the trial. So that where the plaintiff is expected to be disabled for the rest of his life, the starting point is the remaining years of working life. But this figure is then adjusted. In particular, there is a reduction for the fact that the plaintiff receives a capital sum now, rather than periodical payments over the years. The courts also commonly make a reduction for the contingencies of life, for example the chance that the plaintiff might die earlier than expected (although this seems misconceived since the life expectancy already takes account of this risk) or might have become unemployed irrespective of the injury.

The aim is to provide a lump sum which, when invested, will produce an income in terms of interest and withdrawals of capital equal to the lost income over the plaintiff's working life. In practice, the maximum multiplier is about 18 and the norm for a 30-year-old is about 15–16. A young spinster has usually had a smaller multiplier applied than a young man to take account of her otherwise having had workless years bringing up a family.[8] But where her injuries mean that she is unlikely to marry, an alternative approach, adopted in *Hughes v McKeown*,[9] is to make no such deduction from the multiplier while not adding on elsewhere for loss of marriage prospects (as a pecuniary loss); the assumption being that the lost earnings during the years raising a family would have been roughly equivalent to the economic support of the never-to-be-husband.[10]

Low multipliers are applied in respect of young children, since they might never have become wage earners. For example, in *Croke v Wiseman*,[11] where the plaintiff was aged seven at trial and was expected to live until 40, a multiplier of five was applied for loss of future lifetime earnings.

This case is also significant as one of several in which Lord Denning took the view that full lost earnings should not be awarded to a totally incapacitated plaintiff.[12] Sometimes this was argued on the ground that different heads of loss overlap so that deduction from earnings is necessary to avoid overcompensation. But this was a weak line of attack in that the law has long taken into account the need to avoid overlapping by, for example, deducting living

8 *Moriarty v McCarthy* [1978] 1 WLR 155.
9 [1985] 3 All ER 284.
10 This alternative cannot be applied where that assumption is unjustified, eg where she was a particularly high earner: see dicta in *Housecroft v Burnett* [1986] 1 All ER 332 at 345.
11 [1982] 1 WLR 71, noted Davies (1982) 45 MLR 333.
12 See also *Fletcher v Autocar and Transporters Ltd* [1968] 2 QB 322; *Lim Poh Choo v Camden & Islington Area Health Authority* [1979] QB 196, CA.

expenses saved from the cost of care; and given that non-pecuniary loss cannot be precisely measured, it is hardly sensible to knock off from it expenses in not having to pay for life's pleasures. However, there is far more force in the deep-lying rationale of Lord Denning's views, namely that there is no justification in awarding damages for full lost earnings to such a plaintiff since he cannot enjoy their use. This is, in effect, a call for the preferable subjective approach to non-pecuniary loss to be applied to loss of earnings; or even more analogous, for the sensible dependant-oriented approach to lost years awards (discussed next) to be extended to the lifetime earnings of a totally incapacitated plaintiff. But whatever their merit, Lord Denning's views have been firmly rejected by other judges, most significantly by the House of Lords in the *Lim Poh Choo* case.

Where the injury has reduced the number of years which the plaintiff is expected to live, the multiplier and hence the damages are calculated according to his life expectancy prior to the accident, with a deduction for the living expenses which he would have incurred during those 'lost years' that he will no longer live through. That damages can be recovered for the 'lost years' was laid down by the House of Lords in *Pickett v British Rail Engineering Ltd*,[13] overruling *Oliver v Ashman*.[14]

What is the reason for allowing a lost years claim when the plaintiff will not himself be alive to suffer any financial deprivation? The formal answer is to say that, by analogy to, for example, *Wise v Kaye*,[15] the plaintiff's subjective enjoyment of his earnings is irrelevant. He has still *objectively* suffered a loss. As with loss of amenity, however, that approach hardly seems satisfactory. An alternative explanation therefore is that a lost years claim is granted not so much because the plaintiff has himself lost out, but rather because his dependants will otherwise lose out. This is highlighted, as in *Pickett*, where the victim dies from his injuries having settled or obtained judgment, thus preventing any Fatal Accidents Act claim by his dependants.[16] But this alternative explanation can only be valid so long as the plaintiff has dependants. In any event it is rather confusing to represent the loss as the plaintiff's, if it is in reality the dependants'. As such, the main problem could be better solved, without relying on lost years awards, if dependants under the Fatal Accidents Act could be awarded damages even though the victim had settled or obtained judgment. But this would not prevent the dependants losing out if the plaintiff were to live on but with his life

13 [1980] AC 136.
14 [1962] 2 QB 210.
15 [1962] 1 QB 638.
16 *Infra*, p 210. See also *McCann v Sheppard* [1973] 2 All ER 881.

expectancy and earnings reduced. So perhaps the best solution of all, albeit a rather radical one, would be to abolish the lost years award, and for legislation to be passed allowing dependants a claim for pecuniary loss where the person on whom they are dependent has been injured as well as where he has been killed.

No award for the lost years is likely to be made where the plaintiff is a young child. So for example, in *Connolly v Camden and Islington Area Health Authority*[17] a four-year-old with over 20 years life expectancy was given nothing for the lost years; nor was the seven-year-old with a life expectancy of 40 in *Croke v Wiseman*.[18] On a formal level, the justification for such decisions is that to assess the value of the lost years claim in respect of young children involves too much speculation. On a deeper level, as stressed particularly by Griffiths LJ in *Croke v Wiseman*, they are justified by the fact that where a child's injuries render it unlikely that there will ever be any dependants, the policy reason for awarding the lost years damages is non-existent.

How the deductible living expenses in a lost years claim are to be calculated has given rise to controversy which reflects the tension between the formal objective reason and the alternative policy justification for the lost years award. In some first instance decisions[19] it was held that the same approach should be adopted as where calculating damages under the Fatal Accidents Act 1976, ie living expenses are what the plaintiff would have spent *exclusively* on himself (the theory being that the dependants would have benefited from the rest of the plaintiff's money). But these decisions were overruled in *Harris v Empress Motors Ltd*[20] where the Court of Appeal considered that one should deduct as living expenses what the plaintiff would have spent in maintaining himself (the theory being that he would have the rest of his income free to spend as he wished). In contrast to an assessment under the Fatal Accidents Act 1976, a pro rata amount of his family expenditure, eg expenditure on housing, heat, light should therefore be deducted. This decision takes the objective approach. On the alternative view, as the justification for allowing the plaintiff damages for the lost years is to benefit his dependants, who are the ones who will otherwise lose out, calculation of the living expenses should be on the same basis as under the Fatal Accidents Act 1976.[1]

17 [1981] 3 All ER 250.
18 [1982] 1 WLR 71.
19 Eg *Benson v Biggs Wall & Co Ltd* [1982] 3 All ER 300; *Clay v Pooler* [1982] 3 All ER 570.
20 [1983] 3 All ER 561.
 1 Evans and Stanton (1984) 134 NLJ 515.

More recently in *Housecroft v Burnett*,[2] where a 16-year-old girl was very badly injured, the Court of Appeal considered that a simpler way to proceed than deducting notional living expenses from notional earnings, and multiplying by the lost years multiplier, was to add one or half to the multiplier for the lost years and then to multiply the full multiplicand with no living expenses deduction.

(ii) Loss of earning capacity

In some situations, particularly where the plaintiff has not yet lost any earnings, instead of talking in terms of compensating future loss of earnings,[3] the courts prefer to talk of compensating the plaintiff's loss of earning capacity. This is sometimes alternatively described as compensating the plaintiff for his handicap in the labour market, or as awarding '*Smith v Manchester Corpn* damages', that being the leading case.[4] The loss primarily in mind is that, as a result of his injuries, the plaintiff may find it more difficult to find another equally well paid job if he loses his present one. However, this head has also been used for the situation where a child's future employment prospects have been reduced because of injury, either at a very young age[5] or during school years.[6] In all such cases, it is difficult and often impossible to fix a multiplicand, and hence the multiplier approach is generally abandoned in favour of a direct attempt to estimate the loss, taking into account the likelihood and gravity of the plaintiff's earnings-handicap.

(iii) Loss of pension

As a result of his injury the plaintiff may have lost his rights to a pension or may be entitled merely to a lower pension. As shown in the *Lim Poh Choo* case[7] and *Auty v National Coal Board*,[8] the plaintiff is entitled to damages for this loss. The courts appear to put a present value on it by taking the price an insurance company would demand for a pension providing equivalent rights to those lost.

---

2 [1986] 1 All ER 332.
3 In an appropriate case the two claims could be combined.
4 (1974) 17 KIR 1. See also, eg *Moeliker v Reyrolle & Co Ltd* [1977] 1 All ER 9.
5 *Mitchell v Liverpool Area Health Authority* (1985) Times, 17 June.
6 *Joyce v Yeomans* [1981] 1 WLR 549.
7 [1980] AC 174.
8 [1985] 1 All ER 930. See also *Dews v National Coal Board* [1988] AC 1 (where there was no loss of pension).

(iv) Future cost of care

Medical, nursing, hospital and related expenses that the court considers will be reasonably incurred in the future are recoverable, and the points made earlier in respect of pre-trial expenses of this kind are equally applicable here. It should also be noted that in assessing the future cost of care the courts generally use the multiplier approach, multiplying the present annual cost (the multiplicand) by the number of years that care will be required, subject to the usual adjustments.

(v) Other pecuniary losses

All other pecuniary losses that the court estimates will be incurred in the future should be recoverable subject to the usual limiting principles. So, for example, loss of housekeeping capacity is recoverable in accordance with the *Daly* case,[9] as is loss of a female plaintiff's future marriage prospects, that is loss of a husband's economic support[10] (unless, as in *Hughes v McKeown*,[11] this is already taken into account in assessing loss of future earnings). One exception, however, is that according to the *Pritchard*[12] case loss from a divorce is irrecoverable.

(d) Compensating advantages provided by third parties in response to the personal injury ('collateral' benefits)

The important question of whether these benefits should be deducted in assessing the damages has been fully dealt with in chapter 2.[13]

(e) Addendum—damages for wrongful birth[14]

Recently damages have been awarded against health authorities or doctors for losses consequent on having an (originally) unwanted child. Although the losses are not quite the same as personal injury losses, they are sufficiently similar to be included as an addendum to personal injury.

Applying the general compensatory principle, all pecuniary and non-pecuniary loss suffered by the parents as a result of the wrongful birth is recoverable, subject to the usual restrictions like

9 Supra, pp 195–6.
10 *Moriarty v McCarthy* [1978] 1 WLR 155.
11 [1985] 3 All ER 284.
12 [1988] Fam 22, criticised supra, pp 196–7.
13 Supra, pp 124–32.
14 See generally Taylor (1985) 15 Fam Law 147; Symmons (1987) 50 MLR 269.

remoteness and mitigation. So in *Emeh v Kensington Area Health Authority*,[15] where a sterilisation operation had been performed negligently, the mother was awarded damages for the pain and suffering and loss of amenity of having and looking after the child, who had congenital abnormalities, plus the pecuniary loss of maintaining her. Similarly in *Thake v Maurice*[16] the defendant surgeon had failed to warn the plaintiffs, in breach of his contractual and tortious duty of care, that the vasectomy operation would not be a 100% guarantee against pregnancy. Consequently the mother had not sought an abortion at an early stage. The parents were awarded damages for their pecuniary loss (loss of earnings and the cost of the child's upkeep) and ante-natal pain and suffering, subject to a deduction from the latter for the fact that the pain and suffering of an abortion had not been suffered. But post-natal non-pecuniary loss (ie the time and trouble in bringing up the child) was not claimed, and was in any event non-recoverable since it had been fully mitigated by the joy of a having a (normal) child.

Again in *Salih v Enfield HA*[17] the defendant negligently failed to warn the plaintiffs of the risk that their child would be born handicapped by rubella syndrome, as turned out to be the case. In assessing damages for the unwanted birth (the mother would have had an abortion had she been properly warned), it was held by the Court of Appeal that the basic (as opposed to special) cost of maintaining the child was irrecoverable because, on the balance of probabilities, if the plaintiffs had not had that child they would have had another and this they had now decided not to do because of the strain of looking after the handicapped child. In *Allen v Bloomsbury HA*[18] Brooke J carefully summarised and applied the principles of assessment for wrongful birth and also drew attention to the point that compensating the pecuniary loss consequent on bringing up the child constitutes an example of the recovery of pure economic loss for tortious negligence so that, eg limitation periods for personal injury would seem inapplicable. And in *Fish v Wilcox*[19] the Court of Appeal held that a mother could not recover both her loss of earnings and the value of the nursing care provided by her to her handicapped child. That would amount to double compensation as the plaintiff could not carry on in her original employment and look after her child at the same time.

15 [1984] 3 All ER 1044.
16 [1986] 1 All ER 497. See also *Gold v Haringey Health Authority* [1988] QB 481; *Benarr v Kettering HA* [1988] NLJR 179.
17 [1991] 3 All ER 400; criticised by Glazebrook (1992) CLJ 226.
18 [1993] 1 All ER 651.
19 (1993) 13 BMLR 134.

Although not involving a wrongful birth, the controversial decision in *Kralj v McGrath*[20] can also be conveniently mentioned here. The defendant doctor's negligence during the birth of one of the plaintiff's twins had caused the baby's death. The plaintiff wanted three children and hence would have to undergo another pregnancy and workless years which would not have been necessary had that baby not died. Inter alia, Woolf J awarded the plaintiff mother damages for the non-pecuniary and pecuniary loss of another pregnancy and child-birth and the pecuniary loss of initial workless years looking after another child. But the force of this decision is diminished because the only objection to those damages that was examined in the judgment was remoteness and there was no discussion of the fact that this claim was entirely novel and that the loss could not really be regarded as consequent on the personal injury to the mother. If followed to its logical conclusion the decision would mean that a mother whose baby is killed by the defendant's negligent driving should also be awarded damages for the non-pecuniary and pecuniary loss of pregnancy and workless years if she will want to have another child to replace the one lost. Yet such damages are presumably irrecoverable in a claim under the Fatal Accidents Act 1976 where the most the mother would be awarded would be £7,500 bereavement damages (plus any funeral expenses incurred).

(2) Claims by the deceased's estate

The Law Reform (Miscellaneous Provisions) Act 1934, s 1(1), provides that on the death of any person all causes of action vested in him, subject to certain exceptions,[1] survive for the benefit of his estate. The most important consequence of this, and the one with which we are here concerned, is that the deceased's action for personal injury survives for the benefit of his estate. It should be stressed that the action brought by the estate is not for death caused by the defendant. The defendant may or may not have been responsible for the deceased's death. Rather the action is for the deceased's personal injury caused by the defendant.[2]

Thus the estate can be awarded damages for all the deceased's recoverable loss,[3] both non-pecuniary and pecuniary, but only until

---

20 [1986] 1 All ER 54. See also *Kerby v Redbridge HA* [1993] 4 Med LR 178 (damages awarded for the non-pecuniary rigours of an additional pregnancy).
1 Ie defamation (s 1(1) of 1934 Act) and the right to bereavement damages (s 1(1A) of 1934 Act as inserted by s 4(1) of Administration of Justice Act 1982).
2 Ogus *Damages* p 116.
3 Ie subject to the usual principles, eg contributory negligence. Interest can also be awarded according to the usual principles.

the time of his death, applying the normal principle that all events up to trial are taken into account. So in *Rose v Ford*,[4] *Murray v Shuter*[5] and *Andrews v Freeborough*[6] damages for the deceased's loss of amenity were awarded, and in the first two of these cases for his pain and suffering: in *Murray v Shuter* damages for the deceased's loss of earnings were recovered and in *Rose v Ford* for the medical expenses he had incurred.

It has often been argued that a damages claim for non-pecuniary loss should not survive for the benefit of the deceased's estate, as such loss is personal to the deceased. Indeed this is the law in several other countries, including Scotland. But while the estate clearly cannot itself suffer any non-pecuniary loss, there is still good reason for allowing the estate's claim in that the deceased died without having recovered the compensation for non-pecuniary loss to which he was entitled and which would have enured to the estate's benefit.

In one respect, however, the principles governing compensatory[7] damages for the deceased's estate differ from those governing the injured plaintiff's damages. By s 4(2) of the Administration of Justice Act 1982, amending s 1(2) of the Law Reform (Miscellaneous Provisions) Act 1934, no damages may be awarded for loss of income in respect of any period after the death of the injured person; that is, the claim for loss of earnings in the 'lost years' does not survive for the benefit of the estate and *Gammell v Wilson*[8] is thereby overruled. This is a sensible reform.[9] Other than on a formal 'objective' view, the justification for allowing a lost years claim is that the plaintiff's dependants will otherwise lose out. But where the victim has already died from his injuries prior to trial, the dependants are satisfactorily compensated by their Fatal Accidents Act claim and to allow his estate also to claim damages for the lost years potentially benefits persons other than his dependants, who take under his estate, thus providing a 'windfall' to those whom the lost years claim is not intended to benefit. Similarly, to allow the lost years claim to survive means that potentially the defendant may have to pay large damages both under the 1934 and 1976 Acts. Section 4(2) removes

4 [1937] AC 826.
5 [1976] QB 972.
6 [1967] 1 QB 1.
7 Exemplary damages cannot be claimed by the estate—s 1(2) of 1934 Act.
8 [1982] AC 27.
9 Cf Cane and Harris (1983) 46 MLR 478. They criticise the reform, inter alia, because if the victim dies other than from his injuries the estate, and hence dependants, will lose out. But factual causation principles (see *Jobling v Associated Dairies Ltd* [1982] AC 794) dictate that they should lose out because they would have done so if there had been no wrong.

such problems.[10] It should also be realised that an effect of this reform is that where the deceased dies instantly, no claim for damages for personal injury survives for the benefit of his estate.[11]

Where 'provisional damages' have been awarded under s 32A of the Supreme Court Act 1981,[12] does the right of the injured plaintiff to return to court for further damages survive for the benefit of his estate? And is it caught by the 'lost years' bar? Tentative dicta of the Court of Appeal in *Middleton v Elliott Turbomachinery Ltd*[13] suggest that the claim is treated as if a judgment for damages to be assessed. Consequently in assessing those damages the court would be able to take account of the worsening of the plaintiff's condition, including death caused by that condition. Section 4(2) of the 1982 Act would be inapplicable. This is a controversial approach, and it seems preferable to apply s 4(2) while clarifying (by amendment to s 1(1) of the Fatal Accidents Act 1976) that the dependants may bring an action under the Fatal Accidents Act 1976 for the loss attributable to the death.[14]

By s 1(2) (c) of the 1934 Act, where the deceased's death has been caused by the act or omission which gives rise to the cause of action, damages recoverable by the estate 'shall be calculated without reference to any loss or gain to his estate consequent on his death, except that a sum in respect of funeral expenses may be included'. The main part of this is intended to emphasise that even where the defendant has been responsible for the death, the estate can recover only what the deceased himself could have recovered and hence neither loss, such as cessation of an annuity, nor gain, such as an insurance payment consequent on the death, is of any relevance. However, where the defendant has been responsible for the death, the courts are empowered to award the estate funeral expenses incurred. This is exceptional in that it does not represent the survival of a claim the deceased would have had.

10 Waddams (1984) 47 MLR 437 explores the alternative method of solving the overlap problem; ie to repeal the Fatal Accidents Act, to allow the lost years claim to survive and to allow dependants to recover from the estate. See also *Gammell v Wilson* [1982] AC 27 at 80–1 (per Lord Scarman). But this seems satisfactory only if one considers that the 'objective loss' reasoning justifies the injured plaintiff's lost years claim, rather than it resting on compensating the dependants.

11 Furthermore, in *Hicks v Chief Constable of the South Yorkshire Police* [1992] 2 All ER 65 it was held that where injury, pain and suffering are in reality part of the death itself, albeit endured for a very short time before death, no damages are recoverable.

12 Supra, pp 101–2.

13 (1990) Times, 29 October.

14 This is provisionally proposed by the Law Commission in its Consultation Paper No 125 (1992) para 5.20.

4. LOSSES ON DEATH

At common law no action could be brought for loss suffered through the killing of another. But this was altered by the Fatal Accidents Acts 1846–1959, now the Fatal Accidents Act 1976 (as amended by s 3 of the Administration of Justice Act 1982) which gives a statutory action '. . . if death is caused by any wrongful act, neglect or default . . .'[15] Most such statutory actions are founded on a tort by the defendant but the basis may be breach of contract.[16]

(1) Dependants

As laid down in s 1(2) the action under the 1976 Act is for the benefit of the dependants of the deceased (subject to a narrower restriction on who can be awarded bereavement damages). By s 1(3) 'dependant' means wife, husband, child, grandchild, father, mother, grandparent, brother, sister, uncle, aunt, or (as regards the last four) their issue, or, as inserted by the Administration of Justice Act 1982, ascendant beyond grandparent, descendant beyond grandchild, former husband or wife,[17] person treated by the deceased as a child of the family or parent, or person living with the deceased as husband or wife immediately prior to the death and for at least two years before. Under s 1(5) the above list includes in-laws, half-brothers and sisters, and stepchildren. By s 2(1) 'The action shall be brought by and in the name of the executor or administrator of the deceased', but by s 2(2), where there is no such personal representative, or no action is brought by him within six months, the action may be brought by and in the name of all or any of the persons for whose benefit a personal representative could have brought it. Although the loss and damages must ultimately be separately assessed for each dependant, the usual practice is first to determine the total liability of the defendant and then to apportion the damages between the dependants.

This approach of limiting actions to a restricted range of claimants is presumably based on the desire to discourage frivolous claims and to refuse recognition to 'illicit' relationships. But it would seem preferable if anyone who could establish a non-business pecuniary loss resulting from the death were entitled to recover, subject to usual limiting principles like remoteness and the duty to mitigate. Judges are well able to decide whether a real loss has been suffered and the very fact that the list has had to be extended

---

15 Special statutory regimes differing from the 1976 Act (eg under the International Transport Conventions Act 1983) are not examined here.
16 *Grein v Imperial Airways Ltd* [1937] 1 KB 50.
17 Including under a marriage that has been annulled or declared void: s 1(4).

shows its potential arbitrariness. Nor should the deceased's non-conformity to usual family relationships deprive his factual dependants of compensation. As such, the most glaring injustice produced by the present list is that homosexuals who have lived together for many years are unable to claim for loss of dependency.

(2) Actionability by injured person

By s 1(1), an action can only succeed if the wrongful act, neglect or default which caused the death '. . . is such as would (if death had not ensued) have entitled the person injured to maintain an action and recover damages in respect thereof'. Therefore if the deceased was killed entirely through his own fault, if the defendant had validly excluded all liability to the deceased, if the deceased's action had become time-barred before his death, or if the deceased had settled his claim or obtained judgment against the defendant[18] (probably including a settlement or judgment for 'provisional damages' under s 32A of the Supreme Court Act 1981),[19] the dependants will have no action. Similarly by s 5 where the deceased was contributorily negligent in relation to his death, and hence his damages would have been reduced by a certain amount under the Law Reform (Contributory Negligence) Act 1945, the damages recoverable by the dependants under the 1976 Act are to be reduced to a proportionate extent.[20]

(3) The three heads of recoverable loss

(a) The first head—pecuniary loss attributable to the non-business relationship between deceased and dependant

(i) Pecuniary loss

This most obviously refers to the loss of support from the deceased's earnings.[1] But it is important to realise that it also

---

18 It was this that produced the injustice to the dependents of denying the 'lost years' claim to an injured plaintiff, who then died from his injuries: see supra, p 201.

19 This point was left open in *Middleton v Elliott Turbomachinery Ltd* (1990) Times, 29 October. Legislation amending the 1976 Act on this point is desirable: see supra, p 208.

20 In accordance with normal principle a dependant who has been contributorily negligent in relation to his tortious loss (ie was partly responsible for the death) should have his damages reduced. See *Mulholland v McCrea* [1961] NI 135.

 1 It can also include loss of support from the deceased's future retirement pension: *Auty v National Coal Board* [1985] 1 All ER 930.

includes the loss of a mother's or wife's 'services'.[2] So in *Berry v Humm & Co*,[3] a husband was able to recover damages for the loss of his wife's housekeeping 'services' which she had performed gratuitously.[4] Similarly, in *Hay v Hughes*,[5] children were able to recover damages for the loss of their mother's 'services' calculated according to the cost of engaging a housekeeper or nanny, even though on the facts this expense was not incurred because the children's grandmother was looking after them gratuitously. In *Regan v Williamson*,[6] Watkins J stressed that a mother's 'services' should be widely interpreted to take into account the fact that a mother is not just a housekeeper; on the other hand he reluctantly accepted that no damages could be given simply for the loss of a mother's love and care for this was not a pecuniary loss. As laid down in *Spittle v Bunney*,[7] a deduction must be made from the notional commercial cost of a full-time nanny (which was taken to be the net wages a nanny would receive rather than the expense of engaging her) because older children do not require the same looking-after as young children. In *Mehmet v Perry*,[8] the loss to the family of the deceased's services as wife and mother was mainly calculated according to the wages lost by the father by giving up work to look after the children. And, as established in *Stanley v Saddique*,[9] lower damages should be awarded if the mother was unreliable and unlikely to have looked after the child properly.

(ii) Business pecuniary loss

The pecuniary loss caused to the dependant by the deceased's death is not recoverable if it flows from the business relationship between them;[10] business pecuniary loss is clearly outside the Act's scope for

2 See, analogously, *Clay v Pooler* [1982] 3 All ER 570 compensating for the loss of a husband and father's services as a handyman around the house.
3 [1915] 1 KB 627.
4 This has not been affected by s 2 of the Administration of Justice Act 1982 abolishing the action for loss of the wife's services.
5 [1975] QB 790. See infra, pp 218–9.
6 [1976] 1 WLR 305.
7 [1988] 3 All ER 1031.
8 [1977] 2 All ER 529. See also *Cresswell v Eaton* [1991] 1 All ER 484 (value of mother's services based on wages given up by children's aunt to look after them).
9 [1992] QB 1.
10 A further restriction is that there can be no recovery if the deceased earned his living by crime for the claim then arises *ex turpi causa*—*Burns v Edman* [1970] 2 QB 541.

otherwise there would be no sense in the restriction of claims to dependants which excludes, for example, an employer's claim for the pecuniary loss caused by the wrongful death of his employee. So in *Burgess v Florence Nightingale Hospital For Gentlewomen*[11] a husband could not recover damages for his loss of income as a dancer resulting from the death of his dancing-partner wife. Similarly in *Malyon v Plummer*[12] a wife who had been employed by her husband could not recover that part of her lost salary, which represented a true commercial payment for her services.

(iii) Proof of loss

In accordance with general principle there will be no award if the loss is entirely speculative or if there is no 'reasonable expectation of pecuniary benefit as of right, or otherwise, from the continuance of the life'.[13] So in *Barnett v Cohen*[14] the parent of a four-year-old child was held to have no cause of action under this head and in *Davies v Taylor*,[15] where a wife had deserted her husband five weeks before his death and he had instructed a solicitor to begin divorce proceedings, she was held to have no action as she had failed to prove that there was a significant prospect of reconciliation with her husband and hence a reasonable expectation of pecuniary benefit. On the other hand, in *Taff Vale Rly Co v Jenkins*,[16] a parent recovered damages under the Act when his 16-year-old daughter died having almost completed her unpaid dressmaking apprenticeship and in *Kandalla v British European Airways Corpn*[17] the elderly parents of two young women doctors were awarded damages on proof that the doctors had intended to flee from Iraq (where they had been working) to England, where they would have supported their parents.

(iv) Multiplier method

As with future pecuniary loss for personal injury, the calculation of damages for loss of dependency is not easy, and the points made earlier[18] on actuarial evidence, periodic payments and inflation

11 [1955] 1 QB 349.
12 [1964] 1 QB 330.
13 *Franklin v South Eastern Rly Co* (1858) 3 H & N 211 at 213–4. Supra, pp 31–6.
14 [1921] 2 KB 461.
15 [1974] AC 207.
16 [1913] AC 1.
17 [1981] QB 158.
18 Supra, pp 197–9.

apply *mutatis mutandis* here. Again the courts' approach is generally[19] to use the multiplier method.

In this context, the multiplier method is used to assess all the pecuniary loss and not merely the post-trial pecuniary loss. In *Cookson v Knowles*[20] the House of Lords laid down that the dependants' pecuniary loss prior to trial should be assessed separately from that after the trial. This is essentially because the former is less speculative and because no interest is to be paid on the future loss but is payable on the pre-trial loss, normally from the date of death until the time of trial at half the average rate on the special investment account over that period.[1] In *Graham v Dodds*[2] it was clarified that that itemisation does not mean that the multiplier method should be abandoned for pre-trial loss. Rather the multiplier should continue to be calculated from the date of death (rather than from the date of trial) on the basis that, in contrast to a personal injury case, there can be no certainty even that the deceased would have survived until trial. So if, for example, the multiplier is 14, and four years have elapsed between death and trial, the pre-trial loss will be calculated using a multiplier of four and the post-trial loss, using a multiplier of ten. But a separate pre-trial and post-trial *multiplicand* is generally appropriate to take account of facts known at trial: eg the rate of wages for the job that the deceased had.[3]

More controversially it was decided by the Court of Appeal (Ralph Gibson LJ dissenting) in *Corbett v Barking, Havering & Brentwood HA*[4] that it did not contradict *Graham v Dodds* to increase the normal multiplier, calculated from the date of the death, where there had been a long delay between death and trial (11½ years) so that it was a known fact that the child dependant had survived to the age of 11½. That case shows that there is much to be said for departing from *Graham v Dodds* (and *Cookson v Knowles*) and calculating the multiplier from the date of trial. Pre-trial loss would then be calculated in much the same straightforward way as in personal injury cases, with the qualification that there would need to be a general discount for the uncertainty as to whether the deceased would have lived to trial.

Under the present multiplier method, therefore, the *multiplicands* will be the pre-trial and post-trial annual pecuniary loss to the

---

19 But this would not be appropriate, for example, where there is as yet no dependency and hence it is not possible to calculate an appropriate multiplicand.
20 [1979] AC 556.
1 For discussion, see infra, pp 256–60.
2 [1983] 2 All ER 953.
3 See especially Lord Fraser's judgment in *Cookson v Knowles* [1979] AC 556, 575–6.
4 [1991] 2 QB 408.

dependant calculated by, for example, deducting from the deceased's notional annual net[5] earnings his living expenses; and living expenses here means expenses for the deceased's own purposes exclusively. There is then an adjustment to take account, for example, of the prospects of promotion that the deceased had.

But one has to be careful not to include what may at first sight appear to be a loss but on closer analysis turns out not to be. Two cases can be used to illustrate this. In *Auty v National Coal Board*[6] one of the plaintiffs was a widow claiming under the Fatal Accidents Act 1976. She claimed as part of her loss of dependency the lost chance of gaining a widow's 'death-after-retirement' pension, and argued that the widow's 'death-in-service' pension that she was actually receiving was non-deductible under s 4(1) of the 1976 Act (not then amended though the same argument would hold under the new wording). The Court of Appeal rejected this argument and held that, as she was only ever entitled to one or other pension and was receiving one, it was false to say that she had lost the chance of gaining the other. As Waller LJ said, '. . . she cannot claim for loss of an opportunity to obtain a widow's pension because she is already in receipt of a widow's pension.'[7]

Again in *Malone v Rowan*[8] Russell J held that in assessing a widow's pecuniary loss on the death of her husband the courts should not take into account that the couple planned to have a family so that, on giving up work, the wife's pecuniary dependency on her husband would have increased from the position at his death. Russell J was reluctant to so hold and did so only because he felt bound by the unreported Court of Appeal decision in *Higgs v Drinkwater*. But it is submitted that the decisions are correct and that Russell J's reluctance was ill-founded: for the increase in dependency that would have occurred was offset by the change of circumstances brought about by the death, namely that the plaintiff would now not suffer a loss of earnings in giving birth to and bringing up the deceased's children.

There is also some confusion on the authorities as to whether the dependant's (typically a widow's) own earning capacity should be taken into account to reduce the pecuniary loss.[9] Applying the

---

5 Eg tax is deducted—*Zinovieff v British Transport Commission* (1954) Times, 1 April; *British Transport Commission v Gourley* [1956] AC 185.
6 [1985] 1 All ER 930.
7 Ibid at 938.
8 [1984] 3 All ER 402. See Jones (1985) 101 LQR 20.
9 *Howitt v Heads* [1973] QB 64 (ignored). *Cookson v Knowles* [1977] QB 913 (taken into account). Presumably the Fatal Accidents Act 1976, s 4, is irrelevant to this sort of 'benefit'.

duty to mitigate plus the principle that direct compensating advantages should be deducted, subject to a good policy reason to the contrary (like not discouraging private benevolence), earning capacity should be taken into account provided first, it is sufficiently likely that the dependant will work or it is reasonable for her to do so; secondly, she would not have worked but for the death; and thirdly it is reasonable to suppose that her earnings would have reduced the pecuniary benefit from the deceased had he lived.

The starting point for the *multiplier* is the estimated number of years from the date of death that the dependant would have received the deceased's pecuniary support. Most importantly, this depends on the deceased's and dependant's life expectancies. When the deceased was unmarried and supporting his parents account must also be taken of the possibility of the deceased's marriage.[10] And in *Owen v Martin*[11] it was held that the prospects of a divorce between a plaintiff widow and the deceased are to be taken into account in assessing the widow's damages. Again s 3(4) of the 1976 Act, as amended by the Administration of Justice Act 1982, lays down that in the case of a claim by a cohabitee, the court must take into account '. . . the fact that the dependant had no enforceable right to financial support by the deceased as a result of their living together.' This is presumably designed to impress upon the courts that there is even less certainty of continued future support in the case of cohabitees than in the case of married couples, particularly since legal obligations of support continue after the breakdown of marriage.

The starting figure is then adjusted. In particular, there is a reduction because the plaintiff is receiving a capital sum now, which he can invest, rather than periodical payments over the years. A reduction is commonly made for the contingencies of life, such as the deceased's unemployment or earlier than expected death (although the latter seems misconceived, since his life expectancy already takes this risk into account). The aim is to award a capital sum, which when invested will produce an income in terms of interest and withdrawals of capital, equal to the dependant's lost income over the period intended to be covered (ie the period of dependency).[12] The multiplier is in practice no more

10 *Dolbey v Goodwin* [1955] 2 All ER 166.
11 [1992] PIQR Q151.
12 *Taylor v O'Connor* [1971] AC 115; *Cookson v Knowles* [1979] AC 556, 576–7; *Robertson v Lestrange* [1985] 1 All ER 950, 955–8.

than about 18 and the norm in relation to a 30-year-old deceased is 15 or 16.[13]

However, by s 3(3) of the Fatal Accidents Act 1976, as amended by the Administration of Justice Act 1982, in assessing a widow's claim in respect of her husband's death, 'there shall not be taken into account the re-marriage of the widow or her prospects of re-marriage'. Parliament introduced this provision to put a stop to the degrading judicial 'guessing game' of assessing a widow's prospects of re-marriage. But this is at the expense of not deducting what is a direct compensating advantage and the effect can be grotesque; eg a widow who marries a millionaire, even prior to trial, is still entitled to a large sum of damages in respect of the death of her former husband. Certainly there is no good reason, as the Pearson Commission stressed,[14] why a marriage that has already taken place should not be taken into account, since no guessing is then required. It should further be noted that the provision applies only to a widow's claim and therefore a mother's prospects of re-marriage must still be taken into account in assessing a child's claim.[15] Similarly, where the claim is brought by a 'common-law wife' her prospects of marriage are to be taken into account.[16] All in all it is hard to dissent from Atiyah's view that this law reform 'must be one of the most irrational . . . ever passed by Parliament'.[17]

(b) The second head—damages for bereavement

By s 1A of the Fatal Accidents Act 1976, as inserted by the Administration of Justice Act 1982, damages for death are for the first time to be awarded for the mental distress, ie the sorrow, grief, and loss of enjoyment, consequent on the death.[18] Called 'damages

---

13 In *Cookson v Knowles* [1979] AC 556 at 574–6 the argument was rejected that Fatal Accident Act multipliers (calculated from death) are too small in comparison with personal injury multipliers for loss of future earnings (calculated from trial). For rejection of the similar argument that personal injury multipliers are too high, see *Pritchard v J H Cobden Ltd* [1988] Fam 22.

14 Report, paras 409–12.

15 The Law Commission Report No 56 paras 251–2 recommended reform of this.

16 Further, a widower's prospects of remarriage are relevant—the Law Commission Report no 56 paras 251–2 recommended reform of this; see also Pearson Commission Report, para 414.

17 *Atiyah's Accidents Compensation and the Law* (5th edn) p 115.

18 For cases denying such damages prior to the 1982 Act, see *Franklin v South Eastern Rly Co* (1858) 3 H & N 211; *Davies v Powell Duffryn Associated Collieries Ltd* [1942] 1 All ER 657, 665.

for bereavement', a fixed sum, of at present £7,500,[19] can be claimed for the benefit:

(a) of the wife or husband of the deceased; and
(b) where the deceased was a minor who was never married—
   (i) of his parents, if he was legitimate;[20] and
   (ii) of his mother, if he was illegitimate.

This rightly brings English law into line with most other countries, although not all have a fixed award, nor restrict so severely those entitled to claim.

(c) The third head—funeral expenses

By s 3(5) of the 1976 Act, as amended by the Administration of Justice Act 1982, 'If the defendants have incurred funeral expenses in respect of the deceased, damages may be awarded in respect of those expenses.'

(4) Section 4 of the Fatal Accidents Act 1976

By s 4 of the Fatal Accidents Act 1976, inserted by the Administration of Justice Act 1982, 'In assessing damages in respect of a person's death in an action under this Act, the benefits which have accrued or will or may accrue to any person from his estate or otherwise as a result of his death shall be disregarded.'

Under the former s 4(1) any benefit—defined to mean social security benefit, or payment by a trade union or friendly society—insurance money, pension or gratuity was not to be deducted. This was criticised by the Law Commission[1] and the Pearson Commission[2] for not also ordering the non-deduction of benefits derived from the deceased's estate; the benefits in mind being the acceleration and certainty of the inheritance of the deceased's property and awards for non-pecuniary loss[3] under the Law Reform (Miscellaneous Provisions) Act 1934. The new s 4 was passed in

---

19 The Lord Chancellor's power to alter the amount, so far exercised once, is conferred by s 1A(5). In principle interest should be payable as for personal injury non-pecuniary loss: ie 2% from the date of the service of the writ until trial. In practice it has been awarded at the full special investment account rate from the date of death until trial: Kemp and Kemp *The Quantum of Damages* paras 16-015 to 16-016.
20 By s 1A(4) if both parents claim, the fixed sum is to be divided equally between them.
1 Report no 56, paras 254–6.
2 Report, paras 537–9.
3 Infra, p 220.

response to that criticism. This is unfortunate since that criticism lacked force. Compensation dictates the deduction of compensating advantages, the benefits in mind arise directly from the death, and there is no question of deduction discouraging benevolence or undermining the deceased's prudent spending of money in providing for his dependants after death.

The new s 4 (as well as the old s 4(1)) is also inconsistent with the approach advocated in chapter 2 for compensating advantages rendered by third parties in response to the consequences of a tort or breach of contract.[4] According to that, while life assurance payments, gratuitous payments and probably pensions should continue not to be deducted, social security benefits should be deducted. Indeed this was a further reform of s 4(1) recommended by the Pearson Commission.[5]

There also seems no good reason why the provisions for the recoupment of social security benefits contained in the Social Security Administration Act 1992 Part IV[6] have not been made applicable to damages under the Fatal Accidents Act.

A further difficulty is the actual wording of s 4. For the natural interpretation of 'benefits [accruing] . . . as a result of his death' is that all compensating advantages (that is, all benefits factually caused by the death applying the 'but for' test) are covered. But if so, a widow's remarriage or her earnings from starting work after the death or gratuitous services rendered by a relative may all be benefits accruing as a result of the death and therefore non-deductible under the Act. Yet s 4 was clearly not intended to introduce such a wide reform.[7] Indeed if it had been, s 3(3) of the Act ordering remarriage to be ignored in assessing a widow's damages would now be unnecessary and criticism of that provision for not also applying to a child's claim, and for not being matched by an equivalent provision regarding a widower's remarriage, would now be unfounded.

Of course the way out of this difficulty is to take a narrow interpretation of s 4. Indeed, somewhat ironically, the same narrow construction has often been taken at common law—a good example being *Hay v Hughes*[8] concerning gratuitous services rendered by a relative—in deciding that benefits did not result from the death and were therefore *non-deductible* under the general principle of *deduction* laid down in *Davies v Powell Duffryn*

---

4 Supra, pp 124–32.
5 Report, paras 480–3.
6 Supra, pp 127–9.
7 See, eg 428 HL Official Report (5th series) col 28.
8 [1975] QB 790. See also, eg *Peacock v Amusement Equipment Co Ltd* [1954] 2 QB 347.

Associated Collieries Ltd.[9] But it seems clear that the narrow interpretation taken in cases like *Hay v Hughes* is artificial and that the decisions were really justified on policy grounds such as not discouraging private benevolence. Yet now that s 4 has used similar wording, that artificial narrow construction must live on if the section is not to have a far wider effect than intended.

This exact dilemma has surfaced in the apparently contradictory interpretations of s 4 taken in two Court of Appeal decisions. In *Stanley v Saddique*[10] it was held that, in assessing a child's damages for the death of his mother, the advantages to the child from the father's marriage to a woman who provided excellent motherly services to the child (and better care than the child's natural mother would have provided had she lived) were benefits accruing as a result of the death under s 4 and were to be disregarded. Section 4 was not to be given a narrow interpretation. In contrast the majority of the Court of Appeal in *Hayden v Hayden*[11] (McCowan LJ dissenting) decided that, where the tortfeasor was the father of the infant plaintiff and had given up his paid work to look after the plaintiff, the value of his services was not a benefit accruing as a result of the death under s 4 and was to be deducted in assessing the plaintiff's damages for the death of her mother.

It is submitted therefore that s 4 would have more sensibly achieved its purpose if it had excluded from deduction further defined benefits (leaving the very few remaining compensating advantages to be dealt with at common law) rather than laying down a rule of complete non-deduction, which depends for its intended effect on a narrow and questionable interpretation of 'benefits [accruing] . . . as a result of his death'.

(5) The relationship between actions under the Law Reform Act 1934 and the Fatal Accidents Act 1976 where the defendant's wrong has caused death

It seems appropriate finally to clarify this relationship because, where the defendant's tort or breach of contract has caused death,

9 [1942] AC 601.
10 [1992] QB 1. For more straightforward applications of s 4 leading to the non-deduction of benefits, see, eg *Pidduck v Eastern Scottish Omnibuses Ltd* [1990] 2 All ER 69 (widow's pension); *Wood v Bentall Simplex Ltd* [1992] PIQR P332 (inheritance of the deceased's assets).
11 [1992] 1 WLR 986. Section 4 was not discussed in *Watson v Willmott* [1991] 1 QB 140 where a child's loss of dependency was treated as the difference between the pecuniary support that the plaintiff's natural father (as bread-winner) would have provided and that provided by his adoptive father.

an action may be brought under both the 1934 Act and the Fatal Accidents Act 1976 and the two are commonly combined. The former is for the benefit of the deceased's estate and the latter for the benefit of his dependants. Usually, however, a person benefiting from the estate and hence from the 1934 Act will also be a dependant under the Fatal Accidents Act. The former law, embodied in *Davies v Powell Duffryn Associated Collieries Ltd,* was that an award made or likely to be made under the 1934 Act to a dependant was to be deducted from the Fatal Accidents Act damages, although not vice versa. But as held in *Murray v Shuter*[12] an award under the 1934 Act for pre-death loss of earnings (and analogous reasoning applied to awards for other pre-death pecuniary loss) should not be deducted because the dependants would have benefited from those earnings. In other words such an award compensates the dependants for their pre-death loss consequent on the deceased's injury and does not constitute a compensating advantage. Under the old law therefore it was, in any event, only awards for non-pecuniary loss (and, while they lasted, 'lost years' earnings awards) that were deducted. The new s 4 of the 1976 Act now means that even non-pecuniary loss awards under the 1934 Act are not to be deducted.

Thus where the death is not instantaneous the action under the 1934 Act enables the estate to recover damages for the deceased's pre-death personal injury losses, both pecuniary and non-pecuniary (plus any property damage), while the action under the 1976 Act enables dependants to recover their pecuniary loss as a result of the death and a spouse or parent(s) to recover damages for bereavement. Damages to cover the funeral expenses may be awarded under either Act depending on whether incurred by the estate or by the dependants (though clearly the courts would not award them twice over). On the other hand, where the death is instantaneous and there has been no property damage, there is no point bringing an action under the 1934 Act, other than where the estate (and not a dependant) has incurred the funeral expenses.

5. LOSS OF REPUTATION

Loss of reputation is a non-pecuniary loss, which is traditionally regarded as distinct from mental distress in that it deals with society's feelings towards the plaintiff, rather than with the plaintiff's own feelings. But often, particularly in defamation cases where the award of damages is made by a jury, mental distress consequent on

12 [1976] QB 972.

loss of reputation is not clearly separated from the award for loss of reputation itself. Indeed on a preferable view, alternative to that traditionally taken by the courts, all non-pecuniary loss, including loss of reputation, is ultimately regarded as a loss only in terms of the distress or loss of happiness caused to the plaintiff.[13] However, where a plaintiff complains of a loss of reputation he is generally concerned not only about loss of reputation itself, but also and often primarily about the pecuniary loss flowing from it and both will be considered.

In order to put the plaintiff into as good a position as if the tort or breach of contract had not occurred, as the general compensatory aims dictate, damages should be awarded, subject to the usual limiting principles, wherever loss of reputation and consequential pecuniary loss result from a tort or breach of contract. But the courts have taken a more restrictive approach especially where the plaintiff is suing for breach of contract.

(1) Are damages awarded for loss of reputation?

(a) Breach of contract

Addis v Gramophone Co Ltd[14] is the leading authority for the rule that no damages can be given for loss of reputation for breach of contract. In that case the House of Lords held that in the plaintiff's action for wrongful dismissal he should be confined to damages for his direct pecuniary loss, such as loss of salary, and should not be compensated for any loss of his reputation or for the fact that the dismissal might make it more difficult for him to get another job. So the decision appears to deny damages both for loss of reputation in itself—ie as a non-pecuniary loss—and for the pecuniary loss flowing from it. Lord Atkinson said:

I can conceive nothing more objectionable and embarrassing in litigation than trying in effect an action of libel or slander as a matter of aggravation in an action for illegal dismissal, the defendant being permitted, as he must in justice be permitted, to traverse the defamatory sense, rely on privilege, or raise every point which he could raise in an independent action brought for the alleged libel or slander itself.[15]

Addis was recently applied by the Court of Appeal in *O'Laoire v*

---

13 See supra, p 137. On this view too, only a person and not, eg a company, would be able to recover for loss of reputation as a non-pecuniary loss.
14 [1909] AC 488.
15 Ibid at 496.

Jackel International Ltd (No 2)[16] to deny damages for the fact that the wrongful dismissal of the plaintiff, who was managing director designate of the defendant company, would act as a 'black mark' making it more difficult for him to obtain alternative employment. While expressing considerable sympathy for the plaintiff on this point, the Court of Appeal considered itself bound by *Addis* 'unless and until the House of Lords reconsiders that decision . . .'[17]

Yet in many cases subsequent to *Addis*, while damages for loss of reputation in itself have continued to be denied—for example, in *Groom v Crocker*[18] damages were held irrecoverable for any loss of the plaintiff's reputation as a careful driver, caused by his defendant solicitor's breach of contract in wrongfully admitting that the plaintiff had been negligent in his driving—pecuniary loss flowing from loss of reputation has been held recoverable. This distinction was particularly clearly applied in *Aerial Advertising Co v Batchelors Peas Ltd*.[19] There the defendants had contracted with the plaintiffs to advertise their peas by trailers from a plane. In breach of contract the plaintiffs flew the plane with the advertising trailers over a city centre during minutes of silence in armistice services. The public was horrified and the defendants' sales dropped. Atkinson J held that, while following *Groom v Crocker* the defendants were not entitled to damages for loss of reputation in itself, they were entitled to damages for loss of sales following on that loss of reputation.

There are four groups of cases in which damages for pecuniary loss flowing from loss of reputation have been awarded for breach of contract.

First, where the defendant's breach comprises a refusal to allow an actor's appearance or to publish an author's book, the actor or author has been held able to recover for the lost income flowing from the loss of the chance to enhance his reputation or, as it is often termed, the 'loss of publicity'. The leading cases are *Marbé v George Edwardes (Daley's Theatre) Ltd*[20] and *Herbert Clayton v Oliver*,[1] which concerned actors, and *Tolnay v Criterion Film Productions Ltd*[2] and *Joseph v National Magazine Co*[3] concerning

---

16 [1991] ICR 718. See also *McLeish v Amoo-Gottfried & Co* (1993) 137 Sol Jo LB 204 (damages for loss of reputation denied but mental distress damages included a sum for distress consequent on loss of reputation).
17 Ibid at 175.
18 [1939] 1 KB 194. *Bailey v Bullock* [1950] 2 All ER 1167.
19 [1938] 2 All ER 788.
20 [1928] 1 KB 269.
 1 [1930] AC 209.
 2 [1936] 2 All ER 1625.
 3 [1959] Ch 14.

authors. In *Withers v General Theatre Corpn Ltd*[4] the Court of Appeal stressed that while an actor can recover income lost from the loss of a chance to enhance his reputation he cannot recover that lost from damage to his existing reputation. This distinction is not only very difficult to justify in terms of policy but also in *Marbé v George Edwardes* the Court of Appeal had earlier specifically said that damages could be given for lost income flowing from damage to the actor's existing reputation.[5] Since *Marbé* was later applied by the House of Lords in *Herbert Clayton v Oliver*, and since it seems preferable in principle, it is submitted that the *Withers* distinction should be regarded as incorrect.

Secondly, where the breach of contract comprises a mismanagement of advertising, the plaintiff can recover for pecuniary loss flowing from the loss of reputation. This is particularly well illustrated by the *Aerial Advertising v Batchelors Peas* case. Similarly in *Marcus v Myers and Davis*,[6] where the defendant in breach of contract failed to insert an advert in a newspaper, the plaintiff was awarded damages for loss of business. Although loss of reputation was not mentioned, the loss of business can be regarded as analogous to pecuniary loss flowing from the loss of a chance to enhance one's reputation.

Thirdly, where a bank in breach of contract refuses to honour the plaintiff trader's cheque, as in *Rolin v Steward*,[7] or fails to supervise the plaintiff's business as agreed so that the plaintiff goes bankrupt, as in *Wilson v United Counties Bank Ltd*,[8] the plaintiff can recover damages for the pecuniary loss flowing from the damage to his credit and reputation.

Fourthly, where in breach of contract the defendant supplies goods or provides services that are not of the standard required by the plaintiff's customers, the plaintiff can recover damages for the pecuniary loss flowing from the loss of reputation. In *Anglo-Continental Holidays Ltd v Typaldos Lines (London) Ltd*,[9] travel agents were awarded damages for loss of goodwill when the shipowner, with whom they had arranged a cruise, substituted a smaller less attractive ship and a less satisfactory timetable of ports of call. Similarly in *GKN Centrax Gears Ltd v Matbro Ltd*,[10] where the plaintiffs had supplied defective drive axles for fork-lift trucks

4 [1933] 2 KB 536.
5 [1928] 1 KB 269, 281, 288.
6 (1895) 11 TLR 327.
7 (1854) 14 CB 595.
8 [1920] AC 102.
9 [1967] 2 Lloyds Rep 61.
10 [1976] 2 Lloyds Rep 555.

that the defendants had then sold to their customers, the defendants, on their counterclaim, were awarded damages for the loss of repeat orders. Somewhat similar is *Foaminol Laboratories v British Artid Plastics Ltd*[11] where the plaintiffs, who were putting a sun-tan cream on the market in attractive containers, had secured the co-operation of certain editors of ladies' magazines. The plaintiffs had ordered 10,000 of the containers from the defendants who, however, failed to deliver most of them. Hallett J held that damages for loss of profit flowing from the loss of future co-operation with the editors could in theory be recovered, although here they would not be because the pecuniary loss was, first, too speculative and, secondly, too remote. Neither of these grounds of denial is convincing and in the *GKN Centrax* case Lord Denning doubted the actual decision in this case.[12]

The courts have therefore been prepared to compensate pecuniary loss flowing from loss of reputation. Indeed, in terms of policy there is no good reason why those four groups should be regarded as exhaustive: whatever one may say about loss of reputation as a non-pecuniary loss there is no convincing argument for leaving the plaintiff undercompensated by refusing to recognise this kind of pecuniary loss. As Hallett J said in *Foaminol*, '. . . if pecuniary loss be established, the mere fact that the pecuniary loss is brought about by the loss of reputation caused by a breach of contract is not sufficient to preclude the plaintiffs from recovering in respect of that pecuniary loss'.[13]

The recent decision in *O'Laoire* is therefore most unsatisfactory, especially as none of the above cases was even referred to. Nevertheless it serves as a warning that, until formally overruled, it is dangerous to assume that the approach in *Addis* to a pecuniary loss of reputation will always be ignored.

What about the continued denial of damages for loss of reputation in itself, that is as a non-pecuniary loss? While perhaps less crucial there is again no justification for this restriction. Adherence to full compensation dictates recovery, and although proof of this loss may be difficult, as may assessing damages, these are not reasons for a blanket refusal, particularly given the judicial willingness to compensate other types of non-pecuniary loss. Nor, if allowed, is there any reason to think that the courts would be swamped with claims. Furthermore, Lord Atkinson in *Addis* was misguided in fearing that the intricacies of defamation law would be incorporated

11 [1941] 2 All ER 393.
12 [1976] 2 Lloyds Rep 555 at 573.
13 [1941] 2 All ER 393 at 400.

into breach of contract claims, for the simple reason that the issue here concerns damages, not liability. Defences of privilege, truth and so on, are thus irrelevant. It is therefore to be hoped that, just as the courts have often departed from *Addis*, as regards pecuniary loss consequent on loss of reputation, and as regards mental distress,[14] they will also feel able to depart from it as regards damages for loss of reputation in itself.

(b) Torts

Although the term 'loss of reputation' is often not referred to, and although the damages are generally not itemised, loss of reputation in itself, and pecuniary loss flowing from it, are both recoverable for some torts.

The tort of defamation, for example, largely exists in order to protect reputations, and damages there can compensate for both the non-pecuniary and pecuniary loss caused.[15] In *McCarey v Associated Newspapers Ltd*,[16] for example, £9,000 damages had been awarded by the jury in a libel action. The Court of Appeal overturned this as being too high; no exemplary damages could here be awarded, and as the plaintiff had not proved any consequent pecuniary loss, he should be restricted to general loss of reputation as a non-pecuniary loss, plus mental distress damages for grief and annoyance. The judgments do recognise, however, that pecuniary loss flowing from the loss of reputation, as well as the non-pecuniary loss itself, can be compensated. Diplock LJ said, for example:

Under head (1)—that is to say, the consequences of the attitude adopted towards the plaintiff by other persons—it may be possible to prove pecuniary loss, such as loss of practice or employment, or inability to obtain fresh appointment . . . But the major consequences under head (1) may be purely social and lie in the attitude adopted towards the plaintiff by persons with whom he comes into social or professional contact.[17]

Damages for loss of reputation and for consequential pecuniary losses have further been awarded for false imprisonment[18] and have been recognised to be recoverable for malicious prosecution.[19]

14 Infra, pp 232–7.
15 There is some doubt whether loss of reputation in itself is recoverable for slander actionable only on proof of damage. But once liability is established it would seem that it is—*Dixon v Smith* (1860) 5 H & N 450.
16 [1965] 2 QB 86.
17 Ibid at 108.
18 *Childs v Lewis* (1924) 40 TLR 870; *Walter v Alltools Ltd* (1944) 61 TLR 39; *White v Metropolitan Police Comr* (1982) Times, 24 April.
19 *Savile v Roberts* (1699) 1 Ld Raym 374; *Childs v Lewis* (1924) 40 TLR 870.

In contrast it was held by the Court of Appeal in *Lonrho plc v Fayed (No 5)*[20] that, while consequential pecuniary loss is recoverable for lawful means conspiracy, loss of reputation itself is not. In other cases damages for pecuniary loss consequent on loss of reputation have been awarded without any question being raised as to compensating the non-pecuniary loss.[1] For example, damages have been held recoverable where goods infringing the plaintiff's intellectual property rights are so inferior to the plaintiff's that his reputation was diminished and sales were lost.[2] And in *Mulvaine v Joseph*,[3] where a professional golfer was injured in a car accident, his damages for negligence included compensation for the lost opportunity to enhance his golfing prestige by competing in a number of European tournaments.

All this indicates that there are no particular restrictions on tortious recovery for pecuniary loss consequent on a loss of reputation but that for some torts loss of reputation itself is irrecoverable. This can be criticised for the same reasons as have been put forward above in relation to the denial of compensation for non-pecuniary loss of reputation caused by breach of contract.

(2) Assessing damages for loss of reputation

Pecuniary loss consequent on loss of reputation generally comprises lost earnings—as, for example, in *McCarey v Associated Newspapers Ltd* or *Marbé v George Edwardes*—or lost profits, as in the *Aerial Advertising* or *Anglo-Continental Holidays* cases. It is usually not possible to offer precise proof of those losses, although of course the more precise the proof the less the court (be it judge or jury) needs to resort to educated guesswork.

Loss of reputation in itself is, like all non-pecuniary losses, very difficult to assess and all that the courts can aim for is a fair and reasonable sum and some degree of uniformity between awards. Clearly the greater the loss of reputation the greater the damages should be, and in order to prove anything other than general loss of reputation a plaintiff would presumably need to bring evidence to

---

20 [1994] 1 All ER 188. Cf *Pratt v British Medical Association* [1914] 1 KB 244, 282 (unlawful means conspiracy).
 1 In addition to the cases cited below, see *GWK Ltd v Dunlop Rubber Co Ltd* (1926) 42 TLR 593 (inducing breach of contract); *Worsley & Co Ltd v Cooper* [1939] 1 All ER 290 (injurious falsehood).
 2 *Sykes v Sykes* (1824) 3 B & C 541 (passing-off). See similarly *Spalding Bros v Gamage Ltd* (1918) 35 RPC 101 (passing-off).
 3 (1968) 112 Sol Jo 927.

indicate the difference between his present and former reputations. It is submitted that one of the best statements relating to the assessment of damages for loss of reputation is that of Diplock LJ in *McCarey v Associated Newspapers Ltd*,[4] where he made the point that there should be some degree of uniformity not only between loss of reputation damages but also between damages for all non-pecuniary losses. He said:

> In putting a money value on these kinds of injury, as the law requires damage-awarding tribunals to do, they are being required to attempt to equate the incommensurable. As in the case of damages for physical injuries, it is impossible to say that any answer looked at in isolation is right, or that any answer is wrong. But justice is not justice if it is arbitrary or whimsical, if what is awarded to one plaintiff for an injury bears no relation at all to what is awarded to another plaintiff for an injury of the same kind, or, I would add, if what is awarded for one kind of injury shows a wrong scale of values when compared with what is awarded for injuries of a different kind which are also incommensurable with pounds, shillings and pence.[5]

And he later went on:

> If, as I have said, figures much lower than that awarded in this case are the proper compensation for the loss of an eye or limb, or for other life-long disabling injuries, a sum of £9,000 as compensation for this injury . . . is a figure that no reasonable jury, applying correct principles which included a proper scale of value, could have reached.[6]

Unfortunately, this approach has been rejected. For example, in *Blackshaw v Lord*[7] the jury had awarded £42,000 to the plaintiff, a former civil servant, for a libellous newspaper article alleging gross incompetence by the plaintiff resulting in the loss of huge sums of public money. Although the award was regarded as very high, the Court of Appeal held that it was not one which no reasonable jury could have reached. Each of the three judges stressed that no analogy should be drawn with awards for pain and suffering and loss of amenity in personal injury cases, and Stephenson LJ specifically disapproved Diplock LJ's dictum.

Similarly in *Rantzen v Mirror Group Newspapers*[8] the Court of Appeal held that, while a jury could be referred to awards made by

---

4 [1965] 2 QB 86. See also *Coyne v Citizen Finance Ltd* (1991) 172 CLR 211, 221 (per Mason CJ and Deane J dissenting).
5 Ibid at 108.
6 Ibid at 110.
7 [1983] 2 All ER 311. See also *Cassell & Co Ltd v Broome* [1972] AC 1027, 1070; *Sutcliffe v Pressdram Ltd* [1991] 1 QB 153.
8 [1993] 4 All ER 975.

the Court of Appeal in exercising its powers[9] to substitute a proper sum for that awarded by a jury, it was inappropriate to refer to awards in personal injury cases. Neill LJ said:

> We see the force of the criticism of the present practice whereby a plaintiff in an action for libel may recover a much larger sum by way of damages for an injury to his reputation, which may prove transient in its effect, than the damages awarded for pain and suffering to the victim of an industrial accident who has lost an eye or the use of one or more of his limbs. We have come to the conclusion, however, that there is no satisfactory way in which the conventional awards in actions for damages for personal injuries can be used to provide guidance for an award in an action for defamation.[10]

No satisfactory reasoning was offered for so preferring inconsistency and uncertainty. Of course, the root difficulty is the anachronistic survival of jury assessment in defamation cases. Jury awards are notoriously unpredictable and inconsistent and thereby undermine the essential justice of like cases being treated alike. This, plus the expense and length of a jury trial, explains why jury assessment has declined since the middle of the nineteenth century. It also accounts for *Ward v James*,[11] where the Court of Appeal laid down that in personal injury actions, the court's discretion to allow trial by jury should be exercised only in very exceptional circumstances. There are no convincing grounds for treating defamation cases differently. It is therefore most unfortunate that the recommendation of the Faulks Committee on Defamation[12]—that the right to jury trials in defamation cases should be replaced by the usual judicial discretion—has not yet been implemented. But until it is, a trial judge should be encouraged to give to the jury examples of damages for non-pecuniary loss awarded in personal injury cases. Hence it is regrettable that the Court of Appeal has approved the practice of rejecting those analogies.

---

9 Under s 8 of the Courts and Legal Services Act 1990 and Ord 59, r 11(4). In the *Rantzen* case the Court of Appeal approved a more interventionist use of those powers so as properly to protect freedom of expression as required by the European Convention on Human Rights.

10 [1993] 4 All ER 975, 997.

11 [1966] 1 QB 273. This was followed in *H v Ministry of Defence* [1991] 2 QB 103. The legislation governing jury trials is s 69, Supreme Court Act 1981.

12 Report (1975) Cmnd 5909, ch 17.

6. PHYSICAL INCONVENIENCE (EXCEPT WHERE RESULTING FROM PERSONAL INJURY)[13]

Physical inconvenience is a non-pecuniary loss. Traditionally, and especially in the contract realm, it has been regarded as distinct from mental distress and as an objective loss analogous to loss of amenity in a personal injuries claim. But now that the courts are more willing to award mental distress damages (particularly significantly for breach of contract)[14] the distinction between physical inconvenience and mental distress is arguably becoming less important. If so this is to be welcomed for all non-pecuniary loss is ultimately best regarded as a loss only in terms of the distress or loss of happiness caused to the plaintiff.

Subject to the usual limiting principles it seems that physical inconvenience can always be compensated. This is most obviously shown in breach of contract cases, where the head of physical inconvenience is expressly recognised. In *Burton v Pinkerton*,[15] for example, a sailor left a ship at a foreign port, when in breach of his contract of employment, the captain of the ship decided to take it into war. The sailor was able to recover damages for the non-remote physical inconvenience caused by the captain's breach of contract. Similarly in *Hobbs v London and South Western Rly Co*,[16] a man and his family were set down at the wrong station by the defendant railway company in breach of contract. As it was late at night, there was no available transport or accommodation and so, despite rain, they had to walk five miles home. They were able to recover damages for that physical inconvenience. Again in a plethora of cases damages have been awarded for the physical inconvenience of living in a house requiring repairs (including the inconvenience while the repairs are carried out) when the house would not have been bought, or at least not in that condition, but for a breach of the contractual duty of care by the plaintiff purchaser's surveyor or solicitor.[17] Similarly damages for physical inconvenience have been

---

13 Damages for loss of amenity will usually include some damages for physical inconvenience.
14 Infra, pp 231–41.
15 (1867) LR 2 Exch 340.
16 (1875) LR 10 QB 111.
17 Eg *Hill v Debenhams Tewson & Chinnock* (1958) 171 Estates Gazette 835; *Moss v Heckingbottom* (1958) 172 Estates Gazette 207; *Hipkiss v Gaydon* [1961] CLY 9042 (where the defendant was the vendor-builder); *Sinclair v Bowden* (1962) 183 Estates Gazette 95; *Collard v Saunders* [1971] CLY 11161; *Perry v Sidney Phillips & Son* [1982] 1 WLR 1297; *Cross v David Martin & Mortimer* [1989] 1 EGLR 154; *Bigg v Howard Son & Gooch* [1990] 1 EGLR 173; *Watts v Morrow* [1991] 1 WLR 1421. In the last four cases mental distress consequent on the

awarded to tenants against landlords for breach of their covenants to repair.[18] A solicitor was also held liable for physical inconvenience damages in *Bailey v Bullock*[19] where he had delayed in bringing an action for possession of a house. As a result the plaintiff and his family were forced to live in one room of his parents-in-law's small house. A final example is *Perera v Vandiyar*,[20] where the defendant landlord, in an attempt to evict the plaintiff tenant, cut off the supply of gas and electricity to his flat, leaving the plaintiff without alternative means of heat or light. After two days' discomfort, the plaintiff left with his wife and child to stay with friends for five days until the gas and electricity supply were restored. The plaintiff was awarded physical inconvenience damages for breach by the landlord of his tenancy agreement.

As regards tort, while usually not classified under the head of physical inconvenience, damages for the tort of false imprisonment must always include some compensation for the plaintiff's physical inconvenience. The same must generally be true for nuisance; in *Bone v Seale*,[1] for example, each of several plaintiffs was awarded damages for the 'inconvenience, discomfort and annoyance'[2] caused by the smells from the defendant's pig farm which constituted a nuisance. In *Mafo v Adams*,[3] damages for physical inconvenience were expressly awarded to a tenant in an action for deceit against his landlord, who had induced him to leave protected premises, and in *Millington v Duffy*[4] a tenant was awarded damages for inconvenience and distress primarily for trespass to land, his landlord having wrongfully evicted him. In *Saunders v Edwards*[5] damages for inconvenience and disappointment were awarded to the tenants of a flat who had been induced to buy the lease by the defendant vendor's fraudulent misrepresentation that it included the roof terrace. And in *Perry v Sidney Phillips & Son*[6] damages for the physical inconvenience (and consequent distress)

physical inconvenience was also held recoverable: infra, pp 233–5. *Piper v Daybell Court-Cooper & Co* (1969) 210 Estates Gazette 1047 and *Trask v Clark & Sons* [1980] CLY 2588 are analogous (lack of privacy).

18 *Calabar Properties v Stitcher* [1983] 3 All ER 759; *Lubren v London Borough of Lambeth* (1988) 20 HLR 165. In both, consequential loss of enjoyment was also held recoverable.

19 [1950] 2 All ER 1167. See also *Buckley v Lane Herdman & Co* [1977] CLY 3143 in which consequent mental distress was also held recoverable.

20 [1953] 1 WLR 672.

1 [1975] 1 WLR 797.

2 Ibid at 804.

3 [1970] 1 QB 548.

4 (1984) 17 HLR 232.

5 [1987] 2 All ER 651.

6 [1982] 1 WLR 1297. See also, eg *Roberts v Hampson* [1990] 1 WLR 94.

of living in a house with defects that had been negligently omitted from the defendant surveyor's report were awarded in an action brought for both the tort of negligence and breach of contract. Finally in *Ward v Cannock Chase District Council*[7] damages were awarded for the discomfort and consequent distress of living initially in a house with a hole in the roof and later in overcrowded temporary accommodation, all of which was caused by the defendants' tortious negligence.

As regards the assessment of damages for physical inconvenience, then, as with all non-pecuniary loss, no precise compensation is possible and all that can be hoped for is some measure of uniformity both 'internally' between awards for this loss and 'externally' with awards for other non-pecuniary losses. Significantly the majority of the Court of Appeal in *Bone v Seale*, in assessing the physical inconvenience damages, drew an analogy with assessing damages for loss of amenity in a personal injury action. Generally the courts have given low awards for physical inconvenience although clearly the greater the inconvenience the greater the damages.

7. MENTAL DISTRESS (EXCEPT WHERE RESULTING FROM DEATH OR THE PLAINTIFF'S PERSONAL INJURY)[8]

Mental distress covers, for example, disappointment, worry, anxiety, fear, upset, grief and annoyance. It should, however, be distinguished from physical or mental *illness*, such as nervous shock, which the law regards as a type of personal injury. On the traditional approach taken by the courts, mental distress, along with pain and suffering under personal injury and bereavement under the Fatal Accidents Act 1976, are the heads of non-pecuniary loss covering the plaintiff's loss of happiness and distress in contrast to the other 'objective' non-pecuniary losses. On an alternative and preferable view,[9] all non-pecuniary loss is regarded as ultimately dealing with distress or loss of happiness and 'mental distress' is seen as a residual head for distress not falling within any of the other heads.

In order to put the plaintiff into as good a position as if the tort or breach of contract had not occurred, as the general compensatory aims dictate, damages for mental distress should be awarded,

---

7 [1985] 3 All ER 537.
8 For damages for pain and suffering consequent on personal injury and for bereavement see supra, pp 190–1, 216–7.
9 See supra, p 137.

subject to the usual limiting principles, whenever mental distress results from a tort of breach of contract. Traditionally, however, the courts have been reluctant to award mental distress damages, particularly for breach of contract, and despite recent developments they are still sometimes irrecoverable for both torts and breach of contract.

(1) When are damages awarded for mental distress?

(a) Breach of contract[10]

Traditionally *Addis v Gramophone Co Ltd*[11] was regarded as barring any damages for mental distress in an action for breach of contract. There the plaintiff had been wrongfully dismissed. The House of Lords confined damages to his direct pecuniary loss and refused to award any damages for the injury to the plaintiff's feelings following the 'harsh and humiliating manner'[12] in which he had been treated. Similarly in *Groom v Crocker*,[13] in which a solicitor in breach of contract had wrongly admitted negligent driving on the part of the plaintiff, the plaintiff's claim for damages for the humiliation of being branded a negligent driver was denied and *Addis* applied. Further illustrations of the traditional denial of damages for mental distress are provided by cases on physical inconvenience, which drew a distinction between recoverable damages for physical inconvenience and non-recoverable damages for mental distress. For example, in *Hobbs v London and South Western Rly Co*[14] Mellor J said 'For the mere inconvenience, such as annoyance and loss of temper or vexation . . . you cannot recover damages. That is purely sentimental and not a case where the word inconvenience, as I here use it, would apply.'[15]

But this traditional denial was departed from by the Court of Appeal in *Jarvis v Swan's Tours*,[16] where the plaintiff was compensated for his disappointment at not getting as good a holiday as he had contracted for. Since then, mental distress damages have been awarded in many cases, primarily but not only for ruined holidays. However, contrary to what has sometimes been said—most notably

---

10 See generally Veitch (1977) 16 UWOLR 227. For a comparative account, see
   Treitel *Remedies for Breach of Contract* pp 194–201.
11 [1909] AC 488.
12 Ibid at 493 (per Lord Atkinson).
13 [1939] 1 KB 194.
14 (1875) LR 10 QB 111.
15 Ibid at 122. Also see *Bailey v Bullock* [1950] 2 All ER 1167.
16 [1973] QB 233.

by Lawson J in *Cox v Philips Industries Ltd*[17]— it is clear that mental distress damages are recoverable only in certain restricted types of situation; to use Lord Denning's words in *Jarvis v Swan's Tours*, these damages are recoverable only in a 'proper case'.[18] What then is a 'proper case'?

First and most important is where the predominant object of the contract, from the plaintiff's point of view, was to obtain mental satisfaction, whether enjoyment or relief from distress. The ruined holiday cases, such as *Jarvis v Swan's Tours* and *Jackson v Horizon Holidays*[19] most obviously fall within this. So does *Heywood v Wellers*,[20] where the defendant solicitors, in breach of their contractual duty of care, had failed to gain an injunction to stop molestation of the plaintiff by her former boyfriend. She was awarded damages for the mental distress resulting from being further molested. The same principle can also be said to underpin the influential Scottish case of *Diesen v Samson*[1] in which mental distress damages were awarded for the defender's breach of contract in failing to appear at a wedding to take photographs. Furthermore this first category was expressly recognised as an exception to the general bar on mental distress damages by the Court of Appeal in *Bliss v South East Thames Regional Health Authority*:[2] in a well-known, oft-cited, statement Dillon LJ said, 'There are exceptions now recognised where the contract which has been broken was itself a contract to provide peace of mind or freedom from distress.'[3]

A second situation in which mental distress damages can be awarded is where the plaintiff's mental distress is directly consequent on physical inconvenience caused by the defendant's breach of contract. In *Perry v Sidney Phillips & Son*[4] the plaintiff bought a house on the faith of a survey report prepared by the defendants, a

---

17 [1976] 1 WLR 638 at 644.
18 [1973] QB 233 at 238.
19 [1975] 1 WLR 1468. See also *Hunt v Hourmont* [1983] CLY 983; and for unreported Court of Appeal decisions, see (1983) 80 LS Gaz 1429.
20 [1976] QB 446. See also *McLeish v Amoo-Gottfried & Co* (1993) 137 Sol Jo LB 204. Cf *Dickinson v Jones Alexander & Co* [1990] Fam Law 137 (which is controversial because the wife's mental distress consequent on the negligent handling of her *financial* claims surely fell outside this first category).
1 1971 SLT 49. See also *Reed v Madon* [1989] 2 All ER 431 (contract for exclusive burial rights).
2 [1985] IRLR 308.
3 Ibid at 316.
4 [1982] 1 WLR 1297. See also *McCall v Abelesz* [1976] QB 585; *Buckley v Lane Herdman & Co* [1977] CLY 3143; *Calabar Properties v Stitcher* [1983] 3 All ER 759; *Lubren v London Borough of Lambeth* (1988) 20 HLR 165; *Cross v David Martin & Mortimer* [1989] 1 EGLR 154; *Bigg v Howard Son & Gooch* [1990] 1 EGLR 173.

firm of chartered surveyors. The report had been negligently made, in breach of the defendants' contractual and tortious duty of care, and did not mention several serious defects including a leaking roof and a septic tank which produced an offensive smell. The plaintiff was held entitled to mental distress damages for the 'anxiety, worry and distress'[5] caused and this mental distress is best viewed as directly consequent on the physical inconvenience of having to live in a house that was in a poor condition; for having emphasised that the mental distress here was recoverable because reasonably foreseeable, Lord Denning, with whom Oliver LJ apparently agreed, went on to cite with approval that part of the judgment at first instance where no clear distinction was drawn between the plaintiff's physical inconvenience and mental distress consequent on it. Sir Patrick Bennett QC had there said:

> I think it was reasonably foreseeable that, if Mr Perry bought the house in such a condition that he was exposed to the incursion of water, the anxiety resulting from the question of when the repairs should be done and the odour and smell from the defective septic water tank would cause him distress and discomfort which I have gathered together under the term 'vexation' . . . In my view, the plaintiff is entitled . . . to damages for such discomfort, distress and the like . . .[6]

Furthermore, Kerr LJ, in upholding the trial judge's decision on damages for vexation and inconvenience, emphasised that those damages were recoverable because, '. . . the physical consequences of the breach were all foreseeable at the time.'[7]

Similarly in *Watts v Morrow*[8] a husband and wife were each awarded £750 for the physical inconvenience and directly related mental distress of living (at weekends) in a house undergoing extensive repairs. The repairs were necessitated by defects that had been negligently omitted from the defendant's survey report upon which the plaintiffs had relied in buying the house. The Court of Appeal stressed that such mental distress damages belonged to an exceptional category separate from that recognised by Dillon LJ in *Bliss*. Bingham LJ neatly summarised the position as follows:

> A contract-breaker is not in general liable for any distress, frustration, anxiety, displeasure, vexation, tension or aggravation which his breach of contract may cause to the innocent party. The rule is not, I think, founded on the assumption that such reactions are not foreseeable, which they

5 Ibid at 1303 (per Lord Denning).
6 [1982] 1 All ER 1005 at 1016–17.
7 [1982] 1 WLR 1297 at 1307.
8 [1991] 1 WLR 1421.

surely are or may be, but on considerations of policy. But the rule is not absolute. Where the very object of a contract is to provide pleasure, relaxation, peace of mind or freedom from molestation, damages will be awarded if the fruit of the contract is not provided or if the contrary result is procured instead. If the law did not cater for this exceptional category of case it would be defective. A contract to survey the condition of a house for a prospective purchaser does not, however, fall within this exceptional category. In cases not falling within this exceptional category, damages are in my view recoverable for physical inconvenience and discomfort caused by the breach and mental suffering directly related to that inconvenience and discomfort.[9]

Beyond those two situations, mental distress damages are irrecoverable. In particular, a case seemingly opening up a less restricted approach, namely *Cox v Philips Industries Ltd*,[10] was overruled in *Bliss v South East Thames Regional Health Authority*.[11] In the former, the defendants had contracted to give the plaintiff a better job with greater responsibility and an increased salary but having initially complied with this, they later, in breach of contract, relegated him to a position of lower responsibility with very vague duties. Lawson J thought that there was '. . . no reason in principle why, if a situation arises which within the contemplation of the parties would have given rise to vexation, distress and general disappointment and frustration, the person who is injured by a contractual breach, should not be compensated in damages for that breach.'[12] Applying this, he awarded the plaintiff mental distress damages despite *Addis v Gramophone Co Ltd*,[13] where the plaintiff had similarly been humiliated by his employers' treatment of him and yet the House of Lords had refused mental distress damages. Lawson J purported to distinguish *Addis* as a case of wrongful dismissal, whereas the contract in issue in *Cox* was one for promotion. But this was hardly a convincing distinction.

For several years *Cox* went unchallenged judicially and was at the centre of much of the academic discussion of the new approach to mental distress damages. But then in *Shove v Downs Surgical plc*,[14] Sheen J refused to apply it. The plaintiff, who had served the defendant company for 40 years, was its chairman and managing director. By his contract of employment he was entitled to 30 months' notice of dismissal. Whilst he was convalescing from a

9 Ibid at 1445.
10 [1976] 1 WLR 638.
11 [1985] IRLR 308.
12 [1976] 1 WLR 638 at 644.
13 [1909] AC 488.
14 [1984] 1 All ER 7.

heart operation, the defendant company, which had lost confidence in him, repudiated his contract, the directors telling him that they wanted him to leave forthwith. The plaintiff accepted that repudiation as terminating the contract and sought damages, inter alia, for the distress caused by the manner and circumstances of the defendant's breach. Sheen J refused to award those damages, applied *Addis* and distinguished *Cox* on the ground that there, unlike here, the mental distress had been caused by the relegation of the plaintiff to a position of lesser responsibility *during his employment.* This was as unconvincing a ground of distinction as that drawn by Lawson J in *Cox*, and in essence *Shove* was disapproving *Cox.* But it was left to the Court of Appeal in *Bliss v South East Thames Regional Health Authority* to seal *Cox*'s fate. Here the defendant health authority in breach of contract had suspended the plaintiff, a consultant surgeon, on the unfounded grounds that he was mentally unfit for his job. At first instance, Farquharson J applied *Cox* and awarded £2,000 mental distress damages. This was overturned by the Court of Appeal, which held that *Cox* was wrongly decided and that, until altered by the House of Lords, *Addis* largely remains good law.

Subsequent to *Bliss*, the most important case in which mental distress damages have been denied (because the facts did not fall within the two exceptional categories) has been *Hayes v James & Charles Dodd.*[15] The plaintiffs were a husband and wife in the motor car repair business and they bought a yard and workshop on the faith of their solicitors' advice that there was a right of access to the rear of the workshop. This was untrue. The yard and workshop were therefore useless for the plaintiffs' business plans and they were forced to sell them. In an action against the solicitors for breach of their contractual duty of care the plaintiffs were awarded £92,000 for their pecuniary losses. But the Court of Appeal overturned Hirst J's award of £1,500 each for mental distress (largely comprising the anxiety and vexation of the dispute itself). *Bliss* was applied and it was stressed that mental distress damages were inappropriate where the contract was merely a commercial one entered into with a view to profit. Reflecting a widely-held fear that, unless heavily restricted, mental distress damages would feature in almost every award of contractual damages, Staughton LJ said:

I would not view with enthusiasm the prospect that every shipowner in the

---

15 [1990] 2 All ER 815. See also, eg *Rae v Yorkshire Bank plc* [1988] BTLC 35 (dishonouring of cheque); *O'Laoire v Jackel International Ltd (No 2)* [1991] ICR 718 (supra, pp 221–2); *Branchett v Beaney* [1992] 3 All ER 910 (breach of covenant of quiet enjoyment).

Commercial Court, having successfully claimed for unpaid freight or demurrage, would be able to add a claim for mental distress suffered while he was waiting for his money.[16]

In terms of policy the return to traditional thinking marked by *Bliss* is unsupportable. For while the first exceptional category perhaps presents the strongest claim for such relief, since mental distress damages there reflect the 'consumer surplus'[17] (namely the particular value to the plaintiff of the contractual performance over and above its objective market value), the compensatory principle dictates that mental distress caused by the breach of contract should always be compensated, subject to the usual limiting principles, and this was Lawson J's approach in *Cox*. After all, the confusion between exemplary and mental distress damages has been clearly exposed in cases like *Rookes v Barnard*[18] and, while assessing damages is difficult for mental distress, it is no more difficult than for other non-pecuniary losses. Similarly, the fact that mental distress is difficult to prove should not deter the courts, since if the plaintiff cannot establish that he has suffered mental distress that is not *de minimis*, he should recover no damages. Certainly in many other jurisdictions there has been a greater willingness to award mental distress damages.[19] Finally it should be realised that even if mental distress damages were freely available, it would not be correct to imagine that they would figure in almost every contractual damages claim, for often the plaintiff is not a human person, but is, for example, a company which is incapable of experiencing mental distress.[20]

(b) Torts

The law has traditionally been more favourable to the distressed plaintiff in tort than in contract. So there has been compensation, often under the head of 'aggravated damages',[1] for mental distress caused by torts such as false imprisonment,[2] malicious

16 Ibid at 823.
17 Harris, Ogus and Phillips (1979) 95 LQR 581.
18 [1964] AC 1129.
19 For Canadian cases, see Waddams *Damages* paras 3.1310–3.1450. For the US, see Chmiel (1957) 32 Notre Dame LR 482, Second Restatement of Contracts, s 353. And for New Zealand, see the excellent decision of Thomas J in *Rowlands v Collow* [1992] 1 NZLR 178.
20 Contra is *Messenger Newspapers Group Ltd v National Graphical Association* [1984] IRLR 397.
1 Infra, p 241.
2 Eg *Walter v Alltools Ltd* (1944) 61 TLR 39; *White v Metropolitan Police Comr* (1982) Times, 24 April.

prosecution,[3] assault and battery,[4] defamation,[5] nuisance[6] and even trespass to goods.[7] Furthermore the Copyright, Designs and Patents Act 1988, s 97(2) (formerly s 17(3) of the Copyright Act 1956) appears to empower the award of mental distress damages for copyright infringement, although there has as yet been no case clearly awarding such damages;[8] and by s 66(4) of the Sex Discrimination Act 1975 and s 57(4) of the Race Relations Act 1976[9] the courts are empowered to award damages for 'injured feelings' where the plaintiff sues for breach of statutory duty laid down in Part III of those Acts.

Recent decisions have further extended the recovery of mental distress damages for torts.[10] In *Perry v Sidney Phillips & Son*,[11] in an action brought for both the tort of negligence and for breach of contract, the plaintiff was awarded damages for the mental distress consequent on the physical inconvenience of living in a house with several defects which the defendant surveyors had failed to report. In *Drane v Evangelou*[12] and *McMillan v Singh*[13] aggravated damages were awarded to a tenant for his landlord's trespass to land or nuisance in wrongfully evicting him. In the former, the Court of

---

3 Eg *Savile v Roberts* (1698) 1 Ld Raym 374; *White v Metropolitan Police Comr*, ibid.
4 Eg *White v Metropolitan Police Comr*, ibid; *Ballard v Metropolitan Police Comr* (1983) 133 NLJ 1133; *Barbara v Home Office* (1984) 134 NLJ 888; *George v Metropolitan Police Comr* (1984) Times, 31 March; *W v Meah* [1986] 1 All ER 935.
5 Eg *McCarey v Associated Newspapers Ltd* [1965] 2 QB 86 (libel).
6 Eg *Bone v Seale* [1975] 1 WLR 797; *Dunton v Dover District Council* (1977) 76 LGR 87. The damages for 'loss of amenity' in *Carr-Saunders v Dick McNeil Associates Ltd* [1986] 2 All ER 888 presumably also included some compensation for mental distress.
7 *Owen and Smith v Reo Motors Ltd* (1934) 151 LT 274. See also *Piper v Darling* (1940) 67 Ll L Rep 419—sentimental value taken into account in fixing the value of the plaintiff's yacht, destroyed by the defendant's negligence.
8 But see *Nichols Advanced Vehicle Systems Inc v Rees and Oliver* [1979] RPC 127. As to whether s 97(2) authorises exemplary damages, see infra, chapter 5. The Law Commission recommended that mental distress damages should be available for its proposed new statutory tort of breach of confidence, see Report No 110, rec 29.
9 See, eg *Alexander v Home Office* [1988] 2 All ER 118; *Deane v Ealing LBC* [1993] ICR 329 (in which the compensation was ordered by an industrial tribunal for discrimination under Pt II of the 1976 Act).
10 In addition to the cases cited below, see *Reed v Madon* [1989] 2 All ER 431 (breach of the statutory duty not to infringe exclusive burial rights).
11 [1982] 1 WLR 1297. See also *Gobolinscy v Hamilton City Corpn* [1975] 1 NZLR 150 at 163; *Ward v Cannock Chase DC* [1985] 3 All ER 537; *Roberts v Hampson* [1990] 1 WLR 94.
12 [1978] 2 All ER 437.
13 (1984) 17 HLR 120. See also *Millington v Duffy* (1984) 17 HLR 232; *Guppys (Bridport) Ltd v Brookling and James* (1984) 269 Estates Gazette 846 at 942; *Ashgar v Ahmed* (1984) 17 HLR 25.

Appeal emphasised the worry and stress of being deprived of a roof over one's head and in the latter Sir John Arnold stressed also the tenant's outrage at the landlord's actions. In *Archer v Brown*,[14] in which the plaintiff had been induced by the defendant's fraudulent misrepresentation to buy shares from the defendant which the defendant did not own, mental distress damages were awarded to the plaintiff in his action for deceit. Peter Pain J examined the issue in some detail and, having considered a contract case like *Jarvis v Swan's Tours Ltd*[15] and a tort case like *Ichard v Frangoulis*,[16] he concluded that there was no reason why damages for the plaintiff's injured feelings or aggravated damages (he used both phrases) should not be awarded for deceit. In *Whitmore v Euroways Express Coaches Ltd*[17] in an action against a holiday coach firm for negligent driving, the plaintiff's wife was awarded damages for the 'ordinary shock'[18] suffered at seeing her husband's injuries both at the time of the accident and in the weeks afterwards. Finally in *Bagley v North Herts Health Authority*,[19] where the defendant's medical negligence resulted in the plaintiff giving birth to a still-born child, damages were awarded for the plaintiff's loss of satisfaction in bringing her pregnancy to a successful conclusion and for her acute disappointment and loss of pleasure in not being able to have her desired number of children.

However, the above decisions do not mean that damages for mental distress are now always recoverable in tort.[20] The first and major restriction is that, leaving aside statutory bereavement damages, there is no tortious recovery for grief, anguish, upset, worry or strain suffered by a person as a result of the personal injuries tortiously inflicted on that person's spouse or child.[1]

14 [1984] 2 All ER 267. See also *Saunders v Edwards* [1987] 2 All ER 651.
15 [1973] QB 233.
16 [1977] 2 All ER 461. Supra, p 191.
17 (1984) Times, 4 May.
18 As opposed to nervous shock which is a recognised psychiatric illness.
19 [1986] NLJ Rep 1014. *Bagley* was not followed in *Kerby v Redbridge HA* [1993] 4 Med LR 178 on the ground that at least the first head of mental distress there recognised is merely a facet of bereavement distress, which is compensatable under s 1A of the Fatal Accidents Act 1976 (where a child has been born alive and then died as in *Kerby* but not in *Bagley* where the child was stillborn) but not at common law.
20 In addition to the restrictions discussed below, see *Lonrho plc v Fayed (No 5)* [1994] 1 All ER 188 (no damages for injured feelings for lawful means conspiracy).
1 *Hinz v Berry* [1970] 2 QB 40, 42; *McLoughlin v O'Brian* [1983] 1 AC 410 at 418, 431; *Whitmore v Euroways Express Coaches Ltd* (1984) Times, 4 May; *Kralj v McGrath* [1986] 1 All ER 54 at 62; *Bagley v North Herts Health Authority* [1986] NLJ Rep 1014; *Alcock v Chief Constable of South Yorkshire Police* [1992] 1 AC 310, 401, 409–10, 416; *Kerby v Redbridge HA* [1993] 4 Med LR 178.

Secondly, there can be no recovery (except under the tort of assault) for the mental distress of being frightened for one's own safety. This is vividly illustrated by *Behrens v Bertram Mills Circus Ltd*,[2] where the plaintiff, a midget, was in a booth when an elephant went out of control and knocked the booth over. Devlin J found that the plaintiff must have been very frightened and 'shocked'. He said, 'I should like to award him a substantial sum under this head, but I am satisfied that I cannot do so except to the extremely limited extent that the shock resulted in physical or mental harm';[3] and he went on to explain that apart from shock resulting in physical or mental harm (ie nervous shock) damages could not be given '. . . infringing the general principle embedded in the common law that suffering caused by grief, fear, anguish and the like is not assessable'.[4] Similarly in *Hicks v Chief Constable of the South Yorkshire Police*[5] Lord Bridge said:

> Those trapped in the crush at Hillsborough who were fortunate enough to escape without injury have no claim in respect of the distress they suffered in what must have been a truly terrifying experience. It follows that fear of impending death felt by the victim of a fatal injury before that injury is inflicted cannot by itself give rise to a cause of action which survives for the benefit of the victim's estate.

Thirdly, the extension of tortious negligence to the negligent performance of services causing pure economic loss[6] presumably does not also allow the recovery of mental distress damages, unless those damages would be recoverable in that situation for breach of a contractual duty of care. In other words, one will need to show, for example, that a predominant object of the services was to provide mental satisfaction, or that the mental distress results from physical inconvenience. Worry and upset caused by negligent performance of the services will presumably not be recoverable.

As with breach of contract, however, it is difficult to see why mental distress should not be recoverable whenever it is caused by a tort. Certainly Comyn J and Devlin J in the *Whitmore* and *Behrens* cases considered that the restrictions that the law imposes are unsatisfactory, and it is submitted that all such restrictions should be removed.

---

2 [1957] 2 QB 1.
3 Ibid at 27–8.
4 Ibid at 28.
5 [1992] 2 All ER 65, 69. See also *Nicholls v Rushton* (1992) Times, 19 June.
6 Eg in *Junior Books Ltd v Veitchi Co Ltd* [1983] 1 AC 520.

A final word is merited on 'aggravated damages'.[7] In *Rookes v Barnard*[8] those damages were stressed to be compensatory—albeit compensating for mental distress—and not exemplary. But the confusion between the two lingers on.[9] This is not surprising since aggravated damages have traditionally been regarded as a sub-category of mental distress damages to be awarded only where the defendant's behaviour has been particularly reprehensible. Now that mental distress damages are more freely recoverable this link to the especially bad conduct of the defendant seems unhelpful and unnecessary. All confusion would be avoided by abandoning the notion of aggravated damages and by referring only to 'mental distress damages' or 'damages for injured feelings'.[10] This sort of approach has been provisionally supported by the Law Commission: '. . . we have . . . formed the provisional view that the exceptional conduct requirement should be abandoned and that aggravated damages should be assimilated within a compensatory framework.'[11]

(2) Assessing damages for mental distress

As with all non-pecuniary losses the aim must be to award a fair and reasonable sum, which is in line with other mental distress awards. It would also be sensible to maintain 'external consistency', most obviously with damages for pain and suffering in personal injury cases, but as yet there has been little sign of judicial recognition of this. Clearly, however, the courts do not regard mental distress as that serious (although of course the worse the distress the higher the damages should be) for they have often stressed that awards should be kept at a moderate level.[12]

---

7 See, generally, Law Commission Consultation Paper No 132 (1993) 'Aggravated, Exemplary and Restitutionary Damages' esp pp 30–50, 150–4.
8 [1964] AC 1129.
9 Eg *Messenger Newspapers Group Ltd v National Graphical Association* [1984] IRLR 397.
10 Burrows (1993) 109 LQR 358, 361 (noting the striking out of the claim for aggravated damages in *AB v South West Water Services Ltd* [1993] QB 507). See also *Joyce v Sengupta* [1993] 1 All ER 897, 908.
11 Law Commission Consultation Paper No 132 (1993) p 153.
12 Eg *Perry v Sidney Phillips & Son* [1982] 1 WLR 1297; *Archer v Brown* [1984] 2 All ER 267; *Watts v Morrow* [1991] 1 WLR 1421.

Chapter 4

Compensatory damages III: miscellaneous issues

This chapter considers two types of less common compensatory damages—equitable and contractual reliance damages—and two factors of relevance to, while not concerning the assessment of, compensatory damages—awards of interest and limitation periods.

1. EQUITABLE DAMAGES

(1) When may equitable damages be awarded?

Prior to 1858 there was probably some power, albeit very restricted, to award damages in equity in addition to specific performance.[1] But this is of merely historical interest, because by s 2 of the Chancery Amendment Act 1858 (Lord Cairns's Act) the Court of Chancery was given power to award damages in addition to or in substitution for an injunction or specific performance. This power to award equitable damages is now vested in the High Court by s 50 of the Supreme Court Act 1981. As regards damages in addition, the power is self-explanatory—whenever an injunction or specific performance is granted, damages can be added. But when may damages in lieu be awarded?

By s 50, this will depend on whether the court 'has jurisdiction to entertain an application for an injunction or specific performance.' But there is difficulty in deciding when this is satisfied. The traditional approach has been to decide whether the particular reason for denying specific performance or the injunction is jurisdictional or discretionary and only if it is the latter can damages in lieu be awarded. For example, in *Price v Strange*[2] the Court of Appeal in dicta considered that the want of mutuality bar to

---

1 *Todd v Gee* (1810) 17 Ves 273.
2 [1978] Ch 337.

specific performance was discretionary so that damages in lieu could have been awarded had specific performance been refused. Both Buckley and Goff LJJ also thought that the denial of specific performance in contracts for the sale of non-unique goods was jurisdictional, but they disagreed as to whether the personal service bar was jurisdictional or discretionary, Buckley LJ thinking that it was the former and Goff LJ that it was the latter. This disagreement tends to support the view that, given that the bars to specific performance are nowadays rarely absolute,[3] the approach of categorising them as either jurisdictional or discretionary is unhelpful.

A simpler and preferable approach to s 50—and one which can equally well justify past decisions— is to ask whether the plaintiff had an arguable case for specific performance or an injunction at the time the claim was brought; if so, equitable damages can be awarded.[4] In *Ferguson v Wilson*,[5] for example, specific performance of a contract for the allotment of shares to the plaintiff had been refused because, as the shares had already been allotted to third parties (in fact that had been done prior to the claim being brought) compliance would be impossible. It was further held that no equitable damages could be awarded and this can be best justified by saying that the plaintiff had no arguable case for specific performance at the time the claim was brought. On the other hand, in *Miller v Jackson*,[6] where the Court of Appeal refused an injunction but granted damages in lieu, the plaintiff clearly had an arguable case for an injunction—indeed Geoffrey Lane LJ dissented and considered that an injunction should be granted.

Two further points are noteworthy. First, it has traditionally been thought that s 50 does not allow the award of equitable damages in the unusual case where the plaintiff would have been granted specific performance or an injunction had he claimed it but he has made no such claim (since he wants damages in lieu).[7] Secondly, the fact that a court has power to award equitable damages does not mean that it will necessarily use that power. For example, where a plaintiff's conduct has debarred him from specific relief, the court may refuse him even damages in lieu.[8]

3 Infra, chapter 8.
4 There is also jurisdiction where specific performance was ordered but has since been abandoned because of the defendant's non-compliance: eg *Biggins v Minton* [1977] 1 WLR 701; *Malhotra v Choudhury* [1980] Ch 52.
5 (1866) 2 Ch App 77. See also *Proctor v Bayley* (1889) 42 Ch D 390.
6 [1977] QB 966.
7 *Horsler v Zorro* [1975] Ch 302. Also see Jones (1970) 86 LQR 463, 491. Contra is Albery (1975) 91 LQR 337, 352–3.
8 See infra, pp 448–9. For delay barring equitable damages, see infra, p 268.

(2) When are equitable damages more advantageous than common law damages?

As s 49 of the Supreme Court 1981, embodying the fusion provisions of the Judicature Acts 1873–5, allows the plaintiff to combine a claim for common law damages with an action for specific performance or an injunction, equitable damages generally offer no advantage to a plaintiff. This is particularly so since *Johnson v Agnew*[9] in which it was clearly laid down, following doubts in, for example, *Wroth v Tyler*,[10] that the assessment of equitable damages—and in this case the particular dispute concerned the time for assessing market value—is no different to that for normal compensatory common law damages.[11]

However, there remains one major advantage:[12] equitable damages may be awarded even though there is no cause of action at common law and hence no possible award of common law damages. A number of illustrations can be given of the application of this advantage in relation to torts, breach of confidence, and breach of contract.

(i) In *Eastwood v Lever*[13] it was first recognised that a third party can be awarded damages in addition to or in lieu of an injunction, available under the *Tulk v Moxhay*[14] principle, for the breach of a restrictive covenant concerning land, although he would have no cause of action at common law because of the privity of contract rule. A more recent instance of this is *Wrotham Park Estate Co v Parkside Homes Ltd*[15] where houses had been built by the defendants in breach of a restrictive covenant. While Brightman J refused to grant a mandatory injunction to demolish them, he did award substantial damages in lieu.

(ii) In *Hasham v Zenab*[16] it was held by the Privy Council that while an anticipatory breach that has not been accepted gives rise to no cause of action at common law, specific performance can be ordered. It had to follow that equitable damages could be awarded

---

9 [1980] AC 367. See also *Surrey CC v Bredero Homes Ltd* [1993] 3 All ER 705: infra, pp 313–4.
10 [1974] Ch 30.
11 So the principles discussed in chapters 2 and 3 apply also to equitable damages. See also *Malhotra v Choudhury* [1980] Ch 52 (the duty to mitigate, *Bain v Fothergill* restriction).
12 A minor advantage is that equitable damages may be awarded even though not claimed—*Betts v Neilson* (1863) 3 Ch App 429 at 441.
13 (1863) 4 De GJ & Sm 114.
14 (1848) 18 LJ Ch 83.
15 [1974] 1 WLR 798.
16 [1960] AC 316.

in this situation, even though common law damages could not, and this has since been confirmed by the decision in *Oakacre Ltd v Claire Cleaners (Holdings) Ltd.*[17]

(iii) In the classic case of *Leeds Industrial Co-operative Society v Slack*[18] it was held by the House of Lords that damages can be awarded in addition to or in lieu of a *quia timet* injunction, which is an injunction to prevent a threatened wrong where no wrong has yet been committed. So on the facts damages were held recoverable in lieu of a *quia timet* injunction preventing the defendant constructing buildings which, when complete, would have obstructed the plaintiff's ancient lights but as yet were causing no obstruction.

It should also be realised that in respect of torts or a continuing breach of contract equitable damages in lieu of even an ordinary (ie not a *quia timet*) injunction are more advantageous than common law damages in compensating prospective loss. Common law damages, in contrast, compensate only for prospective loss caused by a tort or breach of contract that has already been committed.[19] So, for example, in *Bracewell v Appleby*[20] where damages were awarded in lieu of an injunction to prevent the defendant continuing to trespass by using the plaintiff's road, there was no question of compensatory damages being assessed only for loss caused by past, as opposed to future, acts of trespass. In this context Lord Upjohn's much-discussed statement in the classic mandatory injunctions case of *Redland Bricks Ltd v Morris*[1]—that Lord Cairns's Act had nothing to do with the case—plainly seems wrong. Damages could have been awarded in lieu of a mandatory injunction to restore the support to the plaintiff's land, albeit that on the facts it was arguably preferable to leave the plaintiff to bring fresh proceedings should a new cause of action arise, since the probability of further landslips and their likely extent were both in doubt, and the plaintiff could not carry out effective preventive work on his own land.

In all these situations the normal compensatory aims of putting the plaintiff into as good a position as if no tort or breach of contract had been committed must of course be modified to include the aim of putting the plaintiff into as good a position as if the threatened or continuing tort or breach of contract were not to be committed or continued.

---

17 [1982] Ch 197.
18 [1924] AC 851. See also *Hooper v Rogers* [1975] Ch 43 (damages in lieu of *quia timet* mandatory injunction).
19 Supra, p 99, fn 17.
20 [1975] Ch 408.
 1 [1970] AC 652. Infra, pp 414–6. Jolowicz (1975) 34 CLJ 224, 242–5; Pettit (1977) 36 CLJ 369.

(iv) On the best view of the authorities, while common law damages cannot yet be awarded for breach of confidence, since that is an equitable wrong and not a tort, equitable damages can be.[2]

So in *Saltman Engineering Co Ltd v Campbell Engineering Ltd*,[3] having established that the defendants were in breach of an equitable obligation of confidence in using drawings to make special tools, the Court of Appeal refused an injunction to restrain use or sale of the tools, but ordered an inquiry as to damages, Lord Greene MR saying that damages could be awarded under Lord Cairns's Act '. . . to cover both past and future acts in lieu of an injunction.'[4] Again in *Seager v Copydex Ltd*[5] the Court of Appeal ordered damages to be awarded by the master for breach of confidence in manufacturing a carpetgrip invented by the plaintiff. Although no explanation was offered as to the jurisdiction to award damages, the most natural interpretation, given the plaintiff's application for an injunction, was that they were granted in lieu of that injunction under Lord Cairns's Act.

Similarly there are several cases in which the courts have accepted that damages in addition to an injunction can be awarded for breach of confidence. In *Peter Pan Manufacturing Corpn v Corsets Silhouette Ltd*[6] for example, Pennycuick J said that, in addition to an injunction, the plaintiff had the option to claim damages or to take an account of profits (in fact the plaintiff chose the latter) and in *Ackroyds (London) Ltd v Islington Plastics Ltd*[7] Havers J, in addition to granting an injunction, ordered an inquiry into damages for breach of confidence. Although there was no explanation of the basis for the damages in these cases, it is natural to assume that they were additional to an injunction under Lord Cairns's Act.

However, in *Nichrotherm Electrical Co Ltd v Percy*[8] no application for an injunction had been made by the plaintiffs and yet at first instance Harman J ordered an inquiry as to damages for breach of confidence. Unless one can make something of the fact that the plaintiffs were also given leave to apply for an injunction it would seem that the damages cannot be regarded as equitable and that the

---

2 See Gurry *Breach of Confidence* (1984) pp 431–2; also see supra, p 11, fn 6.
3 [1948] 65 RPC 203.
4 Ibid at 219.
5 [1967] 1 WLR 923.
6 [1963] RPC 45. See similarly the Australian case *Ansell Rubber Co Pty Ltd v Allied Rubber Industries Pty Ltd* [1972] RPC 811.
7 [1962] RPC 97. See also the Australian cases *Interfirm Comparison (Australia) Pty Ltd v Law Society of New South Wales* [1977] RPC 137; *Talbot v General Television Corpn Pty Ltd* [1981] RPC 1.
8 [1956] RPC 272.

decision is out of line with the other authorities. As Jones writes, 'Harman J's suggestion is mildly revolutionary in that, by implying that a damages claim can succeed independently of any prayer for equitable relief, it presupposes a fusion of law and equity.'[9] Significantly the Court of Appeal[10] left open the question of whether there was jurisdiction to award damages in such a situation for breach of an equitable duty of confidence and instead upheld Harman J's decision on the ground that there had been a breach of a contractual duty of confidence where the jurisdiction to award damages was indisputable.

But the above interpretation of the cases is not the only one that can be offered. In particular it has been argued that, other than in respect of future loss, the damages in the above cases were ordinary common law, rather than equitable, damages; and from that it is reasoned that the courts were recognising breach of confidence as a tort.[11] Apart from the first instance decision in *Nichrotherm* the strongest point in support of this approach is that 'at first blush' one would expect damages in lieu of an injunction to cover only future and not past loss and if so the damages awarded for past loss, where no injunction was being granted, must have been given at common law. But Lord Greene MR in the *Saltman* case considered that damages in lieu of an injunction can cover past loss and ultimately this seems a preferable view.[12] For it avoids the anomaly of the courts being able to grant equitable damages to cover past loss in addition to an injunction, but only damages to cover future loss where no injunction is granted.

Finally, Meagher Gummow and Lehane have strenuously argued that even the award of equitable damages in these cases was incorrect because 'wrongful act' in Lord Cairns's Act referred only to legal and not equitable wrongs.[13] But if there was ever any force in this narrow view, the re-enactment of the Lord Cairns's Act power in the Supreme Court Act 1981, s 50, has surely removed it; for that omits any reference to the detailed circumstances in which there is jurisdiction to entertain an application for an injunction or specific performance so that the term 'wrongful act' is no longer included.

9 (1970) 86 LQR 463 at 491.
10 [1957] RPC 207.
11 North (1972) 12 JSPTL 149. Law Commission Report (1981) *Breach of Confidence.*
12 This is supported by, cg *Elsley v J G Collins Ins Agencies Ltd* (1978) 83 DLR (3d) 1.
13 *Equity—Doctrines and Remedies* (3rd edn, 1992) pp 649–50.

2. DAMAGES FOR BREACH OF CONTRACT PROTECTING THE RELIANCE INTEREST

(1) Introduction

The term 'reliance interest' was coined by Fuller and Perdue, whose classic article 'The Reliance Interest in Contract Damages'[14] first clarified and explored the different possible objectives of damages for breach of contract. The aim of damages protecting the reliance interest is, according to Fuller and Perdue, '. . . to put the plaintiff in as good a position as he was in before the promise was made'.[15] This can alternatively and preferably be expressed as aiming to put the plaintiff into as good a position as he would have been in if no promise had been made.

As regards damages for breach of contract, the previous two chapters have been concerned to examine in detail the application of the central principle that damages protect the expectation interest by aiming to put the plaintiff into as good a position as if the contract had been performed; this is indisputably what compensation normally requires in this context. But the question now being asked is, can a plaintiff alternatively recover damages protecting his reliance interest[16] which, in a sense, can also be regarded as compensatory?

(2) Protection of the reliance interest where protection of the expectation interest is barred

While the English courts have generally not adopted Fuller and Perdue's interest terminology, there are decisions which can be viewed as protecting the plaintiff's reliance rather than his expectation interest.

First, there are those cases to which the (now abolished) rule in *Bain v Fothergill*[17] applied. By this if, because of a defect in his title, a vendor without fault broke a contract for the sale of land by failing to complete or delaying in completion, the purchaser could

---

14 (1936–7) 46 Yale LJ 52, 573.
15 Ibid at p 54.
16 Ie as an overall interest, see supra, p 21.
17 (1874) LR 7 HL 158. Abolished by the Law of Property (Miscellaneous Provisions) Act 1989, s 3.

not recover damages for the difference between the market value of the land and the contract price. Rather he was restricted to damages in respect of at least some expenses incurred in relation to the contract; and those damages could be viewed as at least partially protecting the plaintiff's reliance interest.

Secondly, there are cases where the plaintiff cannot directly recover damages protecting his expectation interest because he cannot prove what position he would have been in if the contract had been performed.[18] The Australian case of *McRae v Commonwealth Disposals Commission*[19] affords an excellent illustration. The plaintiffs bought from the defendants an oil tanker together with its contents which the defendants had advertised as lying off a named reef. The plaintiffs went to considerable expense to reach and salvage the tanker but it turned out that neither tanker nor reef existed. The plaintiffs successfully sued the defendants for breach of contract, it being held that the contract contained a term that the tanker and reef existed. The plaintiffs were not given damages based on the value of the ship and its contents, for this was considered too speculative. Rather they were given damages in respect of the price paid for the tanker and for what it had cost to send out a salvage expedition to look for the tanker. Such damages can be viewed as protecting the plaintiffs' reliance rather than their expectation interest.

A similar English authority is *Anglia Television Ltd v Reed.*[20] Here the plaintiffs, with the intention of mounting the film production of a play, sought to engage the defendant for the main part. For the purposes of the production they incurred expenditures to the extent of some £2,750, including fees for a director, designer, stage manager and supporting artists. The contract between the plaintiffs and the defendant was made but a few days later he repudiated. In an action for breach of contract, the plaintiffs did not claim profits that the play would have made since they conceded that these could not be ascertained. They sought instead to recover the £2,750 expenditure in organising the production. The Court of Appeal affirmed the lower court's judgment awarding the full £2,750. This can again be viewed as the award of the reliance loss to plaintiffs who could not prove their expectation loss.

18 See supra, pp 31–6.
19 (1950) 84 CLR 377.
20 [1972] 1 QB 60. See also *Nurse v Barns* (1664) T Raym 77.

(3) Can the plaintiff claim protection of his reliance interest even when protection of his expectation interest is not barred?

Dicta of the majority in *Cullinane v British Rema Manufacturing Co Ltd*[1] and of the Court of Appeal in *Anglia Television Ltd v Reed* supported the view that the plaintiff is always free to claim protection of his reliance interest. As Lord Denning said in the latter case, '. . . the plaintiff . . . has an election; he can either claim for loss of profits or for his wasted expenditure'.[2] The decision in *Lloyd v Stanbury*[3] could also be regarded as supporting this although it concerned a contract for the sale of land and such contracts could, arguably, be regarded as special particularly given the *Bain v Fothergill* rule. But the answer to this question has now been put beyond doubt by Hutchison J's comments in *CCC Films (London) Ltd v Impact Quadrant Films Ltd*.[4] The defendants had there granted a licence to the plaintiffs to exploit three films and the plaintiffs had paid the agreed consideration of $12,000 for that licence. By the contract the defendants were to send to the plaintiffs video tapes of the films and were to insure them. In breach of contract the defendants sent the video tapes by ordinary post and uninsured and they were lost. The defendants were also in breach of contract in failing to deliver replacement tapes. The plaintiffs could not prove any loss of profits and instead claimed damages in respect of the expenses of $12,000. Hutchison J held that they could recover those damages. Moreover he squarely addressed the question of whether the plaintiff's choice to claim reliance expenses is unfettered and said:

. . . the plaintiff has an unfettered choice; it is not only where he establishes by evidence that he cannot prove loss of profit or that such loss of profit as he can prove is small that he is permitted to frame his claim as one for wasted expenditure . . . I consider that those cases [*Cullinane v British Rema Manufacturing Co Ltd* and *Anglia Television Ltd v Reed*] are authority for the proposition that a plaintiff may always frame his claim in the alternative way if he chooses.[5]

But the crucial question that then arises is whether this means that the courts will allow a plaintiff to escape from what is clearly a bad bargain by recovering damages protecting his reliance interest. The

1 [1954] 1 QB 292.
2 [1972] 1 QB 60 at 63–4. Clearly the profits referred to were gross and not net.
3 [1971] 1 WLR 535.
4 [1984] 3 All ER 298.
5 Ibid at 306.

answer, as laid down in *C & P Haulage v Middleton*[6] and *CCC Films (London) v Impact Quadrant Films Ltd*, is that they will not. In the former case, the respondents had granted a contractual licence to the appellant to use their yard for his car-repair business. With ten weeks remaining of a second six-month licence the respondents, in breach of contract, terminated the licence. Proceedings were begun by the respondents but the real controversy centred on the appellant's counterclaim for reimbursement of £1,767.51 to cover labour and material used in building a wall enclosing the yard, laying on electricity and transferring a telephone. The Court of Appeal refused to award the appellant anything beyond nominal damages. If we adopt the reliance interest interpretation, the reasoning was that a court will not award damages protecting a plaintiff's reliance interest if this will knowingly put him in a better position than he would have been in if the contract had been performed. To have awarded the appellant the damages he claimed would have contravened this because the respondents could have lawfully terminated the licence at the end of the next ten weeks and presumably the appellant could not during that period of time, nor indeed during a full six months, have recouped in profits his expenditure on the yard: but, in any case, as the local authority had permitted him to work from home the appellant had been able fully to mitigate his loss of profits during those ten weeks. Indeed his profits would be higher working at home since he was spared paying for the use of the yard.

In deciding that a plaintiff cannot escape from a known bad bargain by claiming protection of his reliance interest, the Court of Appeal took the same view as that prevailing in the United States and Canada. Indeed Ackner LJ, giving the principal judgment, relied heavily on the decision of the British Columbia Supreme Court in *Bowlay Logging Ltd v Dolmar Ltd*[7] which in turn had cited with approval *L Albert & Son v Armstrong Rubber Co*[8] the classic United States authority on this point. In the former, Berger J admirably summarised the underlying rationale of these cases in the following passage:

Where it can be seen that the plaintiff would have incurred a loss on the contract as a whole, the expenses he incurred are losses flowing from entering into the contract, not losses flowing from the defendant's breach . . . The principle contended for . . . would entail the award of damages not to compensate the plaintiff but to punish the defendant.[9]

6 [1983] 3 All ER 94.
7 (1978) 4 WWR 105.
8 178 F 2d 182 (1949).
9 (1978) 4 WWR 105 at 117.

C & P Haulage v Middleton was applied in *CCC Films*, where Hutchison J went on to stress, relying on the same Canadian and US authorities, that where the plaintiff claims reliance damages, the burden of proving that he has made a bad bargain, that is that he would not have recouped his expenses if the contract had been performed, is on the defendant.

The upshot of all this is that where the defendant (D) cannot prove that the plaintiff (P) has made a bad bargain and P's reliance loss exceeds the expectation loss that P can prove, it will be to P's advantage to claim reliance damages. But where D can prove that P has made a bad bargain P's 'free choice' to claim protection of the reliance interest is of no advantage to P because he will be confined to his lower expectation damages.

Ultimately, then, the reliance interest bows to the expectation interest. This is only right since it is the breaking of the promise, disappointing the plaintiff's expectations, that renders the defendant's conduct wrongful.[10] As such, damages for tortious misrepresentation provide an interesting contrast.[11] The very objection to misrepresentation is that the defendant ought not to have induced the plaintiff to rely on an untrue statement. If in reliance on the misrepresentation the plaintiff has, for example, entered into what is a bad bargain, he can and ought to be able to escape from it by recouping all his losses because if the defendant had not wrongfully made the representation the plaintiff would not have entered into the contract. In other words, unlike a contract-breaker who acts wrongfully when he breaks his contractual promise and not when he induces the plaintiff to enter into the contract, the misrepresentor commits a wrong when he induces the plaintiff by his statement to act to his detriment by, for example, entering into a losing contract.

In the important but difficult case of *Commonwealth of Australia v Amann Aviation Pty Ltd*[12] the primary question in issue was the standard of proof faced by a defendant who seeks to discharge the burden of showing that the plaintiff has made a bad bargain (ie that the plaintiff would not have recouped his reliance loss).

The plaintiff had won a contract to conduct aerial coastal surveillance for the defendant. It committed large sums of money in acquiring the necessary specially-equipped aircraft. Several months after the contract commenced, and at a time when the plaintiff was itself in breach by having insufficient aircraft available, the

10 See supra, p 20.
11 See supra, pp 171–8.
12 (1991) 66 ALJR 123; Treitel (1992) LQR 226.

defendant committed a repudiatory breach by serving an invalid termination notice. That breach entitled the plaintiff to terminate the contract and sue for damages, which it did. The majority (Mason CJ, Dawson J, Brennan J, Gaudron J) held that it was entitled to full reliance damages of some $5.5 million (plus interest). Although the defendant had shown that there was a 20% chance that the defendant would otherwise have validly terminated the contract for the plaintiff's own breach, in which event the plaintiff's reliance losses would not have been recouped, the majority felt that no discount should be made for that chance because it was unlikely. A balance of probabilities, all or nothing, standard of proof therefore seems to have been applied. In contrast, the three minority judges thought that a discount should be made. Intriguingly each of them adopted different reasoning and conclusions. Deane J thought the appropriate discount from full reliance damages should be the 20% chance that the defendant would have validly terminated. Toohey J considered that, taking account of all the contingencies in the case, the discount should be 50%. On the other hand, McHugh J thought that reliance damages were inappropriate and that instead normal expectation damages, reduced by the 20% chance, should be awarded.

It is submitted that, while the majority was correct to award reliance damages, Deane J's preference for a 'proportionate chances' approach to the defendant's standard of proof is to be supported. This is because the uncertainty in issue related to hypothetical events and not past facts.[13] As Deane J said:

In circumstances where damages are being assessed on the basis of what would have happened in a hypothetical situation and where it is a matter of speculation whether the Secretary would, in the exercise of the wide discretionary power entrusted to him, have actually cancelled the contract . . ., it would be inappropriate and unjust to go beyond the determination that what Amann lost was an 80% chance and, by reference to a balance of probability test, require the Commonwealth to pay damages assessed on the basis that there had been no possibility of cancellation and that Amann had lost not an 80% but a 100% chance of recoupment.[14]

(4) An alternative interpretation?

As the courts will not knowingly award reliance damages which put the plaintiff into a better position than if the contract had been performed, it is possible to interpret the cases, which have so far been

13 Supra, pp 31–5.
14 (1991) 66 ALJR 123, 151.

interpreted as protecting the plaintiff's reliance interest, as in fact
protecting the plaintiff's expectation interest, albeit in a different way
than the expectation interest is normally protected; that is, one can
say that the law accepts an alternative way of putting the plaintiff
into as good a position as if the contract had been performed,
because it allows the plaintiff the benefit of a presumption, rebuttable by the defendant, that he has not made a bad bargain. Hence
where the plaintiff can prove his reliance expenses, this rebuttable
presumption enables him to recover that amount on the ground
that if the contract had been performed he would at the very least
have made gains to cover those expenses. This was the interpretation strongly favoured by at least five judges of the High Court of
Australia in *Commonwealth of Australia v Amann Aviation Pty Ltd.*

It is submitted, however, that it is preferable to stick to the
reliance interest approach adopted so far. This is for two main reasons. First, it seems an easier way to present and understand the
question of whether this alternative method of measuring damages
should be preferred to that traditionally adopted, which has been at
the centre of so much academic controversy.[15] Secondly, the
reliance interest approach accords with there being a particularly
strong case for legal intervention, resting on underlying 'tort'
notions of corrective justice, when the plaintiff has been left not only
less well off than if the contract had been performed, but also worse
off than if no contract had been made. In contrast, taking the expectation interest approach, there is no obvious explanation for why the
law should allow the plaintiff the benefit of a rebuttable presumption that he would have recouped his expenses.

(5) Pre-contractual expenses

Where a plaintiff can recover reliance damages, can he recover for
expenses incurred before the contract with the defendant was made?
In *Lloyd v Stanbury* pre-contractual expenditure was indeed recovered, and Brightman J said that this should be so, so long as the
costs were of '. . . performing an act required to be done by the contract.'[16] Given doubts about whether contracts for the sale of land
are exceptional, however, the clearest authority is *Anglia Television
Ltd v Reed*. Here many of the expenses recovered were pre-
contractual. Lord Denning, with whom the other two judges
agreed, said:

15 See supra, pp 17–21.
16 [1971] 1 WLR 535 at 546.

If the plaintiff claims the wasted expenditure, he is not limited to the expenditure incurred after the contract was concluded. He can claim also the expenditure incurred before the contract, provided it was such as would reasonably be in the contemplation of the parties as likely to be wasted if the contract was broken. Applying that principle here, it is plain that, when Mr Reed entered into this contract, he must have known perfectly well that much expenditure had already been incurred on directors' fees and the like. He must have contemplated—or at any rate, it is reasonably to be imputed to him—that if he broke his contract, all that expenditure would be wasted, whether or not it was incurred before or after the contract. He must pay damages for all the expenditure so wasted and thrown away.[17]

But this is a most controversial approach for, taking the reliance interest interpretation, pre-contractual expenses would in any event have been wasted if no contract had been made with the defendant. Moreover a denial of such damages accords with sensible policy; if the plaintiff cannot (or is choosing not to) show that those expenses would have been recouped if the contract had been performed, there seems no justice in holding the defendant liable given that he in no sense induced the plaintiff to incur them. As alternatively expressed, the causal connection for corrective justice is missing, and the plaintiff freely undertook the risk that the expenses would be wasted. Significantly in the United States pre-contractual expenses have been held irrecoverable.[18]

However, rigid adherence to the recovery only of post-contractual expenses may go too far, in that the defendant may induce the plaintiff to incur expenses even though no formal contract has yet been concluded. Ogus should therefore be supported when he writes:

Perhaps the best solution would be for the reliance interest award to comprise those expenses incurred as from the time when there was substantial agreement between the parties.[19]

In contrast, if one rejects the reliance interest interpretation in favour of there being a rebuttable presumption that the plaintiff would at least have recouped his expenses if the contract had been performed, pre-contractual expenses would be recoverable. A plaintiff could not be said to have broken even, if he recouped only post-contractual expenses.[20]

17 [1972] 1 QB 60 at 64.
18 Eg *Chicago Coliseum Club v Dempsey* 256 Ill App 542 (1932).
19 *Damages* p 350.
20 *Commonwealth of Australia v Amann Aviation Pty Ltd* (1991) 66 ALJR 123, 161 (per Gaudron J); Waddams *The Law of Damages* paras 5.200–5.250; Owen (1984) OJLS 393, 396–9; McLauchlan (1984 5) 11 NZULR 346.

(6) Reliance losses other than expenses, and general principles of assessment

Although expenses are the primary form of reliance loss, the reliance interest theoretically embraces all other types of loss, whether pecuniary or non-pecuniary; for so long as the loss would not have been suffered if no contract with the defendant had been made, it is a reliance loss. For example in *Lloyd v Stanbury*, in addition to recovering his expenses, the plaintiff was given damages for his lost earnings during the time he had been preparing for or involved in moving home.

Presumably most of the general principles governing the assessment of normal compensatory damages examined in chapter 2 also apply to reliance damages, albeit that the focus is on a different compensatory aim. Although authorities are scarce, an example is provided by *Anglia Television v Reed* where Lord Denning's stress on the defendant's reasonable contemplation of the expenses being wasted shows that remoteness is relevant to reliance as well as to expectation loss.[1]

3. AWARDS OF INTEREST

(1) Introduction

When damages have been awarded then as a 'judgment debt' they automatically carry interest until paid under the Judgments Act 1838.[2] But what we are here concerned with is whether the court will award interest on damages (that is, whether at judgment a sum of interest will be ordered to be paid forthwith along with the damages) and if so, how much interest will be awarded.[3]

Prior to 1934 the courts had no power to award interest on damages, but this has subsequently been altered by statute, the law now being contained in s 35A of the Supreme Court Act 1981.[4] By

---

1 But Lord Denning's judgment in *Parsons (Livestock) Ltd v Uttley Ingham & Co Ltd* [1978] QB 791 indicates that on reflection he would apply the *Wagon Mound* rather than the *Heron II* test to reliance expenses.
2 Where, eg there is a split trial, the judgment debt rate of interest runs from the damages judgment and not from the liability judgment: *Thomas v Bunn* [1991] 1 AC 362.
3 Interest (and its rate and period) may be provided for by a contract term, but it is being assumed here that there is no such term.
4 Inserted by the Administration of Justice Act 1982, Sch 1. Analogous provisions are contained in the County Courts Act 1984, s 69. Generally speaking, the same principles apply to interest on an agreed sum; but see supra, p 98.

s 35A(1), the High Court has discretion to award interest on damages; and by s 35A(2) the High Court must award interest on damages for personal injuries or death (exceeding £200) unless satisfied that there are 'special reasons' why it should not do so.[5]

(2) Why should interest be awarded?

The answer to this is typified by Robert Goff J's statement in *BP Exploration Co (Libya) Ltd v Hunt (No 2)*:[6] 'The fundamental principle is that interest is not awarded as punishment but simply because the plaintiff has been deprived of the use of the money which was due to him.' The money due to the plaintiff comprises either the money that the plaintiff would have had but for the defendant's wrong, or, where the wrongful loss was not of money, the damages themselves which it is felt the defendant should have paid to compensate the loss as soon as it occurred. In commercial cases it is then generally assumed that as a result of being deprived of that money the plaintiff has had to borrow it, whereas in non-commercial cases the assumption is simply that the plaintiff has lost the interest from investing that money.[7]

(3) When do the courts award interest?

As regards personal injury and death, the statute leaves no discretion—interest must be awarded subject to special reasons. But in *Jefford v Gee*[8] and *Cookson v Knowles*[9] it has been held that the different types of loss must be itemised, since no interest is payable on damages for future pecuniary loss for the reason that that loss has not yet been suffered and hence the plaintiff has not been deprived of the use of money due to him.

Outside the realm of personal injury and death, the courts are generally willing to exercise their discretion to award interest on

---

5 But s 35A gives no power to award compound as opposed to simple interest; see Mann (1985) 101 LQR 30, 42–6; Bowles and Whelan (1986) 64 CBR 142.
6 [1982] 1 All ER 925 at 974. See also *Jefford v Gee* [1970] 2 QB 130 at 146; *General Tire and Rubber Co v Firestone Tyre and Rubber Co Ltd* [1975] 2 All ER 173 at 192; *Tate & Lyle Food and Distribution Ltd v Greater London Council* [1981] 3 All ER 716 at 722; *Wentworth v Wiltshire County Council* [1993] 2 All ER 256, 269.
7 For this distinction see especially the *Tate & Lyle* case, ibid at 722–723.
8 [1970] 2 QB 130.
9 [1979] AC 556.

258   *Compensatory damages III: miscellaneous issues*

damages for pecuniary loss:[10] but interest on damages for non-pecuniary loss is denied. So in an action for deceit in *Saunders v Edwards*[11] the Court of Appeal refused to award interest (even at the low 2% rate used in personal injury cases)[12] on damages for inconvenience and disappointment. This denial was thought to be correct in principle because in Bingham LJ's words, 'the damages [cannot] be realistically seen as having accrued due to the plaintiff at a certain time in the past and as having thereafter been wrongly withheld from him.'[13] It was also pointed out that no interest has traditionally been awarded on damages for non-pecuniary loss in defamation cases. The inconsistency with the approach to non-pecuniary loss in personal injury cases was put to one side as a product of the statutory requirement of awarding interest in such cases.

(4) For what period is interest payable?

Under the statute, the courts have the discretion to choose the period for which interest is payable, although the maximum is between the date when the cause of action arose and the date of judgment (or the date of payment in respect of a sum paid before judgment). The date *to which* interest is payable causes little difficulty and is almost always fixed as the date of judgment or trial. More interesting is the date *from which* interest is payable. This was carefully examined by Robert Goff J in *BP Exploration v Hunt (No 2)*, albeit in the context of an award under the Law Reform (Frustrated Contracts) Act 1943 rather than an award of damages. His conclusion was that the general rule is that interest runs from the date of loss, but that there are three main exceptions to this. The first is where it would be unfair on the defendant to make him pay interest from the date of loss: for example: '. . . if the defendant neither knew, nor reasonably could have been expected to know, that the plaintiff was likely to make a claim, and so was in no position to tender payment, or even to make provision for

---

10 In *Edmunds v Lloyd Italico e L'Ancora Cia di Assicurazioni e Riassicurazioni SpA* [1986] 2 All ER 249, interest was awarded even where the damages claimable for breach of an insurance contract had been paid in full before proceedings. And in *Metal Box Ltd v Currys Ltd* [1988] 1 All ER 341 interest was awarded on damages for loss of goods that were not income-producing.
11 [1987] 1 WLR 1116. See also *Holtham v Metropolitan Police Comr* (1987) Times, 28 November.
12 Infra, pp 260–1.
13 [1987] 1 WLR 1116, 1135.

payment if the money should be found due.'[14] The second is where the plaintiff's conduct is such that he should not have interest awarded from the date of loss: for example, where he has unreasonably delayed in pursuing his claim. Finally interest will not be awarded from the date of loss where it would otherwise be unjust in all the circumstances of the case to do so. The most obvious example of this is that, as laid down in *Jefford v Gee*,[15] interest on damages for non-pecuniary loss in a personal injury action is payable from the date of the service of the writ until trial, the reasoning being that, as the loss is spread over a long period of time, it is more just to award interest from when the damages were first formally demanded.

It should further be noted that interest on damages for pre-trial pecuniary loss in personal injury and Fatal Accident Act cases is normally payable from the date of the accident or death until trial, as laid down in *Jefford v Gee* and *Cookson v Knowles*[16] respectively. But this is not an exception to the date of loss rule. Rather it represents half of a formula, considered more fully below, designed as a rough substitute for detailed calculations of the interest on each pecuniary loss from the date it was suffered.

(5) What is the rate of interest?

In commercial cases, where the focus is generally on the plaintiff having to borrow replacement money, the courts usually take the average clearing bank base rate plus 1%, this being the borrowing rate for big companies.[17] Smaller less prestigious companies may be awarded more, corresponding to the higher borrowing rate charged to them.[18]

In personal injury and death cases (and commercial cases where it is unrealistic to think that the plaintiff has had to borrow) the focus is on the lost interest from investment. So for personal injury

---

14 [1982] 1 All ER 925 at 975. See also *Allied London Investments Ltd v Hambro Life Assurance Ltd* [1985] 1 EGLR 45.
15 [1970] 2 QB 130.
16 [1979] AC 556.
17 *BP Exploration v Hunt (No 2)* [1982] 1 All ER 925; *Tate & Lyle Food and Distribution Ltd v Greater London Council* [1981] 3 All ER 716; *International Military Services Ltd v Capital & Counties plc* [1982] 1 WLR 575; *Polish SS Co v Atlantic Maritime Co* [1985] QB 41; *Metal Box Ltd v Currys Ltd* [1988] 1 All ER 341; *Shearson Lehman Hutton Inc v Maclaine Watson & Co Ltd (No 2)* [1990] 3 All ER 723.
18 *Catnic Components Ltd v Hill & Smith Ltd* [1983] FSR 512.

non-pecuniary loss[19] interest is payable at a fixed rate of 2%, as is examined further below. For pre-trial pecuniary loss, interest on the whole amount of loss is normally payable from the date of the accident or death until trial at half the average rate on the special investment account over that period.[20] This represents a rough substitute for awarding interest on each pecuniary loss for the period from when it was suffered until trial at the full average rate (on the special investment account) over that period. As recognised in *Dexter v Courtaulds Ltd*,[1] it may be more appropriate in exceptional cases, for example where all the loss has been incurred years before trial, to award interest on the whole amount of loss for a period from half-way through the time when the loss was suffered until trial at the full average rate (on the special investment account) over that period. But, as stressed, it would be for the plaintiff to plead and prove that such an alternative method of calculation is more appropriate than the normal method.

(6) The relationship between the date for assessment of damages and interest

(a) Liabilities other than foreign currency liabilities

Traditionally the date for assessing damages, ie the date at which the value of money, goods or services is assessed, is the date of loss. But in recent cases, particularly in response to inflation, the courts have assessed damages at a later date.[2] What effect does this have on the award of interest?

The main judicial discussion of this has been in relation to non-pecuniary loss in personal injury actions. One view is that since interest rates contain a large inflationary element (an element to preserve the real value of money) it would overcompensate the plaintiff to award him both damages assessed according to the internal value of sterling at the date of judgment plus full interest on those damages from the date of service of the writ. Put another way, in times of high inflation an investor cannot generally expect to do much more than maintain the real value of his money; an award of interest designed to compensate for the plaintiff being kept out of money to which he is entitled should therefore not be given if damages are already based on the real value of money. This lay behind

---

19 For interest on bereavement damages, see supra, p 217, fn 19.
20 *Jefford v Gee* [1970] 2 QB 130; *Cookson v Knowles* [1979] AC 556.
1 [1984] 1 All ER 70.
2 See supra, pp 107–14.

the decision of the Court of Appeal in *Cookson v Knowles:*[3] since damages for non-pecuniary loss, in contrast to, for example, damages for pre-trial loss of earnings, are now based on the value of money at the time of judgment, it was held that no interest should be awarded on them. But in *Pickett v British Rail Engineering Ltd*[4] the House of Lords overruled this and considered that a clear distinction could be drawn between maintaining the real value of money, to which interest was thought to be irrelevant, and being kept out of money, which was the reason for an award of interest. Lord Wilberforce said:

Increase for inflation is designed to preserve the 'real' value of money, interest to compensate for being kept out of that 'real' value. The one has no relation to the other. If the damages claimed remained nominally the same . . . because there was no inflation, interest would normally be given. The same should follow if damages remain in real terms the same.[5]

In *Birkett v Hayes,*[6] while he accepted that *Pickett* meant that some interest must be awarded on the non-pecuniary losses, Lord Denning considered in the spirit of his approach in *Cookson v Knowles* that a low rate of interest of 2% was appropriate and this was agreed with by the two other judges. Eveleigh LJ said that, where interest rates have a large inflationary element:

. . . it cannot be right to apply such interest rates to an award which already takes into account the need for preserving the value of money. We must look for some other rate of interest.[7]

This low 2% rate of interest was confirmed as correct by the House of Lords in *Wright v British Railways Board.*[8]

There has been little other discussion of the effects on interest of assessing damages at a date later than the date of loss.[9] But the clear message from the above cases is that wherever damages are assessed at a date later than the date of loss, the courts must be careful not to award interest at a rate which will overcompensate the plaintiff.

(b) Foreign currency liabilities

Under the former sterling-breach-date rule, interest was awarded on an agreed sum of damages at sterling rates. But what effect has the

3 [1977] QB 913, CA.
4 [1980] AC 136.
5 Ibid at 151.
6 [1982] 2 All ER 710.
7 Ibid at 715.
8 [1983] 2 AC 773.
9 But see dictum in *Perry v Sidney Phillips & Son* [1982] 3 All ER 705 at 708.

reversal of that rule in *Miliangos v George Frank (Textiles) Ltd*[10] had on the award of interest?

In *Shell Tankers (UK) Ltd v Astro Comino Armadora SA, The Pacific Colocotronis*[11] the Court of Appeal held that, where *Miliangos* applies and judgment is expressed in a foreign currency, interest should be awarded, prima facie, at the rate applicable to that currency. Judgment had there been expressed in US dollars and the rate of interest applied was therefore the dollar rather than the sterling rate. This approach should be supported as effecting true compensation; for example if sterling has declined in value, then since interest rates generally increase in response to a decline in the value of currency, it would usually overcompensate the plaintiff to express judgment in foreign currency (with a conversion into sterling at the date of payment) and then to award interest at the sterling rate.

4. LIMITATION PERIODS

It has been said to be '. . . trite law that the English Limitation Acts bar the remedy and not the right'.[12] It therefore seems appropriate to include a brief outline of limitation periods in a book on remedies.[13] For damages the periods are mainly laid down in the Limitation Act 1980.

It should be stressed at the outset that the periods are to some extent arbitrary and cannot be precisely rationalised, for it is the certainty of having a cut-off point at some time that is of primary importance rather than whether the actual period of years happens to be three or six or even longer.

(1) The normal time limits

By s 5 of the 1980 Act, 'An action founded on simple contract shall not be brought after the expiration of six years from the date on which the cause of action accrued.' By s 8(1), 'An action upon

---

10 [1976] AC 443. Supra, pp 114–9.
11 [1981] 2 Lloyds Rep 40 at 45, 77. See also *Miliangos v George Frank (No 2)* [1976] 2 Lloyds Rep 434.
12 *Ronex Properties Ltd v John Laing Construction Ltd* [1982] 3 WLR 875 at 879 (per Donaldson LJ). But this is not always the case: see, eg s 11A (3) of the Limitation Act 1980.
13 For a detailed account see, eg McGee *Limitation of Actions*.

a specialty shall not be brought after the expiration of twelve years from the date on which the cause of action accrued.' The reason for this difference is not obvious but perhaps it relates to a contract by deed being easy to prove. The date of the cause of action accruing for breach of contract, and hence the date from which the six or twelve years run, is the date of the breach of contract.[14]

By s 2 of the 1980 Act, 'An action founded on tort shall not be brought after the expiration of six years from the date on which the cause of action accrued.' The date of the cause of action accruing for torts, and hence the date from which the six years run, is the date of the tort.[15]

In the past the major difficulty regarding limitation concerned latent damage, whether latent personal injury or, more recently, latent economic loss, caused by torts, like negligence, actionable only on proof of damage. But now that special regimes apply to damages for personal injury and death and for negligent latent damage (other than personal injury) there is little controversy left regarding the normal limitation periods.

However one remaining issue of interest stems from the expansion of the tort of negligence to cover pure economic loss (in certain situations) combined with the acceptance of concurrent liability between tortious negligence and breach of contract: for these developments mean that, for example, where a professional person has negligently performed services beneficial to his plaintiff client causing pure economic loss, the latter is now generally given a longer period in which to sue for the tort of negligence (time running from the date of damage) rather than for breach of contract (time running from the date of breach).[16] It is debatable whether there should be this difference: if this expansion of negligence is based on recognising a negligent breach of promise as a tort,[17] it would perhaps be preferable to hold that, as for breach of contract, so for such a negligence action, time runs from the date of the breach of duty.[18]

---

14 The same periods apply to an action for an agreed sum—infra, chapter 7.
15 Where there is more than one conversion of the same chattel time runs from the date of the original conversion: s 3(1), Limitation Act 1980. For patent infringement the action can accrue before proceedings can be instituted; *Sevcon Ltd v Lucas CAV Ltd* [1986] 2 All ER 104.
16 See, eg *Midland Bank Trust Co Ltd v Hett, Stubbs & Kemp* [1979] Ch 384.
17 Supra, pp 5–7.
18 For the opposite solution (that the contractual action should run from the date of the damage) see Cooke *Essays on Contract* (ed Finn, 1987) ch 8.

(2) The main exceptions to the normal time limits[19]

(a) Damages for personal injury and death[20]

The law on limitation periods for damages for personal injury and death is now contained in ss 11–14 of the 1980 Act, which contains the basic time limits, and s 33 of that Act, which gives the courts a discretion to overrule the basic time limits. One exception, as controversially laid down by the House of Lords in *Stubbings v Webb*,[1] is that a personal injury claim, based on trespass to the person as the cause of action, falls outside s 11 and within the normal six year period of s 2.

(i) Basic time limits for personal injury—s 11

Where the action is brought by the injured person the limitation period, as laid down in s 11(4), is three years from either the date on which the cause of action accrued or, if later, the date of knowledge of the person injured.

By s 14(1) the date of knowledge means the date on which the person first had knowledge (including constructive knowledge as dealt with by s 14(3)) of all the following facts: that the injury was significant (as defined in s 11(2)); that the injury was attributable in whole or in part to the act or omission which is alleged to constitute negligence, nuisance or breach of duty; the identity of the defendant; and if it is alleged that the act or omission was that of a person other than the defendant, the identity of that person and the additional facts supporting the bringing of an action against the defendant.

Where the estate is bringing the action under the Law Reform (Miscellaneous Provisions) Act 1934 the limitation period laid down in s 11(5) is three years from the date of death or the date of the personal representative's knowledge, whichever is the later. Section 14(1) again applies to define the date of knowledge. It should also be remembered that a precondition of a claim by the

---

19 Special provisions of the Limitation Act 1980 deal with the defendant's fraud (s 32) and the plaintiff's disability (s 28). See also s 4A, introduced by the Administration of Justice Act 1985, s 57 (2), reducing the basic period for defamation actions to three years; and s 11A which, inter alia, imposes a three-year basic period and a ten-year long-stop for actions under Pt I of the Consumer Protection Act 1987. Other special limitation periods for damages claims are laid down in, eg the Maritime Conventions Act 1911, s 8 and the Carriage by Air Act 1961, Sch 1, Art 29.
20 See generally Davies (1982) 98 LQR 249.
1 [1993] AC 498. See Rogers (1993) NLJ 258; McGee (1993) 109 LQR 356.

estate is that there is a valid personal injury action surviving. Hence no action can be brought if the deceased was himself time-barred.

(ii) Basic time limits for death—s 12

By s 12(2) the limitation period for a claim under the Fatal Accidents Act 1976 is three years from either the date of death or the date of knowledge of the person for whose benefit the action is brought, whichever is the later. The date of knowledge is again defined by s 14(1).

By s 1(1) of the Fatal Accidents Act 1976, an action can only succeed if the deceased would himself have been entitled to damages. Hence, if the deceased's action was time-barred, no Fatal Accidents Act claim lies, and this is reiterated in s 12(1) of the Limitation Act 1980.

(iii) The discretion to overrule the basic time limits for personal injury and death—s 33

In a novel development, s 33(1) gives a court the discretion to overrule the basic time limits under ss 11 and 12 if equitable to do so having regard to the prejudice to the plaintiff of sticking to the limits and the prejudice to the defendant of extending them. In exercising this discretion the courts, by s 33(3), are to have particular regard to certain factors, such as the length of and reason for delay by the plaintiff, the extent to which the cogency of evidence will be impaired, and the defendant's conduct after the cause of action arose.

The discretion is also applicable vis-à-vis a deceased's action (with, by s 33(5), references to the plaintiff in s 33(3) being replaced by references to the deceased) so that a claim under the Law Reform Act 1934 or the Fatal Accidents Act 1976 can succeed even though the basic time limits would have barred the deceased's action.

There have been several legal decisions dealing with the s 33 discretion.[2] Perhaps the most important are those dealing with the question of whether that discretion is unfettered. In *Firman v Ellis*[3] the Court of Appeal thought that it was, but in no less than three cases[4] the House of Lords has accepted that there is one restriction in that, other than in exceptional circumstances, there is no

---

2 A good example is *Brooks v J & P Coates Ltd* [1984] 1 All ER 702.
3 [1978] QB 886.
4 *Walkley v Precision Forgings Ltd* [1979] 1 WLR 606; *Thompson v Brown* [1981] 1 WLR 744; *Deerness v Keeble & Son Ltd* [1983] 2 Lloyds Rep 260.

discretion under s 33 to allow an action to proceed where an earlier action had been commenced within the basic time limits but had been discontinued by the plaintiff's choice or by failing to serve the writ on time or had been struck out for want of prosecution because of the plaintiff's delay. The reasoning put forward for this is that it is not the time limits under ss 11 and 12 which have prejudiced the plaintiff but rather the plaintiff's own conduct. But this is unconvincing, since the plaintiff's conduct is only prejudicial given the time limits. Moreover, it seems rather anomalous that delay subsequent to issuing the writ does not allow the courts to exercise their discretion under s 33, whereas delay prior to issuing the writ does. Lord Diplock purported to explain this in *Thompson v Brown* when he said:

It may seem anomalous that a defendant should be better off where, unknown to him, a writ has been issued but not served, than he would be if the writ had not been issued at all; but this is a consequence of the greater anomaly, too well established for this House to abolish that, for the purposes of a limitation period, an action is brought when a writ . . . is issued . . . and not when it is brought to the knowledge of the defendant by service on him.[5]

But this is hardly a justification and it is submitted that it would be preferable to regard the s 33 discretion as totally unfettered.

(b) Damages for latent damage (other than personal injury) in the tort of negligence

By definition latent damage occurs, and hence for the tort of negligence the cause of action begins to run, at a time when the plaintiff has no reasonable opportunity of knowing of the damage. Indeed the normal time period may have run out before the plaintiff ever had a reasonable opportunity to discover the damage. While for latent personal injury this problem was solved by the provisions examined above, the expansion of the tort of negligence in the 1970s led to a revival of concern over latent damage this time particularly (although not exclusively)[6] in relation to negligently constructed or designed buildings.

In *Sparham-Souter v Town and Country Developments*[7] the Court

---

5 [1981] 1 WLR 744 at 752–3.
6 The problem has also arisen in claims against, eg negligent solicitors or surveyors: eg *Forster v Outred & Co* [1982] 1 WLR 86; *D W Moore & Co Ltd v Ferrier* [1988] 1 WLR 267; *Lee v Thompson* [1989] 2 EGLR 151; *Bell v Peter Browne & Co* [1990] 3 All ER 124.
7 [1976] QB 858.

of Appeal, in seeking to do justice to plaintiffs, held that the cause of action accrued, and hence time began to run, only when the plaintiff discovered or ought to have discovered the damage (or possibly the defect). But this decision was overruled by the House of Lords in *Pirelli General Cable Works Ltd v Oscar Faber and Partners*,[8] which said that, by analogy to the common law rule for personal injury, time begins to run only from when damage to the building occurs, whether reasonably discoverable or not. However, the House of Lords recognised the injustice that such an approach can cause to plaintiffs and called for legislative reform.

The overruling of *Anns v Merton London BC*[9] in *Murphy v Brentwood DC*[10] has cast doubt on whether there is any liability in the tort of negligence for defective buildings, other than for negligent misstatements under *Hedley Byrne & Co Ltd v Heller & Partners Ltd*.[11] Mysteriously the Lords in *Murphy* approved *Pirelli* as falling within the *Hedley Byrne* principle.[12] What can be said with certainty is that, irrespective of whether the cause of action recognised in *Pirelli* survives, *Pirelli* remains valid in so far as it laid down that a cause of action in negligence accrues at the date of the damage and not the date of discoverability.

The calls in *Pirelli* for legislative reform were soon answered. Following the proposals of the Law Reform Committee[13] the Latent Damage Act 1986 was enacted amending the Limitation Act 1980 in respect of negligently caused latent damage (other than personal injury).[14] By s 14A(4)(a) of the 1980 Act the normal six year limit running from the date of the cause of action (ie the *Pirelli* approach) remains but is now subject to two crucial qualifications: first, by s 14A(4)(b) and (5) a plaintiff can bring an action within three years from the date when he first had the knowledge required for bringing an action, including constructive knowledge (as dealt with by s 14A(10)); and secondly, by s 14B there is an absolute

---

8 [1983] 1 All ER 65.
9 [1978] AC 728.
10 [1991] 1 AC 398.
11 [1964] AC 465.
12 For an excellent discussion of this and other related problems thrown up by *Murphy*, see McKendrick (1991) 11 Legal Studies 326. See also *Nitrigin Eireann Teoranta v Inco Alloys Ltd* [1992] 1 All ER 854; *Lancashire and Cheshire Association of Baptist Churches Inc v Howard & Seddon Partnership* [1993] 3 All ER 467.
13 24th Report Latent Damage Cmnd 9390.
14 Negligence here means the tort of negligence and not breach of a contractual duty of care: *Iron Trade Mutual Insurance Co Ltd v J K Buckenham Ltd* [1990] 1 All ER 808; *Société Commerciale de Réassurance v ERAS (International) Ltd* [1992] 2 All ER 82n.

long-stop bar to actions fifteen years from the date of the (alleged) negligent act or omission causing the relevant damage.

These provisions appear to achieve a measure of fairness for both plaintiffs and defendants: by the fifteen year long-stop defendants are protected against actions being brought scores of years after their negligence, such actions being not only hard to defend but rendering insurance difficult and expensive; and on the other hand, in most situations, the discoverability qualification will allow a plaintiff to get to know of and hence to bring an action for the damage before the fifteen year absolute limit expires. Of course, if *Murphy* has largely eradicated liability in negligence for defective buildings, the scope of the Latent Damage Act 1986 has been correspondingly cut back (leaving it as merely applying to other forms of latent economic loss).

(c) Equitable damages

It would appear that the question of what is the limitation period for equitable damages has never been dealt with in the cases. By s 36(1) of the Limitation Act 1980, none of the statutory time limits applies directly to specific performance, injunctions or 'other equitable relief'. As such, the most obvious view is that whether equitable damages are time-barred or not depends in turn on whether the specific performance or injunction, in lieu of or in addition to which the damages are potentially being given, would be barred under the laches doctrine. Alternatively one might consider that, as equitable damages are so similar to common law damages, the statutory limitation periods for common law damages should apply by analogy. Indeed there is express provision in s 36(1) for the statutory limitation periods to be applied by analogy to equitable relief; but only '. . . in like manner as the corresponding time limit under any enactment repealed by the Limitation Act 1939 was applied before 1940' and this would not appear to cover equitable damages. In terms of policy it would certainly seem that if actions for common law damages are basically acceptable before but not after six years, the same should apply to equitable damages. But given that equitable damages rest on the power to award specific performance or an injunction, the former 'most obvious' view is more likely to prove acceptable.

Chapter 5

Non-compensatory damages

Damages for torts and breach of contract usually seek to compensate the plaintiff by putting him into as good a position as if no tort had been committed or as if the contract had been performed.[1] But this is not always so and some awards of damages are non-compensatory. Of these it has been thought preferable to examine restitutionary damages alongside other restitutionary remedies in chapter 6; and since liquidated 'damages', viewed as a judiciary remedy, are an example of the award of an agreed sum rather than being a sum assessed by the courts, they are examined in chapter 7. This leaves to be considered in this chapter nominal, contemptuous and, most importantly, exemplary damages.[2]

1. NOMINAL DAMAGES

Many torts are actionable only on proof of damage. But torts actionable per se, as well as breach of contract, are actionable without proof of damage. One consequence is that even though the court is satisfied that the plaintiff has not suffered any damage, he is still entitled to damages for the defendant's breach of contract or tort actionable per se. Such damages are termed nominal and they comprise a trivial sum of money, usually about £2.[3] Nominal damages are therefore in no sense compensatory and must be distinguished from a small sum of compensatory damages. Their

---

1 A less common 'compensatory aim' for breach of contract is to protect the plaintiff's reliance interest. See supra, chapter 4.
2 Of the law on compensatory damages in chapters 2–4, the form of damages and foreign currency awards examined in chapter 2 and equitable damages, interest and limitation periods examined in chapter 4 apply also to non-compensatory damages.
3 An example of nominal damages being awarded is *C and P Haulage v Middleton* [1983] 3 All ER 94 (£10); supra, p 251.

function is merely to declare that the defendant has committed a wrong against the plaintiff and hence that the plaintiff's rights have been infringed. Given that the remedy of a declaration is specifically designed to serve this purpose nominal damages are superfluous and could happily be abolished. This is particularly so since what was previously an important practical consequence of an award of nominal damages has been removed by Devlin J's decision in *Anglo-Cyprian Trade Agencies v Paphos Wine Industries Ltd*[4] that a plaintiff awarded nominal damages should not necessarily be regarded as a successful plaintiff for the purposes of costs.

2. CONTEMPTUOUS DAMAGES

Rarely awarded other than by a jury in a defamation case, these are damages of a very small amount—usually of the lowest coin of the realm (at present 1p)—whose function is to indicate that, while the defendant has committed the alleged wrong (including a tort actionable only on proof of damage) the plaintiff deserves no more than a technical acknowledgment of the infringement of his rights, because of his own conduct in the matter.[5] In other words the derisory award amounts to a declaration of the plaintiff's rights combined with an admonition of the plaintiff. As it is difficult to see how the grant of a declaration can achieve this 'double-edged sword' effect, contemptuous damages justify their continued, albeit very limited, existence.

3. EXEMPLARY DAMAGES[6]

Exemplary or punitive damages are damages whose purpose is to punish the defendant for his wrongful conduct. The fascinating and crucial question of policy is whether exemplary damages are justified, but before examining that we must look at the details of the present law.

---

4 [1951] 1 All ER 873.
5 Ogus *Damages* p 26; Waddams *Damages* para 10.40. For examples see *Kelly v Sherlock* (1866) LR 1 QB 686; *Dering v Uris* [1964] 2 QB 669. A plaintiff awarded merely contemptuous damages is even less likely to recover his costs than one awarded nominal damages—*Martin v Benson* [1927] 1 KB 771.
6 See generally Anderson (1992) CJQ 233; Law Commission's Consultation Paper No 132 (1993) 'Aggravated, Exemplary and Restitutionary Damages'.

(1) Are exemplary damages awarded for breach of contract?

As laid down in *Addis v Gramophone Co Ltd*,[7] no exemplary damages can be awarded for breach of contract. There the plaintiff had been wrongfully dismissed. The House of Lords restricted damages to his pecuniary loss and refused to award any damages for the harsh manner in which he had been treated.

The same approach has been applied in several subsequent cases. In *Perera v Vandiyar*,[8] for example, the plaintiff was the tenant of the defendant's flat and in an attempt to get rid of him, the defendant cut off the supply of gas and electricity to the flat leaving the plaintiff without alternative means of heat or light. A week later the gas and electricity supply was restored as a result of an interlocutory judgment granted by the county court, and the tenant was able to return. In an action for damages for breach of the defendant's covenant of quiet enjoyment the trial judge awarded inter alia, £25 exemplary damages, but the Court of Appeal overturned this; since damages were here being given for breach of contract (and indeed no tort had been committed) no exemplary damages could be awarded. Similarly in *Kenny v Preen*,[9] which also involved the breach by a landlord of his covenant of quiet enjoyment, exemplary damages were refused, Pearson LJ saying, 'As the claim was only in contract and not tort, punitive or exemplary damages could not be properly awarded.'[10]

On the other hand in *McMillan v Singh*,[11] where again a landlord evicted a tenant, exemplary damages of £250 were awarded. Although parts of Sir John Arnold's judgment seem to indicate that those damages were being given for breach of the covenant of quiet enjoyment, they are better viewed as being given for the tort of trespass or nuisance. This was not only because of his reliance solely on tort cases, but also because no mention was made of the traditional rule barring such damages for breach of contract.

---

7 [1909] AC 488.
8 [1953] 1 WLR 672.
9 [1963] 1 QB 499.
10 Ibid at 513. Stephenson LJ cited these words in *Guppys (Bridport) Ltd v Brooking and James* (1984) 269 Estates Gazette 846, 942. See also *Drane v Evangelou* [1978] 2 All ER 437.
11 (1985) 17 HLR 120. See also *Warner v Clark* (1984) 134 NLJ 763 (CA dubiously finding a tort justification—inducing breach of contract—for exemplary damages awarded at trial for breach of contract).

(2) When are exemplary damages awarded for torts?

(a) The three categories

The situations in which exemplary damages can be awarded for torts were laid down in Lord Devlin's classic speech in *Rookes v Barnard*.[12] The case concerned the tort of intimidation, and at first instance Sachs J had ruled that exemplary damages could be awarded. The House of Lords overturned that ruling.

The general tenor of Lord Devlin's speech, with which the other Law Lords agreed, was that awarding exemplary damages tends to confuse unsatisfactorily the role of the civil and criminal law and that, while precedent and statute prevent their judicial abolition, the ambit of exemplary damages should be restricted. Having extensively reviewed the relevant authorities, and having stressed that aggravated damages are compensatory and should therefore not be confused, as they often have been, with exemplary damages,[13] Lord Devlin laid down the three sole categories in which exemplary damages can be awarded; first, where there is '. . . oppressive or unconstitutional action by the servants of the government';[14] secondly, where 'the defendant's conduct has been calculated by him to make a profit for himself which may well exceed the compensation payable to the plaintiff';[15] and thirdly, where expressly authorised by statute. As the facts of this case did not fall within any of these categories, Lord Devlin concluded that no exemplary damages should have been awarded. Lord Devlin's speech was later confirmed by the House of Lords in *Cassell & Co Ltd v Broome*[16] following an attempt by the Court of Appeal in the case to outflank that restrictive approach. It is therefore now beyond argument that for a plaintiff to be awarded exemplary damages the tortious conduct must fall within one of the three categories.

(i) *'Oppressive, arbitrary or unconstitutional actions by servants of the government'*

In *Cassell v Broome* it was made clear that 'servants of the government' is to be widely construed. As Lord Diplock said, 'It would embrace all persons purporting to exercise powers of government, central or local, conferred upon them by statute or at common law by

---

12 [1964] AC 1129.
13 Supra, p 241.
14 Ibid at 1226.
15 Ibid.
16 [1972] AC 1027.

virtue of the official status or employment which they hold.'[17] But the defendant must be exercising governmental power and in *AB v South West Water Services Ltd*[18] it was felt that that constituted a different idea in this context than in relation to whether a decision can be judicially reviewed or whether a body is an emanation of the State for the purposes of European Community law. The actions of a nationalised corporation in contaminating drinking water and failing to warn the public properly of this were therefore held not to fall within the first category even if exemplary damages could be awarded for the tort of public nuisance (which, it was held, they could not be).

In *Rookes v Barnard* Lord Devlin instanced three eighteenth-century cases within this category. The best known are the two concerning the printing of the *North Briton*.[19] In *Wilkes v Wood*[20] the plaintiff's house in which it was alleged that the paper had been printed was searched under an illegal general warrant issued by the Secretary of State. In the plaintiff's action for trespass, it was held that exemplary damages could be awarded. Similarly, in *Huckle v Money*[1] the plaintiff was held entitled to exemplary damages for false imprisonment, having been detained for six hours by a King's Messenger on suspicion of having printed the *North Briton*.

But until recently this first category was otherwise more or less devoid of examples and one could be forgiven for regarding it as something of a dead letter. The 1980s, however, saw a dramatic turnabout with this category finding its sharpest ever cutting-edge in actions against the police. So in *White v Metropolitan Police Comr*[2] (which was one of the few cases in which Lord Devlin's first category was actually referred to) £20,000 exemplary damages were awarded to each of two plaintiffs for false imprisonment, assault and malicious prosecution by several police officers. In *George v Metropolitan Police Comr*[3] £2,000 exemplary damages were awarded

---

17 Ibid at 1130.
18 [1993] 1 All ER 609. Cf *Bradford City Metropolitan Council v Arora*]1991] 3 All ER 545 where the public/private divide drawn for judicial review purposes was also rejected but so as to *award* exemplary damages. But that decision must now be considered incorrect on other grounds: see infra, p 279.
19 The third was *Benson v Frederick* (1766) 3 Burr 1845.
20 (1763) Lofft 1.
1 (1763) 2 Wils 205.
2 (1982) Times, 24 April. This and the two following cases (but not the third where vicarious liability was denied) also show that vicarious liability may apply where exemplary damages are being claimed, presumably on the ground that the employer deserves punishment and can best prevent future misconduct. See Atiyah *Vicarious Liability* (1967) pp 433–7; Law Commission Consultation Paper No 132 (1993) pp 90–1, 148–9.
3 (1984) Times, 31 March.

for trespass and assault where police officers had unlawfully searched the plaintiff's house looking for her son and had kicked and hit her. In *Connor v Chief Constable of Cambridgeshire*[4] there was an award of £500 exemplary damages for 'assault' where a police officer had without justification hit the plaintiff over the head with his truncheon in the course of crowd trouble outside the entrance to a football ground and had persisted in a baseless defence to the plaintiff's action. And in *Makanjuola v Metropolitan Police Comr*[5] exemplary damages of £2000 were awarded for trespass to the person and intimidation where a police officer had sexually assaulted the plaintiff. Significantly this rebirth of the first category coincided with increased public criticism of the police, and a widespread belief that police powers are often abused at the expense of civil liberties.

(ii) 'The defendant's conduct has been calculated by him to make a profit for himself which may well exceed the compensation payable to the plaintiff'

This category, which until the 1980s was the only really important one of the three, was the focus of attention in *Cassell v Broome*.[6] The plaintiff, a distinguished retired naval officer, brought an action for libel against two publishers of a book presented as an authentic account of a war-time disaster when a British convoy had been destroyed. The jury had awarded the plaintiff £15,000 compensatory damages and £25,000 exemplary damages. The defendants appealed against the award of exemplary damages, but the House of Lords upheld it as falling within Lord Devlin's second category. In construing Lord Devlin's words it was held that while, on the one hand, the fact that the tortious act was committed in the course of carrying on a profit-making business is not sufficient to bring a case within the second category, on the other hand it is not necessary for the defendant actually to have calculated in arithmetical form that the profit to be made from the tort would exceed the damages and costs to which he would make himself liable. Indeed, as Lord Hailsham said, 'The defendant may calculate that the plaintiff will not sue at all.'[7] So, according to his Lordship, what is required is:

4 (1984) Times, 11 April. See also *Holden v Chief Constable of Lancashire* [1987] QB 380.
5 (1989) Times, 8 August.
6 [1972] AC 1027. See also *Manson v Associated Newspapers Ltd* [1965] 1 WLR 1038.
7 Ibid at 1079.

(i) knowledge that what is proposed to be done is against the law or a reckless disregard whether what is proposed to be done is illegal or legal and (ii) a decision to carry on doing it because the prospects of material advantage outweigh the prospects of material loss.[8]

In the words of Lord Morris:

> The situation contemplated is where someone faces up to the possibility of having to pay damages for doing something which may be held to have been wrong but where nevertheless he deliberately carried out his plan because he thinks it will work out satisfactorily for him. He is prepared to hurt somebody because he thinks he may well gain by so doing even allowing for the risk that he may be made to pay damages.[9]

Applying these approaches to the facts, exemplary damages were justified because there was clear evidence that the defendants, in the knowledge that they might be defaming the plaintiff, were still prepared to sell the book in its sensational form.

A crucial additional point made by Lord Diplock is that damages under this second category are not concerned merely to reverse the defendant's unjust enrichment. He said:

> It . . . may be a blunt instrument to prevent unjust enrichment by unlawful acts. But to restrict the damages recoverable to the gain made by the defendant if it exceeded the loss caused to the plaintiff, would leave a defendant contemplating an unlawful act with the certainty that he had nothing to lose to balance against the chance that the plaintiff might never sue him, or if he did, might fail in the hazards of litigation. It is only if there is a prospect that the damages may exceed the defendant's gain that the social purpose of this category is achieved—to teach a wrongdoer that tort does not pay.[10]

Apart from libel, the main use of this second category has been in actions by tenants against landlords for wrongful harassment or eviction founded on the torts of trespass or nuisance. In *Drane v Evangelou*,[11] for example, the jury had awarded £1,000 damages for the landlord's wrongful eviction of his tenant, and the Court of Appeal held that this award was justified as including some exemplary damages[12] for the tort of trespass under the second category.

---

8 Ibid.
9 Ibid at 1094.
10 Ibid at 1130.
11 [1978] 2 All ER 437. See also *Devonshire and Smith v Jenkins* [1979] LAG Bull 114; *McMillan v Singh* (1985) 17 HLR 120; *Millington v Duffy* (1984) 17 HLR 232; *Asghar v Ahmed* (1985) 17 HLR 25; *Ramdath v Daley* [1993] 1 EGLR 82 (also illustrating the point that there can be no exemplary damages under this category where the defendant is acting for another's benefit).
12 Confusingly Lord Denning appears to use the term 'exemplary damages' to describe an award of both compensatory and exemplary damages.

Both Lord Denning and Goff LJ cited that part of Lord Devlin's judgment where he said:

This category is not confined to moneymaking in the strict sense. It extends to cases in which the defendant is seeking to gain at the expense of the plaintiff some object—perhaps some property which he covets—which either he could not obtain at all or not obtain except at a price greater than he wants to put down.[13]

and Lord Denning said:

. . . this category includes cases of unlawful eviction of a tenant. The landlord seeks to gain possession at the expense of the tenant, so as to keep or get a rent higher than that awarded by the rent tribunal, or to get possession from a tenant who is protected by the Rent Acts.[14]

Similarly in *Guppys (Bridport) Ltd v Brookling and James*[15] landlords had set about converting a building occupied by tenants into self-contained flats. They had no intention of offering alternative accommodation to the tenants and wanted to be rid of them as soon as possible. During the building work they removed all the internal sanitary and washing facilities, discontinued the supply of water to the external toilets and cut off the electricity. The trial judge awarded £1,000 exemplary damages to each of the two plaintiff tenants. The Court of Appeal upheld this as awarded not for the tort of trespass, which was here difficult to make out, but rather for the tort of nuisance. The case fell within Lord Devlin's second category as the plaintiffs were content to ignore the rights of the tenants in order to pursue their own profit-seeking alterations. It should be added, however, that the trial judge and the Court of Appeal were almost certainly accepting that part of the £1,000 included 'compensatory damages': if so, to refer to it all as 'exemplary damages' was unnecessarily confusing.[16]

Finally exemplary damages have occasionally been awarded under this second category for tortious interference with the plaintiff's business. The case Lord Devlin principally relied on within his second category—*Bell v Midland Rly Co*[17]—can be regarded as an early example of this. There the defendants had wrongfully prevented trains running to the plaintiff's wharf so as to divert trade to themselves. A jury award of £1,000 was upheld, Willes J saying:

13 [1964] AC 1129 at 1227.
14 [1978] 2 All ER 437 at 441.
15 (1983) 269 Estates Gazette 846.
16 See also supra, fn 12.
17 (1861) 10 CBNS 287.

. . . if ever there was a case in which the jury were warranted in awarding exemplary damages, this is that case. The defendants have committed a grievous wrong . . . for the purpose of destroying the plaintiff's business and securing gain for themselves.[18]

More recently and controversially in *Messenger Newspaper Group Ltd v National Graphical Association*[19] exemplary damages were awarded against a trade union under the second category for the torts of interference with business by unlawful means, intimidation and public and private nuisance, committed in the course of a dispute over the plaintiffs' refusal to operate a closed shop. But this is hard to justify given that the defendants were not directly seeking any material gain from their conduct. Nor does Caulfield J satisfactorily overcome the objection, considered below, that the NGA had already been heavily fined for its conduct, so that the award of exemplary damages amounted to double punishment.

(iii) Express authorisation by statute

In *Rookes v Barnard* Lord Devlin mentioned the Reserve and Auxiliary Forces Act 1951, s 13(2), as a statutory provision expressly authorising exemplary damages. There are no other clear examples. Most discussion has centred on whether what was formerly s 17(3) of the Copyright Act 1956, and is now s 97(2) of the Copyright, Designs and Patents Act 1988, authorises exemplary damages. Prior to *Rookes v Barnard* the Court of Appeal in *Williams v Settle*[20] held that exemplary damages could be awarded for breach of copyright either at common law or as authorised by what is now s 97(2) of the 1988 Act. There the defendant, a professional photographer, following the murder of the plaintiff's father-in-law, sold to the Press certain photographs taken by him at the plaintiff's wedding which were then published in two national newspapers. One thousand pounds exemplary damages were awarded in the plaintiff's action for breach of copyright. However, in *Rookes v Barnard* Lord Devlin left open whether exemplary damages can be awarded under what is now s 97(2) of the 1988 Act[1] and said that the decision in *Williams v Settle* was more easily justified as an example of aggravated rather than exemplary damages.[2] In *Cassell v Broome* Lord Hailsham agreed with Lord Devlin that the question was an

18 Ibid at 307.
19 [1984] IRLR 397, noted Jones and Morris (1985) 14 ILJ 46. See also *Warner v Islip* (1984) 134 NLJ 763 (inducing breach of contract).
20 [1960] 2 All ER 806.
1 [1964] AC 1129 at 1225.
2 Ibid at 1229.

open one,[3] but Lord Kilbrandon considered that what is now s 97(2) did not authorise exemplary damages.[4] Similarly, in *Belloff v Pressdram Ltd*[5] Ungoed-Thomas J considered that, since the subsection is directed to providing 'effective relief' for the plaintiff, it empowers the award of purely compensatory and not exemplary damages.[6]

(b) Restriction beyond the three categories

Exemplary damages will not necessarily be awarded just because the case falls within one of the three categories. Four additional restrictions (or possible restrictions) fall to be considered.

(i) The tort is not one for which exemplary damages were awarded before Rookes v Barnard

There has been much confusion as to whether this is a restriction. Lords Hailsham and Diplock in *Cassell v Broome*[7] were clear that it was, their reasoning being that Lord Devlin's intention was to restrict, not widen, the availability of exemplary damages. In their view, therefore, no exemplary damages can be awarded for the torts of deceit or negligence even though the facts fall within the second category. Sachs LJ in *Mafo v Adams*[8] tended towards the same view, whereas Widgery LJ's judgment shows the reverse approach, according to which Lord Devlin was concerned to restrict the categories but not the torts for which exemplary damages are recoverable. Widgery LJ therefore thought correct the defendant counsel's concession that exemplary damages can be awarded for deceit, although in any event all such discussion was dicta since the facts did not fall within the second category, it being unclear whether the defendant had the motive of making a profit out of the deceit exceeding the compensation payable to the plaintiff. In *Metall & Rohstoff AG v Acli Metals (London) Ltd*[9] Purchas LJ considered, again in dicta, that exemplary damages are irrecoverable for deceit, whereas in *Archer v Brown*,[10] Peter Pain J preferred to leave the

---

3 [1972] AC 1027 at 1080.
4 Ibid at 1134.
5 [1973] 1 All ER 241 at 265.
6 In *Nichols Advanced Vehicle Systems Inc v Rees* [1979] RPC 127 it was held that damages should be awarded under what is now s 97(2) of the 1988 Act but without clarifying whether exemplary or not.
7 [1972] AC 1027 at 1076, 1130–1.
8 [1970] 1 QB 548.
9 [1984] 1 Lloyds Rep 598 at 612.
10 [1984] 2 All ER 267 at 281.

issue open and stressed that there was no binding authority one way or the other.

This question has also arisen in relation to patent infringement, which like deceit is not a tort for which exemplary damages had been awarded pre-*Rookes v Barnard*. In *Morton-Norwich Products v Intercen (No 2)*[11] Graham J thought that in exceptional circumstances, exemplary damages could be awarded: but in *Catnic Components v Hill & Smith Ltd*[12] Falconer J, in what was part of the decision rather than dicta, held that no exemplary damages were recoverable, although the facts came within the second category, his reasoning being the same as that of Lords Hailsham and Diplock.

In *Bradford City Metropolitan Council v Arora*[13] exemplary damages were awarded for sex and race discrimination and no point was taken that such damages could not be given as the statutory torts were created after 1964.[14]

The issue came directly before the Court of Appeal in *AB v South West Water Services Ltd*[15] which decided that *Cassell v Broome* required that the tort be one for which exemplary damages had been awarded prior to 1964. This was thought to be the view not only of Lords Hailsham and Diplock but also of Lords Wilberforce and Kilbrandon and, possibly, Lord Reid and therefore of the majority of the seven Law Lords sitting in that case. A claim for exemplary damages for the tort of public nuisance in supplying contaminated drinking water to inhabitants of Camelford, Cornwall, was therefore struck out as public nuisance was not a tort for which exemplary damages had been awarded prior to *Rookes v Barnard*. The same applied to alternative claims in the tort of negligence and for liability under the Consumer Protection Act 1987 and the Water Act 1945. *Catnic Components v Hill & Smith Ltd* was approved, while *Bradford Metropolitan City Council v Arora* was treated as having been decided *per incuriam*.[16]

Ultimately whether there should be this restriction depends on

---

11 [1981] FSR 337.
12 [1983] FSR 512.
13 [1991] 3 All ER 545. See also the dicta of the Court of Appeal in *Alexander v Home Office* [1988] 1 WLR 968.
14 In *Arora* the award being appealed against had been made by an industrial tribunal. By s 65(1)(b) of the Sex Discrimination Act 1975 and s 56(1)(b) of the Race Relations Act 1976 an industrial tribunal has power to award compensation of an amount corresponding to any damages that could have been awarded by a county court.
15 [1993] 1 All ER 609. See Reed (1993) NLJ 929; Burrows (1993) 109 LQR 358.
16 That exemplary damages cannot be awarded for race discrimination, following *AB v South West Water Services Ltd*, was confirmed in *Deane v Ealing LBC* [1993] ICR 329.

one's view as to whether exemplary damages are justified. If one considers them an anomaly to be restricted as far as possible (this is the view argued for below), then the Court of Appeal's decision in *AB v South West Water Services Ltd* should be welcomed. On the other hand, if such damages are regarded as serving a useful purpose within Lord Devlin's three categories, it would be irrational and artificial to freeze the range of torts as it was in 1964.

(ii) Double punishment

As laid down in *Devonshire and Smith v Jenkins*[17] and *Archer v Brown*[18] where a defendant has already been punished by the criminal law in respect of the facts upon which the plaintiff now founds his tortious action, no exemplary damages should be awarded since a person should not be punished twice for the same offence. In the first of these cases the defendant had already been fined and, in the second, imprisoned for the conduct in question.

(iii) The plaintiff's conduct

In *Rookes v Barnard*[19] Lord Devlin said that the court should take into account all mitigating circumstances. So most obviously, exemplary damages may be refused (or reduced) if the plaintiff has brought the defendant's conduct upon himself. Indeed this is analogous to the principles of causation and contributory negligence applied in relation to compensatory damages. A rare example of its application is *O'Connor v Hewitson*[20] where exemplary damages were refused for trespass to the person under the first category because the plaintiff had provoked the defendant policeman's assault.

(iv) Compensatory damages sufficient

As stressed in *Rookes v Barnard*[1] and *Cassell v Broome*[2] there should be no exemplary damages if it is considered that the compensatory damages awarded are adequate to punish the defendant.

---

17 [1979] LAG Bulletin 114 CA.
18 [1984] 2 All ER 267. See also *Loomis v Rohan* (1974) 46 DLR (3d) 423.
19 [1964] AC 1129 at 1228.
20 [1979] Crim LR 46. See also *Bishop v Metropolitan Police Comr* [1990] 1 LS Gaz R 30.
 1 [1964] AC 1129 at 1228.
 2 [1972] AC 1027 at 1062, 1089, 1096, 1104, 1118, 1121–22, 1134.

(3) Assessing exemplary damages

Assuming exemplary damages are to be awarded (and hence under the present law we are here dealing solely with tort cases) how does the court, be it judge or jury, assess them? While Lord Devlin did stress that awards should be moderate,[3] the basic answer is that there is almost total discretion to award whatever sum is felt necessary to punish the defendant and to set an example to others. In contrast to personal injury compensation for non-pecuniary loss, and even criminal sentencing, there is no sign of any tariff system, and at least in defamation cases, the archaic survival of jury assessment renders such a development unlikely. This is hardly a happy state of affairs and if exemplary damages are to continue, it is submitted that their assessment should be made the sole preserve of the judges, whose first priority should be consistency of awards.

There are three further important points on assessment. First, Lord Devlin said that the parties' means and all mitigating circumstances should be taken into account.[4] The latter most obviously refers to the plaintiff's own contributory blameworthy conduct, and has already been considered. The former is presumably in line with the criminal sentencing principle that there is no sense in fining someone beyond what he can pay.[5]

Secondly, as laid down in *Cassell v Broome*,[6] where there are joint defendants exemplary damages must not exceed the lowest sum that any of the defendants ought to pay; so that if damages are not justified against any one of the defendants, they should not be awarded at all. It follows that if he can identify him the plaintiff is best advised to sue the most blameworthy defendant alone.

Finally, where there are multiple plaintiffs *Riches v News Group Newspapers*[7] makes clear that the total amount of exemplary damages considered fair for the defendant to pay should first be decided on. Then that amount can be divided among the plaintiffs. The Court of Appeal therefore set aside a total award of £250,000 exemplary damages to ten plaintiffs for libel because, inter alia, there had been no direction on this point by the judge and there was the possibility (and on the face of it, surely a high probability) that the jury had considered that £25,000 rather than £250,000

---

3 [1964] AC 1129 at 1227–28.
4 Ibid at 1228.
5 A defendant ought not to be able to insure against exemplary damages just as he cannot insure against criminal fines.
6 [1972] AC 1027 at 1063.
7 [1985] 2 All ER 845.

(£2,500 rather than £25,000 to each plaintiff) should be the total amount of exemplary damages.

(4) Are exemplary damages justified?[8]

It is submitted that exemplary damages should be abolished for torts and that the law should continue not to award them for breach of contract. But before examining the reasons for this view, what are the arguments favouring the retention of exemplary damages?

(i)   The primary argument is encapsulated in the following passage from Lord Wilberforce's judgment (dissenting on some points) in *Cassell v Broome*:

> It cannot lightly be taken for granted, even as a matter of theory, that the purpose of the law of tort is compensation, still less that it ought to be . . . or that there is something inappropriate or illogical or anomalous in including a punitive element in civil damages, or, conversely, that the criminal law, rather than civil law, is in these cases the better instrument for conveying social disapproval, or for redressing a wrong to the social fabric, or that damages in any case can be broken down into the two separate elements. As a matter of practice English law has not committed itself to any of these theories . . .[9]

So the central points being made are that there is no good reason why punishment should not be pursued by the civil law and, moreover, that authority supports the notion of civil punishment.

(ii) It can be argued that if the *Rookes v Barnard* categories are illogical the preferable approach is to extend not abolish exemplary damages. Support for this is derived from the experience in other Commonwealth countries where exemplary damages continue to be awarded for a wide range of torts.[10] Tortious exemplary damages are also freely recoverable in the United States.[11]

---

8 Street *Principles* pp 34–6; Ogus *Damages* pp 32–4; Waddams *Damages* paras 11.10–11.100; Posner *Economic Analysis of Law* (4th edn) pp 191–2; Collins *The Law of Contract* (2nd edn, 1993) pp 385–8; Stone (1972) 46 ALJ 311; Sullivan (1977) 61 Minn LR 207; Mallor and Roberts (1980) 31 Hastings LJ 639; Farber (1980) 66 Va LR 1443; Owen (1989) 40 Alabama LR 705; Chapman and Trebilcock (1989) 40 Alabama LR 741. For a detailed examination of the arguments, see Law Commission Consultation Paper No 132 (1993) Part V.
9 [1972] AC 1027 at 1114.
10 *Uren v John Fairfax & Sons Pty Ltd* (1966) 117 CLR 118; *Taylor v Beere* [1982] 1 NZLR 81; Waddams *Damages* paras 11.190–11.200.
11 Second Restatement of Torts, para 908.

(iii) Even if illogical, exemplary damages serve a useful function within Lord Devlin's categories. This is supported by the following passage from the speech of Lord Devlin himself:

> ... there are certain categories of case in which an award of exemplary damages can serve a useful purpose in vindicating the strength of the law and thus affording a practical justification for admitting into the civil law a principle which ought logically to belong to the criminal.[12]

Significantly in *Cassell v Broome* Lord Reid expressly disapproved this comment, and supported the retention of the categories only on the basis that Parliament alone could remove them.[13]

However the following arguments against exemplary damages are wholly convincing.[14]

(i) Most importantly, exemplary damages, because their primary aim is punishment, confuse the role of the criminal and the civil law and, with respect to Lord Wilberforce, this is unsatisfactory for several reasons. First, punishment is an extreme sanction justifiable only if a law designated as criminal has been broken. Secondly (as under present criminal proceedings), the defendant should have the benefit of more protective procedures, evidential rules and rights of appeal if punishment rather than other (civil) remedies is in issue. In *Cassell v Broome*[15] Lord Reid was particularly critical of jury awards of exemplary damages on the ground that in criminal cases it is never left to a jury to decide the punishment. Thirdly, punishment demands a state–individual relationship rather than being for one individual to exact from another. It follows that the rightful recipient of monetary punishment should be the state, and not a plaintiff. Of course all this in no sense denies that the criminal courts are justified in awarding compensation or restitution to the victim of a crime, for there is no objection to less drastic remedies than punishment being ordered for a crime. The objection is to the more drastic sanction of punishment being used for civil wrongs.

(ii) If it is felt that tortious exemplary damages do serve some useful purpose within Lord Devlin's categories, there are always

---

12 [1964] AC 1129 at 1226.
13 [1972] AC 1027 at 1087.
14 No reliance is here placed on the argument that exemplary damages would deter an efficient breach of contract. As discussed infra, pp 351–2, this is an unsatisfactory argument given the opportunity to bargain round the remedy. Note also that exemplary damages are almost unknown in civil law systems.
15 [1972] AC 1027 at 1087.

other satisfactory means of achieving the same ends. For example, all the cases on actions against the police within the first category also involved crimes, and a criminal prosecution would serve equally well to punish and deter police misconduct. Even better, as many have argued, would be to introduce a new fully independent police complaints system. Similarly, within the second category there are already adequate criminal sanctions against landlords for wrongful eviction under the Protection from Eviction Act 1977.[16] Significantly too, many more serious libels would constitute crimes if the Law Commission's proposals were implemented for a new statutory offence of criminal defamation to replace criminal libel.[17] Moreover, and irrespective of whether criminal punishment is felt justified, the civil law in respect of the second category can justifiably go beyond compensation by awarding restitutionary remedies stripping the defendant of his profits.[18] Compensation alone does not and need not underpin tortious (or, more controversially, contractual) monetary remedies; restitution, occupying a mid-position between compensation and punishment, is an acceptable remedial function for a civil wrong. Arguably, therefore, cases within the second category like *Cassell v Broome* could be satisfactorily dealt with by awarding a restitutionary remedy to the plaintiff. Indeed that there is dispute over the extent of even restitutionary remedies for torts makes pursuit of the more drastic aim of punishment doubly surprising.

(iii) Some reform of the law has to take place, for Lord Devlin's categories lack satisfactory rationale. They represent a compromise between the desire to rid the law of exemplary damages altogether and the belief that precedent and statutes are too firmly entrenched to allow this. Arguably it is also inconsistent to allow exemplary damages for torts but never for breach of contract. Given the need for reform, the only obvious rational alternative to abolition is to allow exemplary damages for all intentional torts (and arguably breaches of contract). Pitted against such a radical alternative the case for abolition appears all the more moderate and sensible.

In the light of these arguments it is submitted that at the very least, where authority leaves the issue open—for example as to the scope of the first category or whether exemplary damages are authorised under s 97(2) of the Copyright, Designs and Patents Act 1988—a

16 As amended by the Housing Act 1988.
17 Report No 149 Criminal Libel (1985) Cmnd 9618.
18 Infra, chapter 6.

restrictive interpretation should be adopted and exemplary damages denied. But the ideal solution is to reform the law by abolishing exemplary damages altogether.[19] As the House of Lords will probably continue to consider that the authorities are too firmly entrenched for it to overturn them, it is up to the law reform bodies and the legislature to achieve this. To echo Stephenson LJ's words in the *Riches* case,[20] the law on exemplary damages '. . . cries aloud . . . for parliamentary intervention.'

Unfortunately the Law Commission in its recent consultation paper has provisionally recommended that, while there should indeed be reform, exemplary damages should be retained while being put on a principled basis thereby extending their ambit.[1] Oddly the precise basis of principle is left open. The main possibilities canvassed are where the defendant's conduct has been malicious or outrageous, especially if the parties were in a relationship of inequality at the time of the wrong; and/or that the plaintiff's 'rights of personality' have been infringed. No extension of exemplary damages to breach of contract is proposed. And views of consultees are sought on various more specific issues, such as the burden of proof, vicarious liability, joint defendants, and whether part of the exemplary damages should be made payable to the state or another public fund.

It remains to be seen whether the response to the paper will convince the Law Commission that the more principled approach is to abolish exemplary damages. Indeed the case for abolition is strengthened by the difficulty the Law Commission has encountered in articulating a clear principled basis for such damages. Moreover the emphasis on the plaintiff's intangible personality interests is puzzling. The argument at root appears to be that compensatory damages for mental distress, loss of reputation and the like are inadequate and hence need supplementation by exemplary damages. But surely, if that is thought a problem, the appropriate way forward is to ensure that such non-pecuniary harm is taken more seriously by the judiciary by increasing *compensatory* awards. Indeed one would have thought that the clearest infringement of a personality interest is personal injury and yet the Law Commission seems content with the present system of compensating, without exemplary damages, the pain and suffering and loss of amenity consequent on personal injury.

---

19 This was also the view of the Faulks Committee in relation to defamation, Report (1975) Cmnd 5909, para 10.
20 [1985] 2 All ER 845 at 850.
1 Consultation Paper No 132 (1993) 'Aggravated, Exemplary and Restitutionary Damages' esp Part VI.

Chapter 6

Restitutionary remedies

1. INTRODUCTION

(1) Reversing unjust enrichment

In *Lipkin Gorman v Karpnale Ltd*[1] it was finally authoritatively accepted by the House of Lords that there is an English law of restitution based on reversing unjust enrichment.[2] In this book we are concerned only with a small part of its terrain, namely restitutionary remedies—that is remedies reversing enrichment—where the gain is unjust because acquired by a tort or breach of contract.[3] Generally the injustice of an enrichment does not depend on its having been acquired by a tort or breach of contract, or indeed by any other wrong, and therefore most unjust enrichments, and consequent restitutionary remedies, are best viewed as belonging solely to the law of restitution. But where the enrichment is unjust because made by a tort or breach of contract, the law of restitution overlaps with the law of tort or contract.

As will become apparent the main restitutionary remedies in issue in this chapter are an account of profits, an award of money in an action for money had and received and restitutionary damages.[4]

---

1 [1991] 2 AC 548.
2 See generally Goff and Jones *The Law of Restitution* (4th edn, 1993); Birks *An Introduction to the Law of Restitution* (revsd edn, 1989) hereinafter cited as *Introduction*; Burrows *The Law of Restitution*.
3 Apart from the relevant chapters in the works cited in the previous note, see generally Jackman (1989) CLJ 302; Birks *Civil Wrongs: A New World* (Butterworth Lectures, 1990–91); Law Commission Consultation Paper No 132 (1993) 'Aggravated, Exemplary and Restitutionary Damages' Part VII.
4 See supra, p 269, fn 2.

(2) Unjust enrichment by wrongs, autonomous unjust enrichment and alternative analysis

The primary point stressed in the previous subsection can be expressed, using Birks' terminology,[5] by saying that in this chapter we are concerned with a part of 'unjust enrichment by wrongs', whereas most of the law of restitution deals with 'autonomous unjust enrichment'. The latter comprises 'unjust enrichment by subtraction' (where the defendant's gain must match the plaintiff's loss) and is concerned with factors, other than wrongs, that invalidate a direct shift of wealth from the plaintiff to the defendant. The plaintiff's payment of money or rendering of services to the defendant by mistake or under undue pressure, or subject to a condition being fulfilled that has not been, are examples of prima facie autonomous unjust enrichment.

What it is important to realise, and what complicates this chapter's concern solely with unjust enrichment by wrongs (whether by a tort or breach of contract) is that in some situations where a claim could be based on unjust enrichment by wrongs, there is an alternative claim that does not rely on the wrong, and rather lies within autonomous unjust enrichment. This 'alternative analysis' is best understood by reference to an example. Say the defendant has induced the plaintiff to give him £25 by a deliberate misrepresentation of fact. Irrespective of establishing the tort of deceit, the plaintiff has a good reason for a restitutionary remedy under autonomous unjust enrichment; namely he has paid £25 to the defendant under an induced mistake of fact which taints the validity of the shift in wealth. The fact that the defendant has deliberately lied causing the plaintiff loss is irrelevant to that.

It follows from this discussion that where a wrong does result in an enrichment by subtraction, the fact that there may be some restriction, preventing restitutionary remedies based on the wrong, will not necessarily rule out restitutionary remedies in autonomous unjust enrichment, and vice versa. It also follows that where attention is being focused solely on unjust enrichment by wrongs, as in this chapter, some care must be taken not to include cases based instead on unjust enrichment by subtraction.

(3) The enrichment

By committing a tort or breach of contract, a defendant may either acquire a positive benefit, which in general terms can be described as

5 *Introduction* pp 314–15, 334.

a *profit*, or he may merely be negatively benefited, by *saving expense* that he would otherwise have incurred. But whichever sort of benefit is in question, it is a precondition of restitution—as analogously for compensation—that the tort or breach of contract was a factual cause of the benefit: if the defendant would have made that profit or saved that expense irrespective of the wrong (applying a 'but for' test) there is here no justification for a restitutionary remedy.

Since profits commonly result from various causes, of which the wrong may be just one, the courts may prefer to award merely a fair proportion of the profits gained by the wrong, rather than all those profits. This may be regarded as analogous to the desire to limit compensatory damages for loss, on grounds such as remoteness or intervening cause. The sort of factors that one would expect would influence the courts in deciding whether to award merely a fair proportion, and if so, what would amount to a fair proportion, are the skill and effort the defendant has expended to make the profits, the blameworthiness of the wrong and, perhaps, the maintenance of some sense of proportion between the benefit acquired and the plaintiff's loss or lack of it.

The expense the defendant has saved by a breach of contract generally comprises what the defendant would have had to spend to complete his promised performance (minus any part of the contract price now lost). For torts, the expense saved will commonly comprise what the defendant would have had to pay to acquire a substitute for the property he has tortiously used or, in some cases, the fee that the plaintiff would have charged, if the defendant had negotiated with him for legitimate use of the property. The latter can alternatively be viewed as the fee the plaintiff has lost because of the defendant's tort; that is, in some cases, but by no means all, an alternative compensatory analysis can be taken.[6]

2. ENRICHMENTS GAINED BY A TORT[7]

(1) Introduction

We are here concerned with remedies that reverse gains because the defendant has acquired them by committing a tort against the plaintiff. This is often what is meant by 'waiver of tort', that is, the

---

6 Sharpe and Waddams (1982) 2 Ox JLS 290 go too far by in effect arguing that a compensatory analysis can always be taken in property interference cases.
7 See generally Teller (1956) 2 NY Law Forum 40; York (1957) UCLALR 499; Hodder (1984) 42 UT Fac LR 105; Beatson *The Use and Abuse of Unjust Enrichment* pp 206–43.

plaintiff sues on the tort but seeks a restitutionary remedy rather than usual compensatory damages. But it can be argued that 'waiver of tort' also refers to where the plaintiff ignores the tort, and brings his action within autonomous unjust enrichment. It should further be realised that the judicial usage of 'waiver of tort' appears to be confined to where the restitutionary remedy in issue is the award of money had and received (or one of the other 'quasi-contractual' remedies, like a *quantum meruit*) rather than being an account of profits or restitutionary damages. The term 'waiver of tort' is therefore ambiguous and unhelpful and should be avoided wherever possible.

It is also convenient to stress at this initial stage that rescission of a contract for misrepresentation where enrichments gained are reversed,[8] is better viewed as within autonomous unjust enrichment, rather than enrichment by wrongdoing; that is, the reason for the remedy is essentially that the benefit has been rendered non-voluntarily because of induced mistake.[9] This non-wrong analysis is supported by the facts that first, rescission for misrepresentation is similar to that for undue influence, duress, mistake and non-disclosure, where there is no tort (or wrong as such) involved; secondly, rescission was available for non-fraudulent misrepresentation, before the development of the tort of negligent misrepresentation or the passing of the Misrepresentation Act 1967; and thirdly, for the torts involved, whether deceit, negligent misrepresentation or under the Misrepresentation Act 1967, it is necessary to show damage resulting from the misrepresentation, that is, the torts are actionable only on proof of damage, whereas no damage needs to be proved for rescission.[10]

(2) Why should a plaintiff want a restitutionary remedy for a tort, rather than compensatory damages?

The main and most obvious advantage is that the plaintiff may obtain more by restitution than compensation, since the gain the defendant has made by the tort may exceed the loss caused to the plaintiff by the tort.

But there may be other advantages in that a common law rule or a statutory provision may be regarded as barring compensatory

---

8 Rescission may simply be concerned to allow escape from a contract. For the same reasons as those in the text such rescission is best viewed as not being a remedy for a tort and hence as being outside this book's scope.

9 Birks *Introduction* pp 167–71; Burrows *The Law of Restitution* pp 130–7.

10 *Street on Torts* (8th edn, 1993) p 121.

damages but not a restitutionary remedy for the tort. Birks has argued that there can only be an evasion of a bar where it is the remedy (compensation) and not the cause of action (tort) that is barred.[11] But whether illogical or not, the courts in the past have been willing to allow at least some restitutionary remedies for torts to evade bars on 'tort actions'. The major example concerned the *actio personalis* rule, or what was left of it in the Law Reform (Miscellaneous Provisions) Act 1934, s 1(3), whereby there was a six-month limitation period for 'tort actions' against a wrongdoer's personal representatives; for while this was regarded as barring tortious compensatory damages, it was considered not to be a bar to restitutionary remedies, at least if an award of money had and received or an account of profits.[12]

It is worth adding as a postscript that now that the Proceedings Against Estates Act 1970 has finally removed any trace of the unjust *actio personalis* rule, it is unlikely that the courts will see any reason to allow restitutionary remedies for a tort to avoid the six-year limitation period applicable to tortious compensatory damages.[13] Certainly nothing in the Limitation Act 1980 contradicts this. An award of money had and received is not mentioned and no distinction is drawn between compensatory and restitutionary damages. Moreover by s 23 an action for an account of profits '. . . shall not be brought after the expiration of any time limit under the Act which is applicable to the claim which is the basis of the duty to account', which does appear to mean that if the basis is tort, tort limitation periods should apply.

(3) When are restitutionary remedies available for torts?

A restrictive answer to this question was given in the key case of *Phillips v Homfray*.[14] The background to this was that the plaintiff had won a judgment for 'damages' to be assessed for the defendants' act of trespass in using roads and passages under the plaintiff's land to transport coal.[15] Subsequently one of the defendants had died, and the issue that arose was whether a remedy to reverse the gain made by the deceased defendant's trespass could be

---

11 Birks *Introduction* p 347. Cf Burrows *The Law of Restitution* pp 17–18.
12 *Chesworth v Farrar* [1967] 1 QB 407, and reasoning in *Phillips v Homfray* (1883) 24 Ch D 439.
13 Burrows *The Law of Restitution* pp 447–9.
14 (1883) 24 Ch D 439. See Gummow *Essays on Restitution* (ed Finn) pp 60–7; Burrows *The Law of Restitution* pp 390–2.
15 (1871) 6 Ch App 770.

awarded against his executrix despite the *actio personalis* rule barring 'tort actions'.

In a difficult judgment, the majority of the Court of Appeal (Bowen and Cotton LJJ) held that no such remedy could be awarded on the ground that it is only where the defendant's gain consists of the plaintiff's property or the proceeds of that property,[16] that a common law or equitable remedy reversing that gain can be awarded.[17] As on these facts the gain in question did not comprise the plaintiff's property, but was rather the use of his land, and hence the saving of expense of paying a reasonable fee for that use or of transporting the coal by other methods, no restitutionary remedy could be awarded. It is important to realise that the majority's restrictive view of the nature of the benefit was apparently not limited to actions against an executor, albeit that that was the issue directly in point; rather it was seen as a general restriction on remedies reversing gains applicable even in actions against the wrongdoer himself.[18]

Baggallay LJ dissented. He thought that the nature of the benefit should not matter so long as a benefit had been acquired by the wrongful act:[19]

It has hardly been disputed on the present appeal that a remedy for a wrongful act can be pursued against the estate of a deceased person by whom the act has been committed, when property, or the proceeds of property, belonging to another have been appropriated by the deceased person . . . ; but it has been urged that the principle thus enunciated is limited to cases in which property, or the proceeds of property, have been appropriated by the deceased person, and that it does not apply to a case in which the deceased person has derived any other benefit from his wrongdoing than property or the proceeds of property, and in particular that it does not apply to a case in which the benefit derived has not been in the form of an actual acquisition of property, but of a saving of expenditure which must otherwise have been incurred by the wrongdoer, as in the present case, in which, for the purpose of the present argument, it must be assumed that by the use by the defendants, for the carriage of their minerals, of the roads and passages under the plaintiffs' farm, there was a saving to them of an expenditure, which they must otherwise have incurred . . . I feel bound to say that I cannot appreciate the reasons upon which it is insisted that although executors are bound to account for any accretions to the property

16 This is even more restrictive than saying that the benefit must be positive rather than negative.

17 (1883) 24 Ch D 439 at 455, 460, 462–3, 465.

18 Especially ibid at 460–1.

19 An alternative autonomous unjust enrichment analysis is outside this book's scope: Birks considers that logically that is the only possible analysis, *Introduction* pp 322–5, and supra, fn 11. Cf Burrows *The Law of Restitution* p 391.

of their testator derived directly from his wrongful act, they are not liable for the amount or value of any other benefit which may be derived by his estate from or by reason of such wrongful act.[20]

The majority's restrictive view draws an arbitrary distinction between types of benefit and may reflect a confusion between personal and proprietary rights. It is submitted therefore that the principle of Baggallay LJ's dissent should be adopted and *Phillips v Homfray* overruled.[1]

Indeed one can go further and argue that *Phillips v Homfray* was contrary to existing authority and has since been impliedly overruled; for while there has been no award of money had and received for a tort which contradicts the majority's approach,[2] the same cannot be said of the remedies of an account of profits and restitutionary damages. However, before examining these contradictory areas, it is first useful to examine cases awarding money had and received for torts which are consistent with *Phillips v Homfray*.

The tort of conversion provides the most obvious examples of restitutionary remedies being granted where the benefit comprises the plaintiff's property or its proceeds. So in *Lamine v Dorrell*[3] the defendant, pretending to be administrator of an estate, got into his hands certain debentures belonging to the plaintiff and sold them. It was held that the plaintiff could 'waive the tort' of conversion and recover the price that the defendant had sold the debentures for in an action for money had and received. Again, although the more specific issues of election of remedies and limitation periods were in question in *United Australia Ltd v Barclays Bank Ltd*[4] and *Chesworth v Farrar*[5] respectively, the decisions in each rested on an acceptance that a plaintiff can bring an action for money had and received to recover a gain made by the tort of conversion, the gain comprising the plaintiff's property or its proceeds.

The granting of a restitutionary remedy for the tort of trespass to goods to reverse a benefit comprising the plaintiff's property or its proceeds is shown by *Oughton v Seppings*.[6] Here the defendant, a

---

20 (1883) 24 Ch D 439 at 471–2.

1 See Goff and Jones *The Law of Restitution* (4th edn) p 719.

2 Indeed *Phillips v Homfray* was applied in *A-G v De Keyser's Royal Hotel* [1920] AC 508 and see also *Morris v Tarrant* [1971] 2 QB 143; cf *Mahesan S/O Thambiah v Malaysia Government Officers' Co-operative Housing Society* [1979] AC 374 (bribes).

3 (1705) 2 Ld Raym 1216.

4 [1941] AC 1. On the 'election' issue, it was decided that a plaintiff does not need to choose between compensation and restitution for a tort until judgment for (and probably satisfaction of) one of them.

5 [1967] 1 QB 407.

6 (1830) 1 B & Ad 241.

sheriff's officer, in executing a writ of fi fa against A, had wrongfully seized a horse belonging to the plaintiff, which was later sold. It was held that the plaintiff could 'waive the tort' of trespass and recover the sale proceeds that the defendant had received in an action for money had and received.

A final example is *Powell v Rees*,[7] where the deceased had trespassed on the plaintiff's land to mine coal. The plaintiff was held able to 'waive the tort' and recover the proceeds of the sale of the coal from the deceased's administrator in an action for money had and received. Again, the benefit here comprised the proceeds of the plaintiff's property.

Turning now to cases outside the restrictive view, perhaps the most influential espousal of a wide view of the availability of remedies to reverse gains made by torts was put forward in obiter dicta by Lord Mansfield in *Hambly v Trott*[8] when discussing whether such a remedy would succeed against an executor of the deceased tortfeasor despite the *actio personalis* rule. Lord Mansfield thought that it would and included as examples cases where the benefit did not comprise the plaintiff's property or its proceeds. For example he said, 'So if a man takes a horse from another, and brings him back again; an action for trespass will not lie against his executor, though it would against him; but an action for the use and hire of the horse will lie against the executor.'[9] And later '. . . so far as the act of the offender is beneficial, his assets ought to be answerable: and his executor therefore shall be charged.'[10] In *Phillips v Homfray* Baggallay LJ relied on Lord Mansfield's words, but the majority considered that what Lord Mansfield had said could be narrowly interpreted and did not conflict with their restrictive view.

But there have been numerous cases in which restitutionary damages or an account of profits have been awarded even though the benefit did not comprise the plaintiff's property or its proceeds. It is helpful to divide between those awarding restitutionary damages and those awarding an account of profits.

(a) Restitutionary damages

The suggestion that damages can be restitutionary will appear to many as a heresy, since it is generally taken for granted that, other

---

7 (1837) 7 Ad & El 426. Other examples cited in *Phillips v Homfray* are *Lightly v Clouston* (1808) 1 Taunt 112 and *Foster v Stewart* (1814) 3 M & S 191 ('waiver' of the old tort of seduction).
8 (1776) 1 Cowp 371.
9 Ibid at 375.
10 Ibid at 376–7.

than exemplary or nominal or contemptuous damages, damages are concerned to compensate the plaintiff. However, in some cases, the decision and the reasoning indicate that the damages are better or equally-well viewed as restitutionary reversing the defendant's wrongful enrichment; and this is so, even though the benefit did not comprise the plaintiff's property or its proceeds.[11]

(i) Wrongful interference with goods

In *Strand Electric Engineering Co Ltd v Brisford Entertainments Ltd*,[12] the Court of Appeal awarded damages for the then tort of detinue assessed according to a reasonable hiring charge for the period that the defendant had wrongly kept and used theatre equipment. Denning LJ made it plain that he regarded the damages as restitutionary reversing the wrongful benefit acquired by the defendant:

> If a wrongdoer has made use of goods for his own purposes, then he must pay a reasonable hire for them, even though the owner has in fact suffered no loss. It may be that the owner would not have used the goods himself, or that he had a substitute readily available, which he used without extra cost to himself. Nevertheless the owner is entitled to a reasonable hire . . . The claim for a hiring charge is therefore not based on the loss to the plaintiff, but on the fact that the defendant has used the goods for his own purposes. It is an action against him because he has had the benefit of the goods. It resembles therefore, an action for restitution, rather than an action of tort.[13]

On Denning LJ's analysis therefore, the damages awarded are best viewed as reversing the expense the defendant saved in not having to hire alternative equipment, or in not paying to the plaintiff the fee it would have charged if the defendant had negotiated with it for legitimate hire of the goods. Any actual profits the defendant had made from using the equipment were apparently not considered relevant, although Denning LJ said that he could imagine cases where the '. . . owner might be entitled to the actual profits made by the wrongdoer by the use of the chattel.'[14]

---

11 The restitutionary interpretation is strongly supported by dicta of the Court of Appeal in the contract case of *Surrey CC v Bredero Homes Ltd* [1993] 3 All ER 705, 710–11, 714–15. In addition to the cases below, see dicta of Lord Shaw in *Watson, Laidlaw & Co Ltd v Pott, Cassels & Williamson* (1914) 31 RPC 104, 120. The measure of damages laid down for the statutory tort of unlawful eviction under ss 27–8 of the Housing Act 1988 also appears to be restitutionary: see *Jones v Miah* (1992) 24 HLR 578, 587. There is also a natural restitutionary interpretation of the Copyright, Designs and Patents Act 1988, s 97(2).
12 [1952] 2 QB 246.
13 Ibid at 254–5.
14 Ibid at 255.

While there are passages in the majority's judgments which support Denning LJ's approach, Somervell and Romer LJJ overall preferred to fit their decision within the normal conception of damages compensating the plaintiff's loss.[15] This is an equally acceptable approach for even if the plaintiff would not have hired out the equipment for the full period at the full rate to someone else, as the trial judge had found, it may be realistic to say that it suffered a loss in that it was not paid the fee it would have charged the defendant for its legitimately retaining the goods. Indeed, as we have just observed, on the opposite restitutionary approach, the saving of *that* expense, represents one possible explanation of the reasonable hiring charge measure.

(ii) Trespass to land

Lord Denning, sitting as a single judge in *Penarth Dock Engineering Co Ltd v Pounds*,[16] again adopted a restitutionary approach to the assessment of damages, where the defendants were trespassers in the plaintiffs' dock by failing to remove their pontoon. It was clear that the plaintiffs would not have made any gain by letting out the dock to a third party during that period; nor could it be said that they had suffered a loss, in that they had not been paid the fee they would have charged the defendants for legitimately using the dock, for the plaintiffs were desperately trying to have the defendants remove their pontoon and would not have accepted a price for the defendants to have continued using the dock legitimately. But relying on *Whitwham v Westminster, Brymbo, Coal & Coke Co*[17] and his own judgment in *Strand Electric*, Lord Denning awarded damages reversing the benefit the defendants had acquired by use of the dock:

. . . the Penarth company would not seem to have suffered any damage to speak of. They have not to pay any extra rent to the British Transport Commission. The dock is no use to them: they would not have made any money out of it. But . . . in a case of this kind . . . the test of the measure of damages is not what the plaintiffs have lost, but what benefit the defendant has obtained by having the use of the berth.[18]

Damages were assessed at £32 5s a week. This was apparently based on the evidence that £37 10s a week was what the defendants would have had to pay for an alternative dock of that kind. Why

15 See similarly, *Hillesden Securities Ltd v Ryjak Ltd* [1983] 1 WLR 959.
16 [1963] 1 Lloyd's Rep 359.
17 [1896] 2 Ch 538.
18 [1963] 1 Lloyd's Rep 359 at 361–2.

there was some reduction is not made clear but perhaps the plaintiffs' berth was inferior to the alternatives, or involved the defendants in some expense which the alternatives did not, so that to award the full £37 10s would have gone beyond reversing the defendants' benefit.

Whitwham v Westminster, Brymbo, Coal & Coke Co, which Lord Denning relied on in *Strand Electric* and *Penarth Dock,* concerned trespass by the defendants' tipping soil from their colliery on to part of the plaintiffs' land. The judgments tended to the view that the damages awarded were compensatory. Presumably this was on the assumption that the damages covered the loss the plaintiffs had suffered by not renting out that part of the land, or by the non-payment of the fee the plaintiffs would have charged for the tipping if they had been approached. But the former seems unrealistic, since it was most unlikely that the plaintiffs would have otherwise rented out that part of the land to a third party. Moreover there are passages which support Lord Denning's restitutionary interpretation. For example, Lindley LJ said, '. . . if one person has without leave of another been using that other's land for his own purposes, he ought to pay for such user.'[19] On a restitutionary analysis the damages could be said to represent either a fair proportion of the profits made by the defendants, or the expense they had saved by not having to dispose of the spoil elsewhere, or, if regarded as realistic, the saving of the fee the plaintiffs would have charged them for legitimate tipping.

Again in *Swordheath Properties Ltd v Tabet*[20] damages for trespass by tenants remaining in premises after they should have left were assessed according to the ordinary letting value of the property. The Court of Appeal regarded it as irrelevant whether the plaintiffs would have used the property or not and *Whitwham* and *Penarth Dock* were relied on. Megaw LJ said:

> . . . the plaintiff . . . is entitled, without bringing evidence that he could or would have let the property to someone else in the absence of the trespassing defendant, to have as damages for the trespass the value of the property as it would fairly be calculated: and in the absence of anything special in the particular circumstances it would be the ordinary letting value of the property that would determine the amount of damages.[1]

Such damages could only be compensatory, if it was realistic to assume that the plaintiffs would have allowed the defendants to

19 [1896] 2 Ch 538 at 541–2.
20 [1979] 1 WLR 285.
 1 Ibid at 288.

stay on at that rent if they had approached them. But on a restitutionary analysis, while the saving of that expense is one possible explanation of the damages, the alternative is that they represented the expense the defendants had saved in not having to rent alternative property of that type.

In *Bracewell v Appleby*,[2] where the courts refused an injunction to prevent the defendant continuing to trespass by using the plaintiffs' road to reach his newly-built house, damages in lieu were granted, assessed according to what would have been a fair sum for the plaintiffs to have accepted for granting the defendant a right of way over the road, albeit that the plaintiffs would probably not have been willing to grant the right of way. Such a fair sum can be viewed as compensating the plaintiffs for their 'loss of amenity and increased user'[3] or, on a restitutionary approach, as representing a fair proportion of the profits made by the trespass. The latter seems the preferable analysis since in assessing the fair sum Graham J considered it important to take into account the profits the defendant had made on the house. Ultimately damages of £2,000 out of a notional profit of £5,000 were awarded.

Finally, and most importantly, in *Ministry of Defence v Ashman*,[4] in which a tenant had wrongfully ignored a notice to quit RAF accommodation because she and her children had nowhere else to go, a majority of the Court of Appeal (Kennedy and Hoffmann LJJ) accepted that the plaintiff landlord was entitled to restitutionary damages for the trespass. The *Swordheath* and *Penarth Dock* cases were relied on and it was held that the damages should be assessed according to what it would have cost the tenant to rent alternative local authority accommodation had any been available. Hoffmann LJ said:

A person entitled to possession of land can make a claim against a person who has been in occupation without his consent on two alternative bases. The first is for the loss which he has suffered in consequence of the defendant's trespass. This is the normal measure of damages in the law of tort. The second is the value of the benefit which the occupier has received. This is a claim for restitution. The two bases of claim are mutually exclusive and the plaintiff must elect before judgment which of them he wishes to pursue. These principles are not only fair but, as Kennedy LJ demonstrated, also well established by authority.

It is true that in earlier cases it has not been expressly stated that a claim for mesne profit for trespass can be a claim for restitution. Nowadays I do

---

2 [1975] Ch 408.
3 Ibid at 420.
4 [1993] 40 EG 144. See also *Ministry of Defence v Thompson* [1993] 40 EG 148.

not see why we should not call a spade a spade. In this case the Ministry of Defence elected for the restitutionary remedy.[5]

(iii) Nuisance

The hypothetical bargain approach adopted in *Bracewell v Appleby* was further applied in assessing damages in lieu of a mandatory injunction in *Carr-Saunders v Dick McNeil Associates Ltd*,[6] where the defendants were liable in nuisance for having erected extra storeys to their buildings which interfered with the plaintiff's light. Most significantly for present purposes Millett J said that he was 'entitled to take account of . . . the amount of profit which the defendants would look to in the development of their site.'[7] This indicated his willingness to adopt a restitutionary analysis. However, since no evidence of profit was available, the damages awarded are most naturally viewed as compensating for the plaintiff's loss of use and amenity rather than reversing profit. Only if in reality the plaintiff would have been willing to accept a fee to allow that building had the defendants approached him are the damages explicable as restitutionary, for the damages could then be regarded as either compensating for the lost fee or as reversing the expense the defendants had saved in not paying that fee.

A case in which one might have expected the hypothetical bargain approach to be adopted in assessing damages for the tort of nuisance, and yet it was not, was *Stoke-on-Trent City Council v W & J Wass Ltd*.[8] The defendants had deliberately committed the tort of nuisance by operating a market within a distance infringing the plaintiff's proprietary market right. While an injunction was granted to restrain further infringement, the Court of Appeal awarded merely nominal damages on the ground that the plaintiff had suffered no loss of custom. In so doing the Court of Appeal unconvincingly distinguished the cases discussed above in this section and indeed approached the whole case as if only compensatory damages could be awarded. It was only at the very end of Nourse LJ's judgment that there was any reference to restitution. He said:

It is possible that the English law of tort, more especially of the so-called 'proprietary torts', will in due course make a more deliberate move towards recovery based not on loss suffered by the plaintiff but on the unjust enrichment of the defendant—see Goff and Jones *The Law of Restitution* (3rd edn)

5 Ibid at 146.
6 [1986] 2 All ER 888.
7 Ibid at 896.
8 [1988] 3 All ER 394.

pp 612–14. But I do not think that the process can begin in this case and I doubt whether it can begin at all at this level of decision.[9]

This contrasts with the more enlightened view taken by Peter Gibson J at first instance. He awarded substantial damages on the basis of an appropriate licence fee that the plaintiff could have charged the defendant for lawful operation of its market: that is, he awarded damages applying the 'hypothetical bargain' approach of *Bracewell v Appleby*. On the facts that could have constituted a compensatory measure because the plaintiff might well have granted such a licence. Alternatively those damages could have been restitutionary stripping the defendant of some of the profits made.

(iv) Breach of confidence

In *Seager v Copydex (No 2)*[10] Lord Denning said that if there was nothing special about the confidential information, damages for breach of confidence should be based on the fee the defendant had saved himself by not employing a consultant to acquire that information; whereas if the information was special, damages should be assessed according to what a willing buyer would have paid for it.

The former looks like a restitutionary approach, whereas the latter is consistent with either compensation or restitution; as compensation, it would represent the profit the plaintiff had lost in not selling to a third party or the defendant; as restitution, it would represent a fair proportion of the defendant's profits, or the expense saved in either not buying that information from the plaintiff or equivalent information elsewhere.

However, even assuming restitution was the basis,[11] *Seager v Copydex (No 2)* may not necessarily be inconsistent with *Phillips v Homfray*, because on one view confidential information can be regarded as property. Indeed Lord Denning drew an analogy with conversion and even suggested that by paying damages the defendant would be entitled to 'keep' the information.

(b) Account of profits

This is an equitable remedy by which the defendant is required to draw up an account of, and then to pay the amount of, the net profits he has acquired by particular wrongful conduct. The remedy's label 'account of profits' is therefore shorthand for 'account and

---

9 Ibid at 402.
10 [1969] 1 WLR 809.
11 Supra, p 181, concentrates on the compensation analysis.

award of profits'. The contrast with compensatory damages was clearly stressed in the typically superb judgment of Windeyer J in the Australian infringement of trade mark case, *Colbeam Palmer Ltd v Stock Affiliates Pty Ltd*:[12]

The distinction between an account of profits and damages is that by the former the infringer is required to give up his ill-gotten gains to the party whose rights he has infringed; by the latter he is required to compensate the party wronged for the loss he has suffered. The two computations can obviously yield different results, for a plaintiff's loss is not to be measured by the defendant's gain, nor a defendant's gain by the plaintiff's loss. Either may be greater, or less, than the other. If a plaintiff elects to take an inquiry as to damages the loss to him of profits which he might have made may be a substantial element of his claim . . . But what a plaintiff might have made had the defendant not invaded his rights is by no means the same thing as what the defendant did make by doing so.

As yet, an account of profits is only available for torts involving an infringement of intellectual property rights, whether by the infringement of a patent,[13] copyright,[14] design right[15] or trade mark,[16] or passing off;[17] or for breach of confidence.[18] Confinement of this equitable remedy to those torts is explicable historically because they have their roots in equity; and breach of confidence is still best viewed as an equitable wrong. But this is not a policy justification and it can be argued that the role of an account of profits should be expanded to reverse gains made by any deliberate tort.

Originally the courts would only award an account of profits if ancillary to an injunction. For example, in *Smith v London and South Western Rly Co*[19] and *Price's Patent Candle Co Ltd v Bauwen's Patent Candle Co Ltd*[20] it was held that no account of profits could be

---

12 (1968) 122 CLR 25 at 32.
13 Patents Act 1977, s 61(1)(d), *Siddell v Vickers* (1892) 9 RPC 152. Presumably design infringement is analogous.
14 Copyright, Designs and Patents Act 1988, s 96(2); *Delfe v Delamotte* (1857) 3 K & J 581; *Potton Ltd v Yorkclose Ltd* [1990] FSR 11.
15 Copyright, Designs and Patents Act 1988, s 229(2).
16 *Edelsten v Edelsten* (1863) 1 De G J & SM 185; *Slazenger & Sons v Spalding & Bros* [1910] 1 Ch 257.
17 *Lever v Goodwin* (1887) 36 Ch D 1; *My Kinda Town Ltd v Soll* [1982] FSR 147; revsd on liability [1983] RPC 407.
18 *Peter Pan Manufacturing Corpn v Corsets Silhouette Ltd* [1963] RPC 45; *Ansell Rubber Co Pty Ltd v Allied Rubber Industries Pty Ltd* [1972] RPC 811; *AB Consolidated v Europe Strength Food Co Pty Ltd* (1978) 2 NZLR 515; *A-G v Guardian Newspapers Ltd (No 2)* [1990] 1 AC 109.
19 (1854) Kay 408.
20 (1858) 4 K & J 727.

awarded, because as there would be no further patent infringement, there was no justification for an injunction. But while it is generally the case that an account of profits is awarded in addition to an injunction, this no longer seems to be a requirement. Presumably as with an injunction traditional equitable defences concerning the plaintiff's conduct, such as clean hands and acquiescence, will apply as bars to an account of profits.

There are four remaining issues of importance:

(i) Innocent wrong-doing

There is an interesting difference between these torts as to whether an account of profits will be refused because the defendant was an innocent wrong-doer. So by s 62(1) of the Patents Act 1977, in proceedings for patent infringement, it is a defence to a claim for an account of profits or indeed damages (but not an injunction) that the defendant was not aware, and had no reasonable grounds for supposing, that the patent existed. Somewhat similarly, albeit requiring a higher degree of fault, it was laid down in *Edelsten v Edelsten*[1] and *Slazenger & Sons v Spalding & Bros*[2] that neither damages nor an account of profits can be awarded for infringement of a trade mark, unless the defendant knew of the plaintiff's trade mark. Windeyer J explained this as follows in *Colbeam Palmer Ltd v Stock Affiliates Pty Ltd*:[3]

By [the account of profits] a defendant is made to account for, and is then stripped of profits he has made which it would be unconscionable that he retain. These are profits made by him dishonestly, that is by knowingly infringing the rights of the proprietor of the trade mark.

Again, although there are no decisions on this point in relation to passing off, Lord Parker did say in referring to a passing off representation in *Spalding & Bros v A W Gamage Ltd*,[4] '... the complete innocence of the party making it may be a reason for limiting the account of profits to the period subsequent to the date at which he becomes aware of the true facts'.

It may be that the same distinction is also being drawn for breach of confidence. For while an account of profits was ordered in *Peter Pan Manufacturing Corpn v Corsets Silhouette Ltd*[5] and *A-G*

1 (1863) 1 De GJ & SM 185.
2 [1910] 1 Ch 257.
3 (1968) 122 CLR 25 at 34.
4 (1915) 84 LJ Ch 449.
5 [1963] RPC 45.

v Guardian Newspapers Ltd (No 2) (the *Spycatcher* case),[6] the Court of Appeal in *Seager v Copydex Ltd*[7] considered that only damages and not an injunction or an account of profits was appropriate: and one obvious ground of distinction was that the defendants in the *Peter Pan* and *Spycatcher* cases acted dishonestly with knowledge of their wrongdoing, whereas the reverse was true in *Seager v Copydex*.[8]

But in contrast to the above are ss 97(1) and 233(1) of the Copyright, Designs and Patents Act 1988 whereby, for infringement of copyright and a primary infringement of a design right respectively, it is a defence to damages *but not to an account of profits* that the defendant did not know and had no reason to believe that copyright or the design right subsisted in the work or design to which the action relates. There is no justification for such a difference of approach and the inconsistency should be removed. Whether this should be by adopting the standard of deliberate wrongdoing, as for the common law torts, or negligence, as for patent infringement, or strict liability, as for copyright and design infringement, is a difficult policy issue which ultimately rests on the justification for applying restitution as a mid-position between compensation and punishment.

(ii) Account of which profits?

The courts' approach shows a veiled awareness that the wrong must have been a factual cause of the profits for which the account is ordered. Slade J recently affirmed the central principle in the following classic statement in *My Kinda Town Ltd v Soll*,[9] where the defendants were alleged to be liable for passing off by using a name similar to the plaintiffs' for their own chain of restaurants:

> The purpose of ordering an account of profits in favour of a successful plaintiff in a passing off case is not to inflict punishment on the defendant. It is to prevent an unjust enrichment of the defendant by compelling him to surrender those . . . parts of the profits, actually made by him which were improperly made and nothing beyond this.

It followed that as the alleged tort comprised confusing the public into thinking the defendants' restaurants were the plaintiffs', the profits to be accounted for were only those additional profits caused

---

6 [1990] 1 AC 109.
7 [1976] 1 WLR 923.
8 For another distinction, see infra, p 303.
9 [1982] FSR 147 at 156; revsd on liability [1983] RPC 407. See also *Potton Ltd v Yorkclose Ltd* [1990] FSR 11.

by that confusion, and not all the profits made by the defendants from those restaurants.[10]

Again, in relation to infringement of a trade mark, it is not all the profits from the sale of infringing goods that are gained by the infringement and must be accounted for: rather it is only those made because the goods were sold under the trademark. As Windeyer J said in *Colbeam Palmer v Stock Affiliates Pty Ltd*,[11] 'The profit for which the infringer of a trade mark must account is thus not the profit he made from selling the article itself but . . . the profit made from selling it under the trademark.'

Similarly, as Lord Watson pointed out in dicta in *United Horse Shoe & Nail Co Ltd v Stewart & Co*,[12] it 'would be unreasonable to give the patentee profits which were not earned by the use of his invention.' So where the patent infringement comprises using a particular means of manufacturing goods, but there are other means, the profits to be accounted for are those made by using that particular means; that is, as suggested in *Siddell v Vickers*,[13] one should compare the profits actually made with those that would have been made if the next most likely means of manufacture had been adopted.

Factual causation provides a further possible ground for reconciling the two breach of confidence cases of *Peter Pan*, in which an account of all sales profits was ordered, and *Seager v Copydex* where damages only were awarded; for in *Peter Pan*, the defendants could not have manufactured the article at all without the use of confidential information, whereas in *Seager v Copydex*, the confidential information made a relatively minor contribution to the defendants' product.

It can also be argued that, beyond applying factual cause, a court should restrict an account of profits to a fair proportion of the profits made by the wrong to take account, for example, of the skill and effort expended by the defendant to make the profit. But as yet there has been no such restriction,[14] perhaps because the wrongdoing in issue has generally been deliberate.

---

10 *Lever v Goodwin* (1887) 36 Ch D 1, where the amount of profits included sales to non-confused customers, was distinguished on the unconvincing ground that the sales there were to middlemen.

11 (1968) 122 CLR 25 at 37.

12 (1888) 13 App Cas 401 at 412–3.

13 (1892) 9 RPC 152.

14 But see in support, Robert Goff J's dicta in *Redwood Music Ltd v Chappell & Co Ltd* [1982] RPC 109 at 132 (innocent copyright infringement).

(iii) Difficulty of an account of profits

A point emphasised in many of the cases, particularly those of the nineteenth century, in which an account of profits has been ordered is the difficulty of working out the profits the defendant has wrongfully acquired. For example, in *Price's Patent Candle Co Ltd v Bauwen's Patent Candle Co Ltd*[15] V-C Sir Page Wood said, '. . . the questions involved in taking accounts of the particular instances in which patents have been infringed, and of the profits thereby made, are questions of great nicety and difficulty and never tend to any satisfactory result.'[16] But particularly where all profits on the manufacture and sale of certain goods have to be accounted for, it is hard to see why this is regarded as that difficult. After all in the *Peter Pan Manufacturing* case, which concerned the manufacture and sale by the defendants of bras of a certain design in breach of confidence, Pennycuick J was able to put forward what appears to be a fairly simple formula to apply: 'What has the [defendant] expended upon manufacturing these goods? What is the price which he has received on their sale? and the difference is profit.'[17] Even where only some of the profits from sales of goods have to be accounted for, it is not clear why it is thought more difficult to work out the profits the defendant has made from his wrong, than it is to calculate compensatory damages for, for example, the profits the plaintiff has lost as a result of the wrong.

Perhaps the explanation for this emphasis on difficulty is that traditionally the courts have taken the view that an account of profits requires a very precise calculation of the relevant profits, with an actual account having to be drawn up, showing gains and losses, whereas it has been accepted that damages can be calculated in a rough and ready manner. But there is no reason why an account of profits should not also be roughly rather than precisely calculated and in support of this are Slade J's comments in *My Kinda Town Ltd v Soll*:[18]

. . . the general intention of the Court in making the order [of an account of profits] . . . has been to achieve a fair apportionment, so that neither party will have what justly belongs to the other. What will be required on the inquiry, if it has to be pursued, will not be mathematical exactness, but only a reasonable approximation.

---

15 (1858) 4 K & J 727.
16 Ibid at 730. See also *Crosley v Derby Gaslight Co* (1838) 3 My & Cr 428; *Siddell v Vickers* (1892) 9 RPC 152.
17 [1963] RPC 45 at 60.
18 [1982] FSR 147 at 159. See also *Potton Ltd v Yorkclose Ltd* [1990] FSR 11.

It may be that such recognition that an account of profits does not require absolute exactness will open the way for a greater use of this remedy which traditionally, because of the precision thought to be required, has rarely been claimed in preference to damages.

(iv) Account of profits and damages

It has been laid down that a plaintiff cannot both be awarded damages and an account of profits.[19] The justification for this is not entirely clear. It is hard to see that combining restitution and compensation for a tort is inconsistent or constitutes double recovery: one is concerned with the defendant's gain, the other with the plaintiff's loss. In *Neilson v Betts*[20] Lord Westbury explained the rule on the ground that, 'The two things are hardly reconcilable, for if you take an account of profits you condone the infringement.' But this reasoning is unconvincing, and it has been restrictively interpreted in *Codex Corpn v Racal-Milgo Ltd*,[1] where the actual decision was that the taking of an account of profits for infringement of patent does not amount to a 'franking' of the defendant's products so as to prevent future actions for patent infringement. Indeed Lord Westbury's view is reminiscent of the argument rejected in *United Australia Ltd v Barclays Bank Ltd*[2] that, having 'waived the tort' and sued for an action for money had and received, the plaintiff cannot switch to claiming damages for conversion if judgment on that prior action is unsatisfied. Ultimately, perhaps, the rule simply reflects the view that an account of profits can be a harsh remedy which, if anything, should be cut back rather than added to.

(c) Conclusion

The cases show that while there has been no award of money had and received for a tort that contradicts the restrictive view of benefit laid down in *Phillips v Homfray*, the same cannot be said of restitutionary damages and an account of profits. The sort of torts for which restitutionary remedies can be given are therefore not

---

19 *Neilson v Betts* (1871) LR 5 HL 1; *De Vitre v Betts* (1873) LR 6 HL 319; Patents Act 1977, s 61(2); *Colbeam Palmer Ltd v Stock Affiliates Pty Ltd* (1968) 122 CLR 25. See analogously *United Australia Ltd v Barclays Ltd* [1941] AC 1, supra, p 292, fn 4, in which it was accepted that a plaintiff cannot recover both compensatory damages and an award of money had and received for a tort. See generally Tilbury *Civil Remedies* (1990) paras 2015, 2027. See also supra, pp 11–2.
20 Ibid at 22.
1 [1984] FSR 87.
2 [1941] AC 1.

restricted to those in which the plaintiff's property or its proceeds have been acquired.

Taking all three types of restitutionary remedy together (award of money had and received, account of profits, restitutionary damages) the torts for which restitution have been awarded have involved interference with the plaintiff's property, whether that property be real or personal or intellectual.[3] The cases therefore reveal a judicial desire firmly to deter even innocent interference with the plaintiff's property; that is, merely to compensate for any loss caused appears to be regarded as insufficient to deter that interference. This seems sensible. Applying Jackman's illuminating theory, restitution is justified as a means of deterring harm to the facilitative institution of private property.[4]

A subsidiary feature exhibited in a few of the account of profits cases (eg for passing off, infringement of trademark, breach of confidence) is that the tort must be committed deliberately if restitution is to be awarded. It can be argued that this category should be expanded[5] so that restitution should be awarded to reverse gains made by, eg deliberately inducing a breach of contract or a deliberate libel.[6] This is particularly so, if the courts can rid themselves of the former emphasis on an account of profits being mathematically exact. Indeed on the present law, however unsatisfactory, exemplary damages can be awarded for these torts under the category of deliberately exploiting wrongdoing to make a profit[7] and, since stripping the defendant of his unjust profits by restitution is less drastic than punishment,[8] it is arguable that restitution should follow on the reasoning that the greater should include the lesser.

Whether one's emphasis is on proprietary torts, or on deliberate wrongdoing, the recent denial of restitution in *Stoke-on-Trent City Council v W & J Wass Ltd* was disappointing for the tort in question was not only proprietary but was also committed cynically.

Finally it should be observed that the manoeuvring around *Phillips v Homfray* shown by the present law, and the argument considered for greater expansion of the deliberate wrongdoing category, are both supported by the law in the United States.[9] As

3 This was emphasised in *Surrey CC v Bredero Homes Ltd* [1993] 3 All ER 705.
4 (1989) CLJ 302.
5 See Birks *Introduction* pp 326–7.
6 Street also gave examples for the tort of battery in *Principles of the Law of Damages* p 254.
7 Supra, pp 274–7.
8 *Cassell & Co Ltd v Broome* [1972] AC 1027 at 1130 (per Lord Diplock); Ashworth *Sentencing and Penal Policy* (1983) p 294.
9 *Edwards v Lee's Administrators* 96 SW 2d 1028 (1936) (account of profits for trespass to land) and *Raven Red Ash Coal Co v Ball* 39 SE 2d 231 (1946) (value of

with so much else in the law of obligations, English law can therefore usefully turn for support and impetus to the American
experience.

3. ENRICHMENTS GAINED BY BREACH OF CONTRACT[10]

We are here concerned with remedies that reverse gains because the
defendant has acquired them by breach of a contract with the
plaintiff.

It is initially important to stress that remedies, such as the recovery of money had and received for total failure of consideration
and a *quantum meruit*, which an innocent party can claim once he
has validly terminated a contract for breach, are better viewed as
within autonomous unjust enrichment by subtraction, rather than
unjust enrichment by wrongs: that is, they are not remedies for
breach of contract.[11] Three main features of the law support this
view. First, the plaintiff must have validly terminated the contract,
before he can claim these remedies. If the remedies were simply for
breach of contract, there would be no need for this, whereas on the
autonomous unjust enrichment view this is readily explicable on the
ground that it is only where the contract is terminated that the
direct shift of wealth from the plaintiff to the defendant is invalidated. Indeed under the present law, there is a further restriction on
the recovery of money in that total invalidation of the transfer is
necessary: that is, to recover money, there must have been a total
rather then merely a partial failure of consideration.[12]

Secondly, even though no breach is involved, the same restitutionary remedies governed by the same, or very similar, principles
are available where the contract is unenforceable (for example, for
lack of formality) or is void (for example, for uncertainty) or is

---

use of land) directly depart from *Phillips v Homfray*. See also *Olwell v Nye and
Nissen Co* 26 Wash 2d 282 (1946) (reasonable value of use/expense saved by conversion of egg-washing machine); *Federal Sugar Refining Co v United States Sugar
Equalisation Bd* 286 F 575 (1920) (profits from inducing breach of contract). But
see *Hart v EP Dutton & Co Inc* 93 NYS 2d 871 (1949) (refusing restitution for
libel). See generally Palmer *Law of Restitution* (1978) Vol I, pp 49–140, 157–66.

10 See generally Jones (1983) 99 LQR 443; Farnsworth (1985) 94 Yale LJ 1339;
Birks (1987) LMCLQ 421; Stoljar (1989) 2 JCL 1; Palmer *Law of Restitution* Vol
I, pp 437–52; Maddaugh and McCamus *The Law of Restitution* pp 432–8;
Beatson *The Use and Abuse of Unjust Enrichment* pp 15–17.

11 Birks *Introduction* p 334, (1983) 36 CLP 141, 149 et seq.

12 Surprisingly, the Law Commission favoured retention of this—Report No 121
Law of Contract; Pecuniary Restitution on Breach of Contract (1983). See
Burrows (1984) 47 MLR 76, 83–6.

merely anticipated. Prior to the Law Reform (Frustrated Contracts) Act 1943 this was also true of the remedies available where the contract was frustrated.

Thirdly, it is no restriction on the recovery of money paid in an action for money had and received that the defendant had made a good bargain. Say, for example, the plaintiff contracts to buy a car from the defendant for £900 and pays £100 in advance; the defendant fails to deliver the car: the market price is £700: the plaintiff can recover £100 in an action for money had and received.[13] This cannot be sensibly explained if the recovery is regarded as a restitutionary remedy *for* the breach of contract: for the breach cannot be regarded as a cause of the defendant's gain, since if there had been no breach, the defendant would still have made that gain from the contract. The same may also be the law regarding the plaintiff's *quantum meruit* claim. Certainly in *Lodder v Slowey*[14] on appeal from New Zealand, the Privy Council in assessing the plaintiff's *quantum meruit* considered it irrelevant that the defendant might have made a good bargain so that he would have retained some part of that gain if he had not broken the contract. However, this aspect of the law is readily explicable if one regards such restitutionary remedies as falling within autonomous unjust enrichment by subtraction rather than unjust enrichment by wrongs; for if the basis is not breach of contract, but rather an invalidation of the shift of wealth from the plaintiff to the defendant, there is no necessary reason why the value of the defendant's contractual counter-performance should be regarded as relevant.[15]

But if the remedies just discussed are not restitutionary remedies for breach of contract, are there any restitutionary remedies that are?

Generally speaking, the answer to this is no. On the whole, the law does not seek to reverse enrichments that may be considered unjust because acquired by a breach of contract. The defendant must pay damages compensating the plaintiff according to his expectation interest, but he is not made liable for any profits he has acquired by breaking the contract. So, for example, in the Scottish case of *Teacher v Calder*,[16] the defendant financier broke a contract to invest £15,000 in the plaintiff's timber business, and instead

---

13   *Wilkinson v Lloyd* (1845) 7 QB 27.

14   [1904] AC 442. See also *Boomer v Muir* 24 P 2d 570 (1933).

15   This is not to deny that there may be other good reasons for thinking *Lodder v Slowey* incorrect: eg it can be strongly argued that given 'subjective devaluation' the contract price should often be relevant within autonomous unjust enrichment in assessing the services' value to the defendant.

16   (1899) 1 F 39.

invested the same sum in a distillery. It was held that the plaintiff's damages were to compensate for the loss to his business and were not concerned with a disgorgement of the much higher profits the defendant had gained from the distillery investment.

Similarly, where the benefit gained by the breach comprises a saving of expense, no restitutionary remedy is generally awarded to reverse that benefit. As Megarry V-C said in *Tito v Waddell (No 2)*:[17]

> . . . it is fundamental to all questions of damages that they are to compensate the plaintiff for his loss or injury by putting him as nearly as possible in the same position as he would have been in had he not suffered the wrong. The question is not one of making the defendant disgorge what he has saved by committing the wrong, but one of compensating the plaintiff.

So in that case it was irrelevant that the defendants had saved themselves considerable expense by not replanting Ocean Island as they had covenanted to do. The plaintiff's loss was alone considered relevant, and as the islanders no longer intended to replant the island, and were therefore not entitled to the cost of cure, a small sum of damages for the trivial difference in value of the land was awarded.[18] It is important to stress that while the cost of cure may, in some cases, be equivalent to the expense saved, there is no necessary correlation between the two: for example, where cheaper materials have been used in building, the cost of replacing them is likely to be far greater than the expense the defendant saved. In a nutshell, cost of cure damages are indisputably compensatory and not restitutionary.

Again in the leading case of *Surrey CC v Bredero Homes Ltd*[19] the Court of Appeal refused to award restitutionary damages for a breach of contract whether assessed according to the full profits made by the breach by the contract-breaker or according to the expense saved by the contract-breaker in not seeking a release from its contractual undertaking. The plaintiff councils had sold two adjoining parcels of land to the defendant for the development of a housing estate. The defendant covenanted to develop the land in accordance with the scheme approved by the plaintiffs. In breach of that covenant it built more houses on the site than under the approved scheme thereby making extra profit. Although aware of the breach, the plaintiffs did not seek an injunction or specific

17 [1977] Ch 106 at 332.
18 An interim sum, which it was argued the plaintiffs would have accepted for releasing the defendants from their obligation, was also rejected, ibid at 319: see supra, p 152.
19 [1993] 3 All ER 705. See O'Dair [1993] RLR 31; Burrows [1993] LMCLQ 453.

performance but waited until the defendant had sold all the houses on the estate and then sought damages. Nominal damages only were awarded on the ground that the plaintiffs had suffered no loss and restitutionary damages were inappropriate because this was an action for ordinary common law damages for breach of contract: it did not involve either a tort or an invasion of proprietary rights or equitable damages.

But should the law award restitutionary damages reversing the enrichment gained by a breach of contract? Several commentators have argued that it should. For example, Jones writes, 'It is difficult to accept the justice of the result of such cases as *Tito v Waddell (No 2)*, where the defendant had saved himself considerable expense from failing to execute his promise but where the plaintiff's damages were trivial because he had suffered no "loss".'[20] Jones cites the Louisiana case of *City of New Orleans v Fireman's Charitable Association*[1] as a further striking example of injustice. The defendant had contracted with the plaintiff to provide a fire-fighting service over a number of years and had received the full contract price. After the expiry of the contract, the plaintiff discovered that the defendant had not had available the number of men or horses or the footage of pipe promised under the contract. As the plaintiff had suffered no loss—for example, there was no averment that the defendant had failed to extinguish any fires because of the breach— no substantial damages were recovered, despite the fact that the defendant had saved itself over $40,000 by the breach of contract.

In both those cases, the benefit comprised a saving of expense and in the first edition of this book it was suggested that, while the courts should generally not strip away profits made by a contract-breaker, they should be prepared to award restitution depriving him of the expense saved by breach.[2] That distinction primarily rested on the view that making profit in excess of what the plaintiff would have made requires skill and initiative which arguably deserves reward, whereas this is not so with regard to simply saving expense.

On reflection this may not be the best way forward for two main reasons. First, it is often hard to distinguish clearly between expense saved and profit. On one view expense saved is a type of profit. Secondly, there ought to be consistency between the approach to restitution for breach of contract and for torts and the tort cases do not suggest restricting restitution to expense saved.

20 (1983) 99 LQR 443 at 459.
 1 9 So 486 (1891).
 2 1st edn, at 273.

An alternative approach is to limit restitution to where the breach has been cynical (as on the facts of the above two cases).[3] But in many situations there could be practical problems in trying to draw a line (analogous to the second category of exemplary damages) between the deliberate cynical and the 'innocent' non-cynical contract-breaker.[4] Moreover, it flies in the face of the whole tradition of contract law to differentiate in any way between cynical and innocent breach.

A further suggestion is that restitution should be reserved for where compensatory damages are inadequate.[5] But in itself the notion of inadequacy is a vague and elastic one which leaves unclear the precise reason for restitution. And if the inadequacy is thought to stem from unsatisfactory legal restrictions in assessing compensation, it may be more rational to reform the rules for compensation than to turn to an unrelated restitutionary measure.

Closely linked to this is the idea that restitution should be granted where specific performance (or an injunction) would be granted. So, for example, Beatson sees restitution as 'in reality a monetised form of specific performance.'[6] This is because if a person knows he will be stripped of his profits from breach there is no advantage for him in breaking the contract. Similar rules should therefore govern both types of remedy. This has the attraction of building on existing principles of contract law. However, on closer inspection, it is doubtful whether the restrictions on specific performance (eg that it cannot generally be awarded in contracts of personal service; or the severe hardship bar) are appropriate for, or relevant to, restitution. And different, less severe, restrictions apply to injunctions so that, on the face of it, the theory would lead, peculiarly, to restitution being more readily available for the breach of negative rather than positive promises. As Steyn LJ said, in rejecting this theory in *Surrey CC v Bredero Homes Ltd*: '. . . why should the availability of a restitutionary remedy, as a matter of legal entitlement, be dependent on the availability of the wholly different and discretionary remedies of injunctions and specific performance?'[7]

If all these mid-positions are rejected, one may be driven back to

---

3 Birks *Introduction* p 334; (1987) LMCLQ 421.
4 *Surrey CC v Bredero Homes Ltd* [1993] 3 All ER 705, 715 (per Steyn LJ); and for the Law Commission's rejection of this distinction, albeit in a different context, see Report No 121, paras 2.58–2.60.
5 Maddaugh and McCamus *The Law of Restitution* pp 436–8. See also O'Dair (1993) 46(2) CLP 113.
6 *The Use and Abuse of Unjust Enrichment* p 17. See also Waddams *Essays on the Law of Restitution* (ed Burrows) pp 208–12.
7 [1993] 3 All ER 705, 715. See also Dillon LJ at 713.

the two extreme and clear positions of either never allowing restitution for breach of contract[8] or awarding restitution wherever the
gain would not have been made but for the breach of contract.[9] Of
these two, the former reflects the present case law and is probably
to be preferred on the ground that, without a clear convincing case
for departing from the standard compensatory measure, conservatism should prevail.

It should be stressed that no weight is here being attached to the
argument that to allow the plaintiff a remedy reversing profits made
by breach, would deter economic efficiency. This sort of argument
is considered in detail and rejected elsewhere,[10] and here it is sufficient to point out that restitutionary damages will not necessarily
deter the defendant from an efficient breach—namely one where the
profits to be made from breach exceed the plaintiff's expectation
loss—because it will be in both parties' interests to negotiate the
defendant's release from the contract. Say D contracts to make a
machine part for P for £10,000, which P values at £13,000. X
offers D £15,000 for that part. The fact that P may be entitled to
restitution of say £5,000 for breach, would not deter the efficient
result of D delivering the part to X, because it is in P's interest to
accept between £3,000 and £5,000 to release D from the contract
(because if D sticks to the contract, P will make only £3,000) and
in D's interest to pay up to £5,000 to P to be released to transfer the
part to X.

But while in general the law has not granted restitutionary remedies reversing gains because acquired by a breach of contract there
has been the rare exceptional case. So, for example, in *Penarth Dock
Engineering Co Ltd v Pounds*,[11] the plaintiffs' action was brought not
only for trespass to land, but also for breach of contract, because the
defendants had contracted to move their pontoon by a particular
date; and while one can argue that Lord Denning's restitutionary
analysis was confined to the action for trespass, there is no indication of this in his judgment.

The leading case, however, is *Wrotham Park Estate Co Ltd v
Parkside Homes Ltd*,[12] where the defendants had built a number of
houses on land in breach of a restrictive covenant that was enforceable in equity by the plaintiffs. The plaintiffs were refused an

---

8 This is essentially Jackman's view (1989) 48 CLJ 302, 318–21.
9 Goff and Jones pp 414–7; Jones (1983) 99 LQR 483.
10 Infra, pp 351–2. Cf *Surrey CC v Bredero Homes Ltd* [1993] 3 All ER 705, 715 (per
    Steyn LJ).
11 [1963] 1 Lloyds Rep 359. Supra, p 295.
12 [1974] 1 WLR 798. It was followed in the tort case, *Bracewell v Appleby* [1975]
    Ch 408.

injunction ordering the houses to be demolished but damages in lieu were granted. Brightman J cited the leading authorities on tort restitutionary damages—namely *Whitwham v Westminster Brymbo Coal & Coke Co*,[13] Lord Shaw's dicta in *Watson Laidlaw & Co Ltd v Pott, Cassels & Williamson*,[14] Denning LJ's judgment in *Strand Electric and Engineering Co Ltd v Brisford Entertainments Ltd*[15] and *Penarth Dock Engineering v Pounds*[16]—and stressed that even though the plaintiffs had suffered no loss, in the sense that their land had not been diminished in value, nevertheless the defendants were bound to pay substantial damages for their breach. The damages were assessed according to what would have been a reasonable contract price for the plaintiffs to have accepted for relaxation of the covenant, even though in reality the plaintiffs would clearly never have granted such a relaxation.[17] In deciding what was a reasonable price, a major factor taken into account was the £50,000 profit that the defendants had made from the housing development, and ultimately damages were assessed at 5% of that profit. It would seem, therefore, that the damages were not compensating any loss of the plaintiffs, and are best viewed as restitutionary damages reversing the defendants' unjust enrichment, with the sum awarded representing a fair proportion of the profits made by the defendants and the reference to what the parties would themselves have agreed being a pure fiction.[18]

Of course if that is so the decision is inconsistent with the idea that restitutionary damages should not be available for breach of contract. However it can be justified as an exception on the ground that it is analogous to tort cases awarding restitutionary damages for interference with the plaintiff's property: breach of a restrictive covenant, albeit an action for breach of contract, is enforceable by third parties, contrary to normal privity restrictions, and is closely akin to a 'proprietary tort'.

This 'proprietary' reasoning was Steyn LJ's justification for *Wrotham Park* in *Surrey CC v Bredero Homes Ltd*. Rose LJ also thought *Wrotham Park* to have been correctly decided but Dillon LJ was less sure: while he was content to distinguish *Wrotham Park*

---

13 [1896] 2 Ch 538.
14 (1914) 31 RPC 104.
15 [1952] 2 QB 246.
16 [1963] 1 Lloyd's Rep 359.
17 [1971] 1 WLR 798 at 815.
18 Like the old implied contract approach to quasi-contract. In *Surrey CC v Bredero Homes Ltd* [1993] 3 All ER 705, 714, Steyn LJ said, 'The appellants' argument that *Wrotham Park* can be justified on the basis of a loss of bargaining opportunity is a fiction.'

from *Bredero* on the basis that the former was concerned to award equitable, not common law, damages he rightly observed that, following *Johnson v Agnew*,[19] equitable and common law damages should be assessed on the same principles. As he was rejecting restitutionary common law damages for breach of contract, his reasoning should logically have led him to disapprove *Wrotham Park*.

19 [1980] AC 367. Supra, p 244.

Chapter 7

The award of an
agreed sum

The award of an agreed sum is a remedy which protects the
promisee's expectations by enforcing the defendant's contractual
promise to pay a sum of money. As such, its justification ultimately
rests on the morality of promise-keeping.[1] The remedy can be
regarded as a hybrid, being like damages in that it is common law
and monetary but like specific performance in that its function is to
compel performance of a positive contractual obligation.

The most important agreed sum is an agreed price (or remuneration).[2] Indeed an action for the price is the commonest claim
brought for breach of contract.[3] Yet it is not afforded separate treatment in many standard works on contract, where references to it are
rather uncomfortably contained in sections on damages or discharge.[4] This chapter further differs from most analyses in including
liquidated damages and related sums (generally treated under damages)[5] alongside an agreed price, on the ground that they are also
agreed sums awarded by the courts.[6]

To analyse the main issues raised, each of the three principal
types of agreed sum will be examined in turn, after looking at some
points that apply whichever type of agreed sum is in question.

---

1 Supra, p 20.
2 If the amount has not been expressly agreed, but there is a valid contract for
  goods or services, a reasonable sum is payable and is awarded in a (contractual)
  action for *quantum valebant*, where goods, or *quantum meruit*, where services. See
  the Sale of Goods Act 1979, s 8(2); Supply of Goods and Services Act 1982,
  s 15(1); Treitel *Law of Contract* (8th edn, 1991), pp 933–4.
3 Beale *Remedies for Breach of Contract* p 144; Judicial Statistics (Annual Report)
  1991 (Cmnd 1990).
4 Eg *Cheshire, Fifoot & Furmston's Law of Contract* (12th edn, 1991) pp 616–18;
  Anson's Law of Contract (26th edn, 1984) pp 467–8, 491.
5 Eg Treitel *Law of Contract* pp 883–90.
6 For a similar approach see Waddams *Damages* (2nd edn) paras 7.10–7.20,
  8.10–8.30. Also see RSC Ord 6, r 2(1)(b) which treats all agreed sums together
  as debts or liquidated demands; *The Supreme Court Practice* 6/2/7.

1. GENERAL POINTS

The defendant must be in breach of a valid contractual obligation to pay the agreed sum. So the contract must not be void or unenforceable, and must not have been rescinded; nor must the obligation be one that has been wiped away by termination of the contract for frustration or breach.[7] Also the sum must be due. So an agreed sum payable on breach will only be awarded once that breach has occurred and an agreed sum payable on an event other than breach only when that specified event has taken place.[8] An agreed price is only regarded as due, in the absence of any express provision as to advance payment, where the plaintiff has completed or substantially completed what he is being paid for: for example, a seller of goods is generally not entitled to the agreed price until property in the goods has passed to the buyer, as laid down in s 49(1) of the Sale of Goods Act 1979,[9] and a builder generally not until he has completed or substantially completed the stage of the building to which the payment relates.[10]

Agreed sums are normally awarded after trial of the action. However, by s 32 of the Supreme Court Act 1981 and RSC Ord 29, r 12, the High Court has power to award an interim payment in respect of an agreed sum (or indeed any other monetary sum, other than damages, which are covered by Ord 29, r 11)[11] at an interlocutory stage, provided the claim concerns the use and occupation of land by the defendant or the court is satisfied that at the trial the plaintiff would obtain a judgment for a substantial sum of money, apart from any damages or costs.

The law governing interest payable on an agreed sum, agreed sums payable in foreign currency, and the limitation period for

---

7 In *Hyundai Heavy Industries Co Ltd v Papadopoulos* [1980] 1 WLR 1129, the plaintiffs, builders and sellers of a ship, were held able to recover an agreed sum, payable before termination for the defendant's breach, because the right to that part payment had already accrued. But this can be criticised for denying a contract-breaker's set-off/counterclaim for restitution to reverse the plaintiffs' unjust enrichment. See Atiyah *Sale of Goods* (8th edn, 1990) pp 469–71; Beatson (1981) 97 LQR 389.

8 Eg in *Damon Cia Naviera SA v Hapag-Lloyd International SA, The Blankenstein* [1985] 1 All ER 475, the 10% deposit was not recoverable as a debt because it was only payable on the buyers' signing of the contract.

9 Treitel *The Law of Contract* p 897 takes the view that s 49(1) adds a requirement to the sum being due and that this is explicable as encouraging mitigation. But see also Goode *Commercial Law* pp 351–2.

10 *Hoenig v Isaacs* [1952] 2 All ER 176.

11 Supra, p 102. It is unclear whether liquidated damages fall within Ord 29, r 11 or r 12. Theoretically, it should be the latter, but in practice it does not really matter.

claiming agreed sums,[12] has already been dealt with in chapters 2 and 4.

A difficult question is whether a promisee can enforce a contractual obligation to pay a sum of money to a third party by an action for an agreed sum. In principle there seems no objection to this. The defendant's promise is simply being enforced albeit that, subject to exceptions, the doctrine of privity prevents an action by the third party beneficiary. Yet there is no clear support for this, nor indeed direct discussion of it, in the cases or in academic writings.[13] What has been discussed is whether the promisee can sue for an agreed sum to be paid to him, which should have been paid to a third party. The objection in that situation is that the award of the agreed sum would no longer be specifically enforcing the defendant's promise to pay the third party. Windeyer J's dicta rejecting this idea in *Coulls v Bagot's Executor and Trustee Co Ltd*[14] therefore seems correct. If the promisee wishes to recover a monetary sum for himself he should instead sue for (unliquidated) damages.

2. AWARD OF AN AGREED PRICE OR REMUNERATION

The main issue and one of burning controversy is whether an action for the agreed price may fail where the defendant has clearly repudiated the contract[15] but the plaintiff, instead of accepting the repudiation and suing for damages, has kept the contract open. For example, a builder may have gone on to complete a building even though the owner has repudiated, or a seller of goods, where property in them has passed to the buyer, may have kept the goods for the buyer even though the buyer has refused to take delivery of them.

There are two major and contradictory approaches to this issue. First, one might say that the plaintiff has an unfettered option to hold the contract open and recover the agreed price: that is, that the duty to mitigate does not apply to an action for the agreed price and that it is no bar that damages are adequate. The alternative view is

---

12 But for agreed sums time runs afresh from an acknowledgment or part payment—Limitation Act 1980, s 29(5).

13 However, passages in *Beswick v Beswick* [1968] AC 58, 81, 88, 97 may be thought to suggest that the administratrix could sue for arrears to be paid *to the widow* in her personal capacity.

14 [1967] ALR 385, 411. Cf *Cleaver v Mutual Reserve Fund Life Association* [1892] 1 QB 147; Treitel *The Law of Contract* (8th edn) p 531.

15 The repudiation will almost always, but not necessarily, be anticipatory.

that the plaintiff may not be entitled to hold the contract open and recover the agreed price; the duty to mitigate does apply to an action for the agreed price and, where damages are adequate to compensate a plaintiff for his loss, it is contrary to that duty for him to carry on with his own unwanted performance and to claim the agreed price: rather, he should accept the repudiation, claim damages and make substitute contracts.

The leading case is *White and Carter (Councils) Ltd v McGregor*.[16] The plaintiffs supplied to local authorities litterbins on which they let advertising space. The defendants contracted to pay for the display of adverts, advertising their garage business, but later that day they repudiated the contract, which had been concluded by their sales manager contrary to the wishes of the proprietor. The plaintiffs refused to accept the repudiation, went ahead and displayed the adverts for the three-year period of the contract and claimed the agreed price of £196 4s. The House of Lords held, by a 3–2 majority, that they were entitled to the agreed price. Two of the majority (Lords Hodson and Tucker) simply adopted the first of the two views examined above. The third, Lord Reid, while basically taking that view, suggested a possible qualification:

. . . it may well be that, if it can be shown that a person has no legitimate interest, financial or otherwise, in performing the contract, rather than claiming damages, he ought not to be allowed to saddle the other party with an additional burden with no benefit to himself.[17]

But Lord Reid failed to clarify what having 'no legitimate interest' means. Presumably, though, he had a very narrow notion in mind, since despite the fact that damages would surely have been adequate for the plaintiffs, so that they had nothing to gain by continuing performance, Lord Reid did not think it established that they had no legitimate interest in continuing. On the other hand, Lords Morton and Keith, dissenting, took the second of the two views above. Lord Keith said:

I find the argument advanced for the appellants a somewhat startling one. If it is right it would seem that a man who has contracted to go to Hong Kong at his own expense and make a report, in return for remuneration of £10,000, and who, before the date fixed for the start of the journey and perhaps before he has incurred any expense, is informed by the other contracting party that he has cancelled or repudiated the contract, is entitled to set off for Hong Kong and produce his report in order to claim in debt the stipulated sum. Such a result is not, in my opinion, in accordance with

16 [1962] AC 413.
17 Ibid at 431.

principle or authority, and cuts across the rule that where one party is in breach of contract, the other must take steps to minimise the loss sustained by the breach.[18]

It is interesting to contrast immediately the leading United States case on this issue. In *Clark v Marsiglia*[19] a restorer of paintings, who had completed the restoration contracted for, despite an earlier repudiation of the contract by the owner, was held not to be entitled to the agreed price and was rather restricted to damages. Similarly by s 2–709(1)(b) of the Uniform Commercial Code, the seller of goods may only recover their price if he is '. . . unable after reasonable effort to resell them at a reasonable price or the circumstances reasonably indicate that such effort will be unavailing.'[20]

White & Carter has been both attacked and defended by academics,[1] and the judicial reaction has also been mixed.[2] In *Hounslow London Borough v Twickenham Garden Developments Ltd*[3] Megarry J explained, as Lord Reid had himself observed, that *White & Carter* can only apply where the plaintiff is able to carry on with his performance without the defendant's co-operation. But it is particularly significant, and reveals an underlying antipathy towards *White & Carter*, that Megarry J included passive co-operation within this: he therefore held that *White & Carter* did not apply to the facts before him since an owner of land on which building work is being carried out is required to co-operate with the builder in that he has to allow him to enter his land.

The Court of Appeal also distinguished *White & Carter* in *Attica Sea Carriers v Ferrostaal*.[4] This concerned a demise charterparty. On the assumption that the charterers were bound to repair the vessel before redelivery, it was held that, following repudiation by the charterers, the owners should have taken redelivery and were not entitled to insist on holding the contract open and receiving the agreed hire until the ship was repaired. Most radical was Lord Denning. He did not think *White & Carter* should be followed except in a case on all fours with it. 'It has no application whatever in a case where the plaintiff ought in all reason to accept the repudiation and sue for damages—provided that damages would provide

---

18 Ibid at 442.
19 1 Denio 317 (NY 1845).
20 See Atiyah *Sale of Goods* pp 471–3.
1 Goodhart (1962) 78 LQR 263; Neinaber (1962) CLJ 213; Tabachnik (1972) CLP 149.
2 It was followed very soon after in *Anglo-African Shipping Co of New York Inc v J Mortner Ltd* [1962] 1 Lloyds Rep 81.
3 [1971] Ch 233.
4 [1976] 1 Lloyds Rep 250.

an adequate remedy for any loss suffered by him.'[5] An analogy was then drawn with specific performance to emphasise, in contradiction of *White & Carter*, that, when damages are adequate, specific relief (including the action for the agreed sum) should not be granted. Lord Denning went on to emphasise that what made the plaintiff's refusal particularly unreasonable on these facts was that the repairs would cost four times as much as the difference in value between the repaired and unrepaired ship. The owner's refusal to accept repudiation was, therefore, doubly wasteful. Orr LJ, with whom Browne LJ concurred, while saying that he agreed with Lord Denning, distinguished *White & Carter* on the grounds that here co-operation was needed from the defendants, and the plaintiffs had no legitimate interest in holding the contract open. Unfortunately, no explanation of these points was forthcoming. One can safely assume, however, that on the latter point the majority was also influenced by the cost of repairs being uneconomic; it was this that made the facts of *Attica* so extreme.

There were no such unusual facts in *The Odenfeld*.[6] Charterers had repudiated a charterparty but the owners had refused to accept this and had kept the vessel at their disposal. The plaintiffs, assignees of money due under the charterparty, now claimed the agreed hire for the period in question. Kerr J distinguished *Attica Sea Carriers* and considered that it was only in extreme cases like that that *White & Carter* did not apply. In a statement resembling Lord Reid's, Kerr J said '. . . any fetter on the innocent party's right of election whether or not to accept a repudiation will only be applied in extreme cases, viz where damages would be an adequate remedy and where an election to keep the contract alive would be wholly unreasonable.'[7] Kerr J went on to say that on the facts of the case there was doubt about the adequacy of damages because of the difficulty in their assessment and that, since the owners had obligations to the plaintiffs to keep the charterparty in existence, they were not acting unreasonably in refusing to accept the repudiation.

But it would seem that an important, albeit veiled, departure from *White & Carter* and *The Odenfeld* has been made by Lloyd J in *Clea Shipping Corpn v Bulk Oil International Ltd*.[8] The facts were straightforward and again concerned a charterparty: the charterers had repudiated, but the owners had refused to accept this and had kept the vessel at the charterers' disposal until the expiry of the

5 Ibid at 255.
6 [1978] 2 Lloyds Rep 357.
7 Ibid at 374.
8 [1984] 1 All ER 129.

charter. The charterers in fact paid the hire for the full period, but now sought to recover it on the ground that the owners should have accepted the repudiation and were restricted to damages. The arbitrator's decision in favour of the charterers was upheld by Lloyd J. After a masterly survey of the case law he said the following:

Whether one takes Lord Reid's language which was adopted by Orr and Browne LJJ in *The Puerto Buitrago*, or Lord Denning MR's language in that case ('in all reason') or Kerr J's language in *The Odenfeld* ('wholly unreasonable . . .') there comes a point at which the court will cease, on general equitable principles, to allow the innocent party to enforce his contract according to its strict legal terms. How one defines that point is obviously a matter of some difficulty for it involves drawing a line between conduct which is merely unreasonable . . . and conduct which is *wholly* unreasonable . . . But however difficult it may be to define the point, that there *is* such a point seems to me to have been accepted . . .[9]

Applying this approach to the case before him, Lloyd J considered that the arbitrator could not be said to have been wrong to conclude that the relevant point had been reached, and hence that the owners should be restricted to damages. But ultimately, it is hard to see how this decision can be squared with *White & Carter* and *The Odenfeld*. True, Lord Reid and Kerr J recognised a point at which the plaintiff should accept the repudiation, but what is crucial is that that point was regarded as being reached only on extreme facts, like those in *Attica Sea Carriers*. Yet the facts in *Clea Shipping* were in no sense extreme. It would seem, therefore, that Lloyd J's decision represents a move towards the minority approach in *White & Carter* and the second of the two views set out above.

It should also be noted that in dicta Lloyd J did express tentative 'first blush' support for the view, accepted by the majority in *Attica Sea Carriers* but rejected in *The Odenfeld*, that a charterparty requires such co-operation as to fall outside *White & Carter*. Again this approach cannot be sensibly reconciled with *White & Carter*, and if adopted would similarly undermine that decision.

Should such a move away from *White & Carter* be supported, or is that decision justified? This depends on the extent to which it is felt that economic efficiency, as represented by the duty to mitigate, should counter the plaintiff's wish for specific enforcement of the promise to pay him money. Under *White & Carter* that wish is given overriding importance where the plaintiff can go ahead and fulfil his obligations. It is submitted that that is unsatisfactory. Where the plaintiff can be adequately compensated by damages, so

9 Ibid at 136–7.

that it is of no real benefit to him to carry on with his side of the contract, his wishes should be outweighed by the pure waste of his carrying on with an unwanted performance. Put shortly, where damages are adequate, economic efficiency dictates that the plaintiff should be required to mitigate, by stopping performance and making substitute contracts, rather than holding the contract open and claiming the agreed sum.[10] Indeed it should be realised, as clearly Lord Denning did in *Attica Sea Carriers*, that the *White & Carter* approach runs counter to the traditional approach to specific performance, where if damages are adequate, specific performance will not be granted. The importance of upholding the duty to mitigate, which is the primary argument used in chapter 8 to support the traditional subsidiary role of specific performance,[11] is therefore equally valuable for criticising *White & Carter*.

3. AWARD OF AN AGREED SUM PAYABLE ON BREACH—LIQUIDATED DAMAGES[12]

(1) The distinction between liquidated damages and penalties

Although the award of liquidated damages is conventionally treated as an aspect of contractual damages, it is in reality the same type of judicial remedy as the award of an agreed price, in that it is a common law monetary remedy which specifically enforces the defendant's promise to pay a sum of money. Where it differs fundamentally from the award of an agreed price is that the promise enforced represents the parties' agreed remedy for the (primary) breach of contract, and the important question is whether the courts should uphold what the parties have themselves agreed should be paid for breach rather than assessing what should be paid according to the usual principles of damages. Although strictly speaking this question is concerned with the validity of the promise, rather than the judicial remedy itself, examination of it is essential to understand what is meant by an award of liquidated damages. Moreover, it must be relevant to one's general understanding of damages to

---

10 The same argument has been used to criticise the damages principle—analogous to *White & Carter*, but arising only where the repudiation is anticipatory—that there is no duty to mitigate unless the plaintiff chooses to accept an anticipatory repudiation. See supra, p 75.

11 Infra, pp 350-3.

12 For a comparative account, see Treitel *Remedies for Breach of Contract* pp 208-34.

know whether the courts do award such an agreed sum, rather than damages assessed according to the usual principles.[13]

The short answer is that the courts will award the agreed sum if it is liquidated damages; but if it is a penalty, the promise to pay is invalid and the courts will instead award normal (unliquidated) damages. Wherein lies the difference? Liquidated damages are a sum which represents a genuine pre-estimate of the loss caused by the breach, that is, of what is needed to put the plaintiff into as good a position as if the contract had been performed. A penalty, on the other hand, is a sum which is greater than such a genuine pre-estimate, and is inserted to punish the other party in the event of breach and to pressurise him into carrying out his contractual obligations. The distinction was emphasised in Lord Dunedin's classic judgment in *Dunlop Pneumatic Tyre Co Ltd v New Garage & Motor Co Ltd*,[14] which in addition laid down several principles that are relevant in deciding whether a sum is liquidated damages or a penalty.[15] These will now be examined although some are perhaps so obvious as hardly to merit repetition.

(i)   The parties' use of the words 'penalty' or 'liquidated damages' does not conclusively decide the issue.

(ii)   One must judge the issue according to the circumstances at the time the contract was made and not at the time of breach.

(iii) The sum will be held to be a penalty if it is 'extravagant and unconscionable in amount in comparison with the greatest loss that could conceivably be proved to have followed from the breach.' So, for example, if a contract to carry out building work worth £100 provided that the builder should pay £50,000 if he failed to do the work, this would be a penalty.

(iv)   'It will be held to be a penalty if the breach consists only in not paying a sum of money, and the sum stipulated is a sum greater than the sum which ought to have been paid.' According to this, a clause making a debtor liable to pay £200, if he fails to pay £150 on the due day would be penal. But this point is clearly open to criticism in that a creditor's obligations may mean that his loss exceeds the sum due and the sum stipulated could very well, therefore, be a genuine pre-estimate of loss.

(v)   'There is a presumption (but no more) that it is a penalty

---

13 Forfeiture clauses raise analogous problems, but are outside this book's scope, since they are not directly enforceable by a judicial remedy and the underlying cause of action is not breach of contract but (autonomous) unjust enrichment.
14 [1915] AC 79.
15 Ibid at 87–8.

when "a single lump sum is made payable by way of compensation, on the occurrence of one or more or all of several events, some of which may occasion serious and others but trifling damage".[16]

(vi) 'It is no obstacle to the sum stipulated being a genuine pre-estimate of damage that the consequences of the breach are such as to make precise pre-estimation almost an impossibility. On the contrary, that is just the situation when it is probable that the pre-estimated damage was the true bargain between the parties.'

In the case itself, the defendants bought tyres from the plaintiffs under an agreement that they would neither tamper with the manufacturer's markings on the tyres, nor sell the tyres to the public below list price, nor sell them to persons whose supplies the plaintiffs had decided to suspend, nor exhibit or export them without the plaintiffs' consent. Five pounds was made payable for every tyre 'sold or offered' in breach of the agreement. The House of Lords held that this sum was liquidated damages. Although there were several ways in which tyres could be 'sold or offered' in breach of the agreement, the presumption in principle (v) was rebutted because the loss likely to result from any such breach was difficult to assess and £5 represented a genuine attempt to do so.

In *Philips Hong Kong Ltd v A-G of Hong Kong*[17] Lord Woolf, giving the judgment of the Privy Council upholding as liquidated damages a clause in a road construction contract, considered that the courts should not be too zealous in knocking down clauses as penal. '[W]hat the parties have agreed should normally be upheld.'[18] More specifically it was stressed that a clause can be a genuine pre-estimate of loss even though hypothetical situations could be presented in which the plaintiff's actual loss would be substantially lower. To hold otherwise would be to render it very difficult to draw up valid liquidated damages clauses in complex commercial contracts. Moreover it was thought acceptable to take account of the fact that, as it happened, the actual loss was not much greater than the agreed damages. Although the matter must be judged as at the date the contract was made, what actually happened 'can provide valuable evidence as to what could reasonably be expected to be the loss at the time the contract was made.'[19]

16 Citing from *Elphinstone v Monkland Iron & Coal Co* (1886) 11 App Cas 332 at 342.
17 (1993) 61 BLR 41.
18 Ibid at 59.
19 Ibid.

Hire-purchase and conditional sale agreements are a particularly rich source of illustrations of agreed sums payable on breach.[20] In *Bridge v Campbell Discount Co Ltd*,[1] for example, there was a minimum payment clause in the hire-purchase agreement whereby if the debtor was in breach of contract (or chose to terminate lawfully the contract) he should return the goods to the creditor and make up the payments already paid to two-thirds of the hire-purchase price. This sum was expressed to be 'compensation for depreciation'. The debtor, having made several payments, refused to pay any more and returned the car. The House of Lords, having held that he was in breach of contract, decided that the sum payable under the minimum payment clause was penal and irrecoverable because it did not represent a genuine pre-estimate of loss. In particular, the amount stated could not be regarded as compensation for depreciation because, in Lord Radcliffe's words, the clause:

... produces the result, absurd in its own terms, that the estimated amount of depreciation becomes progressively less the longer the vehicle is used under the hire. This is because the sum agreed upon diminishes as the total of cash payments increases. It is a sliding scale of compensation but a scale that slides in the wrong direction ...[2]

On the other hand, in *Wadham Stringer Finance Ltd v Meaney*[3] an accelerated payments clause in a conditional sale agreement—whereby on default of payment in two or more monthly instalments, the creditor was entitled to call for the unpaid balance of the purchase price plus certain charges, in return for title in the car passing to the debtor—was held to be a valid liquidated damages clause. It did represent a genuine pre-estimate of the creditor's loss, given that title was to pass to the debtor.

Further very common examples of agreed sums payable on breach are the demurrage which the charterer of a vessel agrees to pay for detention of the ship for unloading or loading beyond the lay-days and the compensation for delay provided for in building contracts.

The law on penalty clauses was extended to a clause to transfer shares, rather than to pay money, in *Jobson v Johnson*.[4] The defendant bought shares in a football club for £351,688. The purchase price was payable by an initial sum of £40,000 plus six half-yearly instalments of £51,948. The contract contained a clause that if the

20 And of sums payable on events other than breach.
1 [1962] AC 600.
2 Ibid at 623.
3 [1981] 1 WLR 39 at 48.
4 [1989] 1 All ER 621.

326 The award of an agreed sum

defendant defaulted in paying any instalment he was to transfer the shares back to the vendors for £40,000. Having paid £140,000 the defendant defaulted. The plaintiff, who was the assignee of the vendors, sought specific performance of the agreement for the retransfer of the shares. The Court of Appeal held that the clause for retransfer was an unenforceable penalty clause in that it was not a genuine pre-estimate of the vendors' loss. It did not matter that the clause required a transfer of property rather than a payment of money; nor that this was a rare case where equitable relief against forfeiture might *alternatively* have been sought. Dillon LJ said:

In principle, a transaction must be just as objectionable and unconscionable in the eyes of equity if it requires a transfer of property by way of penalty on a default in paying money as if it requires a payment of an extra, or excessive, sum of money.[5]

One might have expected that the defendant would therefore have been entitled to keep the shares, while compensating the plaintiff for his actual loss (ie for all the unpaid instalments plus interest). But as the plaintiff did not want that, the majority of the Court of Appeal instead gave him the option of insisting on either a sale of the shares by the court out of which his actual loss should be paid or an order of specific performance requiring the transfer of the shares for £40,000 if, on inquiry, that sum would not overcompensate him.

(2) Controversial issues under the present law

(a) Actual or legally recoverable loss?

Since an accepted important function of liquidated damages is to avoid difficulties of assessment, it must be the case that the loss that needs to be genuinely pre-estimated includes loss that is legally irrecoverable because it falls foul of the required standard of proof. But whether the loss referred to is exclusive of other legal restrictions on normal damages is unclear. In *Robophone Facilities Ltd v Blank*[6] Diplock LJ considered that liquidated damages could properly include loss that was beyond the defendant's reasonable contemplation (while a fortiori within the plaintiff's) and which would therefore be too remote under the principles for normal damages. On the other hand, the Law Commission provisionally thought 'that the proper yardstick by reference to which it should be

5 Ibid at p 628.
6 [1966] 1 WLR 1428.

determined whether the stipulated sum is a genuine pre-estimate is the damages which a court would award.'[7]

Perhaps the best answer lies in saying that it depends which legal restriction on actual loss is in issue; while there is no obvious objection to liquidated damages circumventing remoteness, or the fact that the type of loss is non-compensatable, it may well be unsatisfactory to uphold an agreed sum estimated on the assumption that the plaintiff will fail to mitigate for, as Beale writes, '. . . this would either encourage wasteful failures to mitigate or would over-compensate the wily party who both claimed the liquidated damages and mitigated.'[8]

(b) Loss greater than penalty

What if the agreed sum is a penalty, but the plaintiff's loss is greater than that agreed sum, so that to refuse to enforce the penalty would actually be to the plaintiff's advantage? Can the plaintiff insist on the penalty being invalid and thereby recover his actual loss? The situation is not as quirkish as may at first sight appear. For example, it is quite likely to occur when the penalty takes the form of one single agreed sum being fixed for the occurrence of several possible breaches. In *Wall v Rederiaktiebolaget Luggude*[9] it was held that charterers could disregard what was construed as a penalty clause (rather than as a liquidated damages or limitation clause) and sue for their greater actual loss. But this is rather weak authority since it is hard to see why the clause in question was penal. In *Cellulose Acetate Silk Co Ltd v Widnes Foundry Ltd*[10] the issue was expressly left open by the House of Lords, and Diplock LJ similarly regarded it as 'by no means clear' in *Robophone Facilities Ltd v Blank.*[11]

Which is the better view? On the one hand, it can be argued that, as matters are supposed to be judged at the time the contract is made, the penalty clause should be held invalid even where this is to the plaintiff's advantage. As against that, it can be argued that, since the refusal to enforce penalty clauses is a rare departure from freedom of contract and is designed to prevent unfairness to the defendant, there is no justification for holding penalties invalid where there is no such unfairness. Moreover, as Hudson has forcefully pointed out,[12] since it is well-settled that where the plaintiff's

---

7 Working Paper No 61 'Penalty Clauses and Forfeiture of Monies Paid' para 44.
8 *Remedies for Breach of Contract* p 57.
9 [1915] 3 KB 66, approved in *Watts Watts & Co Ltd v Mitsui & Co Ltd* [1917] AC 227. See also *Jobson v Johnson* [1989] 1 All ER 621.
10 [1933] AC 20.
11 [1966] 1 WLR 1428 at 1446.
12 (1974) 90 LQR 31; (1975) 91 LQR 25; (1985) 101 LQR 480.

loss is greater than the liquidated damages, he is confined to the liquidated damages,[13] to allow him to recover more than a penalty wrongly treats the plaintiff who has acted unfairly by inserting the penalty clause more favourably than the plaintiff who has acted fairly by genuinely pre-estimating the loss. It also encourages the inclusion of penalty clauses, since the plaintiff can take the advantage of having the clause, without suffering any disadvantage. So in this situation it does indeed seem preferable to uphold the penalty clause and, significantly, this was the view taken in the important Canadian case of *Elsley v JG Collins Ins Agencies Ltd.*[14]

(c) Liquidated damages used to limit damages[15]

While not a genuine pre-estimate of loss, a stipulated sum may be regarded as valid liquidated damages if it seeks to under-estimate and hence limit the plaintiff's damages. In *Cellulose Acetate Silk Co v Widnes Foundry Ltd*[16] a contract for the construction of an acetone recovery plant provided that if completion was delayed the contractor should pay 'by way of penalty the sum of £20 per working week'. The work was completed 30 weeks late and the owners suffered losses of £5,850 as a result. It was held by the House of Lords that the owners were restricted to £20 per week (that is £600) the clause being held valid albeit that its purpose was to limit rather than pre-estimate loss. It is important to realise that while such a clause looks like a limitation clause, the House of Lords was in fact regarding it as a type of liquidated damages clause, the difference being that under a liquidated damages clause a defendant is bound to pay the agreed sum, even if the plaintiff's loss is less, whereas under a limitation clause, he is bound to pay only the plaintiff's loss up to the limit fixed. So Lord Atkin said, 'I entertain no doubt that what the parties meant was that in the event of delay the damages and the only damages were to be £20 a week, *no less and no more.*'[17] But it may be doubted whether it is sensible to take such a hybrid interpretation, and perhaps the clause ought to have been treated as an ordinary limitation clause such that the owners would only have been entitled to their loss if less than £20. Furthermore if it were regarded as an ordinary limitation clause, it would clearly fall within the Unfair Contract Terms Act 1977, whereas it must be doubted whether this is so if the hybrid construction is taken. However, the

13 *Diestal v Stevenson* [1906] 2 KB 345.
14 (1978) 83 DLR (3d) 1 at 14–5.
15 Fritz (1954) 33 Tex LR 196.
16 [1933] AC 20.
17 Ibid at 25 (author's emphasis).

hybrid view is further supported by Lord Upjohn's judgment in *Suisse Atlantique Société d'Armement Maritime SA v Rotterdamsche Kolen Centrale NV*[18] where he said that, even if the demurrage clause in question represented an underestimate of loss, the sum agreed was valid liquidated damages rather than a limitation of liability.

(3) Should penalties, like liquidated damages, be valid?

The initial question is, why is it that the courts allow a plaintiff to recover liquidated damages, thereby ousting the judicial assessment and awarding of damages? The primary answer is that liquidated damages have a number of advantages. They make it less likely that there will be a serious dispute between the parties. They enable the defendant to know in advance what his exact liability will be. From the administration of justice angle, they save judicial time and expense in deciding what the plaintiff's damages should be and, from the plaintiff's point of view, they avoid such evils as the cost of litigation, the risk of inaccurate assessment by the courts, the need to prove one's loss according to the judicially imposed standard and probably restrictions such as remoteness and the non-recoverability of certain types of loss. Further to these advantages, the courts are not hostile to liquidated damages because they reflect the compensatory aim of judicially assessed damages: that is, they are a genuine pre-estimate of the sum needed to put the plaintiff into as good a position as if the contract had been performed.

In contrast, penalties run counter to the central principle that damages are for compensating the plaintiff and not punishing the defendant. They are therefore regarded as substantively unfair. However, in other areas the courts almost always require some procedural unfairness before they will undermine the freedom of the parties to fix their own terms, and hence their refusal to enforce penalty clauses is rather exceptional. This is one of the points made by those who argue that even penalty clauses should be upheld, subject to the usual factors invalidating a contract.[19] Additionally, it is said that there would be important advantages in making all agreed damages clauses prima facie valid. There would be less need for judicial assessment of damages with its attendant expense and, because parties would be more certain as to the validity of an agreed damages clause, litigation costs in testing validity would be reduced and contract making would be encouraged.

18 [1967] 1 AC 361 at 421.
19 Goetz and Scott (1977) 77 Col LR 554; Kaplan (1977) 50 So Cal LR 1055; Beale *Remedies for Breach of Contract* pp 60–1; Muir (1985) Syd LR 503.

On the other hand it has been argued that to uphold penalty clauses would encourage defendants to stick to contracts, which it would be economically efficient for them to break.[20] In other words, the 'efficient breach' theory is against upholding penalty clauses. This theory is discussed in more detail in chapter 8[1] and it will be sufficient here to give a couple of examples and to make a general criticism. Say D contracts to make a machine part for P for £10,000. If X offers D £15,000 for that part, breach by D is efficient if X values the part more than P, and inefficient if X values the part less than P. Let us assume, therefore, that P values the part at £13,000 so that efficiency dictates that D breaks the contract, pays P £3,000 damages and transfers the part to X for £15,000. The argument is that a penalty clause of, let us say, £6,000 in the contract between P and D will prevent the efficient breach, since D will no longer be better off by breaking the contract. However, the flaw in this is that it ignores the possibility of bargaining round the clause. It is in P's interests to accept between £3,000 and £5,000 to release D from the contract (because if D sticks to the contract P will make only £3,000) and in D's interest to pay up to £5,000 to P to be released to transfer the part to X. In other words, the validity of a penalty clause will only undermine efficiency where no bargaining round the clause will take place because the transaction costs are too high. As the transaction costs are unlikely to be high, the efficient breach theory is an unsatisfactory argument for knocking down penalty clauses. As Goetz and Scott write:

. . . the existence of an overcompensation provision is never per se evidence of an efficiency impediment. Absent significant negotiation costs, the pre-stipulation of a penalty still permits . . . efficient solutions in which the efficiency gains are divided between the breacher and the non-breacher in a bargained for manner.[2]

But while the efficient breach theory may be defective, the present refusal to enforce penalty clauses does seem justified.[3] There may even be some validity in the argument of Clarkson, Miller and Muris, that in many cases to uphold penalty clauses will act as an incentive for the plaintiff wastefully to direct resources to induce the

20 Fenton (1975) 51 Ind LJ 189, 191.
 1 Infra, pp 351–2.
 2 (1977) 77 Col LR 554, 568.
 3 As regards consumer contracts, the present law derives some support from para 1(e) of Council Directive 93/13/EEC on Unfair Terms in Consumer Contracts which lists as a possible unfair term one which has the object or effect of 'requiring any consumer who fails to fulfil his obligation to pay a disproportionately high sum in compensation.'

defendant to break the contract.[4] More straightforwardly, it is submitted that compensation rather than punishment is such a central feature of damages, and justifiably so, that it would be wrong to allow parties to oust that regime. Punishment belongs to the criminal and not the civil law.[5] And so while the courts should and do allow the parties to make their own assessment of compensation, it is unjustifiable in a claim for breach of contract for the plaintiff to insist on punishing the defendant.

4. AWARD OF AN AGREED SUM (OTHER THAN AN AGREED PRICE OR REMUNERATION) PAYABLE ON AN EVENT OTHER THAN BREACH

This sort of agreed sum occupies a position between an agreed price and an agreed sum payable on breach. Traditionally it is treated like an agreed price, so that once the event has occurred the sum can be recovered without any type of liquidated damages/penalty analysis. However, the main controversy is whether it is always sensible so to distinguish these agreed sums from those payable on breach.

A colourful example is *Alder v Moore*,[6] where the defendant, a professional footballer, was injured and certified as unable to play football. Under an insurance policy the plaintiffs paid him £500, subject to his agreement to the following term:

In consideration of the above payment I hereby declare and agree that I will take no part as a playing member of any form of professional football and that in the event of infringement of this condition I will be subject to a penalty of the amount stated above.

Four months later, the defendant began to play professional football again, and the plaintiffs claimed the £500, which the defendant resisted on the ground that it was a penalty. The majority of the Court of Appeal held that the plaintiffs were entitled to the £500. The liquidated damages/penalty distinction did not apply since the defendant had made no promise not to play football again. In any case, even if the sum was payable on breach, £500 was a genuine pre-estimate of loss and was therefore liquidated damages rather than a penalty. Devlin LJ dissented because he thought that the sum was payable on breach and was not a genuine pre-estimate of loss, but rather a penalty.

4 (1978) Wisconsin LR 351.
5 Supra, p 283.
6 [1961] 2 QB 57.

Agreed sums payable on events other than breach (as well as on breach) are particularly common in hire purchase and conditional sale agreements. The conventional approach—that the liquidated damages/penalty distinction does not apply if the sum is payable on an event other than breach—is shown in a case such as *Associated Distributors Ltd v Hall*,[7] where the agreed sum was payable on the debtor exercising his option to terminate the contract. In *Bridge v Campbell Discount Co Ltd*,[8] however, some doubt was cast on this where the sum is payable either on breach or on lawful termination by the debtor. It was held that, as on the facts, the debtor was in breach and hence the accelerated payment was payable on breach, the liquidated damages/penalty distinction was applicable in accordance with normal principles, and the sum was held to be a penalty. But Lords Denning and Devlin considered that, even if the debtor had lawfully terminated the contract, so that on the facts the sum was payable on an event other than breach, the liquidated damages/penalty approach should still be applied. The reasoning behind this is that otherwise, as Lord Denning put it, 'It means that equity commits itself to this absurd paradox: it will grant relief to a man who breaks his contract but will penalise the man who keeps it.'[9]

Certainly Lord Denning's approach has much to commend it. Like agreed sums payable on breach, the purpose of agreed sums payable on an event closely allied to breach is either to pre-estimate the plaintiff's loss caused by the 'event' or to punish the defendant for, and hence deter him from, failure to perform. To distinguish them from agreed sums payable on breach does, therefore, produce unsatisfactory paradoxes. On the other hand, it can be argued that, as the refusal to uphold penalty clauses is a somewhat unusual intrusion into freedom of contract, in that it does not rest on inequality of bargaining power, it is not sensible to extend it, particularly since to uphold an agreed sum payable on an event other than breach would not directly oust judicial compensation because there is no liability to pay unliquidated damages for an event that does not amount to a breach. Ultimately though, Lord Denning's approach does seem preferable, and it is therefore submitted that the Law Commission was right to recommend provisionally that the liquidated damages/penalty distinction should be applied to agreed sums payable on events closely allied to breach.[10] Indeed this is in

7 [1938] 2 KB 83.
8 [1962] AC 600.
9 Ibid at 629.
10 Working Paper No 61, para 26. Lord Denning's approach is also strongly supported by Deane J, dissenting, in *AMEV–UDC Finance Ltd v Austin* (1986) 162 CLR 170, 197–201.

essence accepted in the Consumer Credit Act 1974, in respect of regulated hire-purchase and conditional sale agreements. By s 100, where a debtor exercises his statutory right to terminate his maximum liability, despite a higher agreed sum payable on termination (assuming he has taken reasonable care of the goods), is to pay what is needed to bring his payments up to half the purchase price, and the court can further reduce this if the creditor's loss is less.

But the House of Lords decision in *Export Credits Guarantee Department v Universal Oil Products Co*[11] indicates that the common law position remains that the liquidated damages/penalty distinction will not be extended at the expense of freedom of contract. To simplify the very complex facts, a Newfoundland company engaged the defendant building company to construct an oil refinery. Financing of the project was by arrangement between the Newfoundland company and a consortium of bankers. By this, the Newfoundland company were to issue promissory notes to the bankers, in return for their paying the defendants for the work as it proceeded. Payment on the promissory notes by the Newfoundland company was guaranteed by the plaintiffs. The plaintiffs made this guarantee in consideration of a premium paid to them by the defendants, under an agreement, which by clause 7 provided that where the Newfoundland company dishonoured promissory notes at a time when the defendants were in breach of contract the defendants would reimburse the plaintiffs for any sums paid to the bankers under the guarantee. The Newfoundland company subsequently dishonoured many promissory notes and the plaintiffs paid the bankers £39 million under their guarantee. They then claimed £39 million from the defendants under clause 7, as the defendants had been in breach of contract at the relevant time. The defendants argued that clause 7 was invalid as a penalty clause, since it imposed an obligation to repay the plaintiffs no matter how trivial the defendants' breach of contract and the loss caused by it.

On the facts such an argument could never hope to succeed for the simple reason that clause 7 only ever insisted on reimbursement of the plaintiffs' payment to the bankers. So here the plaintiffs had indeed lost the £39 million claimed, and therefore, as stressed by the House of Lords, even if a penalty/liquidated damages analysis were to be applied, the clause had to be valid as liquidated damages. The fact that the defendants would as a result be doing the work for a smaller sum than agreed, such that the Newfoundland company would ultimately benefit excessively, was of no consequence to the

11 [1983] 2 All ER 205.

plaintiffs, who could not be said to be linked to the Newfoundland company, so as to reap the benefit. The defendants were therefore held bound to pay the £39 million.

However, the House of Lords thought that the penalty/liquidated damages distinction was in any case irrelevant because the sum was to be paid on an event other than breach of a contractual obligation owed to the plaintiffs. Lord Roskill, giving the principal speech, confirmed the lower courts' reasoning that:

> The clause was not a penalty clause because it provided for payment of money on the happening of a specified event other than a breach of a contractual duty owed by the contemplated payer to the contemplated payee.[12]

This confirms the traditional common law position of confining the power to strike down terms by a penalty clause analysis. The judiciary's attitude is well summed-up in the observation of Diplock LJ in *Philip Bernstein (Successors) Ltd v Lydiate Textiles Ltd*[13] which Lord Roskill cited with approval:[14]

> I, for my part, am not prepared to extend the law by relieving against an obligation in a contract entered into between two parties which does not fall within the well-defined limits in which the court has in the past shown itself willing to interfere.

---

12 Ibid at 223.
13 Sub nom *Sterling Industrial Facilities Ltd v Lydiate Textiles Ltd* (1962) 106 Sol Jo 669.
14 [1983] 2 All ER 205 at 224.

Chapter 8

Specific performance

1. INTRODUCTION

Specific performance is an equitable remedy which enforces a defendant's positive contractual obligations: that is, it orders the defendant to do what he promised to do. It is therefore a remedy protecting the plaintiff's expectation interest, the justification for such protection resting ultimately on the morality of promise-keeping.[1] Prohibitory injunctions also enforce contractual promises, but differ in that the promises in question are there negative. However, if what is in form a prohibitory injunction, in substance orders specific performance, or if the courts consider that in practice the injunction amounts to specific performance, it is governed by specific performance principles and is dealt with in this chapter.[2]

Strictly speaking, it is not an essential prerequisite of specific performance that the defendant is in breach of contract. Rather as Snell says: '. . . an action for specific performance is based on the mere existence of the contract, coupled with circumstances which make it equitable to grant a decree'.[3] But in practice, it is a breach of contract, actual or anticipatory,[4] that renders it 'equitable' to grant the decree.[5] Theoretically, a threat to break a contract not amounting to an anticipatory breach—for example, where the breach threatened is a minor one—would also justify specific performance[6] (which would then merit the label *quia timet*)[7] but no case on this has been found.

---

1 Supra, p 20.
2 For further discussion of indirect specific performance see inf
3 *Snell's Equity* (29th edn, 1990) pp 585-6.
4 *Hasham v Zenab* [1960] AC 316; Maudsley (1960) 76 LQR
  v Tyndall Holdings plc [1992] 1 All ER 124.
5 An exception is *Bass v Clivley* (1829) Taml 80, but it is un
  equitable to grant the order.
6 Spry *Equitable Remedies* (4th edn, 1990) pp 75-6.
7 Infra, pp 389-90, 422-3.

However, in contrast to damages, specific performance is not available for every breach of contract. Indeed, as in this chapter, specific performance is best approached negatively, that is by examining the numerous restrictions on its availability. Positively, it then follows that if the remedy is not barred by such restrictions, a plaintiff who applies for it will succeed.[8]

Three other introductory points should be made. First, no order of specific performance can be made at the interlocutory stage, where instead the appropriate remedy to enforce positive contractual obligations is the interlocutory mandatory injunction. In so far as the availability of a final order is relevant to the grant of such an interlocutory mandatory injunction, it is of course the principles governing specific performance that are applied.

Secondly, it is often said that, unlike damages, specific performance is a discretionary remedy. But it would be a mistake to imagine that this means that the law on specific performance is not clear and certain. In truth, the expression means no more than that, while there are no bars on damages, which are therefore available as of right for breach of contract (or a tort), there are numerous, albeit clearly established, bars to specific performance. The same contrast can be made of all common law, as against equitable, remedies for breach of contract (and torts).

Finally, a commonly-drawn contrast is between English law's regard of specific performance as a secondary remedy to damages and the allegedly reverse situation under civil law systems. What does this mean? It cannot mean that specific performance is as freely available in civil law systems as damages, for this is plainly not true. It could mean that the bars to specific performance are not as wide-ranging in civil law systems as here, but that this is so is hardly sensibly expressed by referring to specific performance as a primary remedy. It seems rather that the contrast is based on the fact that, deriving from the historical role of equitable remedies as supplementary to those of the common law, a plaintiff in English law will not be awarded specific performance unless he has shown that damages are inadequate whereas in civil law systems there is no such major hurdle. Some recent cases indicate a weakening of this bar, and it has even been argued that specific performance is now the primary remedy in England. This seems exaggerated, but a fascinating theme throughout this chapter is the recent apparent weakening not only of this, but of several other of the traditional

---

8 In addition to the bars discussed in this chapter specific performance cannot be ordered against the Crown—Crown Proceedings Act 1947, s 21(1)(a).

bars, so that specific performance may be more freely available now than it was in the past.[9]

2. THE BARS TO SPECIFIC PERFORMANCE

(1) The primary restriction—adequacy of damages

Specific performance will not be ordered unless damages (and the common law remedy of the award of an agreed sum) are inadequate. This is the major hurdle that a plaintiff seeking specific performance must overcome, but, even having done so, he may still fail because of one of the several other bars.

(a) Availability of substitute—uniqueness

The most important factor in determining whether damages are adequate is whether money can buy a substitute for the promised performance. Most discussion of this has been in relation to a seller's obligation under a contract of sale, where the issue has often been expressed as one of the 'uniqueness' of the subject-matter.

(i) Breach of a contract to sell land

Here specific performance is almost invariably granted where it is sought,[10] the traditional reasoning being that each piece of land is unique and cannot be replaced in the market. However, specific performance is ordered even where this does not reflect reality, for example in the case of a contract for the sale of identical new houses on a housing estate. Nor is the plaintiff's purpose in buying the land considered relevant. In other words, it makes no difference that the purchaser bought the land for resale or long-term investment rather than as a home.[11] The courts are therefore not confining specific performance to where the plaintiff places a subjective consumer value on the land over and above that reflected in the

---

9 For a similar trend in the United States, see Van Hecke (1961) 40 North Carolina LR 1, comment in (1964) 49 Iowa LR 1290. For a general comparative account of 'enforced performance', see Treitel *Remedies for Breach of Contract* ch 3.

10 *Sudbrook Trading Estate Ltd v Eggleton* [1983] 1 AC 444 at 478. Specific performance is also ordered of contracts to dispose of lesser interests in land: in *Verrall v Great Yarmouth Borough Council* [1981] QB 202, it was even ordered of a short-term contractual licence.

11 Brenner (1978) 24 McGill LJ 513, esp 545–8; Jones and Goodhart *Specific Performance* (1986) pp 93–4.

objective market price.[12] Assuming that there is no true substitute land, specific performance for the long-term investor is justified because of the acute difficulty of accurately assessing his profits. But there is no such obvious justification where the plaintiff was intending a quick resale, particularly where the resale contract has already been concluded. All in all, it seems clear that specific performance has simply taken over as the primary remedy for breach of an obligation to sell land, and that the adequacy of damages hurdle is in effect ignored. This is unfortunate as, for reasons later discussed, the adequacy of damages restriction rests on a sound footing.

The seller of an interest in land is also readily awarded specific performance ordering the buyer to accept title and to pay the contract price.[13] Since the seller's interest is purely monetary, damages or, where title has already passed, the remedy of the award of the agreed price would be perfectly adequate, except in a rare case where damages could not be accurately assessed. Nor is it an explanation to say that as the buyer can get specific performance, it is only just, in accord with 'affirmative mutuality',[14] for the seller to be entitled, since no injustice would be caused by the grant of the common law remedies. In truth it seems that on this side of the contract too, the adequacy of the common law remedies is ignored and specific performance is the primary remedy.

(ii) Breach of a contract to sell goods

Section 52 of the Sale of Goods Act 1979 expressly gives the courts a discretion to order the specific performance of the sale of 'specific or ascertained' goods; but the courts have not interpreted this section as removing the adequacy of damages hurdle or as altering their traditional approach to it. Specific performance therefore continues not to be ordered for the sale of most goods, whether 'specific or ascertained' or not, on the ground that money enables substitutes to be bought in the market.[15] On the other hand, specific performance is ordered where the goods are unique.

Goods are most obviously unique where substitutes cannot be bought because the goods possess significant physical characteristics that very few, if any, other goods have. That the courts will order

---

12 Harris, Ogus and Phillips (1979) 95 LQR 581, 588.

13 *Walker v Eastern Counties Rly Co* (1848) 6 Hare 594; *Eastern Counties Rly Co v Hawkes* (1855) 5 HL Cas 331; *Maskell v Ivory* [1970] Ch 502; *Johnson v Agnew* [1980] AC 367.

14 Sharpe *Injunctions and Specific Performance* (2nd edn, 1992) paras 7.820–7.880, 8.160.

15 An extreme example is *Cohen v Roche* [1927] 1 KB 169, refusing the analogous remedy of delivery up in relation to Hepplewhite chairs.

specific performance for the sale of physically unique goods is well-established. So in *Falcke v Gray*,[16] although specific performance was refused on other grounds, the court would have been prepared to order specific performance of a contract to sell two china jars on the ground that the jars were of 'unusual beauty, rarity and distinction';[17] and in *Thorn v Public Works Comrs*,[18] specific performance was ordered of a contract to sell the arch-stone, the spandrill stone and the Bramley Fall stone of the old Westminster Bridge, which had been pulled down. Again the courts are often willing to order specific performance of a contract to sell a ship, because a ship often has characteristics shared by very few, if any, other ships. So, for example, in *Behnke v Bede Shipping Co Ltd*[19] Wright J, in ordering specific performance of a contract to sell the ship *City*, said 'the *City* was of peculiar and practically unique value to the plaintiff . . . A very experienced ship's valuer has said that he knew of only one other comparable ship but that may now have been sold.'[20] On the other hand, in *CN Marine Inc v Stena Line A/B and Regie Voor Maritiem Transport, The Stena Nautica (No 2)*,[1] specific performance was refused because the ship was not sufficiently different from other ships.

While there are few other cases in which the specific performance of the sale of physically unique goods has been ordered, there are analogous examples. First, there are cases where specific performance was ordered of contracts relating to such goods. In *Lingen v Simpson*,[2] for example, in breach of a contract dissolving a partnership one partner failed to release for copying a book of ornamental plates that had been used in the business. The court ordered him to release the book and, although there was no discussion of inadequacy, we can assume that damages were thought inadequate because each of the two books was physically unique. Again when in *Phillips v Lamdin*[3] the defendant, who had contracted to sell his home to the plaintiff, was in breach of that contract by removing an Adam-style door from one of the rooms he was ordered to replace it. Croom-Johnson J said, 'You cannot make a new Adam door. You cannot in these times refashion a door or make a copy . . . I do

---

16 (1859) 4 Drew 651.
17 Ibid at 658.
18 (1863) 32 Beav 490.
19 [1927] 1 KB 649. See also *The Oro Chief* [1983] 2 Lloyds Rep 509 at 521; and *Bristol Airport plc v Powdrill* [1990] Ch 744, 759 (lease of an aircraft).
20 Ibid at 661.
1 [1982] 2 Lloyds Rep 336.
2 (1824) 1 Sim & St 600.
3 [1949] 2 KB 33.

not see how damages can be an adequate remedy.'[4] Secondly, there are several oft-cited and particularly good examples of the analogous remedy of delivery up for wrongful detention being ordered in respect of physically unique goods, such as antiques, heirlooms and works of art.[5]

Analogously to their approach to land, the courts appear not to be concerned with the purpose for which the plaintiff is buying the physically unique goods. In other words, no distinction appears to be drawn between the consumer, with his non-monetary interest, and the businessman who wants the goods for profitable use or resale.[6] The same criticism can be made as in relation to land contracts: namely, that for the reseller damages are adequate, since his interest is purely monetary and, unlike the long-term investor, they can generally be readily assessed.

Will specific performance be ordered for the sale of commercially unique goods? Goods can be said to be commercially unique, a term coined by Treitel,[7] where, although the goods may not be physically unique, buying substitutes would be so difficult or would cause such delay that the plaintiff's business would be seriously disrupted.

Until fairly recently, no case could be confidently cited in which specific performance had been ordered on this ground,[8] although in *Behnke v Bede Shipping*, Wright J did appear to regard it as relevant that the buyer needed the ship immediately for the purposes of his business. There was also Lord Hardwicke's dictum in *Buxton v Lister*[9] that in a supply contract the close vicinity of the goods to the buyer can make damages inadequate. Furthermore in *North v Great Northern Rly Co*,[10] it was accepted that the analogous remedy of delivery up could be ordered for commercially unique goods, here 54 coal waggons; and the interlocutory order for delivery up of 500 tons of steel, made more recently in *Howard Perry Ltd v British Railways Board*,[11] can also be said to have been based on this reasoning.

But commercial uniqueness as a ground for specific performance

---

4 Ibid at 41.
5 Infra, p 454.
6 Eg in *Falcke v Gray* and *Thorn v Public Works Comrs*, the plaintiffs seemed to have merely a commercial interest in the goods. Contra is Sharpe *Injunctions and Specific Performance* (2nd edn) para 8.350 citing *Cohen v Roche* [1927] 1 KB 169 and *Dowling v Betjemann* (1862) 2 John & H 544.
7 *The Law of Contract* (8th edn) p 905; (1966) JBL 211.
8 But see in Australia, *Dougan v Ley* (1946) 71 CLR 142 (licensed taxi-cab).
9 (1746) 3 Atk 383 at 385. But the correctness of this was specifically doubted in *Pollard v Clayton* (1855) 1 K & J 462.
10 (1860) 2 Giff 64.
11 [1980] 1 WLR 1375.

was radically accepted in *Sky Petroleum Ltd v VIP Petroleum Ltd.*[12] Here, an interlocutory injunction amounting to temporary specific performance was granted to enforce the supply of petrol to the plaintiffs' filling stations, at a time when the petrol market was in such an unusual state that the plaintiffs would be unlikely to find an alternative supply and as a result would be forced to stop trading. The reason why this is particularly radical is that petrol is not even 'specific or ascertained' goods within s 52 of the Sale of Goods Act 1979. In *Re Wait*,[13] the majority of the Court of Appeal thought that the Act meant that specific performance could not be ordered of non-specific or unascertained goods and any application of commercial uniqueness to such goods was therefore clearly rejected. But in *Sky Petroleum* Goulding J adopted a different approach. He said:

I come to the most serious hurdle in the way of the plaintiffs, which is the well-known doctrine that the court refuses specific performance of a contract to sell and purchase chattels not specific or ascertained . . .The ratio behind the rule is, as I believe, that under the ordinary contract for the sale of non-specific goods, damages are a sufficient remedy. That to my mind, is lacking in the circumstances of the present case. The evidence suggests, and indeed it is common knowledge, that the petroleum market is in an unusual state in which a would-be buyer cannot go into the market and contract with another seller, possibly at some sacrifice as to the price. Here the defendants appear for practical purposes to be the plaintiffs' sole means of keeping their business going, and I am prepared so far to depart from the general rule as to try to preserve the position under the contract until a later date.[14]

It is noteworthy here that the US 1962 Uniform Commercial Code para 2–716(1) has sought to encourage acceptance of the notion of 'commercial uniqueness' in relation to goods that are not specific or ascertained. The comment to that section reads:

The test of uniqueness must be made in terms of the total situation, which characterises the contract. Output and requirements contracts involving a particular or peculiarly available source or market present today the typical contractual specific performance situation, as contrasted with contracts for the sale of heirlooms or priceless works of art, which were usually involved in the older cases.[15]

---

12 [1974] 1 WLR 576.
13 [1927] 1 Ch 606.
14 [1974] 1 WLR 576 at 578–9.
15 Nichols (1976) 30 Ark LR 65. Output and requirements contracts are the major types of long-term supply contracts. Even where, in contrast to *Sky Petroleum*, there are substitute goods readily available at the time of the supplier's breach, goods in such contracts are typically commercially unique, because the plaintiff is very often unsure of obtaining a substitute supply during the full contract period, and is thereby threatened with disruption to his business.

But while the acceptance of commercial uniqueness for non-specific goods in the *Sky Petroleum* case is important, a degree of caution must be exercised in assessing its effects. Apart from the fact that it was a first instance decision that has not yet been followed or approved, doubt has been cast on the courts' acceptance of commercial uniqueness, even in relation to specific or ascertained goods, by the Court of Appeal decision in *Société des Industries Métallurgiques SA v Bronx Engineering Co Ltd*.[16] Here it was held that an interlocutory injunction restraining the sellers from removing certain machinery from the jurisdiction should not be granted since, even if the sellers were in breach of contract, there was no likelihood of the plaintiff buyers being granted specific performance at the trial, because damages were adequate. This was held to be so, even though the court accepted that the 9–12 month delay in obtaining substitute machinery might substantially disrupt the plaintiffs' business. While one might try to reconcile the cases by saying, for example, that the degree of disruption threatened in *Bronx Engineering* was not as great as in *Sky Petroleum* (or the analogous *North v Great Northern Rly*) the plain truth seems to be that the Court of Appeal was here rejecting commercial as opposed to physical uniqueness. Although *Howard Perry* has since been decided, without any reference being made to *Bronx Engineering*, it is still too early to say that such a rejection will be disregarded. As yet, therefore, even if the goods are specific or ascertained, it cannot be confidently asserted that specific performance will be ordered of a contract to sell goods that are commercially unique for the buyer.

In terms of policy, commercial uniqueness should be accepted, for while theoretically damages for the substantial disruption to a business are adequate, since it is ultimately only money that the plaintiff is losing, in practice in this situation, an accurate assessment of the plaintiff's losses is so difficult that he is likely to be incorrectly compensated; and this high risk of incorrect compensation is a strong justification for accepting commercial uniqueness, whether the goods in question are specific or ascertained or not. Nor, it should be added, is there any need as a matter of construction to take the restrictive exhaustive interpretation of s 52 adopted in *Re Wait*.

It should further be noted that our courts, in contrast again to those in the United States, may not recognise sentimental uniqueness. In Treitel's words, 'It is . . . uncertain whether sentimental

16 [1975] 1 Lloyds Rep 465.

attachment to otherwise ordinary goods makes them unique.'[17] If this is so, it represents an unfortunate failure to take into account the consumer interest, for damages do not enable a satisfactory substitute to be bought for such goods.

Finally, can specific performance ever be obtained by the vendor of goods? The Sale of Goods Act 1979 makes no provision for specific performance being granted against a buyer so as to order the taking of and paying for goods and there is little authority to suggest that a vendor of goods can be awarded specific performance at common law.[18] Normally as the vendor's interest is purely monetary, damages or the award of the agreed price will be adequate. However, in long-term requirements contracts, specific performance may be merited because of the difficulty in assessing the vendor's damages, particularly in view of uncertainty as to the exact quantity of goods being sold and as to the future state of the market.[19] Certainly, prohibitory injunctions are commonly granted in respect of such contracts to restrain the purchaser from buying goods other than from the vendor.[20] But as the courts in such cases have not regarded themselves as in effect ordering specific performance, it is probably misleading to regard such cases as authorities on specific performance.

(iii) Breach of a contract to sell shares or stocks

Where the shares or stocks are freely available on the market, specific performance will generally not be ordered, since damages enable substitutes to be bought. For example, in *Cud v Rutter*,[1] specific performance of a contract to sell South Sea stock was refused, Lord Parker LC saying:

. . . a court of equity ought not to execute any of these contracts, but to leave them to law, where the party is to recover damages, and with the money may if he pleases buy the quantity of stock agreed to be transferred to him; for there can be no difference between one man's stock and another's.[2]

But in the converse situation, where substitute shares are not readily available, an extreme case being where the breach deprives

---

17 (1966) JBL 211, 214.
18 But see *Shell-Mex Ltd v Elton Cop Dyeing Co Ltd* (1928) 34 Com Cas 39; *Elliott v Pierson* [1948] 1 All ER 939.
19 Treitel (1966) JBL 211, 229–30.
20 Infra, p 411.
1 (1720) 1 P Wms 570. Also *Re Schwabacher* (1907) 98 LT 127; *Chinn v Hochstrasser* [1979] Ch 447 at 462, 470.
2 Ibid at 571.

the plaintiff of a majority holding, damages are regarded as inadequate and specific performance will be ordered.[3] Generally this approach is fully justified, although one can imagine situations, for example where the purchaser has bought for a quick resale, where damages can be accurately assessed, and would be adequate.[4] A vendor of such shares has also been awarded specific performance,[5] but as with contracts for the sale of land there rarely seems any justification for this, and at root it probably rests on the unsatisfactory notion of 'affirmative mutuality'.[6]

(b) Difficulty in assessing damages

This head and the previous one (uniqueness) are inextricably linked; difficulty in assessing damages—whether in putting a value on a consumer's interest, or in calculating possible investment profit, or in putting a figure on the serious disruption to a business—lies as the root justification for specific performance, where the contractual subject-matter is unique.[7] But the question now to be examined is, does difficulty in assessing damages in itself render damages inadequate?

The answer would appear to be that it does not for while there are eighteenth- and nineteenth-century cases relying on this, such as *Taylor v Neville*,[8] which concerned a contract for the sale of 800 tons of iron involving delivery in instalments over a number of years, and *Adderley v Dixon*,[9] which dealt with a contract for the sale of debts proved in bankruptcy, later cases, such as *Fothergill v Rowland*,[10] denied the relevance of the difficulty of assessing damages. Indeed this concerned an output contract, where, irrespective of any commercial uniqueness, one would have expected difficulties of assessment to be particularly problematical because not only is there the usual difficulty in long-term contracts of judging future market prices but, in addition, as with requirements contracts, one cannot state in advance the exact quantity of goods to be supplied. Yet Sir G Jessel MR said:

---

3 *Duncuft v Albrecht* (1841) 12 Sim 189; *Langen and Wind Ltd v Bell* [1972] Ch 685; *Harvela Investments Ltd v Royal Trust Co of Canada* [1985] 2 All ER 966.
4 See analogously supra, pp 338, 340.
5 *Odessa Tramways Co v Mendel* (1878) 8 Ch D 235.
6 Supra, p 338, fn 14.
7 Kronman (1978) 45 U of Chi LR 351, 362.
8 Unreported but cited in *Buxton v Lister* (1746) 3 Atk 383.
9 (1824) 1 Sim & St 607.
10 (1873) LR 17 Eq 132. The injunction sought was regarded as amounting to specific performance—see infra, p 412.

To say that you cannot ascertain the damage in a case of breach of contract for the sale of goods, say in monthly deliveries extending over three years . . . is to limit the power of ascertaining damages in a way which would rather astonish gentlemen who practise on what is called the other side of Westminster Hall. There is never considered to be any difficulty in ascertaining such a thing. Therefore I do not think it is a case in which damages could not be ascertained at law.[11]

That the difficulty of assessing damages is irrelevant gains further and more recent support from the judgments in the *Bronx Engineering* case.[12]

This approach is most unfortunate, for where there is grave doubt about whether damages will put the plaintiff into as good a position as if the contract had been performed, specific performance is prima facie a better remedy.[13] Certainly, the difficulty of assessing damages has been expressly regarded as a factor rendering damages inadequate in respect of interlocutory prohibitory injunctions restraining defendants from selling goods other than to or through the plaintiff, their exclusive agent or distributor.[14] But the courts in these cases did not regard themselves as in effect ordering specific performance, and this, plus the ease with which the adequacy of damages hurdle has been traditionally overcome with regard to prohibitory injunctions restraining the breach of negative contractual obligations, probably renders it misleading to use such cases as authorities on specific performance.[15]

(c) Inability to pay the damages

The question of whether the defendant's inability to pay the damages renders them inadequate, has traditionally received surprisingly little attention in the cases. In *Re Wait*[16] though, the Court of Appeal clearly did not consider the defendant's insolvency sufficient to render damages inadequate for failure to deliver wheat, and recently Goulding J appeared to take the same view in *Anders Utkilens Rederi A/S v Lovisa Stevedoring Co A/B*:[17] 'Commercial life would be subjected to new and unjust hazards if the court were to

---

11 Ibid at 140.
12 [1975] 1 Lloyds Rep 465 at 468, 469–70.
13 Similarly it is arguable that damages are inadequate where some of the loss is irrecoverable because of a particular type (eg mental distress) or too remote. But see *The Stena Nautica (No 2)* [1982] 2 Lloyds Rep 336 at 342 (per Parker J).
14 *Evans Marshall & Co v Bertola SA* [1973] 1 WLR 349; *Decro-Wall International SA v Practitioners in Marketing Ltd* [1971] 2 All ER 216. Infra, p 412.
15 Contra is Treitel *Law of Contract* p 904.
16 [1927] 1 Ch 606.
17 [1985] 2 All ER 669 at 674.

decree specific performance of contracts normally sounding only in damages simply because of a party's threatened insolvency.' On the other hand, in the *Bronx Engineering* case, which in all other respects is so anti-specific performance, Lord Edmund Davies did think it relevant in relation to adequacy that the defendants would be able to pay; and in *The Oro Chief*,[18] Staughton J said in dicta that even if a ship was not unique '. . . it may be that in special circumstances, such as when the seller is insolvent and can pay no damages, [the buyer] will still obtain an order for specific performance.' There are also prohibitory injunction cases, expressly stating that damages are inadequate where the defendant is unable to pay,[19] but again it is probably misleading to use them as authorities on specific performance.

In general, the former view seems correct: for where the defendant is insolvent, other creditors may be prejudiced by the plaintiff being granted specific performance, the normal assumption being that specific performance gives priority. But there is no such prejudice, where the plaintiff is the defendant's only creditor or where the performance will not reduce the defendant's assets. In such (unusual) circumstances it is clearly right that an inability to pay damages renders them inadequate and justifies specific performance.

(d) Contractual obligation to pay money

The common law remedies, being monetary orders, are normally adequate where the breach is of a contractual obligation to pay money. However, specific performance has been ordered of a contract to pay an annuity.[20] In dicta in *Adderley v Dixon*,[1] this was justified on the ground of the difficulty of here assessing a lump sum of damages. An alternative justification, put forward in *Beswick v Beswick*,[2] is that specific performance avoids the inconvenience of bringing numerous actions to recover the agreed sum. Specific performance can also be granted to enforce the purchaser's payment obligation in a contract for the sale of land, or for the sale of shares

---

18 [1983] 2 Lloyds Rep 509 at 521. See also *Doloret v Rothschild* (1824) 1 Sim & St 590 at 598.
19 *Evans Marshall & Co v Bertola SA* [1973] 1 WLR 349; *Associated Portland Cement Manufacturers Ltd v Tiegland Shipping A/S* [1975] 1 Lloyds Rep 581. Analogously to these see *Hodgson v Duce* (1856) 28 LTOS 155 (injunction for trespass).
20 *Ball v Coggs* (1710) 1 Bro Parl Cas 140; *Beswick v Beswick* [1968] AC 58.
1 (1824) 1 Sim & St 607.
2 [1968] AC 58 at 81, 88, 97.

that cannot be replaced in the market,[3] but there rarely seems any justification for here regarding the common law remedies as inadequate.[4]

(e) Contracts that can be immediately terminated

A leading case is *Sheffield Gas Consumers' Co v Harrison*,[5] where specific performance was refused of a contract to allow the plaintiff to join a partnership. In Sir John Romilly's words:

> . . . this Court will not enforce the specific performance of a contract to enter into a partnership, which, so far as the defendant is concerned, he may dissolve immediately afterwards. To specifically perform a contract of this description would be merely nugatory.[6]

But if the order would be futile, it would seem that a fortiori damages are adequate, and that the case fails at this initial hurdle.[7]

However, one should not regard specific performance of such contracts as necessarily being ruled out, for one can imagine situations where damages are inadequate and where there is some point from the plaintiff's point of view in being granted specific performance even though the defendant can terminate the contract almost immediately. For example, specific performance of a contract of employment terminable at short notice may be important so as to give the plaintiff an extra period of employment necessary for the accrual of certain rights (eg to maternity leave or to a pension).

(f) Nominal damages and privity

In *Beswick v Beswick*[8] a coal merchant transferred his business to his nephew, who in return promised that, after his uncle's death, he would pay £5 a week to his widow. The uncle died and his widow brought an action for specific performance of the nephew's promise, suing both personally and as administratrix. The House of Lords, upholding the doctrine of privity, held that while the widow could not maintain a successful action suing personally, she could as

---

3 Further examples are the payment obligations in a contract to take up and pay for debentures; in a contract to discharge another's debt; and in a loan agreement collateral to a specifically enforceable agreement. See Jones and Goodhart *Specific Performance* pp 123–9.

4 Supra, pp 338, 344.

5 (1853) 17 Beav 294. See also *Hercy v Birch* (1804) 9 Ves 357; *Tito v Waddell (No 2)* [1977] Ch 106 at 326–7.

6 Ibid at 297.

7 The same reasoning applies to a contract for a lease that has already expired by trial, see *Turner v Clowes* (1869) 20 LT 214.

8 [1968] AC 58.

administratrix succeed in suing for the estate's loss, though not her own personal third party loss. Crucially, however, the Lords held that as administratrix she should be granted specific performance of the nephew's promise rather than being confined to damages.

One aspect of the decision—that specific performance can be granted for failure to pay an annuity—has already been dealt with, and the wider implications of their Lordships' speeches will be considered shortly. But the decision is probably principally well-known for laying down that specific performance can be granted to avoid the injustice that the privity rule can produce. The reasoning was as follows: if a party sues on a contract made for the benefit of a third party his damages, which are assessed according to his own loss, are usually going to be nominal; where this produces injustice, as here where the nephew had got the business and would end up paying almost nothing for it, nominal damages should be regarded as inadequate, enabling specific performance to be granted to enforce the defendant's promise. Only Lord Pearce thought that the administratrix could have recovered substantial damages but, if wrong on this, he too considered nominal damages 'manifestly useless'.[9] It should be added, that, while usually regarded as a pioneering manoeuvre around the doctrine of privity, there were earlier cases ordering specific performance of a contract for the benefit of a third party,[10] and these were relied on by the House of Lords.

(g) *Beswick v Beswick*—the radical interpretation

On a narrow view, *Beswick* lays down merely that damages may be inadequate, and specific performance can be ordered, for breach of a contract to pay an annuity or to benefit a third party.[11] But there is an alternative wide view of *Beswick*, which focuses on the fact that each of their Lordships at some stage described the relationship between damages and specific performance in terms other than the adequacy of damages. Thus Lord Reid, with whom Lord Guest agreed, was concerned with ordering specific performance to produce '. . . a just result.'[12] Lord Upjohn said, 'Equity will grant specific performance when damages are inadequate to meet the justice of the case.'[13] Lord Hodson talked of deciding which was the more appropriate remedy and concluded that, as there had been an

---

9 Ibid at 89.
10 *Keenan v Handley* (1864) 2 De GJ & Sm 283; *Peel v Peel* (1869) 17 WR 586; *Hohler v Aston* [1920] 2 Ch 420.
11 On this, *Beswick* was followed in *Gurtner v Circuit* [1968] 2 QB 587.
12 [1968] AC 58 at 77.
13 Ibid at 102.

unconscionable breach of faith, the equitable remedy was 'apt'.[14] Lord Pearce too said that specific performance was 'the more appropriate remedy',[15] and it is particularly significant that he cited with approval sections of Windeyer J's judgment in *Coulls v Bagot's Executor and Trustee Co Ltd*[16] including the following: 'It is . . . a faulty analysis of legal obligations to say that the law treats the promisor as having a right to elect either to perform his promise or to pay damages. Rather . . . the promisee has "a legal right to the performance of the contract".'[17]

The wide view is that, given such terminology, the Lords were concerned to effect a general change in the relationship between damages and specific performance so that, to use conventional terminology, damages are inadequate in a far wider range of circumstances than in the past. Indeed I Lawson thought that *Beswick* could be interpreted as saying that specific performance replaces damages as the primary remedy in English law. He wrote:

. . . it is not unreasonable to see in it an acknowledgement of a right to specific performance of all contracts where there is no adequate reason for the courts to refuse it. If this is so, we have already in England reached the Scottish principle that specific performance is the normal remedy for breach of contract, and a refusal of it must be justified in specific types of case or on special grounds. In other words . . . the choice between specific performance and damages should in principle rest with the plaintiff, not the court . . .[18]

While *Beswick* can be given such a wide interpretation, and it is hard to interpret Lord Pearce's judgment in any other way, it appears that the courts have taken the narrow view, for they have continued to apply the adequacy of damages bar without even mentioning *Beswick*. However, in *The Stena Nautica (No 2)*[19] May LJ, while not referring to *Beswick*, also preferred a different terminology than adequacy, and cited Sachs LJ's statement in *Evans Marshall & Co v Bertola SA*[20] (a prohibitory injunction rather than a specific performance case)[1] that, 'The standard question . . . are damages

14 Ibid at 83.
15 Ibid at 88.
16 (1967) 119 CLR 460.
17 Ibid at 504, citing *Alley v Deschamps* (1806) 13 Ves 225, 228.
18 *Remedies of English Law* (2nd edn, 1980) pp 223–4.
19 [1982] 2 Lloyds Rep 336 at 346–7. Macdonald (1987) 38 NILQ 244 supports this approach. See also Goulding J in *Anders Utkilens Rederi A/S v O/Y Lovisa Stevedoring Co A/B* [1985] 2 All ER 669 at 674, referring to what 'good conscience' requires.
20 [1973] 1 WLR 349.
1 *Infra*, p 412.

an adequate remedy? might perhaps, in the light of authorities of
recent years, be rewritten: is it just in all the circumstances that the
plaintiff should be confined to his remedy in damages?'[2] Like
Beswick, May LJ's approach can be interpreted widely as advocating
that damages will be held inadequate in a far wider set of circumstances than in the past. But again a narrow view is possible which
regards this new terminology as making no real change; and significantly May LJ went on to apply seemingly traditional reasoning in
denying specific performance: that is, the ship in question was not
unique. The majority reached the same result by the same reasoning without advocating any change of terminology.

(h) Is it satisfactory to maintain an adequacy of damages hurdle?

It is a complex policy question whether the primacy traditionally
given to damages by the adequacy of damages rule is justified other
than historically.[3] On the one hand, it might be said that, subject to
other bars, a plaintiff ought to be entitled to specific performance if
he so chooses, since in accordance with the morality of promise-
keeping, this most closely fulfils his expectations. In particular,
specific performance satisfies a consumer's non-monetary interest in
performance and does not run the risk of inaccurate assessment or
the defendant's inability to pay. Moreover, it saves the costs of a
judicial assessment of damages.

On the other hand, a plaintiff entitled to specific performance has
an incentive to be idle and inefficient, for while a plaintiff seeking
damages has a duty to mitigate his loss, so that his damages will be
reduced if he fails to do so, specific performance requires no reasonable steps to be taken by the plaintiff to put himself into as good
a position as if the contract had been performed. Specific performance is also more of an infringement of individual liberty in that
ordering people to stick to their promises is more coercive of their
behaviour than requiring them to pay damages. Similarly it may be
thought relevant that the sanction to enforce specific performance is
more drastic with disobedience amounting to a contempt of court,

---

2 [1973] 1 WLR 349 at 379. It is unclear which 'authorities of recent years' Sachs
 LJ was referring to.
3 Kronman (1978) 45 U of Chi LR 351; Schwartz (1979) 89 Yale LJ 271; Linzer
 (1981) 81 Col LR 111; Yorio (1982) 82 Col LR 1365; Ulen (1984) Mich LR
 341; Harris *Remedies in Contract and Tort* pp 159–62; Ogus *Contract Law Today*
 (eds Harris and Tallon) pp 243–63; Collins *The Law of Contract* (2nd edn, 1993)
 pp 366–71. See also Laycock *The Death of the Irreparable Injury Rule* (1991) esp
 ch 11.

potentially punishable by imprisonment. Indeed it was one of Dawson's[4] main arguments that specific performance might be more widely used if, as in Germany, the consequences of non-compliance were less severe and more varied. A further argument against specific performance is that it potentially generates undesirable future friction between the parties. Moreover, there is the view that non-monetary remedies generally are less satisfactory than damages, since they give the plaintiff too much of an advantage in pre- and post-judgment bargaining.[5]

Consideration must also be given to probably the most discussed recent argument against specific performance, namely the economic analysis theory of 'efficient breach'.[6] The basis of this is that in a contract in which the plaintiff is to receive a contractual performance from the defendant in return for the payment of money, the plaintiff places a certain value on that contractual performance. This value most simply accords with the profits expected to be made from the performance. The free market produces economic efficiency by moving resources to those who place the highest value on them. In order to support this the law must permit and indeed encourage a defendant to break a contract where this will lead to resources passing to those who place higher values on them while at the same time discouraging breach where the plaintiff has a higher value use than others. The right encouragement and discouragement to breach is produced by awarding, where possible to estimate, expectation damages in preference to specific performance. An example will make this clearer.[7] Say D contracts to make a machine part for P for £10,000. If X offers D £15,000 for that part, breach by D is efficient if X values the part more than P, and is inefficient if X values the part less than P. The regime of expectation damages in preference to specific performance produces the efficient result: if P values the part at more than £15,000, D will not breach, since he will have to pay P expectation damages, which together with the contract price lost, will not exceed the £15,000 offered by X; on the other hand, if P values the part at less

4 (1959) 57 Mich LR 495, 538.
5 Supra, pp 14–5.
6 In addition to the writings cited supra, p 350, fn 3, see Birmingham (1970) 24 Rutgers LR 273; Posner *Economic Analysis of Law* (4th edn) pp 117–26, 130–2; Goetz and Scott (1977) 77 Col LR 554; Farber (1980) 66 Va LR 1443; Macneil (1982) 68 Va LR 947; Craswell (1988) 61 So Cal LR 629; Beale *Remedies for Breach of Contract* (hereinafter cited as *Remedies*) pp 13–14, 142; Harris *Remedies in Contract and Tort* pp 84–7.
7 It is assumed in all economic analysis examples that the parties are rational maximisers of value.

than £15,000, D will breach, since by paying P expectation damages and transferring the part to X, he will be better off. The machine part therefore passes to whichever party, P or X, places the higher value on it.

As it stands, this theory can be challenged on the ground that even if the plaintiff were entitled to specific performance, this would not necessarily prevent the machine part passing to the highest value user. Indeed, according to the Coase theorem,[8] if transaction costs are absent, market forces will ensure that resources go to the person placing the highest value on them, irrespective of the initial assignment of legal rights and remedies. So in the above situation, assuming no transaction costs, D would negotiate from P a release from the specific performance so as to transfer the part to X, if X places a higher value on it than £15,000. Of course, in order to succeed in gaining a release, D will have to offer P more than the latter's expectation damages: as such, it is the distribution of wealth, but not overall efficiency, that is affected by ordering specific performance in the absence of transaction costs.

Ultimately, therefore, the efficient breach theory has to take account of the fact that in the real world there are transaction costs; and it becomes the theory either that the transaction costs of D gaining release from P are often so high as to prevent that release, so that the efficient transfer to X does not result, or that, even if the transaction costs are not so high as to prevent release, nevertheless the efficient transfer to X is more costly under specific performance than damages because of the transaction costs required.[9]

The defect of the former is that, since the parties are already known to each other, the transaction costs are unlikely to be so high as to prevent a release bargain. The latter is also flawed in that it pays insufficient attention to the costs associated with damages. Even though damages allow D to break the contract with P without bargaining for a release, D still has to pay and deciding on the amount will in itself involve transaction costs, or the costs of a judicial assessment of damages, with its attendant risk of inaccurate assessment. Such costs may be greater than the transaction costs associated with specific performance. So for this form of the efficient breach theory to have force empirical data would be needed to prove that the transaction costs of specific performance outweigh the transaction (and other) costs of damages.[10]

8 Supra, pp 12–3.
9 Posner *Economic Analysis of Law* p 131, Beale *Remedies* p 14.
10 Macneil (1982) 68 Va LR 947.

Finally, brief mention must be made of Professor Kronman's 'intention justification' theory,[11] that the present restrictive approach to specific performance is economically efficient, because rational parties stipulating remedies in their contracts would agree to specific performance only where the subject-matter was unique. As the law is in accord with this, initial transaction costs are thereby minimised. But there seems no necessary reason why it cannot be equally plausibly argued that rational parties would stipulate specific performance in a far wider range of cases, particularly where irrespective of uniqueness, damages are difficult to assess.[12] In short, it seems that Kronman's argument could be used for and against the present primacy of damages.

In conclusion, it is submitted that damages should remain the primary remedy: especially convincing is the duty to mitigate objection to specific performance. This conclusion is strengthened by the recent improvements in damages awards from a plaintiff's point of view, brought about, for example, by the modification of the time for assessment and the expansion of compensation for non-pecuniary loss, such as mental distress. Having said that, there is still room for the courts to show a more realistic awareness of when damages will not put the plaintiff into as good a position as if the contract had been performed. As such, the decision in *Sky Petroleum*[13] must be supported. Moreover, difficulty in assessing damages should in itself be regarded as rendering damages inadequate, thereby opening the door to wider specific performance, particularly of long-term supply obligations and of obligations in which the plaintiff has a subjective consumer interest.

(2) The constant supervision objection

Traditionally, specific performance has not been ordered where this would require what is termed constant supervision. This is not an easily understood notion, but what it appears to mean is that, irrespective of the uncertainty bar,[14] specific performance will be denied where too much judicial time and effort would be spent in seeking compliance with the order. Such an objection clearly does not arise where there is an easy method of enforcement without the defendant's co-operation, for example by nominating a person to

11 (1978) 45 U of Chi LR 351, 365–9.
12 Kronman's theory is criticised by Schwartz (1979) 89 Yale LJ 271, 278–84.
13 [1974] 1 WLR 576.
14 For a clear recognition of the difference between these bars, see *Greenhill v Isle of Wight Rly Co* (1871) 23 LT 885.

effect a conveyance of land. It is rather where continuous acts are required of the defendant that the objection bites. In contrast, a lump sum of damages always requires merely a single act and, as Sharpe succinctly puts it, 'enforcement is left to the administrative rather than the judicial machinery of the court'.[15]

The classic authority is *Ryan v Mutual Tontine Westminster Chambers Association*.[16] Here the lease of a service flat to the plaintiff lessee included an obligation on the part of the defendant lessor to provide a resident porter who would be 'constantly in attendance'. The lessor in fact appointed as resident porter someone who absented himself every weekday for several hours. The plaintiff brought an action claiming specific performance of that obligation. The Court of Appeal held that specific performance should be denied because this would involve constant supervision by the courts. Lord Esher MR said:

The contract is that these services shall be performed during the whole term of the tenancy: it is therefore a long-continuing contract to be performed from day to day and under which the circumstances of non-performance might vary from day to day. I apprehend, therefore, that the execution of it would require that constant superintendence by the court, which the court in such cases has always declined to give.[17]

In Lopes LJ's words:

. . . it is clear that it is such a contract, that, in order to give effect to it by an order for specific performance, the court would have to watch over and supervise its execution. But it is a recognised rule that the court cannot enforce a contract by compelling specific performance where the execution of the contract requires such watching over and supervision by the court.[18]

Kay LJ also considered that the court could not here order specific performance because the case fell within the general rule that '. . . the court will not enforce specific performance of works, such as building works, the prosecution of which the court cannot superintend'.[19]

But while *Ryan* is the most important case, there are numerous others in which the constant supervision objection to specific performance has been applied.[20] However, this has not always been so.

15 *Injunctions and Specific Performance* (2nd edn) para 7.480.
16 [1893] 1 Ch 116.
17 Ibid at 123.
18 Ibid at 125.
19 Ibid at 128.
20 *Pollard v Clayton* (1855) 1 K & J 462; *Blackett v Bates* (1865) 1 Ch App 117; *Phipps v Jackson* (1887) 56 LJ Ch 550; *Dominion Coal Co Ltd v Dominion Iron & Steel Co Ltd* [1909] AC 293; *Dowty Boulton Paul Ltd v Wolverhampton Corpn* [1971] 2 All ER 277.

The prime example is *Wolverhampton Corpn v Emmons*,[1] where the Court of Appeal laid down that specific performance could be ordered of contracts to build, provided the order was certain, damages were inadequate and, in accordance with the contract, the defendant had already gained the land on which the work was to be done—that is, the bargain was for the plaintiff to transfer land to the defendant in return for the defendant building something wanted by the plaintiff, such as a road across the land. Traditionally this approach has been explained away by saying that it is a valid exception to the otherwise clearly established rule. But it is hard to see on what rational ground this 'exception' is based. After all, the first two conditions must always be satisfied if specific performance is to be ordered; and the fact that the defendant has already received his part of the bargain, while of relevance to mutuality, in no sense counters the constant supervision objection. Not surprisingly the third requirement has since been modified so that it is now sufficient that the defendant has possession of the land, thereby rendering it possible to carry out the work.[2] But again the possibility of complying with the order is a normal requirement of specific performance. Hence a better explanation of the *Emmons* approach than that traditionally offered is that at root it rests on the view that there is no validity in the constant supervision objection. Certainly this is supported by dicta of Collins LJ and Sir Archibald Smith MR in *Emmons*, the latter, for example, saying quite bluntly that he had never been able to see the force of that objection.

Whatever one's explanation of the *Emmons* approach, it has been the *general* rule that the courts have refused to order specific performance where this involves constant supervision.

Recently, however, Megarry V-C has attacked the validity of this objection. In *Giles & Co Ltd v Morris*,[3] although the actual decision did not turn on the supervision bar, he thought that the refusal of specific performance of contracts for personal service or involving the continuous performance of services could not '. . . be based on

---

1 [1901] 1 KB 515. Prior cases applying the same approach include: *Storer v Great Western Rly Co* (1842) 2 Y & C Ch Cas 48; *Wilson v Furness Rly Co* (1869) LR 9 Eq 28; *Greene v West Cheshire Rly Co* (1871) LR 13 Eq 44; *Wolverhampton & Walsall Rly Co v London and North Western Rly Co* (1873) LR 16 Eq 433; *Fortescue v Lostwithiel and Fowey Rly Co* [1894] 3 Ch 621. *Emmons* has been followed, with the modification discussed below in the text, in *Carpenters Estates Ltd v Davies* [1940] Ch 160 and most importantly in *Jeune v Queen's Cross Properties Ltd* [1974] Ch 97 applying the principles to a landlord's repair covenant, since confirmed and extended in the Landlord and Tenant Act 1985, s 17.

2 *Carpenter Estates Ltd v Davies* [1940] Ch 160.

3 [1972] 1 WLR 307.

any narrow consideration such as difficulties of constant superintendence by the courts'.[4] In *Tito v Waddell (No 2)*[5] his criticisms were expressed even more firmly. One of the many issues raised was whether specific performance should be ordered of a contractual obligation to replant land that had been mined. While Megarry V-C ultimately refused specific performance he thought that it was no longer a valid objection that the order involved constant supervision by the court. He said:

In cases of this kind, it was at one time said that an order for the specific performance of the contract would not be made if there would be difficulty in the court supervising its execution: see, for example, *Ryan v Mutual Tontine Westminster Chambers Association*. Sir Archibald Smith MR subsequently found himself unable to see the force of this objection (see *Wolverhampton Corporation v Emmons*): and after it had been discussed and questioned in *Giles v Morris*, the House of Lords disposed of it (I hope finally) in *Shiloh Spinners Ltd v Harding*.[6] The real question is whether there is a sufficient definition of what has to be done in order to comply with the order of the court.[7]

Megarry V-C also stressed that the courts were particularly willing to overcome such an objection where, as on the facts, the defendants had some or all of the benefit to which they were entitled under the contract; but as has been commented in relation to the *Emmons* case, it is hard to see the relevance of this in undermining the constant supervision objection.

Further support for the removal of this bar is provided by *Regent International Hotels (UK) Ltd v Pageguide Ltd*[8] where the Court of Appeal granted an interlocutory injunction, amounting to temporary specific performance, preventing the defendant company from terminating or hindering the plaintiffs in carrying out their management of the defendant's hotel. In so doing, the constant supervision objection was apparently rejected, reliance being placed on Megarry V-C's comments in *Giles v Morris* and *Tito v Waddell (No 2)*.

Megarry V-C's comments and Lord Wilberforce's judgment in *Shiloh Spinners v Harding* were also cited with approval by Mervyn Davies J in *Posner v Scott-Lewis*.[9] The facts were almost identical to those in *Ryan*. The defendant landlord had broken his covenant to

4 Ibid at 318.
5 [1977] Ch 106.
6 [1973] AC 691.
7 [1977] Ch 106 at 321–3.
8 (1985) Times, 13 May.
9 [1987] Ch 25.

have a resident porter at a block of flats for the purposes of removing rubbish, opening the main door, and controlling the central heating etc. The plaintiff, a tenant of one of the flats, sued for and was granted specific performance ordering the defendant to employ a resident porter for those purposes. Although the actual decision did not contradict the constant supervision objection—since the defendant was not as such ordered to perform, or to ensure performance of, continuous acts but was merely ordered to employ the porter—the judge did indicate his support for the removal of that bar.

Furthermore, although there was no discussion of this objection in *Beswick*[10] or *Sky Petroleum*,[11] these cases support the view that the constant supervision objection is no longer applied because the obligations in question involved continuous acts.[12]

Having said all this, there is still reason to doubt whether the objection has been totally swept away. As late as 1971, in *Dowty Boulton Paul Ltd v Wolverhampton Corpn*,[13] Pennycuick V-C refused an interlocutory injunction, which although prohibitory in form would, if granted, have amounted to temporary specific performance of a covenant requiring a corporation to keep an airfield in operation, and in so doing he cited with approval the following passage from Halsbury: 'The court does not enforce the performance of contracts which involve continuous acts and require the watching and supervision of the court.'[14] Most importantly, however, Megarry V-C's and Mervyn Davies J's reliance on *Shiloh Spinners* seems unjustified: for in that case, Lord Wilberforce appeared to accept the traditional constant supervision objection to specific performance of a contract to do work and was rather stressing that the objection was irrelevant to the requested relief against forfeiture for breach of such a covenant, since all the court had to do was to satisfy itself *ex post facto* that the covenanted work had been done.

But while there is still some doubt on the authorities whether this objection survives, it has little to commend it. In all but a few cases, the fact that the court has ordered specific performance will be sufficient to ensure compliance. In other words in almost all cases defendants do obey court orders. It is hardly sensible to deny the plaintiff the remedy because of problems which arise only

10 [1968] AC 58—unless Lord Pearce had this in mind in his comments at 90.
11 [1974] 1 WLR 576.
12 See also *Luganda v Service Hotels Ltd* [1969] 2 Ch 209 where *Ryan* was distinguished.
13 [1971] 2 All ER 277. See also *Gravesham Borough Council v British Railways Board* [1978] Ch 379, infra, pp 417–8.
14 Ibid at 284, citing Halsbury's Laws (3rd edn) p 627, para 365.

occasionally. Even in a case of non-compliance or alleged non-compliance, there is no need for full judicial machinery to be invoked: for example, a person could be appointed as an officer of the court to ensure enforcement or to investigate the allegations.[15] And even if judicial time and effort are involved, it is still strongly arguable that this is outweighed by the fact that justice otherwise requires the plaintiff to be granted specific performance. In other words, it should be clearly understood that the constant supervision objection rests on denying a remedy to the plaintiff not because as between the parties it is less appropriate than damages but because the costs to society are regarded as too great. Clearly the resources to be devoted to achieving justice between the parties must have some limit, but it may be doubted whether that limit is even approached by the few problematical specific performance cases involving further judicial time and effort. This is particularly so when one bears in mind that specific performance may also save judicial time and effort, namely that involved in the often complex task of assessing damages. Certainly it is unsatisfactory to deny justice on an unsubstantiated hunch about the costs of specific performance,[16] and in any event, it has to be explained why this area should be treated differently from, for example, family law, where the cost of continuing judicial involvement in supervising maintenance, access and custody orders is considered acceptable. In short, the policy justifications for the constant supervision objection to specific performance seem particularly weak and the attempts to remove this bar should therefore be supported.

(3) Contracts for personal service[17]

It is traditionally a well-established rule that the courts will not order specific performance of such a contract, of which the prime example is the contract of employment.[18] Assuming that damages

---

15 Treitel *Law of Contract* p 913; Schwartz (1979) 89 Yale LJ 271, 293–4. The court could also use the power in RSC Ord 45, r 8, to direct another to do the work at the defendant's expense.

16 Kronman (1978) 45 U of the Chi LR 351, 373–4; Schwartz (1979) 89 Yale LJ 271, 292–4.

17 This is shorthand for contract of service or contract for personal services.

18 Specific performance was refused against an employee in *Clark v Price* (1819) 2 Wils Ch 157; *De Francesco v Barnum* (1890) 45 Ch D 430; *Ehrman v Bartholomew* [1898] 1 Ch 671 (injunction amounting to specific performance). And against an employer in *Johnson v Shrewsbury and Birmingham Rly Co* (1853) 3 De GM & G 914; *Brett v East India and London Shipping Co Ltd* (1864) 2 Hem & M 404; *Rigby v Connol* (1880) 14 Ch D 482; *Page One Records Ltd v Britton* [1968] 1 WLR 157 (injunction amounting to specific performance).

are inadequate (and this assumption cannot be made too readily, particularly since many contracts for personal service are terminable at short notice) and that the constant supervision objection is at best very weak, what are the reasons for this rule?[19]

One general reason often given is that such a contract creates a relationship of mutual confidence and respect and that where that has broken down, it cannot be satisfactorily rebuilt by a court order: on the contrary, to force the relationship to continue is only likely to lead to friction between the parties, or at least between the employee and the employer's representative (for example, his foreman). Another reason suggested by Megarry J in *Giles & Co Ltd v Morris*[20] is that where services are of an artistic kind, like opera-singing, it would not be possible to judge whether an order of specific performance against the employee was being properly complied with:

... if ... the singer sang flat, or sharp, or too fast, or too slowly, or too loudly, or too quietly, or resorted to a dozen of the manifestations of temperament traditionally associated with some singers ... who could say whether the imperfections of performance were natural or self-induced?[1]

But whether such reasons are in play or not, more fundamental objections to specific performance may be suggested. From the employee's point of view specific performance would result in involuntary servitude. Thus in *De Francesco v Barnum*[2] Fry LJ said that the courts were afraid of turning 'contracts of service into contracts of slavery.'[3] From the employer's side the analogous rationale, seemingly implicitly accepted by the courts, is that as he has to organise and pay for the work he should have the prerogative to decide who remains employed by him.

As regards an employee being ordered to carry out a contract of service, the bar still applies in full force, being enshrined in the

19 It is sometimes said that repudiatory breach automatically terminates an employment contract and that this is a reason for no specific performance. But rightly this 'automatic' theory was firmly rejected in *Thomas Marshall Ltd v Guinle* [1979] Ch 227 (per Megarry V-C) because, for example, injunctions enforcing negative obligations are still available. See also *Gunton v Richmond-upon-Thames London Borough Council* [1981] Ch 448 (per Buckley LJ); *Dietman v Brent LBC* [1987] ICR 737 (affd [1988] ICR 842); *Marsh v National Autistic Society* [1993] ICR 453. Indeed apparent automatic termination is a consequence of rather than a reason for there being no specific performance.
20 [1972] 1 WLR 307.
1 Ibid at 318.
2 (1890) 45 Ch D 430.
3 Ibid at 438.

Trade Union and Labour Relations (Consolidation) Act 1992, s 236, which provides that:

No court shall, whether by way of—a) an order for specific performance . . . of a contract of employment, or b) an injunction . . . restraining a breach or threatened breach of such a contract, compel an employee to do any work or attend at any place for the doing of any work.

However, on the other side of the relationship, there have recently been some interesting developments.[4] For a full appreciation of these, private law, public (ie administrative) law, and the unfair dismissal legislation must all be examined.

(a) Private law

In *Hill v CA Parsons & Co Ltd*[5], the Court of Appeal confirmed the granting of an interlocutory injunction which amounted to temporary specific performance of a contractual obligation to employ the plaintiff. The defendant employers had made a closed shop agreement with a trade union and gave the plaintiff one month to join that union. When he failed to do so, he was given one month's notice of termination of employment. The plaintiff sought an interlocutory injunction restraining the defendants from implementing their notice of termination. The court held that the defendants were in breach of contract by giving only one month's notice, but the crucial point is that the majority held, Stamp LJ dissenting, that the interlocutory injunction should be granted, even though this amounted to temporary specific performance of a contract for personal service. Both Lord Denning and Sachs LJ stressed that the rule barring specific performance against an employer in a contract for personal service was not absolute. Lord Denning said:

The rule is not inflexible. It permits of exceptions. The court can in a proper case grant a declaration that the relationship still subsists and an injunction to stop the master treating it as at an end . . . It may be said that . . . the court is indirectly enforcing specifically a contract for personal services. So be it.[6]

The majority thought that an exception to the general rule was justified because damages were inadequate and by granting the

---

4 See generally Carty (1989) 52 MLR 449; Ewing (1993) CLJ 405.
5 [1972] Ch 305. See also the comments of Megarry J in *Giles v Morris* [1972] 1 WLR 307, cited with approval in dicta of Goff LJ in *Price v Strange* [1978] Ch 337, 359–60. The actual decision in *Giles* was that the traditional rule is no bar to ordering the employer to make, rather than to perform, a contract for personal service.
6 Ibid at 314–5.

injunction the plaintiff would remain an employee until the coming into effect of the Industrial Relations Act 1971 by which he would be protected if dismissed for not joining the union. Sachs LJ also stressed that there was no breakdown in mutual confidence between employer and employee. On the other hand, Stamp LJ in his dissent thought that there was no justification for departing from the rule that specific performance should not be granted in a contract for personal service.

Hill v Parsons can be and, in some cases,[7] was viewed as a 'freak' case, showing merely that there may be a very rare exception to the usual rule; after all, unfair dismissal legislation has been in force for a number of years, and so there is now no question of continuing employment to catch those provisions. Having said that, there are indications that the majority regarded the case as one of numerous exceptions. Lord Denning spoke of the rule as applying only in the '. . . ordinary course of things'[8] and Sachs LJ thought that, as there had been a recent marked trend towards '. . . shielding the employee', courts must be prepared to modify the traditional rule so as to conform '. . . to the realities of the day'.[9]

That less restrictive interpretation of *Hill v Parsons* has subsequently prevailed. For example, in *Irani v Southampton and South West Hampshire Health Authority*[10] the plaintiff was an ophthalmologist employed on a part-time basis by the defendants at an eye clinic. Following disagreements between the plaintiff and the consultant in charge of the clinic, the defendants gave the plaintiff six weeks' notice of dismissal. As the defendants had failed to go through the disputes procedure laid down in the plaintiff's contract of employment, the dismissal was in breach of contract. The plaintiff sought an interlocutory injunction restraining implementation of the dismissal notice until that disputes procedure had been complied with. This amounted to a claim for temporary specific performance of his contract of employment and, as Warner J described, the defendants had contended that:

7 Eg *GKN (Cwmbran) Ltd v Lloyd* [1972] ICR 214; *Sanders v Ernst A Neale Ltd* [1974] ICR 565.
8 [1972] Ch 305 at 314.
9 Ibid at 321.
10 [1985] ICR 590. See also *Jones v Lee and Guilding* [1980] ICR 310 (injunction amounting to temporary specific performance preventing school managers dismissing a teacher in breach of procedures established in his contract) and *Regent International Hotels (UK) Ltd v Pageguide Ltd* (1985) Times, 13 May (injunction granted amounting to temporary specific performance of a hotel management agreement: but it was doubted that this was analogous to a contract for personal service).

362 Specific performance

. . . there was a clear rule that the court would not grant specific performance of a contract of employment, or in general, grant an injunction to restrain breach of it and that there were no special circumstances which would justify my granting an injunction, the effect of which would compel the defendant authority to continue to employ Mr Irani . . . .[11]

Warner J disagreed, applied *Hill v Parsons* and granted the interlocutory injunction sought. Damages would plainly be inadequate at the interlocutory stage because the six weeks' notice of dismissal would probably have elapsed by trial; in any event, dismissal would make it difficult for the plaintiff to get another job in the Health Service. Warner J was particularly liberal in his application of the two other justifying reasons given in *Hill v Parsons*. He thought that there was still complete confidence between employer and employee in the sense that the defendants had perfect faith in the plaintiff's honesty, integrity and loyalty, and merely considered him an incompatible colleague of the consultant at the clinic; and the fact that the plaintiff was seeking protection under the disputes procedure was regarded as analogous to the protection sought by Mr Hill under the then imminent Industrial Relations Act 1971.

It should be noted, however, that the temporary specific performance granted did not extend to ordering the defendants to allow the plaintiff to attend work (let alone to provide work for him) albeit that this was arguably one of the defendants' contractual obligations.[12] Indeed the plaintiff undertook as a condition of specific performance that he would not present himself for work at any of the defendants' establishments. As such the primary obligations enforced were those of paying the plaintiff his full salary and retaining him on the books as an employee. It would seem that specific performance was similarly limited in *Hill v Parsons & Co Ltd*.[13]

The most important case subsequent to *Hill v Parsons* has been *Powell v Brent London BC*.[14] The plaintiff was appointed principal benefits officer for the defendant local authority. A few days after starting work, she was told that her appointment was invalid because there might have been a breach of the defendant's equal opportunity code of practice in appointing her. She sought an interlocutory injunction requiring the defendant to treat her as if she was properly employed as principal benefits officer and, even though that would amount to temporary specific performance, the Court of

11 Ibid at 597.
12 Freedland *The Contract of Employment* (1976) pp 23–7.
13 [1972] Ch 305 at 314 (per Lord Denning).
14 [1988] ICR 176.

Appeal granted it. Ralph Gibson LJ, giving the leading judgment, relied on *Hill v Parsons* and especially Sachs LJ's judgment, to justify a departure from the general bar to specific performance. In an important statement of principle, he said:

Having regard to the decision in *Hill v Parsons* and the long-standing general rule of practice to which *Hill v Parsons* was an exception, the court will not by injunction require an employer to let a servant continue in his employment, when the employer has sought to terminate that employment and prevent the servant carrying out his work under the contract, unless it is clear on the evidence not only that it is otherwise just to make such a requirement but also that there exists sufficient confidence on the part of the employer in the servant's ability and other necessary attributes for it to be reasonable to make the order. Sufficiency of confidence must be judged by reference to the circumstances of the case, including the nature of the work, the people with whom the work must be done and the likely effect upon the employer and the employee's operations if the employer is required by injunction to suffer the plaintiff to continue in the work.[15]

On the facts there was held to be sufficient mutual confidence between the parties in that the plaintiff had been doing the job satisfactorily, and without complaint, for over four months before the hearing.

Powell has been followed—and interlocutory injunctions, amounting to temporary specific performance, ordered—in *Hughes v London Borough of Southwark*[16] and *Wadcock v London Borough of Brent*.[17] Both concerned attempts by local authorities to reorganise the duties of social workers and, in both, an injunction was granted primarily because there was no breakdown of mutual confidence. The employees were clearly competent at their jobs.

More radical still was the decision in *Robb v Hammersmith and Fulham London BC*[18] in which a director of finance was dismissed without his employers going through the disciplinary procedures required under his contract. As in *Irani*, an injunction was granted requiring the defendants to continue to employ and pay the plaintiff unless and until the procedure had been properly complied with (the plaintiff undertaking not to attend for work unless instructed to do so). Morland J accepted that the plaintiff had lost the trust and confidence of the defendants but regarded the important point as being that the order proposed was perfectly workable. To refuse the injunction would be to allow the defendants to snap their fingers at the rights of the plaintiff.

15 Ibid at 194.
16 [1988] IRLR 55.
17 [1990] IRLR 223.
18 [1991] ICR 514. See also *Jones v Gwent CC* [1992] IRLR 521.

Lest it be thought that, in the light of such cases, specific performance is now the rule rather than the exception, it is helpful to refer to *Alexander v Standard Telephones and Cables plc*[19] in which *Powell* and *Irani* were distinguished. The defendants had made the plaintiffs redundant preferring to keep more skilled employees than applying a 'first in first out' selection. Even if that action by the defendants had constituted a breach of contract, Aldous J held that there was no real prospect of an injunction being granted at trial because, in the context of the rationalisation of the workforce, the employers did not have sufficient confidence in those employees made redundant.

(b) Public law

A further battle-ground on which the bar has been attacked concerns the use of the 'public law' principle whereby certain types of public employee—commonly labelled 'office-holders'—are protected against wrongful dismissal. Traditionally it has been recognised that such a dismissal, particularly where in breach of natural justice, can be declared invalid and may be restrained by an injunction;[20] that is, an 'office' may be specifically protected by the courts.[1] This has traditionally been reconciled with the rule against specific performance by simply regarding an office-holder as not really being an 'employee' under an ordinary or 'pure' contract of personal service.

Since the late 1950s the courts have applied this 'public law' principle to an increasingly wide range of dismissed 'employees' with the result that the area of pure contracts of personal service has been narrowed.[2] But two fairly recent cases have developed this even further by intimating that the very distinction between office-holders and employees under ordinary contracts of personal service is no longer helpful.

In *Stevenson v United Road Transport Union*[3] a regional officer of a trade union was dismissed by the union's executive committee. The Court of Appeal confirmed a declaration that the dismissal was

---

19 [1990] ICR 291. See also *Marsh v National Autistic Society* [1993] ICR 453. The traditional rule was also reaffirmed by the House of Lords in *Scandinavian Trading Tanker Co AB v Flota Petrolera Ecuatoriana, The Scaptrade* [1983] 2 AC 694, 701.
20 Presumably certiorari, prohibition and mandamus may also be ordered.
 1 Early cases are *Willis v Childe* (1851) 13 Beav 117; *Fisher v Jackson* [1891] 2 Ch 84.
 2 Eg *Vine v National Dock Labour Board* [1957] AC 488 (a registered dock-worker); *Malloch v Aberdeen Corpn* [1971] 1 WLR 1578 (a Scottish schoolmaster).
 3 [1977] ICR 893.

void because the committee had acted in breach of natural justice. While the case could presumably have been decided on the traditional principle that the plaintiff held an office, Buckley LJ giving the decision said, '. . . it does not much help . . . to try to place the plaintiff in the category of a servant on the one hand, or an officer, on the other', and he went on to apply the following test:

> Where one party has a discretionary power to terminate the tenure or employment by another of an employment or an office or a post or a privilege, is that power conditional on the party invested with the power being first satisfied on a particular point which involves investigating some matter on which the other party ought in fairness to be heard or to be allowed to give his explanation or put his case? If the answer to the question is Yes, then unless, before the power purports to have been exercised, the condition has been satisfied after the other party has been given a fair opportunity of being heard or of giving his explanation or putting his case, the power will not have been well exercised.[4]

This test was further applied in *R v BBC, ex p Lavelle*.[5] Here Woolf J held that a tape examiner, employed under what would traditionally have been regarded as an ordinary contract of personal service, had the right to be heard, and could be protected by a declaration and injunction, particularly because the employer was required to go through various disciplinary procedures before dismissal, and this took the case out of the pure master and servant category. As such disciplinary procedures are probably incorporated into the contracts of several millions of workers, this approach is clearly of great importance, although on the facts no remedy was granted since Miss Lavelle had in effect waived her rights with regard to the initial disciplinary meeting.

However, it is important to note that Woolf J did not consider Miss Lavelle's case an appropriate one for judicial review under RSC Ord 53 since the BBC was exercising private and not public powers in dismissing her. Therefore the public law notions of an officer and the right to be heard were being relied on, but the procedure for reviewing the exercise of public powers was not.

Of even wider potential significance for the personal service bar is Woolf J's dictum that:

> . . . the employment protection legislation has substantially changed the position at common law so far as dismissal is concerned. In appropriate circumstances the statute now provides that an industrial tribunal can order the reinstatement of an employee. It is true that the order cannot be

4 Ibid at 902.
5 [1983] 1 WLR 23.

specifically enforced. However, the existence of that power does indicate that even the ordinary contract of master and servant now has many of the attributes of an office, and the distinctions which previously existed between pure cases of master and servant and cases where a person holds an office are no longer clear.[6]

In other words, Woolf J seems to consider that irrespective of the contractual incorporation of disciplinary procedures, unfair dismissal legislation has elevated ordinary employees to the status of office-holders, thereby paving the way for their specific protection on traditional principles, But this is clearly a controversial view of the impact of the unfair dismissal legislation, particularly as the legislature there shied away from providing the equivalent of full specific performance.

Perhaps not surprisingly, therefore, this dictum has not been approved since and in the leading case of *R v East Berkshire Health Authority, ex p Walsh*[7] there has been an apparent back-tracking from *Stevenson* and *Lavelle*. The question arising was whether a senior nursing officer could apply for judicial review under Ord 53 to quash his dismissal as being in breach of natural justice. The Court of Appeal answered this in the negative on the ground that it was only if the public law officer principle applied to this plaintiff that he could proceed under Ord 53, and there was no such public law element in his employment, although, like *Lavelle*, there were disciplinary procedures engrafted onto the contract of employment. Without mentioning them, the approach in *Stevenson* and *Lavelle* was impliedly rejected, a narrow view of who is an officer was taken, and the reasoning sought to restore a clear distinction between public officers and private employees.

While on the one hand such a decision prevents the unfair dismissal regime being supplemented, or even by-passed, by judicial review for procedural unfairness,[8] on the other hand a clear distinction between public officers and private employees will be difficult to maintain. In any event cases like *Irani* and *Powell* supplement the unfair dismissal regime irrespective of the officer principle.

6　Ibid at 34.
7　[1985] QB 152. See also eg *R v Home Secretary, ex p Broom* [1986] QB 198; *McClaren v Home Office* [1990] ICR 824 (judicial review unavailable for prison officers); *R v Derbyshire CC, ex p Noble* [1990] ICR 808 (judicial review unavailable for police surgeon).
8　It is unclear whether an application for judicial review may be refused simply on the ground that proceedings before an industrial tribunal would be more appropriate: *R v Civil Service Appeal Board, ex p Bruce* [1989] ICR 171.

It is also of interest that while insisting on a consistency between Ord 53 and the officer principle, which *Lavelle* had rejected, *Walsh*, in contrast to *Lavelle*, frees the right to be heard from its public law confinement to officers. As Purchas LJ said in *Walsh*, commenting on the decision at first instance:

> The importation by direct reference or by implication into a contract of employment of the rules of natural justice does not of itself import the necessary element of public interest which would convert the case from [the pure master and servant category] into one in which there was an element of public interest created as a result of status of the individual or the protection or support of his position as a public officer. With great respect to the judge, it is this distinction which seems to have escaped him.[9]

(c) Unfair dismissal legislation

In providing a full picture of the recent challenges to the rule against specific performance of an employer's contractual obligations, it would be a mistake to leave out of account the unfair dismissal legislation, introduced in the Industrial Relations Act 1971 and now embodied in the Employment Protection (Consolidation) Act 1978. By ss 68–71, an industrial tribunal can order the reinstatement or reengagement of an employee who has been unfairly dismissed. Indeed these remedies are treated in the legislation as the primary remedies although in practice, and presumably for the same reasons as the traditional rule against specific performance, tribunals usually prefer to award compensation, irrespective of the employee's wishes.[10] But even where made, an order of reinstatement or reengagement is not the same as specific performance for breach of contract—an unfair dismissal is not necessarily a breach of contract, and reinstatement or reengagement does not correspond to full specific performance since non-compliance does not constitute contempt and is instead dealt with by an award of extra compensation to the employee. In other words, the legislature accepted that an employer who is prepared to pay can always get rid of an employee. However, the regime is clearly very similar to specific performance for breach, and indeed the sanction of a monetary penalty is somewhat similar to the French 'astreinte' which is there the way of enforcing specific performance.[11]

---

9 [1985] QB 152, 180.
10 Davies and Freedland *Labour Law* (2nd edn, 1984) pp 493–7.
11 Nicholas *French Law of Contract* (1982) pp 215–19.

(d) Conclusion

From the above examination, and particularly in the light of *Hill v Parsons, Irani, Powell,* and *Robb,* it is safe to say that the rule barring specific performance against an employer is less absolute than it once was. But the claim should not be exaggerated. Specific performance will generally still be denied. Moreover, some of the cases carrying the attack on the traditional position have not been concerned to ensure that the employer allows the employee to work or provides work for him,[12] and have primarily been concerned that the correct procedures are complied with before dismissal. In short, the view still holds sway that it is an employer's prerogative to decide ultimately who remains employed by him.

As a matter of policy one might wish to challenge this view, and to support a greater move towards specific performance, which would secure more fully an employee's status.[13] But specific performance can only ever go as far as the contractual terms allow: that is, it can only ensure that dismissal is implemented without a breach of contract. As such, full security of employment can only be brought about by statute. The preference for increased compensation rather than contempt sanctions in the unfair dismissal regime shows that the legislature has as yet been prepared to travel only part way down that road.

(4) Want of mutuality[14]

Fry, in his book on specific performance first published in 1858, stated a rule of mutuality to the effect that a court will not in general order specific performance against the defendant unless from the time the contract was made he could have got specific performance against the plaintiff had the plaintiff been in breach. To use Fry's exact words, 'A contract to be specifically enforced by the court must, as a general rule, be mutual, that is to say, such that it might at the time it was entered into have been enforced by either

---

12 Supra, pp 362–3. The exact effect of nullifying the dismissal of an officer is unclear; but in *Chief Constable of North Wales Police v Evans* [1982] 3 All ER 141 mandamus to coerce reinstatement was refused.

13 Clark (1969) 32 MLR 532; Cohen (1982) 32 U Tor LJ 31; Brown in Reiter and Swan *Studies in Contract Law* (1980) ch 4, pp 100–7.

14 Sometimes referred to as negative mutuality, this is to be contrasted with affirmative mutuality, which is the unsound notion that specific performance will be granted to the plaintiff, simply because it could have been granted against him. See Sharpe *Injunctions and Specific Performance* (2nd edn) paras 7.820–7.880, 10.430–10.570.

of the parties against the other of them.'[15] Over the years many
exceptions to such a rule have been recognised and indeed, on close
examination, the rule has not *necessarily* been supported by any
authority. This has lent support to Ames's view[16] that Fry's formulation overstated the position and that the true rule is that the
defendant will not be ordered to perform unless there is adequate
assurance that the plaintiff will in turn perform. In Ames's words,
'Equity will not compel specific performance by a defendant if after
performance the common law remedy of damages will be his sole
security for the performance of the plaintiff's side of the contract.'[17]
On this approach, in contrast to Fry's, there is no need to view as
exceptional the fact, for example, that a vendor who acquires the
property to be sold subsequent to the making of the contract can be
granted specific performance against the buyer, or that a plaintiff
who has performed personal services in return for a promised transfer of land can compel conveyance. On the other hand, like Fry's
rule, Ames's will support the refusal of specific performance where
the plaintiff's performance is to be subsequent to the defendant's
and will not be specifically enforceable.[18]

The leading case is now *Price v Strange*,[19] where the Court of
Appeal rejected Fry's rule. The defendant, the headlessee of some
flats in a house, orally agreed to grant the plaintiff a new underlease
of his flat in return for the plaintiff's promise to carry out certain
repairs to the house. The plaintiff did half of the repairs but the
defendant refused to allow him to complete them, had them done
at her own expense, and refused to grant the underlease. The plaintiff brought an action for specific performance of the promise to
grant the underlease and this was granted by the Court of Appeal,
subject to the plaintiff compensating the defendant for the expense
she had incurred in having the remaining repair work done. The
defendant had argued that, in accordance with Fry's rule, specific
performance should not be granted because she could not from the
time the contract was made have obtained specific performance
against the plaintiff, since his obligation to repair was not specifically
enforceable. But Fry's rule was held to be wrong and as on these
facts there could be no risk of the plaintiff not performing (since the
work had already been completed) specific performance was
granted. As regards what the correct rule is, however, there appears

15 *Fry on Specific Performance* (6th edn, 1921) p 219.
16 (1903) 3 Col LR 1.
17 Ibid, 2–3, 12.
18 As in *Flight v Bolland* (1828) 4 Russ 298 (infant plaintiff); *Ogden v Fossick* (1862)
    4 De GF & J 426 (plaintiff to employ defendant).
19 [1978] Ch 337.

to be a slight difference between the views of Goff LJ and Buckley LJ: for while the former would seemingly apply Ames's formulation, the latter tentatively indicated that, even if the defendant could not be assured of actual performance by the plaintiff, specific performance might still be granted so long as damages would be an adequate remedy to the defendant for any default on the plaintiff's part. So Buckley LJ's formulation of the true rule was as follows:

The court will not compel a defendant to perform his obligation specifically if it cannot at the same time ensure that any unperformed obligations of the plaintiff will be perfectly performed, unless, perhaps, damages would be an adequate remedy to the defendant for any default on the plaintiff's part.[20]

This formulation (with 'perhaps' omitted) is to be preferred to Ames's; the defendant can have no complaints so long as he is assured of a satisfactory remedy against the plaintiff for any non-performance and it should not be necessary for the defendant to be assured of actual performance; after all, the risk of subsequent non-performance is one that the defendant has contractually undertaken.

Indeed even this watered-down version of mutuality may be too kind to a defendant because rather than refusing specific performance, the courts could grant it on terms that ensure adequate monetary security to the defendant or otherwise provide an incentive for the plaintiff to perform. Even more radical, and yet highly persuasive, is the argument that the defendant merits no such concern at all.[1] A fortiori damages will inadequately compensate the plaintiff, and hence by denying him specific performance, he is, as a matter of certainty, being denied a more appropriate remedy. In contrast, mutuality protects the defendant against a mere *risk* of the plaintiff subsequently not performing, and that is after all a risk which the defendant accepted by entering into that contract.[2]

---

20 Ibid at 367–8.
1 Lewis (1903) 51 Univ of Penn LR 591, 625–9; Schwartz (1979) 89 Yale LJ 271, 301–3. Durfee (1921) 20 Mich LR 289 takes a mid-position: the defence is justified where the defendant's potential hardship is greater than the plaintiff's hardship.
2 Under the Landlord and Tenant Act 1985, s 17, specific performance can be ordered of a landlord's repairing covenant, irrespective of want of mutuality. The courts also allow waiver of the defence—*Price v Strange* [1978] Ch 337 at 358, applied in *Sutton v Sutton* [1984] Ch 184. Also contrast injunctions where want of mutuality is not a defence (see Beale *Remedies* p 138), although the courts may grant an injunction on terms that the defendant can apply for dissolution if the plaintiff does not perform, see infra, p 411, fn 3.

(5) Uncertainty

The terms must satisfy a test of certainty for there to be a valid contract. But even if this is so, and damages are therefore recoverable for breach, specific performance may still be denied where the terms are too vague to allow a clear order to be made. A good example is provided by *Joseph v National Magazine Co*,[3] where the defendants contracted to publish an article by the plaintiff on the subject of jade. In breach of contract, they later refused to publish it without major amendments. It was held that while the plaintiff was entitled to damages, specific performance should be refused because the terms of publication were too vague to allow a clear order to be made. This is also a reason why many building contracts are not specifically enforceable: for example, damages for breach of contract to build a house of a certain value can be readily assessed, but no specific performance will be ordered without building specifications.[4]

There are several reasons for this uncertainty restriction. Most obviously it is only fair to the defendant that he should know precisely what he has to do to comply with the order and avoid being held in contempt, and the courts too must be able to enforce an order and to judge whether there has been compliance with it. Furthermore, there may be a fear that in complying with an unclear order the defendant will perform in a way that does not match the plaintiff's expectations. Finally it can be argued that, as in relation to the constant supervision objection, an unclear order is likely to give rise to future disputes, which will take up judicial time and effort; but this problem in itself could be overcome by appointing a court officer to deal with any subsequent dispute if and when it arises and in any case it is not a strong argument where justice otherwise requires the order.

It is reasonable to expect that the increased willingness of the courts to imply terms will enable them to make clear orders of specific performance and thereby overcome the uncertainty objection. This is supported by *Sudbrook Trading Estate Ltd v Eggleton*[5] where the House of Lords held that if the agreed machinery for

3 [1959] Ch 14. See also *South Wales Rly Co v Wythes* (1854) 5 De GM & G 880; *Greenhill v Isle of Wight Rly (Newport Junction) Co* (1871) 23 LT 885.
4 *Brace v Wehnert* (1858) 25 Beav 348.
5 [1983] 1 AC 444. In *Regent International Hotels (UK) Ltd v Pageguide Ltd* (1985) Times, 13 May, the Court of Appeal suggested that any certainty problems could be avoided by insisting on arbitration of any bona fide disputes prior to court action.

valuation breaks down in a contract for the sale of land a court will ascertain the fair and reasonable price, thereby rendering the contract specifically enforceable.

(6) Contracts not supported by valuable consideration

While the common law remedies are granted for breach of a contract made by deed or supported merely by nominal consideration—that is where there is no true bargain but rather a gratuitous promise—specific performance is not.[6] This is essentially what is meant by the maxim, 'Equity will not assist a volunteer.'

It is hard to see any rational reason for this distinction between the approach at common law and in equity and it is best regarded as a legacy of history. Moreover, since underlying morality justifies upholding gratuitous promises it is submitted that the common law is here to be preferred and that this bar to specific performance should be removed.

Indeed there is now some support for an undermining of this restriction. *Mountford v Scott*[7] concerned an attempt by the defendant to withdraw an option to purchase land granted to the plaintiff for £1. Brightman J regarded the plaintiff as seeking specific performance not only of the contract to sell but also of the option contract and granted the remedy even though the consideration supporting the option was nominal. He said, 'It is not the function of equity to protect only those equitable interests which have been created for valuable consideration.'[8] However, it would be dangerous to place too much weight on this as the Court of Appeal,[9] while upholding the decision, adopted a different analysis under which the question of specific enforcement of the option did not arise; that is, it regarded the grantee of an option as being able to exercise that option, and hence create a valid contract for the sale of the land, without any need for the defendant's co-operation.

(7) Contract unfairly obtained

Specific performance may be denied where there has been procedural unfairness, whether misrepresentation, mistake induced by or known to the plaintiff, undue pressure, or unfair advantage taken of

---

6 *Cannon v Hartley* [1949] Ch 213; *Lister v Hodgson* (1867) LR 4 Eq 30. But it would be surprising, applying usual equitable principles, if specific performance were to be refused where the promisee has detrimentally relied on the promise.
7 [1975] Ch 258 at 263. See also *Gurtner v Circuit* [1968] 2 QB 587 at 596.
8 Ibid at 262.
9 Ibid.

the defendant's weak position. So, for example, in *Walters v Morgan*[10] the defendant contracted to grant the plaintiff a mining lease over land which he had just bought; but specific performance was refused because the defendant had been hurried into signing the agreement in ignorance of the true value of his property. Similarly in *Webster v Cecil*[11] the defendant, due to an arithmetical error, offered his property to the plaintiff for £1250 instead of £2250. The plaintiff accepted this, although since his previous offer of £2000 had been refused, he must have known of the mistake. His action for specific performance was dismissed. Furthermore, while it appears that inadequacy of consideration is not in itself a ground for refusing specific performance,[12] that is, substantive unfairness is insufficient, this will probably tip the balance against specific performance, where there is any hint of procedural unfairness.[13] Finally it should be stressed that *Tamplin v James*[14] lays down the 'modern' approach that unilateral mistake, neither known to nor induced by the plaintiff, is not a defence to specific performance.

However, these days it may be doubted whether a defendant needs to rely on unfairness in obtaining the contract as a defence to specific performance; for, given the expansion of doctrines, such as duress, undue influence, misrepresentation and, though more arguably, unilateral mistake and inequality of bargaining power, the defendant will generally be able to escape from all contractual liability where there is a defence to specific performance because of procedural unfairness. For example, on the facts of *Walters v Morgan*, it may be that the defendant could now escape from the contract, and avoid all remedies for breach, by invoking unilateral mistake or inequality of bargaining power. One can argue that such assimilation is to be supported, on the ground that it is only separate historical development that has led to procedural unfairness that is sufficient to deny specific performance being insufficient to rule out damages.[15] But perhaps some distinction can be rationally defended on the basis that the reasons that justify damages retaining their primacy, under the adequacy hurdle, also justify the courts

---

10 (1861) 3 De GF & J 718.
11 (1861) 30 Beav 62. If damages were available at common law (but cf *Hartog v Colin and Shields* [1939] 3 All ER 566), there would be no advantage here in resisting specific performance, ie damages would probably be £100.
12 *Collier v Brown* (1788) 1 Cox Eq Cas 428.
13 *Griffith v Spratley* (1787) 1 Cox Eq Cas 383 at 389.
14 (1880) 15 Ch D 215. Contrasting with earlier cases, such as *Malins v Freeman* (1837) 2 Keen 25.
15 Schwartz (1979) 89 Yale LJ 271, 300–1. Cf Sherwin (1991) 50 Maryland LR 253.

being more willing to accept wider versions of particular defences where specific performance rather than damages is being claimed.

(8) Impossibility

Specific performance will not be ordered where performance is physically impossible, for there is clearly no sense in ordering the defendant to do something on pain of contempt, which he simply cannot do. So, for example, specific performance will not be ordered against a person who has agreed to sell land which he does not own and cannot compel the owner to convey to him.[16] Similarly, where the defendant has sold property to a third party whose title is unaffected by the plaintiff's prior interest, the plaintiff will not be granted specific performance.[17] Analogous is *Wroth v Tyler*[18] where specific performance of a contract to sell a home with vacant possession was refused because it would require the defendant to embark upon uncertain litigation in an attempt to force his wife to leave the house.

Specific performance will also be refused where this would require the defendant to do something he is not lawfully competent to do. In *Warmington v Miller*,[19] for example, the defendant, a lessee of business premises, agreed to grant an underlease to the plaintiff, even though he was prohibited by his lease from sub-letting. He failed to grant the underlease but specific performance was refused because it would necessitate the defendant breaking the terms of his lease.

Sometimes in these situations, a defendant can escape from the contract and avoid all remedies for breach, by invoking doctrines such as common mistake, frustration or illegality. But those doctrines are clearly narrower than the impossibility bar to specific performance, so that a plaintiff may be able to recover damages if he is denied specific performance.

(9) Severe hardship

Specific performance will be refused where it would cause severe hardship to the defendant.[20] It was on this ground that in *Denne v*

---

16 *Castle v Wilkinson* (1870) 5 Ch App 534.
17 *Ferguson v Wilson* (1866) 2 Ch App 77.
18 [1974] Ch 30.
19 [1973] QB 877.
20 Or, sometimes, to third parties, eg *Thames Guaranty Ltd v Campbell* [1985] QB 210. See Jones and Goodhart *Specific Performance* pp 81–2.

Light,[1] the court refused to order specific performance against the buyer of farming land which was apparently landlocked: that is, there seemed to be no right of way over surrounding land. Similarly, in *Hope v Walter*[2] it was thought unfair to a purchaser to order him to complete the sale of a house that, unknown to both parties, was being used as a brothel by the tenant. Again, in *Wroth v Tyler* specific performance to order the defendant to convey title with non-vacant possession was refused because for the defendant's wife, but not the defendant, to have the right to continue to live in the house could encourage a split-up of the family.

A recent and particularly vivid example is *Patel v Ali*.[3] Here the defendant, a married Pakistani woman who could hardly speak English, had contracted to sell her home to the plaintiffs. In the years after the contract was made, the defendant's husband was sent to prison, she bore two more children and had a leg amputated because of bone cancer. A number of friends and relatives brought her shopping and helped with household chores. However, if she was forced to move it was likely that she would lose this daily assistance. In such circumstances, Goulding J refused to order specific performance and left the plaintiffs to their remedy of damages, even though the defendant's hardship did not exist at the time of the contract and was not in any way caused by the plaintiffs.

On the other hand, specific performance will not be refused simply because the defendant is in financial difficulties[4] or because, on a rising market, the defendant vendor of a house is finding it difficult to acquire alternative accommodation.[5]

Again, it is interesting to see that in many situations of 'severe hardship', the defendant can escape from the contract and avoid all remedies for breach, by invoking doctrines such as common mistake or frustration. But that in this context a clear gap is left for the refusal of specific performance alone is shown by *Patel v Ali*, and by Goulding J's comment that 'Equitable relief may . . . be refused because of an unforeseen change of circumstances not amounting to legal frustration, just as it may on the ground of mistake insufficient to avoid a contract at law.'[6]

---

1 (1857) 8 De GM & G 774.
2 [1900] 1 Ch 257.
3 [1984] Ch 283.
4 *Francis v Cowcliffe* (1976) 33 P & CR 368.
5 *Mountford v Scott* [1975] Ch 258.
6 [1984] Ch 283 at 288. See generally Sherwin (1991) 50 Maryland LR 253.

(10) The plaintiff's conduct[7]

(a) Serious breach

Specific performance will be refused if the plaintiff has committed a serious breach of contract. So for example, in *Australian Hardwoods Proprietary Ltd v Railways Comr*[8] the Privy Council refused specific performance of a contractual obligation to take steps to ensure the transfer of a sawmill licence because, inter alia, of the plaintiff's own breach. Similarly, a plaintiff will not be awarded specific performance if he himself is in breach of a time stipulation where time is of the essence.[9] But since the fusion of the common law and Chancery courts, the defendant rarely needs to rely on this defence, for a breach that is serious enough to justify refusing specific performance should and it seems does entitle the defendant to terminate the contract, rendering him no longer liable to perform. Put another way, the sort of breach necessary to bar specific performance will never be less serious than a breach justifying discharge of the contract.[10]

(b) He who comes to equity must come with clean hands[11]

By this maxim specific performance will be denied to a plaintiff whose past conduct, as revealed by the facts of the dispute, has been highly improper. Indeed, one can regard the previous head of serious breach as incorporated within clean hands, although it is more usually treated separately. As such, clean hands plays a loose and residual role. An example is *Lamare v Dixon*,[12] where the owner of some cellars had orally promised the proposed lessee, prior to the signing of the contract for a lease, that he would make the cellars dry. This he had failed to do and as a result the court refused him specific performance. More recently in *Quadrant Visual Communications Ltd v Hutchison Telephone (UK) Ltd*[13] the defendant contracted to buy the plaintiff's car and portable telephone business. The price to be paid depended on the number of the plaintiff's

---

7 This refers to conduct other than in contract formation. For unfairness in formation see supra, pp 372–4.
8 [1961] 1 WLR 425. In *Dyster v Randall & Sons* [1926] Ch 932 at 942–3, the breach was thought too trivial to be a bar.
9 *Steedman v Drinkle* [1916] 1 AC 275.
10 Farnsworth *Contracts* (2nd edn, 1990) p 856.
11 Generally, see Chafee (1948–9) 47 Mich LR 877, 1065.
12 (1873) LR 6 HL 414. See also *Mason v Clarke* [1954] 1 QB 460 at 472.
13 [1993] BCLC 442.

customers prior to the completion date. Prior to completion, the plaintiff increased the number of its customers through two marketing deals that involved supplying free telephones. The plaintiff informed the defendant of the first but not the second deal. Following breach by the defendant, the Court of Appeal upheld the trial judge's decision not to award the plaintiff specific performance of the agreement because the plaintiff had tricked the defendant and had therefore not come to equity with clean hands.

(c) He who seeks equity must do equity

This means that there will be no specific performance if the plaintiff is not willing and able to perform his own obligations from now on (or is otherwise not willing to do what is fair and right for the defendant). So for example, in *Chappell v Times Newspapers Ltd*,[14] employees were refused an injunction amounting to specific performance of a contract of employment because, inter alia, they could not show themselves ready and willing to perform their contracts without disruption as they were not prepared to renounce their union. Clearly this defence normally rests on similar grounds to that of want of mutuality but it differs in that the court is reacting to a clear indication of the plaintiff's unwillingness to counter-perform.

(d) Laches

By s 36(1) of the Limitation Act 1980, the usual six-year limitation period does not apply to an action for specific performance. But under the doctrine of laches the remedy may be denied for unreasonable delay by the plaintiff in seeking it. Traditionally, the classic authority was *Milward v Earl of Thanet*,[15] where Sir Richard Arden MR said that a plaintiff wanting specific performance had to show himself to be 'ready, desirous, prompt and eager'; and although there were always exceptional situations (for example, long delays did not bar an action merely to transfer the legal estate)[16] delays of more than a few months were generally considered fatal to specific performance, particularly where there was prejudice to the defendant or the subject-matter was property of fluctuating value.[17]

---

14 [1975] 1 WLR 482.
15 (1801) 5 Ves 720n.
16 *Sharp v Milligan* (1856) 22 Beav 606 (18 years); *Williams v Greatrex* [1957] 1 WLR 31 (10 years).
17 *Pollard v Clayton* (1855) 1 K & J 462 (11 months); *Huxham v Llewellyn* (1873) 28 LT 577 (5 months); *Glasbrook v Richardson* (1874) 23 WR 51 (3½ months).

However, *Lazard Bros & Co Ltd v Fairfield Properties Co (Mayfair) Ltd*[18] indicates that in modern times the courts are more tolerant of a plaintiff's delay. There specific performance of a contract for the sale of land was sought over two years after completion was due and was granted. Megarry V-C regarded *Milward v Earl of Thanet* and the idea that specific performance was a prize to be awarded to the zealous and to be denied to the indolent as the wrong approach today; and he went on to say, 'If between the plaintiff and the defendant it was just that the plaintiff should obtain the remedy, the court ought not to withhold it merely because the plaintiff has been guilty of delay.'[19] What exactly this means and hence how far the courts will grant specific performance despite lengthy delays by the plaintiff is left unclear; but it may be expected that in the absence of additional factors, such as prejudice to the defendant, a long delay—and certainly more than a few months—will be needed to bar specific performance.

But while it seems only right to erase the notion that the zealous plaintiff alone can be granted specific performance, it is submitted that the best approach of all—so as to produce desirable certainty and uniformity—would be to amend the Limitation Act 1980 by introducing a limitation period for specific performance.

(e) Acquiescence

Although no case has been found, it has traditionally been assumed that, as with injunctions, acquiescence is a bar to specific performance:[20] that is, that a plaintiff will be denied specific performance where he has encouraged the defendant to believe that he has no objection to the defendant doing what amounts to a breach of contract, and the defendant has acted to his detriment in that belief.

(f) Valid termination of the contract by the plaintiff

Where the plaintiff has validly terminated the contract for the defendant's breach, he can no longer claim specific performance. This was regarded as an 'incontrovertible' principle by Lord Wilberforce in dicta in *Johnson v Agnew*[1] and he later commented, '. . . it is easy to see that a party who has chosen to put an end to a contract by the other party's repudiation cannot afterwards seek specific

18 (1977) 121 Sol Jo 793.
19 Ibid.
20 Meagher, Gummow and Lehane *Equity* (3rd edn) para 2034; *Fry on Specific Performance* p 516.
1 [1980] AC 367 at 392.

performance. This is simply because the contract is dead—what is dead is dead.'[2] An alternative way of expressing this is to say that the plaintiff's election bars specific performance; but the terminology and supposed doctrine of election of remedy is likely to confuse rather than to clarify the law, and it is easier to manage without it.

Sharpe has criticised the present law on the ground that it should only be where the defendant has detrimentally relied on the plaintiff's termination that the plaintiff should be prevented from going back on it.[3] But such an approach would leave the issue too uncertain, hindering the parties' plans for future action. Under the present law the parties know for sure that once the plaintiff has made a clear decision to terminate they are each free to ignore the contract.

Finally, it should be stressed that merely claiming damages for breach does not bar specific performance, as specific performance and damages may be mutually consistent. Rather specific performance is barred where the claim for damages shows that the plaintiff is terminating the contract, that is that he is accepting the defendant's repudiation.[4]

(11) No partial specific performance?

The principle has sometimes been applied that there can be no specific performance of only some of the defendant's obligations under a contract; so if one or more of the obligations is not specifically enforceable, there can be no specific performance of the rest. For example, in *Ryan v Mutual Tontine Westminster Chambers Association*,[5] where the court refused to order specific performance of an obligation to provide a porter who would be constantly in attendance, an alternative claim that the defendants should merely be ordered to appoint a porter was also refused; '. . . when the court cannot grant a specific performance of the contract as a whole it will not interfere to compel specific performance of part of a contract.'[6]

There seems to be nothing in terms of policy to justify such a

---

2 Ibid at 398.
3 Ie the full requirements of estoppel by election are required, Sharpe *Injunctions and Specific Performance* (2nd edn) paras 10.820–10.880.
4 See *Meng Leong Development Pte Ltd v Jip Hong Trading Co Pte Ltd* [1985] AC 511.
5 [1893] 1 Ch 116. See also, eg *Merchants' Trading Co v Banner* (1871) LR 12 Eq 18.
6 Ibid at 123 (per Lord Esher MR).

bar.[7] Damages (or equitable compensation) can be added to compensate the plaintiff for the unperformed part, as they are where performance will be late or where land being bought does not correspond to what was promised. In any event, as it is the plaintiff who is seeking the order, he is clearly prepared to accept the disadvantage of part performance. Nor can the defendant validly complain if he is ordered to do part only of what he agreed.

Fortunately, it is doubtful whether this principle has ever been generally accepted, since there are numerous decisions that conflict with it. In *Lytton v Great Northern Rly Co*,[8] for example, specific performance was ordered of the defendants' contractual obligation to build a railway siding while being refused of their obligation to keep it in repair; and in *Elmore v Pirrie*[9] the defendants' obligation to purchase patent rights was specifically enforced although there could be no specific performance of their obligation to form a company to work the patents and to pay royalties to the plaintiffs. In Kay J's words:

> Why should not the plaintiffs have damages for that part of the agreement of which the court does not grant specific performance? The court has power to order specific performance of the whole of the agreement, or part of it, with damages for the rest.[10]

Moreover in the more recent case of *Posner v Scott-Lewis*[11] Mervyn-Davies J ordered specific performance of a landlord's covenant to appoint a resident porter at a block of flats and, although there was no discussion of the 'no partial specific performance' idea, the decision does appear to be a direct contradiction of *Ryan*.

(12) Conclusion—the trend towards specific performance

Having completed an examination of the various bars to specific performance it is appropriate to take a brief overview of the present availability of the remedy.

In spite of some of the more radical proposals in some cases not finding favour in others, the general picture is one of a trend in

---

7 *Ogden v Fossick* (1862) 4 De GF & J 426 may be justified, but if so this is because of want of mutuality and not because of the 'no partial specific performance' principle relied on.
8 (1856) 2 K & J 394.
9 (1887) 57 LT 333. See also, eg *Peacock v Penson* (1848) 11 Beav 355; *Soames v Edge* (1860) John 669; *Wilkinson v Clements* (1872) 8 Ch App 96.
10 Ibid at 336.
11 [1987] Ch 25.

favour of specific performance. Indeed in relation to no less than eight of the bars there have been recent developments favouring specific performance—adequacy of damages, constant supervision, personal service, want of mutuality, uncertainty, contracts not supported by valuable consideration, laches and, in so far as it was ever a bar, no partial specific performance. So it appears that a plaintiff will now find it easier than ever before to obtain specific performance.

The examination of policy has further shown that, with the exception of the wide view of *Beswick v Beswick*, all such developments in favour of specific performance are either justified or at least unobjectionable. The verdict is therefore one of support for this trend.

Finally it may be asked, why has this trend occurred in recent times? Several answers may be suggested; for example, there is now, arguably, a more flexible approach to precedent; damages are particularly problematical in times of high inflation and when insolvency is common: and the courts are more willing than ever before to intervene in individuals' lives.

3. OTHER ISSUES

(1) Stipulated remedy

There are two issues here. The first, which no English case has yet dealt with, is whether a clause by which the parties indicate that specific performance should be the remedy for breach will be valid so as to ensure the granting of specific performance where it would otherwise not be available. Arguably such a clause, unlike a penalty clause cannot be knocked down as unconscionable, for it cannot be unfair to insist, as at the time the contract is made, that the defendant performs as he promises. Rather such a clause, like a liquidated damages clause, has the merit of saving judicial time and expense, here in deciding between damages and specific performance. However the courts are never keen to allow their jurisdiction to be ousted and, at the end of the day, it is likely that they would take the view that if there are good grounds for otherwise refusing specific performance, an agreed remedy clause is not sufficient to undermine the validity of those grounds.[12]

The second issue is whether a penalty or liquidated damages

---

12 But see the views of Sharpe *Injunctions and Specific Performance* (2nd edn) paras 7.710–7.810. See also Macneil (1962) 47 Cornell LQ 495, 520–3.

clause ousts specific performance. It might be argued, for example, that the insertion of such a clause gives the defendant an option to perform or to pay agreed damages; or, more forceful still, that such a clause indicates that monetary remedies are adequate and that specific performance of the primary obligation is unwarranted. But the courts lean against a construction that would oust a judicial remedy and they have consistently taken the view that the money clause is added as security for performance and/or as clarifying the amount of damages the plaintiff will receive if suing for damages.[13] Specific performance is therefore not ousted.

(2) The flexibility of specific performance—additional damages or compensation and conditional enforcement

(a) Damages in addition to specific performance

The Supreme Court Act 1981, s 49, allows a claim for ordinary common law damages to be combined with an action for specific performance. In the same action therefore, the plaintiff may be awarded specific performance and, where what is ordered is not identical with what was promised,[14] damages to overcome the deficiency. For example, since specific performance seldom results in performance at the time fixed by the contract, damages for delay may be awarded along with specific performance.[15]

Equitable damages may also be awarded in addition to specific performance under s 50 of the Supreme Court Act 1981, the successor to Lord Cairns's Act.[16] But since *Johnson v Agnew*[17] has assimilated the principles of assessment, additional equitable damages are only more advantageous to a plaintiff in the situation where they are available and common law damages are not.[18]

---

13 *Howard v Hopkyns* (1742) 2 Atk 371; *Long v Bowring* (1864) 33 Beav 585; *Magrane v Archbold* (1813) 1 Dow 107. The same approach is taken with regard to injunctions, see infra, pp 413–4.
14 But no order should be made for performance of something entirely different from what was promised: see analogously *Cedar Holdings Ltd v Green* [1981] Ch 129 esp 141–3.
15 *Jaques v Millar* (1877) 6 Ch D 153. See also *Seven Seas Properties Ltd v Al-Essa* [1988] 1 WLR 1272 (specific performance granted against a vendor of land along with an order for the holding back, and retention by the parties' solicitors, of so much of the purchase price as would cover the purchaser's damages claim against the vendor for loss of a sub-sale of the land).
16 Eg *Grant v Dawkins* [1973] 1 WLR 1406.
17 [1980] AC 367.
18 As in example (i), supra, p 244.

(b) Specific performance with compensation or abatement of purchase price[19]

Prior to s 2 of the Chancery Amendment Act 1858 (Lord Cairns's Act) the Court of Chancery had at most a very limited power to award damages in addition to specific performance. This was offset to an extent by the practice of awarding to a purchaser of land that is not as promised, the equitable remedy of compensation or abatement of price along with specific performance.[20] Yet purchasers and courts still respectively claim and award this additional remedy[1] despite the power the courts now have to award common law or equitable damages in addition to specific performance. The continuation of this habit is doubly surprising since, rather than offering advantages over damages, compensation seems less advantageous; for in *Rudd v Lascelles*,[2] several restrictions were placed on the power to award compensation in addition to specific performance and in, for example, *Grant v Dawkins*,[3] it was assumed that the amount of compensation, like abatement, could not exceed the purchase price. Harpum thinks that the practice '. . . perhaps . . . reflects no more than the conservatism of the legal profession who have preferred to stick with the devil they have known for so long.'[4] Seemingly no-one would lose anything and unnecessary duplication and complexity would be avoided if the power to award compensation or abatement of price to a purchaser of land along with specific performance was simply abolished.

(c) Conditional specific performance

To protect the defendant, and to enable the remedy to be as widely applicable as possible, specific performance may be granted on terms. The most common example occurs where the vendor of land seeks specific performance against the purchaser and there is some non-substantial defect[5] in the property; specific performance will be ordered 'with compensation', that is, subject to the vendor paying compensation to the purchaser to cover the defect.[6]

---

19 Harpum (1981) CLJ 47.
20 *Mortlock v Buller* (1804) 10 Ves 292.
1 *Topfell Ltd v Galley Properties Ltd* [1979] 1 WLR 446 is a recent example.
2 [1900] 1 Ch 815.
3 [1973] 1 WLR 1406.
4 (1981) CLJ 47 at 51.
5 The leading case on the meaning of this is *Flight v Booth* (1834) 1 Bing NC 370, but it was actually dealing with rescission.
6 *Re Fawcett and Holmes' Contract* (1889) 42 Ch D 150; *Shepherd v Croft* [1911] 1 Ch 521.

Specific performance on terms has also been commonly adopted as a means of producing a just result for both parties in cases where the defendant is able to resist specific performance because of his mistake. The plaintiff may be granted specific performance if he agrees to conditions reflecting the defendant's understanding of the bargain. For example, in *Baskcomb v Beckwith*,[7] the defendant purchaser had contracted to buy an area of land, without realising—the plans not making it clear—that a small plot of land nearby was to be retained by the vendor, and was not covered by restrictive covenants preventing the building of a public house. The plaintiff was given the choice: no specific performance or specific performance with the restrictive covenant extended to his own retained plot.

Langen and Wind Ltd v Bell[8] shows that where the courts want to protect the defendant against a subsequent failure by the plaintiff to perform they may make specific performance conditional, rather than denying specific performance altogether for want of mutuality. The defendant had there contracted to transfer shares to the plaintiffs for a price that could only be fixed in the future. The defendant was ordered to transfer the shares but as security for future payment they were to be held by the plaintiffs' solicitors until payment.

A more unusual illustration of conditional specific performance is provided by *Price v Strange*,[9] where simply to have ordered the defendant to grant the lease to the plaintiff would have given the plaintiff a windfall, since he had promised in return to carry out the repairs which the defendant had had finished at her own expense. The plaintiff was therefore granted specific performance but subject to compensating the defendant for that expense.

Finally in *Harvela Investments Ltd v Royal Trust Co of Canada Ltd*[10] the House of Lords granted specific performance to a purchaser of shares on condition that it paid the vendor interest from the date fixed for completion until payment.[11] Specific performance by itself would have put the plaintiff into a far better position than if there had been no breach, because it would have had the use of the purchase money during the period of delay, plus taking the rise in value of the shares.[12] Indeed irrespective of such a justification, ordinary equitable principles, generally rationalised in terms of equitable interests or constructive trusts, establish that a vendor is

---

7 (1869) LR 8 Eq 100. See also *Preston v Luck* (1884) 27 Ch D 497.
8 [1972] Ch 685.
9 [1978] Ch 337.
10 [1985] 2 All ER 966.
11 For rates of interest, see supra, pp 259–60.
12 For criticism of the courts for often ignoring this, see Swan (1980) 10 RPR 267.

entitled to interest on the purchase price from the date of completion, while a purchaser is in return entitled to the interim profits from the property.[13]

(3) The effect of specific performance on termination and damages

In *Johnson v Agnew*,[14] the plaintiff vendor of land had obtained specific performance against the purchaser. The purchaser delayed in complying with the order, so that mortgagees of the land enforced their security by selling off the land. With specific enforcement no longer possible, the plaintiff now sought damages for the defendant's breach of contract. The defendant argued, first, that having obtained an order of specific performance the plaintiff had irrevocably forfeited his right to damages—all contractual rights had become merged in the specific performance decree;[15] and secondly, that having 'rescinded' the contract for breach, as the plaintiff had now done, there could in any event be no damages. The House of Lords rejected both arguments. The latter, which is beyond our immediate concern, was held to rest on an incorrect line of authority,[16] that had mistakenly regarded rescission for breach as meaning rescission *ab initio* rather than termination *in futuro*. The former was emphatically rejected, it being held that a contract remains in force after an order of specific performance so that the plaintiff can ask the court to dissolve the decree and revert to his rights to termination and damages.

However, the House of Lords did make one concession to the 'irrevocable election' view, namely that the plaintiff has no *right* to revert to termination and damages. In Lord Wilberforce's words:

Once the matter has been placed in the hands of a court of equity . . . the subsequent control of the matter will be examined according to equitable principles. The court would not make an order dissolving the decree of specific performance and terminating the contract (with recovery of damages) if to so do would be unjust, in the circumstances then existing to the other party, in this case to the purchaser.[17]

---

13 [1985] 2 All ER 966 at 978. See also *Re Hewitt's Contract* [1963] 1 WLR 1298;
   Fry pp 640–1, *Emmet on Title* (19th edn, 1986) paras 7.021–7.033.
14 [1980] AC 367.
15 The terminology of election is often used; but, as in other instances, it is confusing and unnecessary.
16 Eg *Horsler v Zorro* [1975] Ch 302.
17 [1980] AC 367 at 399. See also *Singh v Nazeer* [1979] Ch 474 esp 480–1, *GKN Distributors Ltd v Tyne Tees Fabrication Ltd* (1985) 50 P & CR 403.

This concession would appear to be designed to deal with the situation where it is because of the plaintiff's default that specific performance has not been complied with, so that had the contract been in force in the normal way, it would be the defendant rather than the plaintiff who would be entitled to damages.[18] Beyond this situation, there seems no justification for such a concession.[19]

18 The extent of the concession is discussed by Hetherington (1980) 96 LQR 403, and Jackson (1981) 97 LQR 26.
19 Hetherington, ibid, and Meagher, Gummow & Lehane *Equity* para 2053 do not think the concession is ever justified.

Chapter 9

Injunctions

1. INTRODUCTION

An injunction is an equitable remedy available for both torts and breach of contract,[1] as well as being available in many other situations, outside the scope of this book.[2] The approach adopted in this chapter will be to introduce briefly in this section the three important pairs of contrasting injunctions before going on in the next sections to examine in depth the principles governing the grant of each of the main types of injunction along with the function each performs as a remedy for torts and breach of contract. The plaintiff's conduct as a bar is considered in the last section.

Four further points can be conveniently dealt with at this stage. First, a court will sometimes accept an undertaking from the defendant in substitution for, and in the same terms as, an injunction that it would otherwise have granted.[3] Since, contrary to its non-coercive appearance, such an undertaking plays exactly the same role as an injunction, being enforceable by contempt proceedings,[4] it is hard to see what possible justification there is for this judicial practice.

Secondly, by the Crown Proceedings Act 1947, s 21(1)(a), an injunction cannot be granted against the Crown.[5] But, as explained

1 This presumably includes oral contracts enforceable by part performance: see *JC Williamson Ltd v Lukey and Mulholland* (1931) 45 CLR 282.
2 The Supreme Court Act 1981, s 37(1), gives the High Court power to grant an injunction 'whenever just and convenient to do so', but generally the infringement of a legal or equitable right is required—Hanbury and Martin *Modern Equity* (14th edn) pp 725–31. For treatment of situations outside torts and breach of contract, see Sharpe *Injunctions and Specific Performance* (2nd edn) ch 3 and paras 5.190–5.540..
3 *Evans Marshall & Co Ltd v Bertola SA* [1973] 1 WLR 349.
4 *Camden London Borough Council v Alpenoak Ltd* [1985] NLJ Rep 1209; *Hussain v Hussain* [1986] 1 All ER 961.
5 However an interlocutory injunction can be granted against the Crown to protect the plaintiff's directly effective EC rights: *R v Secretary of State for Transport, ex p Factortame Ltd (No 2)* [1991] 1 AC 603.

by the House of Lords in *M v Home Office*,[6] an injunction, including an interlocutory injunction, can be granted against *an officer of the Crown* when sued in his personal capacity and, in judicial review proceedings (to which s 21 does not apply), when sued in his official capacity. Commonly a plaintiff will be equally satisfied with a declaration against the Crown although, as yet, there is no power to award an interlocutory declaration.

Thirdly, an injunction can affect third parties: ie contempt proceedings can be brought against not only the tortfeasor or contract-breaker for failure to comply with the injunction but also against any person who frustrates the purpose of the injunction.[7]

Finally, it was laid down by the Court of Appeal in *Wookey v Wookey*[8] that no injunction should be ordered against a person whose mental incapacity means that he is incapable of understanding the order; nor, in the vast majority of cases, against a minor who has no earnings from which a fine for disobedience could be paid and is too young to be sent to prison.

(1) Prohibitory and mandatory injunctions

A prohibitory injunction acts negatively, ie it orders the defendant not to do something. A mandatory injunction acts positively, ie it orders the defendant to do something. The distinction is one of substance and not one of form so that, for example, an injunction ordering the defendant not to allow a particular building to remain standing on his land is a mandatory injunction, since in substance the defendant is being ordered to knock the building down. Indeed, prior to *Jackson v Normanby Brick Co*[9] the courts tended to express mandatory injunctions in such a negative form but in that case it was laid down that form should reflect substance and that a mandatory injunction should be expressed in a positive form.

But so long as in substance breach of a negative obligation is being restrained the courts apply prohibitory injunction principles even though *in practice* it is most likely that compliance will necessitate particular positive steps. For example, an injunction restraining a factory-owner from continuing to pollute a river so as to cause a nuisance to the plaintiff is regarded as prohibitory and

6 [1993] 3 All ER 537.
7 *Z Ltd v A-Z and AA-LL* [1982] 1 All ER 556 (Mareva injunction); *A–G v Times Newspapers Ltd* [1991] 2 All ER 398.
8 [1991] 3 All ER 365.
9 [1899] 1 Ch 438.

governed by prohibitory injunction, rather than mandatory injunction, principles. Only on the question of whether to suspend the injunction is any weight attached to the argument that compliance may in practice force the defendant to take particular positive steps, for example, replacing the factory's existing 'waste disposal' system with a new one. The justification for this is presumably that so long as the plaintiff *can* comply with the injunction without positive steps, for example, by not continuing with that business, one cannot be sure that in complying he will take positive steps, and certainly one cannot predict with any accuracy which particular steps he might take. Traditionally the one judicially recognised exception is in the realm of breach of contract, where specific performance generally takes over the role of the mandatory injunction: it has long been recognised that an order which the defendant can comply with only by either not working (or not carrying on business) at all or carrying out particular positive contractual obligations is regarded as indirect specific performance, and is governed by specific performance, rather than prohibitory injunction, principles. The argument later advanced in regard to that area[10]—that, as indicated in some recent cases, the exception should be extended to wherever the order is in practice likely to force the defendant to take particular positive steps—is applicable also to the distinction between prohibitory and mandatory injunctions.

(2) Quia timet[11] injunctions and injunctions where a wrong has already been committed

In *Redland Bricks Ltd v Morris*[12] Lord Upjohn said that a '. . . *quia timet* action . . . is an action for an injunction to prevent an apprehended legal wrong, though none has occurred at present', and Jolowicz has written that a *quia timet* injunction is granted where '. . . no actionable wrong has yet been committed by the defendant.'[13]

Most obviously, therefore, an injunction sought to prevent a continuing wrong is not *quia timet*. But the same can also be said of an injunction sought to prevent a *recurrence* of wrongful acts by the

10 Infra, pp 409, 412.
11 'Since he fears'.
12 [1970] AC 652 at 644.
13 (1975) 34 CLJ 224, 244.

defendant, or a mandatory injunction sought to prevent the defendant's earlier acts causing a *further* wrong. In relation to the latter, Lord Upjohn in *Redland Bricks Ltd v Morris* erroneously treated as *quia timet* a mandatory injunction sought to compel the defendant to restore support to the plaintiff's land. As the land had slipped several times before, so that the same sort of wrong as that now sought to be prevented had previously been committed by the defendant against the plaintiff, the injunction sought should not have been regarded as *quia timet*.[14]

(3) Final and interlocutory injunctions

A final injunction, otherwise known as a perpetual injunction, is one that is granted at the trial of the action or other hearing in which final judgment is given.[15] In contrast, an interlocutory injunction, as normally understood,[16] is one made at an earlier stage in the proceedings which is to last only until the trial at the latest. It is generally expressed to continue in force 'until the trial of this action or further order'. For the plaintiff the great advantage of an interlocutory injunction is that it can be gained quickly, without having to wait for the trial.

Very similar to an interlocutory injunction, and often not distinguished from it, is an interim injunction, made prior to trial, that is to last at the latest until a specified date other than the date of the trial. So an interim injunction will be expressed to continue in force, for example, 'until 10.30 am on Wednesday 25th March (or so soon thereafter as counsel may be heard) or until further order'. An interim injunction is often granted in cases of urgency prior to the plaintiff seeking an interlocutory injunction. The same general principles are applied in deciding whether to grant an interim injunction as are applied to an interlocutory injunction, and hereinafter interim injunctions will not be distinguished from interlocutory injunctions.

---

14 Ibid, pp 244–5.
15 Eg summary judgment under RSC Ord 14.
16 But Mareva injunctions granted after final judgment have been treated as interlocutory because they are ancillary to a final judgment. See *Orwell Steel v Asphalt and Tarmac (UK) Ltd* [1984] 1 WLR 1097; *Hill Samuel v Littauer* [1985] NLJ Rep 57. Also see *Distributori Automatici Italia SpA v Holford General Trading Co Ltd* [1985] 3 All ER 750 (Anton Piller orders made after final judgment).

2. FINAL PROHIBITORY INJUNCTIONS[17]

(1) Torts

(a) The present law

A prohibitory injunction is the appropriate remedy to prevent the continuation or repetition of a tort. By it the defendant is ordered not to perform the acts that constitute the tort. While a prohibitory injunction can be granted in respect of any tort that can be continued or repeated—and has been granted, for example, to prevent trespass to the person,[18] inducing breach of contract,[19] defamation,[20] infringement of copyright,[1] passing off,[2] and the equitable wrong of breach of confidence[3]—it has mainly been sought, particularly at the final rather than interlocutory stage, to restrain torts protecting the plaintiff's real property rights, namely the torts of nuisance and trespass to land.

In relation to these two torts—and, despite the stress often laid on the plaintiff's proprietary rights, there is no reason to suppose that different principles apply to other torts—it is clear that the prohibitory injunction rather than damages is the primary remedy. In other words, the courts rarely exercise their power under s 50 of the Supreme Court Act 1981, the successor to Lord Cairns's Act, to award damages in lieu of a prohibitory injunction sought to restrain the continuation or repetition of a nuisance or trespass to land; and an award of ordinary common law damages is generally not in issue, since in this context such damages are almost inevitably 'inadequate', being available to compensate only for loss caused by past torts.

The classic case indicating the primacy of the prohibitory injunction is *Shelfer v City of London Electric Lighting Co.*[4] Here an electric housing station had been built next to a pub and the vibration and noise caused by the operation of the machines generating the electricity constituted an actionable nuisance to the lessee of the

---

17 *Quia timet* prohibitory injunctions are discussed infra, pp 420–3.
18 *Egan v Egan* [1975] Ch 218 (interlocutory).
19 *Emerald Construction Co Ltd v Lowthian* [1966] 1 All ER 1013 (interlocutory). The availability of the prohibitory injunction contrasts here with the reluctance to grant specific performance of positive obligations in the main contract.
20 *Saxby v Easterbrook* (1878) 3 CPD 339; *Bonnard v Perryman* [1891] 2 Ch 269 (interlocutory).
1 *Performing Right Society Ltd v Mitchell & Booker Ltd* [1924] 1 KB 762.
2 *Erven Warnink BV v J Townend & Sons (Hull) Ltd* [1979] 2 All ER 927.
3 *Peter Pan Manufacturing Corpn v Corsets Silhouette Ltd* [1964] 1 WLR 96; *X v Y* [1988] 2 All ER 648.
4 [1895] 1 Ch 287.

pub. The trial judge had awarded damages in lieu of the prohibitory injunction sought to restrain a further nuisance, but the Court of Appeal reversed this decision and granted the injunction. Particularly important is A L Smith LJ's judgment where he said that damages should only be awarded in lieu of an injunction:

> If the injury to the plaintiff's legal rights is small. And is one which is capable of being estimated in money. And is one which can be adequately compensated by a small money payment. And the case is one in which it would be oppressive to the defendant to grant an injunction.[5]

This statement has been applied many times since, a good example being in *Kennaway v Thompson*,[6] where the Court of Appeal awarded a prohibitory injunction to limit power-boat racing, the noise from which was causing the plaintiff a nuisance.

The primacy of the prohibitory injunction—or, as it is often expressed, the plaintiff's prima facie right to a prohibitory injunction—was also stressed in the well-known case of *Pride of Derby and Derbyshire Angling Association Ltd v British Celanese Ltd*,[7] where a prohibitory injunction was granted to restrain the defendants from polluting a river with untreated sewage so as to constitute a nuisance to the plaintiff angling association which operated a fishery in the river. In Lord Evershed MR's words:

> It is, I think, well settled that if A proves that his proprietary rights are being wrongfully interfered with by B, and that B intends to continue his wrong, then A is prima facie entitled to an injunction, and he will be deprived of that remedy only if special circumstances exist, including the circumstance that damages are an adequate remedy for the wrong that he has suffered.[8]

Similarly in the early case of *Imperial Gas Light & Coke Co v Broadbent*,[9] where a prohibitory injunction was granted to restrain the defendants from operating their gas works so as to cause a nuisance to the plaintiff who carried on business as a market-gardener, Lord Kingsdown said:

> . . . if a plaintiff applies for an injunction to restrain a violation of a common law right . . . he must establish that right at law: but when he has established his right at law, I apprehend that unless there be something special in the case, he is entitled as of course to an injunction to prevent the recurrence of the violation.[10]

---

5 Ibid at 322–3.
6 [1981] QB 88.
7 [1953] Ch 149.
8 Ibid at 181.
9 (1859) 7 HL Cas 600.
10 Ibid at 612.

Finally and more recently, Lord Upjohn in dicta in *Redland Bricks v Morris*,[11] the classic authority on mandatory injunctions, confirmed that a prohibitory injunction to prevent a person withdrawing support from his neighbour's land would be granted 'as of course'.[12]

Naturally all this does not mean that damages will never be awarded instead. Clearly a prima facie right can be lost. The main ground on which this will be so[13] is that, in line with usual equitable principles, the plaintiff's conduct may debar him.[14]

It may also be that a prohibitory injunction will be refused where the interference with the plaintiff's rights is trivial, although there is inconsistency in the authorities on this point. On the one hand, A L Smith LJ's principles in *Shelfer* can be regarded as recognising that, at least where the injunction is also oppressive to the defendant (and this requirement seems to add next-to-nothing) damages in lieu should be awarded where the tortious interference is trivial. Several trespass cases also show the application of a triviality restriction.[15] In *Llandudno UDC v Woods*,[16] an injunction to restrain a clergyman from trespassing by holding services on the plaintiff local authority's seashore was refused, Cozens Hardy J saying that the injunction was '. . . a formidable legal weapon which ought to be reserved for less trivial occasions'.[17] Similarly in *Behrens v Richards*,[18] having decided that the defendants, local inhabitants, were indeed trespassing on the plaintiff's land—an area of the Cornish coast—by crossing it to reach a beach, Buckley J refused a prohibitory injunction because the trespass was causing no real harm to the plaintiff. Nominal damages alone were considered sufficient. A further illustration is *Armstrong v Sheppard & Short Ltd*,[19] where the defendant was trespassing on a small strip of land at the rear of the plaintiff's premises by having a sewer discharging effluent there. An injunction to restrain this trespass was refused, inter

---

11 [1970] AC 652.
12 Ibid at 664. See also *Cowper v Laidler* [1903] 2 Ch 337 at 341; *Wood v Conway Corpn* [1914] 2 Ch 47; *A-G v PYA Quarries Ltd* [1957] 2 QB 169; *Armstrong v Sheppard and Short Ltd* [1959] 2 QB 384.
13 Although rare, uncertainty may also be a bar, ie it must be possible to frame an order clearly specifying what the defendant must not do: *PA Thomas & Co v Mould* [1968] 2 QB 913 at 922–3.
14 Infra, pp 446–51.
15 See also *Lillywhite v Trimmer* (1867) 36 LJ Ch 525 (trivial nuisance).
16 [1899] 2 Ch 705.
17 Ibid at 710.
18 [1905] 2 Ch 614.
19 [1959] 2 QB 384. See also *Woollerton & Wilson Ltd v Richard Costain Ltd* [1970] 1 WLR 411; *League Against Cruel Sports Ltd v Scott* [1985] 2 All ER 489.

alia, because the interference was trivial. The Court of Appeal cited the following useful passage from *Kerr on Injunctions*:[20]

> After the establishment of his legal rights, and of the fact of its violation, a plaintiff is generally entitled as of course to a perpetual injunction to prevent the recurrence of the wrong, unless there be something special in the circumstances of the case, such as . . . where the interference with the plaintiff's rights is trivial.

On the other hand, in granting a prohibitory injunction to restrain a trespass by the defendant's parking of vehicles on the plaintiff's land, the Court of Appeal in *Patel v WH Smith (Eziot) Ltd*[1] preferred the view that an injunction can be granted irrespective of the harm suffered and *Behrens v Richards* was put to one side as an exceptional case. And *Patel* was applied by Scott J in *Anchor Brewhouse Developments Ltd v Berkley House Docklands Developments Ltd*[2] in granting an injunction to restrain the defendants trespassing in the plaintiff's air space by their tower cranes. Scott J said:

> It would be possible for the law to be that the court should not grant an injunction to restrain a trifling trespass if it were shown to be reasonable and sensible that the trespass be allowed to continue for a limited period upon payment of substantial and proper damages. But I do not think it is open to me to proceed on that footing . . . The authorities establish, in my view, that the plaintiffs are entitled as of course to injunctions to restrain continuing trespasses.[3]

There is no obvious way of reconciling those two opposing views. To say that a prohibitory injunction may *exceptionally* be refused where the harm is trivial is of no real help for it is hard to see what was exceptional about a case like *Behrens v Richards*. In terms of policy, the view that triviality of harm precludes a prohibitory injunction is probably to be preferred for, as is discussed below,[4] there are strong arguments for the judiciary making a greater use of damages.

Several points concerning the primacy afforded to the prohibitory injunction merit further consideration. The first is that the courts have often stated that one reason why the prohibitory injunction should be the primary remedy is that otherwise the court would be enabling a defendant who could afford to do so to buy himself the

20 (6th edn, 1927) p 30. See also *Cowper v Laidler* [1903] 2 Ch 337 at 341.
1 [1987] 2 All ER 569.
2 [1987] 2 EGLR 173.
3 Ibid at 178.
4 Infra, pp 399–403.

right to commit wrongs. Typical is Lindley LJ's judgment in the *Shelfer* case in which he said, '. . . the Court has always protested against the notion that it ought to allow a wrong to continue simply because the wrongdoer is able and willing to pay for the injury he may inflict'.[5] In this respect, the courts show themselves to be zealous to protect individual rights, by preventing defendants—and one thinks particularly of large-scale enterprises—riding roughshod over those rights by simply working into their calculations the costs of compensating for wrongs they may commit.

Secondly, and assuming that the interference with the plaintiff's rights is more than trivial, the hardship that compliance with the prohibitory injunction will cause to the defendant has traditionally not been regarded as a reason to refuse it. For example, in *Pennington v Brinsop Hall Coal Co*[6] compliance with the injunction granted would involve closure of the defendant's undertaking at a cost of £190,000, whereas the plaintiff's loss by the nuisance was at most £100 a year. This approach contrasts sharply with the balancing of benefit and burden applied for mandatory injunctions and the 'severe hardship' bar that is a defence to specific performance.

Similarly, so long as any triviality threshold is crossed,[7] the courts are not prepared to deny a prohibitory injunction on the ground that the public interest is more important than the plaintiff's private interest. The *Shelfer* and *Pride of Derby* cases show this.[8] In the former the public interest in having electricity generated was not allowed to override the plaintiff's private interest in living in and running a public house free from undue interference by noise and vibration. Similarly in the latter case the public interest in having the town's sewage cheaply and easily disposed of was not allowed to override the plaintiff club's private interest in being able to fish in the river. A particularly vivid illustration is provided by *A-G v Birmingham Borough Council*,[9] where counsel for the defendant argued, in graphic detail, that if the injunction restraining the corporation from discharging sewage into the river were granted:

5 [1895] 1 Ch 287 at 315–6.
6 (1877) 5 Ch D 769. See also *Redland Bricks Ltd v Morris* [1970] AC 652 at 664, (defendant's financial difficulties irrelevant to prohibitory injunctions).
7 *Llandudno UDC v Woods* [1899] 2 Ch 705 and *Behrens v Richards* [1905] 2 Ch 614, are examples of the upholding of the public interest where interference was trivial.
8 The public interest in the saving of jobs was also ignored in *Pennington v Brinsop Hall Coal Co* (1877) 5 Ch D 769.
9 (1858) 4 K & J 528.

. . . the evil that must ensue . . . would be incalculable. If the drains are stopped . . . the entire sewage of the town will overflow. Birmingham will be converted into one vast cesspool, which in the course of nature, from the great elevation of the town (450 feet above sea-level) must empty itself into the Tame, only in a far more aggravated manner. The deluge of filth will cause a plague, which will not be confined to the 250,000 inhabitants of Birmingham, but will spread over the entire valley and become a national calamity . . . In such cases private interests must bend to those of the country at large. The safety of the public is the highest law.[10]

But to this Sir Page Wood V-C retorted, 'We cannot talk of that in this Court'[11] and in granting the interim prohibitory injunction sought he said, '. . . so far as this Court is concerned, it is a matter of almost absolute indifference whether the decision will affect a population of 250,000 or a single individual.'[12] More recently in *Kennaway v Thompson*[13] the Court of Appeal, in granting the injunction sought, followed *Shelfer* and refused to allow the public interest in having facilities for power-boat racing to override the private interest of the plaintiff in living in her house without excessive interference by noise from the adjoining lake.

But while the courts rarely *refuse* a prohibitory injunction to restrain a continuing tort, they do often suspend or restrict its operation, and it is through this power that some account is taken of the defendant's hardship or the public interest. In Troman's words, the power '. . . can be seen as an uneasy compromise between the traditional fervour for the injunction as the appropriate remedy, and the realisation that an unlimited and immediate injunction may have undesirable effects'.[14]

So, for example, in *Pride of Derby v British Celanese*,[15] the injunction was suspended for two years as it was by the Privy Council in *Stollmeyer v Petroleum Development Co Ltd*,[16] where the defendant's oil-drilling constituted a nuisance by polluting a stream flowing by the plaintiff's land, Lord Sumner saying, 'Their Lordships are of the opinion that it would not be right to enforce the injunction at once. The loss to the respondents would be out of all proportion to the appellant's gain.'[17] Again in *Halsey v Esso Petroleum Co Ltd*,[18] an

10 Ibid at 536.
11 Ibid.
12 Ibid at 539–40.
13 [1981] QB 88.
14 (1982) CLJ 87 at 95.
15 [1953] Ch 149.
16 [1918] AC 498n.
17 Ibid at 500.
18 [1961] 2 All ER 145.

injunction restraining a nuisance constituted by the noise of tankers coming and going from an oil-depot at night was suspended for six weeks. In each of these cases the suspension gave the defendants ample opportunity to sort out how best to comply with the order. A particularly controversial use of the power to suspend was made in *Woollerton and Wilson Ltd v Richard Costain Ltd.*[19] There a crane being used to construct a building was trespassing into the plaintiff's airspace. The plaintiff was granted a prohibitory injunction to restrain this trespass but Stamp J suspended its operation until the date when the building was due to be completed, the crane then being no longer needed. By so doing, the injunction was prevented from having any effect: it might just as well have been refused. Not surprisingly therefore, in *John Trenberth Ltd v National Westminster Bank Ltd,*[20] where an injunction was granted to take immediate effect to prevent the defendant entering the plaintiff's land to erect scaffolding for work on his own property, Walton J considered that *Woollerton* was wrongly decided. If, as seems to be the case, the triviality of the damage was influencing Stamp J to suspend the injunction, it would indeed have been preferable if he had refused the injunction on that ground and awarded damages in lieu. It should also be noted that, as one would expect, given the finding of liability, the defendant will generally be bound to pay damages for the plaintiff's loss during the period for which an injunction is suspended. Indeed, the suspension is likely to be made conditional on the defendant's undertaking to pay such damages.[1]

Cases on nuisance by noise provide the main illustrations of the courts' imposition of restrictions on the operation of a prohibitory injunction. In *Vanderpant v Mayfair Hotel Co Ltd,*[2] for example, an injunction was granted to restrain noise from a hotel between 10.00 pm and 8.00 am; and in *Halsey v Esso Petroleum*[3] the injunction was to operate from 10.00 pm until 6.00 am. In *Dunton v Dover District Council*[4] an injunction was granted allowing a children's playground to be used by under twelves between 10.00 am and 6.30 pm. The injunction granted in *Kennaway v Thompson*[5] is notable for its

---

19 [1970] 1 WLR 411.
20 (1980) 39 P & CR 104; Street (1980) Conv 308.
  1 *Stollmeyer v Trinidad Lake Petroleum Co* [1918] AC 485 at 497; Ogus and Richardson (1977) CLJ 284, 313–14.
  2 [1930] 1 Ch 138.
  3 [1961] 2 All ER 145.
  4 (1978) 76 LGR 87.
  5 [1981] QB 88 at 94–5. This was distinguished in *Tetley v Chitty* [1986] 1 All ER 663 where an unrestricted injunction was granted to restrain a nuisance by go-kart racing.

particularly detailed specifications of what was and was not permitted. The injunction basically restrained 'motor boat racing, water skiing and the use of boats creating a noise of more than 75 decibels on the club's water', but this was made subject to the following restrictions:

... the club is allowed to have, each racing season, one international event extending over three days, the first day being given over to practice and the second and third to racing. In addition, there can be two national events, each of two days, but separated from the international event and from each other by at least four weeks. Finally there can be three club events, each of one day, separated from the international and national events and each other by three weeks. Any international or national event not held can be replaced by a club event of one day.

Additionally the club was '. . . not to allow more than six motor boats to be used for water-skiing at any one time.'

Finally it should be realised that there have been cases that cannot be reconciled with the traditional approach affording the prohibitory injunction such primacy. In *Bracewell v Appleby*,[6] for example, Graham J refused a prohibitory injunction preventing the defendant trespassing on the plaintiffs' private road because to grant it would in effect make the house the defendant had built 'uninhabitable and would put the plaintiffs into an unassailable bargaining position.'[7] But *Miller v Jackson*[8] is the most important recent example, where the majority of the Court of Appeal refused to grant an injunction restraining the defendant cricket club from playing cricket on a ground next to which the plaintiff's house had been built and into whose garden balls were quite often being hit. Cumming-Bruce LJ considered that, in granting the injunction, the trial judge had paid insufficient regard 'to the interest of the inhabitants of the village as a whole':[9] and Lord Denning, who would even have been prepared to decide that there was no actionable nuisance, was clear that the public interest dictated that no injunction should be granted. He said:

The *public* interest lies in protecting the environment by preserving our playing fields in the face of mounting development, and by enabling our youth to enjoy all the benefits of outdoor games, such as cricket and football. The *private* interest lies in securing the privacy of his home and garden without intrusion or interference by anyone . . . I am of opinion that that public interest should prevail over the private interest.[10]

6 [1975] Ch 408.
7 Ibid at 416.
8 [1977] QB 966.
9 Ibid at 989.
10 Ibid at 981–2.

A different Court of Appeal in *Kennaway v Thompson*[11] refused to follow *Miller*, correctly indicating that its approach is irreconcilable with precedent as represented by *Shelfer*'s case.

(b) Is the present law satisfactory?

The present law by which the plaintiff is nearly always able to obtain a prohibitory injunction to restrain the continuance or repetition of a tort seems uncontroversial in respect of torts protecting the plaintiff against personal injury or property damage. But it has recently been criticised in respect of the tort of nuisance,[12] and many of the arguments are equally applicable to other torts, such as trespass to land. Their central thrust is that damages should be awarded far more than they are and that prohibitory injunctions should not be granted 'as of course'. On such an approach, a decision like *Miller v Jackson* is to be welcomed. What then are the arguments for and against greater use of damages in preference to the prohibitory injunction?

(i) *Arguments for greater use of damages*

(i) As the courts weigh the defendant's hardship against the benefit to the plaintiff in deciding whether to grant a mandatory injunction, they should do the same for prohibitory injunctions. But it may be doubted whether this is a valid argument where one is dealing with a truly negative injunction. What is true, however, is that the courts sometimes regard as prohibitory, injunctions that are better viewed as mandatory, because in practice compliance will force the defendant to take particular positive steps.[13] If such injunctions were recognised as mandatory, traditional legal principle would rightly require the defendant's hardship to be considered. Beyond this, change seems unnecessary.

(ii) The courts should be prepared to refuse a prohibitory injunction where the public interest outweighs the plaintiff's private rights. Under the present law, once any triviality threshold is crossed, the courts only take the public interest into account in suspending or restricting a prohibitory injunction. According

---

11 [1981] QB 88. See also *Webster v Lord Advocate* 1984 SLT 13.
12 Ogus and Richardson (1977) CLJ 284; Tromans (1982) CLJ 87; Rotherham (1989) 4 Canterbury LR 185; Sharpe *Injunctions and Specific Performance* (2nd edn) paras 4.60–4.580.
13 Supra, pp 388–9.

to this argument, there is no reason why they should not go further.

(iii) The courts should be wary of awarding injunctions because, like all specific remedies, they allow the plaintiff too much of an advantage in pre- and post-judgment bargaining. So Tromans writes, 'The effect of an injunction may be certainty, but it is certainty achieved by tying one of the defendant's hands behind his back before negotiations begin. This is hardly likely to produce a fair or economic result.'[14]

(iv) The automatic granting of an injunction can be further criticised as absolving the plaintiff from any duty to mitigate his own loss. While, generally speaking, mitigation is less likely to be possible where one is dealing with negative tort obligations than positive contractual promises, there will be situations where a plaintiff could relatively easily take steps to avoid being harmed by the defendant's actions. Automatic injunctions remove the incentive to take such steps.

(v) The fact that an injunction is so routinely awarded may have an unfortunate effect on the substantive law, since the courts may steer clear of finding liability, knowing of the consequent drastic remedy. As Tromans writes in the context of nuisance, '... an unwillingness to give the plaintiff anything other than the best remedy can lead to his getting no remedy at all.'[15] As examples he instances the non-liability for temporary nuisances, and the wide construction courts give to the defence of statutory authority. The latter is shown by *Allen v Gulf Oil Refining Ltd*,[16] where the House of Lords' liberal construction of a private Act of Parliament enabled the defendants to construct and operate an oil refinery without incurring any liability in nuisance to the plaintiffs who were affected by its noise, smell and vibration. No doubt the Lords were influenced by the fact that a finding of liability would inevitably lead to an injunction and hence the potential closure of the refinery. Lord Denning's solution in the Court of Appeal awarding 'damages to cover past or future injury in lieu of an injunction'[17] seems far preferable.

(vi) Calabresi and Melamed[18] have put forward a sophisticated

---

14 (1982) CLJ 87, 105. For detailed discussion of this, see Thompson (1975) 27 Stan LR 1563. Also see supra, p 14.

15 Ibid, p 107.

16 [1981] 1 All ER 353.

17 [1979] 3 All ER 1008 at 1016.

18 (1972) 85 Harv LR 1089. See also Michelman (1971) 80 Yale LJ 647; Ellickson (1972) 40 U Chi 681, esp 738–48; Rabin (1977) 63 Va LR 1299; Harris *Remedies in Contract and Tort* pp 335–9.

economic analysis which would also seem to support a freer use of damages awards in relation to land use conflicts. According to their model, entitlements can be protected by either property or liability rules.[19] Where protection is by a property rule '. . . someone who wishes to remove the entitlement from its holder must buy it from him in a voluntary transaction in which the value of the entitlement is agreed upon by the seller.'[20] Protection is by a liability rule 'whenever someone may destroy the initial entitlement if he is willing to pay an objectively determined value for it.'[1]

It follows that there are four possible outcomes to a land use conflict. If D is polluting P's land, then first, P may have an entitlement to be free from pollution protected by a property rule; that is, P may be granted an injunction to restrain D's nuisance. Secondly, P may have an entitlement to be free from pollution protected by a liability rule; that is, P may be merely awarded damages for D's nuisance. Thirdly, D may have an entitlement to pollute protected by a property rule; that is, D may be held not liable for nuisance, so that P can only prevent the pollution by paying D to stop it. Finally D may have an entitlement to pollute protected by a liability rule; that is, D may be free to pollute unless P pays him a judicially determined price not to: this would most obviously be achieved by a 'compensated injunction', never yet used in England,[2] whereby P would be bound to pay D the costs of D's compliance with the injunction.

In deciding which of these four to choose, Calabresi and Melamed consider that economic efficiency dictates the following results. If transaction costs are low, so that it can be expected that parties will bargain round legal rights and remedies to correct any 'errors',[3] property rules should be chosen, thereby avoiding the costs of a judicial determination of values. Whether the first or third outcome is adopted, depends on whether it is thought D or P is the cheaper cost-avoider. But where transaction costs are high, as they are likely to be in the pollution field, property rules should only be chosen if it is certain which party is the cheaper cost-avoider. No guessing should be undertaken, since the parties will not negotiate round to correct any error. If, as is likely in most pollution

---

19 An entitlement can also be 'inalienable'.
20 (1972) 85 Harv LR 1089, 1092.
 1 Ibid.
 2 But see *Spur Industries Inc v Del E Webb Development Co* 494 P 2d 700 (Ariz, 1972).
 3 Coase (1960) 3 J Law & Econ 1, supra, pp 12–3.

cases, it is uncertain who is the cheaper cost-avoider, a liability rule should be adopted; that is, the second or fourth outcome should be chosen. To decide between these two, the court should make a cost-benefit analysis, mimicking the transaction the parties would themselves have made.

So in a standard land use conflict, where transaction costs are high, and it is difficult to be certain who is the cheaper cost-avoider, this approach indicates that the plaintiff should be awarded damages or a compensated injunction. Clearly this contrasts with the present English judicial preference for a prohibitory injunction.

(ii) Arguments against greater use of damages

(i)   From the plaintiff's point of view an injunction is a better remedy than damages. Damages may be very difficult to assess either because one cannot know the extent of the plaintiff's future loss, or because his loss is non-pecuniary comprising, for example, interference with the enjoyment of land. Moreover the defendant may be unable to pay.

(ii) To allow a defendant to continue with the wrong by paying damages sacrifices to some degree the plaintiff's individual rights. On one view such rights merit absolute specific protection and should not be downgraded in this way.

(iii) An injunction prevents a ruthless defendant simply including the damages in a calculated decision to ride roughshod over the plaintiff's rights. But this objection could be countered to some extent by awarding restitutionary, or even punitive damages, rather than merely compensation.

(iv) The injunction is the best remedy for protecting the environment.[4] Hence the upholding of individual rights and the public interest in environmental control coincide in favouring the injunction as against damages.

(v)   On one view it is not the function of the courts, nor are they properly equipped, to decide what the public interest demands.[5] Their role is and should be one of protecting individual rights which should not be sacrificed for social welfare goals. So, for example, the courts should never involve themselves in deciding whether it is in the public interest to keep open a nuclear power installation that is causing a nuisance by its occasional leaks of radiation.

---

4 McLaren (1972) 10 Osgoode Hall LJ 505, esp 547–61.
5 Dworkin *Taking Rights Seriously* (revised edn, 1978).

But examination of the common law shows that legal decision-making is best understood as a complex mix of principle and policy and that the courts do make decisions on where the public interest lies. So, for example, they judge the public interest in deciding whether to suspend an injunction, and sometimes even in deciding initially whether the defendant is liable. Moreover, this seems perfectly acceptable so long as the courts aim for consistency with the long-term policy goals enshrined in the common law.

(iii) Conclusion

Having weighed up the above arguments, it is submitted that there is a case for damages being awarded more readily than at present for torts involving land use conflicts.[6] However, the case for this should not be exaggerated and generally an injunction should be ordered. But where the defendant is pursuing what is in the long-term public interest, or where the plaintiff could easily take steps to remove the harm, equitable damages in lieu should be preferred to a prohibitory injunction. It is also true that the compensated injunction, whereby the plaintiff pays the defendant the costs of his compliance, would be a useful weapon for the English courts to add to their armoury. For while at first sight it is somewhat alarming to suggest that a plaintiff should pay the defendant for not infringing his rights, on closer inspection, it can be seen that this would add further remedial flexibility and would provide another sensible way of resolving the conflict between the public interest and private rights; and, after all, the plaintiff may well prefer a compensated injunction to no injunction at all.

(2) Breach of contract

(a) Prohibitory injunction as primary remedy

The prohibitory injunction is the appropriate remedy for restraining the breach[7] of a negative contractual promise—that is a promise not to do something: put another way, it enforces a negative contractual promise. It therefore belongs on the reverse side of the coin from specific performance, which enforces a positive contractual promise.

As in relation to torts, and in contrast to specific performance, the prohibitory injunction is the primary remedy as against damages for

---

6 As in the United States and Canada; see Tromans (1982) CLJ 87, 97–9.
7 Including an anticipatory breach.

breach of a negative promise; and here, in contrast to torts, it is generally ordinary common law damages that are in issue as the alternative to the prohibitory injunction—for unless the breach of contract is a continuing one it is not regarded as a prospective wrong and hence common law damages are as advantageous as damages under s 50 of the Supreme Court Act 1981.[8] Since common law damages must be shown to be inadequate before an injunction, being an equitable remedy, can be granted, the primacy afforded to the prohibitory injunction can be expressed by saying that, in this context, adequacy is given a very narrow meaning, so that damages are hardly ever considered adequate.

The classic 'authority' on the primacy of the prohibitory injunction is the dictum of Lord Cairns LC in *Doherty v Allman*.[9] He said:

... if there had been a negative covenant, I apprehend, according to well-settled practice, a Court of Equity would have no discretion to exercise. If parties, for valuable consideration, with their eyes open, contract that a particular thing shall not be done, all that a Court of Equity has to do is to say, by way of injunction that which the parties have already said by way of covenant, that the thing shall not be done; and in such case, the injunction does nothing more than give the sanction of the process of the Court to that which already is the contract between the parties. It is not then a question of the balance of convenience or inconvenience, or the amount of damage or of injury—it is the specific performance by the Court, of that negative bargain which the parties have made, with their eyes open, between themselves.

To similar effect is Sir Page Wood V-C's statement in *Tipping v Eckersley*[10] that, '. . . if the construction of the instrument be clear and the breach clear, then it is not a question of damage but the mere circumstance of the breach of covenant affords sufficient ground for the Court to interfere by injunction.' He went on to grant an injunction whereby the defendant was not to increase the temperature of the water flowing down to the plaintiff's steam engine, such action constituting a breach of the defendant's covenant to allow the plaintiff the free use and enjoyment of the stream.

Why is there this judicial readiness to order prohibitory injunctions

---

8 But equitable damages are the only alternative to a prohibitory injunction restraining breach by a third party of a restrictive covenant affecting land; see supra, p 244.

9 (1878) 3 App Cas 709 at 720. For recent examples of *Doherty* being applied see *Avon County Council v Millard* (1985) 274 Estates Gazette 1025; *A-G v Barker* [1990] 3 All ER 257, 261–2 (per Nourse LJ).

10 (1855) 2 K & J 264 at 270.

to restrain the breach of a negative promise, contrasting as it does with the approach to specific performance, and given that both remedies more closely protect the plaintiff's expectation interest than damages? Perhaps the principal reasons are that prohibitory injunctions do not as commonly contradict a plaintiff's duty to mitigate, and nor do they infringe individual liberty to the same extent as positive orders. Additionally, damages are often less easy to assess for breach of a negative than a positive obligation. Nor do prohibitory injunctions fall foul of the constant supervision objection that has traditionally barred specific performance. But having said all this, the present automatic grant of a prohibitory injunction for breach of contract under *Doherty v Allman* probably goes too far. The arguments examined above in relation to torts suggest that sometimes damages should be awarded in preference to a prohibitory injunction for breach of a negative promise.[11] This is particularly so where the plaintiff could take steps to mitigate his loss.

To say that the prohibitory injunction is the primary remedy does not of course mean that it will never be refused. Two main grounds for refusal[12] are that the plaintiff's conduct debars him,[13] or that the harm suffered by the plaintiff is trivial.[14] But indisputably the most discussed ground for refusal is that to grant the prohibitory injunction would amount to indirect specific performance of a contractual promise for which specific performance would not be ordered. This will now be examined.

(b) Indirect specific performance

Strictly speaking this is not a ground for refusing a prohibitory injunction, but rather an argument that what appears to be a prohibitory injunction enforcing a negative obligation is in reality specific performance of a positive obligation, and should be governed by specific performance principles.

It should be emphasised straightaway that some cases provide no difficulty for it is pellucidly clear that, despite the prohibitory form in which the order is sought, in substance it amounts to specific

---

11 A rare example of a case not following the traditional approach is *Baxter v Four Oaks Properties Ltd* [1965] Ch 816, where Cross J did not want to put the plaintiff into too strong a position in post-judgment bargaining.

12 Although rare, uncertainty may also be a bar: *Hampstead and Suburban Properties v Diomedous* [1969] 1 Ch 248; *Bower v Bantam Investments Ltd* [1972] 1 WLR 1120.

13 Infra, pp 446–51.

14 *Harrison v Good* (1871) LR 11 Eq 338 at 352.

performance. For example, an order to restrain the defendants breaking their positive contractual obligation is specific performance and not a prohibitory injunction. Again in *Sky Petroleum v VIP Petroleum Ltd*[15] and *Hill v Parsons*,[16] the injunctions respectively sought—to restrain the defendants withholding supplies of petrol to the plaintiff and to restrain the defendants implementing their notice of dismissal terminating the plaintiff's employment—were negative in form, but clearly positive in substance.

The interesting and controversial cases are those where, although in substance breach of a negative obligation is being restrained, it is arguable that compliance with the negative obligation will *in practice* force the defendant to comply with his positive obligations. The essential question is to what extent do the courts accede to this argument? Sir George Jessel MR in *Fothergill v Rowland*[17] thought that it was difficult to find any consistent judicial approach:

> I cannot find any distinct line laid down . . . dividing . . . the class of cases in which the Court, feeling that it has not the power to compel specific performance, grants an injunction to restrain the breach by the contracting party of one or more of the stipulations of the contract, and the class of cases in which it refuses to interfere.[18]

It is submitted, however, that a principle has generally been applied, namely that a prohibitory injunction will be regarded as indirect specific performance, and subject to specific performance principles, if compliance with the order will leave the defendant with the 'choice' of either performing his positive obligations to the plaintiff or not being able to work or carry on any business at all. The issue has arisen with regard to two main types of contract—contracts for personal service and contracts for the sale of goods.

(i) Contracts for personal service

Lumley v Wagner[19] is the classic case. Here Mlle Wagner undertook that for three months she would sing at Mr Lumley's theatre in Drury Lane on two nights a week and not use her talents at any other theatre without Mr Lumley's written consent. She then agreed to sing for Mr Gye at Covent Garden for more money. Lord St Leonards LC granted an injunction restraining her from

15 [1974] 1 WLR 576.
16 [1972] Ch 305. See also *Davis v Foreman* [1894] 3 Ch 654.
17 (1873) LR 17 Eq 132.
18 Ibid at 141.
19 (1852) 21 LJ Ch 898. Parks (1918) 66 U of Pa LR 251; Stevens (1921) 6 Cornell LQ 235; Tannenbaum (1954) 42 Cal LR 18.

singing except for Mr Lumley, and considered that this did not amount to indirect specific performance of her obligation to sing for Mr Lumley, which he recognised could not be granted. He said:

It was objected that the operation of the injunction in the present case was mischievous, excluding the defendant . . . from performing at any other theatre while this Court had no power to compel her to perform at Her Majesty's Theatre. It is true, that I have not the means of compelling her to sing, but she has no cause of complaint, if I compel her to abstain from the commission of an act which she has bound herself not to do . . . in continuing the injunction, I disclaim doing indirectly what I cannot do directly.[20]

This approach was followed and explained further in *Warner Bros Pictures Inc v Nelson*,[1] where the film actress Bette Davis had agreed that she would render her exclusive services as an actress to the plaintiffs for a certain period and would not during that time render any similar services to any other person. In breach of that contract she entered into an agreement to appear for another film company. The plaintiffs were granted an injunction restraining her for three years from appearing for any other film company. Branson J reasoned that this did not amount to indirectly ordering specific performance of her contract with the plaintiffs—for while the defendant was being ordered not to work as a film actress for anyone else, she was left free to work elsewhere in any other capacity. Branson J said:

It was also urged that the difference between what the defendant can earn as a film artiste and what she might expect to earn by any other form of activity is so great that she will in effect be driven to perform her contract . . . [but] no evidence was addressed to show that, if enjoined from doing the specified acts otherwise than for the plaintiffs, she will not be able to employ herself both usefully and remuneratively in other spheres of activity . . . She will not be driven, although she may be tempted, to perform the contract, and the fact that she may be so tempted is no objection to the grant of an injunction.[2]

In both these and other cases,[3] it was regarded as important that the negative promise in question was express. This is a red herring, and should not be allowed to cast confusion over the indirect

---

20 Ibid at 902.
1 [1937] 1 KB 209. See also *William Robinson & Co Ltd v Heuer* [1898] 2 Ch 451; *Marco Productions Ltd v Pagola* [1954] KB 111.
2 Ibid at 219–20.
3 Eg *Mutual Reserve Fund Life Assurance v New York Insurance Co* (1896) 75 LT 528; *Mortimer v Beckett* [1920] 1 Ch 571.

specific performance discussion. As other authorities recognise,[4] so long as a clear negative promise can be made out, it should not matter whether that promise is express or implied.

Consistent with the emphasis on the freedom to take up other employment, albeit falling on the reverse side of the line, are *Whitwood Chemical Co v Hardman*,[5] *Ehrman v Bartholemew*[6] and *Rely-a-Bell Burglar & Fire Alarm Co v Eisler*.[7] In each case the injunction sought was to restrain the breach of a promise not to accept any other employment at all. Therefore, if granted, the defendant would have had only the choice of working for the plaintiff or remaining idle. Since this was not a real choice, a prohibitory injunction would in practice amount to specific performance and, as specific performance would not be ordered of a contract for personal service, the injunction was refused.

However, there have been cases in which the courts have taken a different approach. In *Mortimer v Beckett*,[8] for example, the defendant agreed to employ the plaintiff as his boxing manager, to be solely in charge of arranging the defendant's boxing contracts. When the defendant agreed to box for someone else, the plaintiff sought an interlocutory injunction to restrain him; that is, to enforce his implied promise not to box for anyone else. But even though the promise only related to boxing, the injunction was refused, inter alia,[9] because it was thought that it would amount to specific performance of the defendant's personal obligations. Russell J said, 'The effect will be to force the defendant to employ a particular person as his agent, so far as his boxing engagements are concerned, and to accept the agent's services.'[10] Similarly in *Page One Records Ltd v Britton*[11] 'The Troggs' pop group employed the plaintiff as their sole agent and manager for five years, and agreed not to make records for anyone else during that time. In breach of that contract they then entered into an agreement to be managed by someone else. The plaintiff sought an interlocutory injunction to restrain this breach. Stamp J refused to grant it because he thought that it would amount to indirect specific performance of the defendants' personal obligations:

---

4 *Wolverhampton & Walsall Rly Co v London & North-Western Rly Co* (1873) LR 16 Eq 433; *Whitwood Chemicals Co v Hardman* [1891] 2 Ch 416 at 427.
5 [1891] 2 Ch 416.
6 [1898] 1 Ch 671.
7 [1926] Ch 609. See also *Kirchner & Co v Gruban* [1909] 1 Ch 413.
8 [1920] 1 Ch 571.
9 The other, and unsatisfactory, ground was the lack of an express negative covenant.
10 [1920] 1 Ch 571 at 581.
11 [1968] 1 WLR 157.

. . . it was said in this case, that if an injunction is granted, The Troggs could without employing any other manager or agent . . . seek other employment of a different nature . . . I think that I can and should take judicial notice of the fact that these groups, if they are to have any great success, must have managers. As a practical matter . . . I entertain no doubt that they would be compelled, if the injunction were granted, . . . to continue to employ the plaintiff as their manager and agent . . . I should if I granted the injunction, be enforcing a contract for personal services, in which personal services are to be performed by the plaintiff.[12]

Clearly these cases differ factually from *Lumley* and *Warner Bros* in that it was the employee (the manager and agent) rather than the employer who was seeking the injunction. But that cannot account for the difference in result. The better view is that these cases go beyond the general principle in considering it insufficient that the defendant is left free to take up other employment or business. Rather it is the likelihood of his doing so that is important. This is a preferable approach requiring, as it does, a closer examination of the practical realities of the injunction. Applying it to the facts of *Warner Bros v Nelson*, a different decision would be reached, for it was most unlikely that Bette Davis would take up another occupation and abandon making films for the three-year period. On the other hand, *Lumley v Wagner* might well be decided in the same way; for as Mlle Wagner was merely being restrained from singing elsewhere for three months, it was quite likely that she would choose to do something else, or nothing, for that short period, rather than singing for the plaintiff.

Authoritative support for that preferable approach has now been provided by the Court of Appeal in *Warren v Mendy*,[13] in which *Page One Records v Britton* was preferred to *Warner Bros v Nelson* on grounds of 'realism and practicality'.[14] The facts—which concerned a dispute over the management of the boxer, Nigel Benn—differed from the usual restrictive covenant case in that the injunction being sought by the plaintiff was not against Benn for breach of contract but against another manager in a tort action for inducing breach of Benn's contract with the plaintiff. But the Court of Appeal felt that, as the plaintiff would seek an injunction against anyone who arranged to manage Benn, the same principles should be applied as if the injunction had been sought against Benn for breach of contract. The injunction was refused on the ground that to grant it would constitute indirect specific performance of Benn's contract to

---

12 Ibid at 166–7.
13 [1989] 3 All ER 103.
14 Ibid at 112 (per Nourse LJ).

be exclusively managed by the plaintiff for the three-year contract period. While disapproving the approach in *Warner Bros v Nelson*, the Court of Appeal did not doubt the correctness of the decision in *Lumley v Wagner* given the short contract period there in issue. Nourse LJ said:

> Although it is impossible to state in general terms where the line between short and long term engagements ought to be drawn it is obvious that an injunction lasting for two years or more (the period applicable in the present case) may practically compel performance of the contract.[15]

Three final points should be made. First, there has traditionally been some doubt as to the application of the substantive restraint of trade doctrine to the sort of negative obligations in these cases, especially given that they apply during rather than after the employment. The above discussion has assumed the substantive validity of the negative obligation but clearly if it is invalid there is no question of any remedy for breach. Secondly, it has further been assumed above that the plaintiff wants the defendant to perform his positive contractual obligations. Where this is not so, for example where there is a restrictive covenant to take effect after termination of the defendant's employment,[16] or where the plaintiff undertakes to pay the defendant and to give him his other contractual benefits even though the defendant does no work for him,[17] there is no question of an injunction amounting to indirect specific performance. Finally, a prime approach adopted in the United States is to grant an injunction to prevent the defendant working for a competitor of the plaintiff's but not otherwise.[18] So, for example, on the facts of *Lumley v Wagner* an injunction would be granted to prevent the defendant working for Mr Gye, a close rival of the plaintiff's, but would not be granted in respect of a theatre in, for example, northern England; the justification being that the plaintiff had a separate legitimate interest in preventing his audience being diverted to Gye's theatre. This has not found favour in England[19] and, while it will often arrive at the same decision as the preferred approach examined above, it fails to address sufficiently closely the problem of indirect specific performance; for to prevent the defendant working for any of the plaintiff's competitors may in practice leave no real choice but to work for the plaintiff.

15 Ibid at 112.
16 As in, eg *General Billposting Co Ltd v Atkinson* [1909] AC 118.
17 *Evening Standard Co Ltd v Henderson* [1987] IRLR 64; *Provident Financial Group plc v Hayward* [1989] 3 All ER 298. The defendant under such an arrangement is described as being on 'garden leave'.
18 Second Restatement of Contracts, para 367, illustration 4.
19 See especially *Marco Productions v Pagola* [1945] KB 111.

(ii) Contracts for the sale of goods

The question of indirect specific performance has here arisen in relation to obligations not to buy one's requirements of particular goods other than from the plaintiff (requirements contracts), not to sell a particular output of goods other than to the plaintiff (output contracts) or not to distribute goods other than through the plaintiff (sole franchise/distributorship contracts).[20] Traditionally specific performance of the positive obligations in such contracts would not be ordered because of the supposed adequacy of damages. The personal service or constant supervision bars are also sometimes in play. But the courts have generally been willing to grant injunctions restraining breach of the above 'negative' obligations, on the ground that this does not amount to indirect specific performance. Analogously to contracts of employment the unarticulated principle appears to be that so long as the defendant is left with more of a choice than either buying from/selling to the plaintiff or not carrying on any business at all the injunction does not amount to indirect specific performance.

As regards requirements contracts, there are several cases granting a prohibitory injunction restraining defendants from buying petrol for their service station[1] or beer for their pub[2] other than from the plaintiffs. But the best-known authority is *Metropolitan Electric Supply Co Ltd v Ginder*.[3] An injunction was here granted restraining the defendant from breaking his promise not to take electricity from anyone but the plaintiff company. It was reasoned that this did not amount to forcing the defendant to take electricity from the plaintiffs, since the defendant could, if he liked, use no energy at all or burn gas.

Donnell v Bennett[4] shows the grant of an injunction in relation to what was in effect an output contract, being to sell to the plaintiff all the left-overs of fish not used by the defendant in his business. Fry J granted an injunction restraining the defendant from selling those left-overs to anyone else, albeit that he was clearly not totally convinced about the purported distinction between the injunction and specific performance.

---

20 Again it is assumed that the obligation is not invalid under the restraint of trade doctrine.
1 Eg *Texaco Ltd v Mulberry Filling Station Ltd* [1972] 1 WLR 814.
2 Eg *Clegg v Hands* (1890) 44 Ch D 503.
3 [1901] 2 Ch 799. This case also provides the classic example of terms being attached to an injunction to avoid any problems over want of mutuality, the condition attached being that the defendant could dissolve the injunction if the plaintiff failed to supply his requirements.
4 (1883) 22 Ch D 835.

Turning to sole distributorship/franchise contracts, in *Decro-Wall International SA v Practitioners in Marketing Ltd*[5] the plaintiffs had contracted not to sell their goods in the UK to anyone other than the defendants. The Court of Appeal held that the defendants were entitled to an injunction to restrain breach of this negative promise, albeit that Salmon LJ recognised that '. . . the plaintiffs cannot be compelled to continue to supply the defendants until the termination of the contract.'[6] Similarly in *Evans Marshall v Bertola SA*[7] the plaintiffs had been appointed sole agents for the sale of the defendants' sherry in England under a long-term contract. They were granted an interlocutory injunction restraining the defendants from breaking this contract by selling sherry other than through the plaintiffs' agency. Sachs LJ applied *Warner Bros v Nelson* and the *Decro-Wall* case, and said, '. . . the specific performance of such an agreement will not be ordered, but it is no less plain that the courts will grant negative injunctions to encourage a party in breach to keep to his contract.'[8]

However, not all cases have adhered to the thin theoretical distinction being drawn between prohibitory injunctions and specific performance. The classic example is *Fothergill v Rowland*,[9] where the defendants had contracted to sell all of a particular seam of coal to the plaintiffs. The plaintiffs sought an injunction to prevent the defendants selling elsewhere, but this was refused on the ground that it amounted to indirect specific performance of a contract to sell non-unique goods, for which damages were adequate. This case can be regarded as equivalent to *Page One Records* in the employment context, and as taking a more realistic view of the effect of the prohibitory injunction; for surely in almost all the above cases compliance with the prohibitory injunction would render it virtually certain that the defendant would perform his positive obligations to the plaintiff. In practical terms specific performance was being ordered.

But there is a final twist to the tale. It has been argued in chapter 8 that, whether because of commercial uniqueness or the difficulty of assessing damages, specific performance ought to be more readily granted than in the past in respect of long-term supply contracts such as these.[10] Therefore the actual decisions in these cases, now

5   [1971] 2 All ER 216.
6   Ibid at 225. Ultimately no injunction was necessary since the defendants gave an undertaking in the same terms.
7   [1973] 1 WLR 349. See also *Thomas Borthwick v South Otago Freezing Co Ltd* [1978] 1 NZLR 538.
8   Ibid at 382.
9   (1873) LR 17 Eq 132.
10 Supra, pp 340–5, 353.

with the exception of *Fothergill v Rowland*, are to be welcomed, but on the basis that specific performance was in effect being ordered and was justified. Some commentators[11] have indeed used these cases as authorities on specific performance but, with the exception of *Fothergill v Rowland*, this would seem misleading, given that the reasoning took the opposite view.

(c) Stipulated remedy[12]

What effect will be given to a contractual term that the plaintiff should be entitled to an injunction for breach of a negative covenant? One of the few English cases dealing with this was *Warner Bros Pictures Inc v Nelson*.[13] In Branson J's words:

> . . . parties cannot contract themselves out of the law; but it assists, in all events, on the question of evidence as to the applicability of an injunction in the present case, to find the parties formally recognising that in cases of this kind injunction is a more appropriate remedy than damages.[14]

However, it is hard to see the courts attaching any real relevance to such a clause.[15] As has been indicated, true negative obligations are enforceable by prohibitory injunction as of course and hence irrespective of the parties agreeing on that remedy; and where the prohibitory injunction would in effect amount to specific performance of a contract that would not be directly specifically enforced it is hard to believe that the courts would allow such a clause to oust their refusal of the remedy.

A related but converse question is whether the existence of a penalty or liquidated damages clause will oust a prohibitory injunction that would otherwise be granted. Several cases show that the answer to this is in the negative,[16] and that the clause will rather be construed as indicating the amount of damages the plaintiff will recover if he sues for damages rather than an injunction. But in *General Accident Assurance Corpn v Noel*,[17] while this was agreed, it was held that the injunction and liquidated damages were exclusive remedies. While this must be correct as regards future loss, there

---

11 Eg Treitel *Law of Contract* p 904.
12 See analogously supra, pp 381–2.
13 [1937] 1 KB 209. The best known case in the United States is *Stokes v Moore* 262 Ala 5977 (1955).
14 Ibid at 221.
15 But see the views of Sharpe *Injunctions and Specific Performance* (2nd edn) paras 7.710–7.810, and Kyer (1981) 39 U of Tor Fac LR 1.
16 Eg *Jones v Heavens* (1877) 4 Ch D 636; *National Provincial Bank of England v Marshall* (1888) 40 Ch D 112.
17 [1902] 1 KB 377.

seems no reason why liquidated damages for past loss and an injunction should not both be awarded, an approach adopted in the important Canadian case of *Elsley v JG Collins Insurance Agencies Ltd.*[18]

3. FINAL MANDATORY INJUNCTIONS[19]

(1) Torts

The mandatory injunction—ordering the defendant to do something—is the appropriate remedy to remove the effects of a tort committed by the defendant; that is, it compels the defendant to undo the wrong. This function is conveniently and commonly emphasised by referring to the injunction as a mandatory restorative injunction. To give a couple of examples straightaway, in *Kelsen v Imperial Tobacco Co*,[20] the defendants were ordered to remove the advertising sign they had erected which was trespassing into the airspace above the plaintiff's shop; and in *Lawrence v Horton*,[1] the defendant was ordered to pull down buildings he had erected which obstructed the plaintiff's ancient lights. Conceivably a mandatory enforcing injunction could be granted to enforce a positive tort obligation. But given the rarity of such tort obligations, this injunction will be rare indeed, and there is no obvious example of its having been granted.

The classic discussion of the general principles governing mandatory injunctions is Lord Upjohn's judgment in *Redland Bricks v Morris*[2] though his eccentric view that the injunction in issue was *quia timet*[3] means that he includes some principles that are plainly relevant only to *quia timet* mandatory injunctions. The injunction being sought was for steps to be taken by the defendants to restore support to the plaintiff's land. The House of Lords discharged the mandatory injunction that had been granted—that the defendants '. . . do take all necessary steps to restore the support to the plaintiff's land within a period of six months'—because it left as too uncertain what the defendants were required to do. Lord Upjohn said, 'If . . . it is a proper case to grant a mandatory injunction, then

18 (1978) 83 DLR (3d) 1.
19 *Quia timet* mandatory injunctions are discussed infra, pp 420–3.
20 [1957] 2 QB 334.
 1 (1890) 59 LJ Ch 440. See similarly *Allen v Greenwood* [1980] Ch 119.
 2 [1970] AC 652.
 3 Supra, p 390.

the court must be careful to see that the defendant knows exactly in fact what he has to do . . .'[4] So uncertainty is a bar to mandatory injunctions as it is to specific performance and prohibitory injunctions. But in his espousal of the general principles, what is particularly important is that Lord Upjohn clearly accepted that a mandatory injunction is not granted as readily as a prohibitory injunction. He said, 'The grant of a mandatory injunction is, of course, entirely discretionary, and unlike a negative injunction can never be "as of course".'[5] The antipathy of the courts to positive orders is therefore shown in this area, as in relation to specific performance for breach of contract. Again, the desire not to undermine the plaintiff's duty to mitigate, and not to restrict unduly the defendant's freedom of action may be suggested as the root objections. There are also express indications in some cases that the argument that non-monetary remedies give the plaintiff too much of an advantage in pre- and post-judgment bargaining does here weigh with the courts. For example, in *Isenberg v East India House Estate Co Ltd*[6] Lord Westbury, in refusing an injunction to compel the defendant to pull down a building which interfered only slightly with the plaintiff's ancient lights, said that the court would not grant a mandatory injunction which would deliver 'the Defendants to the Plaintiff bound hand and foot, in order to be made subject to any extortionate demand that he may by possibility make.'[7]

So it is the case that, while the injunction may be the better remedy for the plaintiff, damages (in lieu) are generally regarded as sufficient and are the primary remedy. A fortiori, no mandatory injunction will generally be granted where the tortious interference is merely trivial.[8]

Furthermore in contrast to a prohibitory injunction, the hardship to the defendant is here a bar. So, in dicta in *Pride of Derby v British Celanese*,[9] Lord Evershed commented '. . . the court will not impose . . . an obligation to do something which is impossible, or which

---

4 [1970] AC 652 at 666. See also *Kennard v Cory Bros Co Ltd* [1922] 1 Ch 265 at 274 (per Sargant J), [1922] 2 Ch 1 at 13 (per Warrington LJ).

5 Ibid at 665. See also *Durrell v Pritchard* (1875) 1 Ch App 244 at 250, and cases on breach of contract, infra, pp 418–20. It is therefore misleading to say as some judges have—eg in *Smith v Smith* (1875) LR 20 Eq 500, and *Davies v Gas Light and Coke Co* [1909] 1 Ch 708—that the same principles govern mandatory as prohibitory injunctions.

6 (1863) 3 De GJ & Sm 263. See also *Senior v Pawson* (1866) LR 3 Eq 330.

7 Ibid at 273.

8 *Isenberg v East India House Estate Co Ltd*, ibid; *Colls v Home & Colonial Stores Ltd* [1904] AC 179; *Tollemache and Cobbold Breweries Ltd v Reynolds* (1983) 268 Estates Gazette 52. Cf *Kelsen v Imperial Tobacco Co* [1957] 2 QB 334.

9 [1953] Ch 149 at 181.

cannot be enforced, or which is unlawful.' The leading authority is again *Redland Bricks v Morris*, where Lord Upjohn indicated that hardship can here be a very wide restriction since, even in contrast to specific performance, the test can be a relative one; that is, so long as the defendant has acted reasonably, albeit wrongly, the courts can weigh the burden to him against the benefit to the plaintiff. In Lord Upjohn's words:

> ... the amount to be expended under a mandatory order by the defendant must be balanced ... against the anticipated possible damage to the plaintiff and if, on such balance, it seems unreasonable to inflict such expenditure ... then the court must exercise its jurisdiction accordingly.[10]

Applying this to the facts, it was held that a mandatory injunction ordering the defendants to carry out the restoration work as described by the plaintiff's expert, while probably overcoming the uncertainty objection so long as set out in detail, would impose an excessive burden on the defendant who had acted reasonably and should not be granted; such work might cost £35,000, while the value of the plaintiff's land affected by the slip was only about £1,500.

On the other hand, Lord Upjohn made plain that no sympathy will be shown for a defendant who has tried 'to steal a march' on the plaintiff, or who has otherwise acted 'wantonly and quite unreasonably'.[11] Indeed in this situation, the courts appear to go to the opposite extreme, and to be only too willing to grant even an interlocutory mandatory injunction against the defendant, revealing, seemingly, a punitive approach that is hard to justify in a civil law action. For example, in *Daniel v Ferguson*,[12] on receiving notice of the plaintiff's complaint that the building being constructed would interfere with his ancient lights, the defendant doubled his efforts to have the building completed before any court order could be made. In view of this attempt 'to steal a march', the court granted an interlocutory mandatory injunction ordering that that part of the building, which allegedly interfered with the plaintiff's rights, should be pulled down.

10 [1970] AC 652 at 666. See also *Kelk v Pearson* (1871) 6 Ch App 809 at 812; *National Provincial Plate Glass Insurance Co v Prudential Assurance Co* (1877) 6 Ch D 757 at 761; *Rileys v Halifax Corpn* (1907) 97 LT 278; *Sharp v Harrison* [1922] 1 Ch 502 (breach of contract). In dicta in *Gravesham Borough Council v British Railways Board* [1978] Ch 379 at 405, the benefit to *the public* of the injunction was balanced against its hardship to the defendants.
11 Ibid. See also *Colls v Home and Colonial Stores Ltd* [1904] AC 179; *Pugh v Howells* (1984) 48 P & CR 298.
12 [1891] 2 Ch 27. See also *Von Joel v Hornsey* [1895] 2 Ch 774; *Esso Petroleum Co Ltd v Kingswood Motors Ltd* [1974] QB 142.

Consideration must finally be given to the constant supervision objection, which has traditionally been regarded as a bar to mandatory injunctions.[13] As with specific performance, however, the restriction has not always found favour. In this regard *Kennard v Cory Bros & Co Ltd*,[14] the 'moving mountain' case, is instructive, for while the Court of Appeal purported to accept the constant supervision objection, it indicated a lack of genuine support for it. The defendants argued that to order them to unblock a particular drain in the remedial works built to help prevent further landslides would in effect mean that they would be recognised as having a continuing obligation to repair and maintain those remedial works. As such the constant supervision objection would be infringed. While much of the judicial discussion focused on uncertainty, rather than constant supervision itself, the court rejected the above argument and stressed that the limited nature of the order being made meant that the constant supervision objection was inapplicable. But the judges were seemingly not enamoured of that objection. Lord Sterndale MR, after citing *Ryan v Mutual Tontine Westminster Chambers Association*,[15] the classic specific performance authority on constant supervision, could not find '. . . any objection in principle to the imposition of such [a continuous] obligation upon a wrongdoer';[16] and in Scrutton LJ's words, '. . . the Court will in some cases make an order which involves future maintenance . . . when and though that involves that applications from time to time may have to be made to the Court to supervise the carrying out of the order.'[17]

Moreover, even though constant supervision has traditionally been a bar to mandatory injunctions, the recent developments in specific performance suggest, by analogy, that it should no longer be so regarded. This indeed, was part of an argument considered in *Gravesham Borough Council v British Railways Board*,[18] where the cause of action was probably best viewed as tortious. One question was whether a mandatory enforcing injunction should be granted, assuming breach of a common law duty to maintain ferry crossings at reasonable times over the Thames. The objection put by the defendants was that this would necessitate a series of acts requiring the continuous employment of people over a number of years. Although this is not quite the same as just the constant supervision

---

13 *Powell Duffryn Steam Coal Co v Taff Vale Rly Co* (1874) 9 Ch App 331; *A-G v Staffordshire County Council* [1905] 1 Ch 336.
14 [1922] 2 Ch 1.
15 [1893] 1 Ch 116.
16 [1922] 2 Ch 1 at 13.
17 Ibid at 21.
18 [1978] Ch 379.

418   *Injunctions*

objection, counsel for the plaintiffs argued that as recent cases, such as *Tito v Waddell (No 2)*,[19] had shown that there was no longer a constant supervision objection to specific performance so, analogously, the court should be willing to grant a mandatory injunction even though this would require continuously employing people. Slade J's reaction to that argument was not entirely clear. On the one hand, in the light of the authorities, he accepted that '. . . it cannot be regarded, as an absolute and inflexible rule that the court will never grant an injunction requiring a person to do a series of acts requiring the continuous employment of people over a number of years.'[20] But he went on to say that he would still have refused the injunction if there had been a breach of duty inter alia because of the '. . . risk of potential practical difficulties in regard to enforcement arising from the grant of an injunction compelling British Rail to operate its ferry service to a particular timetable.'[1] This ultimately seems to represent an acceptance of the constant supervision objection. If so this is unfortunate, for as discussed in relation to specific performance[2] the policy reasons for this objection are weak and calls for its removal should be supported.

(2) Breach of contract

At first sight, one might expect that the mandatory injunction would be the appropriate remedy to enforce a positive contractual promise—that is, a promise to do something. But other than at the interlocutory stage,[3] this role is entirely taken over by the remedy of specific performance.[4] This leaves the mandatory restorative injunction as the appropriate remedy for removing the effects of, that is for undoing, what the defendant has done in breach of a negative contractual promise, just as it is for undoing a tort.

The leading case in the contractual sphere is *Shepherd Homes Ltd v Sandham*,[5] even though what was there being sought was an *interlocutory* mandatory injunction to remove a fence that the plaintiff alleged had been erected in breach of a restrictive covenant.

19 [1977] Ch 106.
20 [1978] Ch 379 at 405.
 1 Ibid.
 2 Supra, pp 357–8.
 3 Infra, pp 423, 441–2. Specific performance is a final remedy only.
 4 Viewed from this angle, it is perhaps surprising that specific performance developed as a separate remedy, since the mandatory injunction could have fulfilled its entire role.
 5 [1971] Ch 340.

Ultimately the injunction was refused, Megarry J stressing that the courts are particularly reluctant to grant interlocutory mandatory injunctions and would not do so here, where it was unclear whether a mandatory injunction would be granted at trial, and where the plaintiff had delayed in bringing his application.

In discussing the relevant principles—which should be the same as those for torts (set out in the previous subsection)—Megarry J contrasted *Doherty v Allman*[6] and said that a mandatory injunction was not as easy to obtain as a prohibitory injunction.[7] Put another way, damages (in lieu) are generally regarded as sufficient and are the primary remedy. As regards specific bars Megarry J preferred not to try to particularise all the grounds upon which a mandatory injunction might be refused but he said that they at least included '. . . the triviality of the damage to the plaintiff and the existence of a disproportion between the detriment that the injunction would inflict on the defendant, and the benefit that it would confer on the plaintiff'.[8] The former is illustrated by *Sharp v Harrison*[9] where a mandatory injunction to remove a window overlooking the plaintiff's property and built in breach of a restrictive covenant was refused, since little or no interference was being caused. The latter is the important 'hardship' bar, which was also clearly recognised in *Sharp v Harrison* in a passage cited with approval by Megarry J. An example of its application, coupled with a desire to uphold the public interest, is *Wrotham Park Estate Co Ltd v Parkside Homes Ltd*.[10] There a mandatory injunction ordering the defendants to knock down a housing estate built in breach of a restrictive covenant (enforceable by the plaintiff in equity) was refused and damages awarded, because the court wished to avoid 'an unpardonable waste of much needed houses.'[11] By analogy to mandatory injunctions for torts and specific performance one would expect that of the bars not mentioned by Megarry J uncertainty would be the most important; it must be possible for a clear order to be made.

Of course all this does not mean that a mandatory injunction will never be granted to remove the effects of the breach of a negative promise. In *Charrington v Simons & Co Ltd*,[12] for example, the Court of Appeal granted a mandatory injunction ordering the defendant to remove a tarmac farm road the height of which

---

6 (1878) 3 App Cas 709.
7 See also *Sharp v Harrison* [1922] 1 Ch 502.
8 [1971] Ch 340.
9 [1922] 1 Ch 502.
10 [1974] 1 WLR 798.
11 Ibid at 811.
12 [1971] 1 WLR 598.

contravened a restrictive covenant with the plaintiff; and in *Wakeham v Wood*[13] where, in flagrant disregard of a restrictive covenant (enforceable by the plaintiff in equity) and of the plaintiff's complaints, the defendant had erected a building that obscured the plaintiff's sea-view, the Court of Appeal distinguished *Wrotham Park*, albeit not very convincingly, and ordered the defendant to remove so much of the building as obscured the view.

4. FINAL *QUIA TIMET* INJUNCTIONS

(1) Torts

A *quia timet* injunction is granted where no wrong has yet been committed. The commonest type is a prohibitory injunction to restrain wrongful acts which the defendant has not before committed. Although there is no reason why such an injunction should not be ordered to restrain the commission of any tort, most cases concern nuisance. To give a couple of examples of such an injunction being ordered, in *Dicker v Popham Radford & Co*[14] a *quia timet* injunction was granted to restrain the defendant from continuing a building which when completed would infringe the plaintiff's right to light; and in *Goodhart v Hyatt*,[15] where the plaintiff had the right to have water pipes running through the defendant's land, a *quia timet* injunction was granted preventing the defendant from continuing with building work which would interfere with the plaintiff's access to the pipes.[16]

Far less common is a mandatory *quia timet* injunction, ordering positive steps to be taken to prevent earlier actions causing a wrong. The example that most obviously comes to mind is the removal of support from a neighbour's land where no subsidence of that land, and hence no tort of nuisance, has yet taken place.[17] So in *Hooper v Rogers*,[18] where the defendant's work in deepening a farm-track cut out of a slope threatened the foundations of the plaintiff's house

---

13 (1982) 43 P & CR 40.
14 (1890) 63 LT 379.
15 (1883) 25 Ch D 182.
16 More recent examples are *Torquay Hotel & Co Ltd v Cousins* [1969] 2 Ch 106 (inducing breach of contract); *Francombe v Mirror Group Newspapers Ltd* [1984] 1 WLR 892 (breach of confidence). In both, the *quia timet* injunction was interlocutory.
17 See also *Express Newspapers plc v Mitchell* [1982] IRLR 465 (interlocutory injunction ordering a trade union official to withdraw a strike notice that if acted on would constitute the tort of inducing breach of contract).
18 [1975] Ch 43.

standing at the top of the slope, the Court of Appeal held that a mandatory *quia timet* injunction to reinstate the natural angle of the slope could have been ordered and that the trial judge had therefore had jurisdiction to award damages in lieu.

The principles examined earlier dictating whether an ordinary injunction will be granted for tort apply in just the same way where the injunction is *quia timet*. This means, most importantly, that it will be easier to obtain a prohibitory than a mandatory *quia timet* injunction.

But the crucial importance of an injunction being classified as *quia timet* is that, as against ordinary injunctions where these requirements are presumed,[19] the plaintiff must show that the tort is highly probable to occur and to occur imminently. As Lord Dunedin said in *A-G for Canada v Ritchie Contracting and Supply Co Ltd*[20] 'it is not sufficient to say "timeo".'

As regards the first requirement Chitty J in *A-G v Manchester Corpn*[1] said, 'The principle which I think may be properly and safely extracted from the *quia timet* authorities is that the plaintiff must show a strong case of probability that the apprehended mischief will, in fact, arise';[2] and as the plaintiff could not so establish that a smallpox hospital when built would contravene statutory regulations, no *quia timet* injunction was granted. Again in *Pattisson v Gilford*[3] a *quia timet* injunction restraining the defendant from selling, for building, land over which the plaintiff had shooting rights was refused because it had not been shown that building on the land would 'necessarily and inevitably'[4] interfere with those shooting rights; and in *Redland Bricks v Morris*[5] Lord Upjohn said that a mandatory *quia timet* injunction '. . . can only be granted where the plaintiff shows a very strong probability upon the facts that grave damage will accrue to him in the future'.[6] In *Hooper v Rogers*,[7] although it was found on the facts that future damage was a proven probability, Russell LJ criticised the need to show always that the tort is highly probable to occur when he said, 'In truth, it seems to

---

19 The presumption can be rebutted: eg *Proctor v Bayley* (1889) 42 Ch D 390; *Race Relations Board v Applin* [1973] QB 815.
20 [1919] AC 999 at 1005.
 1 [1893] 2 Ch 87. See also *A-G v Kingston-on Thames Corpn* (1865) 34 LJ Ch 481; *A-G v Nottingham Corpn* [1904] 1 Ch 673.
 2 Ibid at 92.
 3 (1874) LR 18 Eq 259.
 4 Ibid at 264.
 5 [1970] AC 652.
 6 Ibid at 665. Presumably 'grave' damage is stressed because a mandatory injunction was in issue.
 7 [1975] Ch 43.

me that the degree of probability of future injury is not an absolute standard: what is to be aimed at is justice between the parties, having regard to all the relevant circumstances.'[8] It can also be argued that a *quia timet* injunction does no harm to a law-abiding defendant. But granting such injunctions too readily may unduly hamper a defendant's freedom of action and may encourage excessive litigation and it is submitted that for such reasons the present high degree of probability should be retained as a requirement.

In other cases the stress has been on the tort being very likely to occur *imminently*. In *Fletcher v Bealey*,[9] for example, the plaintiff sought an injunction to prevent the dumping of 'vat-waste', his fear being that noxious liquid would flow from the waste into a river thereby causing him a nuisance. Pearson J refused the injunction and said that 'imminent danger'[10] must be proved. But his decision could equally be said to rest on the fact that the tort was not sufficiently likely to occur, for he stressed that it was quite possible for the defendants to prevent liquid flowing into the river, and in any case, they might find a means of rendering that liquid innocuous. Again in *Lemos v Kennedy Leigh Development Co Ltd*,[11] the plaintiff's application for a *quia timet* mandatory injunction ordering the removal of his neighbour's tree roots, which he alleged would cause damage to his land, was dismissed because the apprehended danger was not imminent. Finally, in the most recent and, it is submitted, sensible discussion of this requirement in *Hooper v Rogers*,[12] Russell LJ said that it meant that the action should not be premature, and that it would not be where, as in that case (and in contrast to *Fletcher v Bealey*) no other step could be taken to avoid the damage. So although subsidence of the plaintiff's house, following the defendant's removal of support, might not occur for many years, it was held that a mandatory *quia timet* injunction could have been granted and hence damages in lieu were justified.

(2) Breach of contract

There is little if any role for *quia timet* injunctions for breach of contract. This is because a defendant's serious threat to break a contract other than where the breach threatened is a minor one is

8 Ibid at 50.
9 (1885) 28 Ch D 688.
10 Ibid at 698.
11 (1961) 105 Sol Jo 178. See also *Lord Cowley v Byas* (1877) 5 Ch D 944; *Draper v British Optical Association* [1938] 1 All ER 115.
12 [1975] Ch 43.

regarded as an existing wrong, that is, it constitutes an anticipatory breach. As such it would seem that a *quia timet* injunction would only be appropriate where a future breach of contract was sufficiently likely, despite no anticipatory breach. Not surprisingly, no example of this has been found in the cases.

5. INTERLOCUTORY INJUNCTIONS

Interlocutory injunctions, which may be prohibitory or mandatory, *quia timet* or not *quia timet*, are injunctions given prior to trial or other hearing in which final judgment is given, and are intended to last until the trial at the latest. Although temporary in this sense their advantage, as against final injunctions, is that they can be obtained quickly: indeed in some situations, such as where the plaintiff seeks to prevent a particular threatened act, it would be too late for the plaintiff to wait until trial.

In contrast to Mareva injunctions and Anton Piller orders,[13] an ordinary interlocutory injunction is within the scope of this book, since it is not best viewed as being concerned to aid the enforcement of other remedies, that is, as being concerned to enable a final injunction to be effective. Rather it is designed to protect, where justified, the plaintiff's alleged rights during the inevitable delay before trial, and this is so even where an injunction at trial can effectively protect those rights from then on without an interlocutory injunction having been granted.

So as a remedy for torts and breach of contract an interlocutory injunction fulfils analogous functions to a final injunction, but does so more quickly. For example, an interlocutory prohibitory injunction is the appropriate remedy at interlocutory proceedings to prevent an alleged continuing or recurring tort. In one respect, however, an interlocutory injunction plays a wider role than a final injunction; for prior to trial, an interlocutory mandatory injunction is the appropriate remedy to enforce a positive contractual obligation, whereas specific performance rather than a mandatory injunction would be granted at trial.

The fact that an interlocutory injunction is granted at an interlocutory stage of proceedings means that different principles must be applied in deciding whether to grant this sort of injunction than a final injunction. In *American Cyanamid Co v Ethicon Ltd*[14] the House of Lords controversially reformulated the principles

13 Infra, pp 444–6.
14 [1975] AC 396.

governing interlocutory injunctions. However, in order to understand *American Cyanamid*, it is first necessary to consider briefly the law prior to it.

(1) The law prior to *American Cyanamid*

What should be stressed straightaway is that not all cases adopted the same approach to interlocutory injunctions.[15] Nevertheless, as shown for example by the House of Lords in *Stratford & Son Ltd v Lindley*,[16] and at first instance and by the Court of Appeal in *American Cyanamid*[17] itself, a plaintiff generally needed to show: first, a prima facie case[18] both that the defendant was committing or was intending to commit a wrong against the plaintiff and (apparently) that the plaintiff would be entitled to a final injunction at trial for that wrong: and, secondly, that the balance of convenience favoured an interlocutory injunction. Furthermore, given the uncertainty as to whether the granting of an injunction would turn out to have been unjustified, the court almost invariably insisted, as a condition of granting an interlocutory injunction, that the plaintiff should give an undertaking to pay damages for any unjustifiable loss caused to the defendant in complying with the injunction.[19]

While the courts often talked of a prima facie case solely in relation to the defendant committing or intending to commit a wrong, it does appear to have been impliedly accepted that there must also be a prima facie case for a final injunction at trial. Certainly this is how Lord Diplock interpreted the approach of Graham J and of the Court of Appeal in *American Cyanamid*. He said that they had thought there was a rule:

. . . that the court is not entitled to take any account of the balance of convenience unless it has first been satisfied that if the case went to trial upon

---

15 See, eg *Hubbard v Vosper* [1972] 2 QB 84. Interlocutory injunctions pending appeals were also treated differently, as they still are: *Polini v Gray* (1879) 11 Ch D 741; *Orion Property Trust Ltd v Du Cane Court Ltd* [1962] 1 WLR 1085; *Erinford Properties Ltd v Cheshire County Council* [1974] Ch 261.

16 [1965] AC 269.

17 [1974] FSR 312.

18 Often a strong *prima facie* case was required: *Challender v Royal* (1887) 36 Ch D 425; *Smith v Grigg Ltd* [1924] 1 KB 655 at 659.

19 The principles governing such damages are discussed in *Hoffman-La Roche & Co AG v Secretary of State for Trade and Industry* [1975] AC 295 at 361. That case principally lays down that, where seeking to enforce the law, the Crown cannot be required to give such an undertaking. The same applies to other public authorities seeking interlocutory injunctions to enforce the law: *Kirklees Metropolitan BC v Wickes Building Supplies Ltd* [1992] 3 All ER 717.

no other evidence than is before the court at the hearing of the application the plaintiff would be entitled to *judgment for a permanent injunction* in the same terms as the interlocutory injunction sought.[20]

In essence then, the first requirement was that the courts undertook a 'mini-trial' of the dispute, according to the evidence and arguments then available to it.

Assessing the balance of convenience, on the other hand, required the court to do what was most just, on the assumption that it could not at the interlocutory stage decide on the merits whether an injunction was justified or not. The main factors taken into account in deciding this were whether damages would adequately compensate either party for any interim unjustifiable loss, and whether in general terms it would cause greater hardship to grant or refuse the injunction. It was also sometimes said that the courts would prefer to maintain the *status quo*: but this was ambiguous, since any one of several different positions could be regarded as the *status quo*, for example, the position at trial or the position prior to the issue of the writ or the position prior to the alleged wrong. Moreover, there was no obvious justification for such a preference.[1]

What is perhaps particularly significant about the old law is that, at least in more recent times, it was the first mini-trial hurdle that parties regarded as the most important aspect of the interlocutory application. As Hammond writes, 'Counsel began to use the interlocutory injunction as a means of providing a rapid and relatively cheap method of arbitration of disputes.'[2] So even where it would not be too late to challenge the interlocutory decision at trial, cases very rarely proceeded to trial (even as regards a claim for damages) because the parties accepted what was decided regarding the prima facie case as indicative of the trial outcome and settled accordingly. Indeed it has been said that 99% of cases in which the interlocutory injunction was sought did not proceed to trial.[3] The parties' attitude was also reflected or, more arguably, inspired by the courts' refusal to treat the two requirements as rigidly sequential steps, and their consequent tendency to treat the balance of convenience as subsidiary to the strength of the plaintiff's case. So, for example, if the plaintiff had established a very strong prima facie case, the judges seemed happy to ignore the balance of convenience altogether. As Prescott wrote in 1975, '. . . in recent times the tendency has been

---

20 [1975] AC 396 at 407 (author's italics).
1 This remains a problem post-*Cyanamid*; infra, pp 429–30. See Sharpe *Injunctions and Specific Performance* (2nd edn) para 2.550.
2 (1980) 30 UTLJ 240, 251.
3 *Fellows v Fisher* [1976] QB 122 at 133 (per Lord Denning).

to adopt a more robust attitude, and to be guided more and more by the apparent strength or otherwise of the plaintiff's case as revealed by the affidavits.'[4] Moreover, it may well be, as Hammond argues, that all this can be sensibly viewed as a reaction to the specific problem of an overloaded civil litigation system.

(2) *American Cyanamid v Ethicon*[5]

Lord Diplock, in a speech agreed with by the other Lords, here sought to put a stop to the approach of regarding the interlocutory application as a mini-trial. The plaintiffs were seeking an interlocutory *quia timet* injunction to prevent the defendants marketing in Great Britain sterile sutures which they alleged infringed their patent. At first instance Graham J granted the injunction on the basis that the plaintiffs had made out a prima facie case, and that the balance of convenience favoured them. But on appeal this was overturned, the Court of Appeal holding that the plaintiffs had failed to make out a prima facie case. The House of Lords restored the first instance decision but on different reasoning, which was as follows.

First, the plaintiff must establish that there is a serious question to be tried; in other words, that his claim is not frivolous or vexatious. But he should *not* be required to establish a prima facie case.

Secondly, assuming that he establishes that there is a serious question, the plaintiff must go on to show that the balance of convenience favours granting the interlocutory injunction. In assessing this, the following sequential approach should be adopted.

(i)   The court should ask whether damages would adequately compensate the plaintiff for his interim loss and whether the defendant could pay them. If the answer is yes, the interlocutory injunction should not be granted.

(ii) However if the answer is no, the court should ask whether damages payable under the plaintiff's undertaking would adequately compensate the defendant for his interim loss and whether the plaintiff could pay them. If yes, there is a strong case for the interlocutory injunction.

(iii) If however there is doubt as to the adequacy of the respective damages, the case turns on the balance of convenience generally. The main factor is whether it would cause greater hardship to grant or refuse the injunction—or as Lord Diplock

4 (1975) 91 LQR 168, 169.
5 [1975] AC 396. Baker (1977) 42 Sask LR 53.

phrased it, 'the extent of the uncompensatable disadvantage to each party.'[6] Where this and other considerations are evenly balanced, two factors that can be taken into account as a last resort are first, the desirability of maintaining the *status quo* and, secondly, the strength of one party's case being disproportionate to that of the other.

Applying this approach to the facts, an interlocutory injunction was granted because first, it was a serious question whether the defendants were infringing a patent of the plaintiffs so as to entitle the plaintiffs to a final injunction at trial; and secondly, the balance of convenience favoured the grant of the interlocutory injunction, particularly since the plaintiffs' monopoly of the market would effectively be destroyed for ever if the interlocutory injunction were refused.

Consideration of the parties' ability to pay damages, and the sequential structuring of the approach to the balance of convenience, with the adequacy of damages first having to be looked at and in itself possibly resolving which way the balance lies, are two changes *American Cyanamid* has made from the previous law. But the crucial change is that the plaintiff does not first have to establish a prima facie case. The much lower threshold of a serious question to be tried is all that needs to be satisfied, and the strength of the plaintiff's case is relevant only as a last resort within the balance of convenience. In Sharpe's words, '. . . the strength of case consideration of the traditional approach is stood on its head.'[7] The policy behind this is that the interlocutory application should *not* serve as a mini-trial, in which the merits of the dispute are judged, since evidence is merely on affidavit, rather than being oral and subject to cross-examination. Nor are the legal arguments fully presented. The aim is to restore the interlocutory injunction to its supposedly true function of protecting the plaintiff during the period of uncertainty before trial, where this is justified on the balance of convenience. In Lord Diplock's words:

> It is no part of the court's function at this stage of the litigation to try to resolve conflicts of evidence on affidavits as to facts on which the claim of either party may ultimately depend nor to decide difficult questions of law which call for detailed argument and mature consideration. These are matters to be dealt with at the trial.[8]

Subsequent case law has further clarified the *American Cyanamid* principles.

6 [1975] AC 396 at 409.
7 *Injunctions and Specific Performance* (2nd edn) para 2.200.
8 [1975] AC 396 at 407.

So it has been emphasised by Browne LJ in *Smith v Inner London Education Authority*[9] that the three phrases Lord Diplock used to describe the initial hurdle—'a serious question to be tried', 'not frivolous or vexatious', 'a real prospect of succeeding at the trial'[10]—are all ways of phrasing the same test; and although a relatively easy threshold to cross, there have been cases, *Smith* being one,[11] where a plaintiff has been denied an interlocutory injunction for failure to overcome it.

In very few cases has the grant or refusal of the interlocutory injunction been decided by the adequacy of damages for either the plaintiff or the defendant. Even where the courts have been willing to rest their decisions on this—as in *Fosesco International v Fordath*,[12] where it was held that damages would adequately compensate the defendants and could be paid by the plaintiffs, and *Roussel-Uclaf v GD Searle & Co*,[13] where damages were thought adequate for the plaintiff—they have gone on to justify their decision according to the general balance of convenience. This feature is hardly surprising. Adequacy is such an elusive concept that permissible reliance on other factors is almost always to be preferred.

Only factors concerning the parties were traditionally thought to be relevant within the balance of convenience, an approach which was consistent with that for final prohibitory injunctions, where the public interest has not been allowed to override private rights. But in *Smith v ILEA* Browne LJ, in dicta, said that where the defendant was a local authority the court should take into account the interests of the public within the balance of convenience. This has since been applied even where the defendant was not a public authority. In *Roussel-Uclaf v GD Searle & Co* the detriment to the public of being deprived of a life-saving drug was considered the major factor in deciding that the balance of convenience lay against the injunction; and in several industrial dispute cases,[14] the courts have regarded the detrimental impact of strike action on the public as a factor weighting the balance of convenience in favour of granting an

---

9 [1978] 1 All ER 411.
10 [1975] AC 396 at 407–8.
11 Also, *Re Lord Cable* [1977] 1 WLR 7; *Morning Star Co-operative Society Ltd v Express Newspapers Ltd* [1979] FSR 113; *Associated British Ports v TGWU* [1989] 3 All ER 822.
12 [1975] FSR 507. *Laws v Florinplace Ltd* [1981] 1 All ER 659.
13 [1977] FSR 125.
14 *Star Sea Transport Corpn of Monrovia v Slater* [1978] IRLR 507; *Beaverbrook Newspapers Ltd v Keys* [1978] ICR 582; *NWL Ltd v Woods* [1979] 1 WLR 1294; *Duport Steel Ltd v Sirs* [1980] ICR 161.

interlocutory injunction, thereby further curtailing the right to strike. It is also relevant here to mention *R v Secretary of State for Transport, ex p Factortame (No 2)*[15] in which it was held by the House of Lords that, where an interlocutory injunction is sought to restrain the enforcement by the Secretary of State of an English statute on the grounds that it is invalid under European Community law, the public interest in the enforcement of what, on the face of it, is the law of the land requires that no injunction should normally be granted unless the plaintiff establishes a strong prima facie case of invalidity. In contrast to Lord Jauncey, Lord Goff, giving the leading speech, saw this approach as not affecting the initial threshold to be crossed under *Cyanamid* but as going instead to the balance of convenience.

Sir John Donaldson MR in *Francome v Mirror Group Newspapers Ltd*[16] expressed preference for the term 'balance of justice' as against 'balance of convenience'; and May LJ made a similar comment in *Cayne v Global Natural Resources plc*.[17] But it is hard to see what possible advantage there would be in such a change of terminology.

What is meant by the *status quo* has been discussed in several cases subsequent to *American Cyanamid*. In *Fellowes v Fisher*[18] Sir John Pennycuick regarded it as the position prior to the wrong, and this was supported by Geoffrey Lane LJ in *Budget Rent A Car International Inc v Mamos Slough Ltd*.[19] In *Alfred Dunhills v Sunoptic*[20] Megaw LJ took the rather vague view that '. . . the relevant point in time for the purposes of the "status quo" may well vary in different cases.' Lord Diplock attempted to clarify authoritatively what is meant in *Garden Cottage Foods Ltd v Milk Marketing Board*,[1] but his approach is far from simple:

. . . the relevant status quo to which reference was made in *American Cyanamid* is the state of affairs existing during the period immediately preceding the issue of the writ claiming the permanent injunction, or if there be unreasonable delay between the issue of writ and the motion for an interlocutory injunction the period immediately preceding the motion. The duration of that period since the state of affairs last changed must be more than minimal, having regard to the total length of the relationship between

15 [1991] 1 AC 603.
16 [1984] 1 WLR 892. In *A-G v Observer Newspapers Ltd* [1986] NLJ Rep 799 he preferred the term 'balance of inconvenience'.
17 [1984] 1 All ER 225.
18 [1976] QB 122.
19 (1977) 121 Sol Jo 374.
20 [1979] FSR 337.
1 [1984] AC 130.

the parties in respect of which the injunction was granted; otherwise the state of affairs before the last change would be the relevant status quo.[2]

These differences of judicial opinion serve to confirm the view that the preference expressed for maintaining the *status quo* lacks sound justification.

Finally, it has been argued by Gray that, irrespective of exceptions to *American Cyanamid*, 'A judge should be able to reach the same conclusion by applying the *Cyanamid* principles as he would have reached by the previous approach. So the difference between the pre-*Cyanamid* situation . . . and the post-*Cyanamid* situation . . . is superficial, a difference of appearance rather than substance, of approach rather than result.'[3] But while it is true that the *American Cyanamid* principles do allow some flexibility, so that for example a judge eager to bring in his view of the merits of the case can do so by regarding the balance of convenience as equal, the principles *if applied* must affect results because without a prima facie case hurdle to overcome, they must make it easier for a plaintiff to obtain an interlocutory injunction. *Hubbard v Pitt*[4] is a good example, where the majority applying *American Cyanamid*, granted the interlocutory injunction, whereas Lord Denning, applying the old law would have refused it. That many such examples are not forthcoming is best explained by the fact that important exceptions to *American Cyanamid* have been developed, and by the suspicion that, while purporting to apply Lord Diplock's principles, the judges have in fact been distorting them. But the submission is that, if applied, *American Cyanamid* does produce a change of result as well as approach. As Hammond writes:

The classical model has been replaced by a balancing model. A cynic might contend that was merely window-dressing—that judges continued to do the same old things in the same old way—yet the reformulation of the remedy did in some cases affect the case-law results.[5]

(3) Criticisms of *American Cyanamid*

A feature of the post-*Cyanamid* case law has been the reluctance of many judges to follow the Lords' approach. A number of reasons may be suggested for its lack of popularity.

---

2 Ibid at 140. Cf *Graham v Delderfield* [1992] FSR 313 where it was held to be the position at the date of the service, rather than at the date of the issue of the writ, that fixed the status quo.
3 (1980) 40 CLJ 307 at 338–9.
4 [1976] QB 142.
5 (1980) 30 UTLJ 249, 259.

(i) The mini-trial interlocutory application was useful for parties, being a quick and relatively cheap means of achieving rough and ready justice. In Wallington's graphic phrase, 'The House of Lords has effectively closed down the economy-class option: we shall all have to travel in the Rolls—or not at all.'[6]

(ii) In many cases, the time factor and circumstances are such that the decision on the interlocutory application ends the dispute, rendering a trial regarding a final injunction superfluous. In such cases, one cannot fairly decide the interlocutory application on the basis of what is more convenient pending trial, and the merits of the claim must be regarded as decisive.

(iii) The basis of Lord Diplock's reasoning—that there is insufficient evidence and argument at the interlocutory application to come to a sound conclusion on fact and law—appears not to be borne out by experience, for in almost all cases that have proceeded to trial, the decision has gone the same way as at the interlocutory stage.[7]

(iv) *American Cyanamid* is detrimental to civil liberties. This follows from the fact that in assessing the balance of convenience, the courts have traditionally regarded temporary interference with economic interests as more serious than temporary interference with non-tangible interests, such as the right to continue a strike or demonstration, or to speak freely. Where the primary emphasis was on the plaintiff's establishing a prima facie case this mattered less. But Lord Diplock's removal of that emphasis makes it too easy for a plaintiff to infringe the defendant's civil liberties. Wallington has been particularly critical of this aspect of *American Cyanamid*; '. . . failure to bring into account the intangibles is only tolerable where at least an arbitrary assessment of the legal merits has been made, so that the conduct prohibited is at least *probably* unlawful. If there is no determination of the legal issues, it is intolerable that such a vital factor as the defendant's liberties be left out of account in assessing the balance of convenience.'[8]

(v) Under *American Cyanamid*, the fact that the plaintiff appears to have a very strong case as opposed to a merely arguable one has no bearing except as a last resort. This seems unsatisfactory, for a very strong case is a factor that should outweigh whatever the balance of convenience would dictate.

---

6 (1976) 35 CLJ 82, 87.
7 Prescott (1975) 91 LQR 168, 170; Hammond (1980) 30 UTLJ 240, 251.
8 (1976) 35 CLJ 82, 92.

(4) Exceptions to *American Cyanamid*

In view of the above criticisms, it is not surprising that the courts have recognised a number of exceptions to *American Cyanamid*, where the old law, or something similar to it, is applied.[9]

(a) Where no action for a final injunction will reach trial

This, the most important exception, is where the timing and circumstances are such that if the interlocutory decision goes one way or, in some situations, either way it will resolve the dispute relating to injunctive relief without a trial.[10]

It would seem that this is what Lord Denning had in mind when in one of the first cases after *American Cyanamid*, *Fellowes v Fisher*,[11] in a judgment not agreed with by the majority, he said that *American Cyanamid* did not apply and the old law did, where '. . . it is urgent and imperative to come to a decision';[12] and he thought that this would be so in cases of industrial disputes, breach of confidence, covenants in restraint of trade, passing-off, and in many commercial cases. Lord Denning applied the same approach in several subsequent cases.[13]

However, recent cases have established that Lord Denning's approach of listing the sorts of case that would automatically fall within this exception was too wide-ranging. In *Lawrence David Ltd v Ashton*[14] and *County Sound plc v Ocean Sound Ltd*[15] the Court of Appeal has clarified, without doubting the exception itself, that *American Cyanamid* principles apply in the normal way to covenants

---

9 See Martin (1993–4) 4 King's CLJ 52. For an additional exception, not discussed below, see *Re J (a minor)* [1993] Fam 15. Interestingly in Australia there were initial doubts as to whether *Cyanamid* should be followed, given its contradiction of the old law embodied in *Beecham Group Ltd v Bristol Laboratories Pty Ltd* (1968) 118 CLR 618. But more recently *Cyanamid* has been followed in, eg *Australian Coarse Grain Pty Ltd v Barley Marketing Board of Queensland* (1982) 57 ALJR 425; *Tableland Peanuts v Peanut Marketing Board* (1984) 58 ALJR 283; *Murphy v Lush* (1986) 60 ALJR 523. See Meagher, Gummow and Lehane *Equity: Doctrines and Remedies* (3rd edn) paras 2169–73.
10 But it is not sufficient simply that the parties are likely to settle out of court following the interlocutory application, for this is always likely: Newell (1981) 97 LQR 214, 217.
11 [1976] QB 122.
12 Ibid at 133.
13 *Hubbard v Pitt* [1976] QB 142; *Dunford and Elliot Ltd v Johnson & Firth Brown Ltd* [1977] 1 Lloyd's Rep 505, and as agreed with by the other CA judges in *Office Overload Ltd v Gunn* [1977] FSR 39, and *Newsweek Inc v BBC* [1979] RPC 441.
14 [1991] 1 All ER 385. Cf *Lansing Linde Ltd v Kerr* [1991] 1 WLR 251.
15 [1991] FSR 367.

in restraint of trade and passing off cases respectively. Lord Denning's judgment in *Fellowes v Rother* was expressly disapproved as was the approach of the Court of Appeal in *Office Overload Ltd v Gunn*[16] (covenant in restraint of trade) and *Newsweek Inc v BBC*[17] (passing off).

Authoritative support for at least a modification of *American Cyanamid* where no action for a final injunction will reach trial came from Lord Diplock himself; for in *NWL Ltd v Woods*,[18] faced with a legislative reaction embodied in what is now s 221(2) of the Trade Union and Labour Relations (Consolidation) Act 1992,[19] Lord Diplock was forced to concede that *American Cyanamid* could not be straightforwardly applied in industrial dispute cases. He said that this was so because, 'the grant or refusal of an interlocutory injunction generally disposes finally of the action: in practice actions of this type seldom if ever come to actual trial.'[20]

Further support for this exception was given by a strong Court of Appeal, even without Lord Denning, in *Cayne v Global Natural Resources*,[1] where the plaintiff shareholder sought an interlocutory injunction to restrain the directors of Global from allegedly acting in breach of fiduciary duty by merging Global with another company. The plaintiff claimed that the proposed merger was simply a means whereby the directors could resist the attempt by the plaintiff and other shareholders to remove them. In refusing the interlocutory injunction, the Court of Appeal declined to apply *American Cyanamid* and referred to *NWL v Woods*, because in these circumstances the grant of the interlocutory injunction would effectively decide the issue in the plaintiff's favour; for if granted the directors would be unlikely to resist removal by the plaintiff and, as the plaintiff and his supporters would then be directors, the proposed merger would be dropped.[2] As *American Cyanamid* was not being applied, the plaintiff needed to show an 'overwhelming'[3] case, that is a prima facie case, and this he had failed to do. Kerr LJ in

16 [1977] FSR 39.
17 [1979] RPC 441.
18 [1979] 1 WLR 1294.
19 Infra, pp 434–7.
20 [1979] 1 WLR 1294 at 1305. See also *Porter v National Union of Journalists* [1980] IRLR 404 at 406; Newell (1981) 97 LQR 214.
1 [1984] 1 All ER 225. See also *Fulwell v Bragg* (1983) 127 Sol Jo 171.
2 Eveleigh LJ, ibid at 232, thought also that a refusal of the injunction would decide the issue because the merger would then go ahead, the directors would successfully defeat the plaintiff and his supporters, and in practice this could not be reversed by a final injunction.
3 Ibid at 233, 236.

characteristically clear terms stressed that *American Cyanamid* should be restricted to cases where:

> . . . a trial is in fact likely to take place, in the sense that the plaintiffs' case shows that they are genuinely concerned to pursue their claim to trial, and that they are seeking the injunction as a means of a holding operation pending the trial.[4]

It is to be hoped that *Cayne* will be followed and *American Cyanamid* ignored wherever the interlocutory decision, one way or either way, will finally resolve the dispute relating to injunctive relief. This is supported by *Thomas v National Union of Mineworkers:*[5] Scott J, recognising that an action for a final injunction preventing the allegedly unlawful picketing of the plaintiffs, who were working miners, would be unlikely ever to come to trial, followed *Cayne* and, in granting an interlocutory injunction, in effect required the plaintiffs to show a prima facie case that they would be entitled to a final injunction to restrain the picketing.[6] It is also supported by Kerr LJ in *Cambridge Nutrition Ltd v BBC.*[7] But the majority of the Court of Appeal in that case attempted to reconcile *Cayne* and *Cyanamid*[8] by elevating within the balance of convenience the importance of the plaintiff's prospects of success where a trial is unlikely. The Lords Justices were unanimous in discharging an interlocutory injunction restraining the BBC from screening a programme (allegedly in breach of contract) about the plaintiffs' low calorie diet.

(b) Trade dispute defence[9]

In reaction to *American Cyanamid,* the legislature added a new subsection (2) to s 17 of the Trade Union and Labour Relations Act 1974, which is now contained in s 221(2) of the Trade Union and Labour Relations (Consolidation) Act 1992. By this:

> Where (a) an application for an interlocutory injunction is made to a court pending the trial of an action; and (b) the party against whom the injunction is sought claims that he acted in contemplation or furtherance of a trade dispute, the court shall, in exercising its discretion, whether or not to

---

4 Ibid at 234.
5 [1985] 2 All ER 1.
6 Ibid at 25.
7 [1990] 3 All ER 523.
8 See analogously the attempts to assimilate s 221(2) of the Trade Union and Labour Relations (Consolidation) Act 1992 and *Cyanamid* in *Mercury Communications Ltd v Scott-Garner* [1984] Ch 37 and *Dimbleby & Sons Ltd v National Union of Journalists* [1984] 1 WLR 427: infra, pp 436–7.
9 Davies and Freedland *Labour Law* (2nd edn, 1984) pp 765–77.

grant the injunction, have regard to the likelihood of that party's succeeding at the trial of the action in establishing any matter which would afford
a defence to the action under s 219 (protection from certain tort liabilities)
or s 220 (peaceful picketing).[10]

Although this subsection is based on the first exception already
examined—that is, it recognises that *American Cyanamid* would
make it too easy for an employer effectively to end lawful industrial
action for ever, since once stopped industrial action is very difficult
to reorganise—it has given rise to its own interesting jurisprudence
on whether and how the subsection fits in with *American
Cyanamid*; and this issue remains relevant despite the subsequent
development of exceptions to the defence (eg where there has
been no ballot) and the narrowing of what is meant by a trade
dispute.[11]

In *Star Sea Transport Corpn of Monrovia v Slater*[12] Lord Denning
thought that the effect of what is now s 221(2) was 'to restore the
previous law'[13] in cases involving the defence of acts done in contemplation or furtherance of a trade dispute. This should have
meant that the interlocutory injunction would be refused because,
taking this defence into account, the plaintiff could not establish a
prima facie case. But Lord Denning considered that, as there was
an arguable question of law, the balance of convenience should
determine the issue in favour of granting the injunction—an
approach which resembled *American Cyanamid*, rather than the
previous law. The two other judges without clarifying the relationship between s 221(2) and *American Cyanamid* simply thought that
there was insufficient likelihood of the defence succeeding to outweigh the balance of convenience, which was in favour of granting
the injunction.

Lord Scarman in *NWL v Woods*[14] considered that what is now
s 221(2) could not fit within the *American Cyanamid* framework.
But then, rather than simply reverting to the old law, he regarded
the s 221(2) question as a third stage in the inquiry after the serious
question to be tried and balance of convenience issues. This seems
unnecessarily cumbersome, particularly since if the trade dispute
defence is likely to succeed at trial, no interlocutory injunction will

10 Where in contemplation or furtherance of a trade dispute, s 219 affords a defence
   to economic torts, and s 220 to peaceful primary picketing.
11 The meaning of 'trade dispute' is now contained in s 244 of the Trade Union and
   Labour Relations (Consolidation) Act 1992; see *Mercury Communications Ltd v
   Scott-Garner* [1984] Ch 37.
12 [1978] IRLR 507.
13 Ibid at 510.
14 [1979] 1 WLR 1294.

be granted, irrespective of the answers to the first two stages. Nevertheless, Lord Scarman's approach is to be preferred to that adopted by Lords Diplock and Fraser. They considered that s 221(2) could be fitted within the *American Cyanamid* framework with the amendment that in these cases the plaintiff's likelihood of gaining an injunction at trial should be an important rather than a last resort factor within the balance of convenience. While, as we have seen, Lord Diplock's explanation of this modification was eminently sensible—the practical realities of industrial disputes mean that the grant or refusal of the interlocutory injunction generally disposes finally of the claim—confining s 221(2) to a place within the balance of convenience potentially undermines the purpose of that provision: if there is a likelihood of the defence succeeding at trial, no interlocutory injunction should be granted irrespective of other factors.

For a time, however, it looked as if even Lord Diplock was departing from his *American Cyanamid* framework in relation to what is now s 221(2). In *Hadmor Productions Ltd v Hamilton*,[15] in giving the sole judgment, he refused an interlocutory injunction because of the very high likelihood of the trade dispute defence succeeding at trial and, although *Cyanamid* and *NWL v Woods* were mentioned, his approach, with no reference to other factors in the balance of convenience, looked more like that of the old law. Furthermore in *Duport Steels Ltd v Sirs*,[16] the House of Lords, including Lord Diplock, did not even mention *American Cyanamid*.

But any hopes that *American Cyanamid* might be forgotten in the context of what is now s 221(2), particularly with the intervening decision in *Cayne v Global Natural Resources plc*,[17] proved shortlived for in *Mercury Communications Ltd v Scott-Garner*[18] and *Dimbleby & Sons Ltd v National Union of Journalists*[19] the Court of Appeal (under Sir John Donaldson) and the House of Lords respectively, continued to grapple with the assimilation of *American Cyanamid* and s 221(2). The approach adopted in these cases, differing from *NWL v Woods*, was that s 221(2) applies at an initial stage, so that presumably, if the trade dispute defence is likely to succeed, no injunction should be granted. Otherwise *American Cyanamid* applies in the normal way. 'As respects all other issues raised by way of defence to the action the criterion to be applied in order to make recourse to the balance of convenience necessary is the ordinary

15 [1982] ICR 114.
16 [1980] ICR 161.
17 [1984] 1 All ER 225.
18 [1984] Ch 37.
19 [1984] 1 WLR 427.

criterion laid down in *American Cyanamid*—is there a serious question to be tried?'[20] Curiously Lord Diplock thought that the practical realities that in *NWL v Woods* he had regarded as justifying modification of *American Cyanamid* no longer applied in an action against a trade union because now that a trade union could be sued an employer might well be interested in pursuing a claim for damages to trial. This is most misleading, for the important practical reality remains that to grant an interlocutory injunction in an industrial dispute has the drastic effect of ending industrial action without the trial. Therefore, the justification for departure from *American Cyanamid* conceded in *NWL v Woods* remains as valid as ever. Furthermore, Lord Diplock was left without any coherent explanation as to why s 221(2) should have departed from *American Cyanamid*. But having said that, it is an ironic twist that the new approach adopted in these cases is far more acceptable than that adopted by Lord Diplock in *NWL v Woods*, and it seems to come very close to the old law. Indeed it merely serves to strengthen the view, indirectly supported by *Cayne v Global Natural Resources*, that it would have been preferable from the outset to have ignored *American Cyanamid* and to have regarded s 221(2) as restoring the old law in relation to cases involving the trade dispute defence.

(c) Defamation and breach of confidence

Pre-*Cyanamid*, the principles governing interlocutory injunctions in defamation (and injurious falsehood) cases were exceptional. The tradition that juries should hear such cases was one supposed reason for this. But the primary justification was the desire to protect free speech at all costs. As such, interlocutory injunctions were to be refused wherever the defendant raised a defence, whether of justification, fair comment or privilege unless the defence would obviously fail at trial.[1] It has now been established in a series of decisions[2] that these old principles survive *American Cyanamid*, for

---

20 Ibid at 432 (per Lord Diplock).
  1 *William Coulson & Sons v James Coulson & Co* (1887) 3 TLR 846; *Bonnard v Perryman* [1891] 2 Ch 269; *Fraser v Evans* [1969] 1 QB 349.
  2 *Bestobell Paints Ltd v Biggs* [1975] FSR 421; *Trevor and Sons v Soloman* (1978) 248 Estates Gazette 779; *Harakas v Baltic Mercantile and Shipping Exchange Ltd* [1982] 2 All ER 701; *Herbage v Pressdram Ltd* [1984] 1 WLR 1160; *Al-Fayed v The Observer Ltd* (1986) Times, 14 July; *Khashoggi v IPC Magazines Ltd* [1986] 3 All ER 577; *Kaye v Robertson* [1991] FSR 62. See also *Gulf Oil (GB) Ltd v Page* [1987] Ch 327 and esp *Femis-Bank (Anguilla) Ltd v Lazar* [1991] Ch 391 (similarly to defamation cases, the protection of free speech is an important factor in deciding whether to grant an interlocutory injunction to restrain an alleged

as Griffiths LJ said in *Herbage v Pressdram Ltd*,[3] *American Cyanamid* would represent 'a very considerable incursion into . . . [principles] based on freedom of speech'.[4] Indeed Martin has argued that interlocutory injunctions are such an infringement of free speech that they should never be granted. 'If we are committed to the widest possible freedom of discourse on matters of public concern, the jurisdiction to make interlocutory injunctions, this undesirable judicial censorship, cannot on principle be accepted.'[5] Although put forward in respect of Canadian law, the argument is equally applicable here. But it seems to go too far, for very exceptionally the case against the defendant may be clear-cut and indisputable even at the interlocutory stage. Nevertheless the argument does serve to highlight the importance of not weakening the test for interlocutory injunctions in defamation cases, and thereby supports the courts' rejection of *American Cyanamid* in this context.

Is *American Cyanamid* also rejected in respect of breach of confidence, where freedom of speech may again be in issue? The answer is not entirely clear. On the one hand, in *Schering Chemicals Ltd v Falkman Ltd*,[6] concerning a television film, and *Francome v Mirror Group Newspapers Ltd*,[7] dealing with a newspaper article, interlocutory injunctions were granted to restrain breach of confidence apparently on the application of *American Cyanamid*. Similarly in *A-G v Observer Newspapers Ltd*,[8] where an interlocutory injunction was granted to restrain two newspapers publishing confidential information disclosed by a former member of the British secret service in his book *Spycatcher*, the Court of Appeal thought that in this context a proper approach was to grant the injunction unless the court was satisfied that there was a serious defence of public interest which was *very likely* to succeed at trial. Again in *A-G v Guardian Newspapers Ltd*,[9] in a further round of the *Spycatcher* litigation, interlocutory injunctions were upheld by the House of Lords apparently on the application of *American Cyanamid* principles. But

conspiracy to injure so that such an injunction should only be granted where the plaintiff has established a strong prima facie case). And the question of at least modifying *Cyanamid* to protect freedom of speech has also risen in respect of other causes of action such as, eg breach of contract: *Cambridge Nutrition Ltd v BBC* [1990] 3 All ER 523; *Secretary of State for the Home Department v Central Broadcasting Ltd* (1993) Times, 28 January.
3 [1984] 1 WLR 1160.
4 Ibid at 1163.
5 (1982) 20 UWOLR 129, 140.
6 [1981] 2 All ER 321.
7 [1984] 1 WLR 892.
8 [1986] NLJ Rep 799.
9 [1987] 1 WLR 1248.

on the other hand, in *Woodward v Hutchins*,[10] the Court of Appeal drew some analogy to libel cases in allowing a newspaper to publish articles about the private lives of the plaintiff pop singers, written by their former publicity agent, and this was also Lord Denning's approach dissenting in *Schering*. This latter view is further supported by *Lion Laboratories Ltd v Evans*.[11] The question here was whether an interlocutory injunction should be granted to restrain publication in a newspaper of admittedly confidential information regarding the accuracy of the plaintiffs' intoxication instrument being used by the police to test the breath of drivers. The Court of Appeal refused the injunction because the defendants had satisfied the court that at trial they would have a strong defence of public interest. *American Cyanamid* was not applied, and the approach adopted was somewhat analogous to that for defamation, although the court was anxious to stress that the public interest needed to be far more clearly made out than did the defence of justification for libel. 'To be allowed to publish confidential information the defendants must do more than raise the plea of public interest; they must show "a legitimate ground for supposing it is in the public interest for it to be disclosed".'[12] This seems sensible. For while breach of confidence should probably be easier to restrain by interlocutory injunction than defamation—since once made public, confidentiality is destroyed for ever, whereas a lost reputation can be won back—where free speech is in issue, the courts should again be slow to grant an interlocutory injunction, amounting as it does to prior censorship. Certainly *American Cyanamid* should not be applied.

(d) Little factual or legal dispute

Some judges, like Walton J in *Athletes Foot Marketing Associates Inc v Cobra Sports Ltd*[13] and Bridge LJ in *Office Overload Ltd v Gunn*,[14] have recognised a further wide-ranging exception, namely that *American Cyanamid* does not apply where there is little dispute on the facts and the law is not difficult.[15] This should be supported, for Lord Diplock's reasoning—that there should be no mini-trials on

10 [1977] 1 WLR 760. Prior to *American Cyanamid*, see *Fraser v Evans* [1969] 1 QB 349; *Hubbard v Vosper* [1982] 2 QB 84.
11 [1984] 3 WLR 539.
12 Ibid at 548 (per Stephenson LJ citing Lord Denning in *Woodward v Hutchins* [1977] 1 WLR 760 at 764).
13 [1980] RPC 343.
14 [1977] FSR 39. Bridge LJ's approach was approved by the Court of Appeal in *Lawrence David Ltd v Ashton* [1991] 1 All ER 385, 393, 396.
15 The validity of this exception was left open in *Alfred Dunhill v Sunoptic* [1979] FSR 337.

inadequate evidence and argument—is inapplicable to such a case. In similar vein, Sir John Pennycuick in *Fellowes v Fisher*[16] thought that it was particularly in cases 'depending in whole or in great part upon the construction of a written instrument'[17] that the prospect of success was within the competence of the judge hearing the interlocutory application; and in *Official Custodian for Charities v Mackay*,[18] Scott J thought *American Cyanamid* inapplicable where there was no arguable defence to the plaintiffs' claim. Particularly radical was the Court of Appeal's view in *Bradford City Metropolitan Council v Brown*[19] that *Cyanamid* was essentially concerned only with factual as opposed to legal disputes.

(5) An alternative approach

The present law on interlocutory injunctions can be summed up by saying that, while the approach in *American Cyanamid* is that generally followed, there are important exceptions where the old law, or something very similar, is applied.

While this is a workable compromise, it is submitted that the criticisms made of *American Cyanamid* are valid and that the old law was preferable. But having said that—and this is the positive aspect of *American Cyanamid*—the old law could produce injustice to a plaintiff who failed to satisfy the initial prima facie test. To overcome this, the ideal solution would be to revert to the old law, with its emphasis on the strength of the plaintiff's case, but with the qualification that, if the action for an injunction is likely to go to trial, a plaintiff who can merely show an arguable case, should still be granted an interlocutory injunction if the balance of convenience is overwhelmingly in his favour.[20]

(6) Special types of interlocutory injunction

(a) Interlocutory mandatory injunction

It has been consistently stressed that the courts are particularly reluctant to grant an interlocutory mandatory injunction, a

16 [1976] QB 122.
17 Ibid at 141.
18 [1985] Ch 168. See also *A-G v Barker* [1990] 3 All ER 257, 262 (per Nourse LJ).
19 (1986) 19 HLR 16. This derives some support from the reasoning of Lords Jauncey and Bridge in *R v Secretary of State for Transport, ex p Factortame (No 2)* [1991] 1 AC 603.
20 For other approaches, see Sharpe *Injunctions and Specific Performance* (2nd edn) paras 2.370–2.380; Leubsdorf (1978) 91 Harv LR 525.

reluctance which reflects the fact that while a final mandatory injunction is more drastic than a prohibitory one, an interlocutory mandatory injunction is doubly drastic, being granted where the court cannot be sure of the merits of the dispute. In *Gale v Abbott*,[1] for example, it was said that an application for an interlocutory mandatory injunction was '. . . one of the rarest cases that occurs, for the court will not compel a man to do so serious a thing as to undo what he has done, except at the hearing.'[2] Cohen LJ in *Canadian Pacific Rly v Gaud*[3] thought than an interlocutory mandatory injunction was a 'very exceptional form of relief',[4] and this reluctance has again been stressed in more recent cases.[5] This is not to say that such an injunction is never granted.[6] In particular, and seemingly reflecting a punitive approach,[7] an interlocutory mandatory injunction has been ordered to undo an alleged tort because the defendant has tried to 'steal a march' on the plaintiff by, for example, speeding up building work allegedly interfering with the plaintiff's light so as to have the building completed before a pending court hearing.[8]

Furthermore, there is perhaps not the same reluctance to grant an interlocutory mandatory injunction enforcing a positive contractual obligation. In this context, the interlocutory mandatory injunction performs the role which, at trial, is performed by specific performance rather than by a final mandatory injunction. It is therefore apt to view the interlocutory mandatory injunction as temporary specific performance. It has fairly recently been confirmed by the Court of Appeal in *Astro Exito Navegacion SA v Southland Enterprise Co Ltd, The Messiniaki Tolmi*,[9] that there is indeed jurisdiction to grant an interlocutory mandatory injunction

---

1 (1862) 6 LT 852.
2 Ibid at 854.
3 [1949] 2 KB 239.
4 Ibid at 249.
5 *Shepherd Homes Ltd v Sandham* [1971] Ch 340; *Hounslow London Borough Council v Twickenham Garden Developments Ltd* [1971] Ch 233; *Shotton v Hammond* (1976) 120 Sol Jo 780; *John Trenberth Ltd v National Westminster Bank Ltd* (1980) 39 P & CR 104; *Taylor and Foulstone v NUM* [1984] IRLR 445; *Locabail International Finance Ltd v Agroexport* [1986] 1 All ER 901; *Jakeman v South West Thames RHA* [1990] IRLR 62.
6 See, eg the injunctions ordering withdrawals of strike notices, which gave rise to contempt proceedings in *Express Newspapers plc v Mitchell* [1982] IRLR 465; *Austin Rover Group Ltd v Amalgamated Union of Engineering Workers* [1985] IRLR 162.
7 Sharpe *Injunctions and Specific Performance* (2nd edn) para 2.650.
8 *Daniel v Ferguson* [1891] 2 Ch 27; *Von Joel v Hornsey* [1895] 2 Ch 774. See also *Esso Petroleum Co Ltd v Kingswood Motors Ltd* [1974] QB 142.
9 [1982] QB 1248.

amounting to temporary specific performance: and in that case, which concerned the sale of a ship, such an injunction was granted ordering the defendants to comply with their contractual obligations by instructing their bank to release the purchase price before their letters of credit expired. To support its view on jurisdiction, the Court of Appeal referred to *Smith v Peters*,[10] where an interlocutory mandatory injunction had been granted ordering the vendor of a house, in accordance with the contract of sale, to allow a named third party to make a valuation of the fixtures and fittings. Not cited, but just as relevant, is the well-known case of *Sky Petroleum Ltd v VIP Petroleum Ltd*[11] where an interlocutory injunction was granted, restraining the defendants from withholding supplies of petrol to the plaintiffs' filling stations. Although the form of the injunction was prohibitory, it was mandatory in substance, as Goulding J's judgment recognises, and amounted to temporary specific performance of the defendants' contract to supply all the petrol required by the plaintiffs.

Prior to *American Cyanamid v Ethicon* the judicial reluctance to award interlocutory mandatory injunctions was often reflected by insisting, as a first requirement, that the plaintiff should show a strong or very strong prima facie case.[12] Lord Diplock in *American Cyanamid* can be taken to have disapproved of such a requirement, since although he did not expressly refer to mandatory injunctions, his reasoning criticising mini-trials at the interlocutory stage appears to have been directed to all interlocutory injunctions. However, as the balance of convenience will almost always be against granting a mandatory injunction—since to order the defendant to take positive action, particularly where restorative, is usually more of a hardship to him than the plaintiff's interim hardship—application of the *American Cyanamid* approach would be unlikely to lead to such injunctions being more readily granted.

However, it would appear that the courts continue to apply the

---

10 (1875) LR 20 Eq 511.
11 [1974] 1 WLR 576. Other examples are *Luganda v Service Hotels Ltd* [1969] 2 Ch 209; *Texaco Ltd v Mulberry Filling Station Ltd* [1972] 1 WLR 814; *Shotton v Hammond* (1976) 120 Sol Jo 780; *Peninsular Maritime Ltd v Padseal Ltd* (1981) 259 Estates Gazette 860; *Taylor v NUM* [1984] IRLR 445; *Parker v Camden London Borough Council* [1985] 2 All ER 141.
12 *Hounslow London Borough Council v Twickenham Garden Developments Ltd* [1971] Ch 233; *Esso Petroleum Co Ltd v Kingswood Motors Ltd* [1974] QB 142. It should be remembered that when considering the availability of a final order in deciding whether to grant an interlocutory mandatory injunction enforcing positive contractual obligations—ie in deciding whether there is a strong prima facie case (or, on *American Cyanamid*, a serious question to be tried)—the relevant principles are those of specific performance.

pre-*Cyanamid* approach to interlocutory mandatory injunctions on the ground that they are exceptional injunctions not covered by *American Cyanamid*.[13] Indeed that this should be so was expressly stated by the Court of Appeal in *Locabail International Finance Ltd v Agroexport*,[14] which was followed by Auld J in *Jakeman v South West Thames RHA*.[15] A less conventional approach was taken by Hoffmann J in *Films Rover International Ltd v Cannon Film Sales Ltd*.[16] He considered that the basic question was not so much whether the injunction sought was prohibitory or mandatory but whether the injustice to the defendant if the application were granted and the plaintiff subsequently failed at the trial would outweigh the injustice to the plaintiff if the application were refused and he subsequently succeeded at the trial. And while he appeared to view *American Cyanamid* as inapplicable to mandatory injunctions he regarded the Court of Appeal's insistence in *Locabail* on a strong case for an interlocutory mandatory injunction as merely laying down a guideline rather than a rule, which reflected the fact that mandatory injunctions, if granted at an interlocutory stage, *generally* create greater risks of injustice to the defendant in the manner described than prohibitory injunctions. Applying that approach, Hoffmann J granted an interlocutory mandatory injunction, enforcing a contractual obligation, even though the plaintiff could not establish a strong prima facie case.

(b) Ex parte injunction

An interlocutory injunction can be granted *ex parte*, that is, without notice having been given to the defendant so that he has had no opportunity to be heard. Normally an *ex parte* injunction lasts until a named day (ie it is an interim injunction) when an *inter partes* application can be made. Nowadays the most common *ex parte* injunctions are Mareva injunctions and Anton Piller orders,[17] which are governed by their own special principles.

---

13 Indeed since granting the injunction will almost invariably finally resolve the claim without a trial, the exception discussed supra, pp 432–4, is applicable.
14 [1986] 1 All ER 901. See also *De Falco v Crawley Borough Council* [1980] QB 460 at 481 (per Bridge LJ); *R v Kensington and Chelsea Royal LBC, ex p Hammell* [1989] QB 518. Contra are *Meade v London Borough of Haringey* [1979] 1 WLR 637 at 657–8 (per Sir Stanley Rees); *Peninsular Maritime Ltd v Padseal Ltd* (1981) 259 Estates Gazette 860 at 868 (per Stephenson LJ).
15 [1990] IRLR 62.
16 [1986] 3 All ER 772. This is supported by Meagher, Gummow & Lehane *Equity: Doctrines and Remedies* (3rd edn) para 2178.
17 Infra, pp 444–6.

But to justify an ordinary *ex parte* injunction the plaintiff, in addition to satisfying the usual requirements for an interlocutory injunction, will need to show that the matter is one of urgency.[18] Delay, whereby an opportunity to apply *inter partes* has been unjustifiably lost, will bar an *ex parte* injunction. In *Bates v Lord Hailsham*,[19] for example, the plaintiff applied for an *ex parte* injunction at 2 pm to prevent a committee, due to meet at 4.30 pm, from making an order concerning the abolition of solicitors' scale fees. The injunction was refused because the plaintiff had known of the meeting for some weeks and had had ample opportunity to make an *inter partes* application. A further requirement of an *ex parte* application is that the plaintiff should act in good faith by disclosing all relevant facts to the court, including those prejudicial to his case, and failure to do so will lead to the injunction being discharged.[20]

An important additional restriction is imposed by statute on the power to grant *ex parte* injunctions in industrial disputes. By s 221(1) of the Trade Union and Labour Relations (Consolidation) Act 1992, no injunction shall be granted against a defendant who is absent and is likely to raise the defence that he was acting in contemplation or futherance of a trade dispute unless all reasonable steps have been taken to give that person notice and an opportunity to be heard. In practice plaintiffs appear to give, and courts accept as sufficient, about 24 hours' notice.

(c) Mareva injunction

This is an interlocutory[1] prohibitory injunction, which is almost always granted *ex parte* and usually restrains a person from removing assets from the jurisdiction or otherwise disposing of assets within the jurisdiction. In rare circumstances it may also extend to restraining the defendant from dealing with his assets outside the jurisdiction (so-called 'world-wide Marevas'). Regarded by Lord Denning as 'the greatest piece of judicial law reform in my time',[2] the Mareva injunction[3] has the purpose of preventing a defendant frustrating the satisfaction of a monetary judgment that the plaintiff may get against him. Typically it leads to the freezing of a person's

---

18 RSC Ord 8, r 2(1), Ord 29, r 1(2).
19 [1972] 1 WLR 1373.
20 *R v Kensington Income Tax General Comrs* [1917] 1 KB 486; *Beese v Woodhouse* [1970] 1 WLR 586. Presumably there will usually also be a costs penalty.
 1 This can include an injunction granted after final judgment, see supra, p 390, fn 16.
 2 *The Due Process of Law* (1980) p 134.
 3 Named after *Mareva Cia Naviera SA v International Bulkcarriers SA* [1975] 2 Lloyds Rep 509.

bank accounts. The injunction is governed by its own special principles, developed in the case law, and *American Cyanamid v Ethicon* does not apply. As it is designed to ensure that monetary remedies can be effective, rather than itself being a remedy for torts or breach of contract,[4] the Mareva injunction lies outside the scope of this book, and no further consideration will be given to it.[5]

(d) Anton Piller order

Described by Donaldson LJ as 'one of the law's two nuclear weapons',[6] the other being the Mareva injunction, an Anton Piller order[7] is an *ex parte* interlocutory mandatory injunction, which usually basically orders the defendant to allow the plaintiff to enter his premises for the purposes of searching for, inspecting and seizing property infringing the plaintiff's rights, or documents relevant to the plaintiff's claim against the defendant. It is given where speed and secrecy are vital to prevent the destruction or disposal of such property or documents. While developed to deal with cases involving intellectual property, an Anton Piller order has been granted in other contexts such as matrimonial[8] and ordinary commercial cases.[9] Special principles have been formulated to govern Anton Piller orders and *Cyanamid* does not apply.

Like the Mareva, the Anton Piller order is best regarded as outside this book's scope. Primarily it is a means of ensuring that essential evidence is not destroyed. In this role it most obviously belongs alongside orders of discovery,[10] and is a means by which the plaintiff is enabled to prove his case.[11] A subsidiary function is to preserve goods[12] that are likely to be the subject matter of an action brought by the plaintiff and are endangered. In this, the

---

4 It may also be granted in other contexts, eg family law.
5 Ie the Mareva assists enforcement. Hence it is best viewed alongside that large body of law dealing with the enforcement of monetary judgments. For detailed consideration of Marevas, see Gee *Mareva Injunctions and Anton Piller Relief* (2nd edn); *Clerk and Lindsell on Torts* (16th edn) para 7–14; Zuckermann (1993) 109 LQR 432. Neither a Mareva injunction nor an Anton Piller order can generally be ordered by a county court: County Court Remedies Regulations 1991.
6 *Bank Mellat v Nikpour* [1982] Com LR 158 at 159.
7 Named after *Anton Piller KG v Manufacturing Processes Ltd* [1976] Ch 55.
8 *Emanuel v Emanuel* [1982] 1 WLR 669.
9 *Yousif v Salama* [1980] 1 WLR 1540.
10 Ibid at 1543 (per Donaldson LJ); *Rank Film Distributors Ltd v Video Information Centre* [1982] AC 380.
11 Supra, p 3.
12 Hence an undertaking has to be given that articles obtained will be retained by the plaintiff's solicitors in safe custody—*Universal City Studios Inc v Mukhtar & Sons Ltd* [1976] 1 WLR 568.

Anton Piller is like a preservation order made under RSC Ord 29, r 2,[13] and is most sensibly viewed as seeking to ensure that subsequent remedies gained in relation to those goods can be effective.[14]

6. THE PLAINTIFF'S CONDUCT AS A BAR

It has been considered convenient to discuss this as a separate head, since the six doctrines encompassed, apply whether the injunction is final or interlocutory, prohibitory or mandatory, *quia timet* or not *quia timet*.

(1) Serious breach of contract

A good example here is *Telegraph Despatch and Intelligence Co v McLean*,[15] where a prohibitory injunction to restrain a defendant from transmitting news in breach of covenant was refused, because the plaintiffs were themselves in serious[16] breach of their contract with the defendant by selling the news-agency business. However it may be doubted whether a defendant now needs to rely on this equitable defence, since he can simply terminate for breach, thereby also escaping liability for damages.[17]

(2) He who comes to equity must come with clean hands

This is a wide ranging doctrine,[18] whereby the court may refuse an injunction, where it considers that the plaintiff's past conduct, as revealed by the facts of the dispute, has been so improper that he

---

13 Or an interlocutory injunction to preserve property ordered under the courts' general jurisdiction to grant injunctions. See *Redler Grain Silos v BICC Ltd* [1982] 1 Lloyds Rep 435; *Polly Peck International plc v Nadir (No 2)* [1992] 4 All ER 769; Sharpe *Injunctions and Specific Performance* (2nd edn) paras 2.700–2.710.

14 It therefore assists enforcement—supra, p 445, fn 5. Contrast interlocutory delivery up *to the plaintiff*, infra, chapter 10. For general consideration of Anton Pillers, see Gee *Mareva Injunctions and Anton Piller Relief* (2nd edn); *Clerk and Lindsell on Torts* (16th edn) para 7–13; Dockray and Laddie (1990) 106 LQR 601.

15 (1873) 8 Ch App 658. See also *Goddard v Midland Rly Co* (1891) 8 TLR 126; *Litvinoff v Kent* (1918) 34 TLR 298.

16 The breach was not serious enough to bar the injunction in *Western v MacDermott* (1866) 2 Ch App 72; *Chitty v Bray* (1883) 48 LT 860; *Meredith v Wilson* (1893) 69 LT 336; *Hooper v Bromet* (1903) 90 LT 234.

17 Eg *General Billposting v Atkinson* [1909] AC 118.

18 For general discussion see Chafee (1948–9) 47 Mich LR 877, 1065.

does not deserve to be helped by the court's granting of an injunction. Clearly such conduct can take many forms. In *Hubbard v Vosper*[19] Megaw LJ considered that scientologists should be denied an interlocutory injunction restraining publication of defamatory articles because of their own deplorable activities and beliefs; and in *Tollemache & Cobbold Breweries Ltd v Reynolds*,[20] no mandatory injunction ordering the removal of eaves trespassing into the plaintiff's air-space was granted because, inter alia, the plaintiff had acted pettily throughout.

On the other hand, in *Duchess of Argyll v Duke of Argyll*,[1] the plaintiff's own adultery and her own articles revealing some secrets of her former marriage did not prevent her from gaining an interlocutory injunction on the basis of breach of confidence, to restrain her ex-husband publishing in a Sunday newspaper an account of her private life during their marriage. In an important statement, Ungoed-Thomas J said, 'A person coming to Equity for relief . . . must come with clean hands: but the cleanliness required is to be judged in relation to the relief that is sought.'[2] This emphasises that the 'clean hands' doctrine is a relative one, by which an injunction will still be granted to someone whose conduct has been improper, if the defendant's conduct was that much worse.

(3) He who seeks equity must do equity

This maxim is similar to that requiring 'clean hands', but looks to the plaintiff's future rather than past conduct so that, by it, a plaintiff will not be granted an injunction against the defendant, unless he is prepared to do what is fair and right in relation to the defendant. With regard to breach of contract, for example, a plaintiff will be refused an injunction, unless he is ready and willing to perform his own obligations to the defendant. The classic authority is *Measures Bros Ltd v Measures*,[3] where it was held that employers, who had wrongfully repudiated an employee's contract,[4] could not enforce that employee's restrictive trading covenant because, inter alia, they were unwilling and unable to perform their side of the contract in the future.

---

19 [1972] 2 QB 84.
20 (1983) 268 Estates Gazette 52.
1 [1967] Ch 302.
2 Ibid at 332.
3 [1910] 2 Ch 248. *Shell UK Ltd v Lostock Garage Ltd* [1976] 1 WLR 1187 at 1199 (per Lord Denning); *Agricultural Supplies Ltd v Rushmere* (1967) 111 Sol Jo 683.
4 Presumably, the employee could have terminated for breach, rather than relying on the equitable defence.

(4) Acquiescence

In relation to equitable remedies for wrongs,[5] the defence of acquiescence requires that the plaintiff, actively or passively, has encouraged the defendant to believe that he has no objection to the defendant doing what amounts to a wrong against him and that the defendant has acted to his detriment in that belief.[6] So in the leading case of *Shaw v Applegate*[7] the defendant had partly used his property for an amusement arcade in breach of a restrictive covenant with the plaintiff. The plaintiff had made no complaints about this for six years, although he knew about it, and in consequence the defendant had gone on to buy and install more amusement machinery. The Court of Appeal held that acquiescence barred the plaintiff's claim for a prohibitory and mandatory injunction. But damages in lieu were awarded, thereby showing that acquiescence can be a slightly wider defence for an injunction than for damages.[8]

In other cases, however, both an injunction and equitable damages have been barred. For example, in *Sayers v Collyer*,[9] where the defendant had broken a restrictive covenant not to use premises as a shop, but the plaintiff had turned a blind eye to this for three years, no damages, let alone an injunction, were awarded. Similarly in *Habib Bank Ltd v Habib Bank AG Zurich*[10] the plaintiff bank sought an injunction to restrain the defendants from passing off their business as the plaintiffs'. It was held that the tort had not been made out, since there had been no misrepresentation: but even if it had been, the injunction (and presumably, although not mentioned, equitable damages) would be barred by acquiescence, constituted by the plaintiffs' predecessors having worked closely with the defendants and having helped them to set up their bank. As

---

5 There should be no difference in approach whether the wrong be legal or equitable—*Habib Bank Ltd v Habib Bank AG Zurich* [1981] 1 WLR 1265. Acquiescence, often alternatively referred to as equitable estoppel, may also bar the plaintiff's strict rights, and indeed create new rights, in situations where there is no question of wrongdoing by the defendant: eg *Willmott v Barber* (1880) 15 Ch D 96; *Crabb v Arun District Council* [1976] Ch 179; *Taylor Fashions Ltd v Liverpool Victoria Trustees Co Ltd* [1981] 1 All ER 897.

6 *Bulmer Ltd and Showerings Ltd v Bollinger SA* [1977] 2 CMLR 625 at 682 (per Goff LJ). See also *Electrolux Ltd v Electrix Ltd* (1953) 71 RPC 23 at 34 (per Lord Evershed MR); *Habib Bank Ltd v Habib Bank AG Zurich* [1981] 1 WLR 1265 at 1284–5 (per Oliver LJ).

7 [1977] 1 WLR 970.

8 *Sayers v Collyer* (1884) 28 Ch D 103 at 110 (Fry J).

9 Ibid.

10 [1981] 1 WLR 1265.

Oliver LJ said, 'One's initial reaction looking at the history of the matter is that there could hardly be a plainer case of acquiescence than this.'[11]

It should be realised that acquiescence may operate not merely to bar equitable remedies, but also to extinguish the defendant's liability, so that no common law remedies are available either. In a case such as *Shaw v Applegate*, it was indicated that a higher degree of acquiescence amounting to dishonesty or unconscionability[12] would be required to extinguish liability and hence common law remedies. But such a distinction lacks any sensible rationale.[13] The preferable approach is that a lesser degree of acquiescence may bar an injunction than will bar damages, whether they are equitable or common law.

Finally in *Johnson v Wyatt*,[14] it was said that the defence of acquiescence is more likely to apply as a bar to an interlocutory than a final injunction. In particular, this follows because a shorter period of acquiescence will suffice.

(5) Laches

(a) Final injunction

By s 36(1) of the Limitation Act 1980, the usual six-year limitation period does not apply to injunctions. But as the six years runs from the accrual of the cause of action this exclusion is only of real consequence for a non-continuing breach of contract—otherwise where injunctions are in issue the relevant cause of action generally recurs or accrues *de die in diem*.

However, the defendant may claim that under the doctrine of laches, the plaintiff's unreasonable delay in seeking an injunction bars the remedy. While laches has often not been separated from acquiescence, as a distinct doctrine it lays down when delay by the plaintiff in seeking an equitable remedy will bar that remedy, other than where acquiescence can be made out. But in the past it has sometimes been suggested that laches is not a sufficient bar to an injunction, and that the additional requirements of acquiescence are necessary.[15] This, however, has been departed from in more recent

11 Ibid at 1283.
12 [1977] 1 WLR 970 at 978 (per Buckley LJ). *Bulmer v Bollinger* [1977] 2 CMLR 625 at 681 (per Goff LJ).
13 Arguably, *Habib* supports this criticism, although there it was the distinction between legal and equitable *rights*, that was regarded as 'archaic and arcane'.
14 (1863) 2 De GJ & Sm 18.
15 *Fullwood v Fullwood* (1878) 9 Ch D 176.

cases such as *Cluett Peabody & Co Inc v McIntyre Hogg Marsh & Co Ltd*[16] and *HP Bulmer Ltd v J Bollinger SA*,[17] where 'inordinate delay'[18] has been regarded as a bar in itself. In *Cluett Peabody* Upjohn J considered that a delay of 29 years from when the plaintiffs first knew that the defendants were using their trademark barred an injunction restraining the continued infringement of that trademark. On the other hand, in the *Bollinger* case Goff LJ indicated that 16–17 years' delay in bringing an action in respect of a continuing passing off was not 'inordinate'.[19] One would expect that additional factors, such as consequential prejudice to the defendant, will lead to a lesser delay being a sufficient bar (especially where the injunction sought is mandatory).

A sensible reform, producing desirable certainty and uniformity would be to introduce a statutory limitation period barring an injunction after a certain number of years, to run from the date of the initial wrong, or from when the plaintiff knew of the wrong.

(b) Interlocutory injunction

What the court is here assessing is whether the plaintiff has delayed too long in seeking an *interlocutory* injunction and hence much shorter periods of delay will bar this than would bar a final injunction. So in *Church of Scientology of California v Miller*[20] a delay of less than two months was held by the Court of Appeal to bar an interlocutory injunction restraining an alleged breach of confidence; in *Legg v ILEA*[1] Megarry J came close to declining interlocutory injunctions because the plaintiffs had been guilty of 12 weeks' delay; and in *Morecambe and Heysham Borough v Mecca Ltd*,[2] in refusing an interlocutory injunction to prevent the defendants holding a beauty competition, Wilberforce J appears to have been influenced by the finding that the plaintiffs knew of the relevant facts by about mid-December, but did not give notice of motion until April. Again, at the interlocutory stage in *Bracewell v Appleby*,[3] Pennycuick V-C had refused an injunction preventing the defendants trespassing

16 [1958] RPC 335.
17 [1977] 2 CMLR 625.
18 Ibid at 681.
19 Also *Savile v Kilner* (1872) 26 LT 277 (20 years' delay no bar to injunction for continuing nuisance).
20 (1987) Times, 23 October.
 1 [1972] 1 WLR 1245.
 2 [1962] RPC 145.
 3 Referred to at trial by Graham J [1975] Ch 408 at 415. Unfortunately Graham J seemed to regard this as also relevant to the final injunction: contra is *Wrotham Park Estate Co v Parkside Homes Ltd* [1974] 1 WLR 798.

over the plaintiff's road to build a house, because of a few months' delay by the plaintiff. A four-month delay was also regarded as relevant by Megarry J in refusing an interlocutory mandatory injunction in *Shepherd Homes Ltd v Sandham*.[4] Even if the delay does not itself bar the interlocutory injunction, one would expect it to be regarded as strong evidence that the interim harm to the plaintiff is not that serious, which is an important factor, particularly under *American Cyanamid*. Where exactly delay (or acquiescence) fits within the *Cyanamid* principles is unclear. One might think that it would be applied separately, and would not be swallowed up in the balance of convenience. But this is not borne out in the cases.[5]

(6) Valid termination of the contract by the plaintiff

Where the plaintiff seeks an injunction to enforce negative or positive contractual obligations, that injunction is presumably barred where the plaintiff has chosen validly to terminate the contract. Although rarely discussed in relation to injunctions,[6] the law on this in relation to specific performance would seem to apply by analogy—once the contractual obligation has gone there is nothing to enforce.[7]

---

4 [1971] Ch 340.
5 Eg *Roussel-Uclaf v GD Searle & Co Ltd* [1977] FSR 125.
6 But this bar was implicitly accepted in *Thomas Marshall (Exports) Ltd v Guinle* [1979] Ch 227 at 239–43 (per Megarry V-C).
7 Supra, pp 378–9. But this may well not bar a mandatory restorative injunction, which arguably does not depend on the continuing rather than past existence of the obligation.

Chapter 10

Other remedies

'Other remedies' are judicial remedies for torts and breach of contract that have not so far been discussed. As these are not central remedies for torts or breach of contract, and as what needs to be said regarding them is relatively limited, it has been considered preferable to deal with them in this single residual chapter, instead of giving each a separate chapter.

1. DELIVERY UP OF GOODS

(1) Introduction

This is the appropriate remedy for the plaintiff to recover his goods[1] where the defendant is tortiously 'interfering' with them under the Torts (Interference with Goods) Act 1977. By the remedy the defendant is ordered to deliver the goods to, or to allow them to be taken by, the plaintiff. Delivery up therefore belongs alongside the mandatory restorative injunction as a remedy concerned to compel the undoing of a wrong.

Prior to 1854 the common law courts could not make such an order; the most they could do was to order the defendant to return the goods or pay their value at his option. This contrasted with the position in equity, where the Court of Chancery had power to grant delivery up of the plaintiff's goods, which it exercised where there was no adequate remedy at common law. By s 78 of the Common Law Procedure Act 1854 the common law courts too were given the power to order delivery up, in any action for the detention of any chattel, without giving the defendant the option of paying its value and this is now embodied in the Torts (Interference with Goods)

---

1 A co-owner can only obtain delivery up with the written authority of all other owners: RSC Ord 42, r 1A.

Act 1977. By s 3 the following remedies are available in proceedings for wrongful interference against a person in possession or in control of the goods:

a) an order for delivery of the goods and for payment of any consequential damages; or b) an order for delivery of goods, but giving the defendant the option of paying damages by reference to the value of the goods, together in either alternative with payment of any consequential damages; or c) damages.[2]

As the Act has abolished detinue, the actual torts for which delivery up can be ordered are conversion, as statutorily extended by s 2(2), and trespass to goods.

(2) When will the courts order delivery up?

There is no reason to think that the 1977 Act has affected the principles governing when delivery up will be ordered. The primary principle, deriving from the remedy's roots in equity, is that delivery up will not be ordered if damages are adequate. The same approach to adequacy has traditionally been adopted as for specific performance of a contract for the sale of goods and specific performance and delivery up are regarded as directly analogous remedies. For example in *Cohen v Roche*[3] McCardie J said, 'In my view, the power of the Court in an action of detinue rests upon a footing which fully accords with s 52 of the Sale of Goods Act 1893 . . . The law is thus, I am glad to find, consistent in its several parts.' This also explains why cases dealing with delivery up for detinue are often used as authorities on specific performance.

In line with the approach to specific performance,[4] it can therefore be said that delivery up will not be ordered for most goods on the ground that damages will enable substitutes to be bought in the market. An extreme example is *Cohen v Roche* where delivery up was refused to a buyer of some Hepplewhite chairs (to whom property in the chairs had passed) because in McCardie J's view, citing Swinfen Eady MR's words in *William Whiteley Ltd v Hilt*,[5] '. . . the goods in question were ordinary articles of commerce and of no special value or interest.'[6] Again, therefore, the uniqueness of the goods is the most crucial concept in judging adequacy.

2 For the assessment of damages, see supra, pp 167–9.
3 [1927] 1 KB 169 at 180–1.
4 Supra, chapter 8.
5 [1918] 2 KB 808 at 819.
6 [1927] 1 KB 169 at 181.

There are several excellent examples of the Court of Chancery ordering the delivery up of physically unique goods—that is, of goods possessing significant physical characteristics that very few, if any, other goods have. In *Pusey v Pusey*[7] it was the Pusey horn that was ordered to be delivered up; in *Somerset (Duke) v Cookson*[8] it was an antique altarpiece; in *Fells v Read*[9] some ceremonial ornaments; in *Lowther v Lowther*[10] a painting by Titian; and in *Earl of Macclesfield v Davies*[11] an order was made allowing the inspection of an iron-chest on the assumption that if it contained certain heirlooms they must be delivered up.

Goods may also be ordered to be delivered up, if they are commercially unique—that is where, although the goods are not physically unique, buying substitutes would be so difficult or would cause such delay that the plaintiff's business would be seriously interrupted. So in *North v Great Northern Rlwy Co*[12] the commercial uniqueness of 54 coal waggons underlay the acceptance that they could be ordered to be delivered up. Sir John Stuart V-C said:

There can be no doubt that . . . the coal waggons were of special value to him in order to carry on his business. The sudden sale of these waggons, without which the trade could not be conducted, must necessarily have inflicted serious injury by the interruption of his trade . . . It cannot be pretended that the plaintiff could have got on a sudden 54 other coal waggons fit for his business as readily and promptly as he could have purchased 54 tons of coal or 54 bushels of wheat.[13]

Similarly, the even more drastic remedy of interlocutory delivery up under s 4 of the 1977 Act was recently ordered in respect of 500 tons of steel lying in railway depots in *Howard Perry & Co v British Rly Board*[14] because, in view of the steel strike then taking place, the plaintiffs could not hope to acquire any other steel in the short term, and hence non-delivery up of their steel could cause substantial disruption to their business. Sir Robert Megarry V-C said:

. . . at present steel is obtainable on the market only with great difficulty, if at all. If the equivalent of what is detained is unobtainable, how can it be said that damages are an adequate remedy? They plainly are not . . . All that

---

7 (1684) 1 Vern 273.
8 (1735) 3 P Wms 390.
9 (1796) 3 Ves 70.
10 (1806) 13 Ves 95.
11 (1814) 3 Ves & B 16.
12 (1860) 2 Giff 64. See also the Canadian case *Farwell v Walbridge* (1851) 2 Gr 332 (delivery up of sawlogs).
13 Ibid at pp 68–9.
14 [1980] 1 WLR 1375.

the plaintiffs are losing, said counsel for the defendants is the sale of some steel, and damages will adequately compensate them for that. I do not think that this is by any means the whole picture. Damages would be a poor consolation if the failure of supplies forces a trader to lay off staff and disappoint his customers . . . and ultimately forces him towards insolvency.[15]

Although there are no direct authorities, the analogy drawn to specific performance presumably means that factors other than uniqueness, which render damages inadequate for specific performance, such as the difficulty in assessing damages or the defendant's inability to pay (provided other creditors are not prejudiced), also apply to render damages inadequate in relation to delivery up.

An interesting theoretical question is whether the analogy traditionally drawn with specific performance as regards adequacy is a sensible one. As is shown by the ease with which the adequacy hurdle is overcome in relation to prohibitory injunctions for the breach of a negative contractual promise, adequacy is an elastic concept and one would have thought that the wide view of adequacy adopted in relation to specific performance, which confines that remedy to a secondary role, would be inappropriate where the plaintiff's claim is for wrongful interference. Certainly it seems astonishing that if the defendant steals and keeps the plaintiff's goods the plaintiff has no prima facie civil right to recover them but must first overcome a substantial adequacy of damages hurdle. Nor, contrary to the fears of McCardie J in *Cohen v Roche*, would the law be inconsistent if delivery up were to be easier to obtain than specific performance, for the basis of each is fundamentally different. The former rests on interference with an existing proprietary right whereas the latter is simply given for breach of promise.[16]

Even where damages are inadequate, delivery up may still be refused.[17] For example, given its equitable roots, the courts may deny the remedy, while granting damages, because of the plaintiff's conduct, such as his acquiescence or 'unclean hands'. Additionally the normal six-year limitation period for tort actions laid down in s 2 of the Limitation Act 1980 will presumably apply to bar delivery up just as it does damages. Like specific performance and

15 Ibid at 1383.
16 Arguably the Consumer Credit Act 1974, s 100(5), supports delivery up being easier to obtain; on termination of a regulated hire-purchase or conditional sale agreement, delivery up of goods wrongly detained by the debtor must be ordered unless 'it would not be just to do so'.
17 Delivery up cannot be ordered against the Crown—the Crown Proceedings Act 1947, s 21(1)(b).

injunctions, delivery up may also be ordered on terms, for example that the plaintiff compensates the defendant for improvements made to the goods.[18]

(3) Interlocutory delivery up

So far (with the exception of the discussion on the *Howard Perry* case) it has been assumed that delivery up is sought at trial. But delivery up may also be granted at an interlocutory stage.

(a) Torts (Interference with Goods) Act 1977, s 4

By this, and by Rules of the Supreme Court Ord 29, r 2A, the court is empowered to order the delivery up of goods which are or may become the subject-matter of subsequent proceedings for tortious interference. The delivery is to be either to the claimant or to a person appointed by the court for the purpose. In cases of urgency delivery up may be ordered *ex parte* as with interlocutory injunctions.

Delivery up to a person appointed by the court, like a preservation order under RSC Ord 29, r 2, is best viewed as outside the scope of this book, since it seeks to ensure that subsequent remedies in relation to those goods can be effective and therefore belongs alongside the law on the enforcement of remedies.[19] But interlocutory delivery up to the plaintiff is a straightforward remedy for tortious interference. It is the equivalent of delivery up granted at trial under s 3 of the 1977 Act, and from the plaintiff's point of view has the advantage of being available quickly without waiting for trial. There has been little discussion of the principles governing such delivery up but one would expect them to be analogous to those governing interlocutory mandatory injunctions: for example, the plaintiff should have to show a strong or very strong prima facie case and that the balance of convenience favours the remedy.[20] In *Howard Perry & Co v British Railways Board,*[1] which is the leading case on this remedy, Megarry V-C ordered interlocutory delivery up of commercially unique steel kept in the defendant's yards, and stressed that there was no need to show a risk of the goods being

---

18 As expressly laid down in s 3(7) of the 1977 Act.
19 See analogously Anton Piller orders, supra, pp 445–6.
20 Supra, pp 440–3. There is support for this in *Adventure Film Productions Ltd v Tully* (1982) Times, 14 October.
 1 [1980] 1 WLR 1375. See also *Secretary of State for Defence v Guardian Newspapers Ltd* [1985] AC 339.

disposed of, lost or destroyed. He also explained that the order for delivery up could and in this case would require the defendant to permit the plaintiffs to collect the goods.

(b) Replevin

Replevin is an interlocutory procedure of ancient origin by which a defendant can be ordered to deliver up goods taken from the plaintiff. Theoretically replevin is available for any trespassory taking of the plaintiff's goods, but in practice it has been used only where the defendant has taken the goods by wrongful distress. The modern procedure is laid down in the County Courts Act 1984, Sch 1.[2] The plaintiff whose goods have been seized applies to the Registrar, who will order the goods to be 'replevied to that party' provided he gives security to cover, for example, the probable costs of the action and the alleged rent or damage in respect of which the distress has been made, and with a condition of the security being that he will prosecute the action without delay in a county court or the High Court.

Now that s 4 of the Torts (Interference with Goods) Act 1977 provides for interlocutory delivery up, it may be that delivery up in an action for replevin will wither away. Certainly the Law Reform Committee, upon whose report the Act was based, hoped that s 4 would 'pave the way for the abolition of replevin.'[3]

(4) Delivery up of material containing confidential information

It seems appropriate, as an addendum to delivery up of goods, to point out that a plaintiff can be granted delivery up of material containing confidential information belonging to him.[4] This can be regarded as a remedy for the equitable wrong of breach of confidence[5] and, as such, as analogous to delivery up of goods for tortious interference although a fortiori no common law damages, and hence no usual adequacy hurdle, needs to be overcome.

---

2 As amended by the Courts and Legal Services Act 1990.
3 18th Report, Cmnd 4774, para 97.
4 *Alperton Rubber Co v Manning* (1917) 86 LJ Ch 377; *Industrial Furnaces Ltd v Reaves* [1970] RPC 605.
5 See, eg *Industrial Furnaces Ltd v Reaves*, ibid; Gurry *Breach of Confidence* (1984) p 411; Law Commission Report No 110 Breach of Confidence paras 4.102–4.104.

(5) The action for the recovery of land[6]—a contrast to delivery up of goods

This common law action enables a plaintiff to recover possession of his land by ordering the defendant to give up his possession. But interestingly it is not a remedy for the tort of trespass to land as such. So, unlike a claim for that tort, the action for the recovery of land (formerly known as the action for ejectment) is necessarily available to an owner who is out of possession. Moreover, it is available to a plaintiff who was out of possession at the time of the unauthorised entry without any need to rely on the fiction of trespass by relation. Further differences from tortious trespass are that by s 15(1) of the Limitation Act 1980 the limitation period is twelve years rather than six, and that the action rests to a greater extent than does trespass on the plaintiff establishing good title so that, for example, *ius tertii*[7] appears to be a good defence.

All this serves to emphasise the important theoretical point that in contrast (and in some commentators' views,[8] in enlightened contrast) to delivery up of goods, this remedy has retained its identity as a remedy within the law of property without becoming dependent on wrongdoing by the defendant. It also follows that recovery of land falls outside the true scope of this book.

2. DELIVERY UP FOR DESTRUCTION OR DESTRUCTION ON OATH

Where there has been a wrongful infringement of intellectual property rights (whether by infringement of copyright,[9] patent,[10] trademark[11] or design,[12] or by the equitable wrong of breach of confidence[13)] the courts have an inherent jurisdiction to order the defendant to deliver up to the plaintiff or the court for destruction, or himself to destroy, articles made in infringement of the plaintiff's

6 Lawson *Remedies of English Law* (2nd edn, 1980) p 203.
7 'The right to possession is in a third party.'
8 See Weir *A Casebook on Tort* (7th edn, 1992) p 473.
9 *Mergenthaler Linotype Co v Intertype Co Ltd* (1926) 43 RPC 381.
10 *Paton Calvert & Co Ltd v Rosedale Associated Manufacturers Ltd* [1966] RPC 61.
11 *Slazenger & Sons v Feltham & Co* (1889) 6 RPC 531.
12 *Rosedale Associated Manufacturers Ltd v Airfix Products Ltd* [1956] RPC 360.
13 *Prince Albert v Strange* (1849) 2 De G & Sm 704; *Peter Pan Manufacturing Corpn v Corsets Silhouette Ltd* [1963] 3 All ER 402; *Ansell Rubber Co Pty Ltd v Allied Rubber Industries Pty Ltd* [1972] RPC 811; *Franklin v Geddis* [1978] Qd R 72.

rights or even in some cases[14] the means of making those articles. At first sight the function of these alternative equitable final remedies appears most closely allied to that of the mandatory restorative injunction since they generally compel the undoing of what has wrongfully been done.

But as the plaintiff's principal concern is not with the mere continued existence of infringing material (that in itself causing him no harm) but is rather with the harmful *use* of that material, the primary function of the remedies is best viewed as being to prevent acts infringing the plaintiff's rights. As such the remedies go one step beyond, and protect the plaintiff even more effectively than, a prohibitory injunction. The classic judicial statement on the remedies' function is Russell J's in *Mergenthaler Linotype Co v Intertype Co Ltd.*[15] He said:

[The plaintiff] is protected as to further manufacture of infringing articles by the injunction which he obtains, but there remains this, that so long as there is still what I might call infringing stock in the possession of the infringer, he may be subject to too serious and grave a temptation and may therefore be tempted to commit a breach of the injunction which he would otherwise not commit. Accordingly, in order to assist the plaintiff and as a relief ancillary to the injunction he has obtained, the Court may in its discretion make an order for destruction or delivery up of infringing articles.[16]

This passage also supports the view that there is no power to order destruction where a prohibitory injunction has not been granted. But of course just because such an injunction has been granted does not mean that the courts will exercise their power to order destruction. On the contrary there is always greater reluctance to grant positive than negative orders and the courts are also likely to be influenced by the hardship to the defendant and the waste of resources involved. Certainly if the plaintiff's rights can be effectively protected by ordering something less than full destruction, this will be preferred. For example, in *Slazenger & Sons v Feltham & Co*[17] the defendant was ordered merely to erase the plaintiff's trademark from tennis racquets, rather than being ordered to destroy all racquets bearing the trade mark; and in *Rosedale Associated Manufacturers Ltd v Airfix Products Ltd*,[18] where buckets infringing the plaintiff's design and moulds and dies used for making those buckets were ordered to be destroyed, it was explained by Lloyd-

---

14 *Rosedale Associated Manufacturers Ltd v Airfix Products Ltd* [1956] RPC 360; *Wham-O Manufacturing Co v Lincoln Industries Ltd* [1982] RPC 281 at 318.
15 (1926) 43 RPC 381.
16 Ibid at 382.
17 (1889) 6 RPC 531.
18 [1956] RPC 360.

Jacob J that, in respect of the moulds and dies, destruction meant '. . . a modification such as to render them inoperable to make an article of infringing shape.'[19]

When the courts will order delivery up for destruction as opposed to destruction on oath is unclear: but there is support for the view that the choice is essentially a matter for the defendant,[20] unless he has shown himself to be untrustworthy.[1]

It is important to emphasise that these remedies are granted even though the plaintiff does not own the articles ordered to be destroyed.[2] This is the key to avoiding confusion with the different remedy of delivery up of goods or of material containing confidential information, examined above. It follows that, while a plaintiff granted delivery up of goods or confidential information belonging to him is entitled to do what he likes with that property, a plaintiff to whom delivery up for destruction is ordered ought to destroy that property. Unfortunately the distinction between these remedies is clouded by the tendency of judges, practitioners and academics alike,[3] to omit the words 'for destruction' after delivery up to a non-owner. Understanding of the true purpose of the destruction remedies would be further enhanced if delivery up for destruction was always ordered to be made to the court, rather than to the plaintiff.

Although these remedies are clearly ideally suited for the wrongful infringement of intellectual property rights, there are other torts to which one would have thought they might be equally appropriate. The most obvious example is libel, for a plaintiff who has obtained an injunction would be even better protected by destruction (or erasing) of libellous material. The explanation for the present confinement of the remedies is presumably that the intellectual property torts had their roots in equity and these are equitable remedies. But this is clearly not a justification and it is suggested that, although they are drastic remedies, delivery up for destruction or destruction on oath could be usefully extended to other torts.

In relation to infringement of copyright and design right,[4] ss 99

---

19 Ibid at 368.
20 *Paton Calvert & Co Ltd v Rosedale Assoc Manufacturers Ltd* [1966] RPC 61.
1 *Industrial Furnaces Ltd v Reaves* [1970] RPC 605.
2 *Vivasseur v Krupp* (1878) 9 Ch D 351 at 360; *Chappell & Co Ltd v Columbia Gramophone Co* [1914] 2 Ch 745 at 756; *Ansell Rubber Co Pty v Allied Rubber Industries Pty Ltd* [1972] RPC 811.
3 A notable exception is Forrai (1971) 6 Syd LR 382, 391.
4 Analogous provisions apply to infringement of a person's performer's or recording rights by illicit recording: ss 195 and 204 of the Copyright, Designs and Patents Act 1988.

and 230 of the Copyright, Designs and Patents Act 1988 give the courts a specific statutory power (irrespective of the grant of an injunction) to order delivery up of infringing copies or articles, or anything designed or adapted for making infringing copies or articles.[5] Moreover while the courts may require the material delivered up to be destroyed they can also simply order it to be forfeited to the copyright or design right owner.[6] That represents a difference from the remedies available under the inherent equitable jurisdiction: delivery up and forfeiture to the copyright or design owner (of material that is owned by the defendant) may be regarded as occupying a mid-position between delivery up of (one's) goods and delivery up for destruction.[7]

3. APPOINTMENT OF A RECEIVER AND MANAGER

In broad terms a receiver and manager is a person appointed to take in property (such as rents and profits), to recover property, and to carry on or superintend the business for which that property has been employed. There has long been an equitable jurisdiction to appoint a receiver and this power is now embodied in s 37(1) of the Supreme Court Act 1981: 'The High Court may by order (whether interlocutory or final) . . . appoint a receiver in all cases in which it appears to the court to be just and convenient to do so.' In the past such a power was hardly ever used to remedy a tort or breach of contract.[8] But a change may have been heralded by recent cases; for in *Hart v Emelkirk Ltd*[9] and *Daiches v Bluelake Investments Ltd*[10] receivers were appointed in interlocutory actions to collect rents and to organise the repair of flats, which defendant landlords had allowed to fall into a serious state of disrepair in breach of their repairing covenants. In the former, Goulding J said:

5 The courts' inherent jurisdiction is unaffected: see ss 99(4) and 230(7) of the 1988 Act. By s 233(2) damages only can be awarded for innocent secondary infringement of a design right.
6 Section 114 (copyright); s 231 (design right). In effect the same remedy was previously available for infringement of copyright under s 18 of the Copyright Act 1956 (now repealed): the copyright owner was treated as the owner of infringing copies and plates used to make infringing copies and could therefore seek delivery up of (his) goods for the tort of conversion.
7 The primary function of delivery up and forfeiture is probably to compel the undoing of a wrong: cf supra, p 459.
8 Rare exceptions were *Riches v Owen* (1868) 3 Ch App 820; *Leney & Sons Ltd v Callingham and Thompson* [1908] 1 KB 79.
9 [1983] 3 All ER 15.
10 (1985) 275 Estates Gazette 462.

I know of no precedent for such relief, but I also know of no authority that forbids it under the provisions of . . . the Supreme Court Act 1981, s 37 . . . It clearly appears to me to be just to appoint a receiver in this case because it is done to support the enforcement by the court of covenants affecting property. It is also convenient because . . . the properties are in a condition that demands urgent action.[11]

That there is an unfettered jurisdiction to appoint a receiver and manager was confirmed in *Parker v Camden London Borough Council*[12] which also concerned a breach of repairing covenants. But the Court of Appeal there refused to exercise its discretion to make an appointment because it thought that, as the flats were mainly sheltered homes provided by the local authority for the elderly and infirm, an appointment would contravene Parliament's intention under the Housing Act 1957 that only a local authority should have responsibility for the management of such homes.

The appointment of a receiver and manager is clearly a convenient remedy to 'enforce' many continuing positive obligations, and it is therefore surprising that greater use has not been made of this remedy for breach of contract. Perhaps any judicial reluctance is explicable as resting on similar ideas to those underpinning the now increasingly criticised constant supervision objection to specific performance. It remains to be seen whether the recent cases will act as a catalyst for much greater use of this remedy.

4. DECLARATION[13]

While all remedies impliedly declare what the parties' rights are, a declaration is a remedy, generally regarded as statutory[14] albeit with equitable roots, by which a court simply pronounces on the rights or even the remedies of the parties. Available in relation to any sort of legal right, a declaration can quickly and easily, and without invoking any coercion, aid the resolution of a dispute or prevent one from arising. As Lawson wrote:

If persons dispute among themselves as to their legal position, but are

11 [1983] 3 All ER 15 at 16.
12 [1985] 2 All ER 141. See also *Evans v Clayhope Properties Ltd* [1988] 1 WLR 358, 361 (although the actual decision was that the defendant could not be ordered at an interlocutory stage to meet the receiver and manager's expenses or remuneration).
13 See generally Zamir *The Declaratory Judgment* (1962); Young *Declaratory Orders* (1975); Lawson *Remedies of English Law* (2nd edn) ch 16.
14 *Chapman v Michaelson* [1908] 2 Ch 612; *Tito v Waddell (No 2)* [1977] Ch 106 at 259.

perfectly willing to respect and act upon it once they know what it is, there is no need to order them in any way. A mere declaration stating authoritatively their legal relations will suffice.[15]

Prior to 1883, the Court of Chancery alone had the power to grant a declaration, and then this was exercised only where consequential relief was or could have been claimed. But by the Judicature Acts 1873–5 and the accompanying Rules of the Supreme Court 1883 Ord 25, r 5,[16] all divisions of the High Court were given power to make declarations 'whether or not consequential relief is or could be claimed'. It was this 'innovation of a very important kind'[17] that paved the way for the modern widespread use of declarations.

Early this century it was said that the discretion to grant a declaration should be exercised 'with extreme caution',[18] but in Lord Radcliffe's words giving the Privy Council's judgment in *Ibeneweka v Egbuna*:[19]

. . . it is doubtful if there is more of principle involved than the undoubted truth that the power of granting a declaration should be exercised with a proper sense of responsibility and full realisation that judicial pronouncements ought not to be issued unless there are circumstances that call for their making. Beyond that there is no legal restriction on the award of a declaration.

Denning LJ earlier spoke in similar vein in *Pyx Granite Co Ltd v Ministry of Housing and Local Government*:[20] '. . . if a substantial question exists which one person has a real interest to raise and the other to oppose, then the court has a discretion to resolve it by a declaration, which it will exercise if there is good reason for so doing.' So in modern times a declaration is readily granted.

This of course does not mean that a declaration will never be refused. The plaintiff must have a real interest in the matter and must not be merely an interfering busybody. Nor will it be granted where no dispute or infringement of legal rights has yet taken place and the chances of that occurring are regarded as too hypothetical.[1] Moreover it has recently been clarified that the dispute must be as between the parties. In Lord Diplock's words in *Gouriet v Union of*

---

15 *Remedies* p 231.
16 Now RSC Ord 15, r 16.
17 *Ellis v Duke of Bedford* [1899] 1 Ch 494 at 515 (per Lindley MR).
18 *Faber v Gosworth UDC* (1903) 88 LT 549 at 550.
19 [1964] 1 WLR 219 at 225. See also *Guaranty Trust Co of New York v Hannay & Co* [1915] 2 KB 536, 572 (per Bankes LJ); *Hanson v Radcliffe UDC* [1922] 2 Ch 490, 507 (per Lord Sterndale MR); *Booker v Bell* [1989] 1 Lloyd's Rep 516.
20 [1958] 1 QB 554 at 571.
1 *Mellstrom v Garner* [1970] 1 WLR 603.

Post Office Workers,[2] '. . . the jurisdiction is not to declare the law generally or to give advisory opinions; it is confined to declaring legal rights, subsisting or future, of the parties represented in the litigation before it and not those of anyone else.' And in *Meadows Indemnity Co Ltd v Insurance Corpn of Ireland Ltd*[3] a declaration sought by a reinsurer as to the invalidity of a claim made under the head insurance was refused by the Court of Appeal on the ground that there was no contested issue between the reinsurer and the head-assured. Given its equitable roots, it would also appear, although there is little authority on this, that equitable defences relating to the plaintiff's conduct, such as laches, acquiescence and 'unclean hands', further bar a declaration.

As a remedy for a tort or breach of contract a declaration is generally concerned to pronounce authoritatively that the defendant's conduct did or does amount to a tort or breach of contract. So in *Harrison v Duke of Rutland*[4] the defendant, on a counterclaim, was granted a declaration that the plaintiff was trespassing when he rode his bicycle along the defendant's road as a means of interfering with the defendant's grouse-shooting; and in *Louis Drayfus et Cie v Parnaso Cia Naviera SA,*[5] the plaintiffs were at first instance granted, but on appeal refused, a declaration that the defendant shipowners were in breach of a charterparty. A plaintiff may also seek a declaration of the defendant's duties to him, so as to counter a threatened tort or breach of contract. In *Rajbenbach v Mamon,*[6] for example, the plaintiff tenant was granted a declaration of the defendant landlord's contractual obligations to him following the defendant's anticipatory repudiation of a contract under which the defendant was to pay the plaintiff £300 for vacating premises by a certain date. It is especially where the plaintiff is seeking to enforce obligations in a continuing contractual relationship that the declaration shows its advantages, for as Borchard writes:

> The declaration rather than the more drastic and definitive coercive decree enables the parties to re-establish their questioned relations without irreparable injury. The declaration thus has a social advantage which should not be underestimated as an element in the administration of justice.[7]

---

2 [1978] AC 435, 501. See also Lord Wilberforce at 483.
3 [1989] 2 Lloyd's Rep 298.
4 [1893] 1 QB 142.
5 [1959] 1 QB 498; revsd [1960] 2 QB 49. See also *Burdett-Coutts v Hertfordshire County Council* [1984] IRLR 91.
6 [1955] 1 QB 283.
7 *Declaratory Judgments* (2nd edn, 1941) p 554.

Two final points are noteworthy. First, in some cases the courts have found it useful to be able to grant a declaration, while refusing or suspending the more drastic remedy of an injunction.[8] Secondly, the courts have no power to award an interim declaration.[9] In the past this was felt to leave an unfortunate lacuna in respect of actions against the Crown.[10] However, since the decision in *M v Home Office*,[11] it is not at all clear that in practice there is such a gap although Lord Woolf did say that, 'To avoid having to grant interim injunctions against officers of the Crown, I can see advantages in the courts being able to grant interim declarations.'[12]

5. ARE ANY NEW REMEDIES NEEDED?

Having evolved over a long period of time in response to changing conditions, attitudes and demands, the judicial remedies for torts and breach of contract fulfil a wide range of functions and, with the possible exception of interim declarations, there are no obvious omissions. 'New' remedies that have been suggested turn out on closer inspection to be merely calls for modification of the form existing remedies take, for example periodic payments of damages, or calls for the judiciary to exercise their existing powers in a particular way—for example the so-called 'compensated injunction' is but a type of conditional injunction which the courts have long had power to grant.

A good general example of this point was the Law Commission's advocacy of a new 'adjustment order' for breach of confidence.[13] In reality no new remedy was being proposed; rather parties were being encouraged to seek, and/or courts to use their existing powers to grant, declarations of the parties' rights over confidential information, conditional injunctions (whereby the plaintiff should pay fair compensation for wasted expenses incurred by the defendant before he knew or ought to have known that the information was

---

8 *Llandudno UDC v Woods* [1899] 2 Ch 705; *Stollmeyer v Trinidad Lake Petroleum Co* [1918] AC 485; *Race Relations Board v Applin* [1973] QB 815.

9 *Underhill v Ministry of Food* [1950] 1 All ER 591; *International General Electric Co of New York Ltd v Customs and Excise Comrs* [1962] Ch 784; *R v IRC, ex p Rossminster Ltd* [1980] AC 952; *Riverside Mental Health NHS Trust v Fox* (1993) Times, 28 October.

10 Law Commission Report No 73 Remedies in Administrative Law (1976) paras 51–2. See also Consultation Paper No 126 (1993) 'Administrative Law: Judicial Review and Statutory Appeals'.

11 [1993] 3 All ER 537. Supra, p 388.

12 Ibid at 564–565.

13 Report No 110 Breach of Confidence paras 6.110–6.112.

confidential) and compensatory damages for wasted expenses incurred. In addition it was recommended, and here legislation would be needed, that the courts should have the power to award damages in the form of a royalty; but like provisional damages in personal injury cases this would represent merely a break with the traditional lump sum form of award.

But while one can rest content with the types of judicial remedy available for torts and breach of contract, there are numerous ways in which the present law on judicial remedies could be improved. These have arisen for discussion at various stages of the book, and it is sufficient at the close, whether in jogging memories or in whetting appetites, to recap on just a few of them: clarification of the contractual remoteness test and its relationship to the tort test; acceptance of contributory negligence as a defence to breach of contract; taking into account of resale prices in calculating sale of goods damages; abolition of damages for non-pecuniary loss for an unconscious plaintiff; basing of multipliers on the rate of return on index-linked investments; widening of the recoverability of mental distress damages; abolition of exemplary damages; overruling of *White & Carter (Councils) Ltd v McGregor*; removal of the constant supervision objection to specific performance; greater willingness to award damages in preference to injunctions in land use conflicts; and restoration, subject to a few qualifications, of the pre-*Cyanamid* law on interlocutory injunctions.

Index

467